WEFA Industrial Monitor 1997

Subscription Notice

This Wiley product is updated on a periodic basic with supplements to reflect important changes in the subject matter. If you purchased this product directly from John Wiley & Sons, Inc., we have already recorded your subscription for this update service.

If, however, you purchased this product from a bookstore and wish to receive (1) the current update at no additional charge, and (2) future updates and revised or related volumes billed separately with a 30-day examination review, please send your name, company name (if applicable), address, and the title of the product to:

Supplement Department
John Wiley & Sons, Inc.
One Wiley Drive
Somerset, NJ 08875
1-800-225-5945

For customers outside the United States, please contact the Wiley office nearest you:

Professional & Reference Division
John Wiley & Sons Canada, Ltd.
22 Worcester Road
Rexdale, Ontario M9W 1L1
CANADA
(416) 675-3580
1-800-567-4797
FAX (416) 675-6599

John Wiley & Sons, Ltd.
Baffins Lane
Chichester
West Sussex, PO19 1UD
UNITED KINGDOM
(44) (243) 779777

Jacaranda Wiley Ltd.
PRT Division
P.O. Box 174
North Ryde, NSW 2113
AUSTRALIA
(02) 805-1100
FAX (02) 805-1597

John Wiley & Sons (SEA) Pte. Ltd.
37 Jalan Pemimpin
Block B # 05-04
Union Industrial Building
SINGAPORE 2057
(65) 258-1157

WEFA Industrial Monitor 1997

Edited by Priscilla Trumbull

JOHN WILEY & SONS, INC.
New York • Chichester • Weinheim • Brisbane • Singapore • Toronto

This text is printed on acid-free paper.

Copyright © 1997 by John Wiley & Sons, Inc.

All rights reserved. Published simultaneously in Canada.

Library of Congress Cataloging in Publication Data:

ISBN 0-471-19946-X
ISSN 1093-6580

Printed in the United States of America

10 9 8 7 6 5 4 3 2 1

About the Editor

Priscilla Trumbull is Executive Vice President of Industry Services at WEFA, a Primark Company. Her responsibilities include the supervision of 25 analysts supporting a broad range of industrial forecasting services and consulting engagements. She is widely quoted in the business press, and speaks frequently to audiences ranging from small upper management presentations to groups of 200 and more.

Ms. Trumbull's particular area of expertise is in comparative industry analysis, tracking the relative performance, inter-relationships, and geographic characteristics of the various components of the industrial spectrum. Her current areas of active research include industry risk analysis for portfolio management and measurement of global market opportunities for producers of industrial materials.

She has been with WEFA since 1978, working in a number of industrial and consulting groups, as well as contributing regularly to the WEFA macroeconomic forecasts for more than 10 years. Her undergraduate work was split between Swarthmore College and the University of Delaware, and her Bachelor's degree is in Economics and Mathematics from the University of Delaware. She has pursued graduate coursework in econometrics at the University of Pennsylvania.

List of Contributors

Daniel Bachman is Director of U.S. Long-Term Macro Forecasting at WEFA. He is a former Assistant Professor at Temple University, and holds a Ph.D. from Brown University.

Harry S. Baumes is Senior Vice President Agriculture Services at WEFA. He has over 20 years of experience in analysis of agricultural policy, commodity, price and trade analysis, and the fertilizer, pesticides, and farm equipment (manufactured input) sectors.

Mohsen Bonakdarpour is Vice President of Industry Services Development and Consulting. He has more than ten years of experience in statistical and input-output modeling.

Ron Denhardt has over 20 years of experience in the energy industry, focusing primarily on the natural gas and electric industries. His experience includes strategic, market, and fuel planning; acquisition and regulatory analysis; supply contracting; transportation logistics; and pricing.

David K. Eaton is an Economic Analyst in Agriculture Services for WEFA, providing support and analysis for U.S., Canadian, and International Agriculture services.

Jocelyn A. Hansell is an Associate Economist for Industry Services at WEFA, analyzing the U.S. and world steel industry.

Gregory L. Harnish is an Associate Economist in Agricultural Services at WEFA. His primary responsibilities include supply, use, and price forecasts for U.S. crops.

Dixon Hawkins is WEFA's Chief European Economist. He coordinates WEFA's Global Outlook Committee, and has more than 25 years of experience as an international economist.

Michael Hoover is Manager of WEFA's U.S. Agriculture Service, focusing on commodity and price analysis.

Steve Jing is an Economic Analyst in the Industry Services group at WEFA, supporting research in industrial inflation and non-ferrous metals.

Kurt Karl is Executive Vice President of WEFA's U.S. Macroeconomic Services. He has 20 years of experience in modeling and forecasting, and has worked in Europe and Africa as an economist and statistician.

Kate A. Knox is a Senior Administrative Assistant at WEFA, and has responsibility for coordinating and preparing forecast documents and proposals.

Kenneth J. Kremar is Director of Capital Goods and Freight Transportation for WEFA. He has more than 25 years of experience in monitoring and analyzing these markets.

Shirley Lau is an Economist in WEFA's Industry Services group. She has more than 20 years of experience in building and managing economic data bases.

Rick L. Lazasz is a Senior Economic Analyst at Industry Services of WEFA Inc. He monitors and forecasts the aluminum and copper markets.

Teresa M. Luetjen, A.P.P. is Manager of Market and Cost Analysis in the Industry Services group at WEFA, with responsibility for forest products and other sectors.

George M. Magliano has been a professional economist for almost 30 years and is Director of WEFA's Automotive Research. He was Chief Economist at J.P. Stevens and Director of Consumer and Automotive Research for Economic Consulting & Planning.

Andrew March is an Economic Analyst in WEFA's U.S. Financial Service, monitoring bond and equity market trends and analyzing the market impact of economic data.

Amy Matthews is an Economic Analyst for WEFA's Agriculture Services, providing support and analysis for U.S. and International Agriculture services.

James A. McCune is an independent economic consultant who was formerly Global Forecast Coordinator for WEFA and Senior International Economist for the ITT Corporation.

Nicholas Neuheimer is an Associate Economist in WEFA's U.S. Macroeconomic Services, and is a former associate of the Financial Research Institute.

Mary Novak is Senior Vice President of Energy Services at WEFA. She has almost 20 years of experience in energy industry analysis and consulting.

Frantz R. Price is Senior Vice President of Market and Cost Analysis at WEFA. He has over 20 years of experience in industry and economic consulting, including materials cost management, strategic planning, and market research. Prior to WEFA, he held managerial positions at Ingersoll-Rand and Union Carbide.

Pasquale J. Rocco, Jr. is Senior Economist, U.S. Macroeconomic Services at WEFA and a former economist at the Bureau of Labor Statistics.

Thomas Runiewicz, CPA is Director of WEFA's World Steel Services and Senior Economist for other industry services at WEFA. He has more than 18 years of experience in economic forecasting and consulting, and he is a Certified Public Accountant at Brinker, Simpson & Company, L.L.P.

Marlene Scargill is an Administrative Assistant for the Industry Services group at WEFA.

Daniel P. Schleiniger is an Economic Analyst in Agriculture Services at WEFA.

Robert C. Shaw is Manager of Automotive Production Forecasting at WEFA. He analyzes production by make and model in North America, and supports forecasting of sales and global automotive trends.

Arbin Sherchan is an Economic Analyst in WEFA's U.S. Macroeconomic Service.

Allen Shiau is Executive Vice President of WEFA's International Services group. He has more than 20 years of experience in modeling and forecasting in the areas of agriculture, the U.S. macroeconomy, and the global economy.

Richard Simons is an Economist with WEFA's Energy Services Department. He has a master's degree from the University of New Hampshire.

Ronald J. Talley, Ph.D., is Director of the U.S. Financial Service at WEFA. He has more than 25 years of experience as a professional economist, including positions with the Federal Reserve, a major commercial bank, and as an independent consultant.

Lilly P. Teng is an Economist in Energy Services at WEFA.

Arlean Worthy is administrator for WEFA's U.S. Macroeconomic Services. With a BA in journalism, she has previous experience in the publishing business.

Contents

CONTENTS

Foreword

This volume serves an important function for the economic analyst who needs a quick but comprehensive overview of some particular sector or industry, including main characteristics such as production, acreage, main producers, recent historical trends, and plausible projections for the medium term. For most sectors covered in this *Monitor*, the projection horizon is to some point early in the next century, which is about the limit of credible, useful forecasting.

The industry or economic sector breakdown is quite natural, going from major primary sectors (agricultural crops, livestock, dairy, mining, construction, manufacturing, and services). In all, there are 30 chapters and several sectors within each chapter.

This is not a set of sectoral projections rigidly bound together within a large model, but is a series of individual sector analyses, with both quantitative tables and expert narratives. The latter are provided by sector specialists who know their subject well and are able to bring relevant highlights to the reader. Mutual consistencies among the series projected are preserved by input–output analysis.

All these separate sector tabulations are made individually, yet they are mutually consistent within WEFA and are compatible with national and world projections that are regularly made from self–contained models of interrelated sectors.

The commentaries highlight such items as seasonal variations, *specific* cycles, new technologies, rising industries, declining industries, major firms within some industries, regulatory effects, and other aspects of our overall economy which have significant influence on specific industries. It should prove to be invaluable to readers who want ready–reference information on such topics as:

> *supply–demand balance for important crops*
> *major sources of inputs or destinations of output of individual sectors*
> *unusual price or output or input movements in specific sectors*
> *domestic vs. international markets for individual industries*

Generally speaking, historical annual data reflect cyclical and disturbing (or unusual) factors present in each sector's evolution. The time shapes of historical values often have highly visible fluctuations, but in most cases the future looks smooth, in the sense that "point" forecasts of individual series are fairly smooth. Many are extrapolated by steady growth rates, although there are noteworthy cases of sectors growing with new technologies, as well as some that are declining in importance. These movements are all interpreted by a knowledgeable sector analyst.

The reference analyses can be very helpful in getting informed judgments about directions and average magnitude of growth in a dynamic economy, sector by sector.

L.R. Klein

Preface

This book is a comprehensive review of the major industries in the U.S. economy, prepared by the industry analysts at WEFA, the top economic forecasting and consulting firm in the world. Each of its sections is designed to paint a picture of the economic health of an industry over the last ten years, in the very near term future, and looking forward to the year 2006.

The industries are evaluated in terms of: demand, both from domestic customers and export markets; supply conditions, including the structure of the domestic producing sector and imports; the links of the industry to the economy and to product and technology trends; pressures and opportunities in product pricing and production costs; profitability; and issues such as business cycle sensitivity, environmental issues, and consolidation trends that shape each industry and its companies. The issues discussed are key to the formulation of WEFA's forecast for the industries' sales and international trade volumes, and are vital to the reader's understanding of the forces driving the companies in each segment of the economy. The information will be useful for researchers, financial analysts, portfolio managers, market researchers, corporate planners and strategists, lending officers, purchasing managers, and a host of other people who need information about industry trends.

The book is organized into seven main parts. The introductory material provides the overall economic framework in which the industry forecasts have been developed, with chapters describing WEFA's U.S. macroeconomic forecast, the global economic outlook, and the comparative performance of the various industry sectors in the United States. Parts One through Six serve to organize the chapters into broad industry groups: Agriculture, Mining, and Construction; Non-durable Goods Manufacturing; Durable Goods Manufacturing; Transportation, Communications, and Utilities; Wholesale and Retail Trade; and Finance, Insurance, Real Estate, and Services.

More than thirty-five analysts at WEFA contributed sections to this book. While we have not designated authors' names for the specific sections, each of them brings a rich blend of training, experience, and information sources to their analysis. In addition, they have all developed their forecasts in the framework of WEFA's overall economic view -- each contributes to that view and each evaluates the economic environment for an industry from the WEFA forecast for the macroeconomy and for related industries. This consistency of assumptions and approach is critical for virtually all applications of the forecasts, and it is an advantage derived from producing this work from within a single, tightly-knit organization.

WEFA is pleased to have been approached by John Wiley & Sons to write this book. Richard Crucitt and David Fein at John Wiley & Sons, in conjunction with Linda Buddrius and Douglas Anthony at WEFA, were the team that brought the idea to a commitment. Sheck Cho at John Wiley & Sons taught me all about the publishing. Special thanks go to three people at WEFA: Frantz Price, who diligently edited my edits; Kate Knox, who brought the more than 100 separate documents together and enforced consistency on them; and Bill Mundell, who encouraged us all to put in the extra effort to complete the project.

Readers who would like further information on WEFA's more detailed industry analysis, historical and forecast databases, or industry project capabilities are encouraged to contact our sales organization by fax at (610)490-2848 or by e-mail at wefahelp@wefa.com. Annual updates for the Industry Monitor are planned, and we welcome suggestions for future editions.

Priscilla Trumbull
June, 1997

Introduction: Economic Review and Forecasts

U.S. Economic Outlook

World Economic Outlook

Forecast Highlights: The High Growth Industries

U.S. Economic Outlook

The Federal Reserve Board (Fed) is likely to continue raising interest rates through the course of 1997. Job increases remain robust, fueling growth in income and consumer spending. It will take the Fed a year to slow down the economy to its target 2% — 2.5% range for GDP growth. Despite the rise in short–term rates, long–term interest rates will remain near their current levels. Although the yield on the 30–year Treasury bond could go as high as 7.5%, it is unlikely to fall below 7% for any sustained period in 1997. Uncertainty over Fed policy, economic growth, and inflation will tend to put a floor under the yield on the long bond.

Housing starts will hold up reasonably well in 1997, but flag in 1998. The strong dollar — sustained by rising interest rates — will boost imports and weaken exports, helping to slow growth in 1997.

In early 1998, employment growth in the interest–sensitive sectors, such as construction, will be less robust. Employment growth in other sectors will also slow down by the end of 1997, but to a lesser extent than finance and construction. The unemployment rate will remain close to 5%, however. The Fed's tighter monetary policy will keep the unemployment rate from falling below 5% for any sustained period of time, which will help to avert rising wage inflation.

Near Term Fed Policy

The Federal Reserve Board began to raise the Fed funds rate after its March Federal Open Market Committee meeting, seeking to restrain the economy before unsustainably strong growth leads to higher inflation. The Fed's target range for real Gross Domestic Product (GDP) growth is 2.0% to 2.5%, with a distinct preference for it being closer to 2%. At year–end 1996 and in early 1997, the economy was growing at a rate significantly above 3%. The Fed views this pace as excessive because, with the unemployment rate around 5% and capacity utilization over 82%, the resources of the U.S. economy are fully utilized. Sustained demand growth in excess of 2.5% is very likely to lead to increased inflation.

Over the course of 1996 and in early 1997, employment growth accelerated and the unemployment rate fell. The employment increase was accompanied by fairly strong income growth, leading to a rise in consumer spending. Since the beginning of 1996, employment growth increased from about 1.5% to close to 2.5%, boosting consumer confidence to very high levels. Higher incomes and increased confidence pushed consumer spending up from about 2% to 3%. It is this pattern of growth acceleration over the past year or so which has the Fed so worried.

Now that the Fed has begun raising interest rates it faces two problems: how fast and how far? First, it takes about one year for interest rates to slow economic activity. Second, it is unclear how high interest rates need to go to reduce growth. Given that the underlying strength of economic growth is probably around 3.0%, the Fed will need to lower growth by about 0.5 percentage point. WEFA estimates that a one–percentage–point increase in interest rates takes about a year to lower growth by that much. Hence, WEFA believes the Fed needs to raise the Fed funds rate to 6.25% by late 1997, which will bring growth down to near 2% in 1998, the lower boundary of the Fed's target range.

Growth has been so rapid that the specter of a wage–price inflationary spiral has increased in probability. The Fed will be monitoring the pace of real GDP growth to gauge the success of its latest monetary tightening. By early 1998, if year–over–year real GDP growth has slowed to below 2%, the Fed will most likely begin to slowly lower the Fed funds rate. If growth is still between 2% and 2.5%, the Fed will leave the rate at 6.25%. If it is between 2.5% and 3.0%, the Fed might continue to raise rates. If it is still above 3.0%, rates will go higher.

Payroll and Household Employment Growth
Accelerating Since Late in 1995

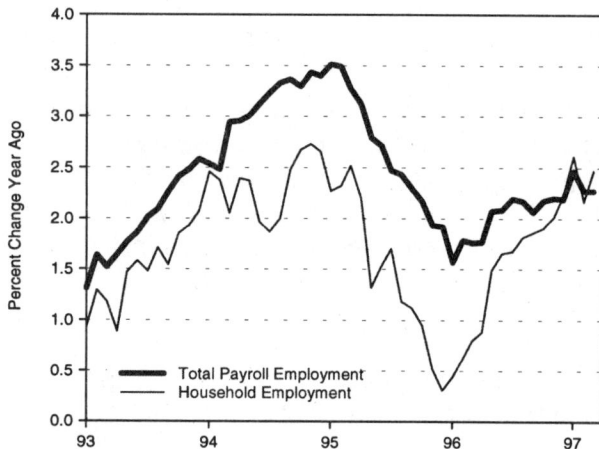

The Fed has drawn the line in the sand — inflation can go no higher. If the Fed's action has come too late and inflation begins to rise, the Fed would need to raise interest rates very rapidly, pushing the Fed funds rate up around 8%. The most likely outcome from such a sharp rise in short–term interest rates would be a recession in 1998. Though WEFA does not think this scenario is very likely — we rate it with a 20% probability — the probability of recession has risen because the Fed is now pushing up interest rates.

The yield on the Treasury's benchmark 30–year bond will fluctuate between 7% and 7.5%, assuming inflation remains under control. There is a great deal of uncertainty surrounding Fed policy, the strength of the economy, and prospects for an acceleration in inflation. This uncertainty will keep the yield on the long bond from falling below 7% in 1997 for any sustained period.

Short–Term Policy Impact: Growth will Moderate

As the year progresses, and interest rates continue upward, economic growth will become less robust. WEFA's model of the U.S. economy reveals a simple rule for the impact of interest rates on growth: a *one*–percentage–point rise in interest rates, *one* year later, reduces the rate of growth of real GDP by *one–half* percentage point.

The rising interest rate environment will gradually affect all sectors of the economy, but the impact and timing will vary. The components which will be most immediately affected are:

- International trade: export growth will be slow, while import growth will be robust. Rising interest rates will support the strong dollar.

- Housing construction will begin to ease off late in 1997.

- Vehicle sales will stall late in the year.

- Household discretionary income will be cut, as adjustable interest rates rise.

The single largest factor in slowing growth in 1997 will be the strong dollar, which will worsen net exports. Net exports are likely to decline by about $30 billion in 1997. Rising interest rates will help to sustain the high value of the dollar despite rising trade deficits. In addition, demand is strong in the United States, increasing the need for imports, while some of our major trading partners, particularly Germany and Japan, are weak. The strong dollar will help to keep inflation tame during 1997, diminishing the need for further Fed tightening.

For the household sector, rising interest rate costs on adjustable–rate credit cards and mortgages will be offset by declining food and energy prices. Adjustable–rate credit card accounts — about 85% of all cards — will become more costly, reducing disposable income by about $5 billion for each percentage point rise in the prime rate. Mortgage interest payments will rise by $10 billion for each percentage point increase on adjustable–rate mortgages. Offsetting this impact on consumers' discretionary income will be declines in gasoline and food prices. The benefit of expected declines in food and energy prices will be about $15 billion, which is about the same amount as the cost to consumers of a one–percentage–point increase in adjustable interest rates.

Long–Term Forecast Summary

Potential real GDP growth should average 2.2% per year over the next decade. In order to clarify the long–run potential of the U.S. economy and its industry sectors, we are using a trend forecast for the macroeconomy. The forecast assumes no external shocks, no major policy blunders, and no boom/bust profile for economic output. Therefore the macroeconomic forecast is recession–free — not as a statement that WEFA does not expect any recessions in the next ten years, but that

■ The current environment does not make a near–term recession likely, and

■ There is nothing inherent in the fiscal and monetary policy situation that will cause a downturn at a specific point in the medium– or long–term forecast period.

Real GDP Growth

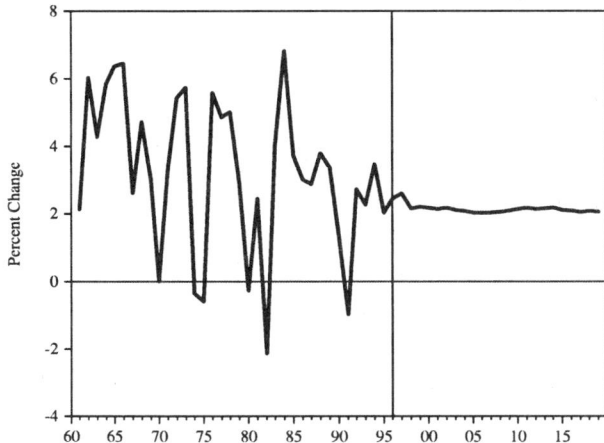

The outlook for inflation remains moderate. Inflation moved modestly higher in 1996, pushed up by higher energy and food prices. Core inflation, however, remains under control at about 2.7%. WEFA expects inflation to remain moderate. Broad measures of inflation should continue at about a 2.7% rate through 1999. Over the longer term, inflation will average about 2.8%.

The path of fiscal policy remains one of the major un-knowns of the long–term outlook. President Clinton and the Congress agree on the desirability of balancing the budget by 2002, and they have agreed upon a compromise plan. However, political reality leaves some of the specifics of its implementation open to change at the hands of future lawmakers. We have assumed that growth in federal spending will be slowed. In particular, current and future efforts will slow growth in medical spending. WEFA forecasts the federal deficit will stabilize, reaching $118 billion, or 1.5% of GDP, by 2000.

Productivity performance for the U.S. economy has been disappointing since the early 1970s. Over the past 25 years measured productivity growth has averaged about 1.1% per year. Continued growth in investment and a more slowly growing labor force should allow for slightly faster productivity growth over the forecast period. Non–farm business productivity growth should average 1.2% per year over the next 10 years, slightly faster than the

recent trend. This productivity growth will support growth in real disposable income per capita of 1.4%.

Long–Term Forecast Highlights

Population and Demographics Population growth is a primary long–run determinant of the potential expansion path of the economy. Population growth affects both the supply and demand sides of the economy. The growth of the population and its composition have profound impacts on the labor force, demand for consumer durables (especially light vehicles), housing, and demand for medical services. The WEFA Long–Term Service is basing its population projections on the Census Bureau's latest middle series assumptions for fertility, life expectancy, and net immigration, which were released in February 1996.

The U.S. population is projected to expand at an annual rate of 0.8% between 1995 and 2006, when the population is projected to reach 288.3 million. Population growth will not be distributed evenly across the population cohorts. Rather, growth in the older age cohorts will be stronger as the baby boomers age.

Productivity and Aggregate Supply It is the economy's ability to increase supply in the long run that determines its potential growth path. Growth in aggregate supply depends on the increase in the labor force, the growth of the capital stock, and improvements in productivity.

Productivity improvement depends on several key factors:

■ Advancement in the education, training, and skills of the work force;

■ The amount that is saved and invested for equipping the labor force with productive capital (tools, machinery, transportation equipment, and other manufactured means of production);

■ The speed with which new technology and improved techniques are introduced into the production, transportation, and distribution of goods and services.

Potential GDP growth will slow in the projection period, expanding 2.2% annually over the next decade. This is in stark contrast to the potential growth path of more than 3.0% that prevailed in the 1960s. Potential growth has been slowing for the past 30 years, and this slowdown is expected to continue.

The most comprehensive measure of productivity growth — real GDP per employee — should grow an average of 1.2% per year over the 10–year projection period. The 1960s witnessed stellar growth in output per man–hour, which averaged 2.9% per year. Productivity growth slumped in the 1970s. Since that time productivity growth has averaged 1.1% per year. WEFA believes productivity growth will quicken modestly in the future.

Government Policy The government sector share of GDP will decline over the next several years, before stabilizing. Spending will slowly be reigned in to reduce the size of the budget deficit. Total government purchases (including state and local) as a share of GDP will decline, from 18.7% in 1995 to 17.5% by 2002, and further decline to 17.0% by 2020. This reduction in the government's share of the economy is concentrated in the federal sector, and the reduction will be concentrated in the defense sector. Scaling back the U.S. defense establishment will result in a 2.4% average annual decline in real defense consumption expenditure between 1995 and 2000. This will reduce the defense share of GDP to only 3.3% by 2000.

WEFA expects the federal budget deficit to stabilize near its current level for several years. The deficit is much lower than its Fiscal Year (FY) 1991 peak — $268 billion on a unified budget basis. The deficit declined to $107 billion in FY 1996 because of assets sales, and will not remain quite so low. Restraint on spending will help the deficit remain near $115 billion through 2000, but rising transfer payments halt further progress on deficit reduction.

We are aware that deficit projections are inherently based more on political, rather than economic, forecasts. Our projections are based on a belief that the public will not accept an escalating debt–to–GDP ratio indefinitely, but we do not explicitly assume major changes to the major transfer payment programs — Social Security, Medicare and Medicaid. Some efforts to reduce the budget deficit are likely. Even so, growing transfer payments make elimination of the deficit extremely difficult.

In addition to reductions in discretionary spending, any effort to control the deficit must include curbs on the growth in health care spending. We have assumed that growth in health care spending is reduced over the next several years through a combination of legislative actions.

Monetary Policy and Financial Markets The Fed will continue to pursue a monetary policy that maintains vigilance against inflation and provides sufficient growth in the money supply to ensure moderate economic growth. A stricter monetary regime would lead to lower inflation, but at the expense of lost output. In order to achieve the "zero inflation rate" that some members of the Federal Reserve Board have advocated, deflation in goods markets would be necessary to offset rising prices of services in such areas as health care. It seems unlikely that the Fed will attempt to implement such a restrictive policy.

Short– and long–term rates are past their peaks for this business cycle. As actual GDP growth recedes to its potential rate of growth, and inflation remains under control, the Fed will gradually reduce short–term interest rates. Long–term interest rates will decline as well. The yield on 30–year Treasuries will begin a steady long–term. Real long–term interest rates will decline, from the more than 4% levels of recent years to near 3%.

Oil Prices After exhibiting weakness in 1993 and 1994, oil prices jumped by more than 10% in 1995. Tension in Iraq, low inventories, and strong demand have pushed oil prices almost 20% higher in 1996. This latest rise in oil prices is expected to be temporary, as Iraq has begun exporting oil, inventories will be adjusted, and non–OPEC production will increase. As a result, oil prices are expected to decline in 1997. Adequate worldwide supply of oil should restrain oil price increases through 2000, with real oil prices rising 7% from 1995 to 2000. The pace of escalation remains moderate after 2000: real oil prices should increase by 1.1% per year from 2000 to 2006.

Foreign Assumptions WEFA maintains a foreign real GDP index based on the GDP growth of the United States' 18 largest trading partners, applying the bilateral trade weights used in the Morgan Guaranty dollar index. Foreign GDP growth will outstrip U.S. growth over the forecast period. Foreign growth will be faster as productivity levels between the United States and the rest of the world converge. Growth outside the United States will decelerate near the end of the projection period as a result of slower population increases. Nevertheless, foreign GDP grows at a rate that is 0.6 percentage point faster than U.S. GDP growth. U.S. export growth will benefit as foreign demand improves faster than U.S. demand does.

The Dollar On the basis of the real Morgan Guaranty index of 18 trade–weighted currencies, the dollar fell 28.6%

between its 1985 peak and 1991. By 1995 the dollar had fallen a further 6.9% from its 1991 level. The dollar has already recovered much of the ground lost in late 1994 and early 1995. Many economists point to purchasing power parity estimates, which indicate that the dollar is undervalued by as much as 50%. This suggests that the dollar may rise. WEFA expects the dollar to continue its recovery from its previous fall, rising through 1998. After declining from 1998 through 2003, the dollar should remain relatively stable in real terms.

Consumption Consumer spending in the long term is primarily determined by the growth of real permanent income, demographic influences, and changes in relative prices. The share of personal consumption expenditures in GDP will stabilize over the forecast interval. Consumer spending as a share of GDP has increased since the early 1980s, reaching 68.0% in 1993. Consumer spending should maintain its share of the overall economy over the forecast horizon. Real consumption expenditure growth averages 2.2% per year through 2006.

The share of consumption devoted to services will rise, while that for goods will fall over the forecast period.

Housing The long-term outlook for housing is based on demographic factors. Underpinning the demand for housing is the growth in the number of households (as opposed to simply population growth). Despite slower population growth, housing starts will rise in the long run, as the number of households increases faster than the overall population does. Housing starts peaked in 1972, at 2.36 million units. The underlying level of starts has moderated to the 1.3 to 1.4 million range in the last several years as a result of the slower growth in the prime

home-buying 25–34 age population cohort. Housing starts are projected to average 1.32 million during the 1990s before they expand to 1.54 million in the 2000s.

Business Fixed Investment The long-run prospects for business fixed investment are very positive. Business continues to strive toward reducing the labor portion of total costs and enhancing productivity growth in order to remain competitive in international markets. Real business fixed investment is projected to rise by average annual rates of 3.9% over the next ten years.

The composition of investment will continue to change in the forecast period: structures' share of investment will decline modestly, while equipment's share rises. This is a continuation of a long-standing trend. One of the fastest growing sectors of the U.S. economy will be producers' durable equipment, concentrated in information processing equipment. The development of advanced electronics, which promise a high rate of return on investment, has led to a massive change in business' priorities for investment.

International Trade The improvement in the United States' real unit labor costs relative to the rest of the industrialized world will promote export expansion and an improvement in the U.S. net export position. A competitive value of the dollar and stronger rest-of-world growth (relative to U.S. growth) will make exports one of the fastest rising components of GDP. WEFA projects that real exports will expand at an average annual rate of 5.4% from 1995 to 2006. By contrast real imports will grow at an average annual rate of 5.0% from 1995 to 2006.

OVERVIEW TABLE 1: FORECAST SUMMARY

	IV 96	I 97	II 97	III 97	IV 97	I 98	II 98	1996	1997	1998	1999	2000	2001	2002
ECONOMIC ACTIVITY														
Real GDP, Bil Chained $92	6994	7046	7086	7119	7147	7179	7213	6907	7100	7231	7399	7562	7720	7884
% Change, SAAR	3.8	3.0	2.3	1.8	1.6	1.8	1.9	2.4	2.8	1.8	2.3	2.2	2.1	2.1
% Change, Year Ago	3.1	3.4	2.8	2.7	2.2	1.9	1.8							
GDP, Bil $	7716	7816	7914	7998	8072	8159	8244	7576	7950	8293	8693	9105	9534	9994
% Change, SAAR	5.3	5.3	5.1	4.3	3.7	4.4	4.2	4.4	4.9	4.3	4.8	4.7	4.7	4.8
% Change, Year Ago	5.0	5.2	4.9	5.0	4.6	4.4	4.2							
Final Sales, Bil Chained $92	6976	7031	7069	7100	7128	7158	7194	6892	7082	7213	7379	7542	7700	7864
% Change, SAAR	4.9	3.2	2.2	1.8	1.6	1.7	2.0	2.7	2.8	1.8	2.3	2.2	2.1	2.1
Industrial Prod, 1992=100	117.1	118.2	119.1	119.7	119.9	119.9	120.3	115.2	119.2	120.8	123.9	127.0	130.0	133.2
% Change, SAAR	4.5	4.0	3.0	1.9	0.9	0.1	1.3	2.8	3.5	1.3	2.6	2.5	2.4	2.4
% Change, Year Ago	3.9	4.5	3.7	3.3	2.4	1.5	1.0							
Employment, Estab, Mil	120.5	121.2	121.8	122.4	122.9	123.4	123.7	119.55	122.10	123.96	125.68	127.41	129.10	130.82
% Change, SAAR	1.8	2.4	2.0	1.8	1.6	1.5	1.3	2.0	2.1	1.5	1.4	1.4	1.3	1.3
Capacity Utilization, Mfg, %	82.3	82.3	82.3	82.2	82.2	82.1	82.1	82.1	82.2	82.1	82.1	82.1	82.1	82.0
Civilian Unemployment Rate, %	5.3	5.3	5.3	5.3	5.3	5.4	5.5	5.4	5.3	5.5	5.6	5.6	5.6	5.6
Lt Vehicle Sales, Mil, BEA	14.8	15.5	15.0	14.7	14.5	14.5	14.6	15.0	14.9	14.7	15.2	15.6	15.6	15.6
Auto Sales, Mil, BEA	8.0	8.6	8.7	8.4	8.2	8.4	8.2	8.5	8.5	8.5	8.8	9.0	9.1	9.1
Lt Truck Sales, Mil, BEA	6.8	6.9	6.3	6.3	6.3	6.2	6.4	6.5	6.5	6.2	6.5	6.6	6.5	6.6
Housing Starts, Mil	1.42	1.44	1.45	1.42	1.42	1.40	1.39	1.47	1.43	1.39	1.42	1.39	1.39	1.40
Disp Pers Income, Bil $92	5147.5	5206.9	5238.9	5265.7	5288.7	5329.3	5356.2	5088.6	5250.1	5371.1	5487.0	5607.4	5732.2	5859.3
% Change, SAAR	2.6	4.7	2.5	2.1	1.8	3.1	2.0	2.9	3.2	2.3	2.2	2.2	2.2	2.2
Personal Saving Rate, %	5.1	5.3	5.1	4.9	4.8	5.0	5.0	4.9	5.0	5.0	4.9	4.8	5.0	5.1
After-Tax Corp Profits, Bil $	408.2	417.1	417.5	423.8	424.5	420.3	415.3	406.8	420.7	418.8	440.8	457.5	475.2	496.1
% Change, Year Ago	5.9	2.0	2.3	5.4	4.0	0.8	-0.5	7.0	3.4	-0.5	5.3	3.8	3.9	4.4
Fed Cur Surplus, NIPA, Bil $	-105.9	-124.3	-109.5	-105.9	-109.2	-127.0	-125.2	-127.2	-112.2	-124.1	-110.6	-99.4	-99.3	-97.9
Fed Surplus, Unified, Bil $	-237.3	-275.1	198.7	-122.2	-247.5	-277.9	183.0	-110.6	-111.5	-123.4	-113.4	-102.2	-102.1	-100.8
COMPONENTS OF GDP														
Consumption Expend, Bil $92	4732.5	4792.3	4831.5	4864.2	4891.3	4913.9	4940.4	4690.7	4844.8	4953.0	5064.0	5178.6	5287.0	5396.1
% Change, SAAR	3.4	5.1	3.3	2.7	2.2	1.9	2.2	2.5	3.3	2.2	2.2	2.3	2.1	2.1
Nonres Fixed Invest, Bil $92	792.0	811.4	819.8	826.4	832.6	839.7	847.0	766.9	822.5	851.1	884.2	913.5	940.3	967.7
% Change, SAAR	5.5	10.2	4.2	3.3	3.1	3.5	3.5	7.4	7.3	3.5	3.9	3.3	2.9	2.9
Prod Dur Equip, Bil $92	593.7	608.1	615.4	621.8	627.8	634.4	640.5	578.6	618.3	644.1	672.8	700.1	726.5	753.8
% Change, SAAR	-0.9	10.0	4.9	4.2	3.9	4.3	3.9	8.3	6.9	4.2	4.5	4.1	3.8	3.8
Structures, Bil $92	199.8	204.8	206.0	206.5	207.0	207.7	208.9	190.0	206.1	209.6	214.9	218.2	220.2	222.1
% Change, SAAR	26.0	10.4	2.4	0.9	0.9	1.3	2.5	4.9	8.5	1.7	2.5	1.5	0.9	0.9
Residential Invest, Bil $92	276.6	279.9	282.6	282.2	281.6	279.8	277.3	276.8	281.6	276.7	283.4	284.5	286.3	289.3
% Change, SAAR	-1.7	4.9	3.9	-0.6	-0.9	-2.5	-3.5	5.3	1.7	-1.7	2.4	0.4	0.6	1.0
Chg Bus Inventories, Bil $92	17.3	15.4	17.7	18.8	18.8	20.5	18.5	14.0	17.6	18.1	19.2	19.6	20.0	19.9
Farm	-2.3	2.8	1.4	0.7	0.6	0.4	0.2	-3.6	1.3	-0.2	0.3	0.3	0.7	0.8
Nonfarm	19.3	12.6	16.3	18.1	18.2	20.1	18.2	17.1	16.3	18.3	18.9	19.3	19.3	19.1
Gov Cons & Invest, Bil $92	1273.4	1274.9	1274.5	1275.6	1277.6	1279.4	1280.7	1270.6	1275.7	1282.2	1295.6	1312.3	1328.9	1346.7
% Change, SAAR	-0.8	0.5	-0.1	0.3	0.6	0.6	0.4	0.8	0.4	0.5	1.0	1.3	1.3	1.3
Net Exports, Bil $92	-98.4	-129.4	-141.8	-151.2	-158.2	-157.8	-153.8	-113.6	-145.1	-152.7	-148.2	-145.5	-139.3	-131.2
Exports, Bil $92	862.9	858.5	863.8	870.4	879.8	894.7	911.6	825.9	868.1	919.4	977.6	1036.5	1098.4	1164.5
% Change, SAAR	25.0	-2.0	2.5	3.1	4.4	7.0	7.8	5.1	5.1	5.9	6.3	6.0	6.0	6.0
Imports, Bil $92	961.3	987.8	1005.6	1021.6	1038.0	1052.5	1065.5	939.5	1013.3	1072.1	1125.9	1182.0	1237.7	1295.6
% Change, SAAR	3.3	11.5	7.4	6.5	6.6	5.7	5.0	6.4	7.8	5.8	5.0	5.0	4.7	4.7
$ Exch Rate, MG18, % Chg, SAAR	3.2	21.9	6.4	0.0	-5.6	-5.7	-5.8	4.9	6.8	-3.2	-0.5	-0.8	-0.9	-0.3
Real Exch Rate, % Chg, SAAR	4.3	20.2	5.3	-2.0	-7.0	-6.2	-7.1	6.6	6.4	-4.4	-1.8	-1.9	-1.7	-0.8
% Change, Year Ago	6.3	8.1	7.5	6.6	3.6	-2.6	-5.6							
Current Account Bal, Bil $	-165.5	-179.0	-179.0	-183.0	-199.5	-202.1	-207.5	-165.1	-185.1	-206.1	-208.0	-203.0	-194.8	-177.7
INFLATION AND PRODUCTIVITY														
GDP Price Index, % Chg, SAAR	1.8	2.2	2.7	2.4	2.1	2.5	2.3	2.1	2.3	2.4	2.4	2.5	2.6	2.6
% Change, Year Ago	2.1	2.1	2.2	2.3	2.4	2.5	2.3							
CPI, All Urban, % Chg, SAAR	3.3	2.1	2.2	2.2	2.5	2.8	2.8	2.9	2.5	2.6	2.8	2.8	2.7	2.8
% Change, Year Ago	3.2	2.9	2.6	2.5	2.2	2.4	2.6							
CPI, Core, % Chg, SAAR	2.6	2.4	2.7	2.8	2.7	2.6	2.5	2.7	2.6	2.6	2.6	2.7	2.7	2.7
PPI, Fin Goods, % Chg, SAAR	3.8	-0.4	1.0	1.3	2.8	1.2	2.4	2.6	1.6	2.0	2.2	1.7	1.8	2.0
% Change, Year Ago	3.0	2.1	1.7	1.4	1.2	1.6	1.9							
PPI, Core, % Chg, SAAR	2.2	1.0	1.5	0.6	1.3	2.2	1.2	1.5	1.2	1.4	1.6	1.4	1.6	1.8
PPI, Ind Comm, % Chg, Year Ago	1.9	1.2	0.1	-0.2	-0.9	-1.4	-0.5							
Comp per Hour, % Chg, SAAR	3.6	3.7	3.7	3.8	3.8	3.9	3.8	3.7	3.7	3.8	3.8	3.8	3.9	3.9
Output per Hour, % Chg, SAAR	1.2	0.2	0.4	0.8	0.8	1.0	1.0	0.8	0.5	0.9	1.1	1.2	1.2	1.2
Unit Labor Cost, % Chg, SAAR	2.6	3.4	3.3	3.0	3.0	2.9	2.9	2.9	3.1	2.9	2.6	2.6	2.7	2.7
FINANCIAL MARKETS														
Treasury Rates														
T-Bill Rate, 3-Month, %	5.0	5.1	5.4	5.8	6.0	6.0	5.8	5.0	5.6	5.7	5.0	4.9	4.9	4.8
T-Note Rate, 10-Year, %	6.3	6.6	6.8	6.9	7.0	6.9	6.8	6.4	6.8	6.8	6.4	6.2	6.1	6.0
T-Bond Rate, 30-Year, %	6.6	6.8	7.1	7.2	7.2	7.2	7.0	6.7	7.1	6.9	6.6	6.4	6.2	6.1
Federal Funds Rate, %	5.3	5.3	5.7	6.2	6.3	6.3	6.0	5.3	5.8	5.9	5.1	5.0	5.0	5.0
Prime Comm Bank Rate, %	8.3	8.3	8.7	9.2	9.3	9.3	9.0	8.3	8.8	8.9	8.1	8.0	8.0	8.0
Moody Aaa Seasoned Bond Rate, %	7.2	7.4	7.8	7.9	8.0	7.9	7.8	7.4	7.8	7.7	7.4	7.2	7.1	7.0
Money Supply (M2), % Chg, SAAR	5.1	4.1	5.4	4.9	4.8	4.4	3.9	4.9	4.6	4.4	4.7	4.7	4.8	4.9

World Economic Outlook

The world economy is expected to continue to expand at a moderate pace, with stable growth in the major industrial economies, and an acceleration in economic activity in Latin America and Africa offsetting somewhat slower growth in the Pacific Basin. Global output growth should gradually rise toward 4% by 1998. Modest world growth, strong global competition, and subdued oil and commodity prices should ensure that inflation remains quiescent.

A renewed acceleration in economic growth in the United States has finally forced the Fed to make a pre–emptive strike against inflation. The Fed funds rate is expected to rise to 6.25% by the end of 1997 to slow growth to a sustainable pace. By early 1998, we expect year–on–year real GDP growth to have dropped below 2%, allowing the Fed to begin to ease up on interest rates.

In Japan, robust growth in the fourth quarter of 1996 will also be followed by a slowdown this year, as tax increases and public spending cuts take effect. However, net exports will lend increasing support to activity as the effects of the yen's depreciation feed through, and the Bank of Japan will maintain an accommodative monetary stance throughout 1997. The support from these sources and the strong finish to 1996 mean that real GDP growth should still average about 2% this year.

The economic recovery in Western Europe continues to follow an uneven course, with another deceleration in growth at the end of last year. Sharp slowdowns in Germany and France and a drop in output in Italy outweighed stronger growth in the United Kingdom, Spain and Sweden. Early indicators for the first quarter are mixed, but the recovery is still expected to gradually gather pace in response to continued low interest rates and improving competitiveness. However, fiscal consolidation to meet European Monetary Union (EMU) qualifying criteria will remain a restrictive influence.

The decision to hold an early parliamentary election in France has increased the risk that EMU may be delayed, but the odds still seem to be in favor of it going ahead on schedule. The political drive behind the project is such that the flexibility allowed in the Maastricht treaty will be fully exploited to try to ensure that the project starts on time. We expect at least eight countries (Austria, Belgium, Finland, France, Germany, Ireland, Luxembourg, and the Netherlands) will participate in the first wave, with other countries being admitted at a later date.

World Economy: Modest Increase In World Growth And Inflation

Economic growth rates in the major industrial economies continued to diverge at the end of 1996 and into early 1997. The United States, Japan, and the United Kingdom experienced an acceleration in growth, while Canada managed to broadly maintain the stronger pace of expansion evident since mid–1996. However, growth in the continental European economies was generally weaker.

The next twelve months should see some convergence in the rates of economic growth of the developed economies, reflecting, in part, their different stages in the business cycle. The current upturn in the United States is now entering its seventh year, and there are signs that the tightening labor market is beginning to exert upward pressure on wage costs. The economy has clearly been expanding at too rapid a pace for the Fed's comfort, and this has resulted in a pre–emptive strike against inflation. Given the momentum that the economy has built up over the past six months, further interest rate rises are likely, which will slow growth to a more sustainable pace in the second half of 1997.

The United Kingdom faces a similar risk of overheating, having moved into a recovery phase some twelve months after the United States. Monetary policy in the United Kingdom has been on hold since last October, due to the imminent election; but a post–election rise in interest rates is firmly in the cards. In Japan and mainland Europe, however, the economic recoveries are of more recent vintage, and more fragile. Fiscal retrenchment will impose a constraint on economic growth in both regions. But monetary policies will remain accommodative throughout 1997, and, together with the benefits of more competitive exchange rates, should promote a strengthening in economic growth during the course of the year.

One of the key developments in the world economy over the past two years has been the resurgence of the U.S. dollar and the U.K. pound. Both currencies have appreciated considerably, particularly over the past six months and especially against the Japanese yen and German mark. This surge reflects the relatively strong growth and positive interest rate differentials of the U.S. and U.K. economies, as well as both currencies' status as safe havens from the uncertainties of the new European currency and the fragility of the Japanese banking system.

In conjunction with a loosening of domestic monetary policy, these exchange rate adjustments have played a key role in reviving economic activity in Japan and in continental Europe. Exports have become one of the main driving forces of economic growth in Japan and many European economies due, in part, to the consequent improvement in their competitiveness. At the same time, the appreciation of the dollar and pound sterling has helped to ease inflationary pressures in the United States and United Kingdom by cutting import costs and by exerting strong competitive pressures on the traded goods sector. This should serve to limit the degree of monetary tightening in these economies in the coming months.

While these shifts in exchange rates appear to have been largely beneficial, there are still some causes for concern. The continued strengthening of the dollar and pound appears to have pushed them into overvalued positions against the Yen and DM. This may exert a stronger than expected contractionary influence on the U.S. and U.K.

The key role that exchange rate adjustments have played in dragging Japan and continental Europe out of recession also calls into question the desirability of the European Union economies irrevocably locking their exchange rates together in 1999.

Japan

Because of the strength during the fourth quarter of 1996 and a likely further pick–up in the first quarter of this year, Japan's economic growth for 1997 is likely to be a moderate 2.0%, in spite of an expected 4.2% decline in real public investment. Output growth is forecast to accelerate to 3.2% in 1998, supported by stronger consumer spending, a rebound in housing investment, and rising business investment.

Although economic growth is forecast to regain momentum next year, the strength of this recovery will still be weaker than the historical average. Consequently, there will still be sufficient slack in the economy to keep inflation in check. Consumer price inflation will gradually increase in 1997 in response to a weaker yen and an increase in the consumption tax rate, but is still forecast to average only 1.6% and 1.5% in 1997 and 1998, respectively.

Western Europe

After expanding by only 1.7% in 1996, real GDP in Western Europe as a whole is forecast to grow by 2.3% in 1997 and 2.5% in 1998, with the strongest expansion this year occurring in Ireland, Finland, Portugal, and Norway. Over the medium term, Western European economic growth should match the long–term trend rate of 2% to 2.5%. Consumer price inflation, which has generally remained on a downward trend since the beginning of the year, is forecast to edge up slightly as the recent currency depreciation feeds through and economic activity picks up. Consumer price inflation in Western Europe (excluding Turkey) averaged 2.4% in 1996, the lowest rate since 1961, and is forecast to rise by 2.2% in 1997 before accelerating back to 2.4% in 1998.

Asia–Pacific

Economic growth in the Pacific Basin is expected to slow further this year, as the rise in U.S. interest rates and the weak yen increase borrowing costs and erode competitiveness. But growth will continue to outstrip that of other regions. The expected recovery in Asia has been hit by a double whammy — rising U.S. interest rates and the continued weakness of the yen. After a dismal performance in 1996, most Asian economies were looking forward to a change for the better this year. The Japanese recovery was expected to gain strength and the yen stabilize. Developing Asia was expected to emerge from an unspectacular 1996 and post respectable growth in exports and output this year. But the persistent weakness of the yen and another expected hike in U.S. interest rates are likely to dampen the recovery, more so in some countries than in others.

To make matters worse, the region–wide slowdown in 1996 revealed serious structural weaknesses in Asian economies — an over–exposed financial sector threatened by an overheated property market and declining stock prices. In the booming first half of the nineties, problem assets could be easily covered by banks flush with cash. But the slowdown in 1996 revealed banks wrestling with mounting bad loans to large companies and property developers.

Economic growth in countries hit by a breakdown of the financial sector will suffer more from rising U.S. interest rates than those where the financial sector is relatively stable, because climbing U.S. interest rates add to the already rising cost of borrowing and raising capital. The weak yen will add to the distress by limiting the room to grow by expanding exports.

Latin America

In Latin America, growth is forecast to accelerate from 3.6% in 1996 to 4.6% this year and 5.2% in 1998. Most economies, apart from Chile and Ecuador, are expected to achieve higher growth rates this year than last, and Chile, despite an anticipated deceleration, is still expected to remain the most rapidly growing economy in Latin America. Over the medium term (1999–2002) regional economic growth is expected to average 5.0%. At the turn of the century, however, we expect slowdowns in Argentina, Brazil, Colombia, Peru, and Venezuela due to "post–election" adjustments.

Despite the strengthening upswing, consumer price inflation is generally expected to decelerate further both this year and next. Venezuela, the only three–digit inflation country in 1996, will see its inflation drop significantly. Ecuador will be the only country with rising inflation in the region in 1997.

Middle East and Africa

In the Gulf region, higher oil revenues have improved external accounts and budget balances, but growth is still sluggish. In the Levant, apart from Israel, growth remains on an upward trend. In Africa, favorable weather and ongoing policy reforms have improved growth prospects. But, the burden of servicing external debt and inability to attract significant amounts of direct foreign investment remain a bottleneck.

Eastern Europe

Eastern Europe should show a further modest improvement in economic growth. Weaker growth in the Czech Republic is expected to be offset by stronger growth in Hungary and sustained expansion in Poland, Slovenia, and Slovakia.

Russia

This year may see the long–awaited revival in economic activity in Russia. The economy's poor performance in 1996 has motivated President Yeltsin to re–energize the stalled market reform process.

Forecast Highlights:
The High Growth Industries

The industries that WEFA forecasts to have the most rapid growth over the next ten years, listed below, fall into the following general categories:

- High-tech industries, where continuing technological change and consumer and business acceptance will bring rapid growth, particularly in volume terms.

- Health services, medical instruments, and drugs, which will benefit from an aging population, advances in scientific research, and world-leading quality that will draw patients from around the globe.

- Air transportation, which will continue to grow modestly in its domestic passenger business, but more rapidly in international flights and in freight.

- Business, engineering, and management services, which will benefit from outsourcing and further expansion into foreign markets.

- In general, services rank higher in the sales ranking, with the exception of telecommunication services, where deregulation and technological change will put downward pressure on prices. Price increases will be considerably more modest for the goods-producing industries, which will continue to have limited pricing flexibility due to expanding global supply. The high-tech goods and services will also face weak pricing, and therefore rank lower in current-dollar sales than in real sales.

Top Sales Growth Industries

	Avg Annual % Change 1996-2006
Health Services	9.5
Electronic Components	9.1
Business Services	8.3
Air Transportation	7.8
Medical Instruments and Supplies	7.0
Computers and Office Equipment	6.9
Engineering and Management Services	6.9
Insurance Services	6.7
Communication Equipment	6.5
Drugs, Soaps, and Toiletries	6.2
Special Industry Machinery	6.1
General Industrial Machinery	6.1

Top Real Sales Growth Industries

	Avg Annual % Change 1996-2006
Electronic Components	9.1
Computers and Office Equipment	8.1
Health Services	5.5
Telecommunications Services	4.5
Communication Equipment	4.3
Air Transportation	4.1
Business Services	3.8
Medical Instruments and Supplies	3.6
Drugs, Soaps, and Toiletries	3.5
Engineering and Management Services	3.3
General Industrial Machinery	3.3
Metalworking Machinery	3.2

Part 1: Agriculture, Mining, and Construction

Chapter 1:   Agricultural Crops

Wheat

The United States typically accounts for 10% to 12 % of global wheat production. Wheat is grown in nearly every state, but most of the acreage and production originates in the Plains and Pacific Northwest. In the 1996/97 crop year (June, 1996 to May, 1997), North Dakota, Kansas, Montana, and Washington accounted for roughly 45% of U.S. wheat acreage and production.

Wheat is not a homogeneous crop, but is divided first into winter wheat and spring wheat, and then into six classes, each with unique flour milling properties. Winter wheat is generally planted from August to November, remains dormant during the winter, and is harvested from late May to July. Spring wheat is planted in April and May and harvested in July and August. Spring wheat yields fewer bushels per acre than winter wheat, and is grown in northern regions where the winters are harsh. In 1996/97, winter wheat accounted for 69% of total wheat acreage and 65% of total production. Winter wheat typically accounts for an even larger share of acreage and production, but yields were poor in 1996/97 and record high wheat prices in 1995/96 resulted in high spring wheat acreage.

Acreage

Since 1975, wheat acreage has ranged between 65.5 and 88.3 million acres. Wheat acreage is determined by expected returns for wheat production relative to other crops, as well as weather prior to and during planting. Grain prices climbed to record levels in the 1970s and early 1980s, and wheat acreage expanded. Less than 50 million acres were planted to wheat in 1970/71, but planted area and production reached a record 88.3 million acres and 2.79 billion bushels in 1981/82.

U.S. wheat exports collapsed in the mid 1980s, falling by nearly 50% between 1981/82 and 1985/86 as a result of a global recession, a strong U.S. Dollar, and stiff export competition. Inventories grew substantially, and prices plummeted to below $2.50 per bushel. The United States made several policy changes aimed at reducing grain inventories. Price supports were lowered to make U.S. wheat more competitive on the world market, and the Conservation Reserve Program (CRP) came into existence as a long–term land retirement program. These programs were effective, and in the late 1980s exports also recovered. Acreage fell to 65.5 million acres in 1988/89, with 11 million acres of wheat land retired under the CRP. Agricultural policy changes resulted in less stock holding by the government, and it made the U.S. wheat market more competitive in the world market.

Since 1990/91, wheat acreage has ranged from 69.2 to 77.0 million acres. Wheat stocks have continued to decline, caused by the government's exit from the business of holding wheat inventories and by poor yields in 1991/92 and 1995/96. Farm level wheat prices recovered to between $3.00 and $4.00 per bushel by 1994/95. The next year saw lower acreage, a spring freeze which damaged winter wheat, and strong exports, including large shipments to China. With wheat inventories equaling only 60 days of use, prices set a new record, averaging $4.55 per bushel. High prices encouraged additional plantings in the U.S. and abroad, which, along with favorable weather, resulted in record or near–record spring wheat crops in the United States, Argentina, Australia, Canada, and the European Union (E.U.). Countries that typically import wheat also experienced production increases, which lowered import requirements. Thus, high prices did their job by promoting increased production, which helped to partially rebuild wheat inventories.

Farm Policy

Prior to April 1996, government agricultural payments were linked directly to production, and expected returns for growing wheat were based on wheat prices and government programs. The wheat program insulated farmers' incomes by protecting them from low prices and yields. In order to participate in the program, farmers were often required to idle a portion of their land and meet other requirements, including conservation measures. Since the late 1980s, up to 23 million acres of wheat land were idled each year. Farmers had little flexibility in planting, because shifting acreage to alternative crops meant forfeiting government payments and reduced ability to receive future support.

Farm policy changed dramatically on April 4, 1996 when President Clinton signed the Federal Agriculture Improvement and Reform (FAIR) Act. The FAIR Act decoupled government support from production decisions. Farmers are now free to plant virtually any crop, and planting decisions do not influence government payments. Farmers will receive cash transition payments to help them adjust to the new policy environment, and the level of payments is set to decline through fiscal 2002 when the FAIR Act expires. On average, eligible wheat farmers will initially receive payments of $20 per acre, with payments declining to $14 per acre by the end of the period. Some form of income support is likely, even after the FAIR Act expires. The implications of the FAIR Act are substantial. Farmers now have the ability to shift land to crops that command the highest returns, and government payments are no longer part of the equation.

The sole remaining supply management policy is the CRP. The CRP was aimed at reducing the grain surpluses of the 1980s by retiring farmland for a period of 10 to 15 years. Since its inception, the Reserve has been transformed to focus on retiring land that offers the most environmental benefits. Enrollment in the CRP is capped at 36.4 million acres, a limit that was reached in the early 1990's. Roughly 11 million of these acres were previously planted to wheat and most of this land was located in the Plains. More than 21 million acres of land currently in the Reserve will expire in September 1997, and some of this land may return to production. Despite recent efforts to re-enroll CRP land and attract additional acres, it appears that on net several million acres will leave the CRP in the fall of 1997 and be available for planting in 1998/99. Because most CRP land is located in the Plains and was once wheat land, the level of the CRP has important implications for wheat area and, in the new era of planting flexibility, acreage of other crops.

Marketing Patterns

Wheat is either milled into flour for human consumption, used for seed, or fed to livestock. Food use is the most stable category of wheat use, accounting for roughly one-third of annual wheat consumption, or disappearance. Flour milling accounts for virtually all food use, with 45 pounds of flour produced from one bushel of wheat. Food use is relatively stable because flour is a high value product, with large changes in wheat prices translating into relatively small changes in flour consumption. The key determinants of flour, and consequently wheat food, use are income and population growth.

Seed use is a relatively small component of total wheat disappearance. Only about 5% of total disappearance is seed wheat, which fluctuates based on the number of wheat acres planted.

Feed use is a volatile category of wheat use, accounting from 2% to 20% of total disappearance. The amount of wheat fed to livestock depends on the demand for livestock feed, the quality of the wheat crop, and the price of wheat relative to prices of other feed grains. The feed value of wheat is roughly 5% higher than that of corn, the primary feed grain.

International Trade

The United States is one of five exporting countries that dominate world wheat trade. Exports generally account for 50% of U.S. wheat disappearance, but this share has varied from 42% to 68% during the last 20 years. Primary trading partners include Egypt, Japan, South Korea, Pakistan, the Philippines, China, Mexico, and the E.U. The Soviet Union was a major importer of wheat in the 1970s and 1980s, but purchases from its successor countries have since fallen sharply. China is now the major wildcard in the international wheat market, accounting for 11% of world trade in 1995/96 and expected to account for less than 4% of world trade in 1996/97.

The other major wheat exporters are the E.U., Canada, Australia, and Argentina. The United States harvests its wheat earlier in the year than the E.U. and Canada, opening a window of opportunity for exports before these competitors' wheat is available for shipment in late summer and early fall. Wheat from Australia and Argentina, on the other hand, is marketed on the world market in the late fall and early winter, before the U.S. harvest. In the case of Argentina, wheat is aggressively marketed during the winter in order to free up storage and transportation resources for the corn and soybean crops which are harvested in the spring.

The United States also imports wheat. Imports are a relatively small but growing component of U.S. wheat supplies. In the early 1980s, less than 3 million bushels of wheat were imported, but import shipments grew to nearly 110 million bushels in 1993/94. Most wheat imports in 1993/94 were from Canada, particularly durum and feed wheat, because U.S. prices were high relative to prices north of the Canadian border. Aggressive use of export subsidies by the United States pushed up domestic wheat prices and lowered international prices. Thus, Canadian wheat flowed south. Politicians from the Northern Plains successfully lobbied for voluntary restraints on Canadian wheat imports. U.S. imports have since fallen, but at roughly 90 million bushels forecast for 1996/97, imports remain high by historical standards. The agreement which restrained Canadian shipments to the U.S. has since expired, leaving the door open for a resumption of Canada imports and perhaps further trade disputes.

U.S. Outlook

Lower wheat production is forecast for 1997/98, but moderate growth is expected during the next ten years. Planted acreage is forecast to decline by more than six million acres in 1997/98 due to wheat's low price relative to alternative crops, planting flexibility provisions of the FAIR Act, and unfavorable weather conditions during planting. The decline in 1997/98 acreage should be partially offset in 1998/99 with a return to normal weather and with former CRP land coming back into wheat acreage. Further strength in planted acreage could come from rising wheat prices. A severe frost struck the Central and Southern Plains in April and dry weather conditions are raising concerns over wheat production in Europe and North Africa. On the demand side, exports are expected to recover in 1997/98 and food use is forecast to increase at about the rate of population growth.

Assuming normal weather, wheat production is expected to grow on the order of 2% per annum. Acreage and yields are expected to grow throughout the next ten years. Wheat acreage will get some additions and some subtractions from fluctuations in CRP acreage through the period. Wheat yields are expected to achieve average annual growth rates of 0.7%, after being stagnant during the last 10 years. Higher growth rates are possible if biotechnology research results in new varieties. Wheat is on the tail end of agriculture's biotechnology revolution, but new varieties are in the works that could result in double–digit yield gains. Future multilateral and bilateral trade agreements should raise U.S. export opportunities and spur additional wheat acreage and production. Farm policy reform in the E.U. will also affect U.S. wheat acreage and production.

The Corn Belt and Lake States are expected to account for a smaller proportion of wheat acreage, as farmers shift to corn and soybeans. Some acreage growth in the Southeast and Mississippi River Delta is expected because of growth in double–cropping practices. Higher wheat acreage is expected in the Plains, Mountain, and Pacific regions, mainly as a result of land expiring from the CRP. However, wheat acreage may decline in areas where alternative crops offer higher returns.

Wheat Supply and Use

Marketing Year	1995/96	1996/97	1997/98
Acreage & Yield			
Planted (Million Acres)	69.13	75.64	69.47
Harvested (Million Acres)	60.95	62.85	61.04
Yield (Bu/Acre)	35.80	36.29	37.72
Supply (Million Bushels)			
Beginning Stocks	507	376	452
Production	2,183	2,282	2,303
Imports	68	89	88
Total Supply	2,757	2,747	2,843
Disappearance (Million Bushels)			
Food & Industrial	884	902	911
Seed	104	102	98
Feed & Residual	152	299	235
Totals Domestic Use	1,140	1,304	1,244
Exports	1,241	990	1,121
Total Disappearance	2,381	2,294	2,365
Ending Stocks	376	452	478
Stocks/Use Ration (%)	15.79	19.70	20.21
Farm Level Price ($/Bu)	14.76	4.30	3.69

Wheat Prices and Stocks to Use Ratios

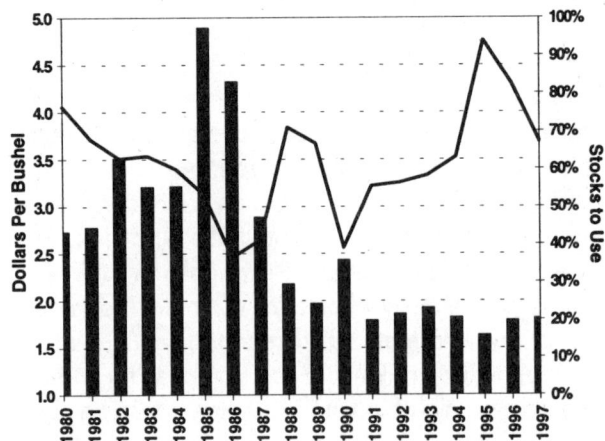

Wheat Planted Area

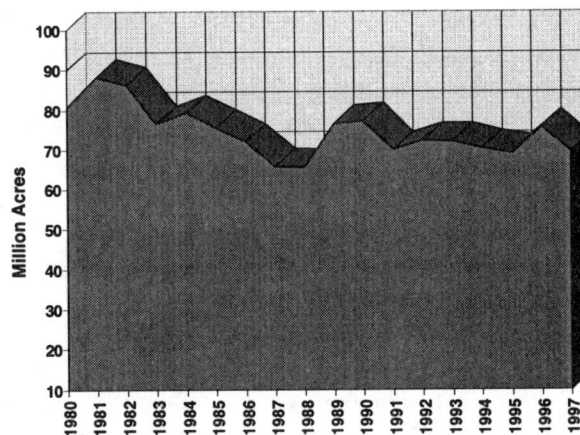

Wheat Use and Ending Inventories

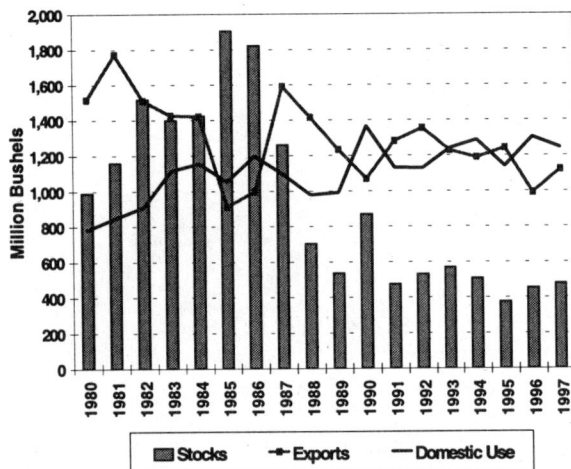

Rice

Rice production is relatively small in the United States as compared to other field crops. In 1995, rice planted acreage was 3.1 million acres, accounting for slightly under 1% of the total planted area for major crops. In 1996, rice planted acreage is expected to drop to 2.8 million acres. Production should not decline as much, as average yields should continue to trend upward.

The U.S. rice marketing year runs from August to July, with most of the crop planted in the spring and early summer and harvested in the summer and the early fall. Over 95% of U.S. rice production occurs in five states. Rice is produced mainly in the South, in the Delta region of the Mississippi and along the gulf coast, in Texas, Arkansas, Louisiana, and Mississippi. Rice is also produced in California.

Acreage

U.S. planted acreage for rice for the 1995/96 (August 1995 to July 1996) season was 3.1 million acres, with nearly 99% of that being harvested. This was only slightly below the record of 3.35 million acres, which was reached in the previous season. In the 1996/97 season, planted acreage is expected to drop off even further, slipping to 2.8 million acres. This 10% decline from the previous year is primarily due to changes in farm program provisions that separated program payments from the requirement to plant rice, resulting in greater planting flexibility. High prices for alternative field crops also contributed to this decline in rice acreage, and would have hurt more if rice prices had not remained relatively high. The decline in acreage is almost exclusively in long grain rice, which is estimated to be down 12% from its 1995/96 total. Among the six major rice producing states, only California, which grows primarily medium grain rice, increased its planted acreage in 1996/97.

Changes to the rice program provisions in the 1996 farm act were the most significant factors contributing to the lower planted acreage. Both target prices and deficiency payments were eliminated, and in their place annual contract payments for participants were created. These payments are completely independent of planting decisions made by farmers, giving them complete freedom to choose what crops to grow. Returns to rice production are expected to decline in the next few years, which should lead some farmers to plant alternative, lower cost crops such as soybeans or corn.

Despite the lower planted acreage in 1996/97, total domestic production should decline by only 1%. This is primarily due to expected record yields, which are forecast to reach 61.2 hundredweight (cwt) per acre, surpassing the 1994 record yield by 0.6 cwt/acre. Yields were especially high in the South, with all southern states except Missouri reporting record yields. Yield in Texas is forecast to be the highest among the southern states, at about 61.5 cwt/acre. California typically has the highest yields and should once again, with yields surpassing 76 cwt/acre in 1996/97. These record yields have three main sources.

- The first is the favorable weather that the southern states have experienced this year.

- The second is the increased plantings in Arkansas of medium grain rice, which typically has higher yields than long grain rice.

- Third, the increased acreage in California has helped pull up the national average yield, since California produces mostly medium grain rice.

Beginning stocks are also down in 1996/97, dropping from 31 million cwt the year before to 25 million cwt. This 20% decline is primarily due to extremely tight long grain rice stocks, which were only 10.1 million cwt, down from 14.5 million cwt the year before. Medium and short grain rice beginning stocks, however, were about the same as they were the previous year. The shift in planted acreage from some southern states, where long grain rice is grown, to California, where medium and short grain rice is more abundant, is a major reason for this shift. The stocks–to–use ratio for long grain rice in 1995/96 was 7.6%, while for medium and short grain rice it was 25.8%.

Imports

The United States imported 7.4 million cwt of rice in 1995/96, virtually the same amount as in the previous year. In 1996/97, however, rice imports are expected to jump to 10.8 million cwt. Although imports account for only a small portion of the total U.S. rice supply, imports have been increasing steadily over the past 15 years, rising from 0.2 million cwt in 1980/81 to 7.4 million cwt in 1995/96. Most of the rice imported into the United States is jasmine rice from Thailand, while the rest is basmati rice from India and Pakistan.

Total Supply

Overall, total supplies of rice in 1996/97 are forecast to be 207 million cwt, down 3% from the previous year. This is also nearly 25 million cwt lower than the peak year of 1994/95. The most significant drop is expected in Mississippi, where production is estimated to be down 15–20% in 1996/97.

Farm Policy

Unlike in the past, under the Federal Agriculture Improvement and Reform Act (FAIR Act), producers with a program crop base now receive transition payments regardless of what crops they plant. This means that planting decisions should be more responsive to expected profitability and market conditions. For rice farmers, this means alternative crops with less risk, such as corn and soybeans, may be planted now. Rice returns over total cash expenses are forecast to decline in 1997, dropping from $237 per planted acre last year to only $194. In the near term, rice returns are expected to continue to decline.

In the past, rice producers have been foremost among major program crop producers in the consistency of program participation. Since 1986, participation has been between 93 and 97% each year, regardless of acreage limitation requirements. In 1997, 99% of rice acreage was enrolled in the program. Base acreage enrolled in the rice program has consistently been 4.1–4.2 million acres each year in this decade. Rice acreage set aside and idled under the Rice Program totaled 210,000 acres in

1995/96, or 5% of the total base acreage. From 1985 through 1995, total government payments to rice program participants ranged from $400–$800 million annually. These payments were based on the difference between market price and target price levels. With the new provisions, government payments are much more consistent and will stay around $450 million. In 1997, payments are forecast to be $464 million.

Rice Supply and Use

Marketing Year	1995/96	1996/97	1997/98
Acreage & Yield			
Planted (Million Acres)	3.12	2.82	2.85
Harvested (Million Acres)	3.09	2.80	2.82
Yield (Bu/Acre)	56.21	61.21	59.90
Supply (Million Bushels)			
Beginning Stocks	31	25	24
Production	174	171	169
Imports	7.4	10.8	8.3
Total Supply	213	207	201
Disappearance (Million Bushels)			
Totals Domestic Use	105	105	107
Exports	82	78	68
Total Disappearance	188	183	175
Ending Stocks	25	24	26
Stocks/Use Ration (%)	13.3	13.1	15.1
Farm Level Price ($/Bu)	9.15	9.98	8.87

Marketing Patterns

Domestic demand for rice should increase at the same pace as population in the next few years. Since 1990/91, the domestic market, which has nearly doubled in the past 15 years, has been growing at about 3% annually. In 1995/96, total domestic use was a record 105.4 million cwt. In 1996/97, rice demand is expected to remain at prior year levels.

Domestic rice demand is composed of food use, brewer's use, seed, and residual. Out of the projected 105 million cwt of domestic disappearance (consumption) in 1996/97, a record 80 million cwt of rice is expected to be consumed as food. Food use has accounted for all of the growth in domestic demand, while brewer's use, seed, and residual categories have shown either no sustained growth or have experienced a decline.

Over the past 15 years there has been a gradual change in culinary preferences toward grain–based foods in the United States, which accounts for a share of the substantial growth in domestic rice food demand. Much of the expansion in rice's food use, however, is due to large increases in the Asian and Hispanic segments of the U.S. population over the past two decades. Per capita consumption of rice by these two groups exceeds the U.S. average.

Per capita consumption of rice has been growing steadily in the United States for the past decade. In 1984/85, 15.75 pounds per capita was consumed; in 1995/96, that figure rose to 25.65 pounds per capita. Almost all of this increase in per capita consumption comes from food use, which has risen 9.8 pounds per capita over that period, while brewer's use has remained steady at 4.1–4.2 pounds per capita each year. In the past three years, per capita consumption of rice has grown at a rate that is 8.6 times greater than the rate of population growth.

Brewer's use of rice is projected to be 15.1 million cwt in 1996/97, approximately the same as it has been the past five years. Peak brewer's use was in 1991/92, when 15.5 million cwt was used. The reasons for this slight decline include lower per capita beer consumption and the increased demand for light beers, which contain less rice than normal beers.

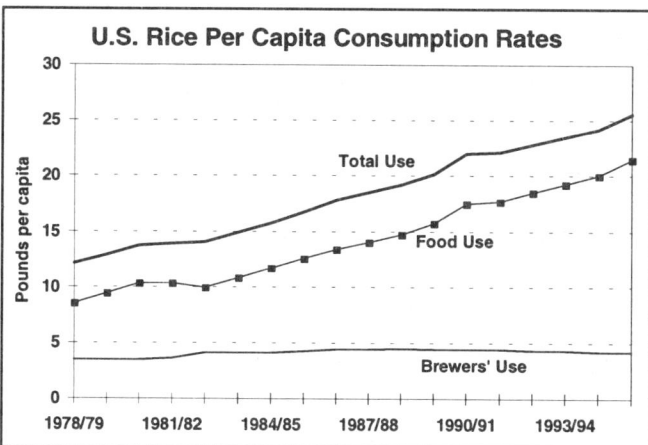

U.S. Rice Per Capita Consumption Rates

International Trade

Over 40% of total U.S. annual rice demand is accounted for by exports, making U.S. rice producers susceptible to factors that influence the international market. With domestic rice production forecast to decline in 1996/97, and the total supply of rice expected to do the same, rising domestic demand will hurt export levels. U.S. exports of rice for 1996/97 will also be dependent on the price premium of U.S. rice as compared to foreign competitors' prices, especially those in Thailand. Unlike many other rice exporting countries, the United States services a large, high–valued domestic market which pushes the U.S. price above international levels. As the price premium rises, price–sensitive markets such as Latin America and the Caribbean switch to lower cost rice. In 1995/96, rice exports from the United States totaled 82 million cwt. In 1996/97, rice exports are forecast to drop 5% to about 78 million cwt.

Latin America, the Middle East, and Europe are expected to remain the most important export markets for U.S. rice in the upcoming years. Canada and the Republic of South Africa are also slowly growing U.S. markets. In addition, under agreements reached at the Uruguay Round of the General Agreement on Tariffs and Trade (GATT), Japan and South Korea have begun to open their markets to rice imports. Japan's minimum access criteria will rise from 379,000 tons in 1995/96 to 758,000 tons in 2000/01. This is an increase of 76,000 tons annually for five years, pushing their imports from 4% of total domestic use in 1995/96 to 8% of total domestic use in 2000/01. In South Korea, 57,000 tons of rice was the minimum import requirement in 1995/96, or 1% of total domestic use. By 2004, imports should be increased to 205,000 tons, or 4% of total domestic use. The United States is expected to compete with Australia to supply medium grain rice to these newly opened East Asian markets.

The agreement also maintains access to the European Union (E.U.), one of the largest markets for U.S. rice. The E.U. has agreed to convert its import levies into tariffs and reduce them by at least 15% for every commodity, with an average across all commodities of 36% over six years. This should lead to increased trade in the rice market. Additionally, the E.U. has agreed to bind the margin between the import price and its support price so that protection will not be increased in the future. Overall,

U.S. rice producers should fare well under the Uruguay Round Agreement.

International Perspective

Global production and consumption in 1996/97 are both projected to reach record highs, with production slightly exceeding consumption, raising world ending stocks for the first time since 1990/91. Global consumption is estimated to be 377.9 million tons, approximately 2 million tons less than production. Ending stocks are expected to reach 49.5 million tons. However, the global stocks–to–use ratio for 1996/97 is forecast to be 13.1%, the lowest since 1974/75. This means that any disruption in consumption or production in a major importing or exporting country could have a large impact on international rice prices.

World rice trade is expected to decline in 1996/97 to 19.1 million tons, dropping 9% from the record 21 million of the previous year. However, this trade volume is still the second highest ever. The slowdown in world rice imports is a direct result of the large harvests experienced in most Asian countries this year. These large harvests have reduced import demand while simultaneously increasing export supplies. In 1995/96, Bangladesh, China, Indonesia, and Iran imported 8.3 million tons of rice; in 1996/97, they are expected to import only 4.3 million tons. Japan and South Korea, however, still have to complete their minimum access agreement purchases for this season, as mentioned earlier. International rice prices should fall some in 1996/97 due to large harvests and the subsequent rise in ending stock levels.

U.S. Rice Outlook

In 1996/97, U.S. rice planted acreage is expected to decline 10% to 2.8 million acres. This is due to some farmers opting to plant lower cost, lower risk, alternative crops such as soybeans or corn in place of rice. Production levels, however, should not suffer as much as record national yields are expected, topping last season's yield by nearly 5 cwt/acre. Beginning stocks are expected to decline nearly 20%. Despite import levels jumping from 7.4 million cwt in 1995/96 to 10.8 million cwt in 1996/97, the declines in beginning stocks and domestic production will lead to a lower total supply level than the previous year. This comes at a time when domestic consumption will have risen for the thirteenth consecutive year, and is forecast to continue to rise into the next century.

In the short term, WEFA expects domestic rice production to continue to decline. Planted acreage is forecast to increase slightly in 1997/98, but then decline in the following year and continue to trend downward in the following years. National yield levels should remain in the 59–61 cwt/acre range. Although imports of rice in the next few years are not expected to top the record 10.8 million cwt of this year, import levels will not fall off substantially. Import levels should rebound back to the 11 million cwt range by the year 2000.

The U.S. season average farm price for rice in 1995 was $9.15 per cwt. In the 1996/97 season, the average farm price should be closer to $10.00, as tight domestic long grain supplies and continued strong international demand for high–quality rice continue to put upward pressure on rice prices. Increasing domestic demand should also keep U.S. prices strong throughout the 1996/97 year. Because domestic demand continues to rise and production is forecast to decline slightly, rice prices should remain at high levels. These high U.S. rice prices should remain higher than international rice prices, thus adversely affecting U.S. export levels. In 1997/98, the rice price should fall slightly, dropping closer to 1995/96 levels. In the short term, rice prices should trend downward from the record high experienced this year.

Corn

Corn is the number one feed grain in the United States and in the world. Over the last ten years, the United States has produced an average of 7.6 billion bushels per year, and in 1994 the United States produced a record 10 billion bushels of corn. As incomes increase around the world, the demand for meat products increases as well. Corn is one of the primary components of animal feed, and the number of animals has been steadily increasing in the U.S. and throughout the world. With animal numbers and incomes increasing worldwide, it is not surprising that the second–largest segment of demand for U.S. corn is export markets. Growth in U.S. corn production and utilization over the last 20 years has been relatively steady, and it appears that continued growth in production will be necessary to meet the demand for corn in the future.

Acreage

Corn is grown throughout the United States, but most U.S. corn production occurs in a region bounded by Ohio to the east, Nebraska to the west, Missouri to the south, and Minnesota to the north. This region, known as the Corn Belt, produces approximately 80% of the corn grown in the U.S. Iowa and Illinois are the top producing states, typically accounting for more than a third of the U.S. corn crop.

Since 1950 the United States has planted between 60 and 85 million acres of corn. In the past, government programs have influenced planted acres dramatically by requiring producers who participate in government programs to idle land. By idling land, the government was attempting to manage supplies and in turn, support prices. The precedent for idling acreage was set in the 1930s. Idle acreage was heavily used in the late 1950s, the 1960s, and sporadically during the 1970s. During the 1980s and early 1990s, government set–asides continued to exist, but were replaced with more commodity–specific programs. The 1985 farm bill included the establishment of the Conservation Reserve Program (CRP), which by 1996 had idled more than 34 million acres of farm land for conservation purposes. Most recent farm legislation has moved away from the concept of acreage set–asides, and now the only way the government can idle acreage is through the CRP.

Under the 1996 Federal Agriculture Improvement and Reform Act (FAIR), producers have the freedom to plant crops as demanded by the markets. Historically, shortfalls in planted acreage were caused by a combination of weather problems and government set–asides. In the

future, annual corn plantings are not expected to fall below 80 million acres and could reach 84 million acres in some years, assuming favorable weather conditions.

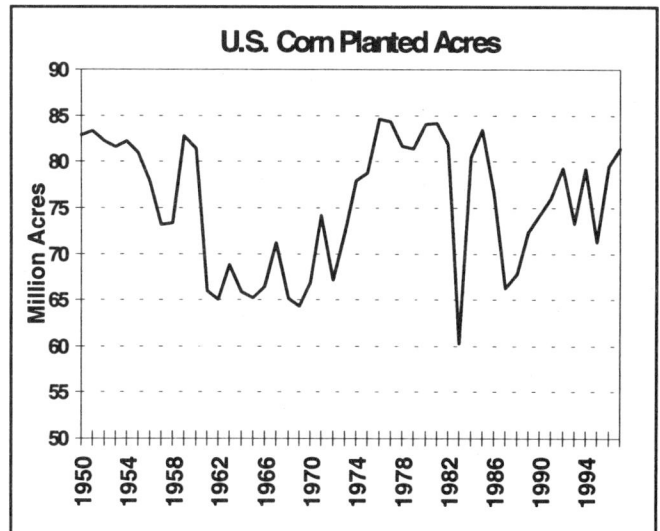

U.S. Corn Planted Acres

Despite relatively small fluctuations in corn acreage, corn supplies have steadily increased since 1950. Increases are largely due to improved yield technologies and management techniques. Yields are expected to increase over the next decade by at least 1 bushel per acre annually. Changes in weather patterns from year to year can cause yields to be either lower or higher than expected. It is important to take notice that annual corn supplies have become more variable over the last decade. Some of this variability is a function of government programs and the rest is weather related. As the use of chemical fertilizers and pesticides has increased over the past three decades, crop yields, although increasing, have become more sensitive to weather patterns. Some crop scientists believe new genetically altered seeds will reduce some of this variability in corn yields in the future, although they are not necessarily expected to improve yields.

U.S. Corn Supply

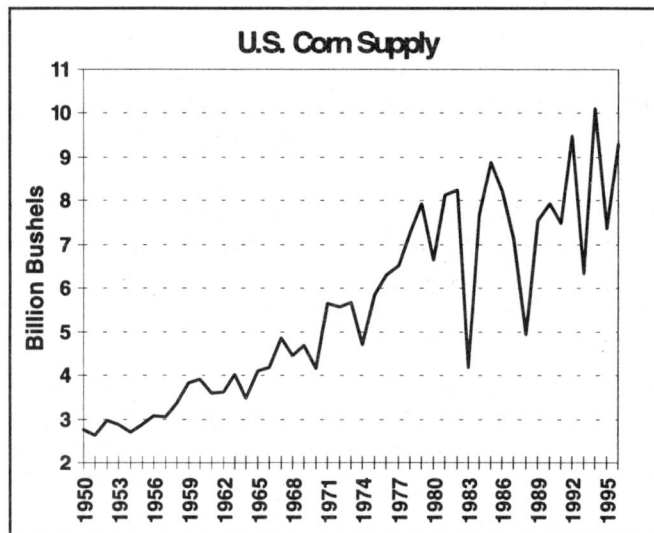

Farm Policy

As mentioned in the previous section, government farm programs have influenced corn acreage dramatically by requiring producers who participate in government programs to idle land. Farmers who participated in corn programs would receive a deficiency payment when prices fell below predetermined target prices. To control program cost, acreage set–asides were used to decrease supplies and increase market prices, which in turn would decrease deficiency payments. Since 1990, acres set aside have ranged between 4 and 8 million acres each year and deficiency payment levels have ranged between 50 and 70 cents per bushel.

Under the 1996 FAIR Act, producers have very few planting restrictions and no longer have to adhere to base acreage requirements and acreage reduction programs. Producers who have signed up for Production Flexibility Contracts under the new farm legislation will receive a transition payment that is decoupled from planting decisions. Corn producers will receive $16.5 billion in transition payments by 2002. Some form of government support for corn farmers is expected to continue after 2002, but it will likely be in the range of $1 billion to $2 billion per year.

Marketing Patterns

Corn used in animal feed rations represents, on average, 75% of domestic corn use. Over the last decade, corn used as feed has averaged 4.8 billion bushels a year. The 1994/95 crop year represented record feed use of over 5.5 billion bushels of corn. The crop year for corn starts September 1 and ends August 31. Feed and residual use of corn is positively related to the number of cattle on feed, as well as the number of hogs and poultry. Variation in corn feeding represents adjustments made by livestock and poultry producers in response to relative prices and the availability of corn and competing feed grains or feed ingredients. Feed substitutes for corn include sorghum, barley, oats, and wheat. Nonetheless, as the demand for meat animals continues to increase in the future, animal numbers will increase and corn for feed will be in high demand. Over the next five years, feed use of corn is expected to grow by 100 to 200 million bushels a year. Growth is expected to slow to 50 to 100 million bushels per year towards the latter part of the next decade.

Although accounting for only 20 to 25% of domestic use, food, seed, and industrial (FSI) use has been steadily increasing over the years. In general, corn FSI demand is related to population growth and the general health of the economy. However, legislation and government policies play a critical role in the use of corn for ethanol, and indirectly in the use of corn sweeteners.

Demand for corn sweeteners is stimulated indirectly by U.S. sugar policies. Import fees, duties, and restrictive import quotas used to administer the current sugar program keep domestic refined sugar prices at an artificially high level, making high–fructose corn syrup attractive to the soft drink industry and other users. Use of corn sweeteners will likely continue to grow, but future growth is unlikely to match the very rapid growth of the early 1980s. Future adjustments in sugar policy could lead to some shifts in corn sweetener use.

Fuel alcohol use of corn depends largely on a mix of government incentives, technology, and prices of corn and substitute products. An income tax credit of 54 cents per gallon of alcohol is allowed to blenders of alcohol and gasoline for use as a fuel, assuming a blend of 10% alcohol and 90% motor fuel. Use of corn for fuel has been growing rapidly in recent years. Such use is expected to sustain levels above 500 million bushels over the next few years, which represents between 4 and 6% of total corn use, up from less than 1% just 14 years ago. Production of fuel alcohol from corn and other feed grains has become more efficient, reducing the need for large government support and tax incentives. However, some government support, either directly or indirectly, to the ethanol industry is needed to sustain growth in corn demand for industrial uses.

International Trade

The United States is the world's largest exporter of corn. Corn exports experienced their greatest growth in the 1970s, during which time U.S. exports more than tripled reaching a record high of 2.4 billion bushels during the 1979/80 crop year. While the former Soviet Union's (FSU) recent retreat from the corn market has removed a large source of export volatility, China has appeared as a new source of export growth potential. Income growth in China and other developing countries will offset the recent sharp drop in corn exports to the FSU. Given the contraction in the FSU livestock sector, there is little chance the FSU will rebound as a major importer of corn in the near future.

Growth in U.S. corn exports is indirectly and directly supported by Uruguay Round Agreement of GATT (the General Agreement on Tariffs and Trade) and the North American Free Trade Agreement (NAFTA). Both agreements are expected to directly boost U.S. agricultural exports through reducing trade barriers and indirectly raise exports through raising global income. NAFTA will have the most noticeable effect on U.S. corn exports. Corn exports to Mexico are expected to grow under NAFTA as corn tariffs decline and Mexican import quotas are lifted, and as Mexican meat consumption rises with stronger income growth. NAFTA included a 2.5 million metric ton duty–free access for U.S. corn in calendar year 1994 that has increased by 3% each year. Mexico's 215% over–quota tariff for corn will be reduced by 24% in the first six years of NAFTA, then phased out in the following nine years.

The greatest uncertainty surrounding U.S. corn exports concerns China. During the 1994/95 crop year, China began to import corn for the first time since 1989/90. Over time, China is expected to import more corn as its livestock sector expands. However, it is difficult to forecast the specific amount of corn that will be exported to China over the next few years, since it is largely dependent on Chinese government policy and weather. Despite the uncertainty surrounding Chinese corn imports, total U.S. corn exports to China and the rest of the world are expected to increase by around 100 million bushels per year over the next few years.

Japan and Taiwan receive more than 46% of U.S. corn exports. Exports to Taiwan are expected to fall by almost a million metric tons in the short–term, due to the recent outbreak of hoof and mouth disease in Taiwan's hog sector. The time it will take and the extent to which Taiwan is able to rebuild its hog sector will determine when exports of corn to Taiwan will begin to increase, but we expect at least a three year rebuilding period.

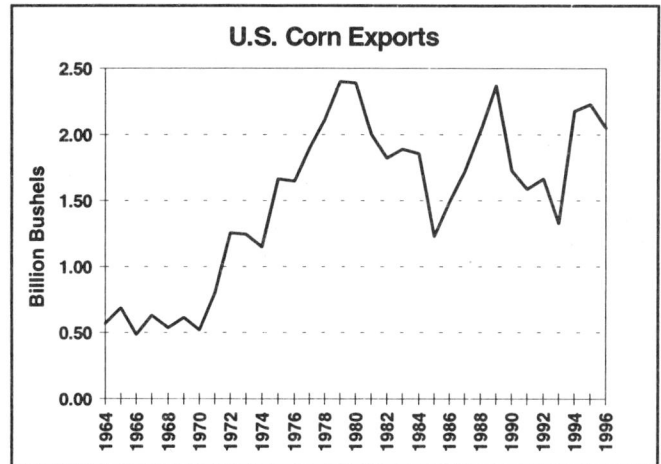

U.S. Corn Exports

U.S. Corn Outlook

The U.S. corn outlook can be characterized as positive. Producers now have the freedom to meet market demands with minimal government interference. Corn acres in the U.S. are not expected to fall below 81 million acres over the next three years, assuming favorable weather patterns. Production and total supplies are expected to increase, and stock levels should increase to 1. 2 and 1.5 billion bushels over the next three years. As a result of stock rebuilding, corn prices will most certainly weaken. It is not necessarily clear how far prices need to decline before producers take land out of production, but it is clear that relative price strength between commodities competing for the same land will determine what crops are planted. Soybeans are the main competitor for corn acres, and the price of soybeans relative to corn is expected to remain strong in the near future. As a result, there will be limited upward potential for corn acreage.

Corn exports will make or break the positive outlook for the U.S. corn market. China's role in international corn markets appears fuzzy, but China will probably need to import corn and other feedstuffs to support its growing livestock sector. Events in major corn importing countries like Japan and Taiwan will also have an impact on U.S. corn export markets. Historically, Japan and Taiwan have represented more than 46% of U.S. corn exports. The recent outbreak of hoof–and–mouth disease in Taiwan's hog sector will decrease Taiwan's feed demand and lower U.S. corn exports to Taiwan over the next three years. Once Taiwan's hog sector is back in order, U.S. exports to Taiwan will pick up pace, but will depend on Taiwan's ability to regain market share in world pork exports.

Corn Supply and Use

Marketing Year	1995/96	1996/97	1997/98
Acreage & Yield			
Planted (Million Acres)	71.25	79.49	81.33
Harvested (Million Acres)	65.00	73.15	73.83
Yield (Bu/Acre)	113.50	127.10	128.55
Supply (Million Bushels)			
Beginning Stocks	1,558	426	893
Production	7,374	9,293	9,491
Imports	16	10	6
Total Supply	8,948	9,729	10,390
Disappearance (Million Bushels)			
Food & Industrial	1,561	1,650	1,661
Seed	22	20	21
Feed & Residual	4,711	5,314	5,205
Totals Domestic Use	6,294	6,984	6,886
Exports	2,228	1,852	2,209
Total Disappearance	8,522	8,836	9,095
Ending Stocks	426	893	1,295
Stocks/Use Ration (%)	5.00	10.11	14.24
Farm Level Price ($/Bu)	3.53	2.89	2.60

Summary

Corn production in years to come will not be affected by government acreage set–aside programs, and producers are expected to respond to market forces and produce enough corn to meet growing domestic and export demand. Evidence of U.S. farmers' willingness to increase production in response to higher prices can be seen in the increases in planted corn and soybean acres during the 1996 and 1997 planting seasons. Corn producers are expected to rebuild corn stocks from the record lows of 426 million bushels in 1995/96 to levels of 1.5 to 1.8 billion bushels over the next decade. Improvements in yield technologies and management techniques are expected to be the main source of production growth in the United States. Some land suitable for planting corn will be released from the CRP over the next decade, which will also increase corn production. The future role of biotechnology in corn production will be an important factor in future production levels of corn.

Demand for U.S. corn will come primarily from animal feed demand worldwide. Animal numbers are expected to increase as the demand for meat increases with income growth. Food and industrial uses are forecast to grow at rates similar to population growth. However, the growth in industrial uses of corn, primarily ethanol, could exhibit some variability due to changes in government policies. Overall, the potential for corn's continued growth is excellent.

Soybeans

The market for the soybean complex (soybeans, soybean meal, and soybean oil) has undergone a number of changes in recent years.

U.S. planted acreage is on an upswing after falling from the record level set in 1979. Soybean area is expanding farther north and west of the main production area, as growers react to strong prices and increasing demand in the United States and abroad. The sector will, however, face international competition in the expanding global market for oilseeds. In particular, policy changes will make South American crops more competitive with those produced in the United States.

Technological improvements in the sector have led to some controversy, especially concerning herbicide residue and genetically altered soybeans. Critics have fears about the risk of allergies and general food safety, but this is not expected to stop the marketing of genetically altered crops. Soybeans may be the first of a new generation of genetically altered agricultural products to reach consumers.

U.S. stocks are tight in 1997 and crushing demand remains extremely high, causing pressures in the market that may persist until the U.S. crop is made available in October. Yields are expected to improve over the next few years. Improved yields should combine with the highest area planted since 1980/81 to increase U.S. production for the 1997/98 marketing year, which runs from the fourth quarter of 1997 to the third quarter of 1998). The medium–term prospects for the U.S. soybean market remain good.

Acreage

- Over half of U.S. soybean farms and production are located in the five Corn Belt States (Illinois, Iowa, Indiana, Ohio, and Missouri). Illinois and Iowa are, by far, the largest U.S. soybean producers accounting for 34% (815 million bushels) of total U.S. production of 2.4 billion bushels.

- Soybean area has been expanding north and west into Wisconsin, Michigan, Minnesota, and the Dakotas. New high–yielding, short–season soybean varieties have displaced flax, oats, sunflowers, dry beans, alfalfa, and land that would normally be fallowed. Rotating soybeans with corn or spring wheat has positive agronomic attributes and has aided their northwestern expansion.

- In the South, the best land was historically devoted to the crops grown under the Federal government's former acreage reduction and price and income support programs, meaning that soybean acreage has increasingly been on substandard soils. This contributed to slower yield growth in the South when compared to the mid–western region.

- Another factor that contributed to slower yield growth in the South is double cropping. Soybeans are often planted on double–cropped fields. These fields are typically planted later than optimal, thus leading to lower yields.

- Southern acreage will greatly depend on future world demand for soybean oil, soybean meal, and other oilseeds such as rapeseed and sunflowerseed. Southern farmers' ability to improve yields and control currently high production costs will also influence soybean acreage in that region.

U.S. planted acreage for soybeans has been growing since 1990 after falling through most of the 1980s. Soybean area reached 71.4 million acres at its peak in 1979, but with the implementation of government payments for corn, soybean acreage fell to approximately 58 million acres by 1990. In 1996, however, acreage was between 64 and 65 million. Most of the decline in acreage between 1979 and 1990 occurred in the lower–yielding, higher–cost southern regions. According to the USDA, of the 29 soybean producing states, farmers in 26 states intend to plant more acres in 1997 than in 1996. North

Dakota growers expressed their intent to devote approximately 35% more land to soybeans in 1997 than in 1996. However, growers in Indiana and Ohio (two of the major producers) are expected to reduce their soybean acreage by about 4%.

Yield improvements have partially offset acreage reductions, so production has remained relatively stable since 1980. Average U.S. yields rose from approximately 32 bushels per acre in 1979 to a high of between 41 and 42 bushels per acre in 1994. In 1996, yields stood between 37 and 38 bushels per acre.

As U.S. producers begin to react to increased international demand and currently strong prices, soybean production should increase over the coming years. Acreage increases will account for most of the expected increase in production in 1997, but yields are also expected to improve.

Farm Policy

In the United States, there are no government support programs directed at soybeans except loan programs. In fact, outside of the E.U., oilseed production is relatively unsupported worldwide. World trade in oilseeds is relatively free of high tariffs and non-tariff barriers and subsidized trade is relatively unimportant. As mentioned above, soybean area and production in the U.S. have been affected mostly by support programs for other crops, particularly corn, which have sometimes encouraged producers to plant other crops even when market prices favored soybean plantings.

Neither the NAFTA nor GATT trade agreements are likely to have much impact on soybean production and trade, since soybeans have not received significant support in the past. Improved market access will provide direct trade opportunities for soybeans, and soybean meal trade may increase as a result of the Uruguay Round. The main opportunities seem to be the East Asian developing countries and China, due to increasing income levels in those regions. Trade is expected to increase only marginally with Mexico, Eastern Europe, Korea, and Japan.

Technology

One of the more interesting developments in the soybean market in recent years was the introduction of Roundup Ready soybeans. These plants are genetically altered to protect them from the herbicide Roundup. Using the old technology, farmers were required to treat the soil before planting and react to weeds as they emerged. Roundup Ready soybeans give farmers the ability to spray their fields indiscriminately without damaging the crop.

There is concern from environmental groups that indiscriminate spraying of the crop will result in a residue on harvested soybeans, but resistance from the international community has been limited. In fact, Roundup Ready soybeans have already been reviewed and approved by regulatory bodies in Argentina, Mexico, Canada, Japan, the E.U., and the United States. On the other hand, French and German farmers are not permitted to use the Roundup Ready technology. Despite this, soybeans may be the first of a new generation of genetically altered products to reach consumers.

Other research has focused on ways to genetically alter soybeans in order to increase the oil and protein content. Such a soybean could be used as a high-protein feed source for poultry or dairy feed. This technology is also likely to bring protests from environmental groups if it comes to market.

Another interesting development for soybeans is the biodiesel market, which is a potential new market despite its higher price relative to traditional diesel fuel. Common Agricultural Policy (CAP) reform limits on European oilseed acreage for food have spurred increasing interest in biodiesel in the European Union since the reform allows additional limited production for industrial uses.

Marketing Patterns

Soybeans undergo a thorough selection process before being converted into edible products. They are first graded, screened, and cleaned. They are then dried to reduce their moisture content and to allow the hull to separate easily from the bean. Soybean hulls can be further processed into edible fiber for livestock feeding. The soybean meat is then rolled into a full fat flake, and soybean oil is extracted from the flake. The result is a white flake containing about 52% protein.

Crude soybean oil first undergoes a degumming process which separates crude lecithin from soy oil. The crude lecithin is further refined for use in both industrial and dietary products. The degummed oil is also further refined to produce salad oil, margarine oil, frying oil, and a number of other soy oils which can be derived through further processing.

Edible defatted flakes provide the basis for a variety of soy products. These flakes can be ground to specific granulations to produce soy grits or soy flour for use in baking. Sugars may be removed from the flakes to produce a soy concentrate containing about 70% protein on a dry basis.

Soy concentrate can be moisturized and processed through an extruder using high temperature and pressure to produce a textured soy protein product with a fibrous, meat–like texture. Finally, the edible defatted flakes can be put through a series of protein precipitations to produce a soy protein isolate with a protein level of about 90%.

- Soybean meal is the most valuable component obtained from processing the soybean, ranging from 50% to 75% of the soybean's value. It is by far the world's most important protein feed, representing around 60% of world protein meal.

- Edible soybean oil use in the United States has increased by about 3% per year over the last decade. This growth rate is on par with the consumption growth rate for all edible oils, but it lags behind the growth of canola and corn oil. Edible oil use could be revolutionized with the development of no–calorie "fat mimics" and engineered fat substitutes.

International Trade

World soybean production has increased dramatically in the last thirty years. Five countries account for approximately 90% of the world's soybean production. The United States leads all producing countries, despite the fact that the 90% production share it enjoyed in 1970 has fallen to about 50% of world production today. The other four key producing countries are Brazil, Argentina, China, and India, in order of importance.

The United States accounts for about 60% to 70% of world soybean exports. Brazil and Argentina combine to export another 20% to 25% of the world total for soybeans. In recent years, raw soybean trade was stagnant due to declining food expenditures as a percentage of income in developed countries and the availability of inexpensive soybean meal from South America.

U.S. soybean exports are closely tied to U.S. production and consumption. Production outpaced consumption in the 1970s, increasing the availability of soybeans for export. In the 1980s, production remained relatively stable due to lower prices and high government support for grains and cotton. Consumption continued to grow in the 1980s, however, and soybean export capacity suffered as a result.

Worldwide oilseed demand has been strong despite higher prices. China has imported substantial quantities of both soybeans and soybean meal, and the E.U. continues to import large quantities of soybeans. U.S. competitiveness in this market depends on a number of external factors, including domestic trade policies in key importing/exporting countries, relative prices and yields, transportation and infrastructure costs, and exchange rates.

One of the most important recent policy developments affecting U.S. soybean exporters' competitiveness is the elimination of the Brazilian government's value–added tax on soybean exports. This tax was levied on exports of soybeans but not on the exports of its products. The tax put Brazilian soybeans at a price disadvantage on the international market and as a result, it was often necessary for Brazilian soybean producers to sell directly to the domestic crushing industry. However, with the removal of the value–added tax, soybean products no longer enjoy such a large advantage over raw soybeans. With this in mind, Brazilian exporters are now poised to challenge U.S. exporters in the soybean market.

A key advantage enjoyed by U.S. exporters is the country's efficient transportation and marketing systems, which reduce the cost of exporting with respect to the other producers. However, cost differentials and competitiveness are always dependent on exchange rates. As the global economy continues to grow and developing countries work to stabilize their economies, developing countries' exchange rates may not be as volatile as they have been in the past.

U.S. Soybean Outlook

Soybean supplies were tight in the United States in the middle months of 1997. As of April 1997, the USDA reported that soybean stocks were at 1.06 billion bushels, down from 1.19 billion in the previous year. Cumulative crushings were running 3% ahead of the previous year's pace and exports were averaging nearly 10 million bushels per week. Prices are expected to move higher over the spring and summer in order to ration available supplies. South America is a potential source for additional supply if short stocks and high demand cause major problems before the U.S. crop is available in October.

Soybeans: Distribution of Use

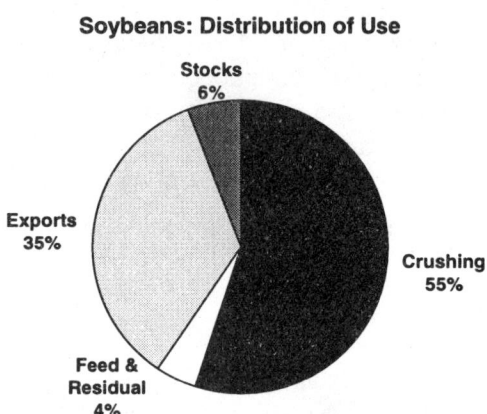

Plantings for 1997/98 are expected to be at their highest level since 1980/81. The high level of intended plantings is attributed to strong returns for growing soybeans relative to alternative crops, and the outlook for soybean acreage over the next five years is favorable. Under the Federal Agriculture Improvement and Reform Act of 1996, producers have the flexibility to plant the crops which they expect to be the most profitable. In the past, planting soybeans often meant potential losses in program benefits from not planting program crops.

- Intended soybean plantings in the Northern Plains show strong growth likely in 1997/98. In this region, projected soybean returns are much more favorable than spring wheat, and farmers anticipate problems seeding spring wheat because of wet soil conditions and flooding.

Yield improvements can also be expected over the next few years. In the U.S., greater pesticide and fertilizer use has made the highest soybean yields in the world possible. Soybeans rank second (behind corn) in pesticide use for all U.S. field crops. This pesticide usage is concentrated in an almost 100% treatment with herbicides, while insecticides and fungicides are rarely used.

Increased supplies, due to the increased acreage and yields, should put downward pressure on prices, which should also stimulate domestic and export use. While prices in 1996/97 are in the $7–8 range, they are expected to fall in 1997/98 to about $6.40 due to increased domestic supplies.

Soybeans	1995	1996	1997
Acreage & Yield			
Planted (Million Acres)	62.58	64.21	68.07
Harvested (Million Acres)	61.62	63.41	66.90
Yield (Bu/Acre)	35.30	37.60	38.03
	-----Million Bushels-----		
Supply (Million Bushels)			
Beginning Stocks	335	183	140
Production	2,177	2,382	2,544
Imports	4	6	6
Total Supply	2,516	2,571	2,690
Disappearance			
Total Domestic Use	1481	1544	1554
Exports	851	887	863
Total Disappearance	2332	2431	2417
Ending Stocks	183	140	274
Stocks/Use Ration (%)	7.9	5.8	11.3

Demand from the livestock industry will continue to influence soybean prices. As long as the poultry and hog sectors continue to expand production, demand for soybean meal will remain strong. The improvement of economies around the world has led to an increase in global demand for meat and consequently for livestock feed. Soybean meal exports are in position to improve due to the increased foreign demand for protein feeds. However, in the short term, domestic demand is strong and stocks are low, so much of the increased production will be consumed in the domestic market.

The long–term forecast for soybeans is for a slight decrease in area. Production is expected to rise, however, due to improving yields. Both domestic and international demand are expected to increase in the long run as a result of higher incomes. U.S. exports should benefit from this increased international demand. Prices will also probably move higher, in the long term, in response to the increased demand.

Cotton

The cotton sector has undergone significant changes in the last three decades. The next five years appear to hold many changes as well. Some major issues cotton producers will continue to face include the impact of pest control on the cost of production, impacts of the 1996 Federal Agriculture Improvement and Reform Act (FAIR Act), changing trends in domestic demand, and the impact of international trade agreements and global demand on exports.

Acreage

U.S. planted acreage for cotton grew from 10.6 million acres in 1989 to a peak of 16.9 million acres in 1995, only to drop back to 14.7 million acres in 1996. It is important to note that for the 1989/90 crop year, 3.5 million acres went unplanted due to the federal Acreage Reduction Program policy.

■ The majority of the acreage gain in the 1990s came in the Southeast, where planted acreage grew from 0.85 million acres in 1989 to 3.46 million acres in 1995, and 3.09 million acres in 1996.

■ While acreage in the Southwest did increase to 1.77 million acres in 1995 from 1.64 million acres in 1989, 1996 acreage fell to only 1.59 million.

Major Cotton Producing Regions

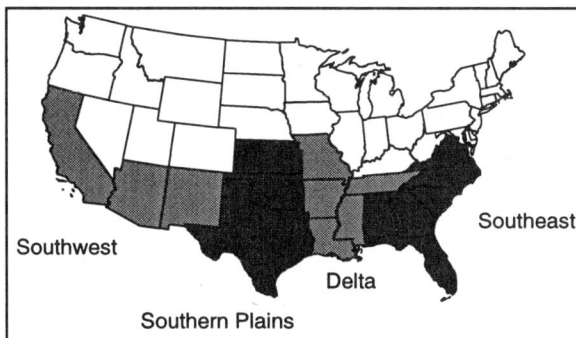

■ The Delta also saw an increase in cotton planted acreage from 2.98 million acres in 1989 to a peak of 4.87 million acres in 1995, before settling at 3.94 million acres in 1996.

■ The Southern Plains region increased from 5.10 million acres in 1989 to 6.82 million acres in 1995 before dropping back to 6.03 million acres in 1996.

This increase in acreage and yields boosted production from 12.2 million bales in 1989 to 19.0 million bales in 1996. Even with this increase in domestic supply, the seasonal average farm price has remained relatively strong due to the increase in domestic use. U.S. domestic mill use of raw cotton increased from 8.7 million bales in 1990 to 11.1 million bales in 1996, while U.S. exports dropped from 7.8 to 7.1 million bales over the same period. Developments in the technologies of textiles, such as wrinkle resistant fabrics, and fashion trends to natural fibers have contributed to increased domestic demand.

The change of emphasis from the Southwest to the Southeast in the 1990s is in line with the downward shift in total cash expenses in the Southeast during that time. Based on data from the USDA, total cash costs dropped from $359.36 per acre in 1990 to $326.35 in 1991. In 1991, chemical cash costs paralleled the downward shift in total cash costs, dropping from $108.80 per acre in 1990 to $70.27 in 1991. This significant decrease in chemical control costs can be partially attributed to the success of the Boll Weevil Eradication Program. Producers in the Southwest, on the other hand, are facing rising irrigation costs and new pest pressures.

Technology

Recent developments in biotechnology could have a significant impact on chemical control costs in the future. There are two major types of biotechnology impacting the cotton industry: Bt Cotton, in which the plant becomes toxic to pests; and Roundup Ready, in which the plant is resistant to the herbicide Roundup.

'Bt Cottonseed' has been genetically engineered to include the *Bacillus thuringiensis* gene, which delivers a natural insecticidal protein that is toxic to the tobacco budworm, bollworm, and pink bollworm. The development of transgenic Bt cotton varieties have the potential to drastically reduce the amount of chemicals needed to control these pests. Roundup Ready and similar technologies are also expected to have an impact on production.

Biotechnology, whether it is for corn, cotton, or soybeans, seems to be readily accepted by the majority of producers. Although it is difficult to foresee the impact these products will have on consumer acceptance and pest resistance, the level of acreage planted with these new varieties is expected to increase in the future. However, this new technology also brings with it the risk of future litigation based on product performance.

Farm Policy

Past farm policy legislation included supply-management programs such as the Acreage Reduction Program, and price support programs such as target prices and deficiency payments, which provided price safety nets and income support to producers. However, the 1996 Federal Agriculture Improvement and Reform (FAIR) Act has reshaped the face of U.S. farm policy. Two key provisions of the 1996 FAIR Act were the elimination of both programs restricting planting and price and income support programs.

Government support of the cotton sector has been extremely important over time. Direct price and income support averaged close to $840 million per year over the 1985-89 period and $870 million over the 1990-95 period. These figures exclude diversion, disaster assistance, commodity loan operations, and Conservation Reserve Program payments. Over the 1996 -2002 fiscal years, the upland cotton sector is scheduled to receive $466 million to $675 million per year in transition payments. Support is expected to be extended beyond 2002 and be maintained at $466 million per year. Under FAIR, price support is provided to participants through nonrecourse loans.

Price and income support programs were replaced in FAIR with transition payments which are not tied to production of specific crops. This program will give producers more planting flexibility, and will encourage more market-based production decisions. However, it will also significantly increase price risk for producers, who will have to place more emphasis on risk management than

they have in the past. Minimizing cash costs will be one of the simplest ways for producers to manage risk, and this may lead to a shift from cotton to other field and row crops with lower production costs, primarily corn and soybeans. This shift was actually evidenced in 1996, in repsonse to cash exposure patterns. The U.S. average total cash cost for cotton producers was $360.42 per planted acre in 1995, compared to $207.33 for corn, $122.51 for sorghum, and $121.17 for soybeans.

Marketing Patterns

Marketing cotton from farms to domestic textile mills and foreign markets is a complex process. Cotton marketing begins when seed cotton is harvested and hauled from farms to local gins. At the gin, the lint, seed, and trash are separated, and the lint is compressed into bales. Most bales of lint are moved directly to warehouse from the gin. The bales are weighed, sampled, and tagged and then placed in storage. The samples are sent to a USDA cotton classing office for quality determination. In some areas of the Cotton Belt, bales are shipped directly from farms to warehouses known as reconcentration points. The shipment of cotton from interior warehouses to reconcentration points is primarily in order to consolidate bales into larger lots of like qualities.

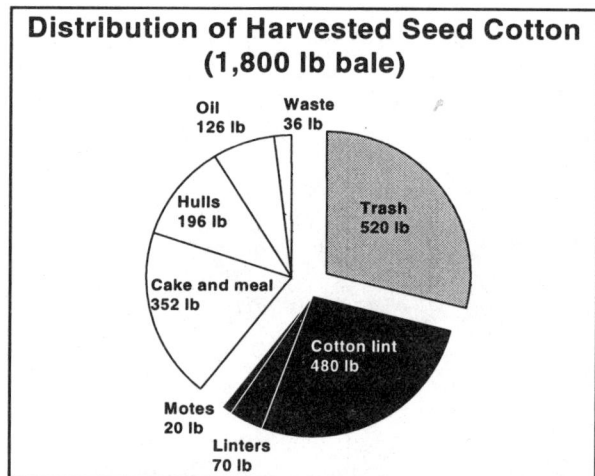

Distribution of Harvested Seed Cotton (1,800 lb bale)

Oil 126 lb
Waste 36 lb
Hulls 196 lb
Trash 520 lb
Cake and meal 352 lb
Cotton lint 480 lb
Motes 20 lb
Linters 70 lb

Domestic textile mills typically maintain only a 30- to 45-day supply of cotton. Bales are shipped from warehouses to mills in fairly even volumes throughout the year to replenish mill stocks. Exports are more seasonal, with January, February, and March being the heaviest export months. The United States is one of the two largest cotton exporters in the world. In 1996 the United States exported 7.1 million bales. Major markets include China (1.8 million bales), Japan (0.9 million bales), Indonesia (0.8 million bales), and South Korea (0.8 million bales).

Aside from waste and tare (bagging and ties), all of the original cotton bale ends up in one of three major end use categories: clothing, home furnishings, and industrial uses. Men's and boy's apparel is by far the largest individual market for cotton fiber. In 1993 about 4.1 million bales were used in men's and boy's apparel.

International Trade

Many important developments in the cotton market are the result of agricultural and economic development policies of various governments around the world. The impacts of the Uruguay Round of the General Agreement on Tariffs and Trade (GATT) will be relatively small in the near to medium term, but could become significant early in the next century because of increased income growth and increased efficiencies in markets.

Much of the impact of GATT on the cotton sector will come from its phase-out of the Multi-Fiber Arrangement (MFA), which will open up textile markets after the turn of the century. The MFA is a system of bilateral trade agreements that has allowed signatories to place quotas on textile imports to prevent market disruption. The primary goal for its phase-out is the expansion of textile trade through liberalizing world textile trade and reducing trade barriers.

A major impact of the Uruguay Round should be an increase in demand for textiles and apparel from increased efficiencies and lower prices, and the resulting expansion in income, particularly in the long run. In addition, the opening of textile and clothing markets will create trade opportunities for exporting countries, many of which are in the developing world. This liberalization will increase over time and become significant early in the next century.

As a result of these agreements and their effect on textile and apparel demand, some countries will reduce their production of cotton because of reduced domestic support. However, changes in the relative levels of cotton prices as compared to crops that compete for acreage, especially grains, are likely to have a larger impact on cotton production. Higher relative grain prices should lead to increased grain production and reduced cotton production, especially in the former Soviet Union and China.

Rising incomes will support demand increases for cotton and textiles in the future, resulting in expanding export markets for U.S. producers. However, U.S. exporters will also face increasing competition in these expanding markets. In general, the United States will benefit from an expanding world cotton market, but there will be considerable competition and shifting trade patterns.

- Nations that are rapidly increasing mill capacity, including India and Turkey, are also implementing programs to increase domestic cotton production or investing in cotton growing regions in other countries. This will limit the demand for cotton imports from other exporters.

- A recovery in mill demand in Russia will likely be at least partially met with trade from central Asian republics, but these republics' ability to increase cotton exports will be limited by their attempts to increase grain production.

- Declining area in Brazil is likely to lead to an increase in cotton imports by this country, a market easily accessible to western hemisphere exporters.

- Countries that are developing primary industries will increase cotton imports as textile industries grow because of relatively cheap labor. This group includes many Asian and Latin American countries.

- However, newly industrialized countries, especially those in Asia, are working to develop secondary and tertiary manufacturing. As competition in the labor pool increases with growth in industries further up the value-added chain, textile production may stagnate as labor becomes more expensive.

U.S. Cotton Outlook

Average cotton yields reached 709 pounds per acre in 1996. The increase in 1996 yield over 1995 levels more than offset the 2.2 million acre decline in plantings, resulting in a 6.1% increase in production. Cotton imports are expected to be at 0.4 million bales and cotton exports at 7.1 million bales for 1996. The farm-level cotton price is estimated to decline to $0.7021/lb. for the 1996/97 year.

Cotton	1995	1996	1997
Acreage & Yield			
Planted (million acres)	16.93	14.67	14.00
Harvested (million acres)	16.01	12.83	13.29
Yield (pounds/acre)	537.00	709.00	675.40
	----- million bales -----		
Supply			
Beginning Stocks	2.7	2.6	3.8
Production	17.9	19.0	18.7
Imports	0.4	0.4	0.3
Total Supply	21.0	22.0	22.8
Disappearance			
Total Domestic Use	10.6	11.0	11.6
Exports	7.7	7.1	6.7
Total Disappearance	18.3	18.1	18.3
Ending Stocks	2.6	3.8	4.5
Stocks/Use Ratio (%)	14.3	21.1	24.8

Cotton acreage is likely to decline over the next two years as profitable corn and soybean crops compete for acreage historically planted in cotton. Demand is expected to remain steady. Over the next year, cotton stocks are expected to increase to 4.5 million bales, keeping downward pressure on cotton prices.

Cotton production has seen incredible growth since 1990, but acreage appears to have peaked in 1995. Cotton acres are expected to decline through 1999. After 1999, cotton acres will rebound modestly in response to firming prices. Although there is downward pressure on acreage planting decisions, farmers still have major investment in cotton equipment. This investment will prevent acreage from dropping below 13.6 million acres. Domestic demand for cotton was stagnant at around 10 million bales per year during the early 1990s; it is expected to increase by an average of 2.4% per year to approximately 14 million bales by the year 2006. Currently, cotton exports are roughly 7 million bales. Growth in cotton exports is expected to remain above 2% per annum, reaching 9 million bales by the end of 2006.

Cotton prices will ultimately dictate the amount of acreage dedicated to cotton, the amount of cotton used in the United States, and the volume exported. The FAIR Act has placed some downward pressure on cotton acreage expectations. As producers respond to market forces, cotton acreage is not expected to climb above 15 million acres in the next five to ten years. Cotton has a relatively high cost of production and relatively high cash outlays, so competition from corn and soybeans, which have lower costs of production and lower cash flow requirements, will influence producers' planting decisions. In addition, market returns will be a key factor as well. Market returns are expected to favor corn and soybean production over the next three years.

Summary

The U.S. cotton sector is poised for additional change over the next five years. The sector is adjusting to the FAIR Act of 1996, and producers must now manage risks differently than they have in the past as the Federal government retreats from intervening in agricultural markets. The agreement from the Uruguay Round of GATT offers opportunity for growth in world and U.S. cotton trade, but U.S. producers will face competition. As growers attempt to manage risk, they are expected to do so by controlling costs and minimizing cash exposure. In addition, elimination of acreage reduction programs will enable producers to respond to market prices and plant accordingly. Minimizing cash exposure and the ability to plant more freely suggest that producers could shift easily to corn or soybean production in a given year.

Farm numbers will continue to decline, although cotton production in the Southeast and Delta will likely be maintained. Western producers are expected to face increasing costs of irrigation, while completion of boll weevil eradication in the Delta area is likely.

The biotechnology revolution also indicates change for the cotton sector. Bt cotton, Roundup Ready technology, and other new products are here and producers are responding favorably to this technology. How insecticide manufacturers respond with new product offerings, lower-cost insecticides, and marketing strategies will affect how quickly biotechnology–based products are adopted. The next ten years will pose challenges to farmers, agribusiness, consumers, and governments. Those challenges will be met in different ways, but change is guaranteed.

Chapter 2: Livestock, Dairy, and Poultry

Livestock (Except Dairy and Poultry)

Red meat production in the United States represents the largest sector of the agriculture economy in terms of cash receipts received by farmers. Both the beef and pork sectors have seen significant structural changes over the past decade, and important changes are likely to be seen in the future. Historical trends in consumption patterns and current market conditions will play an important role in the future of the red meat industry. Increasing incomes around the world and more health conscious consumers will dictate the path of beef and pork production in the future. Exports of beef and pork, particularly to Asian markets, are expected to expand at robust rates for a sustained period.

Beef production has lost significant market share to the poultry industry. Relative price competitiveness of broilers and health concerns over red meat consumption are the main causes in per capita declines in red meat consumption. The decline in per capita consumption of beef has slowed recently, however, and export markets have picked up steam. Modest growth can be expected in the beef industry as long as exports continue to increase and consumer demands are met. More concentration of the beef sector is likely as the industry learns how to improve the genetic stock and the quality of beef produced.

The pork sector has some interesting opportunities in the future. Although U.S. per capita consumption has declined, the industry has been able to change its products and to a large degree its image. The other white meat has hit the 1990s and consumers are buying leaner and healthier pork products. The increased vertical integration of the pork sector has resulted in improved management techniques and improved herd genetics. Improvements are expected to continue, and per capita consumption of pork is expected to increase over the next decade. U.S. pork exports will also provide growth opportunities for the pork industry in years to come.

Demand Conditions

Over the past two decades, meat consumption in the United States has been shifting away from red meats in favor of poultry. Despite the decline in red meat consumption and the increase in poultry consumption, consumers are still consuming more beef and pork than broilers and turkeys, albeit the gap is narrowing and in 1996, per capita broiler consumption surpassed beef consumption by more than 6 pounds and surpassed pork by more than 24 pounds. The trend of increasing broiler consumption and decreasing beef and pork consumption will play an import role in the future direction of the red meat industry.

Per Capita Meat and Poultry Consumption
Pounds Retail Weight

	1970	1980	1990	1996
Beef	84.4	76.4	67.6	67.5
% change		*-9.5%*	*-11.5%*	*-0.1%*
Pork	55.2	56.8	49.4	49.1
% change		*2.9%*	*-13.0%*	*-0.6%*
Broilers	40.1	47.3	60.7	73.2
% change		*18.0%*	*28.3%*	*20.6%*
Turkey	8.1	10.2	17.5	19.1
% change		*25.9%*	*71.6%*	*9.1%*
Total	187.8	190.7	195.2	208.9
% change		*1.5%*	*2.4%*	*7.0%*

Beef and pork prices have risen relative to broiler prices, contributing to the decline in red meat consumption. Health concerns have also played an important role. In addition, the poultry industry has also been more innovative than either the beef or pork industries in the introduction of new products. The steady growth in poultry per capita consumption has also been aided by addition of poultry products to the menus of fast food restaurants and the introduction of "poultry specific" restaurant chains. Although total meat consumption will continue to grow slowly over the next decade, the continuing substitution of poultry for red meat is evidence of important changes in the way U.S. consumers select and consume foods.

While total growth in meat consumption will be slow in the United States, export markets will continue to increase in importance in upcoming years. Rapid increases in per capita income in Asia have provided significant growth opportunities for U.S. grain fed beef and pork. U.S. beef exports totaled 611,456 tons in 1996, 3% above the record export level of 1995. Japan is the primary importer of U.S. beef, receiving more than 50% of U.S. beef exports. Mexico, Canada, South Korea, and Taiwan combined receive about 25%. Increased exports can also be attributed to GATT and NAFTA, international trade agreements that have created new market potential for U.S. agricultural commodities.

Australia is the world's largest beef exporter, and its exports have gained market share in Japan and South Korea. However, rising incomes in Japan and South Korea are helping to shift consumer preferences toward U.S. grain–fed beef over Australia's grass–fed beef. The United States also has an opportunity to develop an export market in Europe, pending the World Trade Organization's ruling on the European Union's ban on the import of beef from cattle treated with growth hormones. Since 1989, the E.U. has banned such imports, which effectively excludes 90% of U.S. beef. Under provisions of GATT, such prohibitions must be supported by credible scientific evidence.

U.S. pork exports continue to gain strength due to increases in production, decreases in the relative price of pork to beef, and European production difficulties which are limiting E.U. supply of fresh product to Asian markets. Pork producers have been able to improve the consistency of their products, which also provides opportunities for export growth. Pork export sales reached a record level of $1 billion in 1996, a 21% increase over 1995. Japanese pork imports represented almost 60% of total U.S. pork exports. U.S. pork exports to Japan are expected to see more growth in the near future due to an

outbreak of hoof–and–mouth disease in Taiwan's swine sector. For the most part, Taiwan will be out of the pork export business until the year 2000, after which Taiwan will need to scramble to regain lost market share. In addition, improved exports to Canada and Mexico are evidence that NAFTA has had a positive effect on U.S. pork exports.

Food safety is an emotionally charged area. The Federal government has a system of regulatory, inspection, and enforcement measures designed to insure the safety of red meats. Concentration in the industry and an industry trend toward a wider variety of products have led to vertical integration and greater control of some food safety risks and greater potential for the spread of contamination in others. In order to keep meat contamination at minimum levels, some firms are providing food safety training for workers, investing in equipment to reduce microbial contamination, and hiring more workers on trim lines for detection of visible contamination on carcasses.

Food safety issues will continue to play an important role in consumption patterns of red meat. Europe's struggle with BSE, bovine spongiform encephalopathy, and the worldwide battle against E. coli will continue to haunt the beef industry in the future. Beef consumption is down 30 to 40% in the E.U. due to the BSE crisis. It is widely believed that the United States could win a significant share of the E.U. market with BSE–free beef if issues surrounding the use of growth hormones can be settled.

Supply Conditions

Beef

In the United States, the beef cattle industry is specialized into two sectors. Cow–calf producers maintain herds of beef cows and produce calves which graze on grassy range lands. These cow–calf producers, or ranchers, sell year–old calves, known as feeder cattle, to feedlot operators. The feedlot operators feed cattle intensively with corn and concentrated feeds for 5 to 6 months before slaughter. Cattle going to slaughter are often referred to as slaughter cattle, fed cattle, or live cattle. More than 75% of the cattle slaughtered in the United States come from feedlots, a proportion that has increased over the past three decades and is much higher than ratios in every other cattle producing country.

The cow–calf sector is made up of more than 900,000 operations, primarily in the Great Plains and Midwest regions of the United States Measured by the population of beef cows, the top five cow–calf states in 1996 were Texas, Missouri, Oklahoma, Nebraska, and South Dakota. Smaller operations remain important in this sector, as ranches with fewer than 100 cows account for more than 90% of the cow–calf operations, and more than half of the cow inventory. Farms with fewer than 100 cows are usually supplementary enterprises on commercial crop farms or major enterprises on part–time farms or ranches. Due to the prevalence of many small operations and the low cash outlays typically required by cow–calf operations, the sector tends to react slowly and weakly to market prices.

Despite slow reaction times to price signals, the industry has been able to improve averaged dressed weights and the quality of beef produced via better management and genetics over the past decade. Average dressed weight for total cattle slaughter has increased from 600 pounds in the mid–1970s to over 700 pounds in the mid–1990s. Part of the increase in dressed weight is due to the decline in the number of dairy cows included in total slaughter, a trend which will continue. More producers pay attention to consumer demands for leaner and more consistent beef products, and some improvements have been made. However, the beef industry's biggest obstacle will be to continue improvements in quality and consistency, either by forming strategic alliances among producers or moving toward some form of vertical integration similar to the poultry and pork industries.

The beef industry has become more concentrated over time, especially the feeding and packing sectors. Out of 50,000 feedlots in the United States, the 390 largest lots account for 65% of the nation's fed cattle marketed, and the 89 largest of those market 35% of all fed cattle. Concentration in the packing sector has been even more dramatic. In 1980, the top four companies slaughtered 41% of the nation's fed cattle. In 1996, the top four slaughtered 83%, and the largest company 35%. Producer and feeder concern over packer concentration and captive supplies led to two recent U.S. Department of Agriculture studies on the issue. Preliminary results indicate there has been no illegal price control on part of the packers, but more studies can be expected in the future.

Pork

The 1990s have been a period of significant structural transformation for the hog industry. What some have called the "industrialization of the pork industry" began in North Carolina in the late 1980s. Industrialization has been characterized by the appearance of very large operations, the rapid growth of contract production, movement toward vertical coordination of production and processing, and an inflow of capital from outside investors. Some early enthusiasts speculated that the "industrial model" would replace the traditional industry, with 50 producers supplying all the hogs needed by the United States. However, events since the early part of the decade have been somewhat more complex than anticipated. In the traditional Midwestern hog producing states, contract production and mega–integrators have not succeeded as they have in North Carolina for a number of reasons.

In the Midwest, "medium–sized" producers, those with 250 sows or more have adopted a variety of strategies to remain competitive with the mega–integrators from North Carolina. In Minnesota, the state school of veterinary medicine has included business training for its animal doctors, many of whom have gone on to organize production networks. In such networks, hog producers may build a shared farrowing facility and own breeding stock in common, finishing their pigs at their respective locations. In Illinois, marketing networks are popular. Farmers pool their pigs into semi–loads, and negotiate improved prices for reliable supplies to packers. In Indiana, producers learned from a study by Purdue University that many of the technologies employed by the large integrators can be adopted, at least in part, by smaller operators. Artificial insemination, phased feeding, segregated early weaning, and other technologies can be applied to reduce production costs and improve competitiveness.

According to a study of the industry based on 1994 data, there were 149,000 hog farms in the United States. Operations that marketed fewer than 1,000 hogs per year accounted for 120,000 of the farms and 18% of the hogs marketed. This implies, then, that 29,000 farms accounted for 82% of hogs marketed. Sixty–six mega–operations accounted for 16.8% of the hogs marketed. The number of small operators continues to decline, and dropped 12% from December 1994 to December 1995. The contraction of the breeding herd which began in late

1994 was most severe in states with large numbers of small operators such as Iowa.

What then, has been the result of the industry's transformation? Clearly, significant efficiencies have been achieved. The national average of pigs saved for litter has increased 10% in the last decade to 8.46 in 1996, with more significant improvement by large modern operations. According to the September 1996 Hogs and Pigs report, operations with more than 2,000 hogs averaged 8.8 pigs per litter. As smaller operations continue to disappear and technology advances, pigs per litter will continue to increase. Reproductive efficiency has also improved with more intensive management of the breeding stock. Closer management of breeding and increased use of artificial insemination results in higher rates of conception. Sows require less "down time" between gestations, resulting in more farrowings per year.

Greater reproductive efficiency has resulted in greater productivity. From 1970 to 1995, the amount of meat produced per breeding animal annually has increased 66% in the hog sector as compared to a 23% increase in the cattle sector. Technological advances have also increased feed efficiency in the hog sector. Improved genetics, weaning practices, and feeding practices have all reduced the amount of feed necessary to produce a pound of pork. Superior management provided by contract or voluntary networks has allowed producers to search for improved rations and to implement techniques such as split–sex feeding and phased feeding where the ration is more specifically tailored to the individual hog.

The pork industry has also been successful in improving the quality and consistency of its product to please the consumer. Most packers offer a system of discounts and premiums to encourage the production of lean and consistent pork. Over the last several years the true and perceived quality of the pork product has improved in the domestic market. Together with an improved product, the pork industry has improved its marketing presence with advertising campaigns and the development of branded products.

Issues

In addition to food safety issues discussed above, a major concern facing cattle and swine producers is the disposal of animal waste. The trend toward larger operations of both feedlots and hog producers have created some very localized problems. Retaining lagoons for hog waste have broken in a number of states including Iowa, North Carolina and Missouri, and the waste has contaminated surface water and water supplies. Nitrate seepage into well and other water supplies from feedlots is also a problem. Historically, operators were able to dispose of waste by spreading it on fields. With today's larger operations, there is too much waste in small areas for the absorptive capacity of the land.

The Federal Agriculture and Improvement Reform Act of 1996 has provisions to begin to address this issue. Under the Environmental Quality Incentives Program, livestock producers are eligible for educational, technical, and financial support (including cost sharing for adopting certain practices and incentive payments for animal waste facilities) to address issues such as livestock waste management.

U.S. Livestock Outlook

The future of the U.S. livestock will be increasingly dependent on export demand. Exports will fluctuate over the coming years due to production cycles, growth in foreign income, and price movements, but will most certainly increase. Due to improved economic performance globally and the Uruguay Round Agreement's improvements in market access, the United States is projected to be a net exporter of beef in the future.

The U.S. beef industry has lost a significant amount of market share since the mid–1970s in the United States and will have to work hard to maintain the current levels of consumption. Some people believe that per capita consumption of beef has leveled off and future changes will be minimal. Whether or not this is true, the beef industry still has opportunities to improve quality and lower retail prices, both of which would help beef to maintain market share. Market share could also increase if significant advances are made in quality control.

Over the next three years, beef consumption is not expected to fall below 67 pounds per capita per year on a retail weight basis, and it is expected to remain above 65 pounds per capita over the next decade. Interestingly, some slight increases will be seen over the next two years as relatively competitive beef prices are realized. Slightly increasing and sustained beef demand will help support prices of slaughter steers and feeder steers over the next few years. Feed prices are expected to decline over the next few years, assuming normal weather and adequate supplies of corn and soybeans. The general health of the livestock sector is currently stable, after a decade of losing market share to broilers. The future of the industry looks good, but more declines in per capita consumption might be seen if the beef sector doesn't learn how to better respond to consumer preferences.

The pork industry is poised to increase exports which, as for beef, will be its main source of growth. Taiwan's problems with hoof–and–mouth disease will increase export opportunities over the next three years, and exports are expected to rise by 11% to 14% per year over the next three years. There is even some upside risk to this forecast due to the problem of cholera outbreaks in the Netherlands. The United States is expected to be a consistent net exporter of pork in the future.

Per capita pork consumption on a boneless weight basis is expected to increase to 50 pounds per year, and if the pork industry positions itself correctly, it could even reach 55 pounds. The industry has done a fine job of improving production efficiencies since 1990. This trend is likely to continue, and the United States should see production rise at about 1.5% a year over the next decade due to increases in pigs per litter and average dressed weight. The cost of feed will definitely decline in the short term, which will help to improve profits in the pork sector.

Poultry and Dairy

The poultry and dairy sectors are moving in opposite directions. Poultry is a dynamic and innovative sector adapting to market changes. The sector is vertically integrated, which has enabled producers to realize market efficiencies, react to changing consumer preferences, and deliver a product that is viewed as being low cost, high quality and low fat, safe, and convenient. Per capita poultry consumption continues to rise, and is expected to grow at the expense of per capita beef consumption. The use of export subsidies and the growth in world economies and trade have opened markets for U.S. poultry in China and Russia. In the future a greater share of U.S. poultry will be exported, but potential disruptions could emerge due to the heavy reliance on the Chinese and Russian markets.

The dairy industry, on the other hand, is not nearly as dynamic. The sector is not competitive in world markets. Commitments made in the Uruguay Round Agreement require that export subsidies be reduced. Although dairy subsidies have been modest, this is not good for export prospects. Domestic per capita demand is expected to decline somewhat from current levels. Due to continued increases in productivity, dairy cow numbers will continue to decline, but at a rate slower than productivity growth. The future consolidation in the number of Federal Milk Marketing Orders should increase competition within the U.S. dairy sector. Prices should trend down from current levels, supporting some growth in total demand.

Demand Conditions

Poultry

Per capita poultry consumption has nearly doubled since 1970. The price of broilers and turkeys has fallen relative to beef and pork, making poultry very popular among cost–conscious consumers. The perception of poultry as a healthy alternative to beef and pork has also contributed to the increase in per capita consumption of poultry. Consumption patterns are still changing, and per capita consumption of poultry could continue increasing by 1.5 to 2% per year over the next few years and by 1% per year on average over the next decade.

Convenience has played a role in the rise of poultry consumption. The amount of time spent in the preparation of food at home has declined, as higher incomes and the increased participation of women in the work force have led consumers to demand more conveniently prepared foods. The poultry industry's ability to develop products for changing lifestyles has increased its popularity among consumers. Producers have increased the attractiveness of their products in the at–home market by introducing precut and prepackaged products that reduce the amount of time for at–home preparation.

Per Capita Meat and Poultry Consumption
Pounds Retail Weight

	1970	1980	1990	1996
Beef	84.4	76.4	67.6	67.5
% change		*-9.5%*	*-11.5%*	*-0.1%*
Pork	55.2	56.8	49.4	49.1
% change		*2.9%*	*-13.0%*	*-0.6%*
Broilers	40.1	47.3	60.7	73.2
% change		*18.0%*	*28.3%*	*20.6%*
Turkey	8.1	10.2	17.5	19.1
% change		*25.9%*	*71.6%*	*9.1%*
Total	187.8	190.7	195.2	208.9
% change		*1.5%*	*2.4%*	*7.0%*

Increased exports are likely over the next decade as a result of GATT and NAFTA, international trade agreements that have created new market potential for U.S. agricultural commodities. Supported by $2 billion exports of broiler meat, the value of U.S. poultry meat exports has increased 22% in 1996 over 1995, to reach a record $2.5 billion. Dominated by export gains to the world's largest broiler meat importers, Russia and Hong Kong/China, U.S. broiler meat passed the 2 million ton mark in 1996. China and Russia accounted for nearly

70% of the value of U.S. chicken meat shipments in 1996. Other smaller markets showing strong growth included Latvia and South Africa. Broiler exports represent more than 15% of U.S. production, and exports are expected to continue to increase.

Dairy

The consumption of dairy products in the United States has been closely tied to age, income, geographic location, and race. In the past, age more than any other factor had an impact on the demand for dairy products. During the baby boom years following World War II and extending through the 1960s, America's adolescent population grew at an average rate of about 3%. This growth in adolescent population was accompanied by growth in fluid milk demand, which fueled production growth in the dairy industry.

Beginning in the 1970s, the adolescent population began to decline for the first time in over 30 years. From 1970 to 1990, per capita consumption of fluid milk declined from 240 pounds to 205 pounds, a 15% reduction. Not only has the consumption of fluid milk declined, the type of fluid milk products consumed has changed. In general, consumers have switched from whole milk to low–fat milk.

New trends in both income growth and lifestyles were seen in the 1980s. Real per capita income reached record levels in the 1980s, partly because of the increasing presence of two–income families. As income rose, the time available for food preparation decreased. As a result, there was increased reliance on partially and fully prepared food and more eating away from home. Both of these trends helped to fuel tremendous growth in per capita consumption of cheese, especially pizza cheese.

Foreign demand for U.S. dairy products has been affected by international trade agreements, notably GATT and NAFTA. Under GATT, the level of subsidized dairy exports must be reduced by 2000. NAFTA, which has been effective since January 1994, sets out separate bilateral agreements on cross–border agricultural trade between the United States and Mexico and Mexico and Canada. U.S.–Canada trade is still covered by the U.S.–Canada Free Trade Agreement. Historically, the United States has not been dependent on foreign markets for a significant portion of the commercial disappearance of milk. Under GATT and NAFTA, U.S. dairy exports could show modest growth.

Policy

The poultry sector has received relatively modest support from the Federal government over time. The sector has benefited from the Export Enhancement Program, which provided export subsidies to combat unfair trade practices of other countries, and from market promotion programs.

The dairy sector has been supported in a number of ways. U.S. dairy products are not competitive in international markets, and as a consequence export subsidies for dairy products are provided under the Dairy Export Incentive Program. The minimum support price for fluid milk is $10.20 per cwt in 1997. The milk price is supported by the Federal government through the markets for other dairy products — if the fluid price of milk were expected to fall below the desired price level, the Federal government would enter the market and purchase butter, cheese, and powdered milk to prop up the fluid price. The government has not had to do this in recent years. The final component of dairy support is Federal Milk Marketing Orders. Marketing orders basically identify market areas in which producers deliver product at a specified price.

In 1996, Congress passed the Federal Agriculture Improvement and Reform (FAIR) Act. The legislation will eliminate price supports for dairy products by 1999. FAIR also consolidated the number of milk marketing orders from 33 to between 10 and 14. Export subsidies will be reduced for both poultry and dairy products to levels required under the Uruguay Round Agreement of GATT.

Supply Conditions

Poultry

Following World War II, a number of firms known as integrators transformed the poultry industry. Integrators now contract with growers to raise broilers, providing them with baby chicks, feed, technical advice, and all marketing activities. Growers are responsible for day–to–day care of the birds, as well as the buildings and equipment required to raise them. Integrators pay growers on the basis of the pounds of broilers produced.

Many integrators use a tournament system of contracting, in which a grower's bonus compensation depends on his performance in comparison with other growers. This system is quite effective in an industry undergoing rapid technological change, because integrators do not have to continually recalibrate a system of incentives based on absolute levels of performance. In addition, growers are motivated to continually improve performance. The sharing of responsibilities between integrator and grower allows the integrator to invest in genetic improvements, improved health practices, and managerial innovations, and the benefits of these investments are shared with the network of growers.

Technical and managerial change in the industry resulted in increases in productivity. The number of pounds of feed required to produce one pound of live broiler meat declined from 2.85 in 1955 to under 2 in the 1990s. Stated another way, one ton of feed would produce just over 700 pounds of chicken meat in 1955 and more than 1,000 pounds in the 1990s, a more than 30% increase in productivity. The increase in productivity resulted in a significant reduction in the real price of poultry to the consumer, contributing to the rise in per capita consumption.

The consolidation and integration of the broiler industry have led to geographic concentration in a few southern states. Arkansas, Georgia, Alabama, North Carolina, and Mississippi produce almost 60% of U.S. broiler meat. Through adopting an intensive integrated system of production, the broiler industry gained a significant competitive advantage over the beef and pork sectors.

Dairy

The dairy industry has been consolidating since the 1950s. The number of dairy farms declined from 2.8 million in 1955 to about 162,000 in 1996. Much of the consolidation was recent — the number of dairy farms was cut in half between 1980 and 1995 — and more can be expected in the future due to increased competition. Reduced government support, tightened waste management regulations, and new technologies will all contribute to the process.

A number of factors have led to dairy industry consolidation in the 1980s. Overall demand for milk declined in the early 1980s, although increased demand for cheese products reversed this trend in the mid–1980s. The general decline in milk prices that resulted from declining government support prices forced many inefficient producers out of business. The need for increased investment in dairy equipment to remain competitive, including cooling tanks, improved milking parlor equipment, and

waste management facilities, has also trimmed the industry of producers unwilling or unable to take on debt for such equipment.

The number of dairy farms has declined at a more rapid pace than has the number of dairy cows, which implies that herd size has increased. The average number of cows per farm in 1975 was 25, and by the 1990s it had risen to almost 60. As less efficient producers have exited the dairy industry, and as genetics and management techniques have improved, per–cow milk productivity has greatly increased. The introduction of bovine somatotropin (BST), a natural hormone, which when combined with other inputs can improve productivity, has also supported the process. Between 1980 and the early 1990s, production per cow increased by almost 30%. Larger herds and more productive cows support economies of scale in the dairy industry, and increased capitalization in modern equipment and waste management facilities will continue to fuel consolidation in the dairy industry over the next decade.

Throughout the 1980s, there was a considerable shift in dairy production from the Northeast and upper Midwest to the West and Southwest. The key factors causing this shift in production included a similar shift in U.S. population, cost of production advantages, and price advantages. One of the most striking trends in the dairy industry has been the emergence of California as the leading dairy state. Former leaders, Wisconsin and Minnesota, still produce more than 20% of the nation's milk supply, but California alone produces more than 15%.

Issues

Issues facing the poultry and dairy sectors are similar. Food safety is an emotionally charged issue, and it is linked to environmental concerns. The Federal government has a system of regulatory, inspection, and enforcement measures designed to insure the safety of poultry and dairy products. Concentration and vertical integration in the industry have led to greater control of some food safety risks and greater potential for the spread of contamination in others. In recent years, the U.S. Department of Agriculture has revamped the inspection process and added more inspectors.

In addition to food safety issues, a major concern facing large dairy operations and dairies is animal waste management. Seepage of livestock waste into wells and surface waterways is a problem. Smaller operations also face difficulties if waste is directly discharged into streams.

The Federal Agriculture and Improvement Reform Act of 1996 included provisions to begin to address livestock waste. Under the Environmental Quality Incentives Program, livestock producers are eligible for educational, technical, and financial support (including cost sharing for adopting certain practices and incentive payments for animal waste facilities) to address issues such as livestock waste management.

U.S. Poultry and Dairy Outlook

Past performance of the dairy sector is a good indicator to suggest what the future holds in store. Productivity per dairy cow is anticipated to rise steadily in the range of 1.0% to 2.0% per year. Improved forages, feeds, management, and technology (especially further adoption of BST) should keep productivity on an upward trend. With the reduction in the number of milk marketing orders, we expect further consolidation, which mathematically will improve the average yield per cow. Dairy cow numbers are projected to decline slowly, and by less than the improvement in cow yields. On net, U.S. milk production should expand at an average rate of 1.0% per annum.

Population should grow at a faster rate than total consumption, and as a result per capita milk consumption should decline somewhat. Production levels will increase faster than demand, leading to higher dairy stocks.

The poultry sector is expected to continue to be an agribusiness success story, represented by its vertically integrated operations from contract growers through the processing plant. Because of this high level of integration, the industry is able to perceive and respond to consumer preferences quickly, as evidenced by the wide variety of product offerings. WEFA expects innovation to continue in the industry, allowing convenience, healthy low fat products, and quality and safety to be packaged together and marketed to consumers. Per capita consumption will expand for broilers by 2.0% to 3.0% per year in the near term and then at a slower rate in the long term. Higher broiler consumption will come at the expense of per capita beef and veal consumption.

The export market will become more important to U.S. poultry producers, growing at a rate of 5.0% to 7.0% per year. The export forecast is not without risk. Reduction in export subsidies and the dependence on the Chinese and Russian markets raise the issue of whether these two markets are reliable. To meet these expected demands, broiler and poultry production is projected to expand at annual rates between 2.0% and 3.0%.

Chapter 3   Mining

Metal Mining

Moderate economic growth continued to lift the metal mining industry in 1996. However, the general weakness in prices for the major metals worldwide inevitably took its toll on the U.S. metal mining industry.

While precious metal prices are still on a downward trend because of the strength of the U.S. dollar and low inflation in the United States, the market for base metals seems to have bottomed out, and is poised to make a run in 1997.

Metal mining includes establishments primarily engaged in mining, developing mines, or exploring for metallic minerals (ores). These ores are valued chiefly for the metals contained, to be recovered for use as is or as constituents of alloys, chemicals, pigments, or other products. This major group also includes all ore dressing and beneficiating operations, whether performed at mills operated in conjunction with the mines served or at mills, such as custom mills, operated separately.

The U.S. economy grew at a moderate rate in 1996, and consequently the demand for metals, such as steel and copper, was relatively stable or increased a bit as compared with 1995. For example, the decline in steel consumed in motor vehicle manufacturing (reflecting lower production of motor vehicles and parts) in 1996 was more than offset by an increase in steel consumed in construction during the same period.

U.S. Metal Mining Industry Trends

	Value of Mined Production ($Mil)	Employment (000)	Number of Mines (Metal Ore)
1991	11,000	44	236
1992	11,500	42	222
1993	10,800	40	199
1994	12,100	39	200
1995	14,000	41	174
1996	12,700	41	N/A

Source: U.S. Geological Survey, Mine Safety & Health Administration.

Market Overview

The total sales of metal mining operations in the United States during 1996 were $12.2 billion, down 14.5% from 1995. The decline was completed attributed to the considerable price erosion among major metals that year, which spilled over to ore prices. Without the price drop, volume was basically unchanged from its level a year ago.

Prices of Major Metals

	1995	1996	% Chg.
Gold COMEX 1st Pos., $/TR OZ	384.5	387.8	0.9
Silver COMEX 1st Pos., ¢/TR OZ	518.5	517.8	−0.1
Aluminum MW US Market, ¢/LB	85.9	71.3	−16.9
Copper MW US Prod Cath., ¢/LB	138.3	109.2	−21.1
Zinc MW NA SHG, ¢/LB	53.2	51.1	−4.0
PPI for steel mill products (1982=100)	120.1	115.6	−3.7

Precious Metals

The gold market had a brief price runup early in 1996, before concerns over an upswing in the U.S. inflation rate were overcome in the second half of the year. Gold prices averaged $387 per ounce on the New York Mercantile Exchange in 1996. However, they had been falling steadily during the course of the year, from over $400 at the beginning of 1996 to $350 at the end of the year. Continued strength in the U.S. dollar and low expectations for inflation in the United States were the primary reasons for the fall.

In the near term, additional downward price pressure is expected from sales of gold by central banks, predominantly by European nations in an effort to raise funds to lower their debt levels in preparation for European Monetary Union in 1999. Despite the recent Busang fiasco (this Indonesian gold deposit, thought to be the largest in the world, was found last year to contain only a minuscule amount of gold), world gold mine production is forecast to rise in the next two years. U.S. domestic gold mine production in 1996 was estimated at slightly below the record levels of recent years, but high enough to maintain the U.S. position as the world's second largest gold–producing nation, after South Africa.

Domestic silver production increased 10% in 1996, following the reopening of several mines that were prompted by a rise in silver prices. Domestic silver consumption remained essentially unchanged from the previous year.

Base Metals

World mine production of copper rose significantly for the second consecutive year, increasing by about 5% in 1996. Most of the increase came from expanding capacity in South America, particularly Chile, where more than 400,000 tons of new capacity came on–stream. U.S. copper companies continued to invest in Chilean and Peruvian properties in an effort to expand production and reduce costs. Domestic mine production, which was flat in 1995, resumed its upward trend in 1996 and rose to 1.9 million metric tons. In the meanwhile, both world and U.S. demand for copper rose significantly thanks to growth in industrial production on a global basis.

Nonetheless, copper last year was overshadowed by only one theme – the "Sumitomo Scandal". Copper prices remained relatively high during the first five months of 1996, with the U.S. producer price for refined copper averaging about $1.22 per pound. In June, Sumitomo revealed that its head copper trader had amassed losses in excess of $1.8 billion from unauthorized trades over a ten–year period. As a result, copper prices fell sharply

worldwide; with the U.S. producer price averaging a little over $0.90 for the second half of 1996. The aftershock was also felt in other metal markets for an extended period.

U.S. zinc mine production increased slightly in 1996, because of increased output at the Red Dog Mine in Alaska, the leading U.S. producer. Domestic zinc consumption continued its upward trend. Most zinc metal was used for galvanizing and alloy production. The United States is the largest consumer of zinc and zinc products, but domestic metal production capacity accounts for less than one–fourth of the quantity consumed. Canada and Mexico are the leading importers of zinc to the United States, because of their geographical proximity and low tariffs.

Iron Ore

U.S. iron ore production, consumption, and trade were about level in 1996. The undergoing structural changes in the U.S. steel industry, toward mini–mills that consume steel scrap and away from the integrated mills that consume iron ore, will not bode well for the iron ore sector. Although the mini–mills under construction or proposed are expected to add 10 million to 15 million tons of capacity to the flat–rolled market by the end of the decade, unfavorable cost comparisons and tougher environmental regulations, especially those restricting coke oven gas emissions, are expected to force the closure of some older integrated facilities.

International prices for iron ore are for the most part negotiated between sellers and buyers on an annual basis. Although international ore prices increased for the second consecutive year, prices in 1996 were considerably lower than those of 1991. There is a trend in the international market away from sintering of iron ore toward pelletization. This is driven, in large part, by environmental considerations. Australia and Brazil continued to be the leading exporters of iron ore, with a combined total of about 60% of the world total. The United States continued to be a net importer of iron ore.

Outlook

The U.S. economy is expected to continue to grow at a moderate rate for the near term, providing a mild stimulus to the nation's metals–consuming industries. Inflation is expected to remain low, and although interest rates are rising this year, the increase will be small enough to allow this stimulus to continue. Although motor vehicle output will fall off slightly, the sector's performance over the next few years will be remarkably stable for this stage in the business cycle. Overall, the U.S. metal mining industry is going to enjoy a year of moderate growth in 1997, then grow slowly thereafter.

International Market

In addition to the further delineation of the world–class resource base and development potential of the Voisey's Bay nickel deposit in Labrador, Canada, 1996 was marked by the ongoing capacity of Canadian equity capital markets to generate investments for worldwide exploration and mining development.

Global commodity priorities were focused on gold, nickel, steel, aluminum, cobalt, and other base metals, the latter despite the effect of the Sumitomo scandal. The demand for metal minerals was fueled by new economic growth in Asia and Latin America, along with the need to rebuild aging infrastructure in North America and Europe. Trends in privatization of state–owned mining and processing enterprises in Europe, Asia, Africa, and Latin America continued, with more willingness of governments to take on private joint–venture partners in countries where the national sentiment was to maintain ownership of natural resources.

Regulations and Trade Issues

Legislation to reform the Mining Law of 1872 has been considered by the Congress and the Administration for the past several years; however, legislation to reform the Mining Law was not enacted in 1996. The Mining Law gives U.S. citizens and corporations the right to prospect for certain minerals on particular Federal lands and confers the right to file claims that permit the claimants to mine and sell minerals found. The Mining Law does not provide for a royalty payment to the Federal government for minerals that are mined. Under the Mining Law, claimants also may apply for a patent that transfers ownership of minerals and mineral lands to the claimant.

Metal Mining

Growth in Sales (Line) and Volume (Bar)

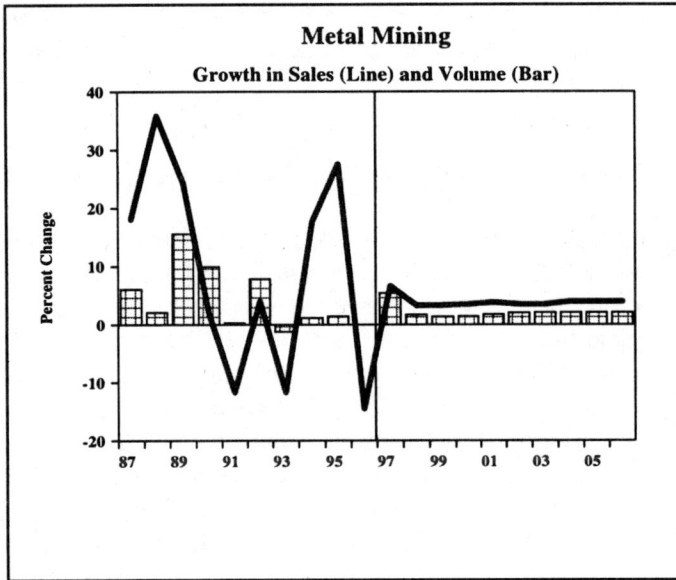

Metal Mining

Growth in Product Prices

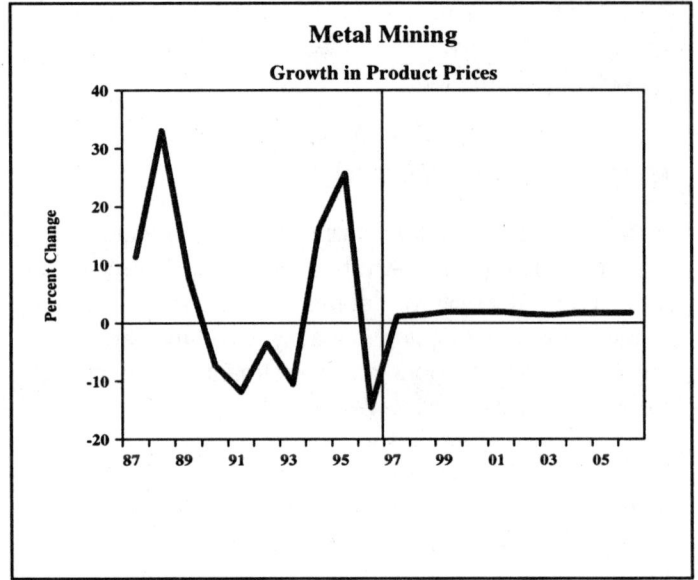

```
Metal Mining
  SIC 10
```

		1990	1991	1992	1993	1994	1995	1996	1997	1998	Compound Ann Avg Growth 1986-1996	1996-2006
Sales												
	Billions of $	11.72	10.35	10.77	9.51	11.18	14.26	12.19	13.00	13.41		
	% Change	1.8	-11.7	4.0	-11.7	17.6	27.6	-14.5	6.6	3.2	7.8	3.9
Volume	% Change	9.9	0.2	7.8	-1.3	1.1	1.5	0.0	5.4	1.7	4.2	2.2
Prices	% Change	-7.4	-11.8	-3.5	-10.5	16.3	25.7	-14.5	1.1	1.5	3.5	1.7
Exports												
	Billions of $	10.71	10.53	10.94	15.44	12.69	14.55	15.11	15.47	16.21		
	% Change	1.6	-1.6	3.9	41.1	-17.8	14.6	3.9	2.4	4.8	4.6	4.5
Imports												
	Billions of $	14.84	14.14	14.15	14.12	17.35	21.28	21.09	21.77	22.67		
	% Change	-8.1	-4.7	0.0	-0.2	22.8	22.7	-0.9	3.2	4.2	3.0	1.3
Apparent Consumption												
	Billions of $	15.84	13.97	13.97	8.19	15.83	20.99	18.17	19.29	19.88		
	Nominal % Change	-7.3	-11.9	0.0	-41.4	93.4	32.6	-13.4	6.2	3.0	4.3	0.1
	Real % Change	0.0	-0.0	3.7	-34.5	66.3	5.5	1.2	5.0	1.6	0.8	-1.5

Iron Ore

There are only 10–15 major iron ore mining companies in the United States and Canada. The vast majority of their sites are in the Great Lakes and St. Lawrence River regions. About 85% of the iron ore consumed in the United States comes from the Great Lakes area, but a significant amount of iron ore is also mined in Utah and Missouri. Many mines are owned by integrated corporations such as Inland Steel, LTV Steel, and USX Corp. Cleveland–Cliffs Inc., the leading U.S. iron ore and pellet producer, is however not directly involved in the manufacture of steel. Its 1996 revenues were about $500 million, out of $1.9 billion for the entire iron ore industry.

Demand Conditions

U.S. iron ore consumption has seen significant growth over the last ten years. Shipments increased from 46.4 million net tons in 1986 to 68.1 million in 1996. Exports have also grown, from 5.0 million net tons in 1986 to 6.9 million during 1996. However, the much larger import category, although up only about 8.0% over the ten–year period, grew more in volume terms. As a result, net consumption increased by more than 25% from 1986 to 1996. This growth has been driven by the resurgence of the U.S. steel industry.

Iron ore consumption can be broken down into blast furnace, steel furnace, and sintering plant demand. The entire growth in consumption from 1986 through 1996 was attributable to blast furnace consumption, which rose 33.6% over the ten years. Demand from the steel furnace and sintering plant segments, on the other hand, has declined over the last ten years. Since less than 10% of U.S. iron ore shipments are exported, the future growth of the industry will be based on domestic demand from blast furnaces and integrated steel mills. The new mini steel mills, which have sprouted throughout the United States in recent years, do not consume iron ore directly. Their inputs are limited to steel scrap or direct reduced iron (DRI). Mini mills will be at the forefront of a 20 million ton increase in U.S. steel melting capacity over the next five years. Therefore, demand increases for iron ore are likely to be modest.

While iron ore is not a direct input used by mini mills, it will continue to play a leading role in the manufacture of steel. The electric arc furnace used in mini mills currently produces about 42% of total U.S. steel production. This means the other 58% is produced by basic oxygen furnaces (BOF) or open hearth (OH) furnaces. Over the next five years WEFA expects the production share of BOF/OH to slip only to 55%. As a result, even though this segment will grow more slowly than mini mills, the growth potential of the iron ore industry should still be classified as healthy.

Supporting future ore demand will also be two new DRI plants currently under construction in the United States. These plants will be able to use iron ore or pellets as input, and they will produce direct reduced iron for use in mini mills. The combined impact of DRI and integrated mill demand should be strong enough to increase iron ore demand by 1.5%–2.0% annually over the next five years. Although this growth is significantly lower than the 5.0% annual growth we expect in steel scrap, the alternative input in steelmaking, ore will still be the primary input for the production of steel.

U.S. trade in the iron ore industry has been dominated by Canada. In 1996, more than 50% of U.S. iron ore imports came from Canada. Brazil and Venezuela were also major sources, accounting for 28% and 12% respectively. While Canada has a distinct location advantage, Brazil is the world's largest producer of usable ore, and Brazilian producers have been very aggressively pursuing world market share.

Canada also is dominant in the U.S. iron ore export market. In 1996, more than 99% of U.S. iron ore exports went to Canada. Over the next five years Canada will remain our senior trading partner in the iron ore business.

Supply Conditions

Iron ore mining capacity is difficult to forecast because it is based on a number of uncontrollable factors. The discovery of mineral deposits is a process that can be motivated by economic factors, but its potential is determined by strictly physical limits. Another complication lies in the fact that future, yet undiscovered, finds have a strong likelihood of being on Federal lands. Nearly 75% of U.S. metal mining lies in the 12 Western States in which 90% of Federal lands are located. Therefore, ore discovery and capacity expansion are dependent upon access to federal land for exploration and mining, which has become more restrictive in recent years. Mining operations on these lands must also comply with natural resource development regulations specified by the U.S. Forest Service and by the Bureau of Land Management, and must strike a balance between environmental protection and economic use.

There are three major classes of iron ore: fines ore, lump ore, and concentrates/pellets. The majority of the production in the rest of the world is categorized as fines. The United States is the largest producer of pellets with approximately 30% of world production. Pellets are a con- centrated iron ore product used in basic oxygen or open hearth furnaces and in the manufacture of direct reduced iron. Production capacity for pellets in the United States is roughly 70 million tons. We expect little change in this capacity by the year 2000, since the steel industry's more rapid growth lies with mini mills. In addition, the size of Canada's large iron ore reserves and the freedom of trade that exists between the two countries make Canada a convenient pressure valve should U.S. producers be unable to meet demand. By the year 2005, we expect U.S. pellet capacity will increase to only 73 million tons.

In summary, North American supplies of iron ore are readily available to meet the expected needs of the steel industry. However, the raw material focus of the steel industry is not with iron ore but in steel scrap. As a result, little growth in iron ore prices is likely over the next five years. WEFA's composite price of ore, defined as direct shipping ore, concentrates, agglomerates, and by–product ore, increased by 5.0% to $30/ton in 1996. Over the next five years we expect average prices to increase by about 2.5% annually. In contrast steel scrap prices are expected to grow between 3.0% and 4.0% annually.

Iron Ore
Growth in Sales (Line) and Volume (Bar)

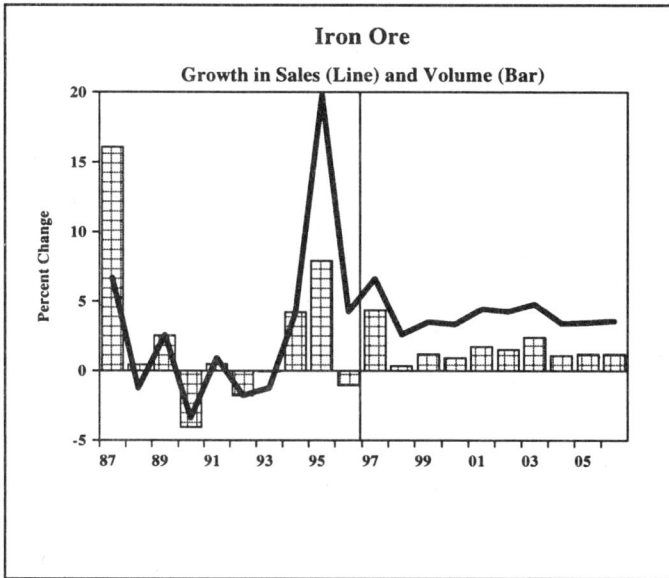

Iron Ore
Growth in Product Prices

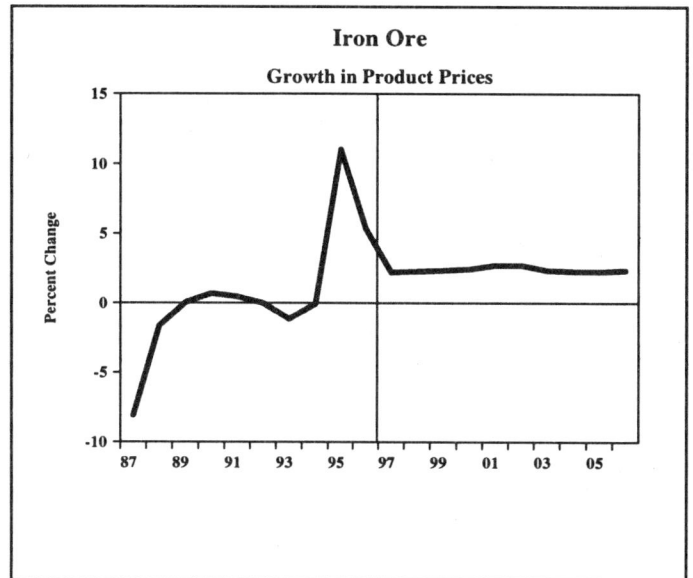

Iron Ore
SIC 101, 106

		1990	1991	1992	1993	1994	1995	1996	1997	1998	Compound Ann Avg Growth 1986-1996	1996-2006
Sales												
	Billions of $	1.49	1.50	1.48	1.46	1.52	1.82	1.90	2.02	2.08		
	% Change	-3.4	0.9	-1.8	-1.2	4.1	19.8	4.2	6.6	2.6	2.9	4.0
Volume	% Change	-4.0	0.5	-1.8	-0.1	4.2	7.9	-1.0	4.3	0.3	2.3	1.6
Prices	% Change	0.7	0.4	-0.0	-1.2	-0.1	11.0	5.3	2.2	2.3	0.5	2.4

3.7

Coal Mining

The coal industry should register steady improvement in 1997. Consumption should increase to levels above one billion tons for the first time, primarily based on growth in the electric power generation sector. Other demand areas, including exports, industrial, coking, and residential/commercial use, are expected to remain generally flat.

The coal industry is composed of establishments primarily engaged in producing and developing bituminous coal or lignite at surface mines, bituminous coal or lignite at underground mines, and anthracite. The industry includes underground mining, auger mining, strip mining, culm bank mining and other surface mining, as well as coal preparation plants engaged in cleaning, crushing, screening, or sizing. It also includes establishments that perform primarily coal mining services for others on a contract or fee basis.

Demand Conditions

Coal consumption reached 982 million tons in 1996. Coal in the United States is sold overwhelmingly in the domestic market, and only about 8.5% of total coal production went to the export market last year.

On the domestic side, electric utilities account for approximately 89% of domestic consumption. Coal is used to generate over 50% of the electric power in the United States, a figure that should remain relatively steady over the next twenty years. Under this assumption, coal use by electric utilities should rise from the 1996 level of 982 million tons to about 1,050 million tons in the year 2015.

Factors favoring increased use of coal in electric utilities include attractive delivered prices, abundant domestic supply, and a declining contribution from nuclear power over the next two decades. Factors which mitigate against coal use include the desire for less capital–intensive fuels by a restructuring electric utility industry, environmental problems associated with coal use, and strong competition from natural gas for electricity generation.

Other domestic coal users include the industrial sector (accounting for 7% of domestic consumption), coke plants employing metallurgical coal (3% of consumption), and residential and commercial uses (only about 0.5% of consumption). Consumption by both coke plants and residential/commercial users are expected to remain stable or even decline in the future. In the case of coke plants, stringent environmental considerations, greater coke–making efficiency, and alternative means of mak-

ing steel will all tend to reduce future consumption. In the residential sector, environmental considerations and the availability of other heating sources suggest there will be no future growth in coal consumption.

Exports are a highly volatile market for U.S. coal. Over the past 25 years, coal exports have varied between 53 and 112 million tons (mt). In 1996, the United States exported approximately 90 million tons, about 37 million tons of which were sent to the international steam coal market and about 53 million tons to world metallurgical coal users. Major countries purchasing coal from the United States include Canada (12 mt), Japan (10mt), Italy (9mt), the Netherlands (7mt), Brazil (6mt), the United Kingdom (6mt), Spain (4mt), France (4mt), and the Republic of Korea (4mt).

The outlook for future exports is bright. In Europe, despite limited growth opportunities for coal, the gradual phasing out of subsidies to domestic coal industries creates extremely attractive markets for U.S. coal, particularly in the United Kingdom and Germany. In Asia, the outlook for strong economic growth ensures a significant increase in coal use in that region. While exports are expected to remain at about last year's level in 1997, they are anticipated to increase to about 112 million tons by the year 2015.

Supply Conditions

The United States possesses enormous coal reserves, which generally results in a market condition of oversupply. Coal companies have been able to offset declining prices for most coals by demonstrating remarkable improvement in productivity.

Compared with the dismal 1970s, when mine productivity (measured as tons per miner–hour) declined, productivity improved at an average rate of 6.6% per year between 1986 and 1995. Productivity from surface mining, which on a national basis is more than twice as productive as underground mining, increased from 3.0 tons per miner–hour (tpm) in 1978 to almost 8.5 tpm in 1995. Deep mining productivity has grown from 1.0 tpm in 1978 to 3.39 tpm in 1995. In terms of production, surface mining has increased by 50% in that time period (1978–95) to 636.7 million tons while deep mining has experienced a 64% increase in that time frame, reaching 396.2 million tons in 1995. Final 1996 data for deep mining versus surface mining are not yet available, but total production in 1996 reached 1.033 billion tons.

Productivity to the coal mining industry is extremely important to meeting the challenge of higher labor and material costs, additional costs borne by consumers associated with more stringent environmental requirements, and strong competition from other fuels, notably natural gas. There are a number of reasons why productivity has improved, but the two most important reasons have been gains in mining technology and more efficient work rules.

In underground mines, productivity has been improved by the expanded use of longwall techniques. Longwalls produce about 48% of underground coal in the United States. In longwall mining, a cutting machine is pulled back and forth across a panel of coal 450 to 750 feet wide and up to a mile long. A conveyor removes the broken coal. Since longwall mining is done under movable roof supports that are advanced as the bed is cut, the roof in the mined–out area is allowed to collapse as mining advances. In 1997, there will be 69 longwalls in operation with an average face width of 824 feet and average panel length of 8,430 feet. Longwall mining typically achieves recovery rates of about 80% to 90% of mineable coal, compared with 50% to 60% with traditional room and pillar methods.

In room and pillar methods, even in the "retreat" phase, when miners try to recover as much coal as possible, some pillars are left because of natural restraints, such as poor mine–roof and floor conditions. However, expansion of the continuous mining techniques used in these methods improved productivity. A continuous min-

ing machine cuts, drills, and loads coal in a single operation, and requires no blasting. By reducing the size of the crew required, from 10 miners to 6 for example, it improves labor productivity. In addition, the expanded use of "supersections" (the use of two or more continuous miners, where traditionally only one was used) has been a capital–intensive approach to expanding productivity.

In surface mines, productivity improved as surface production moved to the west, where major coal seams are thick relative to the amount of overburden that has to be removed and subsequently restored. In addition, the development of more efficient, large–scale equipment, such as gigantic draglines and extremely large haulage trucks, improved productivity. Future use of new mining technology depends in part on the ability of companies, faced with a sluggish market, to finance the large initial investment, and on the availability of mine sites with conditions suitable for employing the new technologies.

Changes in work rules have also contributed to productivity gains. Over the years, as employment in mining declined, the proportion of non–union mines expanded. One result was that non–union operations were sometimes able to take advantage of "alternate" work rules that are more efficient than those provided for in the union contract. Examples include working fewer and longer shifts, cross training miners to do multiple jobs, and permitting supervisors to help out.

Although the United States has nearly 1,700 coal mines with production equal to or exceeding 10,000 tons, 73% of production now comes from 198 large mines, each with annual output greater than 1 million tons per year.

Output west of the Mississippi has increased market share consistently, and now accounts for 47% of U.S. production. Western coal tends to be low–sulfur, low–energy–content coal, produced from huge surface mines. Eastern coal has a higher energy content, but is mined by diverse techniques, and its sulfur content varies widely. It is likely that western coal will account for more than 50% of the nation's supply within the next five to ten years.

Foreign coal, at 7.1 million tons, represents less than 1% of total U.S. consumption. This coal primarily comes from Colombia, Venezuela, Indonesia, and Canada. Most of the coal is used by eastern U.S. electric utilities capable of receiving coal by water. Imports are expected to rise over the next decade, perhaps to as high as 25 million tons, as a result of existing clean air legislation which will promote the use of these lower sulfur coals especially after 2000. The strong price volatility of international coals, however, provides a disincentive to strong reliance by U.S. consumers on these sources.

Pricing

The delivered price of coal varies considerably around the United States, depending on transport costs, the energy content of the coal per unit weight, and its sulfur content. The average real mine price declined an average of 5.6% annually from 1986–95, from $29.52/ton in 1986 to $17.52/ton in 1995. In terms of delivered prices, the average real price of coal has declined by a similar margin, from $41.31/ton in 1986 to $25.12/ton in 1995.

The reasons for these price declines include the significant technology and labor productivity gains identified previously, strong competition from other fuels, and competitive pressures within the coal industry itself. Prices are expected to continue their decline in the future, due primarily to the expiration of older, higher–than–market priced contracts and their replacement with today's more competitively priced coal.

Environmental Issues

The coal industry must contend with some of the most difficult environmental issues in U.S. industry. Power plants built since 1978 are already strictly limited in the amount of sulfur dioxide they may emit. Consequently, they must install costly flue–gas desulfurization equipment (also called "scrubbers"), or burn very low sulfur coal. Additional sulfur emission controls as stipulated in the Clean Air Act Amendments of 1990 are taking effect in two stages. Beginning in 1995, for the 110 power plants built before 1978, emissions are generally limited to 2.5 pounds of sulfur dioxide per million British thermal units (BTU) of energy consumed. The second stage, to take effect in the year 2000, limits emissions for all power plants, old and new, to 1.2 pounds of sulfur dioxide per million BTU of energy consumed.

The plant owners may choose how to achieve these emissions limits. They can retrofit scrubbers, switch to low–sulfur coal, blend low–sulfur coal with high–sulfur coal, co–fire with natural gas, repower with more efficient boilers, or close the plant. Companies that reduce emissions below the required limits can trade "emission cred-

its" within their organization or sell the credits to other firms that can then continue to emit sulfur at levels above the limit. Utilities can also reduce their aggregate emissions below the limit and "bank" emissions credits so they can maintain emissions above the limit in a later year.

Use of these trading allowances or credits, is providing flexibility and cost minimization of compliance while improving air quality. For the majority of older plants, however, the preferred option for the mid–term appears to be switching to low–sulfur coal. Switching allows utilities to hedge between the future cost and availability of emission trading allowances and development of more efficient clean–coal technologies.

The Clean Air Act Amendments also include a list of 150 compounds and classes of compounds deemed "hazardous air pollutants." The Environmental Protection Agency is responsible for developing emissions standards for these substances based upon the "maximum achievable control technology." When burned, both coal– and oil–fired power plants emit several of the listed compounds.

Coal–fired power plants and industrial boilers are likely to become subject to stricter regulation of particulate emissions smaller than 10 microns in diameter. Even though these small emissions receive less attention than other pollutants, recent studies indicate that they are more dangerous than had been thought, and that they should be restricted, as are emissions larger than 10 microns. EPA has proposed stringent standards affecting particulate down to 2.5 microns as well as ozone, and must review thousands of public comments by July 18, 1997.

Another environmental issue of importance to the coal industry is potential global climate change caused by the anthropogenic (man–made) emission of greenhouse gases such as carbon dioxide, carbon monoxide, methane, and nitrous oxides. All fossil fuels, when burned, emit carbon dioxide, the greenhouse gas with the greatest atmospheric concentration after water vapor. However, coal emits 80% more carbon dioxide per unit of energy consumed than does natural gas, and about 20% more than does fuel oil. Hence, coal–fired power stations are prime candidates for controls on carbon dioxide emissions.

Industry Structure

On a national scale, the coal industry is relatively concentrated. The largest producer of U.S. coal, the British–owned Peabody Coal Co., accounted for roughly 143.7 million tons of production in 1995, about 14% of the market, while the top 10 producers accounted for slightly more than 50%. This reflects a very strong trend toward consolidation since five years ago, when it took the output of the top 20 producers to account for more than 50% of production.

Of even greater concern is the trend toward regional concentration of production. Many coal-producing regions in the country are dominated by one or two producers, giving them increasing market power within their geographic areas of competition.

International Trade

The United States has long been considered the "swing supplier" among international coal producers. Whereas the United States typically has had plentiful coal available, its delivered prices have historically been higher than other global suppliers. As a result, significant demand for exports arises only when serious international shortfalls occur, most recently in 1995.

Many international buyers felt that U.S. producers were slow to respond to the 1995 supply shortage. This slowness in responding was due to several factors, some one–time phenomena but others representing more long–term problems. Among the one–time concerns was the fact that 1995 was the beginning of Phase I of the Clean Air Act Amendments, and many producers who were uncertain about domestic requirements decided to remain out of the global market. Moreover, very few producers initially believed the shortfall would last more than a few months, which it did.

There were more structural concerns related to the 1995–96 coal market which must be addressed as the international need for coal increases in the future. First, in sharp contrast to most world coal suppliers, the domestic market remains by far the most important to U.S. producers, so the interest level of U.S. companies in exporting is perceived by many potential importers as being quite low. Second, most international purchases occur on an annual basis, too short a commitment for most U.S. producers, who are more accustomed to longer contract duration.

U.S. Coal Overview, 1987–98

(in million tons)

Year	Production	Stock Changes[1]	Imports	Exports	Total Consumption
			Short Tons		
1987	918.8	6.5	1.7	79.6	836.9
1988	950.3	−25.0	2.1	95.0	883.6
1989	980.7	−13.7	2.9	100.8	889.7
1990	1,029.1	26.5	2.7	105.8	895.5
1991	996.0	−0.9	3.4	109.0	887.6
1992	997.5	−3.0	3.8	102.5	892.4
1993	945.4	−52.0	7.3	74.5	925.9
1994	1,033.5	23.7	7.5	71.3	930.3
1995	1,032.9	−0.3	7.2	88.5	940.6
1996	1,062.8	−13.9	7.1	90.4	982.2
1997	1,093.3	−10.1	7.5	91.9	1,008.5
1998	1,106.9	−3.8	7.5	92.4	1,023.0
			Metric Tons		
1987	883.5	5.9	1.5	72.2	759.2
1988	862.1	−22.7	1.9	86.2	801.6
1989	889.7	−12.4	2.6	91.4	807.1
1990	933.6	24.0	2.4	96.0	812.4
1991	903.6	−0.8	3.1	98.9	805.2
1992	904.9	−2.7	3.4	93.0	809.8
1993	857.7	−47.2	6.6	67.6	840.0
1994	937.6	21.5	6.8	64.7	843.9
1995	937.0	−0.3	6.5	80.3	853.3
1996	964.2	−12.6	6.4	82.0	891.1
1997	991.8	−9.2	6.8	83.4	914.9
1998	1,004.2	−3.4	6.8	83.8	928.1

[1]Includes losses and statistical discrepancies. A negative number indicates a stock drawdown

NOTES: Detail may not add up to totals because of rounding.

SOURCE: U.S. Department of Energy, Energy Information

U.S. Coal Consumption by End Use Sector, 1987–98

(in million tons)

Year	Electric Utilities	Coke Plants	Other Industrial and Transportation	Residential and Commercial	Total
Short Tons					
1987	717.9	37.0	75.2	6.9	836.9
1988	758.4	41.9	76.3	7.1	883.6
1989	766.9	40.5	76.1	6.2	889.7
1990	773.5	38.9	76.3	6.7	895.5
1991	772.3	33.9	75.4	6.1	887.6
1992	779.9	32.4	74.0	6.2	892.4
1993	813.5	31.3	74.9	6.2	925.9
1994	817.3	31.7	75.1	6.0	930.2
1995	768.1	33.0	72.8	5.8	940.6
1996	874.7	31.7	70.6	5.8	982.9
1997	883.7	32.5	71.1	5.8	993.1
1998	888.2	32.7	71.1	5.8	997.8
Metric Tons					
1987	651.3	33.6	68.2	6.3	759.2
1988	688.0	38.0	69.2	6.4	801.6
1989	695.7	36.7	69.0	5.6	807.1
1990	701.7	35.3	69.2	6.1	812.4
1991	700.6	30.8	68.4	5.5	805.2
1992	707.5	29.4	67.1	5.6	809.6
1993	738.0	28.4	67.9	5.6	840.0
1994	741.4	28.8	68.1	5.4	843.9
1995	696.8	29.9	66.0	5.3	853.3
1996	793.5	28.8	64.0	5.3	891.7
1997	801.7	29.5	64.5	5.3	900.9
1998	805.8	29.7	64.5	5.3	905.2

NOTE: Totals may not equal sum of components because of independent rounding.

SOURCE: U.S. Department of Energy, Energy Information Administration.

Other Coal Industry Indicators, 1980–95

Year	Number of Mines[1]	Number of Workers[2]	Productivity (tons per miner per hour)	Productivity Growth (percent)
1980	3,969	228,569	1.93	6.6
1981	4,140	229,302	2.10	8.8
1982	4,098	217,117	2.11	0.5
1983	3,405	175,642	2.50	18.5
1984	3,566	177,848	2.64	5.6
1985	3,355	169,281	2.74	3.8
1986	3,175	154,645	3.01	9.9
1987	3,030	142,667	3.30	9.6
1988	2,915	135,366	3.55	7.6
1989	2,821	131,497	3.70	4.2
1990	2,707	131,497	3.83	3.5
1991	2,394	120,602	4.09	6.8
1992	2,196	110,196	4.36	7.4
1993	2,030	101,322	4.70	7.8
1994	1,898	97,500	4.98	6.0
1995	1,716	90,252	5.38	8.0

[1]Excludes mines producing less than 10,000 tons in the year; silt, culm, refuse bank, slurry dam, and dredge production; and preparation plants with less than 5,000 employee hours. [2]Average number of workers working daily; includes all employees engaged in production, preparation, processing, development, maintenance, repair, shop or yard work at mining operations. Excludes office workers. Includes mining operations management and all technical and engineering personnel.

SOURCE: U.S. Department of Energy, Energy Information Administration.

U.S. Trade Patterns in 1995
Coal Mining
SIC 12
(in millions of dollars, percent)

Exports	Value	Share	Imports	Value	Share
Japan	461	12.9	Colombia	85	34.6
Italy	400	11.2	Venezuela	65	26.4
Canada	316	8.9	Canada	43	17.5
Netherlands	308	8.6	Indonesia	36	14.6
Brazil	279	7.8	Australia	7	2.8
World Total	3,565	100.0	World Total	246	100.0

SOURCE: U.S. Department of Energy: Energy Information Administration.

Export values are based on free alongside ship (f.a.s.) values multiplied by export volume; Import values are based on volume multiplied by customs import value.

Crude Petroleum

U.S. petroleum demand reached a seventeen year high in 1996. In the first half of the year, demand for heating oil largely supported the market, while demand for motor gasoline maintained the momentum during the latter half of the year. Strong demand contributed to the price escalation experienced in 1996.

Petroleum consumption is forecast to grow at an average rate of about 1% between 1996 and 2006. The transportation sector is likely to maintain the largest share of the projected petroleum product demand. Demand for transportation services will expand during the decade on both an aggregate and per capita basis.

Over the next ten years, U.S. crude oil production will continue its slow decline and the country will continue its trend toward increasing dependence on imported supplies. By 2005, the United States will import about 55% of crude and petroleum products.

OPEC has been the dominant force in world oil markets for more than thirty years, supplying approximately 40% of world demand. It has been producing at a quota of 25.33 million barrels per day, although adherence to the quota has been an ongoing problem.

Crude prices are not projected to escalate above $20 in 1996 dollars in the near term. There are factors that exert upward price pressure and factors which will tend to hold prices down. On net, there will be only moderate upward escalation of real crude prices over the next ten years.

Demand

U.S. petroleum demand reached a seventeen year high in 1996, averaging 18.23 million barrels per day. In the first half of the year, demand for heating oil largely supported the market, while demand for motor gasoline maintained the momentum during the latter half of the year. Strong demand contributed to the price escalation experienced in 1996 — the average refiners' acquisition cost of crude oil rose from $17.23 per barrel in 1995 to $20.80 per barrel in 1996. Key market events in 1996 included:

- A cold and long winter. Severe winter weather wiped out much of the stocks on hand by the end of the first quarter. The late arrival of spring exacerbated the situation through continued withdrawals of nearly depleted stocks.

- A prolonged driving season. Mild weather, coupled with strong economic growth, encouraged traveling in the summer and fall of 1996. Motor gasoline demand averaged an all–time high and sustained oil consumption through the second half of the year. This prevented the stock build that usually occurs each year after heating oil demand wanes.

- Backwardation in prices. Persistent backwardation in the futures market — futures prices lower than spot prices — discouraged stock building for all petroleum products. Refiners chose to delay purchases because future replacement costs were expected to be lower.

- Low European stocks. In the fall, distillate stocks in Europe were unusually low. As a result, prices were significantly above those in the United States, which attracted shipments to Europe.

Through the first three quarters of 1996, continuing demand growth, compounded by weather, environmental policy stickiness, and just–in–time inventory management led to supply shortages. Consumers were given a reprieve, however, when mild weather late in the year dampened heating oil demand. By the end of the first quarter of 1997, most petroleum stocks had finally reached normal levels and their effect on oil prices was reduced.

Forecast

Petroleum demand is expected to rise to 18.4 million barrels per day in 1997, driven by strong economic growth, lower crude oil prices, and continuing strength in demand for motor gasoline. The fairly strong growth in the U.S. economy in 1997 will stimulate air travel as well as on–road transport. The advent of the driving season, combined with motor gasoline stocks that are slightly below normal levels, could spur a short–term rise in petroleum prices in the summer months. Coupled with a futures market that is in contango (with spot prices lower than futures), refiners should be more willing to increase inventory purchases.

Petroleum consumption is forecast to grow at an average rate of about 1% between 1996 and 2006. The transportation sector is likely to maintain the largest share of the projected petroleum product demand. Demand for transportation services will expand during the decade on both an aggregate and per capita basis. The demand for travel will be only partially offset by improvements in capital efficiency. Consumers, for example, continue to choose performance, styling, and features over fuel efficiency in their vehicles.

Supply

U.S. crude oil production continues to slide. In 1996, production reached 6.47 million barrels per day, the lowest it has ever been in over twenty years. Alaskan production, which peaked at 2 million barrels per day in 1988, has also been tracking a downward trend, barely reaching 1.4 million barrels per day last year. U.S. production, for the most part, is played out. If prices rise, the long–term decline may be arrestable, but it is not reversible. Over the next ten years, production will continue its slow decline.

With U.S. production on an inexorable decline, the country has become increasingly dependent on imported supplies from OPEC and non–OPEC countries. In 1996, the United States imported 46.6% of its petroleum. Crude oil accounted for the bulk of the imports. However, crude imports were up only 4% in 1996, compared with a rise of 38% (nearly 300 barrels per day) in petroleum products. Demand growth, coupled with limited refinery capacity, triggered the rise. Favorable price differentials between U.S. and European markets also encouraged transatlantic arbitrage.

Motor gasoline accounted for about one–third of the 1996 increase in imports, and brought a secondary impact to the market through its effect on distillates. A barrel of gasoline produced domestically creates one–half barrel of distillate fuel, so high imports of gasoline contributed to low distillate stocks.

OPEC has been the dominant force in world oil markets for more than thirty years, supplying approximately 40% of world demand. It has been producing at a quota of 25.33 million barrels per day, although adherence to the quota has been an ongoing problem. Led by Venezuela, OPEC countries overproduced by nearly 900,000 barrels per day in 1996. OPEC has also had some membership changes of late. Under the United Nations' barter deal (fuel versus food–for–aid), Iraq was allocated 1.2 million barrels per day of the Organization's total goal, about double its production under the embargo that has been in place since the Persian Gulf War. Since the U.N. and Iraq reached an agreement in December 1996, Iraqi production has climbed steadily from 600 million barrels per day to 1.3 million barrels per day in March 1997. OPEC is expected to ignore member overproduction in the short run, so somewhat lower prices are likely for OPEC crude.

Outside the United States, non–OPEC oil production is led by the former Soviet Union, which averaged 6.9 million barrels per day in 1996 — down from a high of 10.3 million barrels per day in 1991. Much of this decline is due to the political and economic uncertainties. Norway and the United Kingdom also contribute significantly to world crude supply from their offshore fields in the North Sea. Together, they averaged 5.8 million barrels per day in 1996, but this was 300,000 barrels per day below market expectations. Seasonal maintenance and delayed startups of new fields accounted for most of the problems. Other major non–OPEC oil producers include China, which averaged 3.1 million barrels per day, Mexico, and Canada.

Forecast

U.S. petroleum supply is projected to fall over the coming decade. Depletion of aging deposits will lead to the downward trend. Alaskan crude production will be declining at a rate of about 4% per year for the next ten years, while lower–48 production will be falling at a more moderate rate. President Clinton lifted the ban on Alaskan exports last year, which will tend to hold up production in the state. However, exports will also increase, and the net effect is that the United States will rely even more heavily on imports. By 2005, the United States will import about 55% of crude and petroleum products.

Three–quarters of the world's oil reserves belong to OPEC countries, most of which are located in the Persian Gulf. OPEC's reserves–to–production ratio is almost 80 years, compared with 42 years for the world as a whole and just 17 years for non–OPEC countries. In addition, OPEC has another competitive advantage in its low marginal costs of production. Supplies from this source are expected to be more than adequate.

The full return of Iraqi exports to the oil markets is expected in 1998. The current oil–for–aid deal is the only channel for Iraq to sell oil during 1997. However, the deal will end in June 1997, and it is questionable whether the current agreement will be renewed or extended. Due to the recent slump in crude prices, Iraq is considering its short–term options: renewing the current oil–for–aid deal, asking for increased volumes, or pushing for the removal of all sanctions. Iraq has continuously been seeking international support for the removal of all sanctions in order to restore its oil development and exploration programs, but the internal pressures for restoring sovereignty are growing. With pressure coming from the United States, the United Nations is not likely to renegotiate or remove sanctions until all of Iraq's U.N. resolutions related to weapons inspections and human rights are fulfilled. Current expectations are for a negotiated settlement between the parties in 1998, which would restore Iraq's crude production and exports to earlier levels.

Non–OPEC supplies are also burgeoning. New technology will play a significant role in the availability of supply by increasing the amount of oil that can be extracted from depleted fields, thereby lowering costs. With three–dimensional seismic and horizontal drilling, operators can reach new producing horizons. For example, it is estimated that offshore Norway could realize an additional 3.1 billion barrels of oil per day from currently producing fields and fields already approved for development by using these new drilling techniques.

The Keys to Supply Development: Technology and Investment

A tremendous amount of investment will be required to meet growing worldwide oil demand. According to official estimates, the cost of expanding capacity by one barrel per day ranges from $3000 for Saudi Arabia, Iran, Iraq, and Kuwait to $10,000 for U.S. and North Sea producers.

Costs to expand are the lowest for the four OPEC producers because they have the largest reserves. Venezuela has large reserves, but the low flow rates in its wells make production costlier. Nigeria, and to a lesser extent Libya and Algeria, have sizable reserves, but unstable political conditions have deterred external investment in these countries. U.S. and North Sea producers tend to benefit from technologies much earlier than OPEC producers, but low reserve–to–production ratios make supply prospects less promising.

Although investments in OPEC capacity expansion are economically viable, official financing may not be forthcoming, since oil industry investments are no longer the top priority for some governments. In response, some OPEC countries, especially Kuwait and the United Arab Emirates, are changing the laws that govern the oil sector in order to attract investment by foreign companies. Iraq has also been proactive in upstream deals with international companies in order to gain support for the lifting of sanctions. The ability to finance expansion will vary according to creditworthiness of the country. Saudi Arabia, the United Arab Emirates, and Kuwait are in the best positions, in terms of both external credit ratings and investment attractiveness. Conditions in countries like Algeria, Iran, Iraq, and Nigeria are less favorable because of their poor balance of payments, bad credit ratings, and political instability.

Non–OPEC production has captured much of the growing oil market due to investment in new technology, which has enabled producers to lower costs and extend the lifetime of existing fields. For instance, offshore drilling was limited to a depth of 1,000 feet, but new technology now allows oil production from basins more than 2,000 feet deep, and further advances are likely.

Prices

U.S. crude and petroleum product markets were remarkably strong in 1996. Oil prices broke records unseen since the Persian Gulf War. Distillate product prices were the most volatile, jumping by 18%. Residual fuel and motor gasoline prices also showed considerable strength, rising 14% and 10% respectively. Product prices relative to crude prices (ratios to crude) shrank, however, as crude prices shot up further and faster than product prices. In short, 1996 was a year marked by strong prices as well as contra–seasonal price patterns.

Uncertainties over the oil–for–aid deal with Iraq accounted for two crude price rallies during the year, in the spring and the summer, as the United Nations and Iraq engaged in several rounds of talks. These discussions caused prices to be extremely volatile early in the spring, when the failure to close the widely anticipated deal caused prices to spike. Tensions rose again near the end of the summer, when Iraq attacked a Kurdish town in Northern Iraq. In response to this violation, the United Nations suspended the oil–for–aid deal. Again, the market responded by pushing prices up. A settlement was finally reached early in December which allowed Iraq to sell $2 billion of oil in a 6–month period.

U.S. refiners also had to deal with domestic problems, including high demand and low stocks that supported prices. A prolonged 1995–1996 winter season depleted crude stocks to all time lows. Distillate fuel stocks also fell significantly below normal levels. A persistently backwardated NYMEX futures market caused buyers to treat crude oil like a depreciating asset. As a result, inventories did not recover until after the heating oil season. To exacerbate the situation, an extended driving season fueled a surge in motor gasoline demand.

Business leaders and consumers voiced their concerns over the rapid increase in prices, which resulted in a request by President Clinton for the Department of Energy to investigate reasons for the runup and to sell approximately 12 million barrels of crude oil from the Strategic Petroleum Reserve. The industry was also worried about disruptions in the market, and refiners undertook measures to boost inventories.

Mild weather, coupled with the return of Iraqi crude into the oil markets, finally caused oil prices to collapse in the first quarter of 1997. U.S. refineries also underwent one of their heaviest turnaround seasons in many years. The lack of refiner demand for crude oil caused a glut of crude supplies in the marketplace, which depressed petroleum product prices. West Texas Intermediate (WTI) futures markets twisted into contango, with spot prices trading at a discount to forward, for the first time in two years. This turn of events indicates that a market correction is underway.

Forecast

Crude prices are projected to see–saw between $19 and $20 per barrel through the end of 1998. The continuing but slow escalation in world oil demand growth, counterbalanced by increases in both OPEC and non–OPEC production, will result in prices that remain fairly constant in nominal dollars.

In general terms, we characterize four trading ranges for crude oil: low prices ($14–$17 per barrel), moderate prices ($17–$20 per barrel), moderately high prices ($20–$23), and high prices ($23 and above). The moderate prices of the last few years resulted from limited world demand growth as other fuels gained the lion's share of the stationary fuel market, and steadily increasing non–OPEC production. While OPEC producers grumbled, they were able to exert little control over a market where technology has radically changed the prospects for supplies. A temporary reversal of these effects occurred in 1996, but WEFA forecasts prices will drop to the moderate range and stay there through 2000.

The rate of world economic growth is the key driver for mid– and long–term oil demand growth. The mid–term outlook calls for economic growth of approximately 4% per annum for developing countries and 2.5% per year for industrialized countries. Growth rates of this magnitude will bring significant increases in global oil demand.

However, despite these building demand pressures, prices are not projected to escalate above $20 in 1996 dollars in the near term. Two key factors will help to hold prices down.

- First, oil demand growth is not increasing in tandem with world economies. While transportation services and petrochemical feedstocks still require petroleum, economies worldwide are working to diversify their energy needs, actively seeking partners to develop their non–oil resources.

- Second, technology has maintained steady improvements in supplies from non–OPEC sources. Supply developments have exceeded all expectations, and over the near to mid–term will play a large role in limiting price increases.

However, there are also factors that will put upward pressure on prices. These include steady declines in supply from the OECD countries and the resource poor countries of OPEC, as well as the fast plays of the reserves of some non–OPEC sources. On net, there will be only moderate upward escalation of real crude prices over the next ten years.

Crude Petroleum
Growth in Sales (Line) and Volume (Bar)

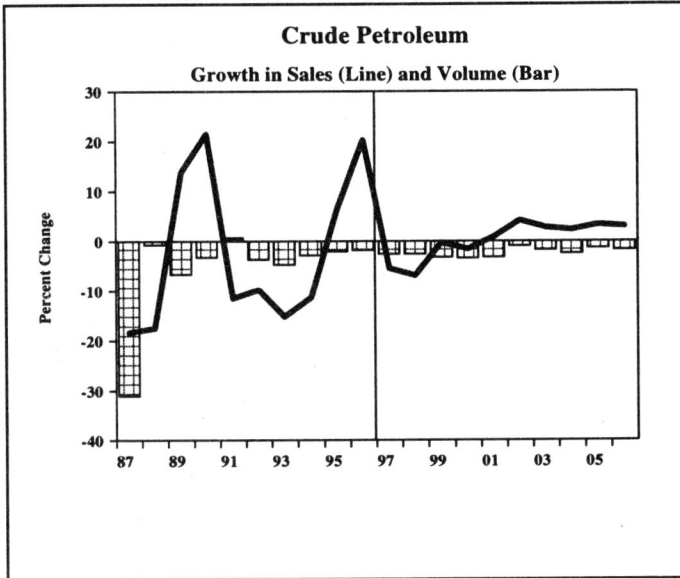

Crude Petroleum
Growth in Product Prices

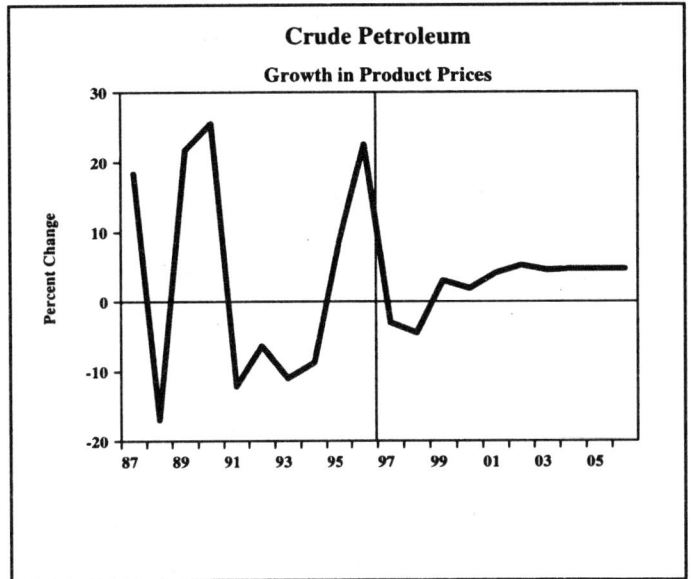

```
Crude Petroleum
  SIC Part of 13

                                                                                        Compound Ann Avg Growth
                        1990    1991    1992    1993    1994    1995    1996    1997    1998    1986-1996  1996-2006

Sales
         Billions of $  67.22   59.51   53.66   45.51   40.37   42.92   51.66   48.82   45.45
             % Change    21.5   -11.5    -9.8   -15.2   -11.3     6.3    20.4    -5.5    -6.9      -3.3       0.1

  Volume    % Change     -3.3     0.7    -3.7    -4.7    -2.9    -2.0    -1.8    -2.6    -2.5      -6.1      -2.3
  Prices    % Change     25.6   -12.1    -6.4   -11.0    -8.7     8.5    22.5    -3.0    -4.5       2.9       2.5

Imports
         Billions of $  43.95   36.90   38.55   38.47   38.48   42.81   50.48   47.42   46.95
             % Change    23.7   -16.0     4.5    -0.2     0.0    11.3    17.9    -6.0    -1.0       8.6       6.5

Apparent Consumption
         Billions of $ 110.97   96.37   92.17   83.93   78.79   85.72  101.66   95.85   92.05
      Nominal % Change   22.4   -13.2    -4.4    -8.9    -6.1     8.8    18.6    -5.7    -4.0       0.8       3.8
         Real % Change   -2.5    -1.2     2.2     2.3     2.8     0.2    -3.2    -2.8     0.5      -2.1       1.3
```

Natural Gas

U.S. natural gas demand is expected to grow by about 2% per year. Environmental and economic advantages will cause natural gas to gain market share in almost all sectors of the energy industry. Efficient gas–fired combined–cycle electric generation units will force the retirement of old dual–fired steam units. Gas is also displacing oil in the residential and commercial sectors.

Gas prices at the wellhead will increase at less than the rate of inflation from the high price level reached in 1996. Gas prices in 1996 were abnormally high because of cold weather and a low level of gas storage at the beginning of the year. The United States will continue to rely on Canadian imports to supplement its gas supply requirements.

Demand

Natural gas demand in 1996 increased by 2.6% from the 1995 figure of 21.58 trillion cubic feet. U.S. consumption of natural gas exceeded 22 trillion cubic feet in 1996, amounting to the highest consumption since 1974. Natural gas demand and prices are very sensitive to weather, and demand growth from 1995 to 1996 was caused by an extremely cold winter in 1996.

■ Residential and commercial demand increased approximately 9% as a result of strong demand for natural gas for heating.

■ The industrial sector experienced more modest growth of 2% in 1996.

■ However, natural gas demand by the electric utility sector declined 9% during the first 11 months of 1996.

The lower 1996 demand for natural gas in the electric utility sector was a result of a cool summer which reduced the demand for air conditioning and fuel switching caused by high gas prices. The strong demand in the residential and commercial sectors, coupled with the declining demand of the electric utility sector, resulted in modest natural gas demand growth for the nation.

Over the next ten years natural gas demand is expected to grow at about 2% per year. The share of natural gas used for home heating is increasing. Also, deregulation of the electric utility industry will result in the replacement of older dual–fired steam generation units with efficient combined–cycle natural gas units. Finally, natural gas

generation is attractive because of environmental considerations.

Natural Gas Consumption
Percent Change

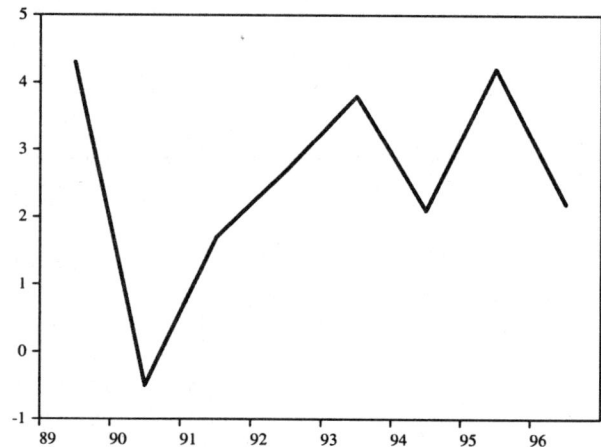

Supply

Domestic production of natural gas was greater than 19 trillion cubic feet in 1996, an increase of more than 2% from the previous year. Growth in production is expected to continue at a similar pace throughout the forecast period. The natural gas rig count for 1996 was 20% higher than in 1995 as a result of strong gas prices. Also, substantial additions of gas supply will come from projects in the deepwater area of the Gulf Coast. Many of these projects are likely to be developed regardless of gas prices because they are being driven by the desire to develop oil supplies in this area.

Indicators of Exploration and Development

	Wells Drilled		Rig Count	
	Thousands	% Change	Wkly. Average	% Change
1988	31.80		936	
1989	28.06	−12%	869	−7%
1990	31.47	12%	1010	16%
1991	29.27	−7%	860	−15%
1992	23.77	−19%	721	−16%
1993	25.32	7%	754	5%
1994	21.03	−17%	775	3%
1995	18.66	−11%	723	−7%
1996	22.04	18%	779	8%

Natural Gas Production and Prices

	Tcf	%Change	$/Mcf	%Change
1988	17.10		1.69	
1989	17.31	1.2%	1.69	0.0%
1990	17.81	2.9%	1.71	1.2%
1991	17.70	−0.6%	1.64	−4.1%
1992	17.84	0.8%	1.74	6.1%
1993	18.10	1.4%	2.04	17.2%
1994	18.82	4.0%	1.85	−9.3%
1995	18.60	−1.2%	1.55	−16.2%
1996	19.09	2.6%	2.25	45.2%

Tcf (Trillion Cubic Feet), Mcf (Thousand Cubic Feet)

In 1995, U.S. imports of natural gas reached 2.84 trillion cubic feet (tcf), an increase of almost 120% from 1988. Natural gas imports are estimated to have been 2.86 trillion cubic feet during 1996. Ninety–nine percent of U.S. natural gas imports during 1995 originated in Canada. In order for the United States to continue receiving significant imports from Canada, pipeline capacity will need to be expanded.

Longer term, an increasing portion of U.S. gas supplies will come from the western half of the United States and Canada. In addition, technological advances will make it feasible to develop additional supplies in the deepwater areas of the Gulf Coast.

Prices

Natural gas prices increased sharply in 1996. This was a result of three factors.

■ First, natural gas prices in 1995 were low because of mild weather.

■ Second, natural gas in storage was abnormally low at the beginning of 1996.

■ Finally, gas demand was strong in 1996 as a result of a cold winter.

Prices for residential and commercial users varied much less than those for industrial users and electric utilities because a larger part of the delivered cost of gas to the residential and commercial sector is for distribution cost. Unlike wellhead prices, distribution charges do not change a great deal from year to year.

The average price of natural gas delivered to residential users was $6.28 per thousand cubic feet for the first 11 months of 1996. This was an increase of 16.5% over the same period in 1995. Similarly, the average price for natural gas delivered to commercial consumers was $5.27 per thousand cubic feet, an increase of only 4% from the previous year. Industrial prices, on the other hand, reached an average of $3.26 for the first 11 months of 1996, which amounted to an increase of nearly 26% from the previous year. Electric utilities experienced an increase of similar magnitude; their average price for the first 10 months of 1996 was $2.60 per thousand cubic feet, an increase of nearly 32% from the previous year.

Prices are expected to decline in 1997 from their 1996 level as a result of a return to more normal weather, higher storage at the end of the 1996–97 winter heating season, and increased natural gas wellhead deliverability resulting from strong drilling for natural gas. Prices are expected to continue to decline in 1998, assuming normal weather, as growing U.S. production capability and a return to more normal storage levels increase available supplies. In the long term, natural gas prices at the wellhead are expected to grow at very close to the overall rate of inflation, as technological advances offset much of the upward price impact of reserve depletion.

Investment

During 1995, three major pipelines came on–line.

- The Tuscarora pipeline, which serves northern California and parts of Nevada, has a capacity of 110 million cubic feet per day.

- The Crossroads pipeline, which serves Indiana and western Ohio, has a capacity of 250 million cubic feet per day.

- Finally, the Bluewater pipeline, which is bidirectional and has a capacity of 250 million cubic feet per day, transports gas between Michigan and Ontario.

There are a number of planned pipeline projects that if brought on–line would increase inter–regional capacity 7% by 1999. In total, nearly $7 billion in investment is planned for pipeline capacity additions through 2000.

In addition to pipeline investments, there are a number of planned additions to storage capacity. In fact, there are 58 projects planned to add storage capacity through 1999. In 1995, working gas capacity was estimated to be 3,828 billion cubic feet. By 2000, proposed underground additions would add storage of 268 billion cubic feet, an increase of 7%.

Industry Structure

Hubs, Market Hubs, and Market Centers

A natural gas hub acts as a physical transfer point, into which several pipelines flow and from which gas is redirected. Generally, such facilities are unidirectional, with little gas flowing back and forth. A market hub includes all the capability of a hub but also provides services for the buying, selling, and trading of natural gas. Both Henry Hub, Louisiana and the Katy Hubs, Texas are market hubs. In operation since 1988, Henry Hub has 12 direct pipeline interconnections and 3 storage sites.

Market centers can exist without the physical infrastructure of a hub or a market hub. They act to arrange storage and transportation from a supply region. Union Hub, Ontario and Columbia Market Center in the Northeast are both market centers.

In recent years, the industry has developed these facilities to ease the transfer and distribution of natural gas. As of September 1996, the United States and Canada had 39 operating facilities, 27 of which have been in operation only since 1994. In addition, there are 6 proposed sites in the United States. In an effort to reduce exposure to risk, futures markets have also developed at a number of hubs, including Henry Hub, Louisiana (NYMEX) and West Texas (NYMEX and KCBOT).

Although hubs and market centers have proliferated in recent years, they remain underutilized. Storage at these centers is often below 40% of capacity. Ostensibly, one of the key roles of hubs and market centers is to ameliorate price volatility. By releasing gas into the system, increases in demand can be met. However, judging by the consistent daily volatility of prices, hubs and market centers are not performing this task. This will continue to be an important factor to watch throughout 1997 and into the forecast period.

Storage

Natural gas demand is very seasonal because of weather–sensitive heating demand. Consequently, large amounts of gas are stored in depleted gas reservoirs. However, as a result of the deregulation of the gas industry, less gas is kept in storage. At the start of the 1995–96 heating season (November 1, 1995), working gas storage in the U.S. was 2.958 billion cubic feet (Bcf). At the start of the 1996–97 season, storage was at 2.725 Bcf, a decline of nearly 8% from the previous year.

The use of high–deliverability storage or salt cavern facilities has increased the speed with which gas can be brought from storage to the market. Roughly 66% of the storage brought on–line in 1995 was of this high–deliverability type. Moreover, such facilities are capable of handling increased cycling, which means that gas can be put into and taken out of storage in rapid bursts. This increased cycling allows for more efficient use of storage facilities and for better response to short–term changes in demand.

Pipeline Contracts

As a result of the changing regulatory environment and the construction of excess pipeline capacity, contracts between natural gas distribution companies and their pipeline transportation providers have come under pressure. In a desire for greater flexibility and less cost, many gas shippers have decided to "turn back" or reduce their commitments when contracts expire.

By the end of 2001, half of the current gas pipeline transportation contract reservations will expire, and 90% will come due by 2010. Transportation providers are therefore facing significant uncertainty. In some regions, capacity exceeds demand, due to increased energy efficiency and conservation efforts. Immediate concerns are greatest in the Southwest, Central, and Midwest regions, because the majority of their contracts expire before 2001. In the Northeast, on the other hand, the greater portion of the contracts range from 20 to 30 years in commitment length.

These contract turnbacks may indicate a transitional period for the natural gas industry, similar to the shift from long–term to spot and short–term contracts in the wellhead market during the 1980s. However, pipelines in areas with excess capacity are likely to be under strong financial pressure. Transwestern Pipeline and El Paso have already been victims of excess capacity in the California market. Excess capacity to the Midwest may signal the advent of similar pressures for pipelines in this region.

The Effect of Electricity Market Restructuring On Natural Gas Markets

Following the issuance of Order 888 in April 1996, more choices have been created for consumers and producers of electricity. Order 888 mandated electric utilities to give all generators equal access to transmission facilities, thereby increasing the competitiveness of the electric generation business. High–volume customers will be the first beneficiaries of the new regulations. It is possible that lower prices for electricity could lead to substitution of electricity for natural gas, specifically in the industrial sector. It is unlikely, however, that significant substitution will occur in the residential sector given the wide disparity in price and efficiency between gas and electricity.

Order 888 has created a more competitive wholesale market. However, initiatives are still underway at both the state and federal levels to increase retail competition. At the state level, the strongest initiatives are in areas where electricity costs are high, such as California and the Northeast. In expectation of deregulation of the retail market, a large number of gas–fired generation units are being proposed to take advantage of the current high cost of generation. This will force the retirement of older plants and increase the demand for natural gas in these areas.

Environmental Issues

Gases, including carbon dioxide, methane, and various nitrous oxides, the main sources of which are the combustion of fossil fuels, are suspected to contribute to an increase in global temperatures. In 1995, carbon emissions from total energy consumption were approximately 1,400 million metric tons. Petroleum products have remained the largest single source of carbon emissions from energy use, with approximately 600 million metric tons in 1995. The second highest source of carbon emissions in the energy sector is coal, with total carbon emissions of almost 510 million metric tons in 1995. Natural gas, however, has remained the lowest contributor to carbon emissions of the three major sources, with total emissions in 1995 of about 320 million metric tons. Moreover, average emissions per unit of input for gas are roughly half those of coal.

In terms of electricity generation, coal remains the leading contributor of greenhouse gases, accounting for over 440 million metric tons of carbon emissions in 1995. Petroleum produced over 14 million metric tons and natural gas produced over 50 million metric tons through electricity generation in 1995. On the whole, natural gas continues to be the most environmentally benign of the three major fossil fuels.

U.S. methane emissions from stationary combustion sources totaled 475,000 metric tons in 1995, down nearly 30% from 1988. Natural gas was the most significant producer of methane emissions of the three major fossil fuels, with 25,000 metric cubic feet in 1995. This should not be surprising given that natural gas is primarily composed of methane.

The largest source of nitrous oxide emissions is energy use. Energy use accounted for 184,000 metric tons of nitrous oxide emissions in 1995, down 4,000 metric tons from 1990. Coal accounted for 29,000 metric tons of nitrous oxide emissions from stationary sources in 1995; fuel oil accounted for 7,000 metric tons; and natural gas emissions were 2,000 metric tons. Nitrous oxide emissions have remained relatively stable since at least 1988.

Natural Gas
Growth in Sales (Line) and Volume (Bar)

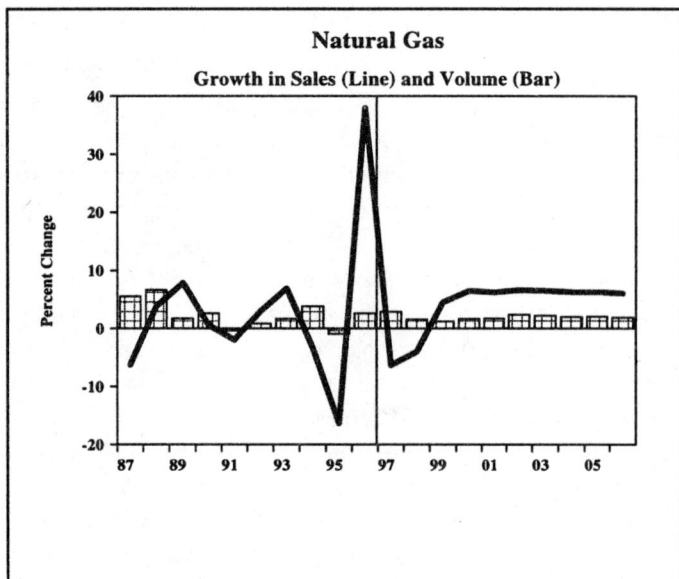

Natural Gas
Growth in Product Prices

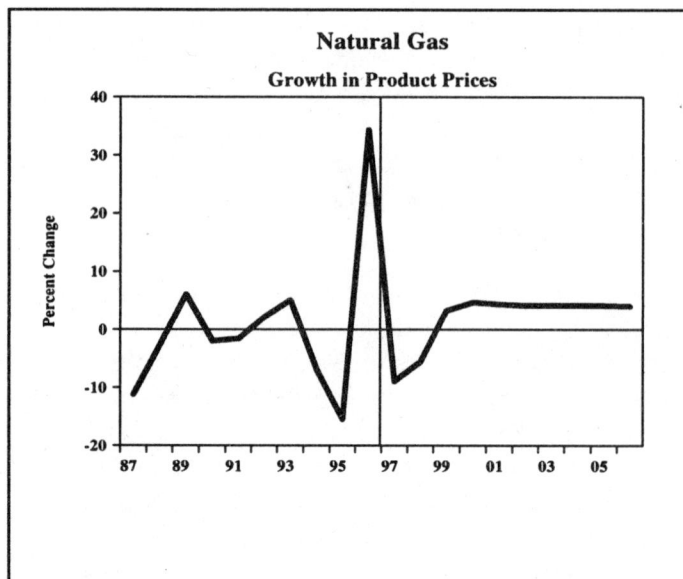

Natural Gas
SIC Part of 13

		1990	1991	1992	1993	1994	1995	1996	1997	1998	Compound Ann Avg Growth 1986-1996	1996-2006
Sales												
	Billions of $	28.47	27.91	28.73	30.71	29.64	24.79	34.20	32.03	30.74		
	% Change	0.6	-2.0	2.9	6.9	-3.5	-16.4	37.9	-6.3	-4.0	2.4	3.8
Volume	% Change	2.7	-0.4	0.8	1.7	3.9	-1.0	2.6	2.9	1.6	2.4	2.0
Prices	% Change	-2.1	-1.6	2.1	5.1	-7.1	-15.5	34.4	-9.0	-5.5	-0.0	1.7
Exports												
	Billions of $	0.55	0.72	0.78	0.62	0.57	0.79	0.78	0.81	0.86		
	% Change	-2.7	30.6	8.3	-20.9	-8.5	39.7	-0.9	3.7	6.1	7.3	5.8
Imports												
	Billions of $	5.55	5.20	4.99	6.22	6.64	6.29	8.02	8.21	8.49		
	% Change	37.4	-6.3	-4.1	24.8	6.7	-5.2	27.4	2.4	3.4	7.9	0.5
Apparent Consumption												
	Billions of $	33.48	32.38	32.93	36.32	35.71	30.29	41.43	39.43	38.36		
	Nominal % Change	5.3	-3.3	1.7	10.3	-1.7	-15.2	36.8	-4.8	-2.7	3.2	3.2
	Real % Change	7.5	-1.7	-0.4	4.9	5.8	0.4	1.8	4.6	3.0	3.2	1.4

Nonmetallic Mineral Mining and Quarrying

The nonmetallic minerals mining and quarrying industry includes minerals such as dimension and crushed stone, sand and gravel, clays, phosphate rock, potash, salt, soda ash, and boron. The largest sector of this industry by far is crushed and broken stone, comprised of limestone, granite, and others. The crushed stone industry is geographically diverse, with quarries in every state except Delaware, Louisiana, New Hampshire, and North Dakota. The size of these operations also varies widely.

Demand Factors

The most important markets for crushed stone are construction and highway and road building, with the former being by far the largest. Moderating employment and disposable income growth along with rising interest rates in the near term will likely cause housing in particular and construction in general to grow more slowly over the next few years. The boost to housing starts in 1996 was fueled by a sharp drop in interest rates a year earlier; and since that kind of stimulus to housing is not expected to recur in the next few years, starts are expected to remain somewhat below their 1996 total level.

This weakness in housing, and the quite slow growth expected for construction in general, will ease the growth of demand for construction–related inputs. Highway and road construction activity is also likely to suffer moderately from a slowing economy. Spending there may not advance much over the forecast period as moderating employment growth — and therefore moderating state and local revenue growth — is expected to result in pressure on state and local budgets. Overall, the demand for crushed stone and gravel will not advance strongly in either 1997 or 1998.

Demand for phosphate rock — 60% of which is sold to the agriculture industry for fertilizer — will depend on crop plantings. Worldwide consumption of these fertilizers has been increasing since the mid–1970s, but the rate of growth has slowed. Demand has eased somewhat in the United States and Europe as agricultural support programs have been reduced. The best prospects for phosphate fertilizers in the future are likely to be in the Middle East and Asia. The second largest segment of demand for phosphate rock is that for detergents. This market has been negatively affected by the belief that phosphates lead to increased water pollution.

The fate of potash demand also depends largely on agricultural output, as roughly 95% of output is used for fertilizer for such crops as soybeans, tobacco, potatoes, sugar beets, and corn.

Borax and other boron compounds are used as intermediate chemical supplies in a wide variety of industrial applications. Expect overall demand for these mineral products to vary with the health of overall industrial production, which is forecast to grow by 2.5% to 3.0% per year over the next ten years.

Soda ash is used in glass containers, chemicals, flat glass, and soaps and detergents. Use by the glass container industry has declined in recent years, as producers have turned more toward recycled glass as a raw material. However, during the same time, demand has been stimulated by growth in detergent use.

Looking at the overall demand for nonmetallic minerals, gains will likely moderate from about 2.5% per year over the past 10 years to roughly 1.5% per year through 2006, as a result of WEFA's very modest growth expectations for the industry's end–markets.

Supply Conditions

In the past, most crushed and broken stone was mined from open quarries. Recently, however, the trend has moved toward underground mining. Underground mining reduces the cost of land for the producer, since it requires less surface space. Given the high cost of transporting crushed stone to its final destination, it is important for the quarrying process to be located near the product's market. The small size and large number of operators in the industry keep competition keen and pricing competitive. Moreover, large volumes and weights make for high transportation costs, which prevent imports from making significant inroads into the industry.

Phosphate rock is produced in only a few countries, and the United States is the largest producer. Since new sources of supply are expensive to develop, prices should firm over the long term as the supply/demand balance tilts more in favor of producers.

Pricing Factors

Almost all businesses that depend on the construction industry encounter tremendous cyclicality in both the volume of demand and product pricing. Soft prices for nonmetallic minerals hurt producer margins during the 1990–91 recession and immediately thereafter. Since then, however, prices have risen at a rate roughly in line with the all–industry average.

Prices for phosphate rock are expected to gain relative to the all–industry average in the longer term, however, due to the high cost of developing new supplies.

Trends Affecting The Outlook

Environmental concerns are growing in numerous industries in the United States and abroad, and crushed stone operators are not immune to such concerns. Many states now require operators in this industry to submit environmental impact reports before starting new facilities. These pressures will add to the cost of opening new supply facilities and for closing old ones.

Demand for soda ash is dominated by glass production. Glass containers represent about 27% of industry demand for soda ash with flat glass accounting for 14%. Recycled supply has cut into soda ash demand for glass container production, and this trend is likely to increase.

Risks To The Outlook

The largest sector of the nonmetallic minerals mining and quarrying industry is crushed stone, and the largest market for crushed stone is construction. Rising interest rates always pose a threat to construction spending, and that risk is all the more present now that the current economic recovery is in its sixth year. Consumer confidence also is very important to construction, and can change rapidly.

All nonmetallic mineral products used as inputs to fertilizer production are susceptible to short–term fluctuations in the weather.

Nonmetallic Minerals, except Fuels
Growth in Sales (Line) and Volume (Bar)

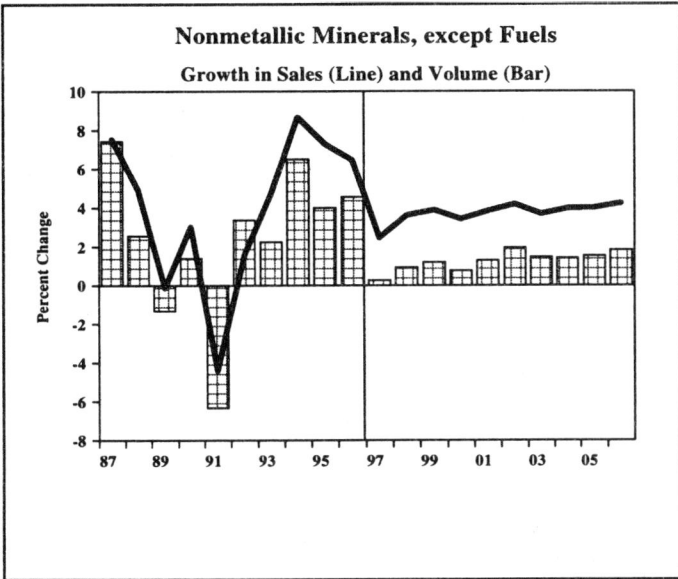

Nonmetallic Minerals, except Fuels
Growth in Product Prices

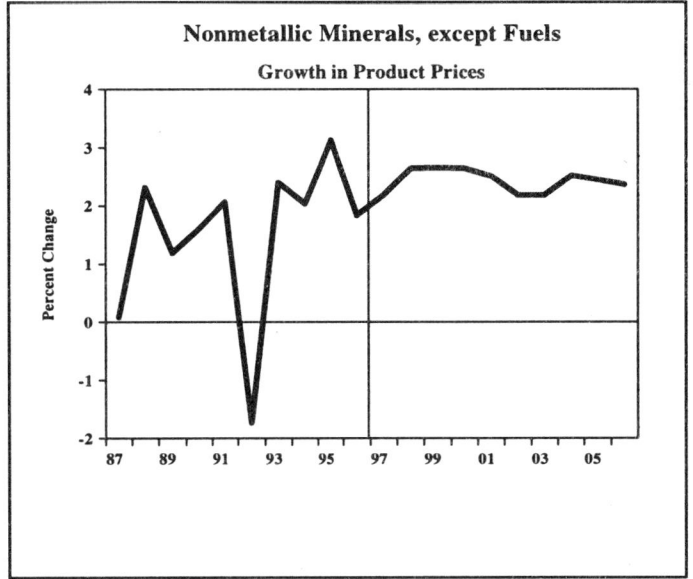

```
Nonmetallic Minerals, except Fuels
 SIC 14
```

		1990	1991	1992	1993	1994	1995	1996	1997	1998	Compound Ann Avg Growth 1986-1996	Compound Ann Avg Growth 1996-2006
Sales												
	Billions of $	13.99	13.38	13.59	14.23	15.46	16.59	17.66	18.09	18.74		
	% Change	3.0	-4.4	1.6	4.7	8.7	7.3	6.5	2.5	3.6	3.9	3.7
Volume	% Change	1.4	-6.3	3.4	2.2	6.5	4.0	4.5	0.3	0.9	2.4	1.3
Prices	% Change	1.6	2.1	-1.7	2.4	2.0	3.1	1.8	2.2	2.6	1.5	2.4

Chapter 4: Construction

Residential Construction

Since 1991 the U.S. residential construction market has made a major comeback. Five years ago, total housing starts were only 1.01 million units. During 1996 about 1.47 million units were started, up more than 45% from the 1991 level. Residential investment in real terms, which includes renovations as well as new construction, climbed by more than 43% during the 1991–96 period.

Mortgage rates are expected to remain favorable for residential construction activity over the next ten years. Income will continue to rise, and affordability will improve, offsetting some of the demographic trends that will tend to slow growth in housing.

Regional diversity is key in the residential construction industry. For example, the Northeast has seen only an 18% increase in housing starts over the last five years. The West and South, on the other hand, have experienced growth of 42% and 59%, respectively. Consequently, the outlook for the U.S. residential housing market must consider not only the health of the general economy, but also demographics, migration patterns, and regional economic issues.

Demand Conditions

The two primary drivers behind the demand for new home construction are affordability, which includes home pricing, interest rates, and buyer income, among other factors, and demographic trends. Demographic factors are certainly key in the long run, and the aging of the baby boom generation through the prime years for buying a first home helped to propel housing starts through the 1980s. The peak year for housing starts in the 1980s was 1986, when starts reached 1.81 million units.

Housing Starts

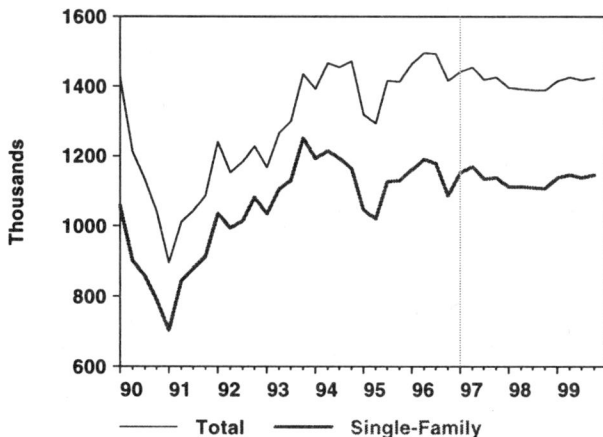

Total ——— Single-Family

Single unit housing starts stood at 852,000 units in 1980 and peaked at 1.18 million in 1986. In 1996 that peak was challenged, as single–unit starts hit 1.15 million. Multi–unit housing starts increased from 440,000 in 1980

to 628,000 in 1986. However, in 1996 they totaled only 308,000. Baby boom demographics certainly played a role in these divergent trends: baby boomers were having families and benefiting from higher disposable income, and therefore preferred more costly single family housing over apartments and condos. Tax laws also enforced the divergent trends — multi–unit housing was encouraged in the early 1980s by the investment tax credit, and its repeal later in the decade caused a major break in the market. A key affordability factor also helped single–unit housing — mortgage rates fell from an effective rate of 12.9% in 1980 to 10.3% in 1986, and then dropped to 7.7% by 1996. During the next ten years, effective mortgage rates will hover in the range of 7.5% to 8.0%.

WEFA expects housing activity to remain relatively strong through the next five years. Total starts are forecast to reach 1.43 million units during 1997 and then vary in the range of 1.39 to 1.54 million units from 1998 through 2006. Single unit starts are projected to be 1.14 million and then range between 1.10 and 1.22 million during the next ten years, accounting for about 80% of total starts.

In addition to favorable mortgage rates, employment and disposable income should also be supportive of the residential construction sector. Real disposable income is expected to grow by 2.6% per year on average through the year 2006. The combination of low mortgage rates with income trends will result in a 5.5% increase in affordability, according to WEFA's affordability index calculations.

Mortgage Interest Rates

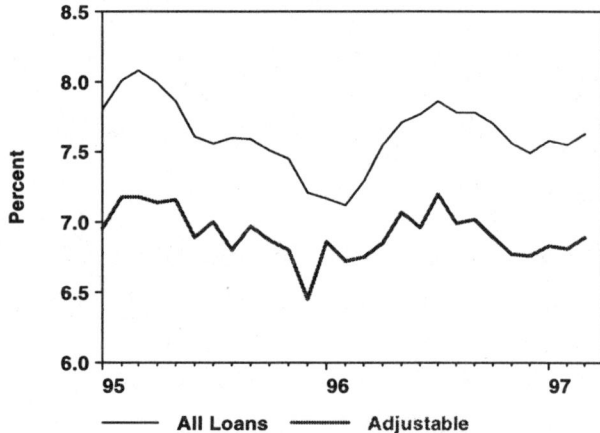

From a regional perspective, residential construction activity will continue to be diverse. Those areas of the country that experience strong job growth are likely to see the largest increase in housing starts. WEFA forecasts that the Mountain, South Atlantic, and Pacific regions will have the highest rates of employment growth through the year 2006, and housing starts in these regions are expected to grow by 2.4%, 2.9%, and 1.2%, respectively, on average during the period. Slowest residential construction growth is expected in the East South Central and West South Central regions.

Upkeep and improvements as well as expenditures on maintenance and repairs for residential property are also classified under residential construction. While it is difficult to capture the full value of do-it-yourself projects, professional construction figures are readily available. In 1980, about $46 billion was spent for residential alterations and repairs in current-dollar terms. This spending was over $100 billion in 1990, and it reached $112 billion in 1996. This 8.4% average annual rate of growth over 16 years is quite strong, given that price increases accounted for only 2% per year.

The economic factors driving growth in renovations, upkeep, and alterations are similar to those behind housing starts. The need for baby boomers to increase living space to accommodate expanding families, and the desire to upgrade homes as disposable incomes increase, are the two main factors supporting residential alterations and repairs. The fact that Federal tax laws allow the interest on home equity loans to be deductible has also stimulated residential renovations, since a large percentage of these loans are at least partially used for renovation work. In addition, the low interest rates of the early 1990s encouraged many homeowners to refinance their mortgages, often including an additional loan for home improvements. The forecast for spending on residential alterations and repairs is moderately bullish. Income and job growth will help, as will relatively low mortgage rates, and growth of 2.0% to 2.5% per year on average is likely over the period from 1997 to 2006.

Material Costs

The building materials used for residential single family structures are significantly different from those used in multi-unit housing, commercial structures, and public projects. Single unit residential structures use a large amount of lumber and wood products, prepared paints, and plastic construction products. They may also use a significant amount of brick or stone, cement, or insulation materials. Unlike larger structures, very little steel is used. However, steel bracing is increasingly finding use as a substitute for lumber in homebuilding. In addition, the large amount of pumps, electrical equipment, and glass products that is used in multi-unit and commercial structures are not necessary in single residences.

Labor is the largest cost component in homebuilding. Since the early 1980s, construction wages have averaged less than 2.0% growth annually. Cement costs have also been stable over the past fifteen years. Lumber and wood products have been the most volatile cost element among residential building materials. Lumber prices have swung up and down over the period, but averaged a hefty gain of 6.4% per year. These increases are in fact the force behind the inroads made by steel bracing.

From a cost standpoint, WEFA expects few shocks in the residential housing sector over the next ten years.

- Labor costs are projected to continue to increase at only about 2% per year.

- Cement costs are expected to increase by only a fraction more.

- Plastic construction product prices should be generally flat.

- Softwood lumber prices will rise more rapidly than the other cost items, averaging hikes between 3% and 3.5%.

Building Construction - Private Residential
Growth in Sales (Line) and Volume (Bar)

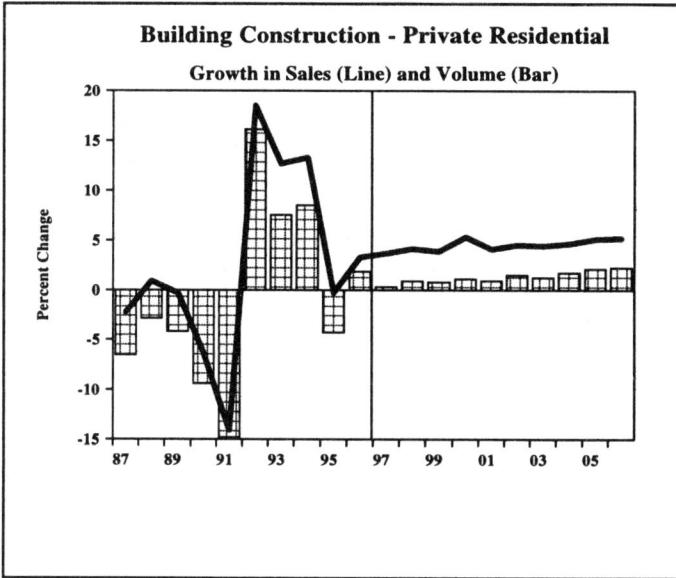

Building Construction - Private Residential
Growth in Product Prices

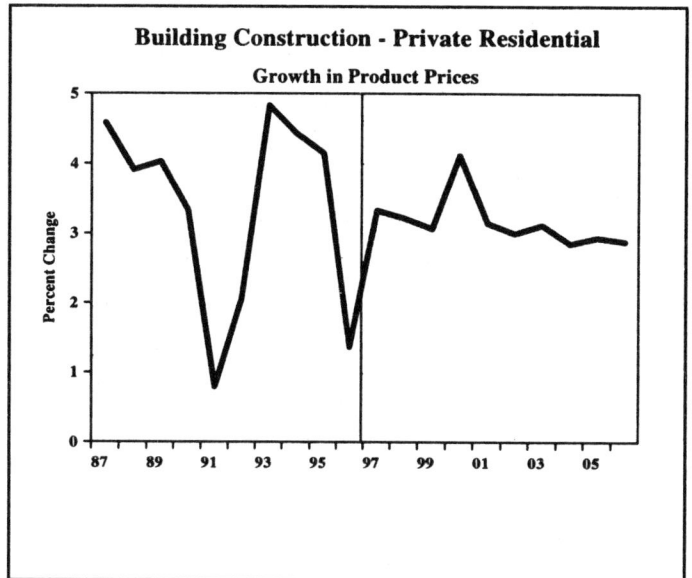

```
Building Construction - Private Residential
SIC Part of 15-17

                                                                                    Compound Ann Avg Growth
                          1990    1991    1992    1993    1994    1995    1996    1997    1998   1986-1996  1996-2006

Sales
         Billions of $  145.68  125.11  148.30  167.16  189.43  188.89  195.09  202.24  210.65
         % Change        -6.4   -14.1    18.5    12.7    13.3    -0.3     3.3     3.7     4.2      2.1        4.5

 Volume  % Change        -9.4   -14.8    16.1     7.5     8.5    -4.3     1.9     0.3     0.9     -1.2        1.3
 Prices  % Change         3.3     0.8     2.1     4.8     4.4     4.1     1.4     3.3     3.2      3.3        3.2
```

Nonresidential Construction

With more than $23 billion in new nonresidential building projects put in place during the beginning months of 1997, the market is already more than 13% ahead of the strong pace of 1995. Four major sectors of the nonresidential construction market are expected to register healthy increases in 1997 and beyond: transportation, technology, buildings, and industrial.

Transportation Construction

One of transportation's hottest markets is airport construction. Lawmakers once again wrestled with the problem of expired airport taxes at year-end 1996, but now that the tax has been reinstated projects can resume at full speed, and most major airports have some form of development underway. Grants from the Airport and Airway Trust Fund provide capital for some of these projects, but bonds still remain the most important revenue source.

Roads and bridges remain a state priority and a construction staple. Of course, nature's capriciousness has predetermined much of the 1997 to-do list for the West Coast and the Midwest. Initiatives in mass transit and the push to get the United States into the high speed rail market continue but at a much slower pace than highway construction.

The progress for many of these projects was contingent upon how well and how fast Congress tackled transportation funding issues. The heavy construction sector was pleased when U.S. House and Senate conferees reached agreement on the FY1997 appropriations bill for the Department of Transportation. Although the bill was still awaiting approval in the spring, it appears that highway, mass transit, and aviation programs will all see funding increases.

Technology Construction

The technology market is another area projected to grow steadily over the next few years. Telephone vendors and carriers note that less than 30% of standard U.S. telephone lines are sufficient to carry the communication required by the latest modems on the market, which run with speeds up to 33.6 kilobits per second. Since much of the growth in sales and profitability experienced by the local telephone companies in the last year or two has been tied to additional phone lines for fax and modem access, the infrastructure for this key new demand area will not be ignored.

Spending on technology infrastructure is a high priority for companies that are not telecommunications providers too. Any company seeking a technological competitive advantage moving into the next century sees the need for technology structures investment. In addition, office buildings must have upgraded hardware, software, cabling, and high electrical capacity in order to attract the best tenants.

Office Buildings

The office market, which has been dormant the past few years, started to pick up at the end of 1996, and is expected to grow further in 1997 and 1998. Builders are seeing the need to fill firms' desires for "back office space" — i.e. sound usable space rather than a corporate magnum opus.

One source of growth in corporate offices can be attributed to small, fast-growing companies that initially need only a small amount of space. However, given twelve to eighteen months to grow, these companies then discover that they need to increase their staff, up their resources, and double the size of the space in which they are located.

The pick-up is most evidently taking place in suburbia. A number of design-to-build projects that are springing up require large areas (some over one million square feet). Many corporations are choosing to move their headquarters out of the inner city to the more serene, and less costly, surroundings of suburbia. Companies are using a "softscape" environment — low rise buildings, landscaping, grass, lakes, etc. — as one more way to attract and retain employees.

Government and Educational Buildings

Government buildings are also expected to rebound sharply in the next few years, and the key areas of growth will be courthouses and education buildings. The education sector has grown at a 3% annual rate over the last ten years.

Due to demographic trends, the rush right now is for elementary schools — districts are struggling to find the space to house children of the baby boom generation. This same cohort will be moving on to secondary school in the years ahead, and WEFA expects this to stimulate additions and new building at the high school level. Other factors driving the educational buildings include the need to upgrade facilities built immediately following World War II — including making them internet–compatible. In addition, the advent of vouchers and other school choice plans has prompted further competition and therefore more upgrades and enhancements to facilities in an effort to draw enrollment.

Industrial Construction

Industrial markets are also projected to register healthy construction numbers. Higher revenues are now the focus versus the bottom line. Industrial construction is projected to turn around from an almost 8% decline in 1996 to about 6% growth in 1997. The 1996 decline was largely the result of overly–zealous construction gains in 1995, rather than an indication of underlying weakness in the industrial marketplace. For the most part the action is in renovation and upgrading of facilities, although greenfield plants are in the works in a few areas and industries.

Most of the action, however, is expected to remain abroad. Petroleum and chemical markets are looking overseas to expand. A tremendous amount of growth in the pulp and paper and petrochemicals sectors is coming from Asia and Latin America. Also, the food processing industry is doing very well overseas. The U.S. nonresidential construction sector includes a few world–class firms whose services are in demand for some of these projects.

Hotels and Recreational Facilities

Hotels, gaming centers, and sports facilities are other markets of steady growth for the nonresidential construction market. Convention centers and sports stadiums are viewed as great vehicles for urban renewal, particularly in the smaller cities. If a city does not have a convention center or a sports team, it wants one; if it has either, the city wants to expand it. Some cities are experiencing a resurgence of hotel activity, particularly in the business class niche, but as with office space, suburban projects are hotter.

The San Francisco 49ers unveiled a model for a new stadium and shopping center proposed for Candlestick Point. Los Angeles is also hoping to be another entry in the sports construction sweepstakes. A developer is negotiating with the city to build a $250 million, 22,000–seat home for basketball's Lakers and hockey's Kings. Quite a number of other professional teams are in the bidding for new homes. Whether or not these projects are successful will depend upon financing plans that do not place the majority of the financial burden on the home city.

Retail Space

One sector of the nonresidential construction market that is not expected to see much growth is retail facilities. A decade of overbuilding has created a surplus of undifferentiated property. Regional malls have been subjected to the competition of big–box, get–it–all–in–one–place stores. Despite some strip mall activity, tied mainly to newly developed suburban towns, the demand for additional retail space is forecast to be weak.

The International Market

The large construction companies of North America are increasingly chasing work overseas as competition intensifies in domestic markets with restrained public spending. Over the long run, construction growth in mature economies is expected to be modest.

Size is important is this market. The large companies with healthy balance sheets are able to make investments in power, water, and transportation projects. These companies also have the scale to provide a full range of skills for customers unmatched by smaller competitors. Also, these large groups are better positioned to set up cross– border takeovers, mergers, and joint ventures with foreign construction companies.

Building Construction - Private Nonresidential
Growth in Sales (Line) and Volume (Bar)

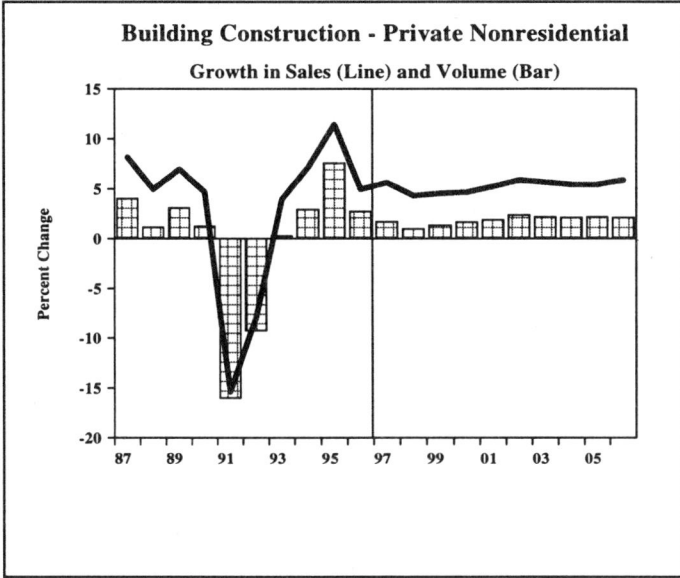

Building Construction - Private Nonresidential
Growth in Product Prices

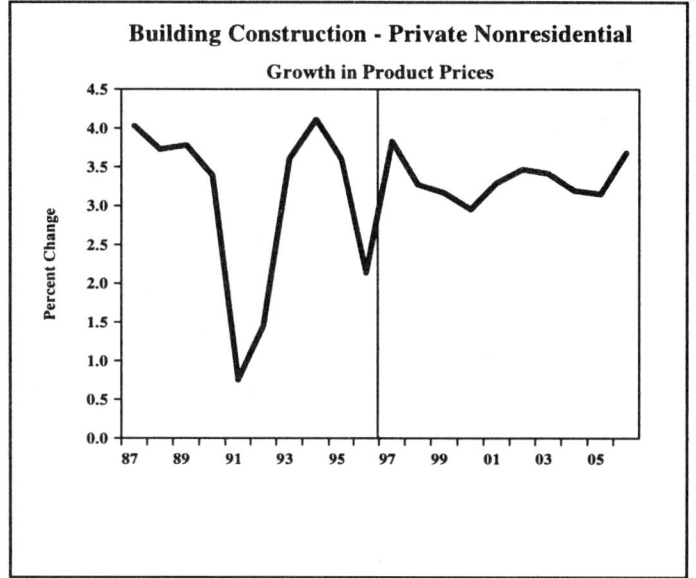

```
Building Construction - Private Nonresidential
 SIC Part of 15-17

                                                                                 Compound Ann Avg Growth
                        1990    1991    1992    1993    1994    1995    1996    1997    1998    1986-1996  1996-2006

Sales
         Billions of $ 450.38  381.13  351.03  364.66  390.77  435.48  456.88  482.33  503.05
             % Change    4.6   -15.4    -7.9     3.9     7.2    11.4     4.9     5.6     4.3        2.6        5.2

   Volume    % Change    1.2   -16.0    -9.2     0.3     2.9     7.6     2.7     1.7     1.0       -0.5        1.8
   Prices    % Change    3.4     0.8     1.4     3.6     4.1     3.6     2.1     3.8     3.3        3.1        3.3
```

Part 2: Nondurable Goods Manufacturing

Chapter 5: Food and Kindred Products

Food and Kindred Products

The food and kindred products industry consists of meat packing plants , poultry processing plants, cheese (both natural and processed), milk, canned fruits and vegetables, cereal and breakfast foods, prepared feeds, bread, malt beverages, wine, and soft drinks. Over half of this industry is made up of red meat and poultry processors and beverage producers. The trend toward less meat and milk consumption and toward healthier foods, particularly those that are easy to prepare, will continue. For the industry as a whole, volume demand should continue at a rate of about 2% per year over the next ten years, while prices will rise an average of about 2.5% per year.

Demand Conditions

Demand for food depends largely on population and income growth. Because the U.S. economy is quite developed and its people on average well–fed, the demand for food is inelastic with respect to income —that is, a 10% increase in income results in less than a 10% increase in food consumption. Changes in income also have an impact on the types of food purchased, with the higher–value and further–processed foods gaining share relative to less expensive raw ingredients in times of income expansion. Another factor that affects the types of food purchased is the continuing growth of two–income families, which value time savings in food preparation more highly than the traditional family unit.

Per capita beef consumption in the U.S. has fallen by 25% since 1975, due largely to publicized concerns over heart disease and excessive weight. The trend leveled off a bit in the early 1990s but the movement away from red meat will continue, although perhaps at a slower pace, as health consciousness rises and the population ages. Pork consumption per capita, however, has remained stable or even gained a bit since 1970. Fish consumption per capita gained in the 1970s and in the early 1980s, only to level off since then. WEFA expects the uptrend in fish consumption per person to resume at a modest pace in the years ahead.

The big gainer in meat consumption has been poultry, where per capita consumption has virtually doubled since 1975. Chicken and turkey are likely to continue to take market share from red meats in the future, but at a slower rate.

The fourth largest segment of the food and kindred products industry, after red meat, poultry, and beverages is milk. Milk consumption per person in the U.S. has declined 20% since 1975, a decline almost as steep as that of red meat. Part of this decline is due to demographic changes and part is due to rising concerns about fat content in the diet. This health trend is observable in the details of consumption by type of milk: per capita consumption of whole milk is currently 60% below its 1975 level while that of low–fat and skim milk has almost doubled. The rising average age of the U.S. population and concerns about health will continue to contribute to a decline in milk consumption per capita, but that decline will slow.

Beverage demand has grown over the last decade, but not all sectors are gainers.

- Demand for soft drinks on a per capita basis has risen rather sharply over the past few years with the economic expansion, but it is not likely to advance so rapidly over the forecast period. Look for soft drinks to grow at a healthy pace in the period ahead, but at a rate somewhere closer to that of the overall population.

- Fruit beverages, at roughly 13% of total beverage volume, should experience solid gains and a rising share of the market as interest in health and nutrition increases.

- The ready–to–drink tea market — already a larger market than those for wine, sports drinks, or spirits — will continue to experience stronger–than–average demand, although the rate of growth will slow.

- Beer consumption per capita continues to decline, and will keep declining as the population ages.

- Wine consumption per capita remains fairly stable, and will probably remain so, or rise modestly in recognition that moderate wine intake may be beneficial to health.

Demand for processed foods that are easy to prepare continues strong. Margins on these products tend to be higher than for more raw foodstuffs, and U.S. companies are also looking to expand these products' markets internationally. Overall food volume demand should continue to grow at a rate of about 2% per year over the next 10 years, while prices rise by about 2.5% per year.

Supply Conditions

The average pork producer has substantially increased in size in recent years, and the number of those producers has declined. Larger operations have led to increased efficiencies and a higher rate of pigs per litter. Cattle producers have less flexibility compared to pork producers, as the longer time required to bring a calf to market as a full–weight marketable steer impedes their ability to respond rapidly to changing market conditions. Such producers can, as a result, be more sensitive to such factors as the price of corn and feeder cattle and the price received per pound of finished product.

Soft drink suppliers don't have the vagaries of the weather to deal with, although the price of sugar and other raw inputs can be quite volatile. Wine and beer producers, however, do have some additional volatility, due to the weather's effects on the price of inputs.

Price Factors

Longer term, prices for processed foods and feeds tend to rise in line with overall inflation, not in line with prices of the raw farm products that serve as the industry's primary inputs. Price surges in farm products due to supply shocks and crop problems are not passed on to consumers dollar for dollar. Consumers can often switch from one type of food which has sharply higher prices to another where prices have not risen. As a result, processors will absorb some raw input price increases in an attempt to remain competitive. On the other hand, when input prices drop, food processors can also retain some savings.

The Outlook

Food processing companies have been devoting increasing energies toward the development and marketing of prepared foods, particularly such items as heat–and–serve products and multi–course meals. The demand for these options has expanded from dinner selections to items for both breakfast and lunch. This trend is likely to continue as no reversal in the trend toward two–income, time–starved families is expected.

Interest in nutrition, which is already a high priority for many Americans, will become even more important to the consuming public. The next step may be demand for vitamin–rich foods that will pit food processors against pharmaceutical companies which currently produce vitamins as supplements. Profit margins for such high–value–added products will make them attractive to food producers, and may put downward pressure on prices of vitamin supplements supplied by the drug industry.

Risks To The Forecast

As mentioned earlier, demand for food products overall tends to be fairly consistent with population growth, not responding in step with all changes in income levels. In the long term, however, changing consumer needs will provide opportunities for new product offerings — for items geared toward ease of preparation and better nutrition — and the success of these offerings will come to some extent at the expense of traditional food products. Increasing restaurant traffic also represents a longer term threat to sales for the food–at–home market. However, eating out and buying ready–to–eat foods is more expensive than preparing meals, so there is a limit to the damage that can be done to the traditional food markets.

Food and Kindred Products

Growth in Sales (Line) and Volume (Bar)

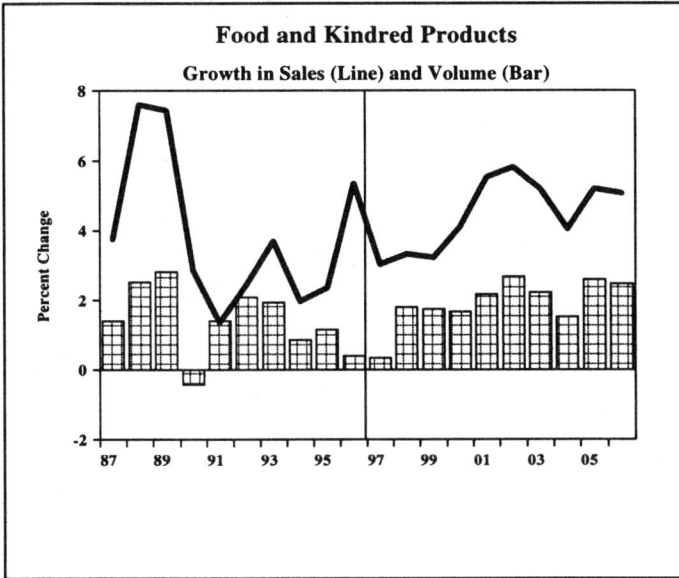

Food and Kindred Products

Growth in Product Prices

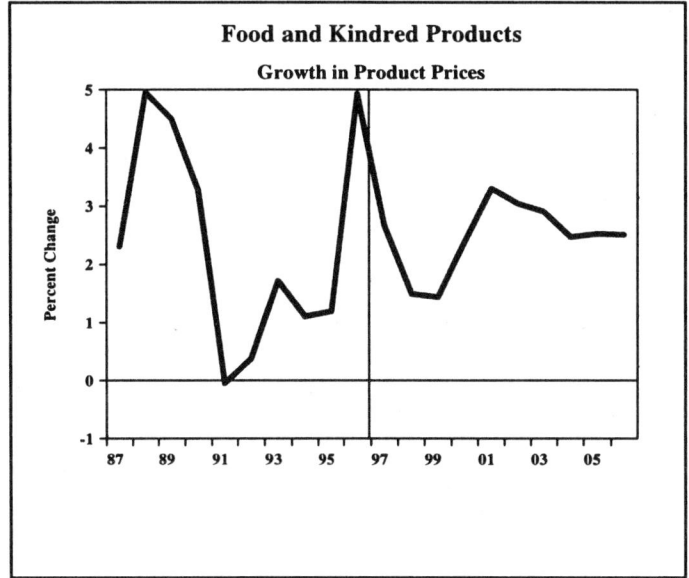

Food and Kindred Products
SIC 20

		1990	1991	1992	1993	1994	1995	1996	1997	1998	Compound Ann Avg Growth 1986-1996	1996-2006
Sales												
	Billions of $	392.20	397.51	407.30	422.32	430.60	440.73	464.25	478.28	494.20		
	% Change	2.8	1.4	2.5	3.7	2.0	2.4	5.3	3.0	3.3	3.9	4.4
Volume	% Change	-0.4	1.4	2.1	1.9	0.9	1.1	0.4	0.3	1.8	1.4	1.9
Prices	% Change	3.3	-0.0	0.4	1.7	1.1	1.2	4.9	2.7	1.5	2.4	2.5
Exports												
	Billions of $	15.83	17.79	20.01	20.65	22.74	24.71	25.78	26.94	29.69		
	% Change	11.7	12.3	12.5	3.2	10.1	8.7	4.3	4.5	10.2	12.3	9.2
Imports												
	Billions of $	22.75	22.60	24.03	24.41	26.29	27.79	29.94	32.79	35.79		
	% Change	8.8	-0.7	6.4	1.6	7.7	5.7	7.7	9.5	9.2	4.8	6.5
Apparent Consumption												
	Billions of $	399.12	402.32	411.33	426.07	434.14	443.81	468.40	484.12	500.29		
	Nominal % Change	2.8	0.8	2.2	3.6	1.9	2.2	5.5	3.4	3.3	3.6	4.3
	Real % Change	-0.4	0.8	1.9	1.8	0.8	1.0	0.6	0.7	1.8	1.2	1.7

Chapter 6:   Tobacco

Tobacco

The tobacco industry is composed of manufacturers of cigarettes, cigars, and chewing tobacco. The industry is an odd combination of sound operating performance and profitability on the one hand, and pervasive and potentially devastating legislative threats on the other. Another interesting feature of the tobacco industry is its size. Due to the massive amounts of capital investment needed to manufacture cigarettes, it is made up of only a handful of companies, roughly a dozen, and is dominated by just two. In contrast, cigar manufacturers are only slightly larger than the average manufacturing establishment and there are more firms in the business — even though their revenues are only 1/100th the size of cigarette manufacturers' revenues.

Demand

The share of the U.S. population that smokes peaked in the mid–1960s at roughly 42%. This share contracted steadily until the beginning of this decade, when it stabilized at around 26%. However, indications are that consumption probably increased somewhat in 1996. In foreign countries, cigarette usage legislation is largely absent, at least for now, and international demand for U.S. blend cigarettes remains high. But anti-smoking legislation is on the rise in Europe, and local manufacturers will fill a growing portion of demand for U.S. blend cigarettes. Also affecting demand has been the return of buying interest to name brand, and more expensive, cigarettes from their cheaper counterparts, the off-brands.

The cigar market has not fared as well as that for cigarettes. From about 9 billion in 1965, the number of cigars smoked has dropped to near 2 billion per year. One consolation, however, is that smokers have traded quantity for quality. Smokers now smoke fewer in number, but are willing to pay more for quality brands.

Overall, tobacco manufacturers experienced erosion in volume from 1991 through 1993, then saw a surge in demand in 1994 in response to the significant price cuts put in place in 1993 and 1994. Since then demand and prices have stabilized, both growing in the 2-3% range. Looking forward, WEFA expects some fallback, as recent volume growth in shipments is not sustainable. For the three years from 1997 through 1999 we expect the volume of tobacco shipments to be modestly down, showing an average decline of just under 1% per year.

Pricing Environment

The rise of discount cigarette brands hurt industry pricing in the early 1990s. Prices received by manufacturers of tobacco products fell 5.5% in 1993 and 13.8% in 1994, in marked contrast to the industry's double-digit price hikes in the three prior years. The return of interest in name brands will help the industry achieve some price growth in the years ahead from their new lower level, and output prices are expected to rise an average 3.5% per year for the period 1996-2006. The ability to push through price increases that are higher than those of the average manufacturer primarily reflects two forces:

- The high capital cost of entrance into the industry, which limits competition, and

- The rather low sensitivity of smokers to price increases.

Supply Conditions

By 1993 discount cigarette brands had captured nearly one-third of U.S. sales volume. The two biggest firms, R.J. Reynolds and Philip Morris, did not sit idly watching their market ebb away — between the two of them they managed to capture roughly 60% of the discount market. However, these product offerings were considerably less profitable than their name brands, so while the strategy may have saved some market share it didn't do much for profit margins.

The cost of entry into the cigarette manufacturing business is prohibitive, which in general allows the few giants to raise prices more effectively than most other manufacturers. Moreover, when this ability to achieve solid price increases (during most periods) is combined with the enhanced productivity of substantial investments of capital, a very favorable profit outcome is to be expected. For example, over the 10 years ending in 1996, hourly wages paid by cigarette manufacturers rose 65%. During the same period, however, total payroll outlays rose by only 11% reflecting a tremendous increase in productivity over the period. These remarkable statistics compare to a 98% increase in total shipment dollars over the same 10 years.

Major Trends Affecting The Outlook

Discount cigarette brands have caused some turmoil in the industry, but that trend may have run its course for now. Sluggish demand for tobacco products, combined with above average price gains, suggest sales growth of roughly 3% per year over the next ten years. Import penetration hasn't been a problem in the cigarette industry as imports account for less than 1% of final sales of tobacco products. Cigar makers, however, have to contend with import penetration of roughly 66% of final sales, and a stronger dollar will make these foreign competitors more attractive to domestic cigar smokers.

Risks To The Forecast

The greatest risk to tobacco manufacturers continues to be the threat of new anti-smoking initiatives. The most devastating such initiative, although carrying a fairly low probability, would be the classification of tobacco as a drug by the FDA and the elimination of over-the-counter sales. Recent speculation about industry deals that might shield tobacco companies from future U.S. lawsuits in exchange for a portion of their profits would serve to stabilize the sector, but the legal outcome of such deals is uncertain at the time of this writing.

Next most threatening is the trend toward ever-rising taxation of tobacco products. Since they have been given the stigma of "evil" by the press, it is popular among government officials needing extra tax revenue to add a few more cents to a pack of cigarettes. Smokers are price inelastic, but just how far can prices go before it starts to have a major impact on demand?

A further threat, of a more moderate degree of forecast risk, would be the return to popularity of discount cigarette brands. This threat may in fact be linked to, and encouraged by, the taxation risks to the outlook.

Tobacco Products
Growth in Sales (Line) and Volume (Bar)

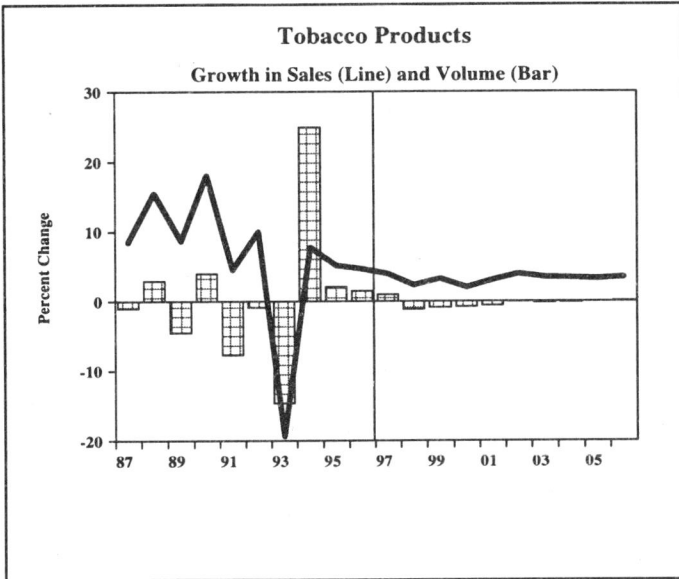

Tobacco Products
Growth in Product Prices

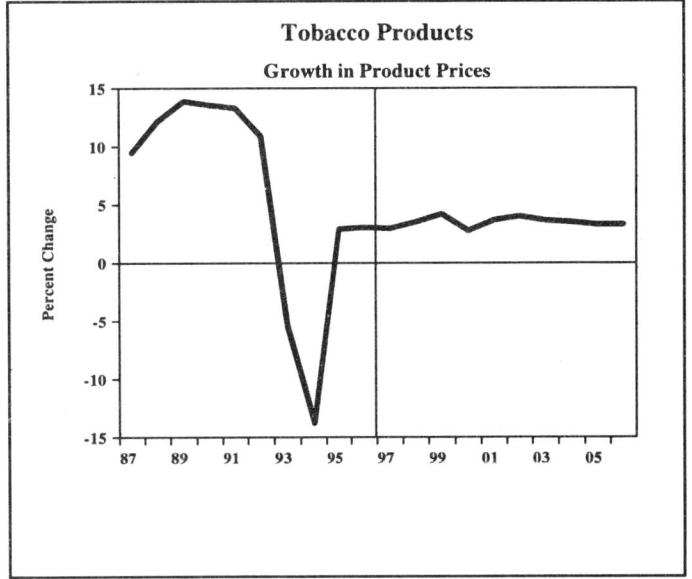

Tobacco Products
 SIC 21

		1990	1991	1992	1993	1994	1995	1996	1997	1998	Compound Ann Avg Growth 1986-1996	1996-2006
Sales												
	Billions of $	30.36	31.73	34.89	28.15	30.32	31.86	33.33	34.65	35.45		
	% Change	18.0	4.5	9.9	-19.3	7.7	5.1	4.6	4.0	2.3	5.8	3.2
Volume	% Change	4.0	-7.7	-0.8	-14.6	24.9	2.1	1.5	1.0	-1.1	0.2	-0.3
Prices	% Change	13.5	13.3	10.9	-5.5	-13.8	2.9	3.0	2.9	3.5	5.6	3.5
Exports												
	Billions of $	5.04	4.59	4.52	4.25	5.42	5.26	5.29	5.80	6.30		
	% Change	37.1	-9.0	-1.5	-5.9	27.5	-2.9	0.4	9.8	8.5	13.3	5.3
Apparent Consumption												
	Billions of $	25.32	27.15	30.37	23.90	24.90	26.60	28.05	28.85	29.16		
	Nominal % Change	14.9	7.2	11.9	-21.3	4.2	6.8	5.4	2.9	1.1	4.9	2.8
	Real % Change	1.2	-5.3	0.9	-16.8	20.8	3.8	2.3	-0.1	-2.3	-0.7	-0.7

Chapter 7:   Textile Mill Products

Broadwoven Fabrics and Other Textiles

Broadwoven fabrics basically consist of three categories: cotton fabrics (37%); wool fabrics (13%); and fabrics made of manmade fibers (polyester, etc.) and silk. Finished output from these manufacturers in turn provide the raw materials input for apparel, home furnishings, and other manufacturers of finished goods. Surging textile and apparel imports in recent years have resulted in substantial downsizing and consolidation within the industry. Volume demand for U.S. manufactures of broadwoven fabrics is expected to continue sluggish over the next three years, rising only about 1.5% to 2% per year — an improvement after two years of declining volume in 1995 and 1996.

Industry Demand

Cotton fabrics are inputs to three general end-product categories: apparel, home furnishings, and industrial products. Within the apparel end-market segment the largest demand is the cotton outerwear market. Cotton outerwear is a mature industry, and has been hit hard by imports. Imported garments are usually cut and sewn from fabrics manufactured in the same country, so a rise in outerwear imports is, more often than not, an import in the raw cotton fabric from which the final product was made. Second only to trade in its impact on demand for broadwoven cotton products is housing starts, which drives the market for home furnishings. The demand for industrial products made of these fibers is driven largely by the auto market and construction activity on new highways and bridges.

In the manmade segment of broadwoven fabrics, demand is impacted by imports as well as a trend toward consumer preference for natural fibers. Massive television ads, promoting cotton products as well as new designs that have reduced wrinkling and are therefore easier to care for and have made cotton clothing easier to maintain, have been effective in promoting substitution of cotton products for those produced with manmade fibers. On the plus side, however, polyester has been making a comeback due to new silk-feel products and a generation of clothes shoppers that don't remember the leisure suit! Moreover, nylon product improvements are boosting sales of women's hosiery, which seem to have bottomed out after several years of decline.

Overall for broadwoven fabric demand, an important development seems to be the recent accord with China which will keep in place almost $20 million in tariff increases imposed on them last September, while annual increases in textile and apparel exports from China will be held to roughly 1%.

High business failure rates, strong unions, and large cyclical swings categorize most segments of the U.S. textile industry, including broadwovens. Another major issue for the industry is trade pacts, including the Multi-Fiber Arrangement (MFA) and NAFTA. With the phase-out of the MFA over the next 15 years and the GATT plan, which will phase in completely by 2010, the industry faces a grave challenge to reshape itself so it can viably face international competition. Concerning NAFTA, many parts of the industry will suffer under the accord finding it difficult to compete on an equal basis with lower wages. The trade pact will likely be positive, however, for the fabric portion of the industry since it requires full sourcing of fabrics from the United States in Mexican apparel production. Volume demand for U.S. manufactures of broadwoven fabrics is expected to continue sluggish over the next three years, rising by only about 1.5–2% per year — an improvement after two years of declining volume in 1995 and 1996.

Supply Conditions

Surging textile and apparel imports in recent years have resulted in substantial downsizing and consolidation within the industry. This pressure can be seen in profit margins as both payroll expense and capital investment per establishment are above the all-industry average, while shipments per establishment is below. The result is lower profit margins than the average U.S. manufacturing establishment. The industry's high usage of capital equipment provides some barriers to entry which protects domestic markets, but in times of sluggish profitability it can hinder the firm's (or the industry's) ability to remain competitive with foreign producers.

Pricing Environment

One of the problems negatively affecting profit margins in this industry has been the difficulty of pushing through price increases. For the three years ending in 1995 output prices for broadwoven fabrics rose only 1.8% per year, and in 1996 they only advanced by an estimated 0.5%. Over the next three years, we expect this trend to continue, with prices expected to advance roughly 1% per year. The level of imports during this period will continue to play an important role in influencing domestic prices.

Major Trends Affecting The Outlook

Our outlook for the U.S. economy over the next two to three years is for modest growth of just over 2% per year. U.S. housing starts are expected to fall by about 1/2 million units in 1997, and remain flat at that level in 1998 and 1999. Moreover, apparel volume sales, discounted for inflation, are likely to rise only 1% per year. All in all, this predicts a rather sluggish outlook for the macro-economic drivers that propel the demand for broadwoven fabrics. Combining our expectation for modest real growth in broadwoven fabric demand and a slight pickup in price markups, overall shipments in this industry should expand by 3% per year over the next three years.

Major Risks In The Forecast

Raw commodity prices for both cotton and wool play an important part in the health of these segments of the broadwoven fabrics industry. Weather or other supply problems can always pop up rather quickly to pose a threat to the stability of both the availability and cost of these important inputs. Pricing discrepancies between input costs and wholesale output prices in synthetic fibers can also pose problems, as was the case in early 1995 when the wholesale price of synthetic fibers rose almost 6% while those for finished fabrics rose only 1 1/2%. Of course a snag could develop in the trade agreement with China causing imports to exceed current estimates, wrecking both demand and pricing forecasts. Add to this the fact that demand from the auto and housing markets is affected adversely by rising interest rates, the level of which remain very uncertain at this time, and you have the recipe for a very cyclical and uncertain outlook.

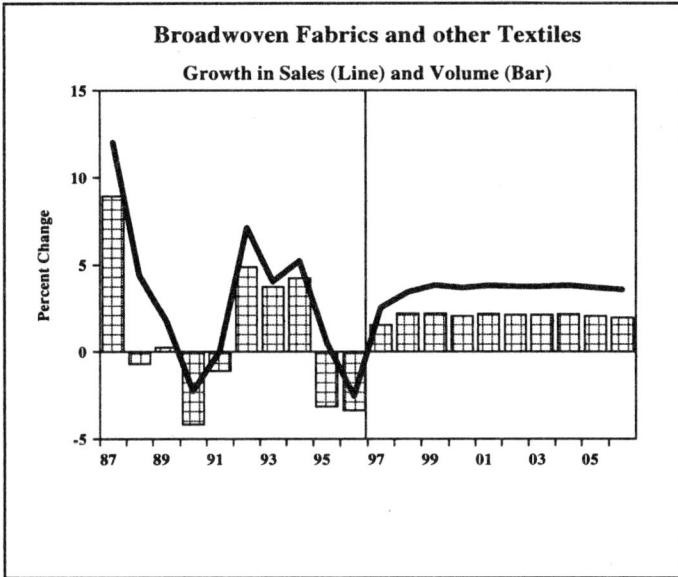

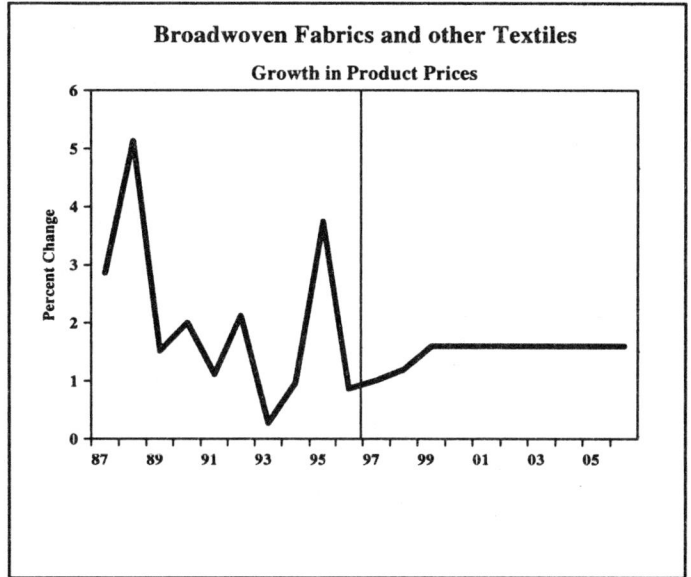

```
Broadwoven Fabrics and other Textiles
  SIC 221-4, 226, 228-9

                                                                                          Compound Ann Avg Growth
                        1990    1991    1992    1993    1994    1995    1996    1997    1998    1986-1996  1996-2006


Sales
          Billions of $ 41.14   41.13   44.06   45.84   48.24   48.47   47.25   48.46   50.12
          % Change       -2.2    -0.0     7.1     4.0     5.2     0.5    -2.5     2.5     3.4       2.9        3.6

  Volume  % Change       -4.2    -1.1     4.9     3.7     4.2    -3.2    -3.4     1.5     2.2       0.9        2.1
  Prices  % Change        2.0     1.1     2.1     0.3     1.0     3.7     0.9     1.0     1.2       2.1        1.5

Exports
          Billions of $  4.05    4.32    4.30    4.32    4.91    5.81    6.17    6.36    6.72
          % Change        9.0     6.7    -0.6     0.7    13.6    18.4     6.1     3.1     5.5      11.3        5.2
Imports
          Billions of $  4.45    4.90    5.47    5.94    6.34    6.58    6.98    7.57    8.29
          % Change       -0.3    10.2    11.6     8.6     6.7     3.9     6.0     8.5     9.4       5.7        6.4

Apparent Consumption
          Billions of $ 41.54   41.71   45.24   47.46   49.67   49.24   48.06   49.67   51.69
    Nominal % Change     -3.0     0.4     8.5     4.9     4.7    -0.9    -2.4     3.3     4.1       2.6        3.8
       Real % Change     -4.9    -0.7     6.2     4.6     3.7    -4.4    -3.2     2.3     2.8       0.5        2.3
```

Knitting Mill Products

Knitting mill products include women's hosiery (9%), hosiery other than women's (16%), knit outerwear (25%), knit underwear & nightwear (6%), weft (circular) knit mills (30%), and lace and warp knit mills (14%).Surging textile and apparel imports in recent years have resulted in substantial downsizing and consolidation within the knit outerwear industry. Much of the final demand for this industry comes from apparel and home furnishings purchases. Overall, the knitting industry is expected to experience a slight bounce back from very modest growth in the past few years, with real volume growth expected to average between 1.5% and 2% over the next three years.

Industry Demand

Outerwear and weft, or circular fabrics, represent 55% of the output of this industry. Outerwear has performed best in terms of industry health due to strong trends in leisure and active wear. The T-shirt market has been one of the fastest growing in the textile industry, especially T-shirts with messages and logos imprinted on them. Weft, or circular fabrics, typically sell their output to manufacturers of outerwear, underwear, or other products in the apparel or home furnishings industries. In the home furnishings industry, carpets and rugs are an important source of demand for knit mill products.

Final demand for the bulk of this industry, therefore, comes from apparel and home furnishings purchases, which in turn depend largely upon consumer income and confidence. The apparel industry is a mature industry, and one that has been hurt by imports: net imports of apparel account for about 50% of personal consumption expenditures on apparel. WEFA's expectations for growth of real disposable income over the next two to three years is about 2.5% per year; and the volume of knitting mill product demand over the same period is expected to increase by about 2% per year.

However, imports are an important factor in this industry, averaging over 17% growth over the last ten years and forecast to continue to grow in the double digits over the next ten years. The phase-out of the Multi-Fiber Arrangement (MFA) and the phase-in of the General Agreement on Tariffs and Trade (GATT) will remove a degree of protection and ensure that domestic production will grow more slowly than demand. A recent accord with China will keep in place almost $20 million in tariff increases imposed last September, while annual increases in overall textile and apparel exports from China will be held to 1%. This should buoy demand for U.S. production over the period immediately ahead. Overall, the knitting mill industry is expected to experience a slight bounce back from declines in the past two years with real volume growth expected to average between 1.5% and 2% per year over the next three years.

Supply Conditions

The surge in textile and apparel imports in recent years has resulted in substantial downsizing and consolidation within the knit outerwear industry. The industry appears to have handled this downsizing rather well, as total payroll costs per establishment are on par with the all-industry average while profitability — due largely to the industry's much lower capital investment cost per establishment — is above the average. Weft knit fabric mills, on the other hand, have not suffered the decline in the number of manufacturing establishments that has occurred in the outerwear segment, but the industry has performed more poorly in terms of operating results. The weft industry (hosiery, underwear, lace, and similar products) has both payroll costs and capital equipment costs well above that of the average in manufacturing. Although sales per establishment are also above average, high costs mean that profit margins within the weft mill industry are below average. Investment for either expansion or modernization will be difficult to finance as a result.

Pricing Environment

One of the problems negatively affecting profit margins in this industry overall has been the difficulty the industry has had in pushing through price increases. For the four years ending in 1996, average output prices for all types of knitting mills rose only 1% per year. Over the next three years, we expect this trend to continue. The level of imports and their pricing in a stronger-dollar environment during this period will play an important role in influencing domestic prices and margins.

Major Trends Affecting The Outlook

WEFA's outlook for the U.S. economy over the next two to three years is for modest growth of just over 2% per year. U.S. housing starts are expected to be essentially flat through this period. Moreover, apparel volume sales, discounted for inflation, are likely to show growth below 1% per year. All in all, the picture is one of a rather sluggish outlook for the macro-economic drivers that propel the demand for knitting mill products. Combining our expectation for modest growth in both volume and prices, overall sales in this industry should expand by about 3% per year over the next few years. In this environment, margins are likely to remain under pressure.

Major Risks In The Forecast

Raw materials prices will play an important part in the health of knitting mill firms in the years just ahead, as will the industry's ability to put through price increases of their own. Weather or other supply problems can always pop up rather quickly to pose a threat to the stability of both the availability and cost of important inputs. Moreover, should a snag develop in the trade agreement with China that would cause imports to exceed current estimates, both demand and pricing forecasts could become optimistic. Finally, the threat of higher interest rates and its effect on both consumer confidence and the crucial outlook for housing remain a source of volatility and uncertainty for this industry in the years just ahead.

Knitting Mill Products
Growth in Sales (Line) and Volume (Bar)

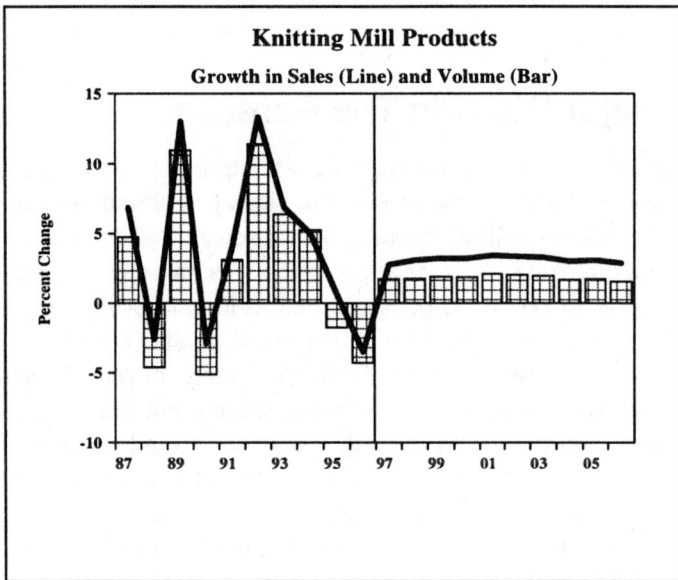

Knitting Mill Products
Growth in Product Prices

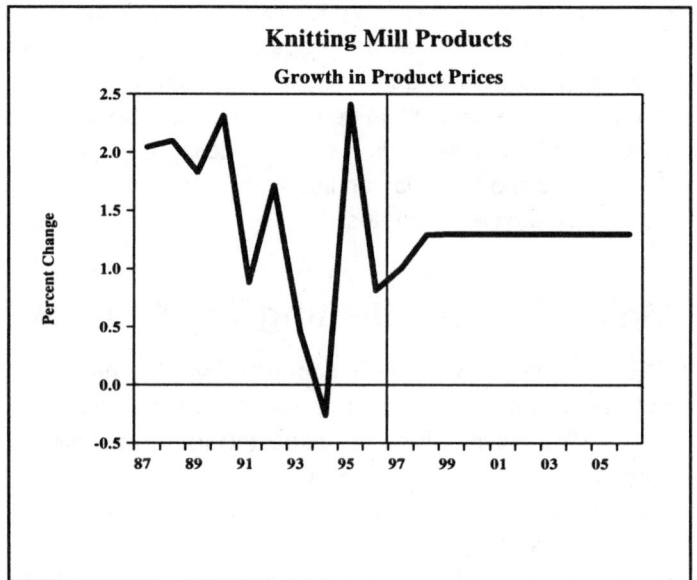

```
Knitting Mill Products
SIC 225
```

		1990	1991	1992	1993	1994	1995	1996	1997	1998	Compound Ann Avg Growth 1986-1996	1996-2006
Sales												
	Billions of $	14.47	15.05	17.05	18.22	19.12	19.23	18.56	19.07	19.66		
	% Change	-2.9	4.0	13.3	6.8	4.9	0.6	-3.5	2.7	3.1	3.9	3.1
Volume	% Change	-5.1	3.1	11.4	6.4	5.2	-1.7	-4.3	1.7	1.8	2.4	1.8
Prices	% Change	2.3	0.9	1.7	0.5	₌0.3	2.4	0.8	1.0	1.3	1.4	1.3
Exports												
	Billions of $	1.43	1.55	1.75	2.03	2.54	2.75	2.61	2.82	3.02		
	% Change	21.3	8.8	12.3	16.5	24.7	8.6	-5.1	8.1	6.9	15.7	3.8
Imports												
	Billions of $	0.75	0.86	0.96	1.06	1.19	1.33	1.41	1.59	1.76		
	% Change	18.8	15.3	11.1	10.5	12.1	11.9	5.9	13.3	10.2	17.7	10.9
Apparent Consumption												
	Billions of $	13.79	14.36	16.27	17.24	17.77	17.81	17.36	17.84	18.39		
	Nominal % Change	-4.0	4.1	13.3	6.0	3.0	0.2	-2.5	2.8	3.1	3.5	3.9
	Real % Change	-6.1	3.2	11.4	5.5	3.3	-2.1	-3.3	1.8	1.8	2.0	2.6

Carpets and Rugs

The carpet and rug industry includes manufacturers of woven, tufted, and other carpets and rugs. It also includes aircraft and automobile floor coverings, except rubber and plastic. The manufacturers included in SIC 2273 shipped roughly $12 billion in 1996, and the United States is the world's leader in tufted carpet and rug consumption and production. Total revenues for the industry are expected to rise about 3% per year, long term, as volume demand and pricing remain sluggish.

Demand

Carpet and rug sales fell sharply during the 1990-91 recession, as is normal in a business cycle given the sector's link to the extremely volatile housing market. The recovery that began in 1992 continued through 1996, but at a much slower pace than occurred during the 1992-95 period. Falling mortgage interest rates and a trend toward home refinancing gave extra impetus to this recovery by making cash available for remodeling.

Looking forward, the carpet and rug industry will follow the economic fundamentals that drive demand. Home-building and automobile production are the two major sources of demand for carpets and rugs. Overall, however, consumer income and spending are the key variables to watch when analyzing market trends. Consumer spending affects both replacement and redecorating demand for the industry's products as well as automotive demand. The most important influence on housing starts, and a key variable in auto sales, is interest rates.

Consumer disposable income, in real terms, is expected to grow at a fairly stable pace over the next two to three years, experiencing modest gains of roughly 2.5% per year. Consumers will, however, remain cost conscious and thrifty — the uncertainty concerning jobs and incomes that used to surface every few years has now become systemic and ingrained in consumer sentiment. Auto sales will be basically flat for the next year or two, then rise modestly with modestly expanding incomes and a new replacement cycle. Housing starts, however, will decline somewhat over the next couple of years after peaking at just under 1.5 million units in 1996. This does not bode well for carpet and rug sales, since the new housing market is the largest source of demand for the industry's products.

Exports also drive the industry. In 1994 the United States supplied roughly 40% of world carpet exports. The country's two largest export markets were Canada and Saudi Arabia. It was, in fact, a surge in exports in 1996 that largely offset weakness in domestic demand for carpets and rugs and allowed the industry to continue to expand. Over the next two years we expect the opposite to happen: domestic demand will remain at fairly strong levels and exports will slump from last year's surge. Overall, WEFA expects volume growth for carpet and rug manufacturers to remain quite weak over the next two to three years. A small decline in volume is likely in 1997, followed by only very modest growth in 1998 and 1999.

Supply

The United States is the world's leader in tufted carpet and rug consumption and production. Shaw Industries is the largest carpet manufacturer in the United States, making tufted carpet for home and commercial use under various labels, including Philadelphia, Cabin Craft, Stratton, Armstrong, Salem, Sutton, and Magee. The company is also the largest carpet maker in the United Kingdom and Australia. Given the firm's size, trends at Shaw often reflect what is going on in the entire industry. In 1996, Shaw added extensively to the retail arm of its operation, not by opening new retail selling space but by acquiring over 50 outlets of existing retailers. In the industry in general, expansion through acquisition has proven much more cost-effective than opening new stores — so it is unlikely that any future expansion will include many new stores.

Shipment dollars per establishment in the carpet and rug industry is roughly 2.5 times those of the average manufacturing firm, as is the number of employees per establishment. The costs of material inputs to the industry, however, are quite high — even though their proportion to total shipments has eased in recent years — and these costs have offset the industry's advantages of lower-than-average hourly wages and capital investment cost per establishment. Steep input costs impede profitability and limit the industry's ability to react quickly to changing market conditions.

Pricing

Price increases within the industry have been rather hard to come by since the late 1980s, although about a 2% industry-wide average price hike in 1996 showed signs of promise. WEFA's expectation is that prices will continue to rise at a similar clip over the next year or two as the industry plays catch-up. Beyond that, however, price gains are expected to fall back in line with their long term trend of about 1.5% average annual growth.

In the long run, therefore, the combination of average volume gains of 1.2% with average price gains of 1.5% will bring annual revenue increases in the carpet and rug industry of roughly 3% per year.

Key Trends Affecting The Outlook

Modest employment and income gains and continued cost consciousness will affect consumer spending patterns for the foreseeable future. These trends will hurt replacement and redecoration demand for both carpets and rugs in the period ahead. Housing starts will drift along without much ability to increase sharply, particularly given the length of the current U.S. expansion. The same is true for auto demand: the big gains are behind and growth will come more grudgingly in the future. Also look for continued consolidation and zeal for cost cutting in the carpet and rug industry.

Major Risks To The Outlook

The major risk to the carpet and rug industry at this point is a resurgence of interest rates. Demand emanating from both of the industry's primary markets — housing and autos — is very interest sensitive, and would retreat quickly in the face of significantly higher rates. Second, consumer sentiment could turn negative if concerns about the long term health of American jobs, and their rate of pay, continues to rise. Of course the risk of recession, or of meaningful economic weakness, is always present, particularly in an economy that has been expanding for six years.

Carpets and Rugs
Growth in Sales (Line) and Volume (Bar)

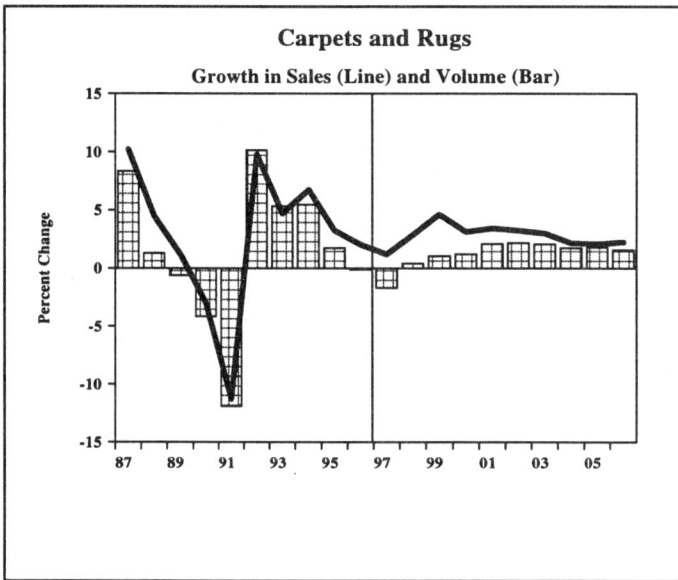

Carpets and Rugs
Growth in Product Prices

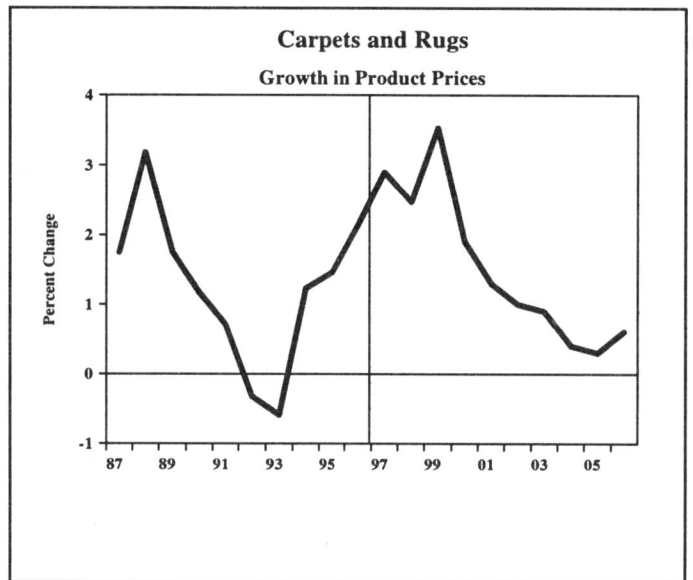

Carpets and Rugs
SIC 227

		1990	1991	1992	1993	1994	1995	1996	1997	1998	Compound Ann Avg Growth 1986-1996	1996-2006
Sales												
	Billions of $	10.09	8.96	9.84	10.30	10.99	11.34	11.57	11.71	12.04		
	% Change	-3.0	-11.3	9.8	4.7	6.7	3.2	2.0	1.2	2.9	2.6	2.8
Volume	% Change	-4.1	-11.9	10.2	5.3	5.4	1.7	-0.1	-1.7	0.4	1.4	1.2
Prices	% Change	1.2	0.7	-0.3	-0.6	1.2	1.5	2.1	2.9	2.5	1.2	1.5
Exports												
	Billions of $	0.57	0.72	0.74	0.73	0.73	0.72	1.37	1.25	1.17		
	% Change	20.3	26.6	3.3	-1.5	0.2	-2.0	90.1	-8.7	-6.4	21.0	0.8
Imports												
	Billions of $	0.61	0.59	0.72	0.68	0.76	0.86	0.85	0.89	0.90		
	% Change	-2.0	-2.8	21.2	-5.6	12.0	14.1	-1.6	4.4	1.6	3.8	2.3
Apparent Consumption												
	Billions of $	10.13	8.83	9.81	10.24	11.01	11.49	11.05	11.34	11.77		
	Nominal % Change	-4.0	-12.9	11.1	4.4	7.6	4.3	-3.8	2.6	3.8	1.7	3.0
	Real % Change	-5.1	-13.5	11.5	5.0	6.3	2.8	-5.8	-0.3	1.3	0.5	1.4

Chapter 8:   Apparel

Apparel

The apparel industry includes the manufacture of men's, boy's, women's, girl's, children's, and infant's apparel and apparel accessories (excluding footwear). Apparel is made by cutting and sewing woven and knit textile fabrics or by knitting from yarn. Most manufacturers produce more than one brand, and in many cases private or store brand labels as well. Roughly half of all apparel sold in the United States is manufactured abroad, and domestic apparel companies have increased the contracting of overseas manufacturers to compete with lower priced imports. WEFA's expectations for apparel sales over the next ten years is for growth of about 3% per year. Volume is forecasted to rise by roughly 1% per year on average, slower than overall consumer income and spending, and prices will average 2% growth.

Demand

Employment peaked in the apparel industry in 1973 at roughly 1.4 million, and is now below one million. Two factors are largely responsible for this trend:

- First is the flood of cheap imported apparel that has found its way into U.S. markets;

- Second is the tremendous gain in productivity that the industry has achieved over the past 20 years.

Price pressure from this competition from low wage countries has unfortunately overwhelmed the productive cost savings for the industry, pressuring margins by preventing meaningful price increases.

What drives apparel sales? Clearly the economy and consumer spending trends matter. Consumer spending is expected to grow by just under 2.5% per year over the next decade. In the 1980s, fashion tended to govern the market, but in recent years, particularly with business downsizing and job uncertainty prevailing, consumers are exercising both caution and a considerable degree of cost consciousness. Women's clothing designers have failed to introduce major trend-setting styles so far in the 1990s. Overall, consumers are shifting down their apparel purchases. They are spending less in total; they are buying less costly items; and they are deserting the department stores for discounters at a steady pace.

Of course it would be meaningless to talk about demand for apparel without mentioning the implications from foreign trade, since apparel imports account for over a third of domestic consumption. Exports, on the other hand, are almost meaningless, accounting for less than 1% of annual U.S. purchases due to high American wages in a labor intensive industry. Last September, the United States imposed almost $20 million in tariff increases on China, one of the key foreign importers into the U.S. apparel market. In addition, China will keep annual increases in textile and apparel exports to the United States close to 1%. However, overall pressure from imports will continue to dampen the outlook for sales of domestically-produced apparel.

WEFA's expectations for U.S. apparel industry sales over the next ten years is for growth of 3.3% per year. Volume is forecasted to rise by 1.2% per year on average, slower than overall consumer income and spending, and prices will average 2%, not too far below the expected average retail price gain for all consumer spending. Wages within the apparel industry are likely to advance a percentage point or two slower than revenue gains over the next few years, so profit margins should advance faster than revenues.

Supply Conditions

There is quite a bit of dispersion within the U.S. apparel manufacturing sector; in fact, it is estimated that there are more than 20,000 firms in the industry. The industry is very cyclical, and it can be whipped around by the whims of fashion and consumer confidence. Apparel manufacturers have a capability, however, that many other manufacturers don't have — the ability to expand or contract output and costs rather easily. This is because the industry is very labor intensive and requires only modest amounts of capital equipment. In addition to their internal flexibility, producers have increased their timely control over output and costs through the use of jobbers and contractors. Increasingly, these jobbers and contractors are foreign, due to cheaper labor costs abroad.

As is the case with many labor intensive industries, apparel manufacturing is very competitive and promotes low wages. Conditions within the industry also provide an environment where labor exploitation is not uncommon.

Important Industry Trends

Consolidation, an ongoing trend in apparel retailing, is leading to larger stores and fewer numbers of retailers in the U.S. marketplace. Larger stores are able to exert more bargaining leverage over prices and conditions of sale from manufacturers. Moreover, the squeeze on wages and jobs in all phases of the apparel industry, as in many other industries, shows no sign of easing. Consumers, therefore, are not expected to return to the free-spending ways of the 1980s at any point in the forecast period. Another important trend is the development of international sourcing capabilities, which have a positive impact on profit margins. One area that shows particular promise over the next several years is sourcing capability in Mexico due to its proximity to domestic markets and the NAFTA accord.

Within the material inputs segment of the apparel industry — broadwoven fabrics and other textiles — high

business failure rates, strong unions, and large cyclical swings make the industry quite volatile. Intense competition from imports at this supplier level as well will continue to play a dominant role in the industry's health and outlook.

Major Risks To The Forecast

There are two major and ever-present risks that might lead the outlook for apparel sales to be less robust than WEFA's already modest forecast:

- The fickle nature of fashion trends, which can turn unfavorable toward any style or brand without notice, and

- The possibility of some loss of confidence on the part of consumers that would simply cause them to stay home more often rather than go shopping.

Fashion trends present the larger risk for companies within the industry — that is, the risk that shopping dollars will go to a competing brand or style rather than to your company's. However, the overall dollar amount spent is less sensitive to specific fashion trends. The consumer confidence risk, however, is a more global risk that total spending will fall and the broad base of retailers and manufacturers will be hurt. At present, WEFA does not forecast any serious confidence threats to the apparel industry in its most-likely scenario.

Apparel and other Finished Textile Products
Growth in Sales (Line) and Volume (Bar)

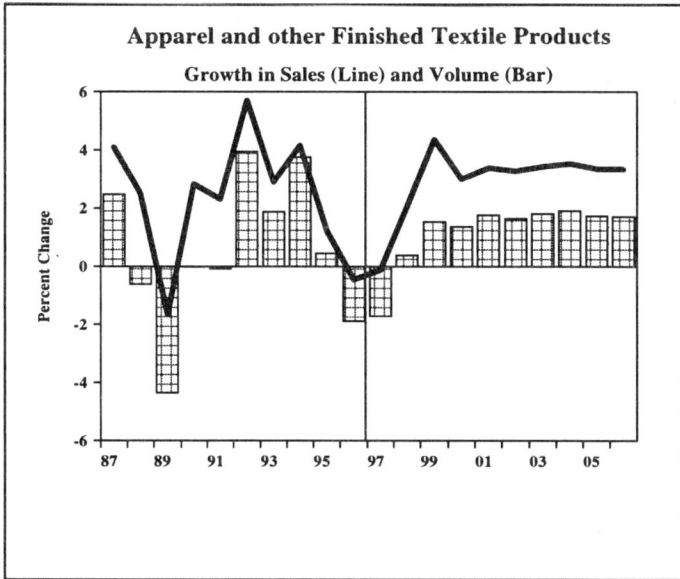

Apparel and other Finished Textile Products
Growth in Product Prices

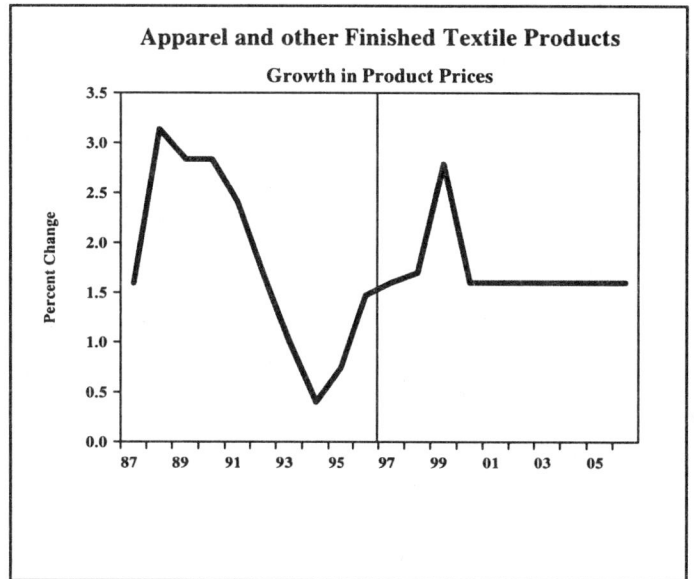

```
Apparel and other Finished Textile Products
 SIC 23
```

		1990	1991	1992	1993	1994	1995	1996	1997	1998	Compound Ann Avg Growth 1986-1996	1996-2006
Sales												
	Billions of $	66.65	68.18	72.08	74.17	77.26	78.19	77.84	77.74	79.36		
	% Change	2.8	2.3	5.7	2.9	4.2	1.2	-0.4	-0.1	2.1	2.3	3.0
Volume	% Change	-0.0	-0.1	3.9	1.9	3.8	0.5	-1.9	-1.7	0.4	0.5	1.2
Prices	% Change	2.8	2.4	1.7	1.0	0.4	0.7	1.5	1.6	1.7	1.8	1.7
Exports												
	Billions of $	0.32	0.42	0.43	0.40	0.46	0.48	0.51	0.55	0.60		
	% Change	41.7	28.9	3.5	-7.1	14.2	5.6	5.3	8.9	7.7	16.7	4.5
Imports												
	Billions of $	27.93	28.86	33.77	36.21	39.25	42.61	44.60	48.90	52.16		
	% Change	7.0	3.3	17.0	7.2	8.4	8.6	4.7	9.6	6.7	8.8	7.4
Apparent Consumption												
	Billions of $	94.25	96.63	105.41	109.98	116.05	120.32	121.94	126.09	130.92		
	Nominal % Change	3.9	2.5	9.1	4.3	5.5	3.7	1.3	3.4	3.8	4.2	4.8
	Real % Change	1.1	0.1	7.3	3.3	5.1	2.9	-0.1	1.8	2.1	2.3	3.0

Chapter 9: Paper and Allied Products

Pulp Mills

The pulp market is global, with large volumes of pulp moving duty–free between net–producing regions and net–consuming regions. While pulp producers have been struggling recently, fundamentals are far from disastrous, especially for the second half of 1997 onward. New pulp capacity additions are not excessive, as minor expansion in North America softens the impact of major projects elsewhere in the world; paper demand has already improved substantially from the drastically low levels of the beginning of 1996; and even producers' pulp stocks are not overly high. A stronger dollar will benefit the economies of Europe and Japan, resulting in a pickup in their paper exports and production.

Market Conditions

The recovery of market pulp prices fizzled in the third quarter of 1996, after staging a remarkable rebound in the preceding three months. Nordic and North American producers unloaded record amounts of pulp and dropped producers' inventories by one million tons — the fastest reduction on record. However, this was accomplished by offering bargain basement prices. As soon as pulp prices moved back up, paper mills began to scale back on new orders, not because paper mills were savvy buyers but because the expected recovery in printing and writing papers never materialized.

By the end of the third quarter of 1996, reality returned to pulp markets, with pulp shipments declining by 1% from the 1995 level and producers' stocks at North American and Nordic pulp mills moving up, increasing by nearly 225,000 tons between the spring and summer months. In the fourth quarter, pulp shipments increased by 12% versus a year earlier, but this was because 1995 shipment levels were highly depressed. Most damaging to pulp producers and price stability was a nearly 200,000 ton increase in producers' stocks, bringing year–end pulp stocks at Nordic and North American mills to almost two million tons — a critical mark for the pulp industry.

At the start of 1997, producers began to discount prices. This, coupled with a stronger U.S. dollar, forced pulp producers in Sweden to lower the dollar-priced northern bleached softwood kraft (NBSK) pulp by $20 to $40/ton by late January, and most other world producers followed suit. With the dollar still appreciating, eucalyptus pulp prices in ECU units were weak and, on a value basis, lower than the prices for southern mixed hardwood. Indonesian hardwoods were selling at a high enough level to destroy old dumping grounds for southern mixed hardwood pulps during oversupply periods.

While the North American pulp market has been struggling, fundamentals are far from disastrous, especially for the second half of 1997 onward. New pulp capacity additions are not excessive; paper demand should improve substantially over the drastically low levels of the beginning of 1996; and even producers' pulp stocks are not excessively high. A stronger dollar will benefit the economies of Europe and Japan, resulting in a pickup in their paper exports and production.

Based on WEFA's current forecasts, pulp prices are expected to slip a little farther in 1997, before regaining solid footing in 1998. We don't expect the price drop to be dramatic, however. During the year prices could drop to the same level as in the 1996 slide.

With increased pulp demand, producers' inventories are forecast to be drawn down by nearly 300,000 tons in the first half of this year from year–end 1996 stocks, bringing total North American and Nordic stocks to 1.6 million tons by the end of June. With producers reducing pulp stocks during that period, operating rates are projected to hover in the high 80% range. With improving pulp demand in the summer months, mill operating rates are forecast to move just above the 90% mark and remain close to this level through year–end 1997.

Industry Structure

The companies in the U.S. pulp, paper, and lumber industries are quite integrated. More than 60 U.S. companies produce pulp of paper grade, but only about 20 of them sell pulp in the merchant market.

About 60% of U.S. consumption of paper-grade pulp is used to produce printing and writing paper. Other key markets include the production of tissue, fluff, and specialty papers. As a result of this customer distribution, U.S. demand for pulp is driven by, and closely linked to, U.S. paper production in general, but especially that of the printing and writing grades.

Since the late 1980s, the link between traded pulp and the printing and writing grades has loosened, largely due to the increased integration of the companies in the forest products industry, as well as a pickup in the use of recovered paper.

Pulp Market Cycles

Characterized by sharp inventory swings and rising or falling prices, the pulp market is highly cyclical, but these cycles do not always coincide with overall economic cycles. In the last twenty years, there have been three sustained runs of market pulp prices followed by a price decline — but the cycle of the last three years is without precedent. This recent cycle peaked in October 1995 with a run–up to almost U.S.$1000 per ton for NBSK, the sharpest rise on record. The collapse to U.S. $500 per ton in March 1996 made the decline of the early 1990s look mild.

A worrisome aspect of pulp markets is that price swings are getting shorter in duration. With any faltering of demand, producers are reluctant to take downtime to correct for oversupply, and instead cut prices to move tonnage, creating unstable markets. For example, during the run–up in producers' inventories in the third and fourth quarters of 1996, producers failed to curtail production enough to keep stocks under control and continued to operate mills at greater than 90%. While prices are expected to firm up through mid–1997, they are likely to take another tumble when demand slackens in late 1997 and early 1998 unless mills recognize the need to curtail pulp supplies when demand weakens.

International Market

The pulp market is global, with large volumes of pulp moving duty–free between net–producing regions and net–consuming regions. North America and the Nordic countries are the largest market pulp producing regions, although nontraditional supplying countries with fast-growing plantations — Brazil, Chile, Portugal, Spain, and Indonesia — are gaining in importance.

During the past decade, world shipments of chemical paper–grade pulp have grown at a greater than 3.5% average annual rate. While shipments by North American and Nordic producers grew by almost 3% during that period, deliveries by nontraditional suppliers, led by Brazil and Portugal, grew at nearly twice that rate. As a result, their share of the world total increased dramatically. The share held by North American and Nordic producers, which declined as a result, is expected to continue to fall as substantial new capacity starts up in regions such as Latin America.

Western Europe (excluding Scandinavia) remains the largest destination for world chemical paper–grade market pulp shipments, accounting for about 40% of total shipments. The United States is the second largest consuming market, while Japan is the third. Consumption by the rapidly expanding regions of the world — Latin America, Asia, and Africa — is growing quickly, however.

As these countries progress further, their demand for consumer products will expand rapidly. The countries with the strongest consumption growth are expected to be China, India, South Korea, and Indonesia. Asia (including Japan) will account for fully one–half of worldwide tonnage growth in printing and writing papers and bleached pulp demand by the year 2000. By the turn of the century, demand for papers will be larger in Asia than in both Western Europe and North America.

Increasing Global Capacity

Market pulp capacity expansions for chemical paper-grade pulp show no signs of slowing down, and pulp producers will likely add over 1.0 million tons per year (tpy) of capacity by 1999. The vast majority of new capacity coming on-line is for hardwood kraft pulp, and nearly all of this is in Southeast Asia, Brazil, and Chile. Of the more than five million tons of chemical paper-grade capacity scheduled to enter the production stream between 1996 and 2001, approximately 4.0 million tons are for hardwood pulp. The projected 1.2 million tons of softwood pulp will come from Chile, Sweden, and Finland. The major unknown factor for the next few years is how much of the huge expansions scheduled and planned for Indonesia and Malaysia will be for open-market sales and what quantity will be integrated.

While the rest of the world is expanding rapidly, the expansion cycle in North America for chemical paper-grade pulp is largely over, and little new capacity is likely to come on-line before 1998. During this time, total market pulp capacity at North American mills is slated to rise by less than 250,000 tons. In the United States, some capacity will possibly even be withdrawn, as producers integrate pulp capacity to support new coated and uncoated free-sheet machines. Even if prices improve, U.S. producers will be reluctant to invest in market pulp capacity, due to a shortage of southern pine pulpwood and to the uncertainty surrounding proposed, new environmental regulations.

Paper Mills

The U.S. printing and writing market is finally beginning to come out of one of the worst downturns in its history. What makes the downturn unusual is the fact that it occurred while the economy was growing; typically, a drop in demand that large has been caused by a serious economic contraction.

The culprit behind much of this falloff in demand was a huge inventory adjustment, driven by unprecedented swings in prices. When prices began their jump from a record low in early 1994 to an all–time high in mid–1995, buyers over–ordered as they tried to head off a run–up in costs. Similarly, once buyers realized that the run–up was over in the second half of 1995, they pulled out of the market so suddenly and in such large measure that prices and orders collapsed across the board. Most of the impact occurred in 1996.

There continue to be small signs of improving market conditions for most of the printing and writing grades. Orders are recovering in the coated grades, and prices have been inching upward. The recovery in un-coated free–sheet prices, however, stalled again late in 1996, and they have moved down in concert with pulp prices. Some uncoated groundwood prices have slipped recently, but the upturn in newsprint prices this year should keep groundwood prices from dropping much below their current levels.

Consumer inventories appear to have returned to more normal levels, so stronger economic growth should translate fairly directly into increased purchases. Shipments of printing and writing grades are rebounding substantially in 1997, helped along by a pickup in economic growth. However, capacity growth in North America and overseas (particularly in Indonesia and Malaysia) will continue to be a damper on prices. The new facilities, based on low manufacturing costs, will allow these nontraditional regions of supply to accept lower prices.

Coated Paper Market Conditions

There is a sigh of relief echoing in the coated paper markets — the market seems to have bottomed out. Still, recovery is going to happen rather slowly. The demand for paper for such applications as annual reports, magazines, directories, and high–end advertising should be modest. Without a dramatic surge in economic growth, end–users will have little reason to spend lavishly on such frills as glossy paper.

The inventory situation has stabilized; and demand is returning to trend levels and exhibiting normal seasonal patterns. Prices should shadow the move upward in demand, and both should continue to pick up throughout 1997 and 1998.

Coated Free–Sheet

The fundamentals of the coated free–sheet market improved greatly last fall. However, prices of publication papers trailed this improvement by several months. Not until the beginning of the new year did prices start to move. Consumers appear to have worked off the excessive inventories they amassed in late 1994 and early 1995. Aided by strong economic growth in the United States, apparent consumption has turned around sharply when compared to year–ago levels.

A number of factors, however, could continue to put downward pressure on prices. First, U.S. annual capacity is slated to grow by more than 7% in the near term. There will also continue to be rapid growth of pulp capacity overseas.

Mill inventories are also a concern. Although they fell rapidly between May and September, inventories rose slightly by the end of 1996, causing a slight drop in the ratio of apparent consumption to mill inventories. The slight rise in inventories was largely caused by higher mill operating rates, which were close to 85% at the end of the year. WEFA does not expect capacity constraints to play a role in determining prices this year. As a result, our forecast calls for only moderate price increases in 1997 and 1998.

Coated Groundwood Papers

A small rise in groundwood paper shipments helped to bring down producer inventories last year, as did a low operating rate, which is estimated to have been about 88%.

December was the first month in 1996 in which shipments were up from year–ago levels. An important indicator of market conditions, the ratio of apparent consumption to mill inventories, also improved ever so slightly toward the end of the year. In keeping with stronger market conditions, the price of light weight calendar (LWC) grades inched forward in early February, as producers were able to cut back on discounting.

Looking forward, prices will receive a boost from limited capacity expansions in the United States. Capacity is estimated to have grown by 1.0% in 1996 and is projected to grow by a similar amount in both 1997 and 1998.

WEFA forecasts rebounding consumption and shipments in 1997. However, these gains will be exaggerated by comparison to an extraordinarily weak 1996. Our projected shipment and apparent consumption levels for 1997 will fall short of those for both 1994 and 1995.

Uncoated Paper Market Conditions

Uncoated Groundwood Papers

The market for uncoated groundwood papers (a step up from newsprint quality) remains tepid heading into mid–1997. Apparent consumption appears to have recovered to trend levels. Even with the dramatic influx of digital technologies, magazines, books, and catalogs still frequently make their way into American consumers' homes.

Since the latter half of 1996, mill inventories have changed little and shipments fell below year–ago levels. The ratio of unfilled orders to mill inventories edged upwards as 1997 began. This ratio usually leads prices by several months. Yet this ratio is still registering a low level, so this is not a terribly bullish sign.

The current strengthening of the newsprint market will help to put a floor under the prices of the near–newsprint grades. In addition, limited capacity growth in 1997 should help pull prices up later in the year. In the United States, combined newsprint/uncoated groundwood capacity is projected to grow by less than 1% in both 1997 and 1998. (Combining the two grades helps to reduce the statistical problem posed by machines that swing between newsprint and the near–newsprint grades.)

Uncoated Free–Sheet

Uncoated free–sheet prices appeared to be on the road to recovery twice in 1996, but by February of 1997 had lost all the ground they had gained. In some cases prices even reached a new low for this cycle.

Not that there wasn't good news. In the fourth quarter of 1996, both U.S. shipments and apparent consumption were up substantially on a year–ago basis. But U.S. producers ran their mills at an operating rate well over 95% in December, which caused mill inventories to rise even as shipments were surging. Combined with seasonal weakness in demand and falling pulp prices, these additional mill inventories helped push free–sheet prices down at the beginning of 1997. Still, WEFA is projecting that conditions will improve and prices will strengthen later this year.

Market conditions for repographic papers, bond papers, envelopes, tablets, carbon/carbonless, and cigarette papers will be helped by steady, albeit moderate economic growth in the United States. Strong growth overseas, as foreign consumers demand more of these paper products, will also help tighten the uncoated free–sheet market.

A low rate of capacity growth in the United States will favor higher prices. On the other hand, there will be fairly rapid capacity growth overseas, in both the uncoated free–sheet and hardwood pulp segments. Low–cost hardwood fiber from the southern hemisphere and southern Asia will continue to be a drag on uncoated free–sheet prices.

Environmental Considerations

Environmental issues and regulations have a profound effect in the paper industry, from forestry practices and pulp production to product marketing and convincing customers to use greener buying patterns and recycle more of what they use.

One long–term global issue is whether the world contains sufficient natural resources to continue on its growth and development path for making and using paper. While the resources appear to be sufficient, their harvesting and renewal will require huge investment. These resources will increasingly come from new pulp–supplying parts of the world.

A key environmental debate has centered around whether paper industry feedstocks (i.e. pulp) should be elemental chlorine–free (ECF) or totally chlorine–free (TCF). Considerable progress has been made by the industry to clean up its effluent by using, for example, hydrogen peroxide rather than chlorine as a bleaching agent. Environmentally friendly feedstock has required the investment of huge sums of money in capital equipment, research and development, and training of industry professionals. The costs associated with these projects have proven to be worthwhile, however — some of the mills that have been upgraded to include advanced pollution abating technologies are now among the lowest–cost facilities in the industry.

A continuing uncertainty for U.S. companies is how much money will be required to comply with "Cluster Rule" regulations expected to be issued by the EPA later this year. Georgia–Pacific estimated that it may have to spend $425 million during the 1996–99 period to comply with the requirements. However, that amount is difficult to estimate, because changes in the regulations are possible, and their proposed implementation deadline of 1999 may be delayed.

Outlook

The threat from the paperless office has yet to materialize. During the past decade, paper producers were rarely intimidated by the dawn of the electronic age and added new capacity quite liberally. Demand for certain grades, such as cut–size repographic, actually increased with the heightened use of computer desktop printers. Also, electronic media actually contributed to the growth in magazines by using advertising to market and sell digital media products.

The number of new paper projects coming on stream in North America has slowed, as implications from the electronic age and modest economic growth have combined to weaken demand for paper products. The next decade promises to show an even greater transformation from paper to electronic media.

In the coming years, some traditional paper end–uses will be progressively replaced in the domestic market by digital media. Mail–order shopping will increasingly go through the Internet, rather than through printed catalogs. Data will be transferred electronically, rather than published and mailed to its user. Letters will be sent electronically, rather than printed and mailed. Banking services will be performed on–line, rather than in the neighborhood branch.

Other segments of the domestic paper market will be endangered by emerging technologies. For example, the largest threat to the coated paper industry is not the initial electronic replacement of print media, but rather the impact on advertising from digital interactive media. Also, technology now allows a combination of computer, fax, and image technologies all in one machine and a paper–free transmission.

The fastest growth in the paper market now and into the next century will be overseas. As consumers in developing economies gain more purchasing power, there will be a great push to advertise and deliver consumer products. There will be a greater demand for magazines, books, and newspapers as higher income is expected to correlate with higher literacy.

Developing countries that are currently producing at the low end of the paper chain are expected to break into the higher value markets within the next five to ten years. This could yield an interesting market situation for U.S. producers, who will be forced to either add greater value to the products they are currently producing, invest in new technologies to ensure they are low cost producers, or lose global share to foreign competitors. The next ten years will prove to be an exciting time in the paper industry as producers around the globe respond to new technologies and new competitors.

Paperboard Mills

The 1997 linerboard market is being assisted by a surge in exports for kraft linerboard. The strength of these shipments is almost worrisome, raising the question of how much of this tonnage is being used and how much is going into user inventory. Export orders were strong at the beginning of 1997, but if inventories in offshore markets are excessive, exports could dwindle as the year progresses.

Markets for bleached board continued to improve through the second half of 1996, as tonnage for both exports and domestic markets moved substantially above those of the beginning of the year. Improved markets pushed mill operating rates to roughly 95% in the latter half of 1996, compared with 90% in the first half. With mill backlogs improving and strong gains being registered in both domestic and export markets, the outlook for 1997 remains promising. The major uncertainty in the near term is whether exports will continue to rebound or will fall off due to a stronger dollar and the onslaught of more Scandinavian capacity, which will make U.S.–produced board less competitive in international markets.

U.S. containerboard demand is expected to bounce back to elevated levels in 1997 and continue at a moderate pace into the next century. The paperboard market is usually able to ride out periods of feeble economic growth better than other sectors of the paper industry. This ability is derived from the fact that its key end–use markets rely more on consumers' purchases of necessity goods, such as food and clothing, than on the sales of more frivolous items.

Containerboard Market Conditions

The U.S. containerboard industry will find it difficult to implement announced price increases in the near term. Buyers perceive that board inventories are high and that the industry is burdened with excess capacity, especially for recycled grades. In late 1996 and early 1997, this remained the case, as inventories stayed at about 2.8 million tons and mills continued to run their machines at relatively full levels. With mills taking little downtime, a modest pickup in box cutups was insufficient to pull down containerboard inventories by the end of 1996.

All of these factors will lead to a tough pricing environment for producers in the near term. The chances of price gains in first–half 1997 are at best 50%, but WEFA's current forecast incorporates a modest price increase in the summer. The pricing outlook through the end of 1997 and into 1998 is better but still uncertain, as the excess supply which continues to be the industry's main problem will remain, although at a lower level.

Continuing growth in the U.S. economy should drive up domestic containerboard demand in 1997 and 1998, but exports remain a question mark over the near term. The linerboard market has been helped recently by a surge in export production for kraft linerboard. The strength of these shipments has even been worrisome, raising the question of how much of this tonnage is being used and how much is going into user inventory, and this information is not generally available outside the United States. Export orders were strong at the beginning of 1997, but if inventories in offshore markets are excessive, exports will drop off as the year progresses.

An additional factor of concern in the export market is the high value of the dollar, which has led to higher effective local currency prices for U.S. products. To keep local currency prices from moving up too much if the dollar keeps rising, U.S. producers will face the prospect of lowering dollar prices.

The high level of exports, coupled with improving board demand from domestic box plants, pushed mill operating rates at kraft linerboard mills into the low– to mid–90% range in late 1996. The strong operating performance for linerboard was not duplicated by corrugating medium, as mill operating rates for semichemical mills were in the low 90% range while recycled mills averaged closer to 89% at the end of 1996.

Probably the most encouraging news for producers has been the moderate to strong rebound in domestic box shipments — however, this has not translated into higher prices. Box demand has steadily improved since second–quarter 1996.

With box cutups rising, the inventory situation looks somewhat more promising, but further reductions will be needed. On a weeks–of–supply basis, stocks were at a still–high 5.1 weeks at the end of 1996.

Boxboard Market Conditions

Markets for bleached board continued to improve through the second half of 1996, as tonnage for both exports and domestic markets moved substantially above those of the beginning of the year. Improved markets pushed mill operating rates to 95% in the latter half of 1996, compared with 90% in the first half. With mill backlogs improving or at least holding up through year–end, board producers were able to reduce price discounts.

Bleached board production in the last half was up by about 2% from the 1995 level and by 4% from the first–half 1996 level. Full–year production in 1996 averaged about 2% below the 1995 level due to domestic and export production being off by about 6% in the first half. In the last half of 1996, production for folding carton stocks increased by 10% from the 1995 level, as converters turned to restocking after a period of inventory reductions.

The worst problem for bleached board producers in 1996 was the poor performance of milk and food service grades, which fell 7% for the year. Even in the second half of last year, production for food service grades was off by 9% from the 1995 level. Some of the problems in this area were due to converters and mills reducing stocks. However, an even greater hindrance to recovery has been weak growth in the retail food sector.

In the second half of 1996, exports of bleached board increased by 3% from the 1995 level. In the first half, export tonnage was off 6%. Export tonnage for milk carton and liquid packaging board has rebounded considerably since the first quarter of 1996, when tonnage was off by 20%.

The outlook for first–half 1997 remains promising, with strong gains being registered in both domestic and export

markets, but this is relative to recent weak performance. The major uncertainty in the near term is whether exports will continue to rebound or will fall off due to a stronger dollar and the onslaught of more Scandinavian capacity, which will make U.S.–produced board less competitive in international markets.

Industry Trends

Recycled Fiber Usage

There is a dramatic change taking place in the container-board industry — a growing number of mills in the United States and other developed economies are producing board from 100% wastepaper. The principal wastepaper grades used are old corrugated containers (OCC) and new double–lined kraft (NDLK) cuttings. Traditionally, recycled liner was viewed as an inferior product, produced by smaller, older mills. New technology, however, now permits production of 100% recycled linerboard that is comparable with kraft linerboard in performance characteristics. U.S. recycled linerboard production is approaching 20% of total linerboard output, up from only about 2% in the 1980s.

The heightened demand for recycled board has prompted many companies to refocus their expansion projects to include recycled mills. Mills that have come on line recently and the ones still projected to come on line are advocating more aggressive recycling programs. The paperboard industry must strive to increase recycling rates if it is to be ensured of a steady stream of feedstock.

Mini–mill Fever

Another new trend has been the rise of smaller "mini–mills" which use recycled fiber. These mills are typically about 250 to 450 tons per day (tpd) in size and are usually located near major urban areas, where wastepaper supplies are plentiful and transportation costs are low. These single–line, bare–bones facilities sometimes use steam from a nearby utility power plant and hook into municipal treatment systems to keep capital costs minimal. Most mini–mill projects are sponsored by independent corrugated converters seeking more control over their raw material supply.

Outlook

U.S. containerboard demand is expected to bounce back in 1997 and continue to grow at a moderate pace into the next century. The paperboard market is usually able to ride out periods of feeble economic growth better than other sectors of the paper industry. This ability is derived from the fact that its key end–use markets rely more on consumers' purchase of necessity goods, such as food and clothing, than on sales of more frivolous items.

WEFA projects economic growth to hover in the 2.5% range over the next ten years. This level of growth will not provide paperboard producers in the United States room for rapid expansion. Nevertheless, moderate growth will ensure that demand for end–use products like beer and soda, soaps and detergents, drugs and cosmetics, cereal and breakfast foods, candy and cookies, and fruits and vegetables will grow modestly but steadily. As a result, so will demand for paperboard.

Considerable growth in the paperboard market will occur overseas. A number of grassroots projects and recycled mills are expected to bring product to market from new overseas facilities within the next five to ten years. Just as in other paper sectors, growing economies and expanding consumer demand will be the drivers behind these projects. More packaged foods and bottled and canned soft drinks will be entering the markets of developing countries. Cigarette producers will be pushing their wares abroad as demand dwindles in the United States. Sanitary paper products and toiletries will be another overseas growth area.

Until these foreign projects are up and running, however, North American and Western European paperboard producers will be called upon to meet worldwide demand. For these regions, this will mean continued growth in exports — as much as a 10% increase (year–over–year) at various times during the coming decade. The need for high–end board products is great news for the integrated producers in mature economies. As various foreign sources of pulp and other crude paper supplies spring to life around the globe, well–established producers will be required to refocus their attention on the value–added products that provide the greatest margins.

Converted Paper and Paperboard Products

Construction and related engineering and architectural services, medical services, and agriculture dominate the end–use markets for converted products — accounting for more than one–third of total sales. The construction market brings cyclical behavior to an otherwise stable industry. Four major sectors of the non-residential construction market are expected to register healthy increases in 1997 and beyond: transportation, technology, buildings, and industrial. This will result in an increase in demand from the construction industry for converted products through the end of the decade. Then, as construction growth weakens, so will the growth for converted paper and paperboard goods.

Converted products will continue to compete for market share with plastic packaging, particularly with returnable plastic shipping crates that are gaining popularity in some distribution channels. However, the higher costs of some of these competitors should help fiber–based products remain a contender in the packaging arena. Principal growth markets are expected to be shipping containers for food products and beverages and consumer goods, and point–of–purchase displays used for product promotions.

Corrugated Containers

Corrugated containers dominate today's worldwide packaging industry. These containers, made by combining two grades of containerboard (linerboard and corrugating medium), are utilized for nearly 90% of industrial and consumer goods shipments. Seventy percent of the industry's output becomes corrugated boxes, while the remainder appears in the form of consumer packaging, printed displays, and cushioning material. Because corrugated containers serve so many markets, their shipments are considered an excellent barometer of economic trends.

Recent trends

Major revisions were made in 1991 to the product protection regulations governing corrugated boxes: Rule 41 of the rail carriers' Uniform Freight Classification and the National Motor Freight Classification Item 222. One key change shifted from the traditional mullen test (bursting strength) for box strength to an edge crush test as the most important measure of box performance. The other change eliminated mandatory basis weight requirements for linerboard and medium.

The revised rules permit the use of more recycled fiber and high–performance linerboard in high–compression boxes that are more durable and can be stacked higher.

These important characteristics have prompted more of the new grades of containerboard to enter the marketplace. In the future, the new rules could increase industry shipments on a square footage basis while reducing paper mill shipments on a tonnage basis.

While corrugated containers are highly efficient and cost–effective, paperboard packaging is being subjected to severe competition from the plastics industry, particularly in the food sector. In Europe, plastic containers have already captured some market share from corrugated. The future of this development in the United States is uncertain. The U.S. subsidiary of Taiwan's Formosa Plastics Group is now making plastic containers and bags at a large new facility in Texas, and the company has plans for rapid growth through market penetration.

Industry structure

The corrugated container industry is highly integrated with paper companies that also produce linerboard and corrugating medium. Vertically integrated firms typically operate between 10 and 40 corrugating medium plants with the ability to use one or more of these plants to produce linerboard. These integrated companies account for about 75% of total U.S. corrugated box shipments. The remainder of the industry is comprised of independent box manufacturers.

Non–integrated producers generally operate sheet plants and depend on integrated producers for their raw materials. Consequently, independent producers are often at a competitive disadvantage, particularly when containerboard is in tight supply. In the past few years, a number of independents have financed small "mini–mills" to supply their box plants with 100% recycled linerboard and corrugating medium. These mills have substantially lower capital and operating costs than large kraft mills.

Changing market requirements

Warehousing and logistics, just as in other industries, have been looking for ways to do more with less and do it faster. Many of the revamped ways of storing and moving product have led to demands for greater box strength and durability. Palletization and automated warehousing has eliminated much of the manual handling of individual corrugated cases in the distribution system. However, automation requires stronger boxes to tolerate rougher handling. The trend towards stacking corrugated boxes to greater heights in warehouses has increased the demand for boxes with greater top–to–bottom compression strength. There is also a shift toward plastic packaging from rigid metal and glass containers, and this switch requires stronger exterior packaging.

As a result of these changes, ring crush (compression strength) is replacing mullen as the most relevant performance requirement for corrugated board. Industry pressure for modifications of existing box specifications, from bursting strength to compression and edge crush, succeeded in early 1990. A number of producers are now marketing high performance linerboard that offers higher strength and yield (surface area per ton) than traditional commodity linerboard.

High–quality printing directly onto corrugated boxes and displays is another trend driving quality changes in the corrugated market. One of the least expensive methods of printing — direct printing with either flexography or letterpress — is used on more than 80% of corrugated products. However, the rough surface of linerboard limits the quality of direct print. As a result, many mills have developed improved linerboard substrates, including mottled white and white–top boards. An alternative way to overcome many printing troubles is preprint linerboard. Its use is growing rapidly due to the increase in point–of–purchase retailing. North American preprint linerboard capacity is estimated to be about 540 million square feet on a total of 18 presses (including two in Canada).

Outlook

U.S. demand for corrugating products has kept pace with the U.S. economy in recent years. This has meant that shipments have increased steadily since 1994. Shipments are expected to slow at the end of 1997, before gathering speed once again in 1998 and 1999.

The United States is the lowest cost producer of corrugated containers in the world. This status will help the United States retain approximately a 35% share of the total number of boxes produced globally over the next three to five years. U.S. exports of containerboard and corrugated boxes should increase to satisfy demand in Mexico, China, Latin America, and the expanding markets in Eastern Europe. In anticipation of greater trade with Mexico, several new box plants are being established on both sides of the border to serve Mexico's growing manufacturing base.

The corrugating industry will continue to experience a number of technological developments in both box design and printing techniques. These developments will include: further development and use of preprint linerboard, increased use of flexography in color printing, improvements in graphics design, more computerization and automation in all phases of box plant operations, better marketing and distribution methods, modifications of box specifications for compression and burst strength, greater emphasis on high–strength boxes for stacking, increased use of laminated board, and improved coatings. Also, the use of recycled materials in all phases of box making will increase.

Converted products will continue to compete for market share with plastic packaging, particularly the returnable plastic shipping crate that is gaining popularity in some distribution channels. However, the higher costs of some of these competitors should help fiber–based products remain a contender in the packaging arena. Principal growth markets are expected to be shipping containers for food products and beverages and consumer goods, and point–of–purchase displays used for product promotions.

Folding Paperboard Boxes

Packaging demand by the U.S. food and beverage industry is the driving force in sales of folding cartons. Folding cartons are the packaging protectors that manufacturers use to ship consumer non–durable goods through distribution channels. Folding cartons are also used to fabricate product displays. They are typically die cut, printed, and shipped flat from folding carton plants to manufacturers. The end–user assembles and fills the cartons on high–speed production lines. The paperboard used for folding cartons must meet technical specifications for scoring, bending, and folding without cracking or breaking; for stiffness and resistance to bulge and surface slack; and for surface smoothness for printing, embossing, or laminating.

Clay coated newsback (CCNB), solid bleached sulfate (SBS), and coated unbleached kraft (CUK) are the three major paperboard grades used to make folding cartons. Coatings such as kaolin clay, polyethylene, wax, and other special treatments are usually applied to the board to improve strength, moisture resistance, and printing surface smoothness.

- SBS has traditionally been the highest quality grade used by the folding carton industry, preferred for its strength and appearance for packaging food products and consumer goods. This grade is also used for high–quality printing and embossing of packaging for cosmetics, toiletries, and tobacco products.

- CCNB is a recycled grade used most often for dry foods, soaps, and detergents, as well as for a wide variety of consumer goods. Markets that have traditionally used bleached board are losing some ground to high quality recycled grades.

- Unbleached kraft board is used mostly for beverage carriers and multi–packs, but has also made gains in traditional folding cartons for both foods and nonfood products. The micro–brewery phenomenon and the thirst for specialty beverages, such as iced teas and fruit juices, provided the coated unbleached kraft sector with the highest growth rate of any boxboard grade during the past decade.

Folding carton volume has suffered during the past decade, mainly as a result of competition from alternatives such as flexible packaging, rigid plastic containers, and E–and F–flute corrugated board. Although many consumer goods switched to plastic packaging over the course of the last five years, there has been some consumer backlash against plastics due to environmental concerns. The folding carton industry has continued to grow through new product introductions, especially those related to food. Food packaging accounts for approximately half of all folding carton purchases.

Market trends

In WEFA's mid–term outlook, the overall industry trend is expected to remain positive, although there has been a significant shift in market share occurring among the three major boxboard grades. According to the Paperboard Packaging Council, recycled paperboard is now used in over 55% of all cartons manufactured, bleached paperboard is used in almost 30%, and unbleached kraft is used in less than 15%. Milk cartons, as well as paper cups and plates (which are made exclusively from bleached paperboard) are not included in these totals.

The number of converting facilities has declined over the past several years. Less efficient and less profitable plants have been phased out, and merger activity has increased. The largest concentration of plants is in the Great Lakes, Northeast, and Mid–Atlantic regions. The Southeast, which also has a concentration of folding carton plants, has been the fastest growing region during the past ten years. The reason behind this growth is that integrated producers have chosen to move closer to their sources of raw materials.

Outlook

Domestic folding carton shipments for specific end–use markets regularly shadow consumer spending trends and real disposable income levels. WEFA projects tempered, yet still healthy, consumer disposable income growth through 1999. This will translate into continued moderate growth in spending on consumer products and food items. The small annual increases in volume of carton shipments, however, will not be a true indication of the industry's real growth potential. Improved technology has enabled the folding carton makers to produce lower–density, lighter– weight, stronger cartons while using less boxboard.

Exports have not been a major factor in the folding carton industry because of the high cost of transportation compared with the value and bulk of folding cartons. It has been more economical to export large paperboard rolls, which can then be easily converted into folding cartons. The principal export markets for folding cartons are Canada and Mexico, which together account for about 80% of the industry's modest export volume.

Other Converted Products

Setup Paperboard Boxes

Setup boxes are custom–made for specific products that require good protection and high–quality appearance. Rigid boxes are used primarily to package high–value products such as liquors, fine stationery, jewelry, toiletries, and specialty foods since traditional rigid boxes are more expensive to produce than folding cartons. Rigid boxes have also found new markets in computer software and video game packaging.

In recent years, the industry has made a number of moves in an attempt to suspend the downward spiral that was occurring. Setup box producers have improved their cost–effectiveness and productivity, diversified their product mix, and entered new markets. Some makers have added folding cartons and paper/plastic combinations and laminations to their product lines. The industry has improved its competitive position through strategic restructuring, mergers, and acquisitions. Now the setup box industry has become a specialty market for the firms that have survived the industry's downsizing.

Annual variations in sales and shipments are largely attributable to U.S. economic trends and to changing disposable income and consumer spending levels. Rigid box shipments are expected to inch up in the near term, provided that the industry continues to adapt its packaging products for new classes of consumer goods. In some traditional markets, setup boxes will be challenged by folding cartons and plastics. However, WEFA projects setup boxes will retain their market share in high–value specialty packaging over the long run. Growth markets for the first decade of the next century are expected to include packaging for cosmetics, pharmaceuticals, confectionery, and electronics and software.

Paperboard Tubes, Cores, and Drums

Sonoco Products Co., Jefferson Smurfit, Caraustar Industries Inc., and Greif Brothers Corp. dominate the business of paperboard tubes, cores, and drums. Sonoco Products and Jefferson Smurfit are also major players in the consumer products sector — an area comprised mainly of composite cans for food products. Except for Greif Brothers, all of these manufacturers are vertically–integrated producers who make nearly 100% of their own paperboard requirements.

In recent years, shipments of tubes and cores have shown modest growth. Consumer and industrial packaging and shipping are the largest markets for tubes. The paper industry, where cores are used for paper mill roll cores, inner cores for towel and tissue products, and office supplies, is the single largest market for cores. The markets for solid–fiber drums account for about one–quarter of industry shipments and include industrial, chemical, and construction sectors. Fiber drums have shown surprising growth in recent years due to growth in the hazardous waste disposal industry. The composite can segment accounts for slightly more than 30% of the converted paper and paperboard industry's total value shipments, down from almost 50% in 1982.

Chapter 10: Printing and Publishing

Printing and Publishing

The printing and publishing industry is made up primarily of commercial printers and newspaper, magazine, and book publishers. These four segments account for three–fourths of the publishing industry's total shipments. The remaining fourth consists of printers of business forms, greeting cards, and bookbinding and typesetting shops. The largest — and fastest growing — segment of the industry is commercial printing. Despite the inroads made by computer–generated printing, growth in population and new businesses, plus a healthy trade balance, will allow commercial printing shipments to advance faster than the industry's other components over the years just ahead.

Newsstand circulation of magazines is soft, but subscription sales remain reasonably strong; adult hardcover books remain weak due to their high prices, but softcovers are doing well — particularly children's and religious books. When forecasted average price gains of 3.8% per year — a rate above the all–manufacturing average — are factored in with reasonable volume growth, WEFA expects revenue in the printing and publishing industry to expand at a healthy 5% to 6% per year rate on average over the next ten years. Please note that the outlook for newspapers is covered separately.

Demand Factors

Commercial printing includes printers using both web and flat sheet technologies. Terms describing these processes include offset printing, photo offset printing, photolithography, and paleography. Two–thirds of the receipts of commercial printers come from work related to advertising — including ad posters, circulars, coupons, and labels — and most jobs are custom. The key to the outlook for this part of the industry is the overall health of U.S. businesses and the economy, for this is what drives advertising. Moreover, population growth and the addition of new businesses will keep demand for printing services rising at a rate somewhat above that of the average industry over the next few years, while a healthy trade balance will allow more comfortable pricing than faced by many manufacturers.

Magazine advertising page counts were fractionally lower than their 1995 level in 1996. Automobile ads — the largest segment of magazine ads — declined, due largely to the automakers' emphasis on advertising in other media in connection with the Olympics. However, 1997 is expected to be a good year for magazines. One key reason for the positive forecast is the growing trend toward brand extensions, which is when a magazine produces goods for sale or licenses its name to a manufacturer. A considerable amount of potential remains for magazine publishers in this area.

Book publishers' net sales are estimated to have risen by about 2.5% in 1996, led by juvenile softcovers and religious books excluding the Bible. Adult hardcovers, however, remain weak because of high cover prices — which are a problem both because prices are between $20 and $23 per hardcover book, up from less than $15 in 1990 and because consumers remain quite price-conscious. Moreover, the rise of book superstores has accustomed customers to the idea that discounts are the norm.

Real consumer disposable income, a key factor in book sales, is expected to grow fairly steadily over the next two to three years, experiencing average gains per year of around 2.5%. Consumers, however, will remain cost-conscious and thrifty. Despite a healthier job market, uncertainty concerning jobs and incomes remains ingrained in consumer sentiment. WEFA's view is that weakness in adult hardcover book sales is probably here to stay — at least through the remainder of the decade.

Another important factor in book sales recently has been the consolidation among independent distributors, which led to some supply disruptions in 1996. Mass market paperbacks were hurt by this confusion in 1996, but sales in this segment of the book market should rise solidly over the next two to three years.

Looking at the printing and publishing industry as a whole, the next 10 years should bring volume growth that is greater than the paltry 0.7% per year rate achieved during the 10 years that ended in 1996 but is less than real consumer spending growth overall. WEFA expects annual volume growth to average roughly 2% over the next 10 years. When forecasted average price gains of 3.8% per year — a rate above the all–manufacturing average — are factored in with this volume growth, WEFA expects revenue in the printing and publishing industry to expand at a healthy 5% to 6% rate per year on average over the next ten years.

Supply Conditions

It is estimated that there are almost 40,000 commercial printing establishments in the U.S. These firms face demands for faster processes, quicker set–up times, better material handling procedures, and enhanced and less expensive color reproduction in order to keep up with rapidly changing technology. The industry also faces a further shift into electronic publishing, and will need to compete in the labor force for increasing numbers of technologically proficient workers.

Healthy gains in revenues and profits were enjoyed in the newspaper industry in both 1995 and 1996. A major factor in the 1996 improvement was the decline in paper prices from the lofty levels reached in 1995. Newsprint and coated paper prices were down 30% to 40% from 1995, and another decline is expected in 1997.

The supply of magazine titles continues to grow even as newsstand sales decline. It is estimated that at least 900 new magazines were introduced in 1996, up from 300 in 1986. This additional supply, when coupled with less shelf space because of lower numbers of both convenience stores and corner newsstands, has significantly increased competitive pressures on magazine publishers.

With the exception of educational titles, book publishing is not highly concentrated. Interestingly, book publishing is one of the few traditional industries that experienced an increase in the number of companies operating over the 1982 to 1992 period, a time of significant consolidation for most manufacturing industries. It is estimated that there were approximately 2,000 companies involved in book publishing in 1982, and roughly 2,500 in 1992. The data does suggest, however, that there has been a small decline in the number of active companies during the years since 1992.

Pricing Factors

Prices for finished products shipped by the printing, publishing, and allied industries group of manufactures, have consistently advanced faster than the overall wholesale price index in recent years. For the 10 year period ending in 1996, overall output prices advanced at an average pace of 4.1% per year. For the three years ending in 1999 prices for this industry are expected to rise at closer to 3.5%.

One factor that accounts for the healthy rate of price gains for the broad industry composite is the trade situation. In many manufacturing industries in the U.S., imports supply a large amount of domestic consumption, and this added supply is preventing significant price increases. Imports of books, newspapers, and magazines, however, remain below exports, giving the United States a trade surplus, and the resulting strength of domestic manufacturers is reflected in their more robust pricing.

Major Trends Affecting The Outlook

Computer technology has eroded the market for commercial printing, as many jobs that used to require the typestyles, clarity, justified margins, and color provided by professional printing can now be produced on a personal computer. As technology evolves and competition intensifies, the growing use of information in non–print formats will also put pressure on the industry.

The type of magazines purchased has changed in recent years. Interest used to be in the glamorous and glossy, and now is centered more on computers and other technical titles, health, and home interest. In addition — as magazine prices have risen — the trend toward cost consciousness observed in so many consumer products in recent years is negatively impacting magazine sales at the newsstand as well.

Concerning the book trade, recent weakness in adult hardcover sales will likely continue due to high cover prices and the ongoing distraction of multimedia products. While some inroads are being made into the demand for books by such products, there is no imminent danger that book demand will collapse as the public switches en masse to computer–screen–generated reading material. The erosion will be slow, and books will continue to provide some advantages that multimedia information cannot yet — particularly portability.

In both the magazine and book trades, WEFA expects consolidation to continue. A longer–term trend that will still plague both segments of the industry is the decline in the American public's desire to read.

Major Risks In The Outlook

Risks in the printing, publishing, and allied industries include many of the risks other manufacturers face. The most important of these risks being sagging sales due to either recession or flagging consumer confidence. WEFA's forecast is for modest growth in consumer disposable income over the next two to three years. The risk posed to print products by multi–media offerings is somewhat overblown, in our opinion, but remains just the same. Should some technological breakthrough occur that dramatically increases the portability and convenience of using these high–tech products, the expected gradual loss in market share suffered by the printing and publishing industry could become a larger loss, and could happen more rapidly.

Printing, Publishing, and Allied Industries
Growth in Sales (Line) and Volume (Bar)

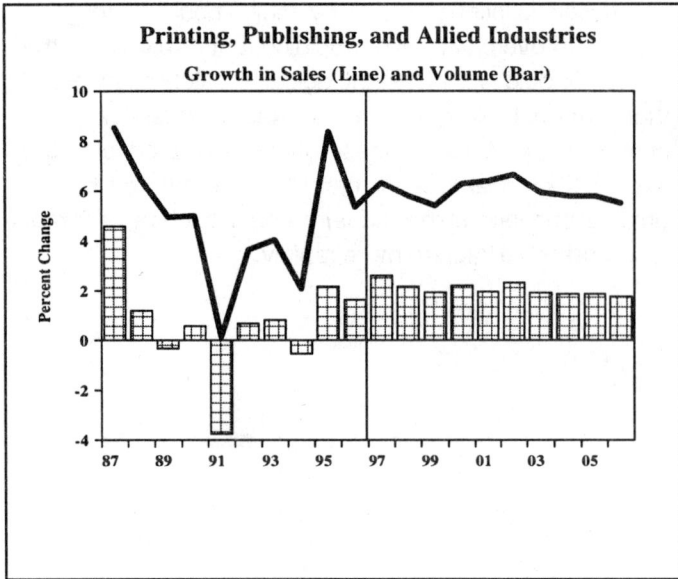

Printing, Publishing, and Allied Industries
Growth in Product Prices

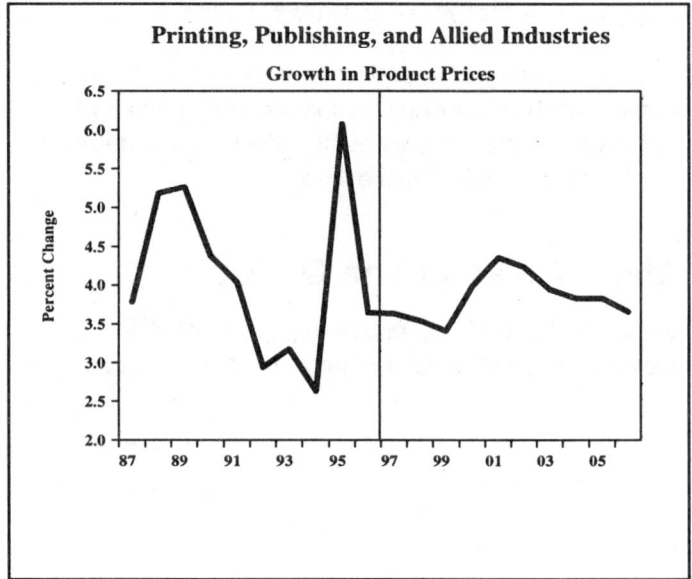

Printing, Publishing, and Allied Industries
SIC 27

		1990	1991	1992	1993	1994	1995	1996	1997	1998	Compound Ann Avg Growth 1986-1996	1996-2006
Sales												
	Billions of $	159.98	160.20	166.03	172.73	176.31	191.09	201.30	214.06	226.45		
	% Change	5.0	0.1	3.6	4.0	2.1	8.4	5.3	6.3	5.8	4.8	6.0
Volume	% Change	0.6	-3.7	0.7	0.8	-0.5	2.2	1.6	2.6	2.2	0.7	2.1
Prices	% Change	4.4	4.0	2.9	3.2	2.6	6.1	3.6	3.6	3.5	4.1	3.8
Exports												
	Billions of $	2.85	3.21	3.43	3.51	3.62	3.95	3.97	4.24	4.49		
	% Change	12.4	12.4	6.8	2.4	3.3	8.9	0.5	7.0	5.8	11.8	2.7
Imports												
	Billions of $	1.55	1.58	1.74	1.84	1.99	2.29	2.39	2.56	2.67		
	% Change	2.5	2.3	10.2	5.4	8.5	15.0	4.6	7.1	4.2	6.4	4.9
Apparent Consumption												
	Billions of $	158.68	158.58	164.35	171.05	174.67	189.43	199.73	212.38	224.63		
	Nominal % Change	4.8	-0.1	3.6	4.1	2.1	8.4	5.4	6.3	5.8	4.7	6.0
	Real % Change	0.4	-3.9	0.7	0.9	-0.5	2.2	1.7	2.6	2.1	0.6	2.1

Newspapers

In 1996, advertisers invested more in U.S. newspaper advertising than in any other medium. The newspaper share of ads was just over one–fifth of all advertising dollars. Nearly 60 million newspapers are sold daily, with an average readership of over 2 readers per copy.

Demand

Newspaper circulation has been declining since the late 1980s. After peaking at just below 63 million copies in 1987, total morning and evening circulation had reached 58 million in 1995. While it may be tempting to blame this decline on the advent of other media, such as on–line services, the truth is that Americans simply don't read as much as they used to. In an age of increasing time constraints, more and more people rely on television to get their news in 30–second bites and 30–minute sessions.

Newspapers have tried to offset declining circulation through expanding related product offerings. Examples of such products are voice services, where customers can access pre–recorded information using a touch–tone phone, voice mailboxes for personal ads, and 1–900 information services. Another new offering by newspaper publishers is access to unprinted material and archives that can be used for research. One area under experimentation that has not yet paid off is electronic services, such as Internet access and CD–ROM information delivery. Such services may take years to become profitable.

Supply Conditions

Although there are over 1400 individual newspapers in the United States, the 20 largest newspaper companies account for almost 25% of total weekday circulation. In the newspaper industry overall, healthy gains in revenues and profits were enjoyed in both 1995 and 1996.

- A major factor in this improvement in 1996 was the decline in raw paper prices from their lofty levels reached in 1995. Newsprint and coated paper prices were down 30% to 40% from 1995 — although the favorable impact on newspaper margins wasn't felt

until the fourth quarter of 1996 — and another decline in paper prices is expected in 1997.

- Another source of profitability in 1996 was higher advertising rates, particularly for classified ads.

Certainly the improvement in margins didn't come from rising circulation. In addition to the secular decline in circulation that has been occurring since the late 1980s, newspaper publishers had deliberately curtailed circulation to marginally profitable geographic areas due to soaring costs. Wholesale prices of pulp, paper, and paperboard products rose an average 12.4% per year over the three years ending in 1995; and the rate of increase in 1995 alone was 26.9%.

In spite of the fact that paper prices fell sharply in 1996 and are likely to fall again in 1997, the cost cutting measures that were enacted by newspaper publishers in response to the price run–up prior to 1996 are not expected to be reversed. Therefore, newspapers are poised to reap better profits in the next few years.

Major Trends Affecting The Outlook

The newspaper industry is dynamic, and it is impacted by a wide range of forces. Perhaps the most important force affecting the future of the newspaper industry is the ongoing decline in the amount of reading done by the American public — particularly for news. Today's young people are particularly attached to "pictures and sound bites" for their information about current events. As this age group matures and replaces the older, non–electronic generation of newspaper readers, the downward trend in newspaper readership will only accelerate.

The plunge in the number of newspaper ad lines sold during the recessionary period of the early 1990s has yet to be fully recovered. Higher classified ad sales have been offset by continuing softness in sales of retail ad lines. Retailers themselves are undergoing a period of stress and consolidation, and they are unlikely to step up newspaper advertising in the near future

Key Risks To The Forecast

The key risks in the newspaper industry are:

- The uncertainty about the degree to which the sector can react to the competitive stresses due to changing technology and information–gathering patterns and

- The speed at which these technologies and preferences change.

As larger proportions of the population become technologically proficient, greater shares of the information delivery market will be electronic. The newspaper industry faces the choice of entering these new media, and thereby transforming into and merging with other industries, or continuing on the consolidation and rationalization process that accompanies a declining market.

Chapter 11: Chemicals and Allied Products

Chemicals and Allied Products

The chemicals and allied products industry is one of the world's most globalized industries. Production is becoming increasingly spread across a large number of countries, and international trade is growing rapidly. The industry produces tens of thousands of products that can be broadly classified into three major groups: basic chemicals (organic and inorganic); chemical products to be used as intermediate materials in further manufacture, such as synthetic materials (plastic resins, fibers, and rubber), as well as dyes and pigments; and finished chemical products ready for consumption (drugs, cosmetics, soaps, and paints) or to be used as supplies in other industries, such as fertilizers, printing ink, and explosives. Together, the categories of basic chemicals and synthetic materials account for 50% to 55% of the U.S. chemicals and allied products industry's shipments. Petrochemicals, defined as carbon-derived products, comprise the vast majority of the organic chemicals and synthetic materials categories. Volume for the overall chemicals and allied products industry is projected to increase by about 4% this year and slightly below 3% on an annual average basis over the next 10 years. WEFA's long-term growth forecast is similar to the increase achieved in the last ten years.

Chemicals is a $1.5 trillion global industry that is characterized by large volumes of international trade. Virtually every country produces chemicals, but just a few countries account for the bulk of the world's total production. In 1995, for example, six countries accounted for more than 60% of global chemical output — the United States, Japan, Germany, France, the U.K., and Italy. With a 25% share of global output, the U.S. chemicals and allied products industry is the world's largest, followed by Japan (16.5%) and Germany (8%).

The chemicals and allied products industry also ranks among the largest and most internationally competitive industries in the United States. Chemicals are essential inputs to the production processes of the construction, manufacturing, service, mining, and agriculture industries. The chemical industry is the single largest purchaser of its own output, with about 25% of its production of basic chemicals used as captive products in the form of raw or intermediate materials. Chemicals range from basic commodities, such as ethylene and sulfuric acid, to the most sophisticated drugs and highly specialized high-tech composites used in aircraft and spacecraft. On a shipment value basis, the U.S. chemical industry accounts for roughly 3% of the nation's total gross production and 11% of its manufacturing sector.

Prices for many chemicals, particularly the commodity products, are set by global supply and demand. World trade reflects an intensely competitive struggle for mar-

kets. Traditionally, the U.S. chemical industry has enjoyed a positive balance of trade. Canada represents its largest single export market, followed by Japan. Chemical exports to Mexico, the third-largest chemical export market for the United States, have more than tripled in the past 10 years. Other large markets include Western Europe, Latin America, and Asia.

The U.S. chemical industry exports much less of its production than many of its foreign competitors. Its exports represent only about 16% of its production, compared to 54% for both Germany and the United Kingdom, and 43% for France. However, the United States is still the world's second-largest exporter of chemicals after Germany. Japan's chemical exports-to-output ratio of barely 12% is even less than that of the United States. By nature, the Japanese chemical industry is not export–oriented, and is geared primarily to supporting the needs of Japan's large manufacturing sector.

In recent years, benefiting from very strong economic growth and an aggressive buildup of its petrochemical industry, the Asia-Pacific region has become a serious contender in the global chemical market. In 1995, it accounted for some 9% of total world chemical exports, roughly half of Germany's share and almost two–thirds that of the United States. In the early 1980s, this region's share was only about 1%. The rapid increases in the export share of the newly industrialized Asian nations and other developing regions have come at the expense of the United States and Western Europe. Over the period 1981-95, the U.S. share of global chemical exports declined from 18.6% to 15.7%, while the Western European share fell from 57.6% to 50.6%. In contrast, during the same time span, the U.S. share of world imports increased from 7.7% to 9.8%, suggesting some loss in competitiveness.

The chemical industry is one of the most capital– and energy–intensive industries in the United States, and one of the least labor–intensive. Ironically, with more than 1 million workers, it still ranks as one of the biggest employers in the domestic manufacturing sector. Reflecting cost-cutting pressures, employment throughout the chemical industry has trended downward since 1980, with most laborforce cutbacks shouldered by the basic chemicals and synthetic materials sectors. These sectors underwent two waves of restructuring during that period that have resulted in a leaner and more competitive business. Drug manufacturing, on the other hand, has seen its head count increase substantially during the 1980s and 1990s, reflecting strong profitability and volume growth.

Successful operation in the chemical industry, where technological and cost advantages are often the key to its members' survival, requires an enormous amount of capital, which makes entrance by newcomers rather difficult. The industry, therefore, tends to be dominated by a relatively small number of very large corporations, such as DuPont, Dow, Johnson & Johnson, Bristol-Myers Squibb, Merck, Abbott Laboratories, Monsanto, and Union Carbide. The high level of capital is essential for building, maintaining, modernizing, and expanding large plant facilities required to achieve economies of scale, as well as for supporting an aggressive R&D program and meeting the government's requirements on health, safety, and the environment.

The chemical industry uses energy not only as fuel and power for its operations, but also as a key raw material in its production process. Natural gas and oil derivatives account for more than 80% of its energy needs. Its overall energy usage amounts to about 7% of this country's total energy consumption. The industry has achieved significant energy efficiency gains during the past 20 years, and energy usage per unit of output has dropped by almost 40%. Continued improvements are required for the industry to maintain its competitive position in the world market.

Complicating the U.S. chemical industry's ability to compete in a global marketplace is a constantly growing regulatory burden. The costs of pollution abatement alone, which represent only a portion of total regulatory costs, have doubled over the past ten years and are currently estimated at about $6 billion. Roughly 75% of this amount is borne by the industrial chemicals segment of the industry, which also faces the fiercest international competitive pressures. Environmental costs are likely to rise further, reflecting not only new regulations but also existing ones which are yet to be fully implemented.

Foreign chemical companies have been playing an increasingly important role in the domestic industry. Foreign direct investment in the U.S. chemical industry has quadrupled since 1985. At the end of 1995, it stood at about $77 billion, with European companies being the dominant investors. In contrast, U.S. investment in foreign chemical industries was $68 billion.

Outlook

Following growth of 3.7% in 1996, total shipments for the U.S. chemicals and allied products industry are forecast to increase between 6% and 7% this year and about 5.5% on an annual average basis over the next ten years. On a constant dollar basis, growth of 4.1% is expected for this year and 2.9% on average through 2006. This compares with average annual growth over the past ten years of 6.2% in nominal terms and 2.7% in real terms.

Chemical prices increased by an average of 3.3% per year during the past decade. Increases on the order of 2.5% are more likely for the next decade, as moderating production cost increases and intensifying global competitive pressures put a damper on pricing. In addition, oncoming capacity for large-volume petrochemicals in Asia, the Middle East, and Latin America will curtail U.S. exports to these regions. This, coupled with an aggressive expansion of our own petrochemical capacity base, will result in an oversupplied domestic market and lower profitability for the rest of the decade. WEFA expects the drug manufacturing sector to continue to post growth above that of the overall chemical industry for both sales and profits.

Industrial Chemicals

The industrial chemicals sector is comprised mostly of industrial organic and inorganic chemicals. Volume for this sector increased at an average annual rate of about 2% during the past ten years, while prices moved up at a 3.4% clip. During the next few years, output growth will be marginally better than the past decade, reflecting moderate growth in domestic demand, but the industry will face lower price growth and a deteriorating balance of trade. Industrial organic chemicals, long a major contributor to chemical industry trade, will experience a period of falling exports and lower prices, as capacity expansions, both in the United States and in the rest of the world, result in global oversupply conditions. The mature industrial inorganic chemicals industry is expected to remain lackluster both in terms of overall demand and prices.

During the past two decades, the U.S. industrial chemicals industry has developed costly programs to reduce the emission of the many types of materials that contribute to air, water, and land pollution. The pollution abatement costs associated with these programs have increased in proportion to the industry's sales, rising from about 1.9% of sales in 1984 to roughly 3% in 1995. Stringent environmental regulations at the federal, state, and local levels will remain a cost burden to the industry and will continue to adversely affect its competitiveness.

Industrial Organic Chemicals

Organic chemicals are defined as those chemicals that are compounds of carbon. Industrial organic chemicals account for about 60% of the industrial chemicals sector. They represent 20% of total U.S. chemical industry shipments, and rank second in importance to the drugs sector. On a trade basis, they account for some 30% of all chemical exports and imports, far more than any other chemical group. They are the most energy– and capital–intensive chemical products, and perhaps those most subjected to environmental regulations by the U.S. Government. The industrial organic chemicals industry employs roughly 145,000 workers. Since 1990, head count has declined by about 1.5% per year, as the industry implements ongoing cost reduction programs aimed at increasing its competitiveness.

Industrial organic chemicals are obtained from many sources, including petroleum and natural gas, coal and coke by–products, fats and oils, and agricultural products. However, more than 80% of the industry's raw material requirements are derived from petroleum and natural gas products, leading to the designation of petrochemicals for most organic chemicals. The basic petrochemicals derived from petroleum and natural gas are primarily building blocks such as olefins (ethylene, propylene, butadiene) and aromatics (benzene, xylene) used to create thousands of downstream products. In

terms of production, ethylene is by far the most important basic petrochemical, followed by propylene and benzene.

In subsequent processing, other chemicals are added to these organic building blocks to form various compounds with certain desired characteristics. The final output may be, for example: polyester fiber or nylon; PVC; anti–freeze; a pharmaceutical product; PET, the plastic resin used in making soda bottles; or the synthetic rubber used in the manufacture of tires. Other organic product groups include cyclic intermediates, dyes, pigments, tar crudes, alcohols, plasticizers, leather tanning agents, rubber processing chemicals, pesticides, and agricultural chemicals.

Most of the major petrochemical producers have a vertically integrated production process, which gives them better control of both raw materials and end–use markets. Industrial organic chemicals are classified for the most part as commodities, and producers face an intense struggle for markets. Cost competitiveness and technology advantage are often the determining factors of success.

Because organic chemicals are transformed into so many products with different properties and applications, their end–use markets are very diverse. They include consumer durable and nondurable goods, as well as capital equipment, construction, and various services. Demand for industrial organic chemicals is particularly sensitive to movements in the highly cyclical construction and automotive markets, the industry's two largest single end–uses. The U.S. economy is the most important factor in determining the industry's profitability and performance. However, global economic conditions have taken on a more significant role in recent years, affecting virtually every facet of the industry, including trade, supply, and prices. WEFA expects foreign competition to intensify in the long run, which will result in a deteriorating balance of trade for the U.S. industry as well as softer pricing conditions.

Lately, the petrochemical trade surplus, long a big contributor to chemical company fortunes, has been shrinking. Exports of organic chemicals declined significantly last year, in part due to soft economic conditions in Europe, Canada, and Mexico. Another key factor is the massive petrochemical capacity buildup in the Middle East and the Asia–Pacific region that has cut into Asian markets for exports from the United States. Meanwhile, imports have surged, buoyed by a strengthening dollar against key currencies.

The largest U.S. markets for chemical exports are in Asia. But, in the past few years places like South Korea, China, Taiwan, Thailand, Malaysia, and Singapore have been aggressively building their own production capacity. South Korea has now the fifth largest ethylene capacity in the world, and China is sixth. Based on announced projects, by the year 2001 Saudi Arabia will have the third largest ethylene capacity in the world after the U.S. and Japan; China will be ranked fifth and South Korea sixth. A large portion of Saudi Arabia's petrochemical production is directed at the Asian market. Saudi Arabia has also targeted the European market, where it enjoys a strong production cost advantage over local petrochemical producers.

Rising feedstock and energy costs and a generally weak pricing environment pushed earnings down dramatically for the major U.S. petrochemical companies in late 1996. However, most of these companies managed to show full–year profit strength thanks to a combination of moderate volume growth in the domestic market, improved productivity, business portfolio restructuring, and generally lower costs during the first half of the year. Prices have rebounded this year for many products, buoyed by strong economic growth in the first quarter

and a generally tight market. The costs of feedstocks and energy have also begun to decline from their recent highs. With demand expected to moderate later in 1997 and new capacity coming onstream, petrochemical producers will have a hard time justifying further price increases. In fact, WEFA expects the second half of 1997 to be the start of a prolonged period of oversupply, soft prices, and poor earnings which may last a couple of years.

Despite the specter of overcapacity looming on the horizon, capital spending is headed for another boost this year, following three years of high expenditures by the industry. Two driving forces continue to propel capital spending.

- First, in order to increase earnings, companies must keep cutting costs because they cannot easily raise prices. One way they achieve these cuts is by investing in new state–of–the–art equipment that boosts production efficiency.

- Second, during the boom years of 1994–95, many companies made aggressive capital spending plans and started major projects. They may not want some of these projects at the moment, but construction in many cases is already under way, and it's simply not economically feasible to stop them.

Canada expects some improvement in its petrochemical business this year, after seeing both chemical shipments and prices drop in 1996. Mexico is experiencing strong demand, as it continues to recover from its recent economic crash. Mexico is also benefiting from an expansion of trade with its NAFTA partners as well as with countries in South America. In this region, sound economic policies and strong growth rates have bolstered investor confidence: $6 billion in chemical investments are scheduled for Brazil alone over the next three years. In Western Europe, a hoped–for expansion in the chemical economy eluded producers last year, but they expect that strengthening exports and improving general economic conditions will set the stage for stronger market activity and financial performance soon. And, in the Asia–Pacific region, although economic growth has slowed, it has only slowed from heady levels in most countries, excepting Japan which continues to struggle along. Asian petrochemical demand is expected to remain strong outside of Japan, while the capacity buildup continues.

To cope with the various challenges of competition both at home and from foreign producers, the major U.S. petrochemical firms have implemented some drastic strategies. First, these firms have rationalized their operations. This means cutting costs, getting out of less promising businesses, and concentrating resources where they have the strongest competitive advantages. The companies that have emerged from restructuring are generally stronger, but in some instances much smaller. Union Carbide is a prime example of such a strategy. Its operations were cut down from a $10 billion revenue base in the early 1980s to $6 billion last year, but it was much more profitable in 1996.

Second, companies are increasingly investing in promising markets such as high technology, or allying themselves with other companies in the industry to take advantage of mutual strengths in markets and technology. Third, they are adding capacity collectively, such as through collective "condo" crackers, to minimize the risk of glutting the industry. Some of these strategies are also being adopted in Western Europe, and lately in Japan.

Industrial Inorganic Chemicals

Industrial inorganic chemicals constitute roughly 25% of the industrial chemicals sector. They are produced from minerals other than hydrocarbons, as well as gases found in the atmosphere, and are used as inputs in the production of other chemicals and finished products. In terms of tonnage, eight of the top ten chemicals produced in the United States are inorganic. Sulfuric acid ranks first, followed by nitrogen, oxygen, lime, ammonia, phosphoric acid, caustic soda, and chlorine.

The industrial inorganic chemicals industry is mature. It is characterized by stagnant growth, overcapacity, and relatively low capital expenditures for new plant and expansions. In spite of the industry's low level of capital spending for capacity additions, the value of its assets per employee is estimated to be four times higher than that for overall manufacturing, an indication of its capital intensity. It also maintains a relatively high ratio of R&D to sales, at between 2.5% and 3.5% of sales annually since 1986, compared to the all–manufacturing average of about 2.2%.

Company expansion is achieved mostly through mergers and acquisitions. Consolidations have taken place frequently in the last few years to permit better use of existing capacity and to tighten supply enough to support price increases. Industrial inorganic chemical companies have also tried to diversify into the production of more profitable and faster growing specially and high–grade products. This trend should continue in the future.

Cost competitiveness is key to survival in the inorganic chemicals business. As a result, companies have devoted much of their efforts to control or reduce their input costs. The industry employs roughly 130,000 workers. Since 1990, employment has declined by about 1.5% per year. Like their organic chemicals counterparts, producers of inorganic chemicals have also been facing increasing costs for pollution abatement. This has added to their cost of production, and there is little hope that these costs will be recouped.

Shipment growth for inorganic chemicals is pegged at about 2% per year. With price increases averaging between 1% and 2% per annum, growth in real output has been less than 1%. This lackluster performance will be maintained over the forecast period.

In the chemical industry, exports have traditionally outpaced imports. But, in 1995 the trade balance for inorganic chemicals turned negative, and estimates for last year showed no improvement. Trade of inorganic chemicals is largely influenced by the value of the U.S. dollar and growth in foreign buyer economies. The major foreign buyers of U.S. industrial inorganic chemicals are: Japan, Canada, Mexico, and Western Europe. These countries experienced slow economic growth over the last few years. This, in conjunction with a strong dollar last year, may have been the culprit behind the deterioration in the trade balance. Exports should pick up again as these economies pick up steam over the forecast period.

There are four major categories of industrial inorganic chemicals: chloralkalis, which account for 9% of total industrial inorganic chemicals shipments; industrial gases, with a 14% share; inorganic pigments, with a 13% share; and inorganic chemicals, not elsewhere classified (n.e.c.), with the largest share of 64%. Over the past ten years, chloralkalis shipments growth has averaged about 1.5% per annum; industrial gases, between 3% and 4%, inorganic pigments, 5 to 6%, and, inorganic chemicals, n.e.c., 1.5%.

The chloralkali industry produces mainly chlorine, caustic soda, soda ash, sodium bicarbonate, potassium hydroxide, and potassium carbonate. Chlorine and caustic soda account for more than 80% of industry shipments, while soda ash represents 15%. Chlorine and caustic soda are manufactured as co–products through the electrolysis of brine.

- Almost 50% of the chlorine produced is used to process organic chemicals, notably ethylene dichlorine, the precursor of vinyl chloride and PVC. The remainder is used to make pulp and paper and other industrial products.

- Caustic soda has a much broader use, finding applications in many industries, including industrial chemicals, soaps and detergents, petroleum refining, textiles, and alumina.

- Soda ash is mainly used to manufacture glass and glass containers. It is also a substitute for caustic soda in certain applications.

The chlorine industry has been adversely affected by environmental regulations in the past several years, particularly in applications such as chlorofluorocarbons (CFCs) and pulp bleaching. However, these setbacks have been partially offset by PVC's growing success in the housing market, increasingly becoming the material of choice for window frames, piping, soffit, and siding.

The industrial gas industry markets gases in compressed liquid or solid form. Such gases include the basic industrial gases (nitrogen, oxygen, hydrogen, acetylene, carbon dioxide) and about one hundred specialty gases that are used in a variety of electronics, aerospace, medical, and communications applications. Specialty gases account for a relatively small portion of industrial gas production, but represent about one–third of the industry's revenues.

The two largest end–use markets for basic industrial gases are the chemicals and metals industries, in particular steel. Other markets include: electronics, oil recovery, fertilizers, refrigeration, petroleum refining, the space program, and beverages. Because of the diversity of their markets, industrial gases are largely dependent on total manufacturing performance. However, growth above that of manufacturing is occurring because of new applications in waste treatment, pulp bleaching, electronics, medical diagnostics, and communications. The industrial gas industry has gone through a period of consolidation in the past twenty years. Four major producers control an estimated 80% of the U.S. market. They are: Air Liquide, Air Products, BOC, and Praxair.

The industrial inorganic chemicals, n.e.c., category includes the basic bulk inorganic chemicals, such as: sulfuric, hydrochloric, nitric, and phosphoric acids; aluminum, potassium, and sodium salts; calcium phosphates, hydrogen peroxide; and sulfur. This industry is very mature and offers no significant prospects of growth beyond that of its end–use markets. Some of its major markets are the fertilizer, metal, petroleum refining, mining, oil and gas production, housing, pulp and paper, and soap and detergent industries.

Inorganic pigments are also a very mature segment of the industrial inorganic chemicals business. It is a fragmented industry with many small players. Pigment growth is largely dependent on activity in the paint and coatings market, as well as the textiles and paper markets. Because of its strong tie to construction and automotive manufacturing, demand for pigments is very cyclical. The most important pigment in terms of volume and also the most widely used is titanium–oxide, a white pigment. It ranks among the top 50 U.S. produced chemicals, based on shipments.

Industrial Chemicals
Growth in Sales (Line) and Volume (Bar)

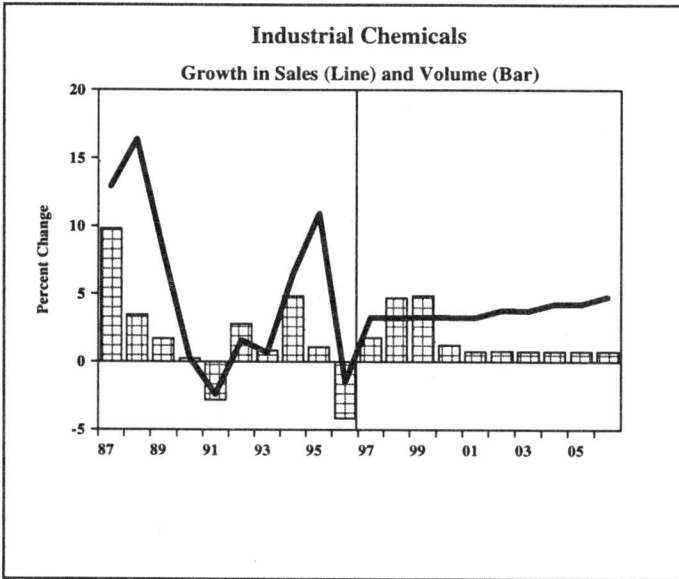

Industrial Chemicals
Growth in Product Prices

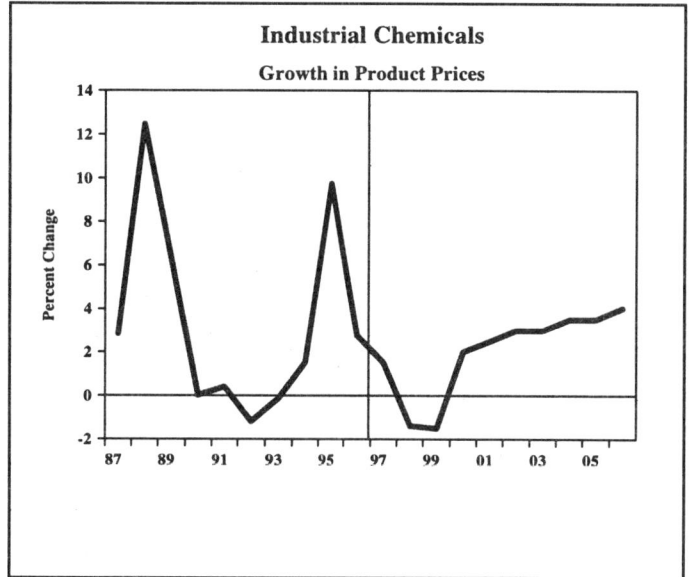

Industrial Chemicals
SIC 281, 286, 289

		1990	1991	1992	1993	1994	1995	1996	1997	1998	Compound Ann Avg Growth 1986-1996	1996-2006
Sales												
	Billions of $	159.17	155.31	157.75	158.79	169.04	187.52	184.71	198.75	196.94		
	% Change	0.3	-2.4	1.6	0.7	6.5	10.9	-1.5	3.3	3.2	5.1	3.7
Volume	% Change	0.3	-2.8	2.8	0.8	4.8	1.1	-4.1	1.7	4.7	1.7	1.7
Prices	% Change	0.0	0.4	-1.2	-0.1	1.5	9.7	2.8	1.5	-1.4	3.4	2.0
Exports												
	Billions of $	12.15	12.95	12.67	12.54	14.48	17.91	17.18	18.22	19.31		
	% Change	-3.1	6.6	-2.2	-1.0	15.5	23.7	-4.1	6.1	6.0	9.8	6.0
Imports												
	Billions of $	9.13	9.16	9.79	9.98	11.72	14.14	14.98	16.48	18.29		
	% Change	5.3	0.3	7.0	1.9	17.4	20.7	5.9	10.0	11.0	11.7	7.9
Apparent Consumption												
	Billions of $	156.15	151.52	154.87	156.24	166.28	183.75	182.51	189.01	195.92		
	Nominal % Change	0.8	-3.0	2.2	0.9	6.4	10.5	-0.7	3.6	3.7	5.2	3.9
	Real % Change	0.8	-3.4	3.4	1.0	4.8	0.7	-3.3	2.0	5.1	1.8	1.9

11.7

Plastic Materials

Plastics constitute the largest category of materials used in the United States. Plastic resins production has grown at an average annual rate of about 5% since 1980, propelled by end–use market growth, but also by new technology–driven applications and plastics' displacement of traditional materials like glass, paper, wood, concrete, and leather in many uses. There are some 45 basic families of plastic resins, and each can be made with hundreds of variations, which gives the industry almost unlimited possibilities in terms of market applications. The bulk of plastic resins shipments is made up of high–volume, low–cost commodity products whose prices are determined by global supply and demand conditions and the cost of feedstocks. Plastic resins are used in the fabrication of plastic products, whose end–use markets span from packaging and construction to transportation, electronics, and toys.

In the past ten years, plastic resins prices have increased at an average annual clip of 2.4%. This rate was 1.5 percentage points below the price gains achieved by their industrial organic chemicals inputs, resulting in a margin squeeze for resins producers. The inability of resins producers to pass through the full increase in their material input costs during that period is a reflection of the intensity of competition that exists both in the United States and overseas. The number of plastic resins producing countries has increased significantly in recent years, mainly among the newly industrialized and developing countries, giving birth to a large amount of new capacity that has eroded U.S. exports. This trend will intensify during the next ten years, as these countries aggressively develop their industrial infrastructure. The quest for larger market share in the U.S. market has also led plastic resins makers to considerably increase domestic capacity. The additional capacity, foreign and domestic, will result in an oversupplied market during the next couple of years that will weaken prices and will limit U.S. plastic resins production to a slower rate of growth, about 3% per annum, in the long run.

Products and Markets

Plastic resins are produced by processing petrochemical feedstocks and intermediate chemicals. Ethylene is the major feedstock, followed by propylene, benzene, xylene, toluene, butadiene, methane, and butylenes. Major intermediate chemicals include vinyl chloride, styrene, ethylene glycol, propylene glycol, and acrylonitrile.

The two major categories of plastics are thermoplastics and thermosets. Thermoplastics can be repeatedly softened or hardened by increasing or decreasing their temperature. Thermosets, on the other hand, cannot be resoftened by heat once they have been fully cured. Thermoplastics account for about 80% of U.S. plastic resins sales and captive use. They are mostly low–cost, high–volume commodity products, which include polyethylene (PE), polypropylene (PP), polyvinyl chloride (PVC), polystyrene (PS), and bottle–grade polyethylene terephthalate (PET).

Percentage Distribution of Plastic Resin Uses

Packaging	27.2%
Bulding and Construction	20.1%
Consumer and Institution	12.7%
Exports	10.9%
Transportation	5.5%
Furniture and Furnishings	4.5%
Electrical and Electronics	4.2%
Adhesives, Inks, Coatings	2.5%
Industrial Machinery	1.1%
All Other	11.3%

Source: The Society of the Plastics Industry, Inc.

Thermosets include: phenolic, unsaturated polyester, urea and melamine, isocyanates, polyether and polyester polyols, and polyurethanes.

Plastic resins, which are produced in small quantities but at a relatively high processing cost, are referred to as engineering or high–performance resins. They represent about 8 to 10% of total plastic resins shipments. These products are typically designed for specific applications which require high ratings for mechanical, thermal, electrical, and chemical properties. Fillers and reinforcements such as glass, carbon, and fibrous glass are often added to improve these properties. Research and development and marketing are the major cost factors in producing engineering resins, with feedstock the least important cost element. Historically, some of these resins have enjoyed double–digit growth rates, spurred by new applications in the aerospace, medical, and electronics industries.

Packaging is the largest single end–use market for the plastics industry, followed by building and construction and transportation equipment. Because of the industry's market dependency on construction and automotive, and durable goods in general, it is quite cyclical. In addition, additional shipments volatility is added by often wide short–term inventory swings, caused either by buyers or producers, as witnessed in late 1994 and early 1995.

Plastic materials shipments were valued at about $40 billion last year. Exports represented roughly $11 billion, and imports $5 billion.

Growth in imports has surpassed growth in exports in the last several years. Since 1989, exports have increased at an average nominal rate close to 10% per year, while imports have surged at a 17% rate. The fast pace of imports reflects an acceleration in shipments in recent years from Canada, Mexico, Western Europe, and Japan, the largest importers of plastic resins into the United States. These countries took advantage of a booming U.S. plastics market during the mid–1990s and generally tight supply conditions to boost their exports. Asia/Pacific ranks first as a foreign buyer of U.S. plastic resins, accounting for 33% of total U.S. resins exports; Canada accounts for 21%, Western Europe 20%, Mexico 9%, and Japan 5%. Asia's biggest buyers of U.S. resins in 1995 were: Hong Kong, Japan, Taiwan, and South Korea. During the next ten years, U.S. exports to Asia/Pacific will be increasingly at risk, as this region continues to frantically develop its local petrochemicals production capacity to meet its fast–growing needs for goods and services.

Plastic products account for about 20% of municipal waste in the U.S. Recycling and disposal of these products have become a growing environmental concern, forcing the use of recycled plastic materials to increase in recent years. Domestic production of recycled material expanded by more than 10% from 1994 to 1995 to about 1.65 billion pounds. About 40% of this volume was PET; 35% was high–density polyethylene (HDPE); and, 10% was low–density polyethylene (LDPE/LLDPE). The remainder consisted of small volumes of the other commodity resins. Recycled plastics are used in a wide variety of products, ranging from automotive bumpers to surfboards. WEFA expects the use of recyclate to increase by 7 to 8% per year over the next few years.

Outlook

Following production gains of close to 10% in 1994, domestic manufacturers of plastic resins started 1995 in a state of euphoria. Despite running their plants flat out, they struggled to produce fast enough to satisfy the domestics market's voracious appetite. Prices jumped by 27% between May 1994 and May 1995. But, in mid–1995 the market peaked. Consumption eased, throwing the supply–demand balance off kilter. Producer inventories snowballed, as buyers worked off the stocks they had built late in 1994 and early in 1995 when prices were surging. As a result, prices began a slide that lasted until the first quarter of 1996 and totaled 14%. The inventory depletion process for buyers ended in the early months of last year, and the rebuilding of their stocks contributed to another rebound in domestic demand. At the same time, numerous upstream plant problems during 1996 kept raw materials like ethylene, propylene, and styrene in short supply, which contributed to an increase in their costs. Skyrocketing energy and feedstock costs added to this upward push. The combination of short materials supply, strong resins demand, and surging energy and feedstock costs led to another wave of plastic materials price increases.

There are growing signs that this most recent party is coming to an end.

- First, energy and feedstock costs have begun a precipitous decline, prompted by growing supplies and moderating demand.

- Second, domestic demand for plastic materials is expected to slow due to decelerating growth in the economy later this year and in 1998, as rising interest rates take their toll on consumer and business spending.

- Third, from the second half of 1997 through 1998, the plastic resins industry will experience massive increases in its capacity. Plastic resins companies have had healthy margins for over two years, and that has inevitably translated into plenty of new capacity, as they position themselves to maintain or grow their market shares. This will result in a flood of material onto the market that will compel these companies to lower their prices during that period.

Over the next five to ten years, growth in overall U.S. demand for plastic materials is expected to slow to a rate of about 3% to 3.5%. This will happen as the industry matures, exports (particularly to Asia) decelerate due to increasing international competition, and imports from Canada continue to increase under the freer trade conditions brought by the NAFTA agreement. On the positive side, U.S. plastic materials manufacturers will be able to take advantage of growing demand from Mexico, South America, and the Caribbean. The domestic industry will continue to be a world leader in engineering plastics, both in terms of R&D and commercialization of new product applications. This area will play a more strategic role in the long run as global competition intensifies in the commodity segment. Additionally, technology licensing, direct investment by U.S. firms in foreign countries, and alliances with domestic and foreign partners will play an increasingly larger role in the long run.

Drugs, Soaps, and Toiletries

The drug industry includes companies engaged in manufacturing or processing pharmaceutical products, medicinal chemicals, botanical preparations, and diagnostic products. The soaps and toiletries industry comprises manufacturers of soaps, detergents, surface active agents, and cleaning and polishing preparations, as well as producers of personal care products including cosmetics.

Sales of drugs, soaps, and toiletries, combined, have increased at an average annual rate of 7.6% in the last ten years, with volume growth of 4.2% and prices up 3.4%. Exports have increased at a faster pace than the domestic market. Last year, they made up 8% of total sales, up from 6% in 1990. Imports have been gaining in importance as well, as their share of consumption almost doubled in the past six years, from 4.8% to 9%. As a group, drugs, soaps, and toiletries have typically enjoyed a positive balance of trade. Despite the recent increase in imports and the strength of the dollar, WEFA expects the United States to maintain its competitive advantage in those markets during the next several years.

The drug industry is the fastest growing segment of the drugs, soaps, and toiletries group. With two–thirds of the group's sales and a consistently strong financial performance, it is also the largest and most profitable. Historically, shipments of drugs have increased at a 10% clip per annum, spurred by new product introduction and expanding overseas markets, compared with increases of 3.5 to 5% for shipments of soaps and toiletries. WEFA's forecast calls for drug sales to maintain their good historical performance over the next several years. Profitability in the drug manufacturing business is also expected to remain the strongest in the chemical industry, and among the best in the U.S. manufacturing sector. Shipments of soaps and toiletries are expected to decelerate to a 3% to 4% pace. The aging of the U.S. population will play a critical role in the outlook for not only the drug market but also the soaps and toiletries business.

Drugs

The drug industry employs about 260,000 employees. It is by far the biggest employer among the major segments of the chemicals and allied products industry, and it is the only category that has increased head count consistently over the past five years, with gains averaging close to 2% per annum. Roughly 20% of its employees are full–time R&D scientists and engineers, compared to 9% for the overall chemical industry and 4% for manufacturing in general.

Research and development require a large share of U.S. drug companies' sales. R&D expenditures amounted to about 9% of sales during the 1980s, and 10% to 12% during the 1990s. In contrast the R&D–to–sales ratio for the overall chemical industry has been relatively steady at 5% to 5.5% for the past ten years. The drug sector's commitment to invest in R&D has been the cornerstone of its strong competitive advantage. This commitment

has led to several new product discoveries in recent years that have contributed to the industry's remarkable performance. Among them are: early–diagnosis products and home test kits, which can reduce cost and increase success in combating disease; nicotine patches; and drugs for prostate enlargement, cardiovascular disease, and AIDS and cancer treatment.

Drug prices increased at a 4.7% average annual rate during the 1986–96 period. However, in the past five years, price gains have slowed to an average rate of 3.3% per annum. Last year's increase was a modest 1.8%. Price deceleration reflects a number of factors, some of which are:

- Increasing public concern over health care costs;

- Combined purchasing by large hospital groups that gives hospitals more buying leverage;

- The need of the drug industry to develop and market lower–cost medications to serve a growing aging population that lives on fixed incomes; and

- The growing trend toward replacing prescription drugs with less expensive over–the–counter and generic drugs.

The cost–containment push throughout the U.S. health care system, including numerous legislative proposals to control drug prices, has also kept the pressure on drug manufacturers to restrain price increases.

Drug industry shipments were estimated at about $85 billion in 1996, representing roughly one–fifth of overall chemicals and allied products shipments in that year, up from 12% in 1980. Drug industry profits relative to overall chemical industry profits also increased considerably in the past fifteen years, from about 30% in the early 1980s to almost 44% last year. Volume and price increases above those realized by the overall chemical industry largely explain the relative gains in shipments and profits during that period, but cost reduction measures have also played a significant role in boosting drug companies' profitability.

Like many other industries, the U.S. drug industry has implemented aggressive cost reduction and management restructuring programs to increase its competitiveness over the last few years. It has gone through a series of mergers and acquisitions, which gave rise to increased foreign ownership in the domestic market. Today, 50 to 60 companies account for the bulk of drug sales in the U.S. These companies include such world giants as Merck, Johnson & Johnson, Abbott Laboratories, Pfizer, SmithKline Beecham, Bristol–Myers Squibb, Rhone–Poulenc Rorer, and Bayer.

Drug exports reached $6.5 billion in 1995, an increase of 6% over the previous year. During the 1990–95 period, exports increased at a 9.4% average annual rate. Western Europe is the largest recipient of U.S. drug exports, accounting for more than 50% of the total. Asia is in second place, with a 24% share, and Canada in third, with a 16% share. In 1995, drug imports were valued at $5.5 billion, up 18.5% from 1994. Roughly 75% of these imports originated from western Europe; 15% were from Asia, with Japan being the biggest contributor to that share; and, about 7% were shipped by Canada. From 1990 to 1995, drug imports surged at an average annual clip of 17%. The United States has run a trade deficit with Europe since 1990. In spite of this, its overall balance of trade in drugs has been positive. Over the next three to five years, WEFA expects the United States to maintain its trade advantage on a global basis, but rising imports from Europe will progressively erode this advantage.

Historically, senior citizens have consumed one–third of all prescription medication dispensed in the United States. With older people in the 50– to 75–year–old bracket expected to comprise 30% of the U.S. population in the next ten years, the drug industry will devote a considerable amount of its resources to making new medicines for the cure and treatment of such diseases as arthritis, Alzheimer's disease, and osteoporosis. This increase in the number of older people with fixed incomes will also boost domestic demand for quality low–cost drugs, forcing the industry to develop more lucrative products for other markets.

The trend to preventive disease treatment is growing rapidly, and with it the development of new bacterial and virus vaccines, as well as home diagnostic kits such as those developed for checking blood cholesterol levels and diabetes. Also, with increasing consumer interest in natural products, drug companies are expected to accelerate their plant research for potential drug applications, and add more herbal ingredients to their products. Cancer treatment, with products like Taxol, is a prime example of successful plant–derived pharmaceutical research by the industry.

The U.S. government has stringent regulations for new drug approval. By law, the Federal Drug Administration (FDA) is required to review and act upon applications for new drugs within six months. However, the average review time for the 28 new drugs approved by the FDA in 1995 was 19.2 months. Reacting to public criticism about the agency's inefficiency, Congress is working on legislation that will require the FDA to meet the existing six–month statutory requirement. The legislation will also make it easier for seriously ill patients to be treated with experimental drugs. Approval of the legislation by Congress would be viewed by consumers, hospitals, and drug producers alike as a remarkable achievement.

Soaps, Detergents, and Other Cleaning Preparations

Shipments for the soaps, detergents, and other cleaning preparations industry are valued at $25 to $30 billion. In the past five years, they have increased at an average annual rate of 2% to 3%, while prices have gone up at a 1.0% clip. Over the next ten years, WEFA forecasts both shipments and prices for this industry to continue rising at their recent historical pace. Soaps and detergents account for more than 60% of total industry shipments, polishing and sanitation goods for 24%, and surface active agents for the remainder.

Exports for the industry are valued at roughly $2 billion, or 7% of total shipments, and imports at $600 million. Although exports represent a relatively small portion of the market, they have increased at double–digit rates in recent years, providing good growth opportunities for the industry overseas.

A handful of companies account for the bulk of the industry's sales. They include Procter & Gamble (P&G), Johnson & Johnson (J&J), Dial Consumer Products, Colgate–Palmolive, Church and Dwight, Unilever, and The Clorox Company. P&G leads the group in laundry and automatic dishwasher detergent sales, with brand names like Tide, Cheer, and Cascade.

Of the soaps and detergents category, detergents are by far the largest component, with about $16 billion in sales. Household laundry detergents are a major segment of the detergents market. Sales of soap, consisting largely of soap bars for personal use, are estimated at about $2 billion.

The U.S. laundry detergents market is divided into liquid products, conventional powder, and superconcentrates. The latter, with built–in bleaching agents, constitute the highest growth sector.

P&G, Unilever, Dial Consumer Products, and Colgate–Palmolive account for the bulk of soaps and detergents shipments in the United States. Mergers and acquisitions in the domestic market have slowed from their frantic pace of a few years ago, as the best opportunities have already been taken. However, producers are very active overseas, as competition in the international market heats up. For example, in the past two years, P&G has acquired several companies in Brazil and Peru, while

Unilever has increased its presence in China through a partnership with a local company and in Israel through an acquisition.

New product introduction and R&D expenditures account for a large part of the cost of manufacturing detergents. In response to environmental concerns over the use of phosphates and trihalomethanes and the ban of these products in many states, detergents manufacturers have turned to zeolites, silicates, and citrates to achieve cleaning performance. In addition, these manufacturers are trying to meet consumer and environmental demands for biodegradable products.

Personal soaps constitute a diversified market that reflects the changing needs of consumers. As a result, product innovation is a key success factor for companies in this business, but it requires the support of high levels of R&D expenditures. Liquid hand soaps with anti–bacterial properties are an example of what consumers have demanded in recent years. Matching consumer preference with the right product characteristics has resulted in the market success of this type of soap, whose sales have increased at a rapid clip. Of the four main producers of soaps in the United States, European–owned Unilever is the largest in terms of market share. This company claimed an estimated 30% share of the domestic soap business in 1995 with brands like Dove and Lever 2000.

Polishing and sanitation goods consist of polishes for furniture and metal, and for household, institutional, and industrial use. They also include industrial disinfectants, dry–cleaning preparations, household bleaches, floor waxes, and solvents. The institutional and industrial (I&I) market accounts for two–thirds of polishing and sanitation products shipments. These markets are broken down further into various segments, which include janitorial, industrial, food service, and laundry applications. Janitorial applications have the biggest share of the I&I market, at about 40%. Total shipments of polishing and sanitation goods are estimated at $6 to $7 billion. The search for more convenience is the common tie that binds the various end users of these goods. Convenience will remain the main driving factor of product sales over the forecast period, as buyers continue to demand multipurpose products that can achieve better cleaning with less time and effort.

Surface active agents, or surfactants, are used as wetting agents, emusifiers, and primary materials in the fabrication of soaps and detergents. Shipments for 1996 are estimated at about $4 billion.

Surfactants are produced largely from petrochemical feedstocks, mostly ethylene, but also from natural products such as vegetable oils and animal fats. Synthetic and natural surfactants are interchangeable in many applications, including laundry detergents. By and large, synthetic surfactants are commodities, while natural surfactants tend to be classified as specialty products. Production of surfactants is concentrated in industrial countries, as is the bulk of global consumption. However, specialty surfactants are increasingly produced by developing countries and newly industrialized countries, such as Malaysia and Thailand, due to the availability in these places of natural materials like coconut and palm kernel oils. Market growth for specialty surfactants has outpaced that for commodities in recent years. This trend is expected to continue in the future as more niche markets develop.

Linear alkyl benzene sulfonate currently holds about 50% of the commodity surfactant market. It has replaced ethoxylated alcohols as the most commonly used surfactant in the production of concentrated powder detergents, and is rapidly increasing its use in liquid detergents preparation.

Drugs, Soaps and Toiletries
Growth in Sales (Line) and Volume (Bar)

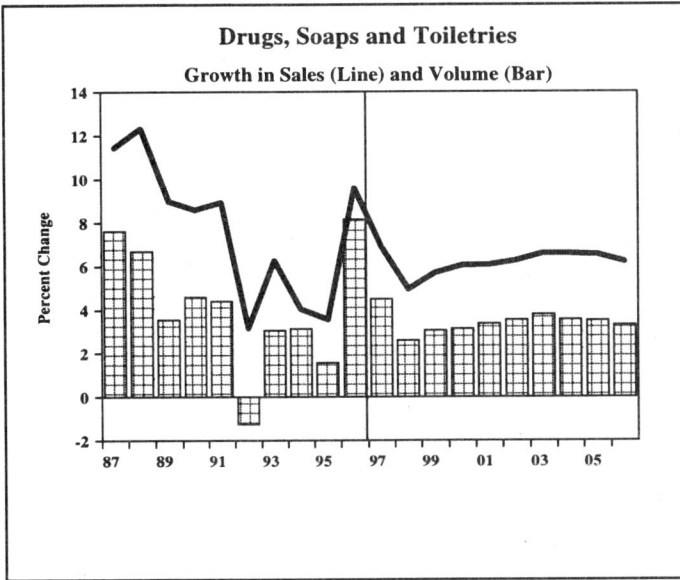

Drugs, Soaps and Toiletries
Growth in Product Prices

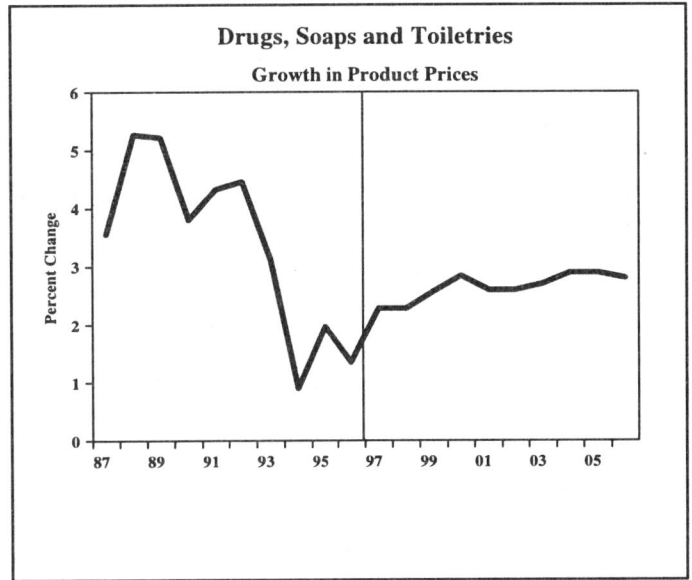

```
Drugs, Soaps and Toiletries
  SIC 283-284

                                                                              Compound Ann Avg Growth
                      1990    1991    1992    1993    1994    1995    1996    1997    1998    1986-1996  1996-2006


Sales
          Billions of $  98.70  107.52  110.92  117.86  122.63  127.01  139.21  148.80  156.15
          % Change      8.6     8.9     3.2     6.3     4.0     3.6     9.6     6.9     4.9         7.6       6.2

  Volume  % Change      4.6     4.4    -1.2     3.0     3.1     1.6     8.1     4.5     2.6         4.1       3.4
  Prices  % Change      3.8     4.3     4.5     3.1     0.9     2.0     1.3     2.3     2.3         3.4       2.6
```

Perfumes, Cosmetics, and Other Toilet Preparations

This industry consists of companies that manufacture a wide range of personal care items, including hair care products, skin care products, fragrances, dentifrices and mouthwash/breath fresheners, deodorants and anti–perspirants, shaving creams, and other cosmetic products such as color cosmetics. Industry shipments are valued at about $20 billion. Hair care, with an estimated 25 to 30% share of these shipments, is the largest business segment. It is followed by fragrances with a 20 to 25% share of the market, and skin care with about a 15% share. The other personal care items make up the remainder.

Growth in the perfumes, cosmetics, and other toilet preparations industry has averaged about 5% per year in nominal terms, and 3% in real terms, historically. Exports represent close to 10% of industry shipments and are growing much faster than the domestic market. Imports are small, and account for less than 5% of sales. Demand tends to be very volatile, particularly for prestige products, as it is highly dependent on discretionary income and the spending habits of consumers. Over the next five to ten years, WEFA forecasts shipments to increase at a 4% average annual clip. The baby–boom generation, which by 2006 will be in the 50 to 75 age group and account for nearly one–third of the U.S. population, will represent a considerable market for anti–aging products. As a result, skin–care products are expected to offer the best growth opportunities for the industry. Other areas of strong growth include various domestic and foreign ethnic markets for makeup, skin care, and hair care.

In the past few years, manufacturers have had to contend with increasingly cost–conscious consumers, rising materials costs, and fewer outlets for their products, as many department stores and specialty drug stores closed. This caused competition to heighten at a time when margins were weakening. To respond to these challenges, the industry restructured and consolidated. As a result, many small and mid–sized firms, including raw materials producers, were absorbed by the larger personal care companies. Today, the top 10 producers control two–thirds of the domestic market. Over the past two years, the industry has witnessed the public offering of two cosmetic giants: Revlon and Estee Lauder. Also, during that period, L'Oreal, another major manufacturer, bought Maybelline, the number–three U.S. mass market cosmetics company, while Unilever acquired Helene Curtis.

Cosmetics are becoming high–tech products. In recent years, research and development expenditures and new product introductions have accounted for an increasing proportion of industry costs, as consumers demand more technically sophisticated and environmentally safe products. In 1996, Johnson & Johnson (J & J) introduced Renova, the first product approved by the FDA that claims to reduce wrinkles. This move to "cosmeceuticals", if successful, could tilt the competitive balance away from the other producers who do not have the same research facilities and regulatory approvals as J & J.

Hair Care Products

Shampoos make up about 40% of all hair care products shipments. Conditioners are estimated to account for about 20%; hair sprays, 15%; and gels and mousses, another 10%. Hair care is a mature industry, with little or no growth left in the overall domestic market. It is also a business where one product cannibalizes another. Typical examples of such a practice are the two–in–one and three–in–one formulations that offer the convenience of shampoo, conditioner, and more recently shine enhancer, in one bottle, displacing those products sold individually. Other examples include styling gels, which have been successful in recent years at picking up sales from hairsprays that have been adversely affected by governmental regulations of VOCs (volatile organic compounds).

Looking for offshore market opportunities and securing a technological advantage over the competition have become important business strategies for U.S. producers. Foreign markets where income is rising rapidly, such as the newly industrialized countries in Asia and Latin America and other developing countries, present attractive alternatives to a mature domestic market.

After several years of promoting the subjective results of hair care products such as manageability, body, and luster, producers are now increasingly emphasizing the development and marketing of results through chemical performance. For example, the industry has developed a complex lipid that has been shown to replace the ceramide in hair, preventing loss of protein from cuticle damage. Other advances include those technologies that have crossed over from the skin care industry, such as alpha hydroxy acids (AHAs) that are used for scalp conditioning, and naturally–derived proteins used to provide moisture and sun protection. Sales of AHAs, which promise rejuvenated looking skin with improved color and texture, have surged since their introduction in the early 1990s.

Fragrances

The average annual sales gain in the domestic fragrance market is normally only 3 to 4% in nominal terms. Competition is fierce in this slow growth environment, where it is very hard for smaller companies to survive. The men's market is growing at the higher end of that range, but represents only about 20% of total industry sales.

Concern over profit margins has caused fragrance producers and retailers alike to rethink their strategies for the future, as cost–conscious consumers increasingly move away from prestige brands to mass market fragrances for value pricing. By promoting mass scents, retailers can also achieve higher margins because they do not have to go through the middleman required for the prestige merchandise. Ten dollars seems to be the magic number for an acceptable fragrance price for consumers in the mass market. With this market traditionally yielding margins of 25 to 30% to retailers, fragrance manufacturers have started to make perfume and cologne gift sets with room to give retailers that kind of margin under $10.

Spurred by the success of specialty outfits, like The Body Shop, fragrance companies are increasingly broadening their market exposure through new and unique channels of distribution, such as the Banana Republic chain of clothing stores, the QVC network, and even the Internet.

The teen generation, which the industry views as a strong potential for its domestic sales, is the next frontier. Various products designed to appeal to this segment are in the offing. For girls, they include: fruity and citrus blends, as well as the fast–growing "edible" fragrances containing vanilla, cappuccino, or coconut. For boys, image–driven scents and a renewed interest in musk are apparent. However, it is the adult category that comprises the lion's share of the market. Fortunately for the industry, product innovation for that segment is not as critical as it is for the teen population. Nevertheless, a certain degree of novelty is important, and mature, sophisticated, and comfort nuances such as leather, cognac, and Cuban cigar are being introduced, as well as transparent fragrances that are lighter and do not wear heavily.

Skin Care Products

With the 50–to–75–year–old baby–boomers expected to represent close to 30% of the U.S. population in the next five to ten years, this segment will be responsible for fashioning a large portion of the domestic skin care industry's product offerings. As these boomers battle the effects of time on their skin, they will constitute a vast market for anti–aging products. And, as their demands upon the personal care industry increase, they will spur further research into slowing or even turning back the aging process.

Any products that deal with wrinkles, sun–damaged skin and skin dryness, and are also biodegradable and multi–functional, are likely to be winners. An example of multi–functionality includes the use of sun protection agents not only in sunscreens but also in moisturizers and make–ups. Such applications will increase the frequency of wear of these products from occasional to routine. Also headed for growth are the manufacturing ingredients that are gentle to older skin. They include: emollients, anti–irritants, conditioning agents, and natural extracts.

Overall, skin care products are expected to offer the best growth opportunities for the personal care industry through at least 2005, with annual sales gains on the order of 8 to 10%. In addition to the baby–boomer population, products designed specifically for darker skin will also contribute to strong growth, as the industry multiplies its efforts to cover the domestic ethnic markets as well as foreign markets in Asia, Latin America, and Africa.

The desire for mildness is increasingly pushing surfactants out of non–cleansing formulations. Surfactants are irritating, and polymeric emulsifiers are used more and more to replace them in applications where emulsification is needed. Additional technological trends include water–based products, as consumers seek out the non–greasy feel. Environmentally improved, natural, and clear prod-

ucts remain big favorites with consumers. But, function is key, as these consumers will reject socially–conscious products if they do not work.

As the demand from baby–boomers plateaus, the younger generation will expect more advanced technologies from the skin care industry. Research and development to improve the beneficial and even therapeutic properties of skin care products will increase, slowly narrowing the gap with pharmaceuticals. As a result, a new regulatory category of "cosmeceuticals" or prescription cosmetics is likely to emerge.

Agricultural Chemicals

The key components of the agricultural chemicals industry are fertilizer, plant protection (pesticides), and the relatively small animal health sector. The outlook for the agricultural chemicals industry is inherently tied to the future prospects of the U.S. agriculture sector, particularly for acreage planted. Agriculture legislation passed in 1996 eliminated annual Acreage Reduction Programs (ARP) and altered the way farmers receive price and income support. ARP idled an average of 21 million acres annually between 1990 and 1995. That land will now be available to plant and will require fertilizer and pesticides. As a result, agricultural chemical sales are likely to continue the expansion that began in 1993 for the next couple of years.

The fertilizer business is a commodity business — fertilizer is fertilizer, and it does not matter which company or which country is producing the product. Farmers typically satisfy their nitrogen needs first, and then if funds are available they purchase phosphatic and potassic fertilizer material. Of the three nutrients, nitrogen accounts for about 50% to 55% of total fertilizer sales and potash and phosphate the remainder. Potash usually accounts for a slightly larger share than phosphate. The United States is a net importer of nitrogen and potash. Canada is a major source for both. Mexico and Trinidad–Tobago are important sources of nitrogen. The United States is a net exporter of phosphate, but is facing increased competition from abroad. Consolidation in the fertilizer industry is continuing, a process that began in the 1980s.

Pesticides are used widely in agriculture production, with herbicides being the most widely used pesticide, followed by insecticides, fungicides, and other pesticides (growth regulators, rodenticides, etc.). Winter wheat receives the smallest amount of pesticides, 8 ounces per acre, compared with more than 60 pounds per acre for potatoes. The continued increase in conservation tillage practices indicates further growth in the herbicide market. Interesting technology issues are facing the pesticide industry. Corn, cotton, soybeans, and potatoes are now being produced from genetically altered seeds that make them resistant either to pests themselves or to herbicides. Questions of consumer acceptance, pesticide residues, efficacy of protection with high pest pressures, and resistance should be considered. It is not clear that future pesticide use will decline with an increase of genetically altered seeds. Consolidation continues in the pesticide industry as well, and most companies operating in the United States are multinational. The United States should continue to be a net exporter of pesticide products.

The U.S. agricultural chemical industry consists primarily of the fertilizer and crop protection subsectors. The animal health industry is another subsector, but it is smaller than the other two and is often a subsidiary of a larger pharmaceutical company. Fertilizer tends to be a commodity with little brand name recognition, and therefore foreign countries can compete effectively with U.S. producers. The plant protection industry, made up primarily of pesticides, does have branded products, and manufacturers may be able to extract price premiums from the market place. Many of the plant protection companies operating in the United States are multinational firms.

Sales of agricultural chemicals have expanded at double digit rates over the 1994 to 1996 period. Apparent consumption has shown excellent growth, but not quite as strong as domestic producer sales, which have also benefited from good export performance. The United States is a net exporter of agricultural chemicals, with exports exceeding imports by $1.0 to $1.5 billion.

Fertilizers

Total sales for U.S. fertilizer producers, including $1.7 billion of crop protection chemicals, equaled $13.9 billion in 1996, about 5% greater than 1995.

There are three primary fertilizer nutrients: nitrogen, phosphate, and potash. In agriculture, nitrogen is typically viewed as the most essential of the three primary nutrients, and farmers purchase their nitrogen first. Then they satisfy their other nutrient needs with their remaining budget. For the 1995/96 (July 1995 — June 1996) fertilizer year, 12.3 million tons of nitrogen, 4.5 million tons of phosphate, and 5.2 million tons of potash were used by U.S. agriculture. Nitrogen typically accounts for between 50 and 55% of total U.S. agriculture demand. Phosphate and potash account for the remainder of nutrient demand, with potash use slightly larger than phosphate.

Corn is the major source of demand for nutrients by the agriculture sector, accounting for about 40% of nitrogen, 43% of phosphate, and 45% of potash use. Corn requires relatively large amounts of nutrient on a per–acre basis, and there were 79 million acres of corn planted in 1996 by U.S. farmers. Wheat accounts for 15% to 18% of the nitrogen and phosphate use and 4% to 6% of potash. Soybeans, a legume which fixates nitrogen from the atmosphere, accounts for about 1% of nitrogen use, between 7 and 9% of the phosphate use, and 13 to 15% of potash use.

There are a number of fertilizer materials which deliver nutrient at differing levels and costs to plants:

- Nitrogenous materials include anhydrous ammonia (82% nitrogen(N)), urea (46% N), ammonium sulfate (21% N), ammonium nitrate (33.5% N), nitrogen solutions (N content varies typically from 28% to 32% N), ammoniated phosphates (N content varies from 16% to 18% N most popular), and mixes.

- Phosphatic materials include normal (single) superphosphate (20% phosphate, or P_2O_5), triple superphosphate (46% P_2O_5), ammoniated phosphates (P_2O_5 content varies, with 46% and 52% P_2O_5 most popular) and mixes.

- Potassic products include muriate of potash or potassium chloride (61% potash, or K_2O), potassium sulfate (50% K_2O), and mixes.

Most of the nitrogen use by U.S. agriculture is delivered by anhydrous ammonia. Muriate of potash is the primary source of K_2O nutrient, and ammoniated phosphates, which deliver both N and P_2O_5, are the primary phosphate source.

Anhydrous ammonia is the basic feedstock for the manufacture of nitrogenous materials. Ammonia is made from the reaction of natural gas and nitrogen. Phosphatic materials are produced through a reaction of phosphate rock and sulfuric acid which results in phosphoric acid.

The acid is further processed to make end product fertilizer materials. Potassium salts are mined.

Through the 1980s and the 1990s, consolidation has occurred in the U.S. fertilizer industry. The commodity nature of the business and foreign competition, particularly for the nitrogen business, and the industry's dependence on agriculture have all contributed to the decline in the number of U.S. producers. U.S. producers are able to satisfy the majority of nitrogen demand, but the United States is a net importer of nitrogen. The phosphate sector is able to meet U.S. needs and export about 40% of production. The United States relies on potash imports, primarily from Canada, to meet domestic needs.

The Outlook

The outlook for the U.S. fertilizer industry is dependent on the amount of acreage planted in the United States. Historically, the federal government exercised supply management practices to balance supplies and demands for agricultural commodities, primarily feed grains, food grains, and cotton. On average, between 1990 and 1995, 21 million acres were idled under annual Acreage Reduction Programs (ARP). Another 36 million acres were idled by the long–term Conservation Reserve Program (CRP). In April of 1996, President Clinton signed the Federal Agriculture Improvement and Reform (FAIR) Act. The FAIR Act eliminated the annual ARP and now provides farmers the opportunity to base planting decisions on market price signals. The Act also continues the CRP, but in all likelihood, the acreage enrolled in the CRP will be reduced to close to 30 million acres. The bottom line is that there will be more acreage available to plant. While there is a trade–off between land and fertilizer, future domestic demand for agricultural chemicals is expected to expand by about 1.0% to 1.5% per annum.

There will be a number of other factors influencing demand for nutrients in the future, including tillage practices, crop rotations, and precision agriculture. Land in continuous corn or soybean crop production tends to receive more fertilizer than land rotated, although for some rotations a greater percentage of the area may be fertilized. The opposite tends to hold for cotton and wheat. Studies on precision agriculture indicate mixed results — some suggest higher nutrient use, but with more precise nutrient placement. Other studies suggest precision reduces fertilizer use.

International Competition

The United States is a major producer and consumer of fertilizer material. Reserves are key to the phosphate and potash business.

The United States has phosphate rock reserves in Florida, North Carolina, and in the West (Idaho, Montana, and Utah). Florida and North Carolina mines account for the bulk of phosphate rock production, which in turn is processed into phosphatic fertilizer materials. Currently, U.S. producers are in a surplus phosphate rock situation — productive capacity exceeds demand by 4 to 6 million tons. The availability of rock reserves, the technology of the industry, and the availability of sulfur (sulfuric acid) enable the United States to compete in world markets. However, competitive forces are increasing. The United States exports phosphoric acid, super phosphoric acid, mono- and di-ammoniated phosphates, and phosphate rock. Morocco holds 50% of the world's phosphate rock reserves and is expanding its downstream processing capacity. Jordan, Senegal, and China are also adding to their productive capacity. In the future, it will be increasingly difficult for the United States to maintain its leadership position in the world phosphate market.

U.S. potash production is relatively modest and occurs in New Mexico, Utah, California, and Michigan. The United States relies on Canada as its primary source of potash, and Israel and Russia ship to the U.S. market as well. Due to limited production, the United States is essentially a non–exporting country.

The cost of natural gas and the efficiency of the facilities converting natural gas to ammonia determines the competitive edge of U.S. nitrogen producers in global markets. U.S. production facilities are older and less efficient than new world class facilities elsewhere. In 1996, U.S. ammonia facilities required between 33 and 34 million btu (MMBTU) of natural gas per ton of ammonia produced, at an average gas cost of $2/btu. New facilities realize economies of scale and require only 26 to 28 MMBTU per ton of ammonia produced. In some developing countries that have natural gas reserves but no developed markets for natural gas, such as Mexico and Trinidad, the cost of gas is extremely low. Canadian gas prices are lower than those in the United States as well. Thus, it is not surprising that these three countries are key nitrogen exporters to the United States. As a consequence, the United States will become increasingly dependent on imports as a source of nitrogen.

Crop Protection

The U.S. crop protection industry is consolidating. Most recently, Ciba–Geigy and Sandoz, both Swiss companies, merged to form Novartis. In addition, most crop protection firms operating in the United States are multinational and some are headquartered outside the United States.

As in fertilizers, the crop protection industry is dependent on agriculture and acres planted. Pesticide use in any one year is also dependent on the occurrence of widespread pest infection or infestation, weather conditions that might increase the probability of pest infection or infestation (including over–wintering of pests), and whether there was an infestation or infection the year before. 1996 was a light pest pressure year, except in some cotton producing areas in Texas.

The pesticide industry may be further segmented into herbicide, insecticide, fungicide, and other chemical business lines. The global business is estimated to be in the range of $26 to $30 billion. Herbicides represent about 47% of the world business, insecticides 29%, fungicides 19%, and other chemicals (rodenticides, growth regulators, etc.) about 5%. The U.S. industry holds about a one–third share of world sales, accounting for $8 to $9 billion in 1995. The composition of output in the United States differs somewhat from the global business in that herbicides are more important, accounting for about 64% of the U.S. industry, followed by insecticides at 24%, fungicides at 7.5%, and the other chemicals category at 5%.

Pesticide use in the United States is measured by active ingredient (a.i.). In the 1990s total active ingredient applied has been increasing, rising from 498 million pounds a.i. in 1990 to 565 million pounds a.i. in 1995. Most of the increase has been in the fungicide and other pesticide market categories. Pesticides were applied to virtually all fields of corn, soybeans, cotton, potatoes, and spring and durum wheat in 1995. Only about 60% of winter wheat fields were treated with pesticides. The corn crop tends to receive the highest level of herbicide and insecticide volume. Grains, cotton, and soybeans receive the majority of herbicide applications. Cotton and corn account for about 90% of the insecticide use.

Fruits, vegetables, and peanuts account for about 90% of the fungicide market. It is not surprising that the fungicide market continues to expand in the United States. A health–conscious population with growing incomes is demanding more fruits and vegetables. This high–valued product area of agriculture is delivering unblemished high–grade fruits and vegetables, and it has contributed to the growth in fungicide use.

A 1995 U.S. Department of Agriculture survey indicated that soybean and corn area accounted for 58% of the herbicide used in the survey. The same survey indicated that 90% of the area surveyed received herbicide applications, but only 17% of the area received insecticides. For the fields in the survey and for the crop production year, the average amount of pesticide applied was 2.4 pounds per acre, but it ranged from a low for wheat area of 5 ounces/acre to a high for potatoes of 60 pounds per acre. Farmers have been responding to growing concerns about pesticide use and acknowledge a greater need to monitor pest pressures in their fields. Nearly 80% of fields in the 1995 survey were scouted for pests, suggesting that growers do not treat fields indiscriminately.

Tillage practices also influence pesticide use. Those acres that were under no–till or minimum till practices received no post–plant cultivation. Those acres planted in narrow rows were treated most intensively with herbicides. Fields with wider rows and conventional tillage practices received less herbicide application.

Technology

Technological developments have a significant impact on the plant protection industry. Some companies have invested heavily in biotechnology and have purchased seed companies. Technological developments in the pesticide area are evolving in two directions, both results of transgenic research.

- The first approach has the technology added to the seed, and the plant becomes toxic to the pest. *Bacillus thuringiensis*, Bt technology, is currently available for cotton, corn, and soybeans.

- The other approach is to genetically alter the plant so that it becomes resistant to the pesticide. This technology is also currently available. For example, soybeans or corn acreage that is resistant to herbicides can be treated with a post–emergent herbicide without fear of damaging the crop. Pesticide residue issues have emerged, as have consumer issues. But, as of this writing, no official action has been taken to prevent the planting of crops with these characteristics.

The efficacy of genetically altered crops will likely be tested in many ways in the coming years. 1996 was a low pest pressure year. How these new crops will fair under varying weather conditions, pest pressures, and other stresses is unclear. Companies with patent rights think that their products will withstand the test of time. Others are not as certain, as evidenced by the cotton growers in Texas in 1996 who filed a lawsuit against the company that provides Bt cotton. The issue of resistance is also not clear. The pest population has shown an amazing ability to adapt to chemical controls over time. With the new technology, the chemistry of control is basically the same, and the difference is in how the control is delivered. Only time will tell.

The Outlook

The outlook for the pesticide industry is unclear. Undoubtedly the elimination of the ARP and the reduced acreage in the CRP suggest that more land will be planted. If historical patterns continue, then this suggests expanded demand for pesticide products. Conservation tillage practices have been growing steadily since 1989, from about 25% of the area planted to field and row crops to about 35% in 1996. No–till acreage has shown the greatest growth over this time period, increasing by more than threefold. This indicates likely growth for the herbicide market. Pest infections and infestations will also pull up demand for pesticide materials on an as needed basis.

The issue of biotechnology is where the uncertainty about the future arises. Will genetically altered products be embraced by consumers? Will genetically altered products and technology be effective during times of high pest pressures and differing environments? Will growers continue to pay premium prices for licensing and technology fees to grow genetically altered crops? Will growers abide by the terms of agreements restricting areas planted, harvesting seed, and using only select products in the production process? Will manufacturers of traditional chemical controls reduce prices sufficiently to compete with genetically altered seeds? The answers to these questions and issues are not obvious.

The United States is the world's largest producer of pesticides. Production facilities in the United States tend to be fairly efficient. Many firms have restructured to control costs and maintain a competitive advantage. The outlook for global agriculture is favorable and the United States should continue to be a net exporter of pesticide materials.

Environmental Issues

The use of chemicals in food production continues to be an emotionally charged issue. First, pesticide residues on food and fiber products raise questions as to the safety of food produced in the United States. Secondly, applications of fertilizers and pesticides do not remain where they are applied, and residual amounts do leech into ground and surface water. Until the mid–1980s, environmentalists and chemical manufacturers were in adversarial positions — one side arguing that people and the environment are at risk and the other side arguing that fertilizer and pesticide use was safe. Since then, there appears to have been a much more cooperative approach, in which industry is working with the public sector and consumers to address issues and concerns that arise from pesticide and fertilizer use.

Pesticides are regulated by the Environmental Protection Agency (EPA). The Food Quality Protection Act (FQPA) of 1996 included pesticide food safety legislation that had broad–based support. The law amended the Federal Insecticide, Fungicide, and Rodenticide Act (FIFRA), which required registration of pesticides for use in the United States, labeling, and other safeguards designed to protect the physical and human environment. The law also amended the Federal Food, Drug, and Cosmetic Act, which regulates pesticide residue tolerance levels in food. Enforcement of food tolerance levels is carried out by the Department of Health and Human Services' Food and Drug Administration and the Department of Agriculture's Food Safety and Inspection Service.

The new legislation eliminated what was known as the "Delaney Paradox", which distinguished between ready–to–eat processed food and raw agricultural commodities. It is possible for higher levels of cancer–causing pesticides to concentrate in processed food than in the raw commodity. If that higher concentration exceeded that of the raw commodity, the Delaney clause regulated zero tolerance. This had paradoxical effects: alternative pesticides could pose higher non–cancer risks; the EPA sometimes allowed the same pesticide in other foods based on negligible risk. The FQPA establishes that tolerances for pesticide residues in all food, raw and processed, will be set under the same provisions and the standards will apply to all risks (carcinogenic and non–carcinogenic). The EPA is also reviewing tolerance levels for pesticide residues.

FIFRA, as amended by the FQPA, requires the EPA to establish a periodic review of all pesticide registrations. In 1988, the EPA began the process of reviews on all pesticides registered before November 1984 and their associated tolerance levels. The review process was not mandated until the FQPA became law. The Act aims at establishing a 15–year review update cycle. A key element of the review process is that the EPA may call for a review at any time, and pesticide manufacturers must supply the data required. Other ways that pesticides and pesticide use are regulated include application and handling procedures, certification of applicators for some pesticides, and pesticide container disposal.

Water quality, like food safety, is an emotional issue. Fertilizer and pesticide run–off does end up in surface and ground water. However, given the non–point source nature of this pollution, it is difficult to regulate. The U.S. Department of Agriculture's Water Quality Program is intended to reduce degradation of the country's water resources. The program, now in its seventh year, provides farmers with educational, technical, and financial assistance and funds research projects designed to result in lower pesticide and fertilizer leeching into ground and surface water.

Agricultural Chemicals
Growth in Sales (Line) and Volume (Bar)

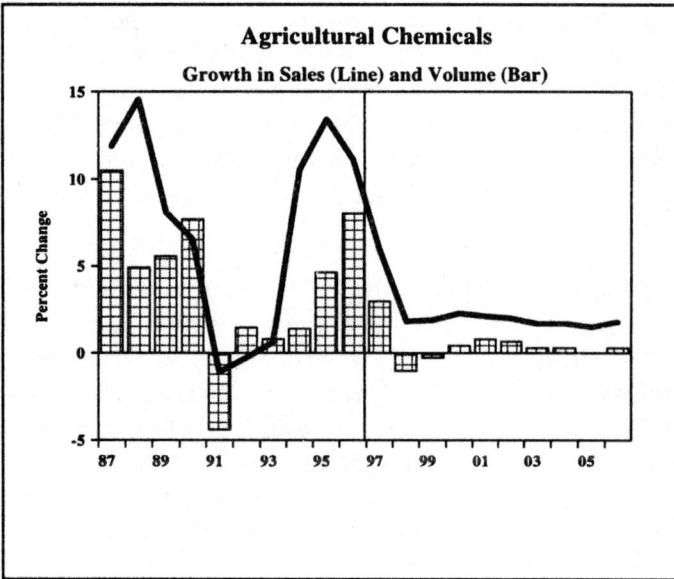

Agricultural Chemicals
Growth in Product Prices

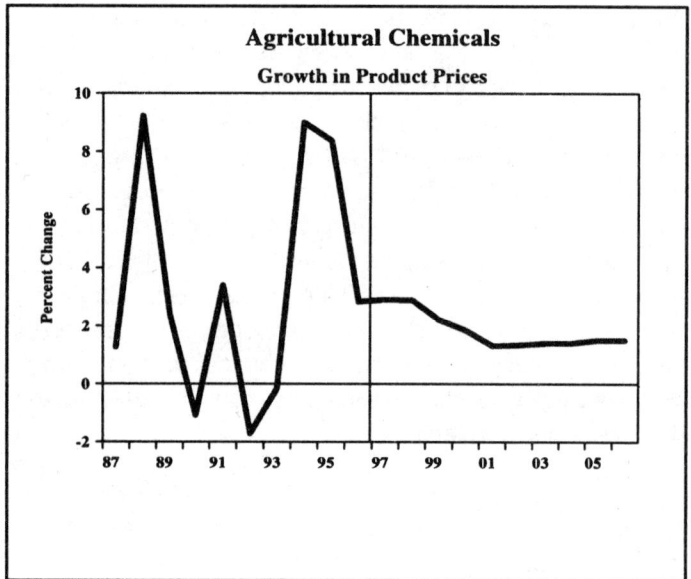

Agricultural Chemicals
SIC 287

		1990	1991	1992	1993	1994	1995	1996	1997	1998	Compound Ann Avg Growth 1986-1996	1996-2006
Sales												
	Billions of $	18.82	18.61	18.56	18.68	20.64	23.41	26.01	27.56	28.07		
	% Change	6.5	-1.1	-0.3	0.6	10.5	13.4	11.1	6.0	1.8	7.4	2.3
Volume	% Change	7.7	-4.4	1.5	0.8	1.4	4.6	8.0	3.0	-1.0	4.0	0.4
Prices	% Change	-1.1	3.4	-1.7	-0.2	9.0	8.4	2.8	2.9	2.9	3.3	1.8
Exports												
	Billions of $	3.91	4.23	3.63	3.06	4.04	4.72	4.64	4.57	4.60		
	% Change	-3.4	8.2	-14.2	-15.9	32.2	16.8	-1.8	-1.5	0.8	2.3	0.5
Imports												
	Billions of $	1.85	1.89	2.05	2.29	2.75	3.22	3.25	3.41	3.60		
	% Change	-5.6	2.3	8.2	11.9	20.0	16.9	1.1	4.8	5.7	6.8	2.7
Apparent Consumption												
	Billions of $	16.76	16.27	16.98	17.91	19.35	21.91	24.63	26.41	27.07		
	Nominal % Change	7.6	-2.9	4.4	5.5	8.0	13.2	12.4	7.2	2.5	8.6	2.6
	Real % Change	8.8	-6.1	6.2	5.7	-0.9	4.5	9.3	4.2	-0.4	5.2	0.8

Chapter 12: Petroleum Refining

Petroleum Refining

U.S. petroleum demand reached a seventeen year high in 1996, averaging 18.23 million barrels per day. In the first half of the year, demand for heating oil largely supported the market, while demand for motor gasoline maintained the momentum during the latter half of the year. Strong demand drained product inventories. By year–end 1996, motor gasoline and distillate fuel remained understocked while a significant recovery in residual fuel stocks was evident.

Petroleum demand is expected to rise to 18.4 million barrels per day in 1997, driven by strong economic growth, lower crude oil prices, and continuing strength in demand for motor gasoline. The healthy U.S. economy in 1997 will stimulate air travel as well as on–road transport.

Along with strong crude prices, high demand and low stocks supported product prices in 1996. A prolonged winter season depleted distillate stocks to record lows. A persistently backwardated NYMEX futures market (with futures prices lower than spot prices) caused buyers to treat distillate fuel oil like a depreciating asset. As a result, inventories did not recover until after the heating oil season. To exacerbate the situation, an extended driving season fueled a surge in motor gasoline demand.

WEFA forecasts that petroleum product prices will track upward with crude oil prices. Refining margins should widen over the forecast horizon as product prices regain and then outpace crude prices. Margins are projected to improve somewhat over the forecast interval, but only for light–end products. Growing demand for clean–burning fuels will enhance their market value, while residual products are projected to maintain at best their current value relative to crude oil. Motor gasoline and jet fuel kerosene prices will be rising faster than the other product prices due to the growing demand for transportation and air travel.

A margin squeeze, caused at least partly by the cost of compliance with environmental regulations, will bring further consolidation to the U.S. petroleum refining industry.

Demand

U.S. petroleum demand reached a seventeen year high in 1996, averaging 18.23 million barrels per day. In the first half of the year, demand for heating oil largely supported the market, while demand for motor gasoline maintained the momentum during the latter half of the year. Strong demand drained product inventories. By year–end 1996, motor gasoline and distillate fuel remained understocked while a significant recovery in residual fuel stocks was evident.

Demand for distillate fuel surged in 1996 due to a harsh winter, low inventories, and a robust economy. Strong demand for heating oil, which wiped out inventories in the first half of the year, followed by inventory purchases in the second half, accounted for most of the rise. Stocks were under 100 million barrels from February to May, about 20 million barrels below normal. By December,

stocks had climbed to 127 million barrels, just 3 million barrels below the level at the start of the drawdown. A growing U.S. economy raised transportation requirements, which contributed to demand, while high natural gas prices discouraged utilities from switching to natural gas.

Demand for residual fuel continued its downward trend in 1996. While this is a long–run trend, attributable to the market's preference for cleaner burning fuels, prices can cause deviations from the trend if they differ significantly from natural gas prices. Although demand was fairly high over the winter months, utilities purchased alternative fuels for the rest of the year. As a result, residual fuel stocks recovered more rapidly than any other fuel. By December 1996, stocks exceeded normal levels by 9 million barrels.

Motor gasoline demand established an all–time record at 7.8 million barrels per day in 1996, boosted by a healthy economy and mild weather that lengthened the driving season. The strong demand growth brought with it many problems. Under current environmental regulations, motor gasoline and other major petroleum products are formulated differently for each season, and for each region of the country. Therefore, stocks are minimized at the close of each season, and there is little supply sharing across regions. In 1996, stronger–than–normal demand for heating oil resulted in the early drawdown of distillate stocks, prompting demand for distillate from refineries and limiting stock build for motor gasoline. With demand roaring, stocks did not catch up to "normal" coverage until late in 1996. Motor gasoline stocks ended the year at 196 million barrels, 6 million barrels below the 1995 level and 19 million barrels below the level in 1994.

Through the first three–quarters of 1996, petroleum product prices reflected continuing demand growth and tight supplies due to economic performance, population, weather, environmental policies, and just–in–time inventory management. Consumers were given a reprieve however, when mild weather late in the year dampened heating oil demand, allowing refiners to rebuild stocks. By the end of the first quarter of 1997, most petroleum stocks had finally reached normal levels, and their effect on oil prices was reduced.

U.S. Consumption of Petroleum Products and Total Energy, 1987–96
(in quadrillions of Btu)

Year	Petroleum Products[1]	Total Energy[2]	Petroleum Products as a Percentage of all energy
1987	32.87	76.89	42.7
1988	34.22	80.22	42.7
1989	34.21	81.33	42.1
1990	33.55	81.27	41.3
1991	32.85	81.12	40.5
1992	33.53	82.14	40.7
1993	33.84	83.86	40.6
1994	34.74	85.59	40.5
1995	34.66	87.19	39.8
1996	35.72	89.94	39.7

[1]Petroleum products include natural gas plant liquids and crude oil burned as fuel.
[2]Excludes wood, waste, geothermal, wind, photovoltaic, and solar thermal energy except for small amounts used by electric utilities to generate electricity for distribution.
SOURCE: U.S. Department of Energy, Energy Information Administration.

Petroleum products are priced according to their viscosity. The lighter the oil, the higher the refinery cost or margin. Thus, prices rise as the product moves from the bottom to the top of the barrel. On the low end, there is residual fuel. Residual fuel oil is valued at less than crude because it is the residue that remains after the extraction of costlier lighter–end products. Since the price of residual fuel rises with declining sulfur content, ratios for low sulfur grades are closer to 1.00. Distillate fuel, motor gasoline, and jet fuel are priced at a premium to crude. Ratios of distillate fuel and motor gasoline are quite similar, but their prices tend to peak in different seasons of the year. Motor gasoline peaks in the spring or summer while distillate fuel peaks during the winter.

Petroleum Products Supplied to the U.S. Market by Type, 1987–96[1]

(in millions of barrels per day)

Year	Motor Gasoline	Jet Fuel	Distillate Fuel Oil	Residual Fuel Oil	Other Products	Total Products[2]
1987	7.21	1.38	2.98	1.26	3.84	16.67
1988	7.34	1.45	3.12	1.38	3.99	17.28
1989	7.33	1.49	3.16	1.37	3.98	17.33
1990	7.24	1.52	3.02	1.23	3.98	16.99
1991	7.19	1.47	2.92	1.16	3.97	16.71
1992	7.27	1.45	2.98	1.09	4.24	17.03
1992	7.48	1.47	3.04	1.08	4.32	17.24
1994	7.60	1.53	3.16	1.02	4.47	17.72
1995	7.79	1.51	3.21	0.85	4.37	17.73
1996	7.85	1.58	3.37	0.84	4.59	18.23

[1]Products supplied to the U.S. market from U.S. production and imports.
[2]Total may not equal the sum of components due to independent rounding.
SOURCE: U.S. Department of Energy, Energy Information Administration.

Forecast

Petroleum demand is expected to rise to 18.4 million barrels per day in 1997, driven by strong economic growth, lower crude oil prices, and continuing strength in demand for motor gasoline. The healthy U.S. economy in 1997 will stimulate air travel as well as on–road transport. With the advent of the driving season, and motor gasoline stocks again below normal levels, higher demand for gasoline could spur a rise in petroleum prices in the next few months. Coupled with a futures market that is in contango (with spot prices lower than futures), refiners should be more willing to increase inventories.

In the long term, petroleum product consumption will increase due to rising demand for transportation services despite slowing requirements for oil in the residential and power sectors. The transportation sector will maintain the largest share of the projected petroleum product demand, and will continue to show healthy growth over the next ten years. Offsetting this growth will be the shrinking role of petroleum products in stationary markets, such as home heating electric generation. The net effect will be a rise in petroleum demand averaging about 1% per year between 1996 and 2006.

The transportation sector is expected to expand on both an aggregate and per capita basis. The demand for travel will only partially be offset by improvements in capital efficiency, as consumers continue to choose performance, styling, and features over fuel efficiency in their vehicles.

This will trigger a rise in motor gasoline demand at an average annual rate of almost 1% per year.

Oil use for home–heating and electric generation purposes is declining. Distillate fuel and residual fuel oil are losing share to natural gas in these markets. More homes and apartment buildings have been built with gas burners than oil burners, and many owners of older housing stock will also convert from oil to gas. Home improvements, including renovations undertaken to increase energy efficiency, will lower demand for heating oil. In the electric utility sector, many utilities are switching from oil–fired turbines to the gas–fired combined cycle turbine because of its energy efficiency, flexibility, and low investment cost. Most of the incremental capacity built for electric generation in the future will require the use of these turbines.

Prices

In the simplest terms, petroleum product prices are comprised of two components: the value of the crude oil and the refinery margin. Product prices tend to move in tandem with crude prices, although unanticipated changes in petroleum product markets can affect crude prices.

Ratios of Petroleum Product Prices to Crude Oil Prices

Petroleum Product	Ratios to crude
Jet Fuel	1.20
Motor Gasoline	1.18
Distillate Fuel	1.17
Crude Oil*	1.00
Residual Fuel Oil (0.3% Sulfur)	0.93
Residual Fuel Oil (1.0% Sulfur)	0.81
Residual Fuel Oil (2.2% Sulfur)	0.75

Lighter → (Jet Fuel, Motor Gasoline, Distillate Fuel)

Heavier → (Residual Fuel Oil products)

*Crude oil = West Texas Intermediate

Market Overview

Petroleum product markets were remarkably strong through 1996. Largely driven by high demand and low stocks, oil prices broke records unseen since the Persian Gulf War. Distillate product prices were the most volatile, jumping by 18%. Residual fuel and motor gasoline prices also showed tremendous strength, rising 14% and 10% respectively. Ratios to crude, however, shrank as crude prices shot up further than product prices. In short, it was a year marked by strong prices as well as contra-seasonal price patterns.

Business leaders and consumers voiced their concerns over the rapid increase in prices, which resulted in a request by President Clinton for the Department of Energy to investigate reasons for the runup and to sell approximately 12 million barrels of crude oil from the Strategic Petroleum Reserve. The industry was also worried about disruptions in the marketplace, and refiners undertook measures to boost inventories.

Along with strong crude prices, high demand and low stocks supported product prices in 1996. A prolonged winter season depleted distillate stocks to record lows. A persistently backwardated NYMEX futures market (with futures prices lower than spot prices) caused buyers to treat distillate fuel oil like a depreciating asset. As a result, inventories did not recover until after the heating oil season. To exacerbate the situation, an extended driving season fueled a surge in motor gasoline demand.

Despite heavy refinery turnarounds, petroleum product prices collapsed in the first quarter of 1997. Starting at year-end 1996, mild weather dampened heating oil demand, diluting the impact of the tight inventory situation, and distillate fuel stocks finally reached normal levels. In January 1997, inventories lagged the year-ago level by 600,000 barrels, but by the end of March, inventories exceeded the prior year's level by 11 million barrels. Residual fuel oil prices came under tremendous pressure as stock levels rose. Not only did the warm winter contribute to increasing prompt supplies, but refiners switched their purchases to cheaper sour crudes which yield more residual fuel oil.

Forecast

WEFA forecasts that petroleum product prices will track upward with crude oil prices. Refining margins should widen over the forecast horizon as product prices regain and then outpace crude prices. Margins are projected to improve somewhat over the forecast interval, but only for light-end products. Growing demand for clean-burning fuels will enhance their market value, while residual products are projected to maintain at best their current value relative to crude oil. Motor gasoline and jet fuel kerosene prices will be rising faster than the other product prices due to the growing demand for transportation and air travel.

Real distillate fuel prices are projected to rise at an average rate of 1.5% to 2% per year over the next decade. This forecast reflects expectations for the crude market, some losses of stationary (home heating and power generation) market share, and some recovery in the industry's abysmal margins over the next ten years as refining consolidations occur. Ratios to crude will shrink as demand for distillate fuel relative to other fuels declines.

Residual fuel prices are projected to rise over the long term. Higher prices are attributed to rising crude prices, increasing demand for lighter products which limits residual fuel production, and a shift toward higher-cost and higher-price low sulfur residual fuel products. While the prices of residual fuel's competitors are projected to remain lower, residual fuel will have some opportunity to increase market share through the potential shutdown of nuclear facilities in the Northeast market. Oil–fired generation may replace some of this lost capacity, which will boost residual fuel prices. In the vessel bunkering market, the outlook for residual fuel prices is bullish since the lack of alternatives will support demand for residual fuel oil.

Motor gasoline prices will be affected in the long term by ongoing environmental debates and more stringent mandates. Reformulated gasoline (RFG) currently represents 16% of the petroleum market. The nine areas in the United States with the worst ozone pollution records are required to join in the RFG program. Others with less severe ozone records, may "opt–in" at the discretion of state governors. However, the EPA has proposed tougher air pollution standards, and a national RFG program is being considered. Growing demand for RFG will translate into higher prices as costs associated with producing this cleaner–burning fuel increase.

Capacity

Total U.S. operable crude oil distillation capacity was 15.4 million barrels per day in 1995, up from 15 million barrels per day in 1993. The total number of operable refineries has declined over the last five years, as many small refineries with capacities under 50,000 barrels per day were unable to survive the cost of the environmental requirements of the 1990 Clean Air Act Amendments (CAAA). The economics of refining are bearish, and as a result refinery output should increase only very slowly. Net imports of refined products, on the other hand, will rise to 1.63 million barrels per day by 2000 from 1.05 million barrels per day in 1996.

Petroleum Products: U.S. Refinery Output, Trade, and Supply, 1987–96
(in millions of barrels per day)

Year	Refinery Output	Gross Imports	Gross Exports	Net Imports[1]	Products Supplied[2]
1987	14.63	2.00	0.61	1.39	16.67
1988	15.02	2.30	0.66	1.64	17.28
1989	15.17	2.22	0.72	1.50	17.33
1990	15.27	2.12	0.75	1.37	16.99
1991	15.26	1.84	0.89	0.95	16.71
1992	15.37	1.80	0.86	0.94	17.03
1993	15.70	1.83	0.90	0.93	17.24
1994	15.78	1.93	0.84	1.09	17.72
1995	15.99	1.61	0.86	0.75	17.73
1996	16.29	1.92	0.87	1.05	18.23

[1]Net imports equals gross imports minus gross exports.
[2]Includes output from natural gas processing plants, refinery gains, crude oil burned directly, and inventory changes.
SOURCE: U.S. Department of Energy, Energy Information Administration.

Mergers and Acquisitions

Downstream restructuring has shaken the U.S. refining industry. There have been more than ten deals reached between refining companies since January 1996 in an effort to overcome poor downstream returns. U.S. refining margins have fallen by a third over the last decade while spending for upgrading plants to meet strict environmental regulations has risen significantly. Consolidation seems to be the quickest way to improve profits, largely through economies of scale. Recently, Valero announced that it will purchase Basis Petroleum and an agreement between Shell and Texaco was reached to combine their refining assets.

Petroleum Products Supplied to U.S. End–Use Sectors, 1987–94
(in millions of barrels per day)

Year	Residential and Commercial	Industrial	Transportation	Electric Utilities	Total[1]
1987	1.33	4.25	10.53	0.55	16.67
1988	1.34	4.39	10.87	0.68	17.28
1989	1.32	4.26	11.01	0.74	17.33
1990	1.14	4.32	10.97	0.55	16.99
1991	1.14	4.25	10.80	0.52	16.71
1992	1.13	4.56	10.97	0.41	17.07
1993	1.14	4.45	11.18	0.46	17.24
1994	1.11	4.69	11.50	0.43	17.72

[1]Total may not equal the sum of components due to independent rounding.
SOURCE: U.S. Department of Energy, Energy Information Administration.

Environmental Regulations

The high cost of compliance with environmental regulations has hindered oil companies' efforts to cut costs. The negligent release of hazardous pollutants into the water is a crime under the Clean Water Act, and release of them into the air is a criminal violation of the Clean Air Act. The Oil Pollution Act of 1992 requires various measures to reduce the likelihood of and damages from oil spills from tankers. It also requires tanker owners to have a substantial amount of liability insurance. These rules have driven some bunker oil dealers out of business.

Clean Air Act Amendments of 1990

The Clean Air Act Amendments created a plethora of regulations that affect the composition and consumption of refined petroleum products as well as the refining process. Most of the regulations are to be promulgated by 2000. Some examples of these regulations are listed below to highlight the costs and constraints facing the industry over the near term. The industry has responded to the environmental challenge by changing processes, valuing input material differently, and changing marketing objectives. The impact of environmental protection on the industry has been substantial, and it will continue to have an effect at least through the end of the next decade.

- Stationary Source Emissions: Phase I, implemented in 1990, has raised the cost of producing heavy fuel oil because of the requirement to upgrade refineries. In addition to refineries, power plants have also been affected since they emit sulfur dioxide (SO2) and nitrous oxide (NOx). The effects so far have been borne by only those plants with the largest sources of emissions. Phase II, to be implemented in 2000, will tighten emission limits imposed on large higher–emission plants.

- Oxygenated Gasoline Program (1990): Aimed at reducing carbon monoxide emissions. The CAAA's winter oxygenated–gasoline requirement mandates that motor gasoline sold during at least four winter months in 39 areas of the country, where levels of carbon monoxide most seriously exceed Federal standards, must have a minimum oxygen content of 2.7% by weight (2% in California). The program began November 1, 1992. The petroleum, ethanol, and petrochemical industries provided large volumes of oxygenates to specific geographic areas.

- Reformulated Gasoline Program (1990): The requirement to meet specifications under this program has driven production costs up. One of the targeted emissions is nitrogen oxide. Beginning in January 1995, the nine areas with populations more than 250,000 and with levels of ozone that most seriously exceed the Federal ozone standard, began using motor gasoline that meets emission and composition requirements. This reformulated gasoline must have a minimum oxygen content of 2% by weight, not more than 1% benzene by volume, and no heavy metals. Nitrogen–oxide emissions may not exceed that of a 1990 summertime baseline gasoline, and there must be a 15% reduction in tailpipe emissions of volatile organic compounds and toxic air pollutants. Aromatics content (benzene, toluene, xylene) may not exceed 25%.

■ Diesel Regulations: As of October 1, 1993, the sulfur content in diesel fuel must not exceed 0.05% by weight, and it must have a minimum cetane index of 40. (The cetane index is a measure of ignition quality.)

U.S. refiners have had to reexamine their operations closely in light of the CAAA requirements. Large, integrated companies with multiple refining operations have committed considerable resources to plant additions and reconfigurations, product reformulations, and research and development in processing technologies. For smaller refineries, the required investments are even higher on a per–barrel basis. As a result, these facilities are unlikely to weather the continuing escalation in environmentally driven costs. Although the large integrated companies are better positioned for this transition, they are not free from difficult decisions, including consolidation.

Increases in environmental costs come at a time of little growth in overall demand for petroleum products. While demand for higher–quality refined products is increasing, the quality of the refiners' crude oil inputs is declining, forcing even more investment spending.

The new or tightened environmental regulations will make the major petroleum products less interchangeable between seasons, geographical areas, and uses. Refiners, shippers, storers, importers, and marketers will all be affected. Distribution costs, as well as production costs, will also increase.

The wave of recent Federal and state environmental legislation has created considerable uncertainty for the refining industry. Details of many CAAA provisions, due to take effect in the late 1990s, have yet to be determined by the Environmental Protection Agency, and discrepancies between Federal and state regulations have yet to be resolved.

Refining operations and capital investments will be affected by pending technological standards to reduce stationary–source emissions. Future regulatory changes will most likely force petroleum refiners to alter refinery configurations and invest heavily in downstream processes. In some instances, it may be more economic for certain refineries to close down partially or entirely, rather than upgrade facilities to meet the new standards.

Despite the resumption of refinery shutdowns in recent years, and the likelihood that these will continue throughout the decade, total distillation capacity should remain relatively stable. Larger refineries will continue to make incremental additions to both crude distillation and downstream capacity. However, it is not expected that these incremental additions to capacity will keep pace with increases in petroleum demand.

Petroleum Refining and Related Industries
Growth in Sales (Line) and Volume (Bar)

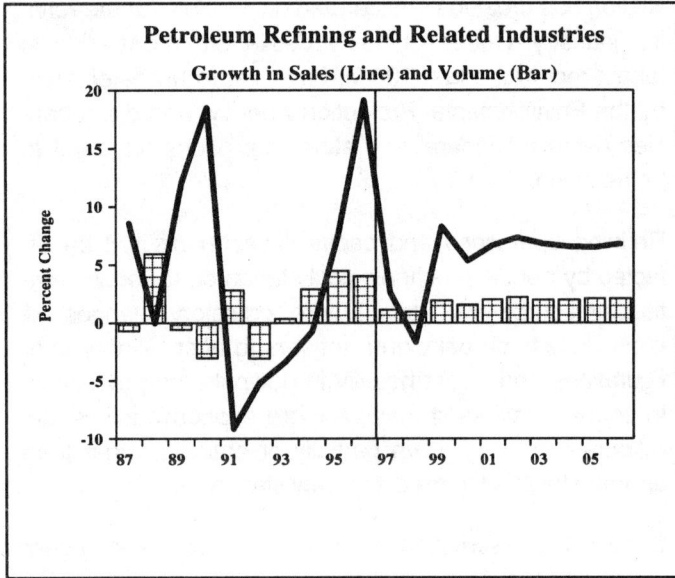

Petroleum Refining and Related Industries
Growth in Product Prices

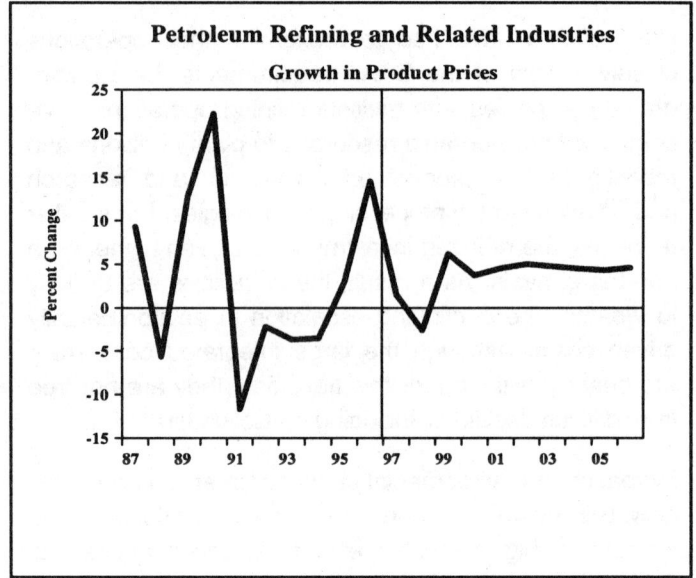

Petroleum Refining and Related Industries
SIC 29

		1990	1991	1992	1993	1994	1995	1996	1997	1998	Compound Ann Avg Growth 1986-1996	1996-2006
Sales												
	Billions of $	174.06	158.14	149.83	144.77	143.68	154.57	184.15	189.01	185.78		
	% Change	18.5	-9.1	-5.3	-3.4	-0.8	7.6	19.1	2.6	-1.7	4.3	5.5
Volume	% Change	-3.1	2.8	-3.1	0.3	2.9	4.5	4.0	1.1	1.0	1.3	1.8
Prices	% Change	22.2	-11.6	-2.2	-3.7	-3.5	3.0	14.5	1.5	-2.6	3.0	3.6
Exports												
	Billions of $	7.81	7.90	7.15	7.08	6.60	7.56	8.51	8.92	9.58		
	% Change	34.1	1.1	-9.4	-1.1	-6.8	14.6	12.6	4.9	7.3	7.9	7.0
Imports												
	Billions of $	15.13	11.58	11.10	10.49	10.11	9.16	13.68	12.90	12.82		
	% Change	19.2	-23.4	-4.2	-5.5	-3.7	-9.4	49.3	-5.7	-0.6	2.8	7.0
Apparent Consumption												
	Billions of $	181.37	161.82	153.77	148.18	147.19	156.17	189.32	192.98	189.03		
	Nominal % Change	18.0	-10.8	-5.0	-3.6	-0.7	6.1	21.2	1.9	-2.0	4.1	5.5
	Real % Change	-3.5	1.0	-2.8	0.1	3.0	3.0	5.8	0.4	0.6	1.0	1.8

Part 3: Durable Goods Manufacturing

Chapter 13: Lumber and Wood Products

Lumber and Wood Products

Because of its strong tie to the residential construction market, the lumber industry is highly cyclical. Years of price increases can be followed by a year or two of significant declines. WEFA forecasts a modest decline in housing starts and other residential construction activity during 1997 and 1998, and therefore lumber demand will be tapering off slightly. However, supply issues focused on the regional shift in lumber production and import restrictions, which have considerably influenced the supply/demand balance and lumber prices in the past few years, will continue to play a significant role.

More than 90% of the homes built in the United States use softwood framing lumber. A typical single–family home requires 16,000 board feet of lumber. New home construction accounts for an estimated 40% of the softwood lumber consumed in the United States; another 30% is used for remodeling and repair.

About 25% of the U.S. west coastal region will be removed from logging over the next ten years, and the cutbacks will be even more extreme in the western inland logging region. Inland mills are more dependent on public timber than the coastal regions, receiving almost half of their log supplies from public lands as compared to about 30% for coastal mills. Based on these figures, we look for coastal lumber production to fall, from a current market share of about 29% to about 26% by 2006. The inland region will see a larger loss. Its market share, estimated at 25% last year is expected to fall to 18% in ten years.

The production lost in the western logging regions will, in part, be made up in the south. Southern production is pegged at a minimum of 15 billion board feet (bbf) and a maximum of about 17 bbf annually, and the region's share in U.S. output should rise from 45%–50% today to over 55% in ten years.

However, Southern supply will be insufficient to fill the gap. As a result, imports will have to rise and exports will fall. Imports, largely from Canada, have been a major component of U.S. lumber supply for well over 25 years. In 1990, Canadian imports comprised approximately 29% of domestic supplies. This year, their share of the U.S. market will approach 37%.

There are two major reasons behind this structural change. First, lumber production levels in the United States were, and still are, limited. Environmental issues such as the spotted owl and overforestation brought about a number of cutting restrictions on government

lands. More than 7 million acres of coastal federal and state timberlands have been taken out of lumber production since 1990. Second, there were a number of major natural disasters (the west coast earthquake, hurricanes, and floods) that coincided with a booming construction market earlier in the recovery.

During the rapid recovery period for lumber demand in the United States (1992–94), there was a very strong economic incentive for Canadian producers to increase their shipments to the United States — lumber prices here surged by 15.8% in 1992, 26.7% in 1993, and 2.8% in 1994. Prices eased a bit in 1995, falling about 8%, but this decline was short–lived. Prices turned up again modestly in 1996. During 1997, despite the fact that housing starts are expected to decline moderately, lumber prices are expected to post a 6.0% overall gain for the year. This price increase is a signal of continuing tight supply conditions, caused in large part by import restrictions placed on Canadian lumber.

Despite slowing growth in economic activity, and lower unit housing starts, over the next two to three years, WEFA expects U.S. supply to fall even further behind demand as a result of environmental issues. As a result, if trade restrictions permit, Canadian market penetration should continue to grow, by about one percentage point each year, and reach a 47% market share by the year 2006.

U.S. lumber exports have fallen consistently since 1992. This year is no exception, as high U.S. prices and a tight domestic market make exporting unattractive. Over the next ten years, U.S. lumber producers will become an even more domestically–focused sector. Supply reductions in the western coastal and inland regions will bring the center of attention to the South and to Canada. Furthermore, as real spending on single unit housing begins to grow slowly again after the next year or two, our dependence on foreign supply will likely expand beyond Canada, possibly to South America.

U.S./Canada Lumber Agreement

There is one issue, however, that can upset the above scenario: the U.S./Canada Lumber Agreement. Under this agreement, Canadian lumber shipments that exceed a quota of 14.7 billion board feet annually, or 4.226 billion board feet quarterly, are subject to export fees. There is also a quota allocation scheme, whereby lumber exporters based in British Columbia will get 59% of the total annual quota, Quebec companies will receive 23%, Ontario companies 10.3%, and Alberta exporters 7.7%. The allocation goes to primary producers and remanufacturers who process lumber further, while wholesalers of lumber are not given direct quotas.

During the course of 1997, this agreement has caused a significant amount upheaval in the U.S. lumber market, and has definitely contributed to the renewed rise in prices. The agreement will likely lead to two short–term effects on U.S. imports from Canada — the volume of imports will be less than the demand for those imports, and Canadian producers will likely shift their shipments to the United States out of low–grade lumber into higher–value material.

Quotas create inequities

The attempt to apply government controls to the lumber trade has created more difficulties than ever existed in the past. For a business that was already highly volatile, participants at all levels have been subjected to increased volatility and uncertainty. For a deal that was supposed to establish a "level playing field," the agreement with Canada has definitely created winners and losers.

The winners

- U.S. softwood lumber producers, who are enjoying price levels of at least $100 per thousand board feet higher than last year.

- Timberland owners whose asset values have risen sharply.

- Canadian lumber producers who received adequate quotas.

- Offshore lumber suppliers who now have the opportunity to increase their U.S. shipments.

- Suppliers of non–wood substitutes, like steel, aluminum, and plastics, which now have an opportunity to increase their market share.

The losers

- Many Canadian producers who received quotas substantially below their needs.

- U.S. wholesalers and retailers who face major adjustments in their supply strategies.

- U.S. homebuilders who have witnessed the price of home construction escalate by $2000 to $3000 per unit.

Material Substitution: Steel?

With the lumber market in tight supply, the timing of the announcement that the National Building Code accepts steel framing couldn't be any better — for the steel industry, that is. Historically, lumber has maintained a stronghold on the residential construction market. With training, design, and construction procedures long established, building with lumber has been more cost effective than nontraditional materials, such as steel. For example, until now, every steel framed house has required a structural engineer — this was a key barrier in making steel framed homes cost–competitive with wood framed homes.

The Council of American Building Officials (CABO) accepted the initial submittal by a coalition shepherded by the American Iron and Steel Institute to have steel framing as part of the one– and two–family building codes. Steel now has exterior wall standards for eight, nine, and ten feet heights, and standards for floor joint systems. These standards apply to areas involving moderate wind loads, yet do not include seismic zones three and four.

Another factor in the cost–advantage clash has been price. Typically, prices have allowed lumber to be the material of choice for framing — assuming prices stay in the range of $200 to $400 per thousand board feet (tbf). When prices of lumber rise above $400/tbf, as they have currently, non–traditional materials look more attractive.

Although steel prices may now be competitive with lumber prices, WEFA expects lumber to remain the material of choice for home builders. Resistance to changing building practices and additional costs, such as retraining builders to utilize steel, will make the switch to steel over the next several years a slow process at best.

Lumber and Wood Products, except Furniture
Growth in Sales (Line) and Volume (Bar)

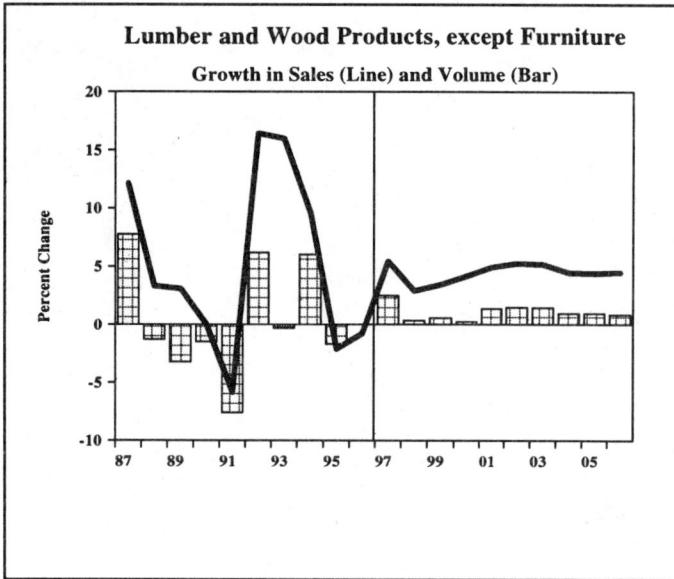

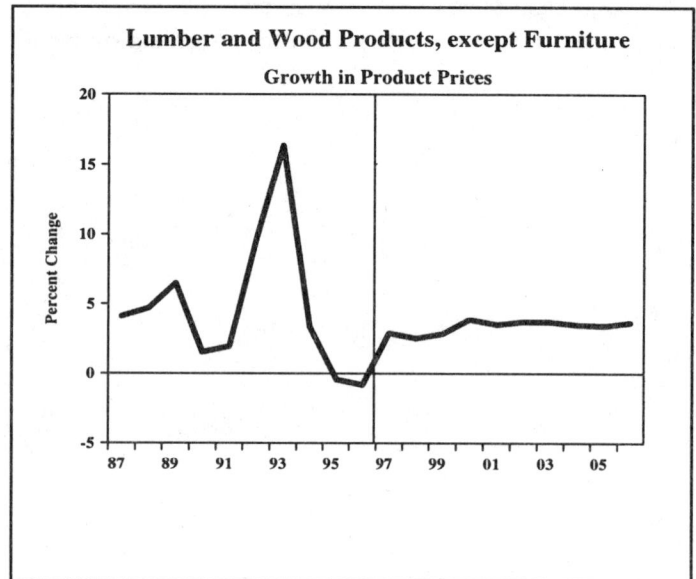

Lumber and Wood Products, except Furniture
Growth in Product Prices

Lumber and Wood Products, except Furniture
SIC 24

		1990	1991	1992	1993	1994	1995	1996	1997	1998	Compound Ann Avg Growth 1986-1996	1996-2006
Sales												
	Billions of $	74.45	70.11	81.62	94.64	103.70	101.51	100.67	106.17	109.24		
	% Change	0.0	-5.8	16.4	16.0	9.6	-2.1	-0.8	5.5	2.9	4.9	4.5
Volume	% Change	-1.5	-7.6	6.2	-0.3	6.0	-1.7	0.0	2.5	0.4	0.3	1.1
Prices	% Change	1.5	1.9	9.7	16.3	3.3	-0.4	-0.8	2.9	2.5	4.6	3.3
Exports												
	Billions of $	5.83	5.65	6.00	6.56	6.39	6.43	6.36	6.69	7.17		
	% Change	1.9	-3.2	6.3	9.3	-2.6	0.8	-1.1	5.2	7.2	8.9	6.9
Imports												
	Billions of $	0.74	0.64	0.80	0.95	1.01	1.03	1.10	1.13	1.17		
	% Change	2.7	-13.3	26.2	18.1	6.5	1.5	7.6	2.6	3.6	2.7	0.7
Apparent Consumption												
	Billions of $	69.35	65.10	76.42	89.04	98.33	96.10	95.42	100.61	103.24		
	Nominal % Change	-0.1	-6.1	17.4	16.5	10.4	-2.3	-0.7	5.4	2.6	4.7	4.2
	Real % Change	-1.6	-7.9	7.1	0.1	6.9	-1.9	0.1	2.5	0.1	0.1	0.9

Chapter 14: Furniture

Furniture

The furniture industry is comprised of producers of household furniture, public building furniture, and office and store furniture and fixtures.

The household furniture manufacturing industry is made up of producers of wood furniture which accounted for an estimated $10.0 billion, or 44% of household furniture industry shipments in 1995; upholstered furniture, $7.6 billion or 31%; metal furniture, $2.2 billion or 10%, mattresses and bedsprings, $3.5 billion or 14%; and wood television and radio cabinets, $0.4 billion or 1%.

Shipments by the U.S. household furniture manufacturing industry grew 10.6% in 1996, the industry's largest increase so far in this recovery. A rise in home sales and residential construction contributed to the gain in 1996. The sales growth was comprised of a substantial real volume increase of 8.6% and a modest price rise of 1.6%. Sales should continue to grow at an average of about 2.5% per year for the next five years.

Public building furniture will be influenced most over the next ten years by educational building requirements, as the primary school–aged children of baby boom parents stress the capacity of the nation's secondary school system. Office building furniture and fixtures should see reasonable growth over the next ten years. Computer furniture, one of the sources of strength in office furniture over the past decade, will continue to grow but at a significantly slower pace.

Demand For Furniture

The demand for household furniture tracks with the sale of new homes and the patterns in remodeling and renovation. New housing starts have held up well for this late stage in the economic cycle, totaling 1.47 million units in 1996. Consumer income gains have also been strong, growing by 2.9% in 1996 and accelerating at the beginning of 1997. Consumer spending for furniture and household goods has been rising rapidly for the last few years, growing by about 9% per year in current–dollar terms. However, this growth pace is expected to slow considerably over the next few years.

One reason for the expected slowing in growth in spending for furniture is the increase in short–term interest rates in 1997. The rate rise will slow both housing starts and remodeling, mainly through their impact on financing of short–term debt and monthly budgets, since mortgage rates will be affected only modestly by the Fed's rate hikes.

The outlook for household furniture in the next two years is for relatively moderate growth. Compared to the first half of the decade, growth should slow considerably and then pick up a bit in the second half of 1998.

In the longer term, demand for household furniture will grow modestly, as slower growth in household formations slows the growth pace of the housing market. In real terms, sales of domestically–produced furniture will average growth of about 2% per year. Consumption will grow a bit more rapidly, at closer to 2.5%. Export growth will slow significantly from the pace of the last decade, and import growth will slow only slightly, indicating a further loss in market share for U.S. producers over the coming decade.

Public building furniture will be influenced most over the next ten years by educational building requirements, as the primary school–aged children of baby boom parents stress the capacity of the nation's secondary school system. Over the next ten years, high school enrollment will advance by 16.7% while that of elementary schools will grow by only 4% — virtually a reversal of the pattern observed over the last decade

Office building furniture and fixtures should see reasonable growth over the next ten years. Office building construction is moving up, responding to rising demand for office space in suburban locations. Computer furniture, one of the sources of strength in office furniture over the past decade, will continue to grow but at a significantly slower pace.

Employment

Employment in the household furniture industry has declined for the past two years by a bit more than 1% per year, from 267,000 employees in 1994 to 260,000 in 1996. Average hourly earnings in the household furniture industry rose from $9.00 in 1994 to $9.60 in 1996, an average increase of 3.2% per year. This increase was a little better than the inflation rate of about 3%. Increased production costs as well as mounting international competition have forced manufacturers to reduce hiring.

Supply: Hardwood Prices Decline

In 1996, wood furniture companies' profits were helped as a result of a general decline in their lumber input costs. Although softwood lumber prices increased by more than 6%, hardwood lumber prices fell by almost 2%, and plywood prices fell 5%. Hardwood lumber is used in producing higher quality furniture.

Steel prices, which are more important to the public and office furniture markets, are forecasted to show little growth over the next decade, as the industry deals with capacity that is increasing more rapidly than demand.

Furniture Industry Faces Continued Restructuring

Consumers' price sensitivity, along with increasing international competition, has made the furniture industry increasingly competitive. Several decades ago the industry was dominated by many small retailers that were supplied in turn by many small manufacturers. However, in recent years retailers have consolidated, and the large furniture store chains have pushed for lower prices and put pressure on producer profit margins. While once there was a large number of local manufacturers, there are now large national manufacturers supplying retailers across the country and the world. Almost half of U.S. furniture output is produced by the top 25 manufacturers. Masco Home Furnishings alone accounts for more than 20% of production.

International Trade

Despite a 15% decline in shipments to Canada, U.S. furniture exports grew by 1% in 1996 to $1.2 billion. Furniture exports have been static in recent years, following sound advances in the late 1980s and early 1990s. Exports to Japan, South Korea, and the United Kingdom all grew by 30% or more in 1995.

Japan is the second leading importer of U.S. furniture, and remains the only Asian country that buys more furniture from the United States than it ships here. Malaysia, Indonesia, the Philippines, China, and Thailand together took in $25 million worth of U.S. furniture while sending $1.8 billion here.

Furniture imports are considerably larger than exports — the trade gap in furniture last year was $4.8 billion. Furniture imports into the United States grew 12% in 1996. Canada continues to be the leading household furniture importer into the United States, and in 1996 imports from Canada grew 22% to $1.3 billion. Aggressive marketing and the weak Canadian dollar helped Canadian exporters. A weak currency and NAFTA were the factors that helped Mexico, as U.S. furniture imports from Mexico rose 39% in 1996. Other big import increases were from China (30%), Malaysia (21%), and the United Kingdom (19%).

Exports

U.S. Furniture Exports by Destination Country 1996 (*millions of dollars*)

	1996	1995	% Change from 1995
Canada	$496.70	$587.2	−15%
Japan	110.3	85.0	30
Mexico	88.2	77.6	14
Saudi Arabia	54.4	56.4	−4
United Kingdom	41.1	29.6	39
South Korea	28.9	18.8	54
Brazil	26.6	20.1	33
Kuwait	18.4	15.2	21
Germany	17.7	22.2	−20
France	16.3	18.5	−12
World Total	**$1,243**	**$1,229**	**1%**

Source: U.S. Customs Service, U.S. Census Bureau, U.S. International Trade Commission

Imports

U.S. Furniture imports by Producing Country, 1996 (*millions of dollars*)

	1996	1995	% Change from 1995
Canada	$1,305.3	$1,067.7	22%
China	887.7	682.1	30
Taiwan	870.8	956.1	−9
Italy	632.9	596.9	6
Mexico	494.4	355.6	39
Malaysia	391	323.5	21
Indonesia	233.7	225.8	4
Philippines	165.8	164.6	1
Thailand	158.7	162.0	−2
United Kingdom	93.1	78.1	19
World Total	$6,045.30	$5,398.60	12%

Source: U.S. Customs Service, U.S. Census Bureau, U.S. International Trade Commission

Environmental Issues

The American Furniture Manufacturers Association (AFMA) has asked the Environmental Protection Agency not to adopt stricter clean air standards, saying they would particularly hurt smaller producers and further encourage imports. The AFMA said the proposal to reduce allowable ozone levels from 12 parts per million to between seven and nine, and to cover for the first time "fine" particulate matter of 2.5 microns and smaller, would cost upholstery and wood furniture facilities $109 million in the first year and about $58 million in each subsequent year. Two likely results of tighter standards are further consolidation in the U.S. furniture–producing industry and loss of market share to lower–cost producers in Asia.

Furniture and Fixtures
Growth in Sales (Line) and Volume (Bar)

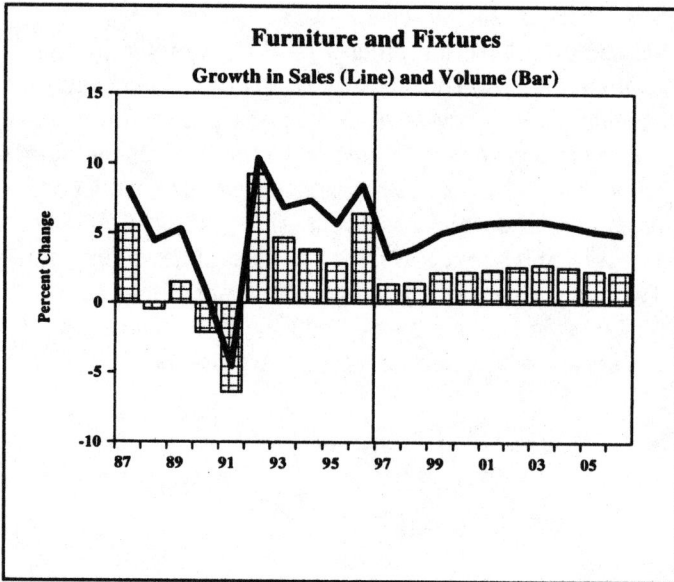

Furniture and Fixtures
Growth in Product Prices

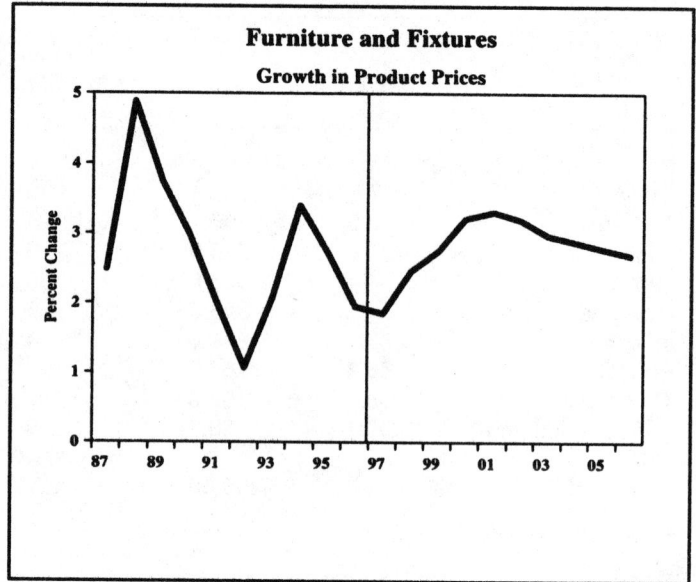

Furniture and Fixtures
SIC 25

		1990	1991	1992	1993	1994	1995	1996	1997	1998	Compound Ann Avg Growth 1986-1996	1996-2006
Sales												
	Billions of $	41.63	39.73	43.86	46.87	50.32	53.17	57.68	59.57	61.91		
	% Change	0.8	-4.6	10.4	6.9	7.4	5.7	8.5	3.3	3.9	5.2	5.1
Volume	% Change	-2.1	-6.4	9.2	4.7	3.8	2.9	6.4	1.4	1.4	2.4	2.2
Prices	% Change	3.0	2.0	1.1	2.1	3.4	2.7	1.9	1.8	2.5	2.7	2.8
Exports												
	Billions of $	1.00	1.27	1.55	1.64	1.76	1.70	1.81	1.99	2.17		
	% Change	20.1	26.9	21.9	6.0	7.4	-3.6	6.3	10.2	8.9	19.8	5.7
Imports												
	Billions of $	4.04	3.99	4.28	4.81	5.65	6.27	7.03	7.63	8.06		
	% Change	4.2	-1.4	7.3	12.5	17.4	11.0	12.2	8.5	5.6	6.7	6.3
Apparent Consumption												
	Billions of $	44.67	42.45	46.59	50.04	54.20	57.74	62.91	65.21	67.80		
Nominal % Change		0.7	-5.0	9.8	7.4	8.3	6.5	9.0	3.7	4.0	5.1	5.2
Real % Change		-2.2	-6.8	8.6	5.2	4.8	3.7	6.9	1.8	1.5	2.4	2.3

Chapter 15: Hydraulic Cement

Hydraulic Cement

In this section, the term cement will refer exclusively to hydraulic cement, which is cement that will harden when mixed with water. It is the overwhelmingly dominant category of cement manufactured in the United States. During 1996, cement was produced in 37 states, fairly evenly distributed by region, and in Puerto Rico, by 46 companies. The top ten producers accounted for over 55% of production and close to 60% of capacity. The top four, in descending size order, are: Holnam, Inc.; Lafarge Corp.; Southdown, Inc.; and Ash Grove Cement Co. As little as seven years ago the cement industry was characterized by shrinking domestic capacity, increasing imports, and flat demand. Since then, capacity has begun to edge up, by about 3%, and demand has begun to recover. However, imports have also grown, by more than 6% over the seven–year period, and account for about 15% of consumption.

Demand Conditions

There is a very strong relationship between cement demand and the construction industry. Data collected by the Portland Cement Association show that 64% of total cement consumption is used in the construction of buildings. About half of that amount is used in residential projects, and the commercial sector consumes about another third. The remainder is used in public construction projects. As a result of this diversification within the three main construction markets, as well as its use in both new construction and renovation work, the cement industry is somewhat less cyclical than, for example, housing starts.

Recently, diversification has not been an issue because all three construction sectors, residential, commercial, and public, grew nicely in 1996. Furthermore, the coincidental growth of these three sectors is expected to continue, although at a modest pace, over the next five years. Real investment on residential structures is projected to experience a 1.5% annual average increase through the year 2001. Commercial structures should see about 2% growth per year. The largest supporter of the cement industry is likely to be public projects, where a 3% average rate of growth is anticipated.

U.S. cement demand has grown little since 1990. However, since the 1993 rebound in construction, it has increased by more than 10%. Cement consumption has never been evenly distributed throughout the United States. For example, the Southeast has seen high growth in cement demand because its population is the fastest growing of the major U.S. regions. The Olympic Games in Atlanta also spurred a construction boom and considerable growth in cement demand. Florida continues to see rapid in–migration. Furthermore, resort and hotel construction in the Southeast has been surging.

Natural disasters have also played a role in determining relative regional cement demand. At times hurricanes in Florida and along the Gulf Coast have caused considerable increases in demand for building supplies. Earthquakes on the West Coast have pushed cement demand upward as buildings, freeways, and bridges are rebuilt.

While natural events are unpredictable, demographic trends are fairly clear. The most dominant cement consumption areas in the country have been the South Atlantic, the West South Central, and the Pacific regions. We believe that these regions will continue to command the largest shares of cement demand in the United States.

Supply

Cement companies in the United States range from small single–plant operations that account for only tiny shares of U.S. production, to large corporations with many plants that produce as much as 13% of U.S. output. More than 50% of U.S. cement companies are foreign–owned, and many of these were bought from U.S. ownership during the 1980s. However, just recently UNICEM SpA of Italy became the 100% owner of RC Cement Co. Inc. proving that ownership of U.S. cement manufacturers is still attractive overseas.

There are 115–120 portland cement producing facilities in the country, with a total capacity of over 93 million metric tons. For years domestic output was inadequate to meet demand, and imports filled the shortfall. The recent combination of only small capacity growth and strong demand has boosted capacity utilization to the 90% range. This has led to price increases and significantly improved corporate revenues. It has also led to an increasing dependence on imports.

Over the last 10 years there have been a number of trade issues involving dumping by Japanese and Mexican cement companies. As a result, antidumping tariffs on imports from Japan and Mexico were imposed. These tariffs have dramatically reduced cement and clinker imports from both countries. In 1990 cement imports represented close to 15% of total consumption. By 1993 they fell to about 13% and expectations were that they would decline further. However, after 1994 the U.S. dollar strengthened and the construction sector began to improve. In response, imports returned to about a 15% share in 1995 and 1996.

Cement imports from Canada account for 5.4 million of the 14.2–million–metric–ton import total. Spain and Venezuela each export another 1.5 million. Mexico exports 1.3 million tons to the United States and Japan's total is now less than 0.1 million tons. It appears that antidumping tariffs have been effective, and have reduced cement imports from Mexico and Japan, but other countries that do not fall under the agreement have simply filled the gap.

Future supplies of cement will come from a combination of domestic and foreign sources. We expect import penetration to average between 15% and 16% over the next five years. These figures are based the assumption that the U.S. dollar will slowly decline relative to the currencies of our major trading partners. This also incorporates WEFA's forecast of continued healthy activity levels in the three construction sectors. Domestic capacity is likely to expand. A new clinker plant with 200,000 tons per year capacity has recently commenced operations in Nevada. Two companies also announced plans to construct new kilns in Florida, with a combined net capacity increase of 1.4 million tons. Their completion is slated for 1998.

Total U.S. cement production increased from 67.2 million tons in 1991 to 80.6 million tons in 1996, an average rate of growth of 3.7% per year. While we do not expect production to continue to grow this rapidly over the next five years, growth in the 2.5% range is quite possible.

Perspective On Prices

Due to transportation costs, portland cement prices vary widely on a regional basis, by as much as $30/ton. Some of the lowest prices can be found in the Midwest. The highest are in Alaska, Hawaii, and Florida. During 1994, portland cement prices averaged $61/ton. Market pressures increased the price to $68/ton and $71/ton in 1995 and 1996 respectively. With additional capacity coming on stream, further price rises will be more modest, most likely in the 2.0% to 2.5% range.

Chapter 16: Primary Metals

Steel Works

The U.S. steel industry has gone through a tremendous transformation over the last two decades. Steelmaking capacity has declined from 127 million tons in 1986 to 109 million in 1995. At the same time production increased from 81.6 million tons to 104.9 million. The primary focal point of this structural change has been the emergence of the mini-mill and the decline of the integrated steel corporations.

The top ten major U.S. mini-mills increased their sales from $2.4 billion in 1986 to $8.0 billion in 1995, an increase in market share from 9.8% to 23.2%. Sales of NUCOR, the world's largest mini-mill, surged from less than $0.5 billion in 1986 to nearly $3.5 billion in 1995. This is in sharp contrast to the integrated steel companies that have been shrinking and restructuring. LTV, one of the noted "Integrated Big Six", has seen their sales decline from $4.5 billion in 1986 to $4.3 billion in 1995. Overall, total sales for the six largest U.S. integrated mills fell from $29.2 billion in 1981 to $22.1 billion in 1995.

Future Trends

The mini-mill is the steel mill of the future. Although it has one major disadvantage — it cannot produce certain quality products — time and advancements in technology will eventually diminish this disadvantage. WEFA looks for output in the U.S. steel industry to grow by approximately 4.8% in 1997 and another 4.9% in 1998. Over 42% of this will be supplied by electric arc furnaces, of which a large percentage are mini-mills. As technology and engineering changes accelerate, the minis' market share could increase by 1.25 to 1.5 percentage points annually over the next ten years.

Overall, the U.S. steel industry is expected to see healthy growth over the next five years. Driven by increases in the sector's end-use markets, steel consumption is forecast to grow at an annual average rate of 3.0% through 2002. Both the non-residential construction and industrial machinery (excluding computers) sectors are

Annual U.S. Steel Forecast

Million Tons	1994	1995	1996	1997	1998	1999	2000	2001
Total Shipments	95.1	97.5	100.5	104.4	109.3	114.4	118.9	122.2
% change, year ago	6.9	2.5	3.1	3.9	4.7	4.7	3.9	2.7
Domestic Sales	91.4	90.4	95.5	99.4	103.9	108.8	113.3	116.5
% change, year ago	7.5	-1.1	5.6	4.0	4.6	4.7	4.1	2.8
% of shipments	96.1	92.7	95.0	95.2	95.1	95.1	95.2	95.3
Exports	3.7	7.1	5.0	5.0	5.3	5.6	5.7	5.7
% change, year ago	-7.0	91.4	-29.7	1.2	6.1	5.1	1.0	1.2
% of shipments	3.9	7.3	5.0	4.8	4.9	4.9	4.8	4.7
Imports	30.1	24.4	29.2	28.5	28.0	27.1	26.5	26.0
% change, year ago	54.4	-18.9	19.5	-2.3	-1.9	-2.9	-2.3	-2.1
market share, %	24.8	21.3	23.4	22.3	21.2	20.0	19.0	18.2
App. Consumption	121.5	114.8	124.7	127.9	131.9	136.0	139.8	142.4
% change, year ago	16.2	-5.5	8.6	2.6	3.1	3.1	2.8	1.9

Historical Source: American Iron and Steel Institute; Forecast Source: WEFA expected to be the leading supporters, with average annual increases of 2.9% each. The motor vehicle industry is likely to provide another 2.5% annual support for demand. Finally, demand for steel products from the electrical machinery sector, thought relatively small from a steel perspective, should grow by about 4.7% per year. Non-residential construction and motor vehicles each account for about 30% of steel demand. The fabricated metal sector consumes 15%, and the metal can/container, appliance, non-electrical machinery, electrical machinery, and oil and gas sectors each consume roughly 5%.

Foreign trade will also have a significant impact on the steel industry. Both steel imports and exports can have huge swings in direction. During 1996 imports grew by close to 20% while exports plunged 30%. As a whole, exports have settled into a position representing approximately 5% of shipments. Imports approached 25% of total demand during 1994, but since have fallen off to a 22% level. WEFA's outlook for steel trade is dependent on the value of the U.S. dollar relative to our major trading partners. It is also contingent on the industrial output of the rest of the world relative to the United States. Applying WEFA's forecasts for a gradual weakening of the U.S. dollar and faster growth for foreign industrial output relative to the U.S. industrial sector, we project the market share of imports to decline by approximately 1 percentage point per year. By the year 2001, look for imports to supply only 18% of total demand.

New Capacity

The steel sector has always had a history of volatile prices. It is not unusual for composite steel prices to decline by over 10% in one year and increase by more than 14% during another. In 1996 the U.S. composite spot price fell by more than 5.0%, despite the fact that consumption increased by almost 9%. Support from the steel industry's end-use markets also proved to be

strong. So why did prices fall? Our answer lies with capacity. During 1996 total U.S. steel melting capacity increased from 112.3 million tons to 116.4 million, a net expansion of over 4.0 million tons. The last time the U.S. steel industry saw growth even close to this amount was in 1989. Prices fell by more than 6.0% that year.

During the next five years, the increase in U.S. melting capacity is expected to be unparalleled. By the year 2001, close to 20 million tons of melting capacity could come on-line. Almost all of this will be in the mini-mills. Mini-mills will rely on a simple formula of low costs and reliable products to register growth. Their low costs will be the result of efficient operating practices, limited product lines, and employee empowerment. Equally important to their future financial success will be their relatively low capital costs (as opposed to integrated mills) and speedy installation of new plant and equipment. Current operating costs of mini-mills are around $342 per output ton, as compared to the integrated mills' per-ton operating costs of $481.

Other relative advantages of mini-mills are their low incidence of unionization, their aggressive management, and the fact that there are virtually no pension fund problems. Mini-mills can also be located close to areas of demand, transportation, or shipping ports, and this flexibility can give them a strong competitive advantage when it comes to delivered pricing.

Perspective On Prices

As discussed earlier, in 1996 steel prices fell in response to significant growth in capacity. As steel capacity expansions accelerate in 1998 and 1999, look for prices to fall further despite healthy growth in steel demand. End-use market activity is expected to grow by 2.6% annually over the next five years. However, capacity is expected to grow at a 3.6% average annual rate. As a result, look for composite steel prices to decline approximately 3.2% annually between 1998 and 2000.

U.S. Steel Market: Annual Price Outlook

Us$/Ton	1994	1995	1996	1997	1998	1999	2000	2001
"Major-6" Average (1)	495	510	498	508	485	475	465	470
% Change	5.5	3.0	-2.3	2.0	-4.5	-2.1	-2.1	1.1
Mini-10 Average (2)	393	420	430	430	430	432	438	442
% Change	8.6	6.9	2.4	0.0	0.0	0.5	1.4	0.9
Steel Ppi (1982=100) (3)	113	120	116	116	111	109	108	109
% Change	4.4	6.3	-3.7	0.3	-4.3	-1.8	-0.9	0.9
Spot Price Composite (4)	458	434	412	426	406	393	386	389
% Change	14.6	-5.3	-5.1	3.4	-4.6	-3.3	-1.8	0.9
Integrated Spot Price (5)	479	450	424	444	421	405	397	401
% Change	15.5	-5.9	-5.7	4.7	-5.3	-3.7	-2.0	0.9
Mini Mill Spot Prices (6)	353	356	364	363	360	357	353	357
% Change	5.6	0.9	2.2	-0.3	-0.8	-1.0	-0.9	1.0
Scrap - No.1 Heavy Melt (7)	127	137	135	138	138	140	145	152
% Change	13.4	7.9	-1.3	2.1	0.0	1.4	3.6	4.8

Mid-month, F.O.B. prices; Forecast Source: WEFA; Unless Otherwise Noted, Historical Source: Purchasing Magazine;

1- Avg. Value/Ton Steel Sold By Major-6 Steelmakers; Historical Source: Company Financial Reports;

2- Avg. Value/Ton Steel Shipped By Birmingham, Bayou, Chaparral, CMC, Florida, Laclede, New Jersey, Northwestern, NS Group, Nucor;
   Historical Sources: WEFA Survey; Independent Market Cross-Check;

3- Composite of all steel mill products; Historical Source: Bureau of Labor Statistics;

4- Composite of HR Sheet, CR Sheet, Galvanized Sheet, Plate, CF Bar, Structurals, Wire Rod and REBAR;

5- Composite of HR Sheet, CR Sheet, Galvanized Sheet and Plate;

6- Composite of CF Bar, Structurals, Wire Rod and REBAR;

7- Historical Source: American Metal Market.

Lead

Although consumption broadly follows trends in economic activity, demand for lead is probably the least cyclical of all the major non–ferrous metals. A large and growing proportion is consumed by the replacement SLI (starting–lighting–ignition) battery market. In the short term, this sector is most directly affected by seasonal weather patterns, and in the long term by trends in vehicle ownership and use.

In the United States, the transportation industry is the principal direct user of lead, accounting for 65% of consumption for batteries, fuel tanks, solder, seals, and bearings. Electrical, electronic, and communications uses (including batteries), ammunition, television glass, construction (including radiation shielding), and protective coatings combine for about 28% of consumption. The balance is used in ballast and weights, ceramics and crystal glass, tubes and containers, foil, wire, and specialized chemicals.

In 1996, continued strength in domestic demand, particularly for replacement batteries, drove up the U.S. lead market and, coupled with steady world lead consumption, sent prices to six–year highs. However, the market slacked in the last quarter of 1996 as battery demand took a break. The market has not yet recovered, and is not expected to do so soon without the help of the all–important battery sector.

Concentration among lead–consuming companies is less marked than among producers. However, the rising share of consumption taken by the battery sector, now accounting for over 85% of the total, together with supply–side changes in the lead industry, suggest that the market power of lead buyers is likely to grow. Battery manufacturers have also integrated backwards into secondary production.

U.S. Lead Industry Trends
(Thousands of tons, unless otherwise noted)

	1992	1993	1994	1995	1996
Mine Prod	407	362	370	394	430
Refined Prod	1,166	1,173	1,228	1,300	1,310
Apparent Consumption	1,270	1,340	1,490	1,540	1,560
U.S. Prod Price (¢/LB)	35.1	31.7	37.2	42.3	48.8

Demand

It is not a surprising fact that the United States, the world biggest automobile market, also possesses the largest consumer market for refined lead, consuming more than one–fourth of the world total. In 1996, the market increased slightly to 1.56 million tons, marking the fifth successive year that lead use in the United States has risen. Consumption in batteries increased by 4.4%, underpinned by increased shipments of both replacement and original equipment batteries. This occurred despite the fact that the automotive industry didn't grow last year. Most of the strength in battery demand came from the replacement lead–acid batteries, especially in early 1996 when the United States was hit by extremely cold weather.

Lead consumption in ammunition fell by 18%, largely due to the tightening of legislation on lead shot. Use of lead by the chemicals sector increased by 16%. In addition, demand for industrial–type batteries, particularly in the telecommunications and computer sectors, increased appreciably. With further growth expected in the U.S. economy in 1997 and a pickup in auto production, WEFA expects the upward trend in lead consumption to continue.

Supply

On the production side, the industry has a handful of large producers. The degree of concentration is similar to that of copper and zinc at the mining stage, but it is less concentrated at the refining stage, owing to the importance of secondary producers.

The recycling of lead is well developed compared to other metals. Secondary production (involving the re-fining of scraps, residues, and wastes) generated about 1 million tons of secondary lead in 1996, an amount equivalent to 64% of domestic consumption. The growing share of batteries in total consumption and the intensification of environmental legislation which has given rise to enforced recycling will ensure that the secondary sector will increase in importance. About 880,000 tons of lead were recovered from used batteries alone in 1996.

U.S. mine production rose about 9% to a value of $445 million, based on the average U.S. producer price in 1996. U.S. production remained in third place globally behind Australia and China. Primary refinery production declined by 8%, mainly due to the closure in June 1996 of Asarco's 60,000 ton–per–year (tpy) Omaha refinery. However, secondary refinery production continued to move up, rising 4% over that of 1995. Each year, the U.S. market has continued to absorb a significant amount of imports, mainly refined lead from Canada and Mexico. These production and market conditions are expected to continue in the near term.

Long–term hopes for the continued demand for lead will be underlined by the launch of Electric Vehicle (EV). The EV battery contains 600 pounds of lead, compared to an average of 20 pounds in a standard automotive lead–acid battery, and it also has a life expectancy of only two years. Although lead–acid batteries are technically advanced, they face potential competition from nickel–hydride or lithium ion alternatives.

Prices

The large share of secondary production in total refined output means that, at least in theory, the short–term price elasticity of refined lead supply is high, with secondary refineries acting as swing capacity during price upturns or downturns. This has tended to reduce the volatility of prices in recent years, at least when compared with other major metals, and on some measures lead is now one of the least volatile.

A North American producer price (as published by *Metals Week*) is based on the average list prices of a number of U.S. and Canadian producers, weighted by their production levels for the previous year. Although this price is normally at a substantial premium over the London Metal Exchange (LME) price, the two markets

often move in parallel, largely because of the influence of secondary producers, many of whom now base their quotations on the LME price.

During 1996, the price for lead increased significantly in the United States and in the rest of world. The U.S. producer price for the first nine months of the year averaged 16% higher than the previous year, as refined lead remained in short supply and stock levels were low because of the weather–led increased demand for replacement batteries. After registering six–year highs, U.S. producer prices ended the year disappointedly. Slack demand combined with slowly–rising stock figures resulted in a continued slide for lead prices during the last quarter of 1996. Part of the problem was that a much–anticipated drawdown in stocks failed to materialize in the final part of the year, despite the Northern hemisphere entering what is usually its strongest period for demand. Prices have since been relatively flat with no uplift given by this year's mild winter. In the near term, price weakness is likely to continue until we see renewed strength in the battery market.

London Metal Exchange Cash Price

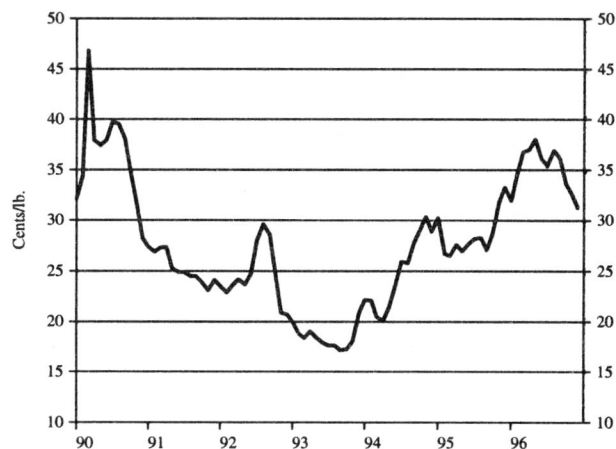

International Markets

Major OECD countries dominate lead consumption, accounting for two–thirds of the world total, but their importance has been declining for many years. The market share of developing countries generally, and the Asian newly industrializing countries (NICs) in particular, has risen dramatically.

1996 was an exciting year for the world lead market, with LME prices rallying to five–year highs, but the market headed down at the end of the year without much support from the demand side. Another important factor that has added to lead market weakness has been China's significant increase in exports. The surge in exports near the end of the year surprised the market and prompted further producer selling as fears of a glut of Chinese exports mounted.

The International Lead & Zinc Study Group (ILZSG) reported an increase in world lead consumption of 2.3% to 5.7 million tons in 1996, taking levels to over 5 million tons for the first time ever to outstrip supply. Demand was particularly strong in both Western and Eastern Europe and Southeast Asian countries (except Japan). WEFA forecasts that industrial production will continue to grow moderately in 1997 in the OECD and the NICs, resulting in increased global lead consumption.

Strong growth in mine production in Canada and Australia contributed to an 8% rise in Western World output to 2.16 million tons in 1996. However, the increase in total world output was limited by a fall in mine production in some Eastern countries, limiting the rise to 0.9% to 2.77 million tons, according to the ILZSG. World mine production is expected to rise in 1997, despite the recent temporary suspension of operations at Anvil's Faro mine in Canada. Total world refined lead output for 1996 dropped back 1.4% to 5.53 million tons, although Western World production rose marginally by 0.8% to 4.67 million tons. Refined production news has been fairly neutral, with capacity expansion reported in Australia balanced by the temporary closure of Metaleurop's Nordenham smelter in Germany.

For 1997, WEFA predicts that lead prices will hover around 30¢/lb on the LME. However, China's lead buying and selling activities constitute a risk to this forecast. Exports of Chinese lead helped to put a lid on world prices in 1996, rising by more than 50% compared to 1995. In the 1990s, China has been the major exporter of refined lead to the West. It will continue to be the big swing producer in the foreseeable future, with exports rising as prices increase and dropping as prices decrease.

Environmental Issues

Two key areas of environmental concern in the lead market are leaded gasoline and lead paint remaining in older housing stock. Both have been under increasing regulation due to health and air quality concerns.

- The U.S. Environmental Protection Agency (EPA) issued a direct final rule prohibiting the introduction into commerce of any gasoline for highway motor vehicle use that is produced with lead additives or contains incidental trace levels of more than 0.05 gram of lead per gallon.

- EPA and U.S. Department of Housing and Urban Development also jointly issued a final rule in 1996 requiring sellers and lessors to disclose the presence of known lead–based paint and/or lead–based paint hazards as part of the sale or lease of their housing.

Zinc

The United States has the largest single–country consumption of zinc. About one–fourth of that demand is supplied from domestic sources, while three–fourths of apparent consumption are imported.

Among all the industrial metals, zinc is the fourth widely used after iron, aluminum, and copper. Most zinc is used for galvanizing and diecasting, brass (as an alloying metal with copper), and in its chemical form in paints and rubber.

Galvanizing represents the largest intermediate use of zinc, and its share has grown rapidly in the last few years, largely at the expense of zinc diecastings. It accounted for 55% of the total U.S. zinc consumption in 1996, and its share is still rising.

The zinc mining industry is quite different from that of other non–ferrous metals. There is a high level of co–product and by–product metal production. These mines also produce lead, silver, copper, or gold as well as zinc, which is normally the main product. Zinc mine output is therefore heavily influenced by price and market developments for all of these metals.

In 1996, zinc production in the United States was flat, owing to limited capacity expansion and weak zinc prices. Despite the mildly bullish prospects for zinc demand, the U.S. zinc industry is not able to really benefit. We have available cheap and easily–accessed imports from Canada and Mexico, and U.S. capacity growth will be limited.

Zinc's Major U.S. Uses, 1996

Galvanizing	55%
Zinc Alloys	20%
Brass	11%
Other Uses	14%

Demand

The United States is the largest consumer of zinc and zinc products, accounting for about one–fifth of Western consumption. However, domestic metal production capacity supports less than one–fourth of the quantity consumed. Canada and Mexico are the leading sources of zinc imports to the United States, because of geographical proximity and low tariffs. Under the North American Free Trade Agreement (NAFTA), which went into effect in 1994, tariffs on zinc and zinc–containing products from Canada and Mexico were either eliminated or lowered significantly. Canada is the largest zinc producer in the world, and Mexico is the sixth–largest.

U.S. zinc consumption has been on a steady upward trend in the 1990s, averaging about 4% growth per year. Consumption has been following the two major zinc end–user industries: motor vehicles and construction. Zinc is used in the form of coatings, diecastings, rubber, and brass in the automobile manufacturing process, totaling about 40 pounds of zinc used on average in a U.S.–manufactured car. Zinc's use in light vehicles continues to rise because of the corrosion protection, the added strength, and the durability offered by zinc–coated steel. U.S. vehicle production fell slightly in 1996, although it remained at a healthy level. This took a toll on zinc demand, however, which grew by only 1%.

However, overall zinc demand is still in good shape, and prospects look fairly bright for the year ahead. An area of particular growth has been galvanized sheet, especially demand for hot–dipped galvanized (HDG) strip, for which prices have increased significantly in the United States. A new potential source of growth for zinc is in steel used in framing of residential construction in place of lumber framing. This use will likely be concentrated in galvanized steel, especially hot–dipped material.

Supply

The value of the zinc mined in 1996 in the United States was about $800 million. Almost all of it came from 22 mines, and about 77% came from only five mines. On a regional basis, Alaska alone accounted for more than half of the output. Domestic mine production increased slightly in 1996, because of increased output at the Red Dog Mine in Alaska, the leading producer in the United States.

Exports of zinc ore and concentrates increased by 430 tons in 1996. The United States is expected to remain the world's largest exporter of zinc concentrates and the world's largest importer of zinc metal for at least the next decade, because of inadequate primary refinery production capacity. The total available primary annual capacity in 1996 was 250,000 tons, at three major smelters – Zinc Corp. of America's Monaca smelter, Savage Zinc's Clarksville smelter, and Korea Zinc's Sauget smelter. U.S. refined zinc (including both primary slab zinc and secondary slab zinc) totaled 360,000 tons in 1996, marginally down from its 1995 level. This output of refined zinc is expected to edge up slightly in the next few years due to minor capacity expansion underway. In 1996, an estimated 355,000 tons of zinc was recovered in waste and scrap, adding a remarkable amount of supply to the market.

Prices

A U.S. producer price (as published by *Metals Week*) is quoted for Special High Grade (SHG) zinc. This is intended to be representative of U.S. list prices for delivered metal, and is traditionally at a few cents per pound premium to the London Metal Exchange (LME) price, reflecting the cost of shipping metal from Europe to the United States and the different market conditions between the United States and Europe. The U.S. producer price SHG averaged 51¢/lb in 1996, finishing the year at 53¢/lb. Since then, the price has jumped 20%, reaching a 4–year high. The LME price has also surged, largely due to a substantial decline of stocks on the LME lately. WEFA does not expect the current strength in zinc prices to be abated in the near term. HDG demand is strong, particularly in the United States, while a recovery in Japan is emerging.

International Market

Large multinational companies have traditionally dominated zinc mining and smelting, and concentration has increased since the early 1990s. The six largest smelting companies, located in Australia, Canada, and Europe, now account for as much as half of Western slab output. In the future, capacity in emerging economies, including China, India, Korea, and Taiwan, will increase, while structural change in the European and Japanese zinc industries continues.

London Metal Exchange SHG Cash Price

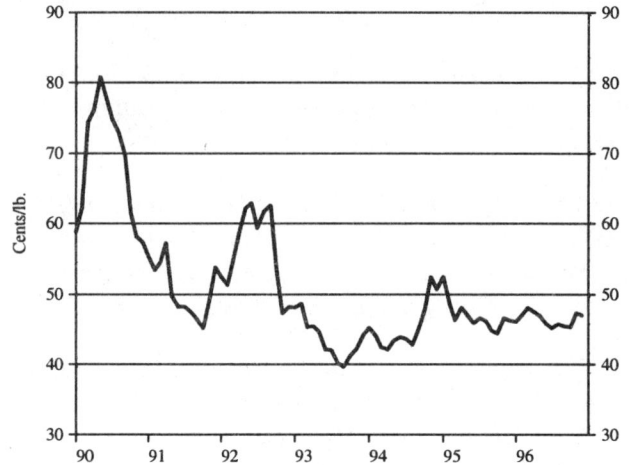

Zinc averaged 46.5¢/lb on the LME in 1996, down marginally from its 1995 level. Meanwhile, the LME stock level was down more than 150,000 tons. The lack of direction of prices throughout the year was not that surprising given that LME stocks finished the year at 506,825 tons – a higher than normal level.

World zinc consumption totaled 7.54 million tons, similar to consumption in 1995, according to the International Lead and Zinc Study Group (ILZSG). Western World zinc consumption totaled 6.28 million tons, also virtually unchanged from 1995 levels. In the years ahead, western world demand growth will be slow, but consumption will grow in the developing countries, with Latin America recovering well and Asian demand remaining buoyant. WEFA expects world zinc consumption to rebound moderately in 1997.

Total world zinc mine output rose 0.9% in 1996 to roughly 7 million tons – the highest production since 1992. This figure includes a 5.5% rise in Western World output to about 5.6 million tons, despite several temporary mine closures at the end of 1996. While Western World mine output grew sharply last year, refined zinc metal production dropped back marginally from the record levels seen in 1995 to an estimated 7.3 million tons. A modest increase is likely in 1997 with smelters expected to produce closer to planned levels, and rising LME prices encouraging higher rates of capacity utilization. Imminent capacity expansions are expected to take place in Japan, Korea, and Australia.

Moderate growth in zinc demand in major economies this year, coupled with a small rise in net imports from the former Eastern Bloc, suggests that stocks will continue to fall in 1997. Against such a background, WEFA expects a modest increase in the spot LME zinc price in 1997. However, Chinese exports of zinc to the Western market could influence the pricing outlook.

Having emerged as a major exporter to the West in 1993, China has had a significant bearing on the zinc market for some years now. China's zinc production is approximately 2 to 3 million tons higher than its domestic consumption, though the latter is rising. The LME zinc price is an important factor in influencing how much material China exports. For example, rising prices in the second half of last year supported a higher level of exports than were seen in 1995. A higher zinc price in 1997 could potentially bring more metal into Western markets, capping any further rise in prices.

Other Industry Issues

The Fate of the Penny

According to a study done by the General Accounting Office(GAO), the penny is no longer profitable because the cost of making it exceeds its value. The 98%–zinc penny uses approximately 35,000 tons of zinc annually. However, some advocacy groups for the poor and charitable organizations strongly favor retention of the penny, as the poor and the elderly make more small cash purchases.

Substitution

There is no effective substitute for zinc in large–volume galvanizing, but in the coating of steel sheet and strip, high–aluminum–zinc alloys such as Galvalume have displaced high–zinc alloys. Aluminum, plastics, and magnesium are major competitors as diecasting materials. Plastic coatings, paint, and cadmium and aluminum alloy coatings are replacing zinc for corrosion protection, and aluminum alloys have been displacing brass in car radiators. Many elements are substitutes for zinc in chemical, electronic, and pigment uses.

Aluminum

The aluminum industry ended 1996 on a somewhat positive note. Prices bottomed out during the last quarter at levels not seen since mid–1994, but quickly rebounded to reach close to the 80 cents/lb. mark. While the first half of 1996 brought increasing aluminum stock levels, weak consumption, and falling prices, the end of the year was marked by relatively strong demand, falling inventories, and a price comeback. Higher–than–anticipated aircraft production contributed to aluminum orders — transportation equipment is the single largest market for aluminum, accounting for nearly one–third of total domestic shipments.

Because of the first half's weakness, overall aluminum shipments for 1996 were down 2.5% from 1995. The renewed strength in demand experienced toward the end of the year should continue over the next five years, spurred by steady growth in virtually all of aluminum's major markets. Demand from motor vehicles and parts, whose decline in production largely contributed to the drop in last year's aluminum shipments, should be fairly stable in the near term, with only small output declines likely. In addition, aircraft and machinery will continue to grow. The aircraft industry is currently benefiting from a surge in orders from both domestic and foreign airlines, as these companies strive to replace their aging fleet. The boom in the high–tech sector of the machinery industry continues, albeit at a less frantic pace than that of the last three years.

In the long run, the desire to manufacture lighter products in a range of industries will allow aluminum to flourish. WEFA forecasts that aluminum shipments will grow at an average annual rate of 3% to 3.5% in volume terms over the next ten years, and price increases should average 1% to 2%. Global aluminum supply is expected to outpace world demand during that period, which should keep aluminum prices under control both in the United States and overseas.

Domestic Market

With production of 3.6 million metric tons in 1996 and a 20% share of the global market, the United States is the leading world producer of aluminum, followed by the former Soviet Union and Canada. The Aluminum Company of America (Alcoa) produces nearly 30% of U.S. aluminum. The second largest domestic producer is Alumax, which accounts for 15% of total U.S. production; it is followed by Reynolds (10%) and Kaiser (6%). The largest agglomeration of aluminum capacity in the United States is in the Pacific Northwest (Oregon, Montana, and Washington); this region boasts 38% of the country's aluminum production capacity. The Ohio Valley accounts for 31% of capacity, and the rest of the United States the remainder.

The huge U.S. aluminum capacity is not sufficient to satisfy the country's appetite for aluminum. The United States is not only the world's largest aluminum producer but also the largest consumer, with a 25% share of global aluminum consumption. This high demand makes the United States the second largest importer of aluminum as

well. Most of the added metal comes from Canada, which supplies about 60% of the U.S. aluminum imports.

The demand for aluminum is attributed mainly to two major industries.

- Leading aluminum consumption is the transportation industry, especially automotive. In 1991 transportation made up only 17% of the aluminum market, and was the second largest consumer of aluminum behind containers and packaging. However, this metal's unique properties (non–corrosive, light weight, and strength), which make it an ideal substitute for steel in several automotive applications, contributed to a rapid increase in its use by the automotive industry. Today, the transportation share of the aluminum market is more than 27%.

- The containers and packaging sector is currently the second largest end user of aluminum in the United States. This sector, which lost its leading position to transportation in the last several years, represents almost a quarter of all aluminum consumed by the

United States. Aluminum cans now control nearly 100% of the beverage can market, having displaced steel. However, aluminum cans are now being threatened by beverage companies heading toward cheaper plastic containers.

U.S. Aluminum Consumption by Industry

Transportation	27.2%
Containers & Packaging	24.0%
Building & Construction	12.7%
Electrical	6.9%
Consumer Durables	6.5%
Machinery & Equipment	6.0%
Other	2.9%

International Markets

China made a dramatic impact in the global aluminum market in 1996 by dramatically increasing its imports — its imports of ingot surged 74%, and it increased imports of other aluminum materials as well. In other areas of Asia, including the ASEAN (industrializing southeast Asian) countries, demand remained strong last year, although we are seeing a slight slowdown from the torrid pace of the past few years. In North America, Mexico is fast recovering from its 1995 economic crisis. Mexico's real GDP grew by 4.5% in 1996; WEFA is forecasting growth above this level for the next several years, which should be favorable for U.S. aluminum exports to this country.

Several countries are adding significantly to their aluminum production capacity, which should result in a slightly oversupplied global market during the next few years. This oversupply will keep aluminum prices largely under control. Among the countries adding capacity are Iceland, Australia, and Dubai. China is also expected to increase its output of aluminum, which will help to satisfy its fast-growing domestic demand and reduce the level of its imports.

Last year, Russia began to really get its product into Western markets. We anticipate that it will export between 2 and 2.5 million tons of aluminum this year. Even though Russia's aluminum industry is now considered an integral part of the global market

economy, a good portion of Russia's contribution to Western supplies has ended up as surplus stashed away in warehouses. Many European and North American companies have backed and/or taken a stake in the Russian aluminum industry. The investment by these companies had added much needed equipment and essential technological improvements that Russia itself could not contribute, leading to a dramatic increase in Russian aluminum exports to countries outside the Commonwealth of Independent States.

Domestic Aluminum Prices

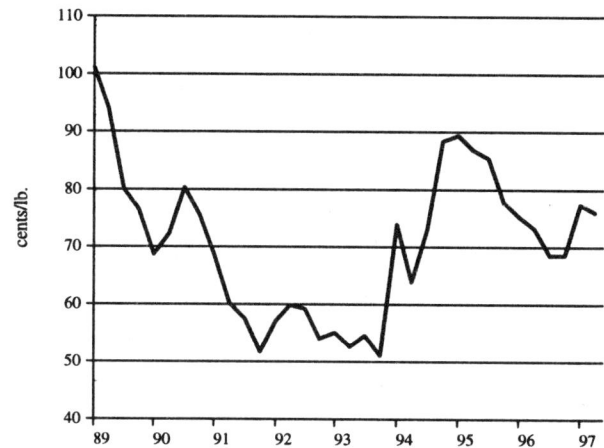

Automotive Uses

Automakers are predicting that aluminum usage in block engines and vehicle frames will quadruple by the turn of the century. Audi, a strong proponent of aluminum usage, is releasing their A8 model, which is made up almost entirely of aluminum, this year. The car is 1000 pounds lighter than a steel sedan counterpart. Ford's management is also moving toward aluminum, and is planning to manufacture aluminum block engines by 2001.

Reducing the cost of producing aluminum–intensive vehicles has provided a great incentive to substitute aluminum for other more traditional metals. The cost gap between aluminum and conventional steel bodies is closing. In the long run, if improvements continue in material and parts manufacturing processes, the cost gap will continue to shrink, and aluminum–intensive cars could be made available at about the same price as steel cars. In addition to better metal production and parts–fabricating methods, the factors that are likely to help reduce the gap include optimized car and component designs and refinements in the recycling process.

Copper

While U.S. consumption of copper was up 4% in 1996, prices fell. Average yearly COMEX Copper prices in 1996 finished down 20% from 1995, but this decline in no way reflected the true market conditions. The past year was led astray by the "Sumitomo Scandal", a big event in a specialized market. Although the scandal happened in Japan, the copper market around the world is heavily interlinked, and it had effects on the United States and other countries.

Copper demand and prices for the next several years look positive, but slower economic growth late in 1997 and early in 1998, thanks to the Fed's interest rate management, may put a damper on copper consumption in the United States in the short term. Construction, definitely an interest–rate–sensitive sector, was a key factor behind higher copper consumption in 1996, and its growth is expected to slow by year–end.

The Year Of The Scandal

Copper prices on the COMEX were trading in the $1.20–per–pound range in June 1996 before news hit that Yasou Hamanaka, the major copper trader for the Sumitomo company in Japan, was hiding copper stocks and falsifying contracts to protect his positions in the market. Mr. Hamanaka was trying to corner the market and had artificially inflated prices by 15 to 20 cents/lb. for over a year. Because he took long positions in the market, Mr. Hamanaka, who held a huge portion of global copper stock, falsely stated the amount of stock that his company controlled and gave the illusion that the market was a lot tighter than it actually was.

The result of the scandal was a price drop of nearly 30 cents/lb. overnight, and the market took nearly 4 months to recover. Prices finally climbed in October by more than 9% and closed the year at $1.09/lb.

The recovery on the price side was greatly aided by high copper consumption in the U.S. market in many industries. Copper buyers enjoyed an unusual situation — high demand for copper products accompanied by low copper prices.

Demand Remained Strong

U.S. copper consumption was in excess of 2.6 million tons in 1996, up more than 4% from 1995. Two key factors drove this healthy performance.

COMEX Copper Prices

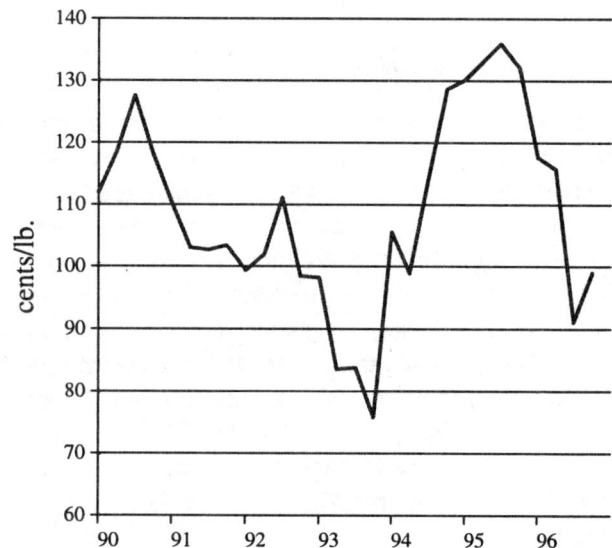

First, construction was solid. Due to low interest rates and moderate weather conditions, housing and commercial building were strong. This construction growth lead to a high demand for copper waterworks, which accounts for more than 20% of all copper demand in the United States. The waterworks industry is made up of valves, water meters, tubes, and pipes. Copper demand from tube producers jumped 11.2% in 1996 and hit a new record of 657 million pounds. Copper tubing benefited specifically from the high demand for air conditioning and cooling devices (ACR). Other areas in the copper sector also benefited from construction in 1996; building wire demand surged 33%.

The second factor helping copper demand in 1996 was the strength from the computer industry and internet access. Demand for copper from data cable producers grew by 9% last year, and is likely to jump 15% — 20%, in 1997. The telecommunication industry was another source of double–digit growth in copper demand. The expansion of home telephone lines, often for internet connection for home computers, was the key source of this growth.

1996 U.S. Copper Cable Demand Growth

	% Change
Building Wire	33%
Magnetic Wire	18%
Telecommunication	12%
Data Cable	9%
Power Cable	8%
Automotive	7%
Miscellaneous	13%

Copper Facts and Players

U.S. output of mined copper ranks second in global copper production only to Chile, the king of the copper world. The United States supplies about 20% of world copper production, and ranks first in production of refined copper. Domestic copper is mined in the Midwest and the Southwest, with Arizona accounting for about 50% of U.S. output and New Mexico about 20%.

The leading copper companies in the United States are Phelps Dodge, accounting for 23% of refined copper with sales in 1996 of $3.3 billion, ASARCO with sales of $2.8 billion and a 25% share of refined copper, Kennecott with sales of $885 million and a 12% share, Southwire Co. with sales of $1.7 billion and a 7% share, and Cyprus, with sales of $1.6 billion.

Outlook

The U.S. copper market is due for a cooling–off period. Production is likely to grow by 4% to 4.5% over the next few years, and consumption by 2.5% to 3.5%. This slowdown in consumption will come from many sources, as the U.S. economy slows, but especially from less buoyant activity in the construction market. Although price pressures will ease a bit as domestic demand moderates, strength in foreign markets will hold prices up. Over the next five years copper prices should average around $1.10 to $1.15 per pound.

Growing foreign markets, especially the rapidly–developing countries of Asia, will be importing an increasing share of the world's copper output. China's imports of copper surged 13% in 1996 in response to last year's low prices but also because its demand for the metal is on a long–term growth path. South Korea and some of the ASEAN nations that are investing in an automobile production base are other likely sources of demand growth.

Japanese demand for copper should pick up, as the weak yen has begun to boost Japanese automakers' competitiveness. Japan is the second largest consumer of copper, but over the last decade produced less than 1% of its requirements.

Chapter 17: Fabricated Metal Products

Fabricated Metal Products

The fabricated metal products industry is made up of a large number of sub–industries, companies which manufacture various types of metal products for both personal and industrial consumption. Over half of the broad industry's shipments, however, are produced by just seven industry categories. In order of shipment dollar size, they are: automobile stampings; sheet metal work; metal cans and shipping containers; non–automotive metal stampings; hardware not elsewhere classified (n.e.c.); fabricated structural metal; and fabricated plate work and boiler shops.

For the fabricated metal products industry overall, we expect modest volume growth of about 2% per year over the next decade with annual price increases of 2% to 3%. Considerable growth variation will exist between the industry's various sub–components, however, and import pressure will continue unabated for many products.

Demand Factors

Automotive stamping plants tend to be large operations, with over 80% of all such firms in the United States employing over 100 workers. Competition is intense from Japanese imports, particularly because Japanese producers can change dies much more rapidly than can U.S. firms. These competitive pressures led to considerable investment by the Big Three U.S. automakers in the last few years for new presses and new stamping plants, particularly those tied to assembly facilities. The health of this industry depends upon the health of North American light vehicle sales, and the share of those sales accruing to North American manufacturers. With the U.S. economy in its sixth year of expansion and interest rates rising, vehicle sales will be a bit slower in 1997 and 1998 than in 1996. North American light vehicle facilities have increased market share dramatically in the 1990s, and while further gains are unlikely, share will not be lost either.

Sheet metal work covers establishments primarily engaged in manufacturing sheet metal work for buildings, stovepipes, light tanks, and other products made of sheet metal. The rate of home–building is expected to slow somewhat in 1997 and 1998 and then remain rather flat for the remainder of the ten year period. The overall growth in industrial production is likely to ease slightly going forward as higher interest rates take hold and the economic recovery ages. Modest gains (1.5% to 2% per year) in real sheet metal work volume are likely over the next few years.

Metal can and container sales have been hurt by trends in the food processing industry. The food market has turned toward easy–to–prepare offerings, especially microwave–ready food products, which are usually packaged in either paper or plastic. Within the industry, however, aluminum containers continue to make gains against those made out of steel. Aluminum has all but taken over the beverage container business due to its environmental attractiveness through easier recycling and its lighter weight. In addition, opportunities exist for aluminum containers overseas where production is still skewed toward steel; this opportunity is due primarily to aluminum's environmental advantages which are increasingly becoming attractive to markets in the developed countries. Due to its packaging properties, however, steel is still dominant in metal food cans and containers, and it still has roughly half the market for non–food containers. The metal container industry is mature and facing a challenge from microwave–ready packaging and other convenience foods. Expect modest growth overall for this industry, with most of the gains going to aluminum.

The fabricated structural metal industry consists of three primary categories. Fabricated structural metal for buildings accounts for roughly half of total output; structural metal for bridges accounts for about 7%; and other fabricated structural metal, both specified and non–specified, accounts for roughly 40% of the total. Residential construction is expected to slow somewhat in 1997 and 1998, then remain on a fairly flat course on a trend basis for the next 5–10 years. Commercial construction will advance strongly in 1997 but will settle back into a longer term pattern of 1% to 2% growth per year. Industrial construction, however, has already weakened, and will likely stay rather flat for the duration of this expansion. Bridge construction will be the beneficiary of the release of moneys from the federal government's transportation funding program and should be a strong sector within the fabricated structural metal industry. These same end–market conditions are also the key factors for demand for pre–fabricated metal buildings.

For the fabricated metal products industry overall, WEFA expects modest volume growth of about 2% per year over the next decade with annual price increases of about 3%. Considerable variation will exist between the growth rates of the industry's various sub–components, however, and import pressure will continue unabated for many industry sectors.

The Outlook

Globalization and competition from countries offering lower wages and less stringent environmental standards will be ongoing issues in the fabricated metal products industry. The pressure to cut costs will continue for the foreseeable future. Consolidation will also continue, as firms attempt to achieve economies of scale and expand by buying competitors in markets that are mature and are expected to show little growth over the next few years. Finally, as production technology continues to advance, manufacturers will need workers with higher levels of technical skills, and they will have to compete for those better trained workers with other industries that have the same need.

The fabricated metal products industry is one of the most diverse of manufacturing sectors; it provides products to a broad range of both consumer and business users. This diversification in end–markets helps to reduce the overall risk to the industry's growth; however, it makes the industry susceptible in a small way to everyone's problems.

Fabricated Metal Products
Growth in Sales (Line) and Volume (Bar)

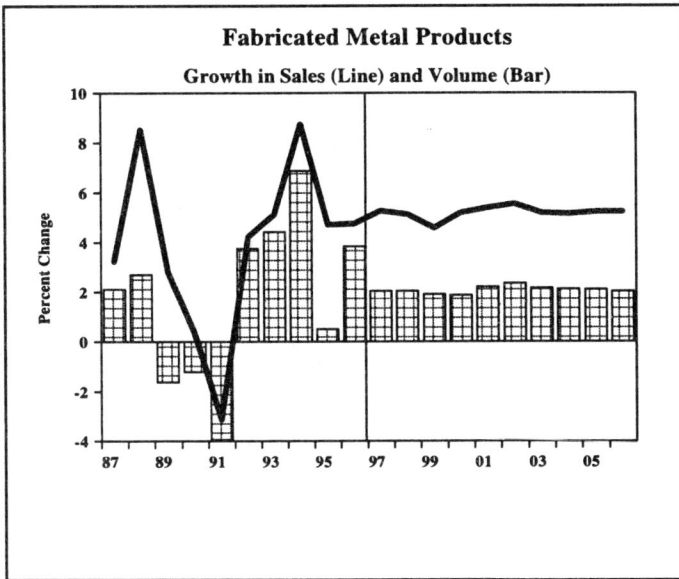

Fabricated Metal Products
Growth in Product Prices

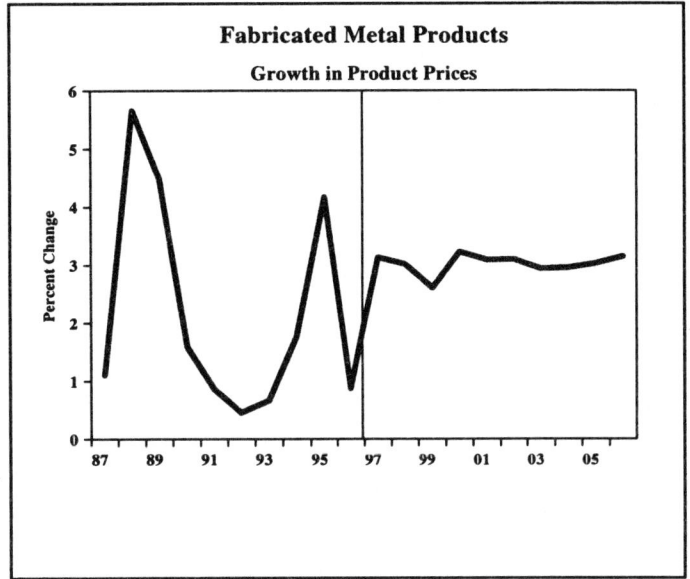

```
Fabricated Metal Products
 SIC 34
                                                                          Compound Ann Avg Growth
                       1990   1991   1992   1993   1994   1995   1996   1997   1998   1986-1996 1996-2006

Sales
         Billions of $ 165.04 159.89 166.64 175.18 190.52 199.48 208.95 219.94 231.23
         % Change        0.4   -3.1    4.2    5.1    8.8    4.7    4.7    5.3    5.1      3.9       5.2

  Volume  % Change       -1.2   -3.9    3.8    4.4    6.9    0.5    3.8    2.1    2.1      1.7       2.1
  Prices  % Change        1.6    0.9    0.5    0.7    1.8    4.2    0.9    3.1    3.0      2.1       3.0

Exports
         Billions of $   5.32   6.02   6.37   6.86   7.92   8.80   9.91  10.55  11.23
         % Change         9.1   13.1    5.8    7.6   15.5   11.1   12.5    6.5    6.5     15.1       5.8
Imports
         Billions of $   7.11   6.91   7.80   8.66  10.26  11.33  12.29  12.90  13.85
         % Change        -1.4   -2.7   12.9   10.9   18.5   10.5    8.4    5.0    7.3      7.3       6.7

Apparent Consumption
         Billions of $ 166.82 160.78 168.07 176.98 192.86 202.01 211.33 222.29 233.85
     Nominal % Change     0.0   -3.6    4.5    5.3    9.0    4.7    4.6    5.2    5.2      3.7       5.2
        Real % Change    -1.5   -4.4    4.1    4.6    7.1    0.6    3.7    2.0    2.1      1.6       2.2
```

Chapter 18: Industrial and Electrical Machinery

Turbines and Generator Sets

Turbine and generator set sales have been growing steadily, as the worldwide appetite for electric power continues to grow. The United States leads the world in production of turbines, and exports are a growing percentage of this business.

As the domestic market tightens in response to deregulation of the electric power generation industry, sales to the expanding economies of the developing world will pick up the slack. Deregulation of domestic electric power generation has forced cost–cutting domestic utilities and non–utility generators to cut back on capital expenditures, including spending for turbine and generator sets. The bright spot in the U.S. market is likely to be applications of the gas turbine for the new class of non–utility generators.

Demand Conditions

Domestic

Over the past decade, growth in prices and shipments contributed to a 6.2% annual average climb in turbine and generator set sales. After gaining ground in 1997 and 1998, sales growth will level off.

Technology is profoundly affecting the character of the turbine and generator set industry, and technical innovation is also driving deregulation of its key customer, the electric power generation industry. Combined cycle gas turbines now boast compactness, fuel–efficiency, and environmental safeguards. This improved technology has spawned a new class of power equipment consumers, non–utility generators (NUGs). Non–utility generators include producers that are exempt from government regulations, independent power producers, and industrial generators. These NUGs were given a boost by the reforms of the Energy Policy Act of 1992. Then, last year, the Federal Energy Regulatory Commission opened the wholesale electricity market to competition. Forty–nine states are also debating reforms to retail electric service.

Competition among power generators will increasingly push them to cut costs, ultimately shrinking domestic orders for turbine and generator sets. Domestic shipments will stall over the next decade, averaging virtually no growth.

Counteracting this trend is the need for new domestic capacity to meet growing energy demands. WEFA estimates that generating capacity will grow at an average annual rate of 1.6% from 773.3 gigawatts (GW) in 1996 to 904.8 GW by 2006. NUG capacity will climb by close to 6.6% per year over the next decade, compared with utility capacity growth of 1.1%. Utilities and non–utility generators both favor combustion turbines, which are replacing steam turbines as the dominant generating source.

Two decades ago, it was profitable for utilities to build large coal–fired, nuclear, or hydro–powered plants to generate electricity. Turbine and generator set advances now give new fossil fuel–fired generating plants an edge: new plants require shorter lead times, have lower investment hurdles, and use cheaper fuel sources. Nuclear fuel costs cannot compete with currently low fossil fuel prices: coal, fuel oil, and natural gas have all stabilized in price and should show only moderate increases, in the 2.0% to 3.0% range, over the next decade.

Nuclear and traditional coal–fired power equipment sales will continue to slump, while expenditure on natural gas–fired facilities grows. In fact, over the next 20 years, the Department of Energy estimates that as much as half of the new power generating capacity added in the United States could be in the form of gas turbine systems. Most of the expenditure on nuclear facilities will be applied to maintenance of existing nuclear–fueled turbines and generator sets.

Coal continues to be the cheapest fossil fuel, so in order to minimize fuel costs, major manufacturers are developing natural gas–fired units that also run on gasified coal. Power equipment sales to renewable resource–powered generators have gained incrementally. Biomass, principally in the form of wood residues, has fueled power generation on a limited scale to date.

Technology improvements also allow more large manufacturers to develop their own generating capacity, providing industrial users with bargaining power in their negotiations with utilities. Thus far paper and chemical manufacturers have set up the most new capacity. Small municipal utilities, households, and small communities may feasibly own their own small generators in the future, further shifting the demand base for turbines and generator sets.

Exports

The strongest component of turbine and generator set shipments has been exports. Exports averaged 14.8% growth over the past decade, while overall shipments grew by 3%. Developing countries have become the export growth source, as many are initiating infrastructure projects. Strong economic growth in developing Asia, Latin America, Eastern Europe, and Russia is expected to continue to drive orders for new power equipment.

Manufacturers cite Asia as the largest power market in the world. Orders for sets to equip Asian power plants should continue their upward trend. The more developed markets of east Asia, in particular Korea, have produced the largest share of orders. Steam turbines dominate developing Asia's orders, reflecting the construction of large solid–fuel–fired and nuclear projects. Central and southern Asia, primarily China and India, also has a pressing need for power generation equipment.

Gross Domestic Product (GDP) growth in developing countries, coupled with acute need for additional power generation capacity in some countries, should translate into greater U.S. exports of turbines and generator sets to developing markets. The establishment of stable financing remains the only real restraint on orders.

Traditional markets of Canada and Western Europe will lend support on a smaller scale. Japan also looks to add capacity, becoming a potential export destination. A leveling off of the U.S. exchange rate will contribute to the expansion of exports as well. WEFA estimates that turbine and generator set exports will climb at a 5.8% compound annual rate over the next decade.

Supply Conditions

The Department of Energy hopes to further improve gas turbine technology by co–sponsoring a program with large domestic turbine manufacturers. The Advanced Turbine Systems program seeks to develop a high efficiency, low cost, environmentally sound gas turbine by 2000. The top domestic manufacturers are represented among the participants — Solar Turbines, Inc., Westinghouse Electric Corporation, General Electric, and Allison Engine Company.

Competitiveness among domestic turbine and generator manufacturers and from abroad has prompted an increasing number of partnerships in the industry. For example, Stewart and Stevenson Services, Inc. recently added to its distribution network by acquiring Sierra Detroit Diesel Allison, Inc.

Strategic alliances with foreign manufacturers or distributors are helping U.S. companies to gain a foothold in export markets. The parent company to Solar Turbines, Inc., Caterpillar, Inc., recently acquired engine production leader MaK Motoren GmbH. General Electric took on two partners in a Mexican project last year, while Westinghouse partnered with Shanghai Electric Corp. to acquire 35% of a Chinese turbine manufacturing facility. Maintained relationships include Westinghouse and Hyundai Heavy Industries in Korea.

In late 1997, Westinghouse Electric Corporation will spin off its industrial businesses including its turbine business, the Power Generation Business Unit, to become CBS Corporation.

New product offerings will also squeeze the market, and applications for turbines continue to expand. Small gas turbines are set to power personal watercraft and small boats.

Pricing

Turbines and generator set prices have averaged 3.0% growth over the past ten years, keeping pace with the overall U.S. economy. The healthy appetite for electricity helped to support steady price growth. Manufacturers have been able to make even moderate price increases stick.

Although prices dipped along with shipments last year, slight gains, in the 1.0% to 2.0% range, are forecasted in the near term. Long term prospects are sound, and prices should average 2.5% growth through 2006.

Some cyclicality still exists in the turbine and generator set industry, however, it is much more subdued than in recent history. The near–equilibrium characteristics of the current U.S. economy mute former whip–saw cycles. A lackluster domestic market and stable prices will likely combine with rocketing growth rates overseas to move turbine and generator set real consumption into the next decade at a modest 1.2% rate

Turbines and Turbine Generator Sets
Growth in Sales (Line) and Volume (Bar)

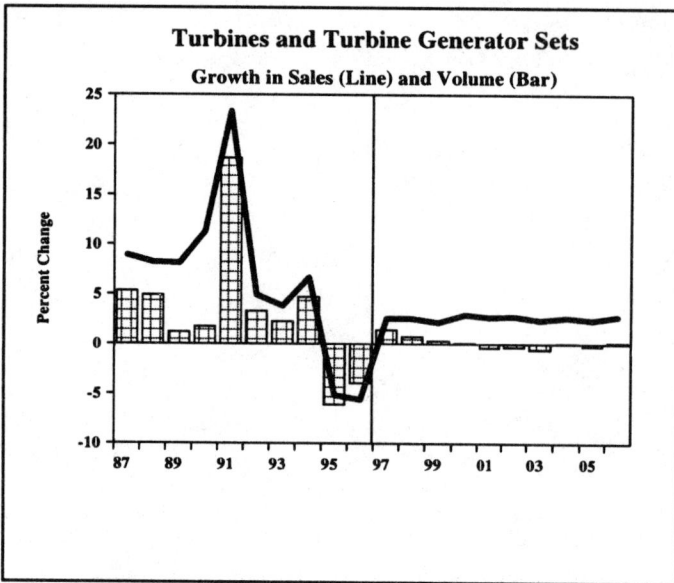

Turbines and Turbine Generator Sets
Growth in Product Prices

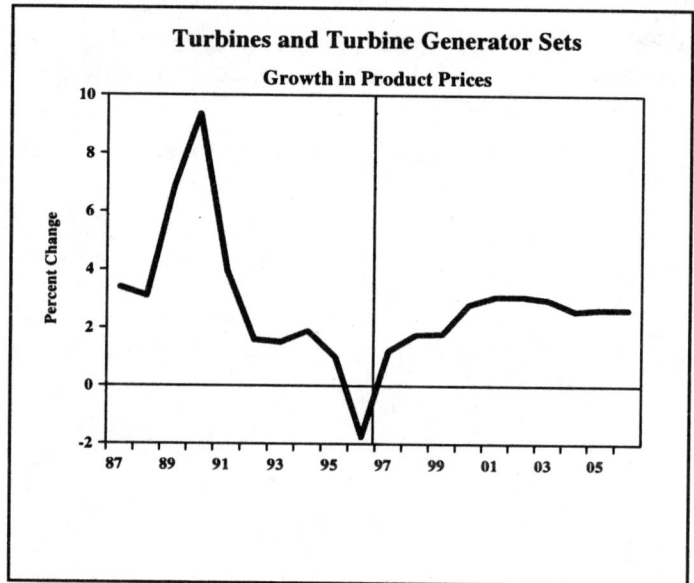

```
Turbines and Turbine Generator Sets
  SIC 3511
```

		1990	1991	1992	1993	1994	1995	1996	1997	1998	Compound Ann Avg Growth 1986-1996	1996-2006
Sales												
	Billions of $	4.45	5.49	5.76	5.98	6.38	6.05	5.71	5.86	6.01		
	% Change	11.3	23.4	4.9	3.8	6.7	-5.2	-5.6	2.6	2.6	6.2	2.6
Volume	% Change	1.7	18.7	3.3	2.3	4.7	-6.1	-3.9	1.4	0.8	3.0	0.1
Prices	% Change	9.3	4.0	1.6	1.5	1.9	1.0	-1.8	1.2	1.8	3.0	2.5
Exports												
	Billions of $	3.08	3.61	4.06	4.51	5.06	5.79	5.67	6.10	6.51		
	% Change	23.1	17.3	12.5	11.0	12.2	14.6	-2.2	7.5	6.8	14.8	5.8
Imports												
	Billions of $	3.68	4.04	4.62	5.28	5.43	7.05	7.24	7.54	7.85		
	% Change	6.7	9.8	14.4	14.3	2.8	29.8	2.7	4.1	4.1	12.1	4.1
Apparent Consumption												
	Billions of $	5.05	5.92	6.32	6.75	6.75	7.31	7.28	7.30	7.35		
	Nominal % Change	2.1	17.2	6.7	6.8	0.0	8.2	-0.3	0.3	0.6	6.1	1.2
	Real % Change	-6.6	12.7	5.1	5.3	-1.9	7.2	1.4	-0.9	-1.1	3.0	-1.2

Internal Combustion Engines

Shipments of internal combustion engines are expected to grow by about 5.0% annually over the next ten years. About half of the sales gain will be due to volume growth, signaling an improvement from virtually no volume growth over the last ten years, and about half will come from price increases.

Key domestic markets such as industrial power generation, construction, farm, lawn and garden, and outboard motors will provide modest support. WEFA expects a replacement cycle to prop up demand in the commercial truck market as the current decade draws to a close. An acceleration in defense–related procurement is anticipated during the latter part of the ten–year period. Exports will become more important in the years ahead as developing nations in Latin America, Asia, and eastern Europe look to improve their infrastructure and industrial base.

Recent History

The demand for internal combustion engines fell 17% in 1990–91. Weakness in the industrial, construction, commercial truck, and marine markets was accompanied by a fall off in consumer demand for outboard motors and lawn and garden equipment. This depressed demand for engines of various sizes. Downsizing at the Department of Defense also hurt demand for engines.

Signs of life in the general economy triggered a rebound in internal combustion engines beginning in 1992, and shipments increased 5.6%. Over the next three years, 1993–95, shipments expanded by nearly 6% per year.

- Industrial plant expansion, construction activity, a record rebound in commercial trucks, and gains in the marine market provided considerable support.

- Better financial conditions in the farm sector boosted demand for internal combustion engines used in agricultural equipment.

- The strength in new home construction bolstered demand for power mowers.

- Improving consumer incomes had a positive impact on outboard motor sales.

- Finally, favorable economic conditions in a number of key foreign markets and a weak dollar boosted U.S. exports of internal combustion engines.

Last year, shipments fell by 6.6%. Industrial plant construction fell back after a very strong 1995, dampening demand for stationary power units. The transportation and farm markets contracted after achieving very impressive gains during the three previous years. Power mower, garden tractors, and snow thrower shipments fell 12%, depressing demand for smaller engines.

The number of production workers involved in the manufacture of internal combustion engines stood at 46,920 in 1988. Weakness in the economy and defense related reductions drove that number down to 37,970 by 1992, a decline of 19%. As the demand for internal combustion engines grew during the recovery, employment expanded to 40,530 by 1995, only to fall back to 39,040 last year.

The Outlook

Shipments of internal combustion engines are expected to grow by about 5.0% annually over the next ten years. About half of the sales gain will be due to volume growth, a marked improvement from virtually no volume growth over the last ten years, and the other half will come from price increases.

Key domestic markets such as industrial power generation, construction, farm, lawn and garden, and outboard motors will provide modest support. WEFA expects a replacement cycle to prop up demand in the commercial truck market as the current decade draws to a close. An acceleration in defense–related procurement is anticipated during the latter part of the ten–year period. Exports will become more important in the years ahead as developing nations in Latin America, Asia, and eastern Europe look to improve their infrastructure and industrial base.

Internal Combustion Engines
Growth in Sales (Line) and Volume (Bar)

Internal Combustion Engines
Growth in Product Prices

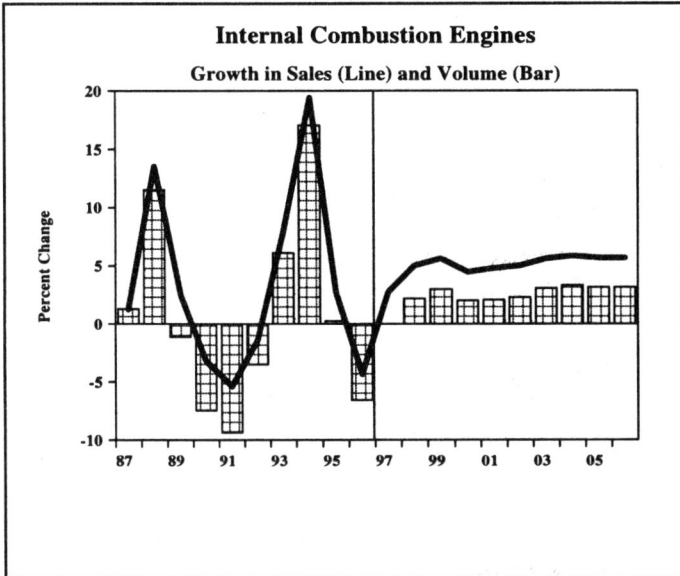

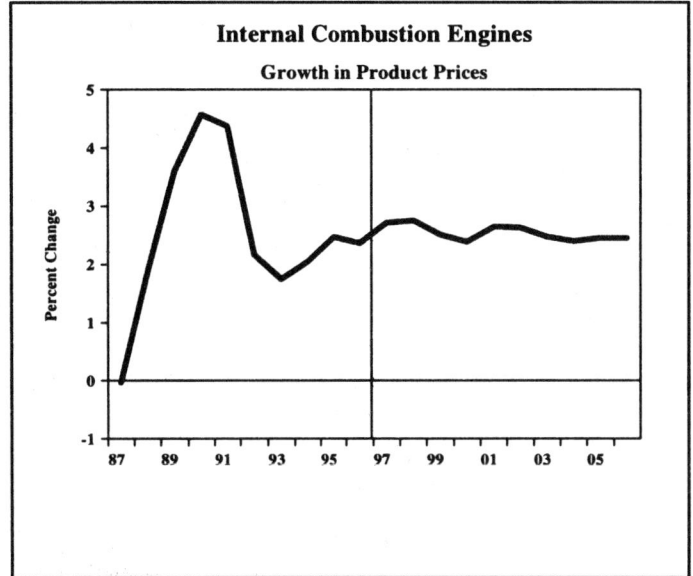

```
Internal Combustion Engines
SIC 3519

                                                                            Compound Ann Avg Growth
                      1990   1991   1992   1993   1994   1995   1996   1997   1998   1986-1996 1996-2006

Sales
       Billions of $  12.55  11.88  11.71  12.64  15.09  15.50  14.83  15.23  15.99
          % Change     -3.2   -5.4   -1.4    8.0   19.4    2.7   -4.4    2.7    5.0      3.0       5.0

  Volume  % Change     -7.5   -9.4   -3.5    6.1   17.0    0.2   -6.6    0.0    2.2      0.5       2.4
  Prices  % Change      4.6    4.4    2.2    1.7    2.1    2.5    2.4    2.7    2.7      2.5       2.5

Exports
       Billions of $   5.36   6.22   6.66   7.51   9.18  10.16  10.21  10.82  11.39
          % Change      4.1   16.1    7.1   12.7   22.2   10.7    0.5    6.0    5.3     13.6       4.3
Imports
       Billions of $   3.46   3.26   3.62   4.09   5.76   6.18   6.26   6.32   6.57
          % Change      1.7   -5.8   10.9   13.2   40.6    7.3    1.3    1.1    3.8      8.8       4.3

Apparent Consumption
       Billions of $  10.66   8.92   8.67   9.23  11.68  11.52  10.88  10.74  11.17
    Nominal % Change   -5.1  -16.3   -2.9    6.5   26.6   -1.3   -5.6   -1.3    4.0      0.0       5.3
       Real % Change   -9.3  -19.8   -4.9    4.6   24.0   -3.7   -7.8   -3.9    1.2     -2.4       2.7
```

18.7

Farm and Garden Equipment

The farm and garden equipment industry is expected to continue to expand in the near term, based on the strength of the U.S. agriculture sector and the general economy. Sales and apparent consumption are projected to increase in the 6.5% to 7.5% range, with the farm machinery industry growing at a modestly faster rate than garden machinery. The strong showing of agriculture from a global perspective is expected to lead to the United States being a net exporter of farm and garden equipment.

In the long term farm and garden equipment growth is expected to slow relative to the growth of the next few years, but there will be conflicting trends in key determinants of demand. Real interest rates are expected to peak in the near term and then gradually trend down. In the farm sector, acreage is projected to rise by 8 to 10 million, farm income is expected to weaken from the 1996 high level, and then improve as prices strengthen in the next decade. Government payments are scheduled to decline through fiscal year 2002, after which WEFA expects that the Federal sector will continue transition payments to agriculture at the $4 billion level.

The farm and garden machinery sector has been expanding steadily since 1993. After two successive years of decline in 1991 and 1992, when sales dropped from $16.8 billion in 1990 to $14.9 billion in 1992, steady growth in the U.S. economy and improvement in the agricultural sector pushed sales to nearly $22.5 billion in 1996. The 1991 and 1992 decline in sales was solely attributed to a cumulative decline of 16% in volume. Prices have been rising at the rate of 2% per annum over recent history and rose nearly 3% in 1991 and 2.3% in 1992.

The farm and garden machinery industry is dominated by the farm equipment segment. Excluding replacement parts, farm machinery accounts for about 60% of the total value of shipments. The largest component of the farm equipment category is wheel tractors, which accounts for between 45% and 50% of farm machinery shipments excluding replacement parts. Harvesting equipment accounts for about 25% of sales, and planting, dairying, and haying machinery each account for about 7% to 8% of shipments excluding parts. In 1996, replacement parts accounted for about $1.24 billion in additional farm machinery shipments.

There are two subsectors that make up the lawn and garden machinery category. One subsector is comprised of commercial turf and ground care equipment and the other is traditional residential lawn and garden equipment. The commercial segment is smaller than the residential component, but has grown at a faster rate over the past decade. Commercial turf and ground care equipment, which accounted for only 11% of the lawn and garden machinery shipments in 1985, grew to a 16% share in 1995.

Lawn and Garden Equipment

There are a number of factors that affect the lawn and garden segment of the farm and garden machinery industry. These factors include personal income, the number of single family housing starts and total units, and interest rates. Between 1985 and 1995, shipments of the lawn and garden segment doubled, rising from $3.5 billion to $7.0 billion, an average per annum increase of 6.6%.

Over the 1990–95 period, real disposable personal income growth averaged 2.8% per year. Income growth was weakest in 1991 (0.2%) and 1994 (1.4%), when total lawn and garden machinery shipments exhibited year–over–year declines. Income should improve at a 2.5% rate between now and 1998. Another economic driver is real interest rates, which were high in 1990 and 1991, at 4.0% or more, then dropped to 1.4% by 1993, and rose to 3.8% by 1996. Over the next two years, real rates are expected to rise by about 509 basis points, returning to the level of 1990 and 1991. The final key factor to consider is housing starts. The general economy was weak

Value of Shipments of Farm Machinery and Lawn and Garden Equipment,
By Type of Equipment: 1985 to 1995
(Value in millions of dollars)

	1985	1986	1987	1988	1989	1990	1991	1992	1993	1994	1995
Wheel Tractors, farm type	1,443.2	893.4	958.6	2/	2/	2/	2/	2/	2/	2/	2/
Farm dairy machines, sprayers, dusters, elevators, and farm blowers	403.6	371.7	364.7	434.8	478.2	516.0	449.2	469.9	588.7	709.0	766.2
Planting, seeding, and fertilizing machinery	453.3	371.2	409.1	508.6	638.2	676.2	601.0	634.1	802.3	949.1	833.1
Harvesting machinery	1,190.8	1,230.1	1,282.3	1,422.8	1,858.8	2,303.5	2,158.0	1,863.7	2,027.6	2,201.4	2,663.2
Haying machinery	498.1	383..4	433.7	574.6	731.1	875.1	659.1	558.2	622.8	784.6	728.3
Plows	111.0	75.3	74.6	117.7	130.8	136.0	119.6	107.4	124.3	144.7	146.2
Harrows, roller, pulverizers and similar	166.0	99.2	99.9	136.9	207.8	212.4	321.6	273.4	289.4	181.0	176.0
All other farm machinery and equipment 2/ 3/	1,051.9	933.1	1,186.5	3,002.8	3,586.6	4,091.1	3,397.2	3,327.8	3,679.9	4,293.2	4,584.0
Commercial turf and grounds care equipment	376.7	412.8	514.6	595.0	633.9	707.9	724.8	781.8	882.8	1,022.0	1,102.2
Lawn and garden equipment	3,155.1	3,385.8	3,979.9	3,937.0	3,708.5	4,101.8	3,972.9	4,251.7	4,763.2	5,750.2	5,869.0

Source: US Department of Commerce

2/ Data for Wheel tractors, farm type are included with All other farm machinery and equipment for years 1988 through 1995
  to avoid disclosing data for individual companies.

3/ Includes irrigation systems

in the early 1990s, and housing starts had been in decline since 1987. From 1987 to 1991, housing starts suffered a cumulative drop of 45%, which contributed to the 1991 downturn in lawn and garden machinery shipments. Starts are expected to weaken somewhat from their 1996 level over the next two years.

Overall, real personal disposable income will be a positive influence on lawn and garden equipment. Although interest rates are expected to rise in real terms, the increase should not be viewed as being too detrimental to shipments. Housing starts, though expected to weaken in 1997 and 1998, are not in a free fall as they were in the late 1980s. The growth in the lawn and garden segment should continue in the near term, but at a slower rate than that of the mid–1990s, likely in the 3% to 4% range.

Farm Equipment

The farm equipment segment of the farm and garden machinery sector has been experiencing a strong resurgence since 1992. Farm equipment shipments dropped 18% over two years, from $8.81 billion in 1990 to $7.26 billion in 1992. By 1995, shipments had grown to $9.9 billion (excluding parts for replacement units). Retail sales of tractors (greater than 40 horsepower) followed a similar pattern, falling from 66,300 units in 1990 to 52,800 units in 1992. Figures for 1996 indicate unit sales of tractors climbed to 66,900, a bit above the 1990 level.

Obviously, the fate of the farm equipment industry depends on the economic well being of the farm sector. The U.S. farm sector has been relatively healthy in the 1990s. A number of factors specific to the farm sector impact the

performance of the farm equipment industry, including interest rates on loans for equipment, farm debt, the farmer's ability to pay, asset value, liquidity, farm numbers, and farm size. The key is the cash farmers have available to spend. The 1991 and 1992 sales declines were due to declines in real net farm income. Farmers' income had fallen since 1987 before bottoming out in 1992. Income rose in 1993 and 1994.

The economic well being of the farm sector may be measured by any of a number of factors: income, cash receipts, asset values (real estate and non–real estate), debt, and debt–to–asset ratios, to mention a few. Income by most measures peaked in 1994 when net farm income reached $48.4 billion and gross cash income exceeded $50 billion. Although income fell in 1995, it rebounded in 1996 and is expected to be in the range of $42–$45 billion over the next two to three years.

Government payments and the new farm policy are significant components to the farm income picture. For the first half of the decade, farmers were eligible for price and income support program benefits if they participated in federal acreage reduction programs. These acreage reduction programs required that producers idle a share of their program crop base in return for price and income support. On a calendar year basis, support payments ranged from a low of $7.0 billion in 1995 to $13.4 billion in 1993. In return, producers idled an average of 21 million acres in the annual acreage reduction programs (ARP) and another 36 million in the long–term Conservation Reserve Program (CRP). Withholding acres from production adversely affects farm equipment demand, but a cash income stream helps farm equipment sales.

Agricultural policy changed significantly with the passage of the Federal Agriculture Improvement and Reform (FAIR) Act of 1996. This legislation eliminated annual acreage retirement programs and price and income support programs directly tied to production. The significance of this act is that the acres idled in annual programs are now free to be planted. Producers, for the most part, may plant based on market prices and not government programs. Producers who are eligible and enroll in the program will receive transition payments over the 1996–2002 period. Transition payments will range between $4.0 and $5.8 billion dollars over the period, and these payments are not tied to production behavior. The only requirement is that the land remain in agriculture. The FAIR Act continued the CRP, but the Administration has some discretion as to the level of acres enrolled. It appears that around 30 million acres will be enrolled in the CRP in the future.

Interest rates for farm equipment loans follow the same type of pattern as general interest rate movements. Real rates were over 8.0% in the late 1980s and 1990 and then declined to the 6.0% to 6.5% range in the first half of the 1990s. Real rates are expected to edge upward through 1998 and become a modest drag on farm equipment demand.

Tillage practices also influence the demand for farm equipment. Concerns over soil erosion and the introduction of highly erodible and environmentally fragile land into agricultural production in the 1970s and early 1980s mobilized environmentalists. Past farm legislation recognized the need for farmers to be stewards of the land, and producers were required to develop and implement conservation plans in order to continue to receive commodity program benefits. This spawned the adoption of reduced tillage, crop rotation, and residue management practices. Since 1989, the use of conservation tillage practices has expanded from about 25% of the area planted to field and row crops to about 35% in 1996. No–till acreage has shown the greatest growth over this time period increasing by more than threefold.

The benefits of adopting reduced tillage practices are many, including fewer trips with tractors across fields, leading to reduced costs for fuel and oil, labor, and wear and tear on equipment, and reduced soil compaction. The adoption of reduced tillage practices will likely continue to grow as farmers strive to control, minimize, and reduce costs. Reduced tillage adversely affects the de-

mand for farm equipment, especially tractors, by reducing the wear and tear on equipment. Equipment lasts longer and repairs are less frequent. Conservation tillage practices also require less horsepower than conventional tillage practices.

Other U.S. farm sector characteristics that are related to farm equipment demand are mixed. Farm numbers and land in farms continue to decline, but at differing rates. The average farm size is increasing, at 469 acres in 1996 compared to 447 in 1986. There are about 2.1 million farms in the United States. Asset values have climbed steadily in the 1990s, and land values jumped more than 8.0% in 1996. Asset values are growing at a more rapid rate than farm debt. As a consequence, debt–to–asset ratios are declining, indicating that farm sector debt is manageable and the sector is creditworthy. These are factors that favorably impact the farm equipment industry.

The farm equipment industry is very concentrated. Four to five companies produce the majority of tractors, combines, and other harvesting equipment, and baling and haying machinery in the United States.

International Trade

The United States has shifted between being a net exporter and net importer in the total category of farm and garden equipment. In 1993 and 1996, the sector was a net exporter of approximately $110 to $150 million of equipment. Over the 1990–95 period, the value of imports exceeded that of exports by $20 to $65 million in all years except 1993. The industry's status of net importer or net exporter has been swung by the volume of garden equipment imports. From 1990 through 1996, the United States has been a consistent net exporter of farm equipment, exporting about $1 billion more than it imports.

Key markets for U.S. farm equipment exports include Canada (about 25% to 30% of the total), Mexico (typically 8% to 10%), Australia (6% to 7%), Germany (5%), France (3% to 5%), and the United Kingdom (3% to 5%). Canada, Germany, Japan, and the United Kingdom each account for between 15% to 20% of U.S. farm equipment imports. Collectively, Italy, France, and Brazil account for between 14% and 18% of imports. The North American Free Trade Agreement (NAFTA) is likely to continue to expand equipment trade with Canada and Mexico. The Uruguay Round Agreement of GATT should also help expand world trade in farm equipment. Japan is a major supplier lawn and garden equipment to the United States.

The United States is a fairly diverse importer and exporter of farm equipment. Between one–quarter and one–third of U.S. exports are gear boxes, axles, and assemblies. Another 25% of exports are new and used tractors of various sizes. Combines and harvesting equipment account for 10% to 12% of U.S. exports. Farm implements, irrigation equipment, and engines make up the bulk of the remaining export categories. On the import side, tractors make up about one–half of imports, and gear boxes and assemblies make up 25%. For the past six years, combines and other harvesters and haying and baling equipment have accounted for $300 million or more of the value of farm equipment imports.

Given the relatively promising outlook for agriculture from both a global and domestic perspective, continuation of trade reforms and improved market access, stability of the U.S. dollar, economic growth globally, and modern and efficient production of farm equipment in the United States, the future looks favorable for trade. The United States is projected to be a net exporter over the near term of garden and farm equipment. U.S. farm equipment exports are projected to inch up over the next few years, while imports stagnate.

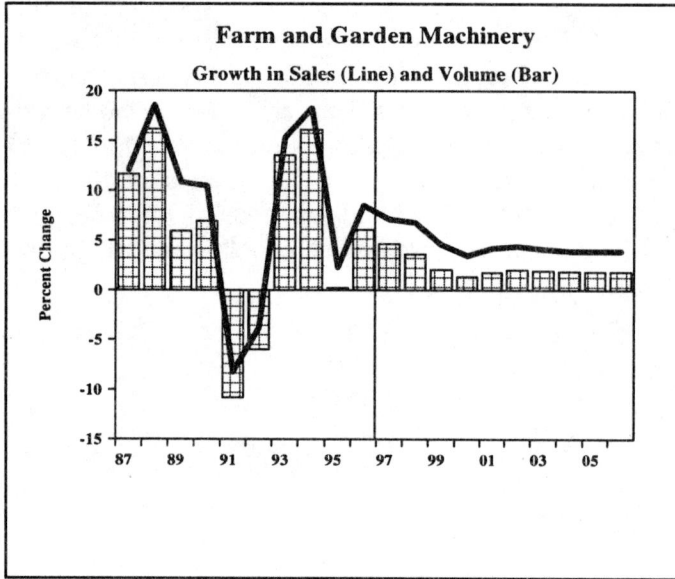

Farm and Garden Machinery

Growth in Sales (Line) and Volume (Bar)

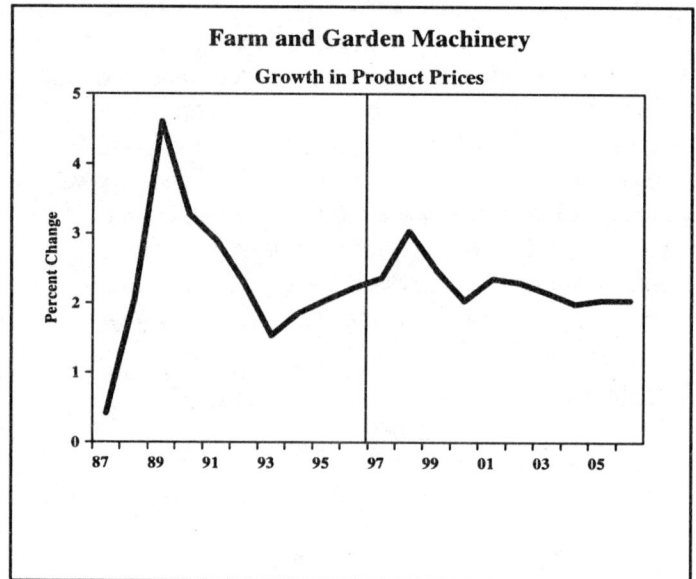

Farm and Garden Machinery

Growth in Product Prices

Farm and Garden Machinery
SIC 352

| | | 1990 | 1991 | 1992 | 1993 | 1994 | 1995 | 1996 | 1997 | 1998 | Compound Ann Avg Growth | |
											1986-1996	1996-2006
Sales												
	Billions of $	16.82	15.44	14.85	17.12	20.24	20.71	22.46	24.06	25.69		
	% Change	10.4	-8.2	-3.8	15.3	18.2	2.3	8.5	7.1	6.8	8.1	4.6
Volume	% Change	6.9	-10.8	-6.0	13.5	16.1	0.3	6.1	4.7	3.6	5.6	2.3
Prices	% Change	3.3	2.9	2.3	1.5	1.9	2.0	2.2	2.4	3.0	2.3	2.3
Exports												
	Billions of $	2.28	2.14	2.35	2.73	2.88	3.12	3.73	3.77	3.80		
	% Change	4.2	-6.0	9.8	16.1	5.4	8.5	19.5	1.2	0.6	8.1	-0.4
Imports												
	Billions of $	2.92	2.23	2.37	2.58	3.51	3.75	3.62	3.59	3.66		
	% Change	12.4	-23.9	6.6	8.6	36.2	6.7	-3.4	-0.8	1.9	6.9	2.4
Apparent Consumption												
	Billions of $	17.47	15.53	14.87	16.97	20.87	21.33	22.35	23.87	25.55		
	Nominal % Change	11.6	-11.1	-4.2	14.1	23.0	2.2	4.8	6.8	7.0	7.9	5.0
	Real % Change	8.1	-13.6	-6.4	12.4	20.8	0.1	2.5	4.4	3.9	5.4	2.6

Construction, Mining, and Material Handling Equipment

Construction, mining, and material handling equipment sales have performed well over the past decade, gaining an average of 5.4% per year. Demand for this type of machinery should continue to expand.

Favorable U.S. economic growth, rising income, and low inflation will prompt housing starts, infrastructure projects, mining activity, and wholesale trade. This, in turn, will cause equipment orders to escalate into the future. Modest strength in domestic markets will be augmented by expanding equipment orders from overseas. To capitalize on global opportunities, manufacturers are making strategic alliances in greater numbers.

Domestic Demand

Construction, mining, and material handling equipment sales registered their highest rate of growth in recent years, 16.1%, in 1995. Vigorous equipment sales from 1993 through 1995 saturated the market with new units. However, following these events, 1996 sales exceeded expectations by growing by more than 8%, driven primarily by solid gains in key construction markets. Given the strength in the market over the past few years, some equipment manufacturers have expressed concern about the sustainability of the growth they have experienced, and a slowdown in shipments is expected in late 1997.

In 1996, total construction contract awards grew by 1%. Demolition, excavation, and heavy and highway contractors were active, making up a large part of equipment sales. U.S. assembly of high volume construction machines rose for the fifth straight year in 1996, and sales rose for the fourth straight year. The Southeast has been the largest and fastest-growing regional market for construction and allied equipment. Airports, sewerage, water control, waterworks, and bridge and tunnel projects gained market share, while construction of power plants continued its four-year decline. Overall government construction dropped off in 1996, while non-residential construction continued its comeback.

Demand from the rental industry pushed up sales of small products. Skid steer loader sales, a mainstay of the construction equipment industry, increased by close to 7% in 1996, and are set to continue to grow in the near term. Backhoe shipments, also a good indicator of

equipment sales, are due to climb as well. Other gainers in the near term will be cranes, crawlers, excavators, and wheel loaders.

The prospects for industry growth look solid. Healthy GDP and income growth, relatively mild interest rates, and stable prices bode well for construction and allied equipment sales. A sizable rise in interest rates could be the only mitigating factor. Current activity, coupled with our expectations for activity in construction, mining, manufacturing, and wholesale markets, supports optimistic equipment demand forecasts.

Non-residential construction should continue to expand at a healthy pace this year and then moderate to a growth rate of 1.5%–2.5% per year, on average. Industrial plant construction will proceed at a modest pace, with above average growth coming from the pharmaceutical, paper, and food processing industries. Office construction will be very slow in urban centers, but much stronger in suburban areas. A boom in hotel and motel construction is now starting to wind down but this market should again pick up some steam beyond the year 2000. Lastly, electric utilities will proceed slowly with new power plant construction as they adjust to a deregulated environment.

Public construction will continue to expand throughout the forecast period. Road, bridge, and other infrastructure projects should remain a staple of the public construction sector, pending Congress' decision on the organization of federal aid. Plans for mass transit and high speed rail development will also stimulate equipment orders, but this category may be more at risk in federal funding. Airport construction will also require equipment for new development. Finally, modest growth is anticipated in public spending for schools, hospitals, and other public buildings.

WEFA expects the residential housing sector to lose momentum through 1997 and into the early part of next year, reflecting the effect of the Federal Reserve tightening of monetary policy. Housing starts should slip to 1.39 million units by 1998, down from 1.47 million units in 1996. Longer term, demographics and economic conditions suggest a new home construction market of roughly 1.4 million units per year.

Coal mining looks to grow only incrementally in the near term, but may show better growth after 2000. As advances in other fuel technologies slow and their prices increase, utilities will demand more coal. The strength in coal mining will remain in the West, primarily the Powder River Basin of Wyoming. This low sulfur coal is surface–mined using steam shovels, drag lines, and other earth–moving equipment that are technically characterized as construction machinery.

Coal production in eastern underground mines will expand at a snail's pace, suggesting limited potential for longwall mining machinery and related equipment. Western coal continues to gain share with eastern electric utilities. Eastern coal demand will depend largely on the export and steel markets. Export sales should benefit from favorable exchange rates and good economic growth. Sales to the steel industry will be dampened as the electric furnace method of producing steel, which does not use coke, continues to gain share.

Metal mining should lend only minor support to the mining machinery market, as metallic ore shipments are expected to grow by only about 2% per year. The electric furnace method of producing steel is gaining share at the expense of the basic oxygen process (BOF), which uses iron ore. In 1990, the BOF process accounted for 63% of total steel production. By the year 2000, we expect its share to fall to 55%, with further declines on tap in future years.

Manufacturing and wholesale trade will contribute to higher volumes of industrial truck, conveyor, and overhead crane sales. Activity in these markets should expand by about 2.5% per year, on average, during the next decade. Regional shifts in production and distribution facilities will also bolster demand. Lifting equipment will directly benefit, gaining by the largest margin of all domestic equipment categories. Finally, office, hotel, department store, retail mall, and public building construction will stimulate demand for elevators and escalators.

Exports

Exports are critical to the construction, mining, and material handling equipment industry. Last year, exports of $16.6 billion accounted for 38% of total industry sales. With imports reaching $9.2 billion, our trade surplus came in at $7.4 billion, an increase of about $1 billion.

Caterpillar, Case, and John Deere, all predict continued increases in their volume of machinery shipments to Eastern Europe, Southeast Asia, and South America. The countries in these regions are expected to experience healthy growth and are already in the process of massive infrastructure expansion. Additional support will come from the more traditional markets of Canada, and Western Europe.

Construction and allied equipment exporters cite Mexico and Chile among the top ten overseas markets for domestic production. In particular, increasing development of Latin American hotel, energy, and factory industries promises future equipment export growth.

U.S. companies are also breaking into the developing Asian market. Last year saw two U.S. firms win contracts at China's Three Gorges Project, although the Export–Import Bank refused funding guarantees upon failure to resolve environmental issues.

Financing has become an integral part of construction, mining, and material handling equipment exports. Some manufacturers report requests for credit from half of their customers. Major mining companies and other large clients can usually afford to arrange their own credit, yet even large clients increasingly require letters of credit and other assistance.

The prospects of developing countries will push exports up in the range of 5% to 6% per year for the next few years. The traditionally strong Canadian market should also absorb more U.S. equipment. Western Europe will continue its support to exports, as well. The near term residential housing sector in the United Kingdom looks to be particularly vibrant.

Over the next ten years, WEFA expects average annual economic growth in China of 9%. Growth in the rest of Asia is put at 6%–7% per year. The economies of Eastern Europe and the former Soviet Union should grow by 5% per year. Mexico, which in recent years has emerged as a major export market for U.S.–produced machinery and equipment, is slated to benefit from economic growth of 5% yearly. The rest of Latin America will chip in with an expansion rate of 4.5% per year. The Canadian economy, the major U.S. market, is slated to expand by 3% yearly. Lastly, growth in Western Europe will be in the 2.5% range per year.

With this as a backdrop, the potential for equipment sales overseas is considerable. Favorable exchange rates and the recognized high quality of U.S.–produced machinery and equipment will add to our overseas sales volume. Total exports of construction and allied machinery should average about 5% growth per year throughout the next decade.

Supply Conditions

Case, Melroe, John Deere, and Caterpillar number among the top players in the industry. New Holland, Komatsu, JCB, Volvo, and Daewoo add to that list.

The construction, mining, and material handling equipment industry continues to globalize. Manufacturers are building empires via acquisitions and joint ventures. Case Corporation acquired four companies in 1996. Three of Case's acquisitions were of companies outside the United States, improving the company's market position in Europe. Most recently, Case acquired Bor–Mor Inc., a manufacturer of directional drills, boosting Case' underground construction machinery offerings.

Volvo Construction Equipment followed a 1995 acquisition of a French firm with the recent purchase of Champion Road Machinery Ltd. of Canada.

Indicative of industry trends, Terex Corporation established a joint manufacturing operation in China in 1996, and plans another in India.

The Buy/Lease/Rent Decision

Financing choices figure prominently in the capital equipment industry. Used equipment sales volume approached half of the 1996 equipment market, from one-third in 1993. Buyers prefer to lease used equipment, rather than buying or renting. Almost 13% more pieces of equipment were leased in 1996 than in 1995.

New equipment purchasers, on the other hand, chose to rent more pieces of equipment in 1996, representing a 25% increase over 1995. These purchase decisions may reflect continuing cost minimization on the part of buyers.

Construction, Mining, and Material Handling
Growth in Sales (Line) and Volume (Bar)

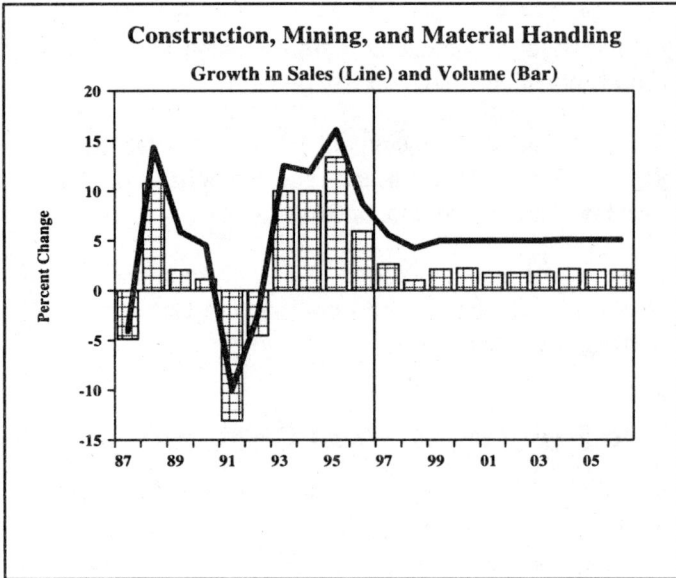

Construction, Mining, and Material Handling
Growth in Product Prices

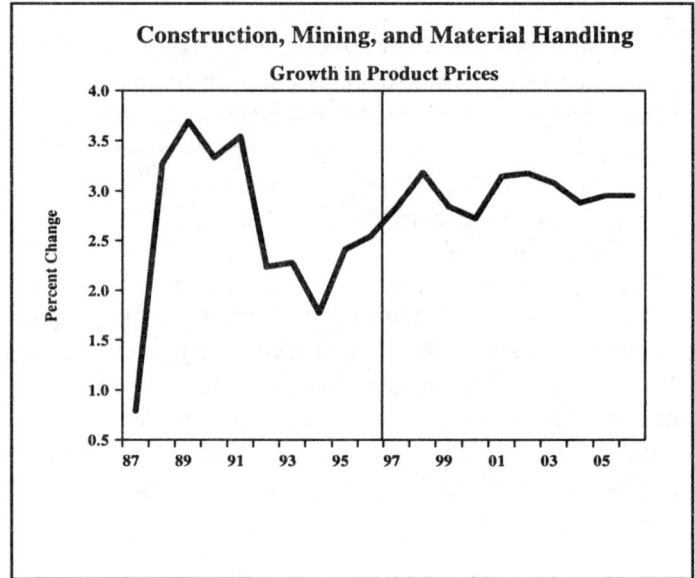

```
Construction, Mining, and Material Handling
  SIC 353
```

		1990	1991	1992	1993	1994	1995	1996	1997	1998	Compound Ann Avg Growth 1986-1996	1996-2006
Sales												
	Billions of $	30.99	27.90	27.24	30.64	34.29	39.80	43.25	45.65	47.59		
	% Change	4.5	-10.0	-2.4	12.5	11.9	16.1	8.6	5.6	4.2	5.4	5.0
Volume	% Change	1.1	-13.1	-4.5	10.0	10.0	13.3	6.0	2.7	1.0	2.8	2.0
Prices	% Change	3.3	3.5	2.2	2.3	1.8	2.4	2.5	2.8	3.2	2.6	3.0
Exports												
	Billions of $	10.66	12.32	12.70	12.17	13.69	15.21	16.60	17.70	18.70		
	% Change	2.0	15.6	3.1	-4.2	12.5	11.1	9.1	6.6	5.6	10.0	5.2
Imports												
	Billions of $	6.20	5.17	5.00	6.59	8.11	8.82	9.20	9.65	9.95		
	% Change	-5.7	-16.6	-3.4	31.8	23.2	8.6	4.3	4.9	3.1	6.2	4.3
Apparent Consumption												
	Billions of $	26.53	20.74	19.53	25.06	28.71	33.41	35.84	37.60	38.84		
	Nominal % Change	2.9	-21.8	-5.9	28.3	14.6	16.4	7.3	4.9	3.3	4.0	4.7
	Real % Change	-0.4	-24.5	-7.9	25.4	12.6	13.6	4.6	2.0	0.1	1.4	1.7

Oil and Gas Field Machinery and Equipment

U.S. oil and natural gas drilling seems to be recovering from its long slump. In 1996, there was a 3% increase in U.S. drilling activity. Modest gains for the drilling industry in the short run should translate to near-term gains for domestic oil and gas field machinery and equipment manufacturers.

Exports remain a critical market for oil and gas field equipment. With the WEFA forecast for energy prices trending upward slowly in the long run, increases in worldwide drilling activity should bolster equipment exports.

Demand Conditions

Domestic

1996 brought a recovery of sorts for the U.S. oil and natural gas drilling industry. The decline in total completions of oil and gas wells decelerated from its 7% average over the past five years to a 4% decline in 1996. Exploratory drilling dropped off last year, while development drilling was mixed. Oil well completions fell off, while the number of completed gas wells rose.

Domestic drilling activity in the mid–Continent, Arkansas–Louisiana–Texas, and Permian basin regions improved last year. Activity in the southern Rocky Mountains, Alaska, California, and Northeastern states fell off. The recent record round of leasing in the Gulf of Mexico should create equipment demand in the long term.

WEFA estimates that 40%–50% of U.S. natural gas is drilled in the Gulf of Mexico, with many of the plays containing both oil and gas reserves. In addition to Gulf reserves, the Rocky Mountains is a growth site for natural gas drilling.

1996 set a record for gas demand, and oil prices hit a six–year high. WEFA expects the West Texas Intermediate crude oil price to drop from this peak in the near term, but average 1.9% annual growth through 2006. Gas prices jumped last year as well, but they have undergone significant downward corrections since then. The long–term outlook for gas prices is for modest rates of growth.

With higher incentives through higher prices, drilling activity has increased. Three new land units were manufactured in 1996, the first produced in the United States for domestic use since 1992. This brought rig utilization rates to 77%, a high unseen since the boom times fifteen years ago. However, the total U.S. rig count declined for the 14th straight year. Oilfield revenues of $2.6 billion, an increase of close to 15%, complete the improved industry picture.

Demand for oil and gas is expected to increase by 1% to 1.5% in 1997. The decline in completions of oil and gas wells will continue to decelerate, dropping by only 2%–3% in 1997.

In response to the more favorable climate, a survey of oil companies recorded increases in capital spending for exploration and production of between 10% and 15% in 1996. Large capital expenditures daunt some rig owners, however: close to one–third of all rigs deleted in 1996 were dropped because they required large capital expenditures. Nevertheless, in the short term, close to half of contractors expected to expand their fleet of rigs, while less than 5% planned to decrease their fleet. The availability of skilled workers tops drill rig owner concerns, but drill pipe replacement and environmental concerns also rank high.

Consolidation is the trend among oil and gas companies. The locus of mergers has moved from the offshore drilling business to land contractors. Almost one–third of contractors were planning to seek merger opportunities in 1996. In addition, 1996 saw the beginning of strategic cooperation between operators and drilling contractors. Such partnerships are slowly increasing in frequency and are moving toward true profit sharing. These trends lend efficiency and market power to the resulting companies, both of which should help equipment sales.

Exploratory work currently underway represents a drop compared with last year. The number of seismic crews working shows a 3.7% decline. The southwestern United States and the Gulf Coast are bright spots of domestic activity, and this action should drive long–term demand for exploratory machinery and equipment in those regions.

Drill rigs are exiting the market at a decreasing rate, and the number of active rigs is set to increase. While this combination seems a sure boon to equipment manufacturers, the benefit may be remote. With the prohibitive costs of capital expenditures, increased rig utilization rates exhausting the equipment may be the real factor determining demand for new capacity.

Exports

Exports are key to oil and gas field machinery and equipment shipments. Drilling in the North and Caspian Seas, as well as in the Persian Gulf, is strong. OPEC is producing at a 16–year high. The North Sea and Latin America are burgeoning export destinations for American–made oil and gas field machinery and equipment, with the North Sea area absorbing the most exports. Africa is also a growing destination.

Despite an upswing in United States drilling activity, increasing numbers of rigs are moving abroad, mainly to South America and Venezuela. Drilling is less expensive outside the United States, and imports of crude oil are climbing. The Department of Energy expects the import share of U.S. oil consumption to reach 60% by 2010. Persian Gulf and OPEC countries imports totaled 8.4% and 22%, respectively.

It follows that overseas sales of domestic oil and gas field machinery and equipment are, and will remain, a significant percentage of U.S. manufacturers' business.

Supply Conditions

Baker Hughes is the top player among domestic producers of oil and gas field equipment, with a 30% worldwide market share in its key market segments. In 1996, all–time high company revenues surpassed $3 billion.

The company has not bucked the drilling industry trend of consolidation. In 1996, Baker Hughes, Inc. made two acquisitions of separation systems makers, Vortoil and Ketema. In addition, the company forged two strategic alliances. This year shows the trend continuing with plans to acquire two more companies. The most recent target, Drilex, is involved in the manufacture, sale, and rental of mud motors for drilling rigs.

Emerging technologies are set to cut drilling costs, as well as improve efficiency. Coiled tubing drilling and re–entry wells are among the new advances.

Pricing

The forecasted tight supply of oil and gas should continue to push up prices of oil and gas field equipment.

Input costs should remain stable, improving manufacturers' profits. Steel products, including casing and tubulars, are required for much of oil and gas field machinery and equipment. WEFA estimates that the producer price index (PPI) for steel will rise incrementally in 1997, before declining through 2000

Metalworking Machinery

Domestic demand for metalworking machinery is influenced by conditions in a number of key sectors of the U.S. economy. Activity and capital spending in the fabricated metal products, appliance, industrial machinery, motor vehicle, and aerospace industries drives the demand for machine tools and related accessories, which include special dies, die sets, jigs and fixtures, and industrial molds. The steel and aluminum industries call the tune for rolling mill machinery. Housing and construction, and assembly operations are critical to the power hand tool market. Finally, the demand for welding equipment is heavily influenced by the automotive, capital equipment, and construction sectors. Exports of metalworking machinery, primarily machine tools and related products, are tied to currency fluctuations and economic conditions in key markets such as Canada, Mexico, Europe, and Asia.

Recent History

The 1990–91 recession took a toll on the manufacturers of metalworking machinery as production fell 3.0% in 1990 and 10.3% in 1991. Business investment in metalworking machinery fell 10% in 1990, and dropped another 9% the following year. On the foreign trade front, U.S. exports of metalworking machinery held steady in 1990 and 1991, and imports were also stable. In the face of faltering end–market activity, producers of metalworking machinery reduced production worker employment by 2% in 1990 and 6.4% in 1991. Within the industry, the largest percentage drop in employment during this 2–year period occurred in metalcutting machine tools, followed closely by machine tool accessories, metalforming machine tools, and special dies, tools, jigs, and fixtures. Producers of power driven hand tools reduced production worker employment by 1.6% in 1990, but boosted it again the following year by 1.3%.

Metalworking machinery came out of the recession with an increase in production of 5.8% in 1992. Business spending for such equipment rose 4%, in real terms. Exports jumped 12.3%, and tumbled by a similar percentage. Over the next three years, metalworking machinery staged an impressive comeback as the metalworking and primary metals industries benefited from expanding demand for consumer goods and new housing, a strong revival in business investment, and considerable progress on the foreign trade front.

Healthy growth in key overseas economies and a favorable exchange rate also helped the metalworking industries directly, allowing exports to advance by 6% in 1993,

and jump the following year by 21% reaching $4.4 billion. Production of metalworking machinery rose 6.2% in 1993, and 6.9% in 1994. On the employment front, the number of production workers employed in the manufacture of metalworking machinery declined by 3.6% in 1992 to 212,700. However, the strong revival in demand eventually prompted an expansion of the workforce which rose very modestly, by 1.8%, in 1993 to 216,600, followed by a more robust 5.1% rise to 227,700 in 1994.

Production of metalworking machinery expanded at a healthy 13.3% clip in 1995, supported by a jump in business spending for such equipment and a 19.7% increase, in nominal terms, in exports to $5.2 billion. Metalworking machinery manufacturers continued to aggressively add to their workforce in that year, boosting the number of production workers by 6% to 241,860.

In 1996, metalworking equipment production growth slowed to 2.9%. A number of major capital projects in the metalworking and primary metals industries, and a moderation in export growth were the main causes of the growth pause. Not surprisingly, employment among producers of metalworking machinery also stalled.

Foreign Trade

The United States has consistently run trade deficits in metalworking machinery since 1980. Between 1986 and 1996 imports of metalworking machinery, primarily from Japan, Western Europe, and Taiwan, expanded from $3.44 billion to $7.48 billion, or roughly 11.7% per year on average. Imports, particularly of machine tools, have been a major factor in the U.S. market for metalworking machinery for some time.

- Aggressive marketing of simple low–priced stand–alone machines allowed the Japanese and Taiwanese to gain a foothold in the U.S. market many years ago. They now offer a broad range of products, from the very simple to the most complex of equipment.

- European producers have long been major producers of high quality complex equipment.

Foreign manufacturers have been very aggressive in courting the U.S. market, gaining ground despite periodic unfavorable currency fluctuations. Imports accounted for 14–16% of the U.S. market during the 1986–1993 period. In subsequent years, the strong performance of the U.S. market resulted in import penetration rising to 18.8% in 1996. Exports, on the other hand, tripled during the 1986–1996 period, rising from $1.92 billion in 1986 to $5.81 billion last year. During this ten–year span the metalworking trade deficit averaged $1.61 billion. The trade deficit last year came in at $1.67 billion.

The Outlook

WEFA forecasts production of metalworking machinery to expand by 1.0% this year and 1.3% in 1998. Longer–term, 1999–2006, output is slated to grow by about 3.2% per year.

We expect domestic demand for metalworking machinery to grow at a moderate pace during the 1996–2006 period. End–market performance this year and next will be generally less than awe–inspiring, but a modest acceleration in activity is expected thereafter. Investment in metalworking machinery will be triggered by pressures to expand capacity and introduce new products for both consumer and business markets, and the need to steadily improve productivity and efficiency.

Primary Metals Markets

Steel industry output is slated to expand by close to 5% per year during the 1997–1999 period, reflecting healthy growth in steel consumption and a downward drift in imports of steel mill products. Longer–term, WEFA forecasts average annual growth of 1–2% per year as progress is limited by the relative stability of the automotive and nonresidential construction markets. We are anticipating additions to capacity during the 1997–2001 period,

and ongoing efforts to improve productivity and efficiency within the steel industry should help to support purchases of metalworking machinery.

Fabricated Metal Markets

The output of fabricated metal products is slated to expand by about 1% this year, down from about 2% in 1996. Structural metal products should benefit from growth in construction. Fasteners and stampings will reflect activity in the automotive and capital goods markets. Growth is expected to taper off next year as construction markets lose some of their forward momentum. Light vehicles and aerospace will remain supportive. As the current decade draws to a close, we anticipate renewed signs of life in the housing sector and a replacement cycle in light vehicles. This, combined with continued progress on the capital goods front, should allow production of fabricated metal products to expand by about 2% per year in the long run.

Industrial Machinery Markets

The growth in domestic demand for traditional capital goods, such as construction, mining, and material handling equipment, farm machinery, and special and general industrial machinery is beginning to stabilize. Over the near term, the investment climate is not expected to turn negative, but modest growth in final demand, some pressure on profit margins, and the absence of a significant need to expand capacity suggest that the pace of investment will be moderating. Export demand should remain solid, however. Production of traditional capital goods is slated to expand by about 3% this year versus 1–2% in 1996, largely because of a swing in farm machinery and engines and turbines. Longer–term, our expectations for general economic conditions in the U.S. and overseas suggest a growth rate of about 3% per year on average.

Appliance Markets

The revival in new home construction and growth in consumer income last year allowed appliance production to expand by almost 6%. The lingering effects of the pickup in housing starts last year, and solid growth in real disposable personal income, will support a rise in appliance production of roughly 3% this year. With little support from the housing sector in 1998, and with income growth slowing, appliance production will slow thereafter, and average in the 1.5%–2.5% range.

Motor Vehicle Markets

North American light vehicle production is expected to hold at a healthy rate of close to 15 million units for the next year or two. A pickup in the replacement cycle will encourage modest growth in 1999 and 2000, and thereafter, light vehicle production will remain relatively stable at about 16.4 million units. New model introductions and major changes to existing models will continue to have a profound influence on the demand for metalworking machinery. The number of new and revamped auto models peaked at 17 in 1994, and then trailed off to 11 in 1995 and 1996. Indications are that the number will be around 10 this year and then jump to 15 in 1998. Thereafter, the number of new and revamped models will fall to 13 in 1999 and then average about 10 per year.

Aerospace Markets

We are still in the early stages of a significant recovery in the commercial aircraft market, driven by increasing pressure to replace older units still in service, the introduction of new models designed to meet the needs of specific traffic corridors, and anticipated strong growth in the Asian and Latin American markets. Deliveries of new aircraft are expected to be on the rise through the end of the decade before tapering off. The defense portion of the aerospace industry has been in the doldrums in recent years, as military downsizing occurred at an aggressive pace. However, discussions on the next generation of military aircraft are underway, and WEFA expects defense–related aerospace to gain ground slowly and then accelerate through the middle of the next decade. On balance, we now expect production of aircraft and parts to show a double-digit increase this year, and grow by about 4.0%–4.5% per year through the year 2000 before tailing off thereafter.

Construction Markets

Building activity is set to grow by about 3.3% this year, slower than the 4.7% rate achieved in 1996. While the residential market is expected to eke out an increase of only 1.1%, nonresidential construction appears headed for an increase of over 6%. Additional support will come from steady, albeit modest growth in public projects spending. Beyond this year we expect a little stronger growth in the residential market, a moderating rate of expansion in nonresidential construction, and relatively stable growth in public construction. With this as a backdrop, we now expect construction sector volume to grow by 2.5% in 1998, 2.3% in 1999, 1.9% in 2000, and about 1.5% per year thereafter.

Export Markets

Exports of metalworking machinery have been on the upswing since 1992, rising 92% during the 1992–1996 period. This occurred despite slumps in the Mexican, Japanese, and Canadian economies. A stronger dollar is expected to take some of the wind from their sails, but a moderately faster pace for world economic growth and an acceleration in economic activity over the near term in a number of key foreign markets should allow metalworking machinery exports to continue to expand during the forecast period. WEFA expects real world economic growth at 3.0% this year, up from 2.6% in 1996, and our current forecast has growth remaining above 3% per year over the long–term.

Canada and Mexico have been major export markets for the metalworking sector largely because of auto industry production, expansion, and retooling, which have required investment in machine tools and power driven hand tools used in the assembly process.

- Canada represents the largest single market for U.S.– produced metalworking machinery. The Canadian economy is in the early stages of a solid recovery, and WEFA expects growth in real GDP to reach 3.1% this year following a scant 1.5% increase in 1996. Average growth is put at about 3.5% over the next three years, and 3% thereafter.

- In recent years, Mexico has emerged as a major market for machine tools and other metalworking machinery. The recovery in Mexico is well underway. After posting an increase of 5.1% last year, we are projecting real growth in the Mexican economy in the 5.5–6.5% range through the next five years.

Other export markets also look promising. Conditions in the rest of Latin America are also improving, with GDP growth put at 4% this year versus 3% in 1996, and an acceleration to about 4.5% over the next few years. The Japanese economy will expand by only about 2% this year, but the longer term growth rate is more along the lines of 2.5%–3.0% per year. China offers great opportunities for metalworking equipment, with economic growth expected to remain close to 9% per year into the next decade. Opportunities will also abound in the rest of Asia. Finally, while economic growth in Western Europe will be modest, there is hope that the former Soviet Union and the rest of Eastern Europe will stage a general recovery during the coming decade.

Metalworking Machinery
Growth in Sales (Line) and Volume (Bar)

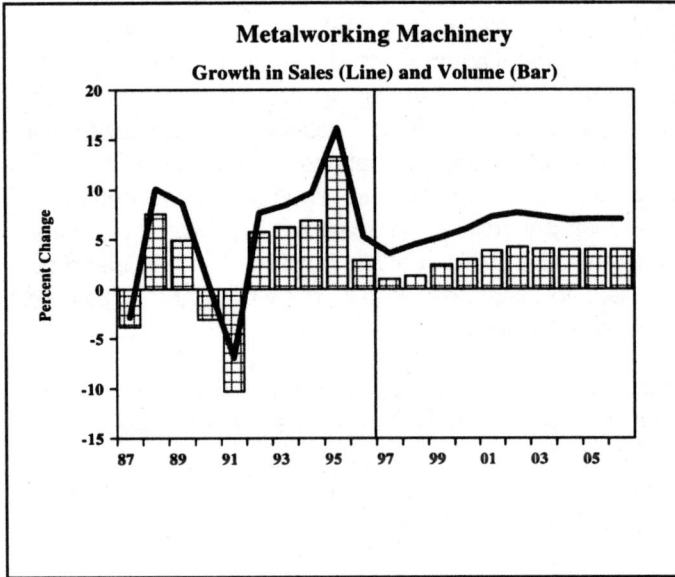

Metalworking Machinery
Growth in Product Prices

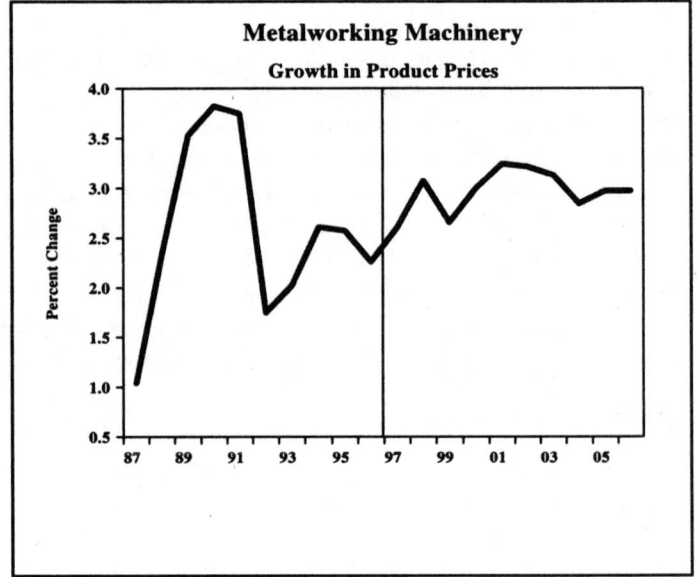

Metalworking Machinery
SIC 354

		1990	1991	1992	1993	1994	1995	1996	1997	1998	Compound Ann Avg Growth 1986-1996	1996-2006
Sales												
	Billions of $	26.36	24.52	26.39	28.60	31.36	36.43	38.35	39.73	41.50		
	% Change	0.7	-7.0	7.6	8.4	9.7	16.2	5.3	3.6	4.5	5.5	6.2
Volume	% Change	-3.0	-10.3	5.8	6.2	6.9	13.3	2.9	1.0	1.3	2.8	3.2
Prices	% Change	3.8	3.7	1.8	2.0	2.6	2.6	2.3	2.6	3.1	2.6	3.0
Exports												
	Billions of $	3.04	3.03	3.41	3.61	4.38	5.24	5.81	6.16	6.49		
	% Change	-0.5	-0.4	12.3	6.1	21.2	19.7	10.9	6.0	5.3	11.7	4.3
Imports												
	Billions of $	4.06	4.10	3.60	4.26	5.16	6.64	7.48	7.48	7.67		
	% Change	-3.5	0.9	-12.2	18.5	21.1	28.7	12.7	-0.1	2.6	8.1	3.1
Apparent Consumption												
	Billions of $	27.38	25.59	26.58	29.25	32.14	37.83	40.02	41.05	42.68		
	Nominal % Change	0.1	-6.5	3.9	10.0	9.9	17.7	5.8	2.6	4.0	5.2	6.0
	Real % Change	-3.5	-9.9	2.1	7.8	7.1	14.8	3.4	-0.0	0.9	2.6	2.9

Special Industrial Machinery

Special industrial machinery includes equipment used by the food and beverage, paper, printing, textile, chemicals, refining, rubber and plastics, and other specific industries. Between 1986 and 1996, production of special industrial machinery grew by 5.2% per year, on average. During that period, activity in the key markets for such equipment expanded by just 2% per year. Business spending for special industrial machinery grew by 4% per year, in real terms. Export growth provided additional support. Going forward, our expectations for activity in key domestic markets, coupled with favorable export prospects suggest that production of special industrial machinery will expand by about 3% per year, on average, during the 1996–2006 period.

Recent History

Production and Employment

The 1990–91 recession triggered a fairly severe contraction in the demand for special industrial machinery. Production declined 1.0% in 1990, and then fell by 5.0% the following year. Domestic demand weakened as key industries reduced capital spending, and export demand limped along. Business spending for special industrial machinery fell 16.7%, in real terms, during the 1990–91 period. Signs of life began to emerge in 1992, but production still managed to end the year down 2.3%.

Demand once again hit its stride in 1993 and grew rapidly through 1995. Domestic business spending for special industrial machinery was strong. Exports of food products, paper, textile, and other special industrial machinery also posted solid gains during these years, providing additional support. Last year brought a slight 1.2% decline in production as major capital programs in key industries began to wind down, offsetting continued growth on the export front.

The number of production workers employed in the manufacture of special industrial machinery peaked at 97,320 in 1989, just prior to the last recession. Weakness in key markets resulted in employment dropping by 3.5% in 1990, 7.8% in 1991, and another 2% in 1992. As the recovery in the demand for special industrial machinery gained momentum, manufacturers boosted employment to 98,570 by 1995, and kept it above 98,000 last year.

Foreign Trade

Exports of special industrial machinery expanded from $2.9 billion in 1986 to $8.9 billion last year, representing an average annual increase of about 20%. Canada, Western Europe, and in recent years Mexico and the rest of Latin America, represent key markets for U.S. produced machinery and equipment.

- Exports of food products machinery totaled only $446 million in 1986, but had risen to over $1.1 billion by 1989 and continued to grow rapidly to over $2.2 billion last year.

- Paper and printing machinery exports exceeded $1 billion in 1986 and had risen to over $3 billion ten years later.

- Overseas sales of textile machinery totaled only $453 million in 1986, but exceeded $1.2 billion last year.

- Finally, exports of woodworking, glassmaking, and other types of special industrial machinery have grown from $960 million in 1986 to almost $2.4 billion in 1996.

Imports of special industrial machinery, primarily from Japan, Germany, and the rest of Western Europe totaled $5.2 billion in 1986, and grew to $11.9 billion by 1995, an increase of 14% per year, on average. Strong demand, aggressive marketing, and generally favorable currency swings have supported the growth in imports. Imports fell by more than 5% last year to $11.2 billion as major capital programs in key industries were completed. The

United States has consistently reported a trade deficit in special industrial machinery. Over the past ten years, the deficit ranged from a low of $1.1 billion in 1991 to a high of $3.5 billion in 1995. Last year, the deficit came in at just under $2.4 billion.

Near–Term Outlook: 1997–1998

Production of special industrial machinery appears headed for a tough year this year. Despite better domestic activity in the food and beverage, paper, printing and publishing, chemical, and rubber and plastic industries, there is little need as yet for renewed equipment spending. However, improving economic conditions in Canada, Mexico, and the rest of Latin America are allowing exports to continue to gain ground despite the strength in the dollar.

We are anticipating a loss of forward momentum next year in the very same industries that are providing support this year, and little, if any, help from the textile and petroleum industries. With this as a backdrop, capital programs in these industries will be restrained. Exports should remain a relative bright spot as key foreign markets continue to expand at a healthy clip. On balance, U.S. production of special industrial machinery is slated to expand by just over 2% in 1998.

Longer–Term Outlook: 1999–2006

The prospects for special industrial machinery are more constructive over the longer term. On the domestic front, we anticipate average annual growth rates of 2.0%–3.0% in the food and beverage, paper, printing and publishing, chemicals, and petroleum industries. Textile industry output is slated to grow by less than 2.0% during the next ten years. Modest growth in industry output, coupled with continuing pressure to improve productivity and efficiency and introduce new products, will stimulate investment in new state–of–the–art machinery and equipment. Additional support will come from a very fertile export market. The prospects for the Canadian economy are generally encouraging with growth in excess of 3% per year likely, and we look for strong support from developing countries, such as Mexico and Latin America. Finally, additional support will come as economic progress in Asia continues, and signs of real life emerge in Eastern Europe.

Special Industry Machinery
Growth in Sales (Line) and Volume (Bar)

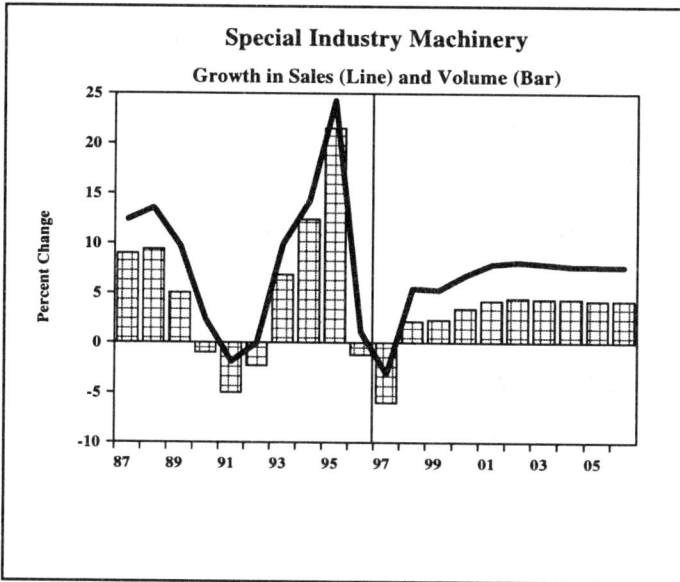

Special Industry Machinery
Growth in Product Prices

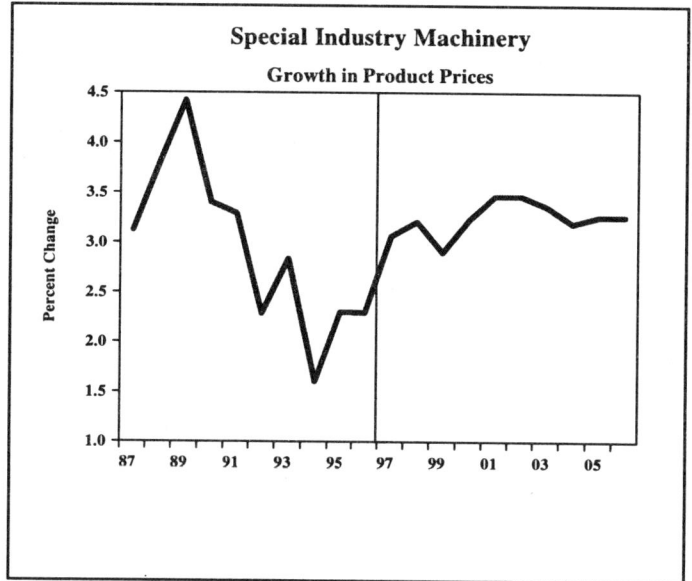

```
Special Industry Machinery
SIC 355
```

		1990	1991	1992	1993	1994	1995	1996	1997	1998	Compound Ann Avg Growth	
											1986-1996	1996-2006
Sales												
	Billions of $	21.87	21.46	21.45	23.57	26.92	33.47	33.82	32.76	34.56		
	% Change	2.4	-1.9	-0.0	9.9	14.2	24.3	1.1	-3.1	5.5	8.3	6.1
Volume	% Change	-1.0	-5.0	-2.3	6.8	12.4	21.5	-1.2	-6.0	2.2	5.2	2.8
Prices	% Change	3.4	3.3	2.3	2.8	1.6	2.3	2.3	3.1	3.2	2.9	3.2
Exports												
	Billions of $	5.82	6.00	6.21	6.67	7.31	8.34	8.86	9.46	10.03		
	% Change	3.9	3.2	3.5	7.3	9.6	14.0	6.3	6.8	6.1	11.8	5.1
Imports												
	Billions of $	7.44	7.14	7.64	8.61	10.52	11.86	11.22	11.62	12.37		
	% Change	0.8	-4.0	7.0	12.6	22.2	12.8	-5.4	3.6	6.4	8.0	6.9
Apparent Consumption												
	Billions of $	23.50	22.60	22.88	25.51	30.12	36.99	36.18	34.93	36.89		
	Nominal % Change	1.5	-3.8	1.3	11.5	18.1	22.8	-2.2	-3.5	5.6	7.5	6.6
	Real % Change	-1.8	-6.9	-1.0	8.4	16.2	20.0	-4.4	-6.3	2.3	4.4	3.2

General Industrial Machinery

General industrial machinery includes a variety of equipment and components that find their way into many segments of the U.S. economy. Pumps and pumping equipment are utilized in the process industries, hydraulics, and construction. Ball and roller bearing production is tied largely to the automotive and capital goods markets. Air and gas compressors find their way into a multitude of industrial applications and are widely used at construction sites. Blowers and exhaust and ventilation fans are used in commercial buildings, industrial plants, and residential buildings. The demand for industrial patterns and process furnaces and ovens is heavily influenced by foundry activity and general manufacturing. Industrial sector activity also drives the demand for speed changers, industrial high speed drives, gears, and mechanical power transmission equipment. Finally, the demand for non-food packaging machinery is influenced by manufacturing sector production levels and capital spending programs.

Recent History

Production

Production of general industrial machinery declined 2.2% in 1991 as the economy weathered the recession, and slipped 0.9% further in 1992. Bearings and gears output actually began to falter in 1989 and continued to contract well into 1992. Between 1989 and 1992, production of bearings and gears fell 15.4%. The general industrial equipment subcategory suffered much less during the last recession, with production rising 2.4% in 1990 and then slipping 0.9% in 1991. Signs of life began to emerge in 1992, but production for the year as a whole was up only 0.5%.

The following three years, 1993-95, saw great strides in general industrial machinery demand. These were the years of very healthy increases in industrial, construction, and motor vehicle sector activity, and capital spending. In addition, favorable economic conditions in a number of key foreign markets and favorable exchange rates allowed exports to gain ground. During this period, production of general industrial machinery rose by over 14%, with significant increases in both bearings and gears and the general equipment subcategory.

The demand for general industrial machinery began to lose momentum last year, as major capital spending programs in the manufacturing sector began to wind down, industrial plant construction declined following a very strong performance in 1995, and production of light vehi-

cles and commercial trucks and trailers declined. Export markets continued to provide support, with stronger growth in the Mexican economy a major factor. For the full year, production of general industrial machinery rose by 3.4%, with bearings and gears output down slightly, and output of other equipment up.

Employment

Last year, the general industrial machinery industry employed nearly 163,000 production workers, an increase of 0.6% from the previous year. Employment has expanded 8.6% since it bottomed out at 149,700 production workers in 1993. The ball and roller bearings segment of the industry was the largest employer with almost 31,000 workers last year. This was followed by blowers and fans with 23,400, pumps and pumping equipment 16,800, air and gas compressors 15,300, power transmission equipment 14,700, and speed changers, drives, and gears with about 12,000.

The Outlook to 2006

The moderate pace that characterized the demand for general industrial machinery throughout much of last year will persist in 1997. Growth in domestic demand for this type of equipment will be modest, but we are anticipating additional gains on the export front, despite the recent strengthening of the dollar. Economic conditions in Canada have been improving, and the recovery in Mexico is continuing apace. This, combined with generally stronger world economic growth, should allow exports of general industrial machinery to continue to gain ground. On balance, WEFA expects production of general industrial machinery to expand by 1.3% this year.

■ The demand for bearings will be influenced positively by a very modest 1% increase in light vehicle production, an acceleration in commercial aircraft assembly, and solid gains in farm and construction machinery production. However, we are anticipating declines in the rail equipment, medium and heavy truck, and truck trailer markets.

■ Pumps and pumping equipment and air and gas compressors will benefit from stronger activity in key process industries, such as food and beverage, paper, and chemicals, modest growth in construction, and continued progress on the export front. However, support from the petroleum production and refining and mining industries will be limited.

■ The outlook for blowers and fans is mixed. Commercial construction is expected to accelerate in 1997, and signs of life have emerged in industrial building. However, we are anticipating a more subdued residential market as housing starts flatten out.

■ Industrial sector activity calls the tune for industrial patterns, speed changers, process ovens, power transmission equipment, packaging machinery, and other types of general industrial machinery. The industrial sector is expected to show more life in 1997 than it did last year, and this will surely provide support. However, we have just recently ended a period of very aggressive industrial sector investment and a return to the robust growth pace that characterized the 1993-95 period is unlikely.

In the longer term, over the period 1998-2006, WEFA projects real growth in general industrial machinery of roughly 3.5% per year. Domestic markets, such as the process industries, capital goods, motor vehicles, aircraft, and construction will be supportive, but exports will become more important in the years ahead.

Growth in domestic and overseas demand for traditional capital goods, such as construction, mining, and material handling equipment, farm machinery, and rail equipment, is forecast to grow by about 3% per year, on average. North American light vehicle production will increase between 2% and 2.5% in 1998 as a replacement cycle gets underway. With the replacement cycle in full bloom production should grow by almost 4% in 1999 and about 3.0% in the year 2000. Thereafter, light vehicle production will remain relatively stable at about 16.4 million units. We are still in the early stages of a significant recovery in the commercial aircraft market, which is being driven by increasing pressure to replace older units still in service, the introduction of new models designed to meet the needs of specific traffic corridors, and anticipated strong growth in the Asian and Latin American markets. Delivery of new aircraft is expected to remain at healthy levels through the end of this decade before tapering off. We expect defense–related aerospace to gain ground in the years ahead, and begin to accelerate through the middle of the next decade.

Process industry output is likely to grow by roughly 2.5% per year, on average, through 2006, with the chemical industry leading the way with growth of 3% per year. Petroleum refining will expand by only about 1.5% per year. Oil and gas extraction will show little or no growth during the forecast period. Construction activity beyond this year will see a little stronger growth in the residential market, a much more modest rate of expansion in nonresidential construction, and relatively stable growth in public construction. WEFA expects construction sector volume to grow by 2.0% to 2.5% in each of the next three years and about 1.5% per year thereafter.

Exports of general industrial machinery should remain on the upswing. WEFA expects real world economic growth to average above 3% per year over the long-term. Canada remains the largest single market for U.S.–produced general industrial machinery, and Canadian economic growth is likely to exceed 3% per year. Mexico will remain a fertile market. We are projecting real growth in the Mexican economy well in excess of 5% through 2002. Conditions in the rest of Latin America are improving, with GDP growth forecast at 4.5% annually over the next few years. The Japanese economy will expand along the lines of 2.5%-3.0% per year. China offers great opportunities, with economic growth expected to remain close to 9% per year into the next decade. Opportunities will also abound in the rest of Asia. Finally, while economic growth in Western Europe will be modest, there is hope that the former Soviet Union and the rest of Eastern Europe will stage a recovery during the coming decade.

General Industry Machinery
Growth in Sales (Line) and Volume (Bar)

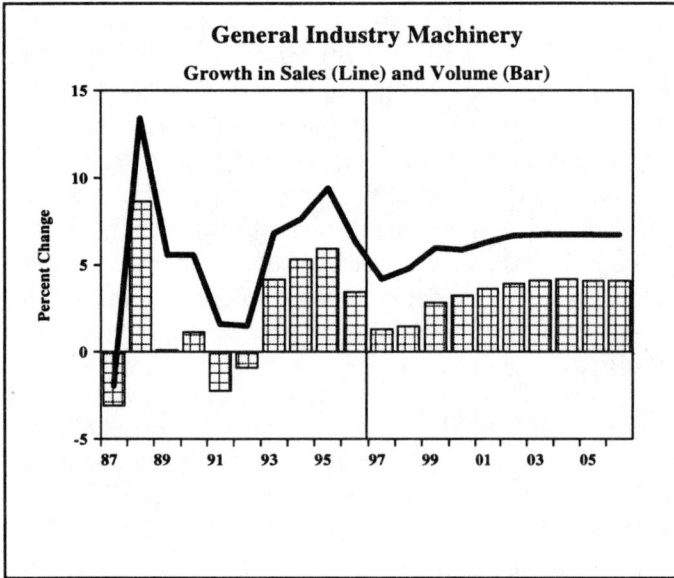

General Industry Machinery
Growth in Product Prices

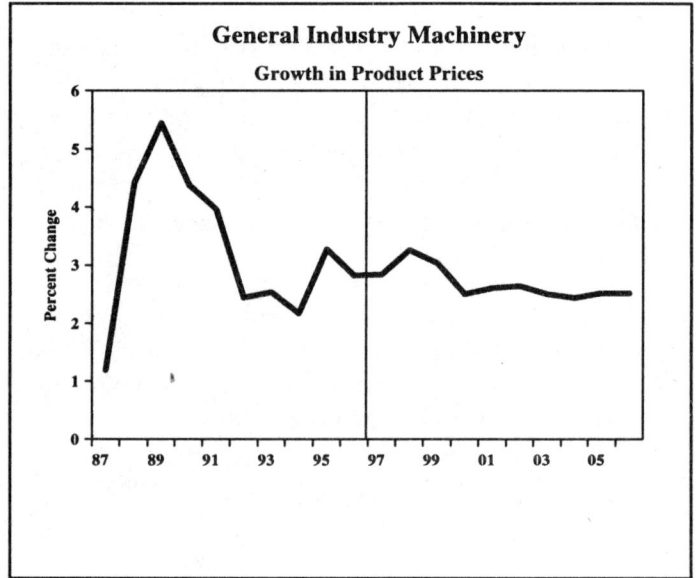

General Industry Machinery
SIC 356

Growth		1990	1991	1992	1993	1994	1995	1996	1997	1998	Compound Ann Avg 1986-1996	1996-2006
Sales												
	Billions of $	30.50	30.99	31.46	33.60	36.16	39.56	42.08	43.84	45.94		
	% Change	5.6	1.6	1.5	6.8	7.6	9.4	6.4	4.2	4.8	5.5	6.1
Volume	% Change	1.2	-2.2	-0.9	4.2	5.3	5.9	3.4	1.3	1.5	2.2	3.3
Prices	% Change	4.4	4.0	2.4	2.5	2.2	3.3	2.8	2.8	3.3	3.3	2.7

Refrigeration, Heating, and Service Industry Machinery

A slump in construction, consumer income, and business investment drove production of refrigeration, heating, and service industry machinery down 9.7% in 1990 and 5.8% in 1991. Business investment in such equipment fell by 7.8% in 1990 and 7.6% in 1991, in real terms. Not surprisingly, equipment manufacturers scaled back production worker employment by 14% or 19,200 workers during this period.

Refrigeration, heating, and service industry machinery emerged quickly from the recession, posting a production increase of 8.8% in 1992, and following that with a 6.3% increase the following year. Business spending for commercial refrigeration and heating equipment and service industry machinery rose by only 2.8% in 1992, but posted a much more robust 6.4% increase the following year. With the economy and most key end–markets hitting all cylinders, production surged ahead in 1994. Production growth slowed to 2.9% in 1995 as new home construction softened, the Canadian economy stumbled, and Mexico fell into a severe recession. Domestic business purchases also lost momentum, advancing by only 4.3%. Production growth accelerated again in 1996 to 7.5% growth, supported by gains in new home construction and exports. Production worker employment expanded steadily during the recovery, growing by over 32,500 workers during the 1992–96 period. Output–per–worker grew by almost 11%.

Given WEFA's expectations for consumer income growth, residential construction, and business investment, we do expect considerably slower growth in domestic demand for such equipment this year and next. However, despite the strong dollar, we believe exports will provide additional support as economic growth in a number of key foreign markets actually accelerates. As a result, growth in the production of refrigeration, heating, and service industry machinery is expected to slow to about 2%–2.5% in 1997 and 1998. Over the longer haul, 1999–2006, a better housing market, steady increases in consumer income, adequate corporate profits, above average growth in service sector activity, and a fertile export market should support production growth of close to 4% per year.

Refrigeration, Air Conditioning, and Heating Equipment

The demand for refrigeration, air conditioning, and heating equipment is tied to both consumer and business spending patterns. New home building, additions and alterations, and replacement buying are the driving factors in the unitary air conditioner and residential heating market. Historically, replacement demand has accounted for about 50% of unitary air conditioner sales. Capital investment calls the tune in the commercial and industrial refrigeration and heating markets. Exports, particularly to Canada and Mexico, but increasingly to the rest of Latin America and to Asia, round out the major markets for refrigeration, air conditioning, and heating equipment.

A solid performance in all of these markets during the 1992–94 period supported growth in production of 7.9% in 1992, 6.5% in 1993, and a whopping 16.9% in 1994. During this period, housing starts in the U.S. grew by 43.6%, and consumer incomes expanded by 15.8% in nominal terms. Industrial and commercial construction remained in the doldrums in 1992, but began to exhibit signs of life in 1993 and grew nicely in 1994. The additions and alterations and replacement markets also supported growth during the 1992–94 period, as consumer disposable income grew by nearly 5% per year and corporate profits expanded by 12% per year.

The transportation market also provided considerable support. Solid demand for meat, dairy, and food products, coupled with a strong replacement cycle, triggered a surge in demand for refrigeration units used in commercial trucks and truck trailers. Between 1991 and 1994, refrigerated trailer production grew by 77%. Growth in world trade involving food products that require refrigeration also had a very positive impact on equipment demand. Between 1991 and 1994 the world leasing company refrigerated–container fleet expanded by 52%. On the export front, the Canadian and Mexican markets, which account for about 40% of foreign sales, provided support, as did the rapidly expanding markets of Latin America.

However, in 1995 production growth slowed to only 1.7%, reflecting a sharp divergence between residential, nonresidential, and export markets for this equipment.

- New housing starts declined, and the additions and alterations market slowed to a crawl. This more than offset the continuing strength in replacement for unitary air conditioners in the residential market.

- Industrial and commercial construction surged in 1995, which bolstered demand for heating and air conditioning equipment.

- Restaurant patronage grew at a solid pace which helped the commercial refrigeration market.

- Sales of commercial trucks and truck trailers also advanced as private carriers and trucking companies continued to aggressively expand and upgrade their fleets. Production of refrigerated trailers rose almost 12% in 1995.

- Sales of refrigeration units to container leasing companies rose by double–digit rates.

- Finally, exports lost some of their momentum as the housing market in Canada dropped by 28%, the Mexican economy fell into a severe recession, and economic growth in the rest of Latin America slowed to 2.5% following a 6.0% increase in 1994.

The industry posted much better numbers last year with production expanding by 8.8%. New home construction showed solid positive growth again and commercial building continued to gain ground supported by office, store, warehouse, and hotel construction. Residential and light commercial unitary air conditioner replacement demand also remained supportive. In addition, leasing companies continued to expand their fleets of refrigerated containers. This more than offset the impact of a slump in

industrial construction and sales of refrigeration units to the on–highway transportation market. On the export front, the Canadian market benefited from a 12% jump in new home construction, and the Mexican market rebounded as the economy grew by 5.1%. Economic conditions in the rest of Latin America proved to be more supportive, and other key markets, such as China, and the rest of Asia continued to expand at a healthy clip.

The producers of refrigeration, air conditioning, and heating equipment also expanded employment as end–market demand gathered momentum. The number of production workers expanded in 1992 to 87,010. By 1996, the number of production workers had reached 108,800. In addition, productivity was growing, with output–per–worker up by 9% from 1992–96.

Near–Term Outlook

Fundamentals suggest very modest growth both this year and next. New home construction is slated to decline slightly during this period. Consumer income should expand by 3.2% in 1997, in real terms, but growth is put at a slower 2.2% in 1998. We are experiencing an acceleration in industrial and commercial construction this year, with growth now pegged at about 8% versus 1% in 1996. WEFA expects a more modest 2.5% increase in this sector in 1998. This year will see another decline in purchases of refrigeration units for use in commercial trucks and trailers, and only a very modest advance in 1998. Production of refrigerated containers is expected to moderate, following a period of very strong growth during the past six years.

Export markets will continue to provide support, as growth in key foreign markets overwhelms the negative impact of the stronger dollar. The Canadian economy is poised to increase between 3% and 3.5% during the 1997–98 period. Canadian housing starts are set to expand rapidly this year and next, and nonresidential construction is also slated to expand after two years of decline. The recovery in Mexico appears to be on solid ground, with GDP growth now pegged at 5% to 6% this year and in 1998. Economic growth in the rest of Latin America is forecast to accelerate to 4.0% in 1997, and 4.8% in 1998. Finally, real growth in China and the rest of Asia will average about 6.5% and 9.5%, respectively, over the next two years.

Longer–Term Outlook

The U.S. market for refrigeration, air conditioning, and heating equipment will expand modestly through the middle of the next decade.

- Housing starts are expected to average about 1.47 million units per year versus our current forecast for 1998 of 1.39 million units.

- Consumer income growth is now pegged at about 2% per year during this period.

- Growth in industrial and commercial construction is set at 1.5%–2.0% per year. Above average economic growth in the warmer climate regions of the U.S., such as California, the South, and the Southwest will have a favorable influence on air conditioning equipment used in residences, schools, office buildings, stores, and other buildings.

- A replacement cycle in refrigerated trucks and trailers and steady growth in the demand for fresh and frozen food items is expected to provide some lift to the market into the early part of the next decade.

- Foreign trade in food products which require refrigeration will continue to support investment in refrigerated containers.

- Exports of refrigeration, air conditioning, and heating equipment will continue to increase in importance. The prospects for the Canadian economy are generally constructive with growth of roughly 3% per year likely. Look for strong support from developing warm–weather regions, such as Mexico, Latin America, Africa, and India, where new housing, industrial, and commercial construction projects will be expanding at a healthy clip. Additional support will come as economic progress in Asia continues, and signs of real life emerge in Eastern Europe.

Service Industry Machinery

Service industry machinery includes commercial laundry and dry cleaning equipment, vending machines, and equipment used by gas and service stations, restaurants, car washes, and commercial cleaning services.

The demand for service industry machinery has been expanding at a robust pace since 1992, coinciding with the general health of the economy and a period of very strong capital spending by small businesses. The strength in new home construction during the past few years and concern about drinking water quality bolstered demand for household water filters and softeners and water purification equipment. Corporate downsizing and restructuring resulted in increased outsourcing of tasks that were previously handled in–house. This boosted activity and investment among business services firms, such as commercial cleaning services. Restaurant patronage grew at a solid pace, particularly from 1993–96, stimulating investment in commercial cooking, food warming, and dishwashing equipment. Gas and service stations benefited from the favorable economic fundamentals that triggered steady growth in motor fuel consumption and vehicle miles driven. Gains in personal income and the trend to more two wage–earner households had a positive impact on consumer spending on services.

Production of service industry machinery grew by 10.8% in 1992, 6.0% in 1993, 6.7% in 1994, 5.6% in 1995, and 4.4% in 1996. In response to the momentum in the market, the producers of service industry machinery steadily boosted employment during the 1992–96 period. The number of production workers in the industry averaged 40,640 last year, up from 34,200 in 1991 and an increase of 18.8%. With industry output expanding by 38.1% over the past four years, worker productivity expanded by roughly 3% per year.

Near–Term Outlook

The demand for service industry machinery will continue to gain ground over the near term. While the major restructuring and downsizing efforts are probably behind us, they are now part of the normal course of doing business. As a result we expect corporations to continue to look at outsourcing as a means of reducing operating costs.

The two wage–earner household will remain the norm stimulating the consumer services sector. Our current forecast has restaurant patronage growing by about 3% in 1997 and 1998, a bit slower than the 4% of 1996, indicating moderating growth in demand for commercial cooking, food warming, dishwashing equipment, and vending machines. However, there are usually eating facilities associated with new commercial and industrial structures, and the growth we anticipate in these markets over the next two years should provide some support.

Declining gasoline prices should have a positive impact on personal and commercial vehicle miles driven and fuel consumption, stimulating service station activity and investment in new equipment.

Longer–Term Outlook

The longer–term outlook for service industry is no less bright. WEFA's view of the overall economic climate suggests a continued focus on corporate cost–containment, and assumes that the two wage–earner household remains the norm. This alone ensures that business and personal service sector activity will expand at a decent clip. An aging population and expanding incomes will have a positive impact on restaurant patronage and related equipment. Additionally, we are anticipating a strengthening of new home construction during this period which, in conjunction with health concerns, will have a positive impact on the demand for water filters, softeners, and purification equipment.

Refrigeration, Heating and Service Industry Equip
Growth in Sales (Line) and Volume (Bar)

Refrigeration, Heating and Service Industry Equip
Growth in Product Prices

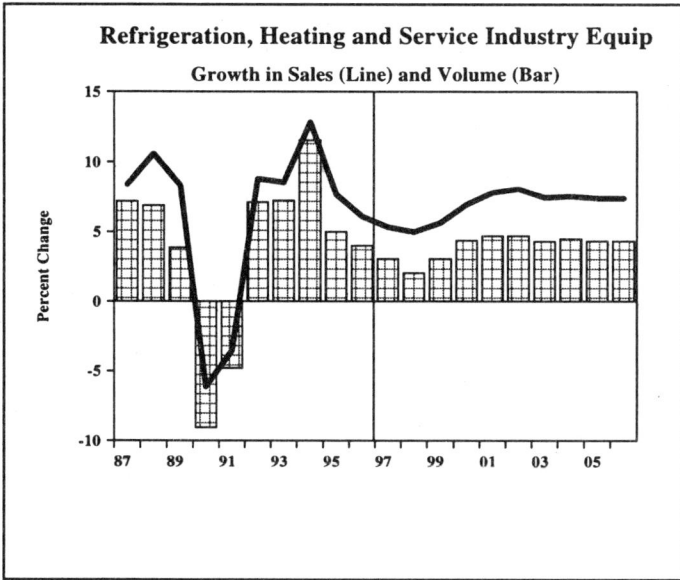

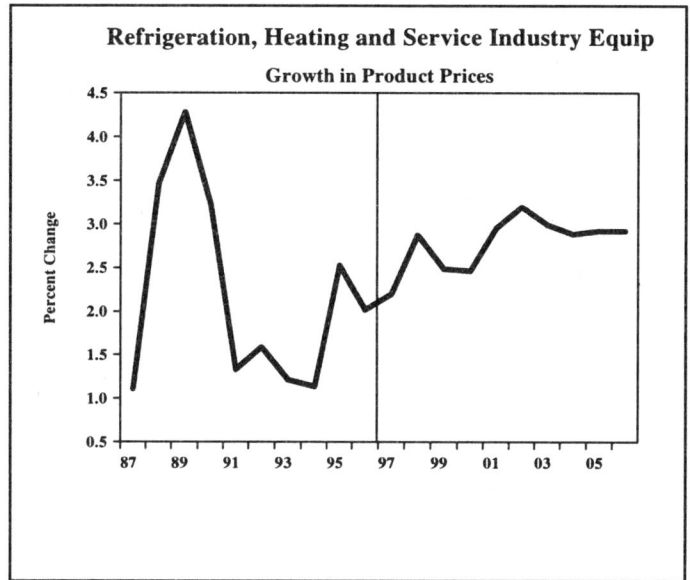

```
Refrigeration, Heating and Service Industry Equip
 SIC 358

                                                                                      Compound Ann Avg Growth
                         1990   1991   1992   1993   1994   1995   1996   1997   1998   1986-1996  1996-2006


Sales
         Billions of $  26.21  25.28  27.50  29.84  33.67  36.24  38.43  40.47  42.48
              % Change   -6.1   -3.5    8.8    8.5   12.8    7.6    6.1    5.3    5.0       6.0        6.8

 Volume      % Change   -9.1   -4.8    7.1    7.2   11.5    5.0    4.0    3.0    2.0       3.7        3.9
 Prices      % Change    3.2    1.3    1.6    1.2    1.1    2.5    2.0    2.2    2.9       2.2        2.8

Exports
         Billions of $   3.54   3.77   4.16   4.40   4.79   5.09   5.42   5.81   6.18
              % Change    2.4    6.6   10.4    5.8    8.8    6.2    6.5    7.2    6.5      13.1        5.4
Imports
         Billions of $   3.28   3.31   3.61   4.12   4.82   5.38   5.90   6.08   6.43
              % Change   -1.5    0.8    8.9   14.1   17.2   11.6    9.7    2.9    5.7      10.1        6.2

Apparent Consumption
         Billions of $  25.95  24.82  26.95  29.56  33.70  36.53  38.92  40.74  42.72
      Nominal % Change   -6.6   -4.4    8.6    9.7   14.0    8.4    6.5    4.7    4.9       5.8        6.9
         Real % Change   -9.5   -5.6    6.9    8.4   12.7    5.7    4.4    2.4    1.9       3.5        4.0
```

Industrial Machinery NEC

This catch-all category includes carburetors, pistons, piston rings and valves, amusement park machinery and equipment, and a whole host of miscellaneous machinery and equipment. Machine shop activity is also included in industrial machinery NEC. Machinery shops are heavily influenced by activity and capital spending in the motor vehicle, aerospace industries, and mobile off-highway equipment industries.

Recent History

During the last recession, real shipments of industrial machinery NEC held up fairly well, inching up by 0.3% in 1990 and declining by only 2.1% in 1991. Employment during this period stalled in 1990 and then fell by nearly 5% in 1991 to 224,000 production workers. Signs of life in the motor vehicle industry and capital investment offset the weakness in the commercial aircraft market between 1992 and 1995, and shipments rose 27%. An additional 13.4% increase was recorded last year as the commercial aircraft market took off once again. Employment actually declined by 5% in 1992 to 212,500 production workers. However, solid gains in key industry segments, particularly the recent rebound in commercial aircraft, saw the number of production workers swell to nearly 253,000 by the end of last year.

Forecast 1997-2006

In the near term, over the next two years, this catch-all category will be influenced by conflicting developments. Slower growth is on tap in business investment, and gains in motor vehicle industry activity will be subdued.

However, the recovery in commercial aircraft is actually accelerating. Our current forecast has real shipments of industrial machinery NEC rising by over 4% this year, with growth slowing to around 3% in 1998.

As the decade draws to a close, a replacement cycle in motor vehicles and growth in the mobile off-highway equipment market will bolster production of carburetors, pistons, piston rings, and valves. These markets will also have a positive impact on machine shops that are tied to automotive and off-highway equipment production. The growth in commercial aircraft will be slowing, however, as the decade draws to a close, but machine shops that are linked to this market will continue to experience healthy levels of business. Modest growth in business investment, and a relatively healthy export market should also bolster demand for miscellaneous industrial machinery. On balance, real shipments are slated to expand by about 3% per year in 1999 and 2000. Longer-term 2001-2006, we are projecting growth in shipments of about 3.5% per year, reflecting our expectations for the general economy, motor vehicle and aerospace industry activity, business investment, and foreign trade prospects.

Industrial Machinery, n.e.c.
Growth in Sales (Line) and Volume (Bar)

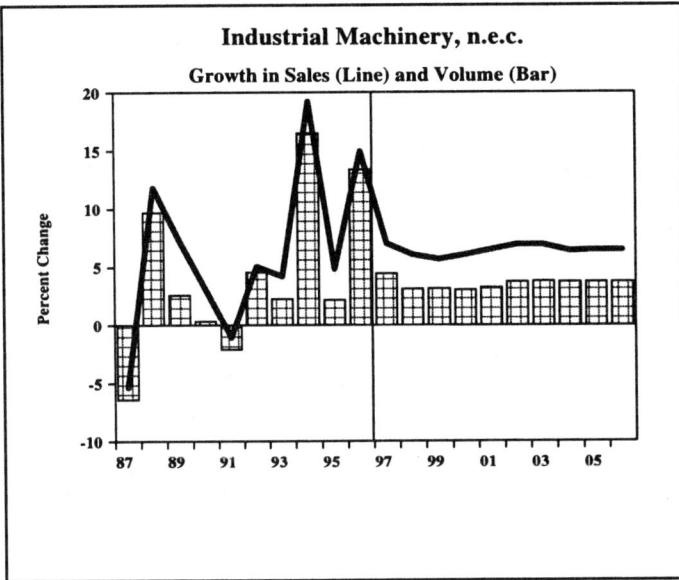

Industrial Machinery, n.e.c.
Growth in Product Prices

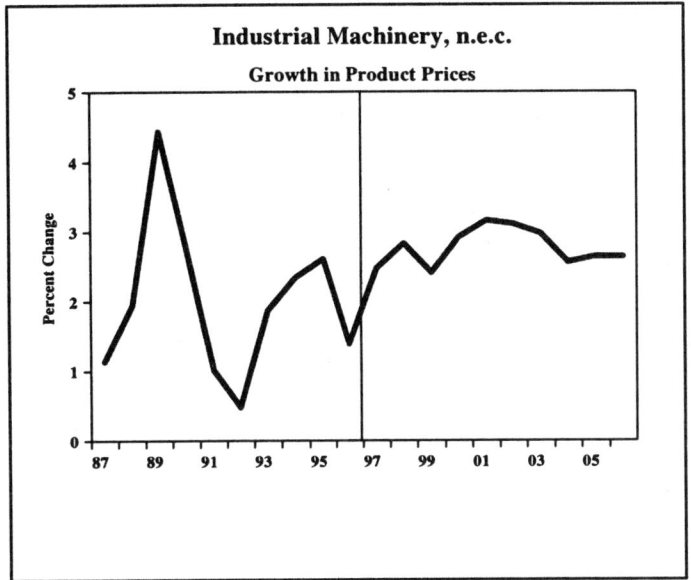

Industrial Machinery, n.e.c.
 SIC 359

Growth		1990	1991	1992	1993	1994	1995	1996	1997	1998	Compound Ann Avg 1986-1996	1996-2006
Sales												
	Billions of $	24.54	24.27	25.50	26.56	31.67	33.20	38.17	40.85	43.31		
	% Change	3.1	-1.1	5.1	4.2	19.2	4.8	15.0	7.0	6.0	6.2	6.4
Volume	% Change	0.3	-2.1	4.6	2.3	16.5	2.2	13.4	4.4	3.1	4.1	3.6
Prices	% Change	2.7	1.0	0.5	1.9	2.3	2.6	1.4	2.5	2.8	2.0	2.8
Exports												
	Billions of $	9.44	10.20	10.43	11.58	13.34	16.57	18.02	19.30	20.55		
	% Change	1.8	8.0	2.3	11.0	15.2	24.2	8.8	7.1	6.4	13.5	5.4
Imports												
	Billions of $	7.09	7.29	7.69	8.57	10.21	12.39	13.33	14.06	15.23		
	% Change	2.6	2.8	5.5	11.5	19.1	21.3	7.6	5.5	8.3	11.2	8.8
Apparent Consumption												
	Billions of $	22.19	21.36	22.75	23.56	28.54	29.02	33.48	35.60	37.99		
	Nominal % Change	3.5	-3.7	6.5	3.5	21.1	1.7	15.4	6.3	6.7	5.0	7.9
	Real % Change	0.7	-4.7	6.0	1.6	18.4	-0.9	13.8	3.8	3.8	3.0	5.0

Home Appliance Manufacturers

Household appliances include both major appliances such as stoves and refrigerators, and smaller items like vacuum cleaners, and hot plates. The industry is subdivided into cooking equipment, refrigerators and freezers, laundry equipment, electric housewares (generally small electrical items such as blenders and can openers), vacuum cleaners, and other appliances including water heaters, sewing machines, and garbage disposal units. The category does not include electronic and entertainment equipment such as televisions and computers.

Demand

Fluctuations in the demand for appliances are closely related to fluctuations in housing demand. Appliance shipments therefore jumped in the early 1990s after the end of the recession. In fact, the rise in appliance shipments was faster than the modest housing recovery would have justified. This was likely caused by the continued increase in sales of existing homes, which have been trending upward since the early 1980s, combined with a rash of home improvement projects in conjunction with refinancing that resulted from low mortgage rates, and pent–up demand caused by the recession. By the end of 1994, appliance shipment growth dropped back down to more normal levels.

Appliance Shipments Follow Housing Markets

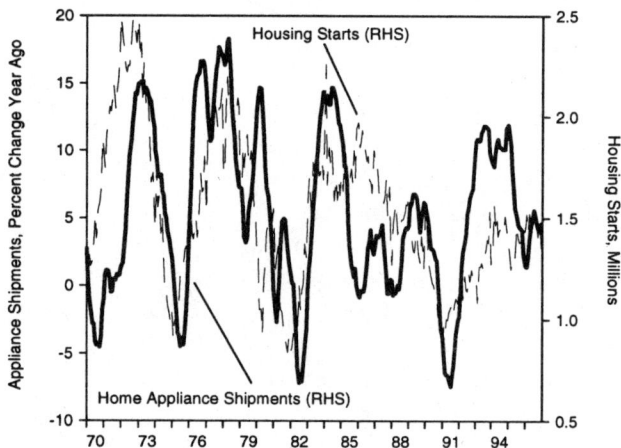

The industry's shipments value is dominated by major appliances. Each of the main types of appliances accounts for roughly one–fifth of total shipments, with refrigerators and electric housewares accounting for a little

more, and cooking appliances a little less. Since 1980, shipments of other appliances have grown faster than average, while shipments of electric housewares and fans have hardly grown at all. This is the result of technological change, which has allowed the price of these appliances to fall as electro–mechanical controls are replaced by electronic controls, and foreign competition, which is greater in this area than in the traditional "white goods" such as refrigerators and laundry machines. Shipments of the "white goods" categories have grown at about the same 4% to 5% rate over this period.

Shipments are not Dominated by One Type of Appliance

Refrigerators & Freezers	22.6%
Electric Housewares	21.9%
Laundry	20.2%
Cooking	16.7%
Other Appliances	18.6%

Supply and Industry Structure

Major household appliance manufacturing is dominated by five large manufacturers. Each manufacturer may have several name brands, the result of past mergers and the desire to provide a broad spectrum of products. Major manufacturers are generally older, established companies, and there are few new entries into this industry. Several (such as GE and Amana) are divisions of large diversified manufacturing corporations.

Because it follows housing, home appliance manufacturing is quite cyclical. Shipments typically drop 30% from year–ago levels during recessions, as both new housing and replacement demand decline. The most recent recession brought a relatively moderate drop of 15%, however.

Foreign Trade Issues

U.S. manufacturers specialize in certain portions of this industry. The United States tends to manufacture and export the so–called "white goods" which include refrigerators, freezers, and laundry machines. Imports are concentrated in electronic–type appliances, such as microwave ovens, and smaller appliances. In aggregate, the value of imports and the value of exports are generally very close, so that the United States runs an approximate trade balance in the overall category.

NAFTA presents a major trade challenge to U.S. manufacturers. "White goods" can clearly be as easily manufactured in Mexico as in the United States or Canada. With the proximity of Mexico to U.S. markets, the major manufacturers will almost certainly move some production there to take advantage of lower costs, resulting in lost production in the United States. On the other hand, high–end appliances (those which are larger and have more features) will continue to be produced in the United States, and NAFTA will likely result in a significant increase in the export market for these goods. On the whole, however, the United States is likely to see its trade position in this industry erode over time because of NAFTA.

Pricing

Appliance prices, like prices of many goods, have risen very slowly over the past few years. Between 1990 and 1996, prices of major appliances rose an average of only 0.3% per year, while all consumer prices rose an average of 3.1% per year. Appliance manufacturers responded by attempting to cut costs even while maintaining shipment levels. Employment in the industry has thus grown more slowly than production. Output per worker has grown at about 6% per year, allowing wages to keep up despite the price pressure on the industry.

Environmental Issues

Aside from normal environmental issues faced by all manufacturing firms, appliance manufacturers must deal with two special concerns:

- *Energy Use.* Both consumers and government regulators desire more efficient appliances. Over the past 20 years, the manufacturers have made important strides in improving the energy use of some appliances (notably refrigerators). U.S. manufacturers are world leaders in this area. Appliance manufacturers are currently negotiating with the Department of Energy about the introduction of efficiency standards for refrigerators, much like the standards that exist for automobiles.

- *Refrigerants.* Until recently, chlorofluorocarbons (CFCs) were considered the ideal substance for refrigerants. Unfortunately, these substances contribute to the depletion of the ozone in the Earth's upper atmosphere. In 1990, the United States and many other countries signed the Montreal Protocol, which required countries to phase out the use of these substances. The industry responded by developing refrigerators using hydrochlorofluorocarbons (HCFCs), but these are due to be phased out by 2030. The industry continues to sponsor research to find new non–chlorine refrigerants that meet the standards of the protocol. The new technology will likely add to costs, however, in an environment where consumers are clearly unwilling to pay more for appliances.

Outlook

The aging of the population and slow growth of households will help to keep growth in the household appliance industry at moderate levels. Production volume will rise at an annual average of less than 1% per year, as the industry continues to experience severe competition from both imports and other spending opportunities. Export growth will not remain as strong as in the past 10 years. Imports, however, will grow rapidly, as U.S. manufacturers take advantage of lower production costs in Mexico and as the heavily imported small electronic appliances grow more rapidly than the market overall.

Household Appliances
Growth in Sales (Line) and Volume (Bar)

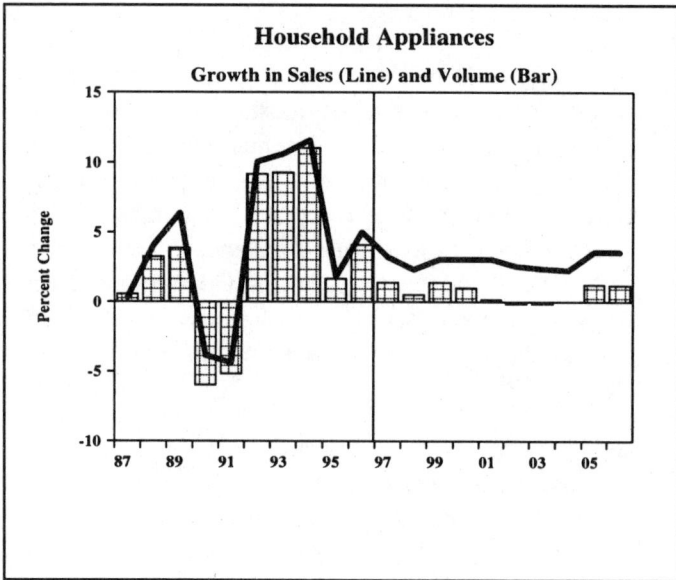

Household Appliances
Growth in Product Prices

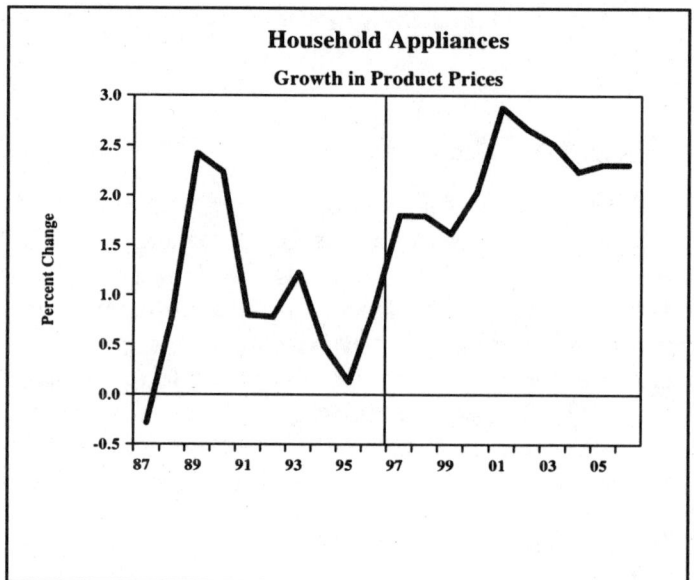

Household Appliances
  SIC 363

		1990	1991	1992	1993	1994	1995	1996	1997	1998	Compound Ann Avg Growth 1986-1996	1996-2006
Sales												
	Billions of $	17.65	16.88	18.56	20.53	22.91	23.32	24.48	25.27	25.86		
	% Change	-3.9	-4.4	10.0	10.6	11.6	1.8	5.0	3.2	2.3	4.0	2.9
Volume	% Change	-6.0	-5.1	9.2	9.3	11.0	1.7	4.1	1.4	0.5	3.0	0.7
Prices	% Change	2.2	0.8	0.8	1.2	0.5	0.1	0.9	1.8	1.8	0.9	2.2
Exports												
	Billions of $	2.99	3.43	3.84	4.13	4.39	4.61	5.01	5.41	5.78		
	% Change	8.8	15.0	12.0	7.5	6.2	5.1	8.6	8.1	6.8	21.5	3.7
Imports												
	Billions of $	3.83	3.80	4.34	4.48	5.13	5.31	5.59	6.12	6.51		
	% Change	-4.4	-1.0	14.3	3.3	14.4	3.5	5.2	9.5	6.5	7.3	7.2
Apparent Consumption												
	Billions of $	18.50	17.24	19.06	20.89	23.66	24.02	25.06	25.98	26.59		
	Nominal % Change	-5.7	-6.8	10.6	9.6	13.3	1.6	4.3	3.6	2.4	3.0	3.9
	Real % Change	-7.8	-7.5	9.7	8.3	12.7	1.4	3.4	1.8	0.6	2.1	1.6

Chapter 19: Computers and Electronic Equipment

Computers and Office Machines

The technology–driven computer and office machines industry has grown at a phenomenal pace since 1992, posting double–digit rates on average. Last year was no exception to this trend. Volume growth has been even more remarkable due in great part to the large price declines that have now been a feature of this industry for the past several years. WEFA expects both volume and shipments to continue increasing at a solid clip during the next ten years.

Growth Continues

Much of the computer and office equipment growth in 1996 was in the area of communication interfaces (fax modems, PCMCIA cards, and ethernet cards). Connection to the world wide web and/or a corporate intranet was definitely last year's flavor of choice for the computer sector, which took advantage of strong demand from businesses and individuals alike. Sales of communication interfaces were up by more than 43% compared to the previous year.

Other strong growth segments were central processing units (CPUs) and memory. CPU and memory chip production led the computer equipment sector in dollar value at over $62 billion. Much of this demand for CPUs and memory was driven by the consumers' and computer manufacturers' need to upgrade, with the installation of chips with ever–increasing performance required to keep up with new operating systems and software. U.S. producers' sales of CPUs for personal computers and workstations was up 16% from 1995, and little slowing in that growth pace is likely for the next several years. There are two major factors behind this trend, both associated with the introduction of new chip technologies from Intel.

The first source of continuing CPU growth is the release of the sixth generation Pentium Pro which, for the first time, allows a true 32–bit compiling processor.

The second source of growth is exciting news for multimedia–hungry users, the release of the MMX chip.

Not all segments of the computer industry were as fortunate in 1996, since the growth of new technology inevitably pushes out the old. The two hardest–hit product groups were large mainframes and minicomputers. The Achilles heel for these markets is the server. Today's technology is providing servers which are lower priced, almost as powerful, and running with easier visual operating systems as compared with the large mainframes and minicomputers.

IBM, the major manufacturer of mainframes, has released their new CMOS (complementary metal–oxide semiconductor) mainframe in an attempt to stall the erosion of the mainframe market that has occurred over the last several years. This new mainframe has some significant advantages over its ancestors, including a 20% cheaper price tag, and lower maintenance costs since it is no longer water cooled. Although this new CMOS technology is delaying the mainframe demand slide, the days of the large mainframes and minicomputers are coming to an end.

In contrast to the stellar performance of the computer equipment sector, other types of office equipment experienced sales growth of only 4% in 1996. This smaller increase is due in large part to a 3% decline in monochrome copiers. Even with this downward slide, sales of monochrome copiers, at $6 billion, were three times larger than the second largest segment, color copiers. Color copiers did, however, post the largest sales advance, up over 40% from 1995, due primarily to businesses taking advantage of lower price tags. Prices finally came down after several years of being out of an acceptable price range for many companies.

Computer and office equipment exports were valued at $46 billion last year. Over 40% of these exports were in computer parts, shipped predominantly to Europe, Canada, and Mexico. Computer peripherals exports were also significant, at a little over $12 billion. The remaining exports were comprised mostly of computer systems, copiers, and printers. Imports were valued at $68 billion, a 10% increase from 1995. The trade deficit is likely to expand over the next few years due to the increasing imports of computer peripherals from Japan, Singapore, Taiwan, South Korea, and Canada.

Outlook

Several factors should contribute to the ongoing growth in computer and business equipment. First, technology improvements and stiff global competition will continue to lead to lower prices. Prices for this sector fell 16.5% in 1996, following declines of 11.4% and 9.6% in 1995 and 1994, respectively. Second, demand for business equipment remains on a fast track. Business investment in computer and office equipment has posted remarkable growth since 1992. Last year, investment was up 18%. Over the next five years dollar spending on computers and office equipment should maintain an upward growth path at close to 10% on average. A good deal of this demand will be from the development of new technology that makes it easier for people to work out of their homes. According to the Electronics Industry Association (EIA), 54% of American homes had home businesses in 1995, and they greatly contributed to the increasing demand for printers, faxes, copiers, and calculators.

Business Investment

Computer and Office Equipment

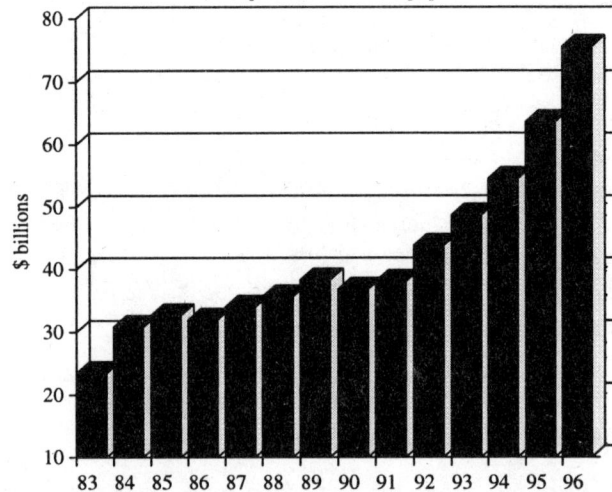

The third factor is the emergence of the information superhighway. It is becoming more apparent that this superhighway revolution is not just a fad. For example, equipment designed for visual and image conferencing is in use today, and will become higher–quality and more accepted for business applications, as faster chips such as the MMX chip from Intel become the standard processor format in computers in the future.

The last factor, and undoubtedly the largest area of growth potential, is the television and telephone market. In the next several years it will become more difficult to distinguish television sets from computers. The recent announcement by the FCC that will make digital television transmission (HDTV) the standard by 2006 may have opened the door to a large market for computer monitor and computer hardware manufacturers. Telephones with digital displays are also likely to become standards as we move into the next millennium.

```
Computer and Office Machines
 SIC 357

                                                                                        Compound Ann Avg Growth
                          1990   1991   1992   1993   1994   1995   1996   1997   1998   1986-1996  1996-2006


Sales
        Billions of $    65.18  60.78  66.55  68.98  79.30  93.38 103.95 116.05 123.57
            % Change      -1.5   -6.8    9.5    3.6   15.0   17.7   11.3   11.6    6.5      6.2        6.9


Exports
        Billions of $    28.03  29.78  31.34  31.70  35.78  42.37  46.66  45.75  46.63
            % Change       4.9    6.3    5.2    1.1   12.9   18.4   10.1   -2.0    1.9     11.0        3.3
Imports
        Billions of $    27.09  30.20  36.59  43.44  52.40  63.14  68.21  73.52  82.47
            % Change       4.7   11.5   21.2   18.7   20.6   20.5    8.0    7.8   12.2     16.9        7.2

Apparent Consumption
        Billions of $    64.25  61.20  71.80  80.72  95.92 114.14 125.49 143.82 159.41
      Nominal % Change    -1.6   -4.8   17.3   12.4   18.8   19.0    9.9   14.6   10.8      8.6        8.2
         Real % Change     9.5    6.9   37.8   29.6   31.4   34.3   31.7   19.5   11.9     22.9        9.4
```

Computer Equipment

For the computer equipment industry, the last several years were ones that most producers in the market would surely like to duplicate. U.S. shipments of computer equipment were up by more than 13% in 1996. This growth was pretty dramatic, considering that in 1995 shipments rose by 17.8%. The factors that have driven the domestic market for computers over the past few years will continue to have a positive tilt, and will continue to stimulate spending for new equipment. WEFA forecasts domestic spending for computers will grow by about 8% per year for the next few years.

Shipments of computers account for about 65% of the sales of the computers and office machines industry, and have risen by about 140% during the 1992–96 period.

Computer costs have been declining for more than a decade, dropping by 12% in 1995 and over 20% last year. Prices of personal computers fell 20% in 1995 and a whopping 30% this past year, even as a succession of more powerful products hit the market.

Computer Prices

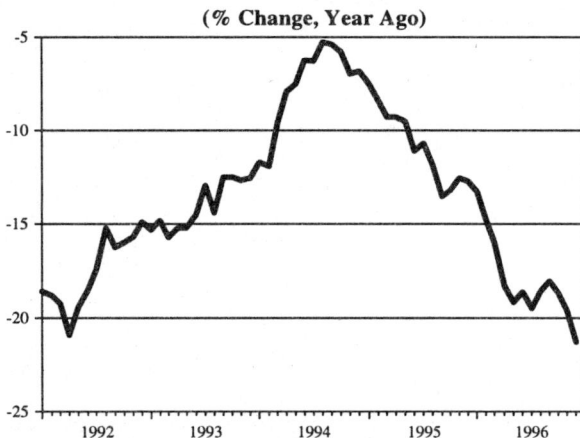

(% Change, Year Ago)

The steady drop in computer prices has been accompanied by an equally steady stream of faster and more capable computer systems and software. This has played no small role in the recent buying binge by corporations, individuals, and the public sector. Since Pentium chips were introduced in 1995, there have been three enhancements or upgrades. Looking at it another way, at the rate new products have been hitting the street, the computer system you buy today will be surpassed by a new and improved model in only about nine months.

Domestic Consumption

Business investment in computers and peripheral equipment grew by 67%, in nominal terms, during the 1992–95 period, and expanded by another 20%–25% last year. Personal and public sector spending for computers and related equipment more than doubled, in nominal terms, during the 1992–95 period, but the growth appears to have slowed in 1996, perhaps as these customers tried to absorb the huge influx of new equipment they have purchased in recent years.

The surge in business spending for computers and related equipment was triggered by a combination of factors, including lower prices, strong growth in corporate profits, low interest rates, intense pressure to improve productivity and efficiency, and advances in computer and software technology. Consumer spending for computers and related equipment was also influenced by declining prices, technological improvements, the explosion of information available on the internet, a greater focus on computer literacy in grammar and high schools and at the college level, and expanding consumer incomes. Public sector investment in computers and related equipment was stimulated by improved finances, particularly at the state and local level, a need to improve the delivery of services and reign in costs, the availability of a lot of computer power at declining prices, and the emphasis on computer literacy in school systems.

The near term prospects for the domestic market remain constructive, although we do not expect a return to the double–digit growth rates achieved during 1992–96. Computer prices will decline further, but we are assuming that price declines will moderate somewhat over the near term. WEFA forecasts that prices of all computers will drop 15% in 1997, and personal computer prices will fall by 23%.

- One sure bet is that computer and software companies will continue to introduce new and more powerful products which will continue to enliven the market.

- The pressures on the corporate and public sector to improve productivity and efficiency will remain intense, keeping these market segments very active.

- The pressure on the education system to boost the computer literacy of students is increasing and this will continue to stimulate personal and public sector outlays for new equipment.

- There is more and more information being made available on the internet every day and the number of internet users will continue to grow rapidly.

- Corporate profits, consumer income, and government revenue growth will be less than robust, but should be adequate to promote additional equipment purchases.

The factors that have driven the domestic market for computers over the past few years will continue to have a positive tilt, and will continue to stimulate spending for new equipment. WEFA forecasts growth of domestic spending for computers to grow by about 8% per year for the next few years.

Foreign Trade

The United States first recorded a trade deficit in computers and office equipment, $416 million, in 1991. Since then the deficit has grown dramatically, exceeding $21 billion in 1996. Imports of computers and accessories expanded by 10% in 1996 to $56 billion. Japan, Singapore, Taiwan, and South Korea continue to be the primary overseas sources. U.S. subsidiaries based in Asia and other overseas locations are also major providers.

Exports of computers and accessories rose by 12% in 1996. Major exports markets include Canada, Japan, Western Europe, Asia, Mexico, and the rest of Latin America.

Exports are forecast to continue to grow, in the range of 8% to 10% per year. Improving economic conditions in Canada, Mexico, and Latin America will provide much of the support, particularly in 1998. Sales to Western Europe, Japan, and other Asian countries will continue to gain ground, but at a more subdued pace. Imports should continue to gain ground over the near term, also rising by about 8% per year. Continued healthy demand for computers, the increasing popularity of mail order companies, such as Gateway, which largely manufacture offshore, and a relatively strong dollar should allow imports to nudge their share of the total U.S. market for computers and office machines to 55.5% by 1999.

Domestic Consumption of Computers and Office Equipment
(Bil.$)

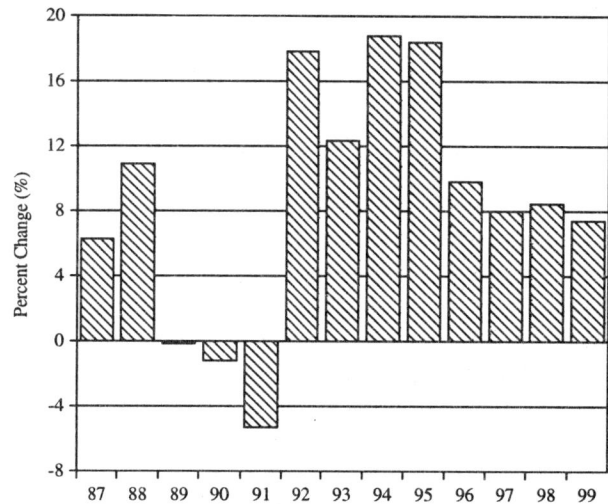

Storage Devices

Shipments of storage devices showed amazing growth in 1996 in all areas: rigid disk drives (hard drives) increased by more than 20%; optical drives (CD–ROM) grew in excess of 30%; disk arrays (RAID) growth was 25%; and removable disk drives climbed 15%. Although the pace of growth that occurred over the last five years may not be sustainable into the future, it is estimated that by the year 2000 shipments of storage devices should be 50% higher than 1996 sales.

While shipments were increasing during 1996, prices were falling unmercifully. Average storage device prices fell 15.3% from 1995. Prices of fixed disks, heavily represented by the 3.5 inch disk drive, fell by more than 25%. Optical drive prices fell 19%.

Optical Drives

The United States was once a leader in the manufacture of optical storage devices, but it has now been overtaken by Asian producers. It is estimated that in 1996 only 10% of world CD–ROM drive output was manufactured in the United States. Worldwide production of companies with U.S. ownership has a higher share, however, of almost 25%.

Since their introduction to the computer market in the early 1990s CD–ROM drives have not skipped a beat. Readable CD–ROM drives accounted for 95% of all optical storage device shipments in 1996. The remaining share was held by writable CD–ROMs, which have been growing in share but whose growth has been limited so far by their higher price. As prices drop on writable CD–ROMs, the read–only CR–ROM will likely fade, and the share of writable CD–ROMs in all optical storage devices is likely to quadruple by 2000.

A new product that will be a source of growth for optical devices is the DVD–ROM drive. This new device provides 3 to 4 times more storage space, as well as smoother delivery of data, particularly for video information.

Removable Disks

Another growth area for storage devices in 1996 was removable storage devices. Shipments in this sector grew 15%, up from 10% in 1995. The demand of removable data storage devices was spurred on by the release of the Iomega Zip Drive. This device lets a user store up to 100 megabytes of information on a removable 3.5 inch disk. Sales of these high capacity disk drives grew by more than 600% last year. Other storage devices are also showing strong growth in this sector. Rigid disk cartridge drives jumped 200% in 1996, and removable small optical drives grew by more than 65%.

Market Share of Storage Devices, 1996

Rigid Drives	39%
Removable Drives	36%
Optical Drives	21%
RAID	4%

Growth in removable data storage is expected to remain on track. Double–digit gains are forecasted into the millennium. Most of the impetus should come from flexible disk drives, as they become a standard part of equipment for PCs, especially for on–the–go users.

Rigid Disks

Rigid disk storage devices had an exceptional year of shipment growth of 22.5% in 1996, following 28% growth in 1995. Most of the upswing in the rigid disk market was from the old reliable 3.5 inch fixed disk drives, which constitute nearly 90% of this market. Sales of 3.5 inch disk drives increased 19% in 1996, while prices fell 27%. The biggest sellers in the 3.5 inch disk market for 1996 were 1 — 2 gigabyte drives.

Demand for rigid disk drives should continue to grow at rates close to 20% per year through the turn of the century. As long as computer manufacturers continue to ship more computer units with ever–increasing software packages demanding up to 100 megabytes of storage space, fixed drive demand will stay at this high level. In addition to the demand from the computer OEMs, users are also constantly upgrading software and requiring more storage and more extra storage devices.

Communication Equipment

Shipments of communication equipment grew at an annual rate of 7.9% during the 1986-96 period, reaching $72.6 billion last year. Strong domestic demand, prompted by favorable economic conditions and dramatic technological advances, combined with a vibrant export market to support this growth.

Over the next ten years, shipments are slated to expand 6.5% per year. Positive economic and market fundamentals in the United States, deregulation of the telecommunications industry, and ongoing efforts to upgrade and modernize voice and data communication systems will bolster domestic sales. U.S. exports will expand steadily, supported by solid economic growth overseas, the efforts of developed nations to follow the U.S. lead in voice and data communication, and developing nation investment programs aimed at establishing a modern communications infrastructure.

Communication equipment can be divided into two major categories, telephone and telegraph apparatus, and radio and television broadcasting and communication equipment.

Telephone and telegraph apparatus includes switching and transmission equipment, telephones, and fax machines. Radio and television broadcasting and communication equipment includes fixed and mobile radio systems, cellular radio telephones, radio transmitters, transceivers, and receivers, fiber optics equipment, satellite communication systems, television equipment, and studio audio and video equipment.

The communication equipment industry employed about 263,000 people last year. The recent low point in employment came in 1992 when the industry employed 238,500 workers. The producers of telephone and telegraph apparatus employed just under 113,000 workers in 1996, up from a low point in the past decade of 109,500 workers in 1994. The radio and television communications equipment industry employed 150,000 workers in 1996 versus a low of 129,000 in 1992.

Domestic Demand

Domestic spending for communication equipment grew at a compound annual rate of 6.2% during the past decade, 1986-96, reaching $66.6 billion last year. Since emerging from the 1991 recession, U.S. consumption of communication equipment has grown by over 76%. This surge in spending is even more striking given that it occurred during a period of very little inflation in communication equipment, with prices rising only about 1% per year on average. Thus, in volume terms the spending for communication equipment grew by 70% during this period.

Most of the growth of the last decade occurred in the last three years. From 1994 to 1996, business outlays for communications equipment surged 55%. Corporate America has made great strides in its efforts to expand and upgrade voice and data communication systems in order to improve operating efficiency and reduce costs. The explosion in spending for computers, the increased use of local and wide area networks, and very strong growth in business activity on the internet, has played no small role in all of this.

Growth in corporate profits and the rebound in new office construction has also bolstered spending for telephone network and on-premises equipment, such as phones, fax machines, voice mail systems, and modems. Finally, the use of commercial satellite communication has expanded dramatically during the past decade.

The communications industry itself has been taking advantage of new technology, strong demand for a widening array of services, and deregulation, and is spending freely. Both local and long-distance telecommunications companies have been investing heavily in an effort to meet the current demands of their customers and position themselves for the future.

- Sprint has been building one of the nation's largest wireless calling networks, using personal communications services technology. In the first quarter of 1997 alone, Sprint's capital spending totaled $600 million, 25% above year–ago levels.

■ GTE's capital spending reached $4.2 billion last year.

■ The pressure on the Baby Bells to boost investment has been more severe after years of operating in monopoly markets left them with outmoded networks ill–suited for the emerging new era in communications.

Broadcast and cable television companies have also been very aggressive on the investment front. Cable companies alone spent about $1.8 billion last year to upgrade their systems for new services.

The progress in new home construction since the last recession has had a positive impact on the demand for phone transmission systems and switches purchased by public and private service providers, and private branch exchanges. Second or third lines have been added in millions of households to link home computers to the internet. In addition, the demand for telephones, including portables and cellular phones, paging systems, modems, and satellite TV dishes has gained ground as consumer income expanded and the prices of new equipment became more attractive.

Department of Defense outlays for communication equipment retreated during the last ten years as a result of the end of the Cold War and major budget cuts. Shipments of military communication equipment totaled only $3.2 billion last year. On the other hand, non-defense federal, state, and local government purchases of communication equipment have been expanding, driven by a pressing need to upgrade communication systems, improved economic conditions which boosted government receipts, technological advances, and attractive equipment and systems prices.

Foreign Trade

U.S. exports of communication equipment grew at a staggering rate of almost 17% per year, on average, during the past decade. Growth last year slowed to just 3%, with exports totaling $20.3 billion, but this followed gains of 22% in 1995, 21% in 1994, and 18% in 1993. Western Europe, Canada, Japan, Mexico, and in recent years China, are the major U.S. markets for communication equipment.

Imports of communication equipment, primarily from Japan, China, other Asian countries, and Canada, grew by 11% per annum during the 1986-96 period, reaching $15.9 billion last year. Foreign manufacturers have a commanding presence in the line and cordless phone, fax machine, and paging systems market. Last year, imports accounted for 21.5% of the U.S. communications equipment market. This represented a low share in the last six years; imports captured an average share of 26% during the 1990-95 period, and the share peaked at 28.6% in 1994. WEFA believes the loss of share for imports reflects a shift in the mix of products being purchased, away from the simpler consumer products toward technology, equipment, and systems purchased by corporate users and the communications industry. These business communications products are largely manufactured in this country.

The United States had a trade deficit in communications equipment of $350 million in 1990. Since then, the industry has moved strongly into a surplus position that reached a peak of $6 billion last year. The United States is still in a deficit position in the customer premises equipment market (telephones, fax machines, etc.) but more than offsets that deficit with a strong surplus in network, transmission, radio communications, broadcasting, and other communications equipment.

Forecast

WEFA is conservatively projecting growth in shipments of communication equipment of 6.5% per year, on average, during the next 10 years. This will put U.S. manufacturer shipments at about $120 billion by the year 2006. There is considerable upside risk to this forecast, but the conservatism is prudent given the continued strength of the U.S. dollar. This exchange rate problem could encourage foreign competition in the business communication equipment market, where overseas producers could make their way into some of the simpler products that could have wide global markets.

Domestic demand is slated to expand by about 5% per year, exceeding $100 billion by 2006. Import growth will moderate to 7% per year, with foreign equipment sales to the United States of roughly $25 billion in 2006. Imports are expected to gain share in the coming decade as the demand for customer premises equipment remains strong, and foreign equipment manufacturers begin to increase their presence in other markets. By the end of the forecast horizon we expect imports to capture about 25% of U.S. demand.

Domestic demand for communication equipment will be favorably influenced by general economic conditions, growth in consumer income and corporate profits, and the steady, if modest, growth in new housing and commercial buildings. The pressure on U.S. businesses to improve productivity and efficiency, and public sector efforts to further improve voice and data communications systems, will lend additional support. The use of computers, LAN and WAN networks, the internet, portable phones, fax machines, paging systems, voice mail, satellite communication systems, etc., will only increase in the coming decade as consumers, businesses, and the public sector continue to embrace new technologies.

Commercial use of Global Positioning System (GPS) navigation systems has been rising and will continue to provide support during the forecast period. Over-the-road truckers, railroads, and the shipping industry have already turned to satellite communication systems that are used to pinpoint the location of equipment. This allows equipment owners to better monitor equipment utilization and more efficiently schedule traffic flows.

Deregulation of the telecommunications industry will result in an interlocking of the various communications industries, including telephone services, cable television, and even information services. The goal is to put together packages of local and long-distance phone, data, and video services. To accomplish this end, it will be necessary for these industries to maintain a high level of capital investment.

The Defense Department and commercial aircraft markets will also provide some support. The big reductions in defense spending are behind us, and there is some hope that procurement will turn the corner in the years ahead.

However, just the fact that we have gone from big declines in defense spending to much more subdued declines, and will eventually see modest increases in procurement, should be viewed as a positive development for communication equipment.

Commercial aircraft did well from 1990 to 1992 and then fell into a slump that has only recently ended. The prospects for commercial aircraft, particularly over the next few years, are very positive. This will also serve to increase the demand for communication equipment.

Strong growth in air traffic worldwide will certainly boost investment in air traffic control and communication systems throughout the next decade, which also will have a positive impact on the communication equipment industry. There is considerable concern about the quality of air traffic control and communication systems in developing regions of the world, which are also expected to experience the most dramatic gains in traffic during the next ten years. We also expect aggressive efforts to modernize these systems in traffic lanes that are currently well traveled and experiencing congestion.

Growth in communication equipment exports will remain strong over the next decade, growing by about 11% per year. With overseas sales reaching $43 billion by 2006, the U.S. trade surplus in communication equipment will hit $18 billion. We anticipate steady growth from our traditional export markets, primarily developed countries, as they continue their efforts to expand and upgrade communications systems, and adopt emerging technologies. However, the real action in the coming decade will be in China, Southeast Asia, India, Mexico, Latin America, Eastern Europe, and the former Soviet Union. These areas of the world have the greatest need to expand and upgrade existing communications capabilities, and in some cases to establish a modern communications infrastructure from scratch.

Communication Equipment
Growth in Sales (Line) and Volume (Bar)

Communication Equipment
Growth in Product Prices

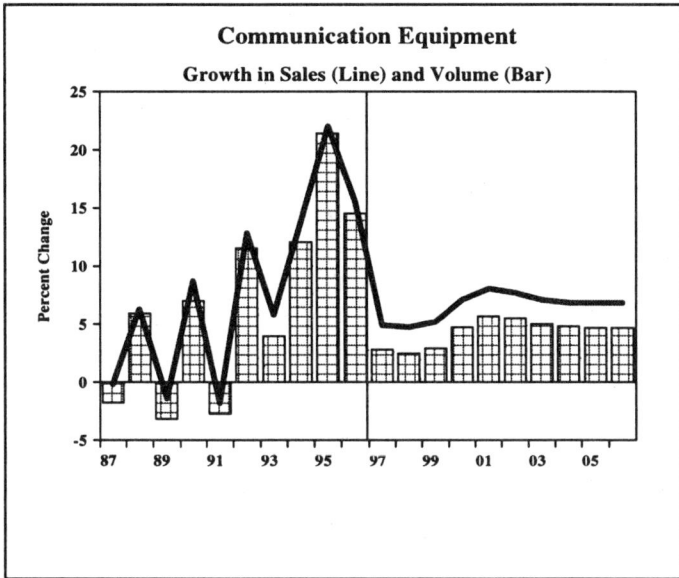

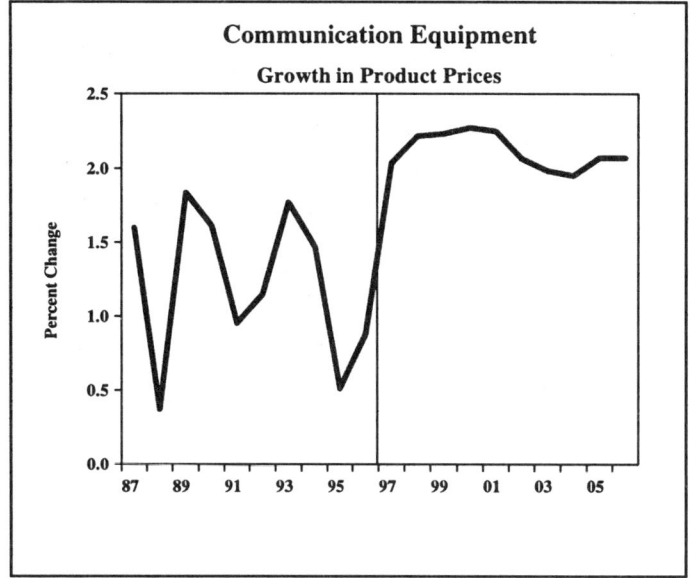

```
Communication Equipment
 SIC 366

                                                                                   Compound Ann Avg Growth
                       1990    1991    1992    1993    1994    1995    1996    1997    1998    1986-1996 1996-2006

Sales
        Billions of $  38.66   37.97   42.83   45.31   51.52   62.87   72.62   76.16   79.75
           % Change      8.7    -1.8    12.8     5.8    13.7    22.0    15.5     4.9     4.7       7.9       6.5

  Volume  % Change       7.0    -2.7    11.5     4.0    12.1    21.4    14.5     2.8     2.5       6.6       4.3
  Prices  % Change       1.6     1.0     1.1     1.8     1.5     0.5     0.9     2.0     2.2       1.2       2.1

Exports
        Billions of $   9.14   10.16   11.36   13.36   16.21   19.81   20.34   22.90   25.66
           % Change     13.4    11.2    11.8    17.6    21.4    22.2     2.7    12.6    12.0      16.8      11.0
Imports
        Billions of $   9.49    9.94   10.78   11.28   14.18   15.33   14.31   14.88   15.89
           % Change     -1.0     4.7     8.4     4.6    25.8     8.1    -6.7     4.0     6.8       7.5       7.2

Apparent Consumption
        Billions of $  39.01   37.75   42.24   43.23   49.50   58.39   66.58   68.13   69.99
      Nominal % Change   5.2    -3.2    11.9     2.3    14.5    18.0    14.0     2.3     2.7       6.2       4.9
         Real % Change   3.5    -4.2    10.6     0.6    12.8    17.4    13.0     0.3     0.5       4.9       2.7
```

Electronic Components

Total sales by the U.S. electronic components industry rose to $125 billion in 1996, double the sales level of 1990. However, the 7.4% growth rate in 1996 was considerably weaker than the two years of tremendous performance in 1994 and 1995.

While the industry is recovering slowly and growth is expected to pick up over the next two years, in the long term the industry will gradually mature, slowing in growth and facing increasing competition from the rest of the world.

Electronic components are the fundamental building blocks for a wide range of electronic products.

Electronic components cover a wide range of products, including electron tubes, printed circuit boards, semiconductors and related devices, transistors, capacitors, resistors, coils, transformers, connectors, and others. They are widely used by many other industries, but the largest sources of direct demand are the computer, telecommunications, instrumentation, medical equipment, and transportation industries.

Market Overview

The overall electronic components market settled down in 1996 after growing at a torrid pace in the previous two years. Oversupply and price declines were common among many electronic products, especially semiconductors. Despite the 1996 correction, the industry managed to increase sales by 7.4% and exports by 4.6%, a performance that many other industries would envy. A steady recovery is currently underway, as overbuilt inventories were for the most part used off during 1996, and prices have been slowly firming.

The outlook for key end–user markets in the United States remains bright. Continuing economic growth will translate into further investment on efficiency–boosting hardware. Demand for computer equipment will likely be strong. Moreover, the personal computer (PC) is an accepted productivity–enhancing tool in corporate philosophy and a mushrooming consumer–entertainment and education product that is increasingly becoming a family focal point. The industry is expected to resume its dou-

ble–digit sales growth in 1997 and extend it into the beginning years of the next decade.

Components prices are forecast to remain weak. Rapid technological improvement – the keystone of the industry – is the main engine putting pressure on prices over time.

Since 1993, the trade deficit in the U.S. electronic components market has widened, reaching a peak at almost $5 billion in 1995. However, the trade deficit narrowed to $1 billion in 1996 – a year of correction, thanks to a 6% decline in imports. The decline in imports was the result of an overstocked domestic market. Meanwhile, exports grew only slightly, a significant decline in growth due to the strength of the U.S. dollar against many world currencies. The prospect in the near term is for little change in the trade balance for the U.S. electronic components industry, with imports growing slightly more rapidly than exports because of the improving domestic market.

Electronic Components Exports and Imports ($ billion)

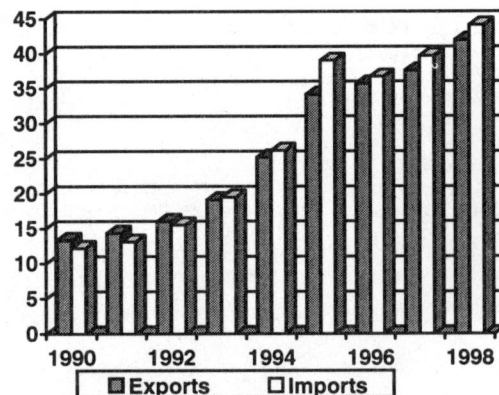

The gathering momentum of worldwide economic activity will create particularly strong growth in developing countries. In addition, many developing countries have adopted plans to dramatically upgrade their telecommunications and other technological infrastructures, and electronic components manufacturers will be the main beneficiaries of these plans during the next few years.

The long–term prospect for the U.S. electronic components industry is a gradual movement to a more mature industry and moderating growth rates. Companies will face continuing demand for higher performance products. The increased complexity of miniaturized, high–performance systems places a premium on compatibility and functionality among components. Nonetheless, the biggest challenge for U.S. companies is how to benefit from productivity and technological advantages to maintain the industry leading role, while facing intensified international competition.

International Competition

The ongoing economic recovery in Europe and more favorable exchange rates will certainly help to propel the European electronic components industry. Also, communication industry reform, deregulation, and the spin–off of state–owned enterprises will boost demand for new communication products, which are rich in electronic components. However, high unemployment and the absence of meaningful structural reform will serve to limit gains in the near term.

The Japanese electronic components industry also received a lift from its nation's recent economic rebound. Additional demand was created due to the partial deregulation of the wireless communication sector. With the Japanese government continuing to be reform–minded, more deregulation down the road seems likely, and it will bring a more competitive market environment and growth opportunities for the Japanese electronic components industry.

The developing countries of the Asia/Pacific region have chalked up economic growth rates in excess of 7% for many years. But weakness in 1996, in part tied to the electronic components industry inventory cycle, slowed growth by about one percentage point. However, this region will continue as the world's premier growth market for both supply and demand of electonic components. Of the less–sophisticated products, this region is the major world supplier with a distinctive advantage – low production costs. On the other hand, it provides one of the largest markets for more technologically sophisticated products, which are the best markets for U.S. producers.

Trade Issues

The electronic components industry is currently working with the Office of the United States Trade Representative (USTR) on identifying existing non–tariff trade barriers. This is in support of the USTR's agreement to work toward elimination of all non–tariff trade barriers by the year 2000 in accord with the implementation of the Information Technology Agreement (ITA). The elimination of non–tariff trade barriers will eventually increase the competitiveness of the U.S. electronic components industry in markets outside North America.

Electronic Components and Accessories
Growth in Sales (Line) and Volume (Bar)

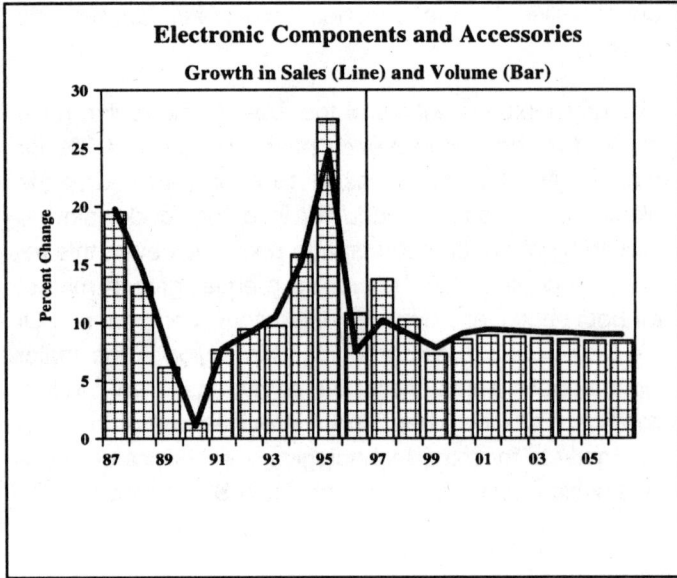

Electronic Components and Accessories
Growth in Product Prices

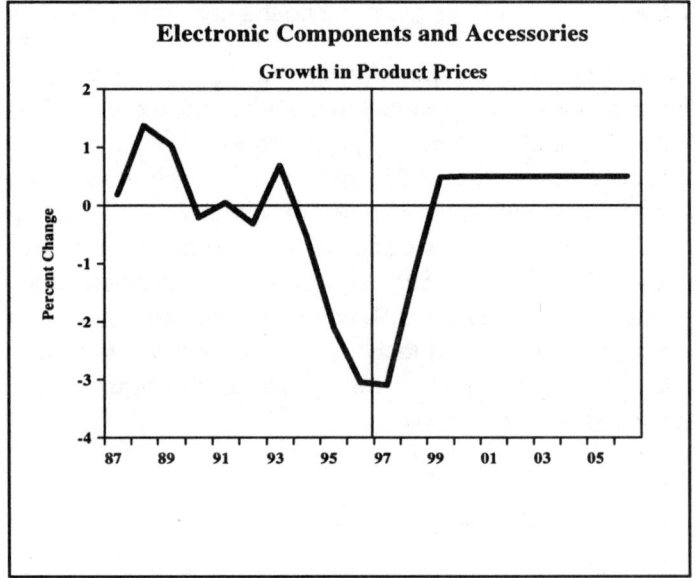

```
Electronic Components and Accessories
  SIC 367
```

Growth 2006		1990	1991	1992	1993	1994	1995	1996	1997	1998	Compound Ann Avg 1986-1996	1996-2006
Sales												
	Billions of $	62.60	67.43	73.55	81.28	93.67	116.89	125.57	138.38	150.74		
	% Change	1.1	7.7	9.1	10.5	15.2	24.8	7.4	10.2	8.9	11.6	9.1
Volume	% Change	1.3	7.7	9.4	9.8	15.9	27.5	10.8	13.7	10.3	11.9	9.1
Prices	% Change	-0.2	0.0	-0.3	0.7	-0.5	-2.1	-3.0	-3.1	-1.2	-0.3	-0.0
Exports												
	Billions of $	13.32	14.35	15.99	19.12	25.18	34.15	35.73	37.58	41.99		
	% Change	13.0	7.7	11.4	19.6	31.7	35.6	4.6	5.2	11.7	22.2	11.7
Imports												
	Billions of $	12.17	13.08	15.48	19.48	26.16	39.04	36.70	39.71	44.12		
	% Change	-1.3	7.5	18.3	25.9	34.3	49.3	-6.0	8.2	11.1	20.0	11.6
Apparent Consumption												
	Billions of $	61.44	66.16	73.04	81.64	94.65	121.78	126.54	140.51	152.87		
	Nominal % Change	-1.6	7.7	10.4	11.8	15.9	28.7	3.9	11.0	8.8	11.3	9.1
	Real % Change	-1.4	7.6	10.7	11.0	16.6	31.4	7.2	14.6	10.1	11.7	9.1

Printed Circuit Boards

After experiencing a boom year in 1995, the U.S. printed circuit board (PCB) industry began a period of consolidation in 1996. Company acquisitions and price consolidations were two major trends within the industry. Further consolidations and a return to slower but more sustainable growth rates are expected in 1997 and for the next few years.

The printed circuit board (PCB) provides both the physical structure for mounting electronic components and the electrical interconnection between these components. Industry professionals often refer to printed wiring boards (PWBs) as the bare circuit board, but in this analysis we will use PCB as the term for bare board. Printed circuit boards are used in a wide range of automotive, aerospace, telecommunications, and specialty applications involving electronics.

PCBs are usually classified into two major categories — rigid boards and flexible boards — depending on the base material used.

In the United States, PCB manufacturers represent a uniquely entrepreneurial business. Approximately 700 independent companies produced over $7.7 billion dollars of PCBs in 1996. Companies ranged in size from under $1 million in sales — often family-owned businesses — to public companies producing $300 million in revenue. PCB manufacturers serve every facet of the electronics industry from boards for industrial and environmental controls to computer central processing units and storage devices. While the large companies dominate the business, small companies can be competitive and successful by focusing on specific customer niches and meeting market demand.

The U.S. Market

The U.S. PCB industry had a boom year in 1995 when production grew by 15.2%. Although nearly double-digit growth rates were racked up in 1996, the pace was slower. Slower output growth coupled with large write-offs for plant start-ups, extraordinary items, and business consolidations caused many domestic PCB manufacturers to show lower earnings, or even losses, in 1996. In the fourth quarter of 1996, a group of 13 major publicly-held PCB manufacturing companies reported a $52 mil-

lion loss compared to a $20 million profit for the same period in 1995. Since business conditions have now improved, profits should increase in 1997.

One of the business realities and factors underlying U.S. PCB manufacturing growth over the past 20 years is the continuing trend for original equipment manufacturers (OEMs) to purchase PCBs from qualified suppliers. This outsourcing has become a key business strategy in the United States, as companies focus on their core business competencies and seek vendor partnerships for key inputs. The percent of OEMs producing their own boards (captives) dropped from 60% in 1979 to 15% in 1995. Likewise, the percent of PCBs produced by independent manufacturers has increased from 40% to 85% today.

**U.S. Rigid PCB Market in 1996
(Current Dollars)**

	Output ($Mil)	Growth Rate
Non-captive Prod	6,487	13.6
Captive Prod	892	-11.5
Total Prod	7,379	9.8
OEM Purchase	7,554	8.8
Consumption	7,547	10.6
Exports	371	17.2
Imports	946	25.0

Source: Electronic Outlook Corporation

Since original equipment manufacturers do not have much more PCB manufacturing business left to outsource, continued U.S. PCB market growth will rely on overall industry growth in the electronics industry and increased competitiveness in capturing that growing global business.

Computers and telecommunications are the largest end users of printed circuit boards in the United States for both captive and independent PCB producers. Almost 60% of all printed circuit boards produced are used in the growing markets of personal computers, cellular telephones, and other computer and communication products. The computer industry is expected to maintain its double-digit pace of growth into the next century, while the prospects for the communication industry also remain bright, with the help of deregulation and growing international markets.

Aside from industry segment growth, a new customer has come onto the scene for U.S. PCB fabricators. The electronics manufacturing services (EMS) industry, which are PCB contract assemblers, represent a growing force in U.S. electronics manufacturing. EMS companies are taking over many of the traditional electronics assembly functions formerly performed by OEMs. Large, medium, and small PCB manufacturers are selling to EMS providers. PCB manufacturers must rise to this growing challenge to their market share by forming new customer partnerships and meeting EMS company needs for high quality and timely delivery. The continuing success of EMS providers and their willingness to source within the U.S. are an additional but strong factor for the U.S. PCB industry's success.

International Markets

PCB imports will continue to exceed exports by a significant margin as long as the U.S. dollar maintains its strength.

The Japanese PCB market is divided into two segments. Price-sensitive boards continue to be weak; while the demand for multi-layer boards (MLBs) remains buoyant. In particular, the demand for boards produced with microvia technology is quite strong. With total output of microvia MLBs estimated at about $400 million in 1996, the market is poised to double in size in 1997.

Taiwan has developed into a leader in electronics and PCBs in Asia, trailing only Japan in terms of quality and level of sophistication. Taiwan is the largest importer of glass-based bare boards into the United States, representing 37% of the dollar volume of all imports of single, double, and multi-layer boards. To maintain competitiveness in the international PCB market, and to keep up with technological trends, manufacturers in Taiwan and in Hong Kong are increasing their investment in production lines aimed at more intricate circuits.

China's electronics and PCB industry, meanwhile, is still in its infancy. Nonetheless, China's growing domestic market and its attraction to numerous foreign investors are the right recipes for the strong development of this industry. The rest of the decade for China will see a slow but steady climb from a manufacturing center for low-end consumer electronic goods to a producer of low-to-medium level products.

Supply and Investment

Total U.S. PCB production exceeded $7.7 billion in 1996, but fell short of total domestic consumption. Rigid board shipments rose 13% in 1996 and 16% in 1995, and flexible circuit shipments were up 16% in 1996 after 18% growth in 1995. Slower equipment growth, increased seasonality, and inventory corrections in PCBs and semiconductors all played a part in slowing down the industry's growth last year.

In the PCB industry, participants are well aware of the need to invest and prepare for the future. In order to better meet customer requirements, increased investment in people and equipment will be necessary. In a series of annual studies, the Institute for Interconnecting and Packaging Electronic Circuits (IPC) has found that PCB manufacturers increased equipment investment from 4.5% of sales in 1992 to 7.5% of sales in 1995. The biggest investment expenditures have been in mechanical (drilling) and wet processing equipment.

Industry Consolidation

Industry consolidation continues. Hicks, Muse, Tate & Furst recently bought the second largest board manufacturer in the UK, the Forward Group, after acquiring Circo Craft and the interconnection business of Lucent Technologies in 1996. It appears that all these companies will be operating under the general banner of "Viasystems Technologies," which boasts an interconnection business of well over $650 million, making it the largest PCB company in the United States.

Hadco has also been in the action, acquiring Zycon in 1996. The combined revenue of the two companies during calendar 1996 exceeded $550 million, creating another world-class contender. Other acquisition activities included the purchase of ElectroStar Inc. by Tyco International, a diversified manufacturer of industrial and commercial products.

The ongoing merger and acquisition spree is radically changing the competitive PCB market environment. The industry is in the final stage of a major change in OEM requirements. Formerly, the most important OEM requirement for PCB production was its physical proximity, but now OEMs want to deal with a financially strong supplier corporation that can provide a full array of PCB products and interconnect services on a global basis. The industry will continue to consolidate due to international competitive pressures.

Semiconductors and Related Devices

The semiconductor industry's slump in 1996 marked its worst performance in over a decade. The year was even more shocking because it followed 10 years of uninterrupted prosperity. The beginning of a recovery toward normal market conditions will bring single-digit growth to the semiconductor industry in 1997.

Despite the recent market fluctuation, the industry's traditional robust growth should resume after 1997 and extend into the next century.

Market Overview

People who enjoy excitement should get a tremendous kick out of the semiconductor industry. Every year, we take one wild ride after another, as new technologies emerge and flex their muscles in the market.

**U.S. Total Semiconductor Sales
(Millions of Dollars)**

	Annual Total	Annual Growth
1991	15377	6.4
1992	18410	19.7
1993	24745	34.4
1994	33564	35.6
1995	46992	40.0
1996	42858	-8.8

For more than a decade, the semiconductor industry grew by an average of 15% a year. Sales jumped by an unprecedented 34.4% in 1993, 35.6% in 1994, and 40.0% in 1995. Then along came the reality check of 1996, when the market put the brakes on the semiconductor's strong ascent. An 8.8% decline in sales in 1996 meant the first bad year for the industry since 1985.

Although end-equipment markets slowed in 1996, the major causes of the sales decline were excess inventories, excessive capacity, a DRAM (Dynamic Random Access Memory) price collapse, and a weakened yen. Prices plunged as much as 75% last year in the DRAM market, which represents 19% of the world chip market.

With end-equipment markets firming up this year, 1997 is expected to be a growth year for the industry.

DRAMs

Over the past few years, the DRAM industry has gone through a number of changes that have drastically affected the outlook for its market. Reduced trade barriers, global fabricator expansions, new vendors, and overcapacity have significantly increased the competitiveness of the DRAM market.

While semiconductors have blossomed with the success of DRAMs, they suffered in 1996 as DRAM prices plunged and DRAM producers' revenues plummeted nearly 40%. Excluding DRAMs, the semiconductor market actually grew 6% in 1996. The heightened competition in the market will continue in the near term, causing more downward pressure on prices and margins for DRAMs. The DRAM market has begun to shown signs of rebounding from last year's oversupply, but supply and demand will still not come into balance in 1997. It now appears that production reductions and product holdbacks by both Japanese and South Korean vendors are helping, but will not be sufficient.

Microprocessors

With most types of semiconductors in decline in 1996, only microprocessors were able to do well, logging about a 20% growth rate. The continued prosperity in this sector can be attributed to the greater market control held by primary manufacturers, and the increasing popularity of PCs for business and home use. Microprocessors are poised for continued growth through the rest of the decade, because new applications will drive demand for higher-performance systems, with most users upgrading their equipment every two to three years. Microprocessors will likely surpass DRAMs and become the largest semiconductor segment during the next ten years.

Demand Situation

Demand from PC manufacturers will continue to drive demand for microprocessors, DRAMs, and other semiconductor products. In the short term, the PC market is expected to proceed with good growth in 1997, which bodes well for semiconductors.

- Following rather weak demand in the last quarter of 1996, it appears that the introduction of the MMX has stimulated consumer interest in PCs in the new year.

- While PC demand from small to mid-size companies has been strong, demand from large corporations remains relatively weak.

- From an international perspective, demand has remained strong in Asia, and demand in Europe appears to have improved somewhat.

Overall, PC demand is expected to continue to grow this year, largely because of the introduction of Windows NT to offices. In the meanwhile, faster speed and higher performance will continue to be required of PCs, as they become the core equipment for the multimedia era. These demands will be made possible by an evolution of semiconductor technology and will result in higher semiconductor content in PCs.

Semiconductor content in electronic products has been increasing over time. In the 1970s, semiconductor content was about 4% of sales. This share grew to 8% in the 1980s and today is about 12% and still growing. In addition, semiconductors are being included in more products, advancing well beyond their initial inroads in automobiles, consumer electronics and household appliances. Emerging applications, including digital video disk (DVD) systems, personal handyphone systems (PHS), personal digital assistants (PDA), network PCs, and set-top boxes will begin to expand, generating additional demand for semiconductors.

In addition, emerging economies will provide new potential markets for semiconductors. These economies will experience rapid growth, which will eventually lead to plans for advances in communications and computer infrastructures, both of which are rich in semiconductor content.

In summary, the semiconductor market will continue to be fueled by tremendous growth and rapid technological change.

Supply and Investment

As a result of the integration of the world semiconductor market, success requires a strategy of global vision and investment on a global scale. Making up one of the most rapidly growing industries in the United States, semiconductor companies are well aware of the importance of investment to expand capacity in anticipation of future growth opportunities.

Although the semiconductor industry may be overbuilt in some sectors, all capacity is not the same. Most semiconductor production facilities are highly specialized and geared to build very specific types of products. Many operating in the United States today are not capable of producing the complex types of chips that are expected to dominate semiconductor demand in the coming years. Although spending for DRAM capacity may have been a bit excessive in recent years, the same cannot be said for capital outlays for leading-edge logic products, such as ASICs, multimedia chips, digital signal processors, microcontrollers and microprocessors. In particular, there is excess capacity in the 0.8-micron and greater range, but there is still a persistent capacity shortfall in the sub-0.5-micron area.

Many companies are currently adopting a balanced expansion strategy in order to maximize their future flexibility in reacting to changing market conditions. Purchases of existing facilities, new construction, additions, and upgrades are all within the capacity expansion mix.

Overcapacity has been blamed for the short-term slump in the market in 1996. However, in the long run, supply is still expected to play catch-up with voracious demand.

The prices of semiconductors have been more or less in line with market conditions. As most excess inventories were used up in 1996, prices are firming up in 1997 and are expected to increase during the course of the next few years.

COMPUTERS AND ELECTRONIC EQUIPMENT

Global Market Share

Although the U.S. semiconductor industry should retain its standing as the world's leading semiconductor producer, supplying about one-third of the world's semiconductors, the structure of production in the rest of the world is changing. This may have a profound impact on the business strategies adopted by U.S. semiconductor companies. Japan suffered a 14.8% decline in semiconductor sales in 1996, but remains the second largest producer, representing 26% of the world market. However, Japan's share of global production is slipping. Asia-Pacific producers outside of Japan are the fastest-growing, and jointly will overtake Japan's No. 2 spot in the next two or three years. Europe currently ties the Asia-Pacific production share with 20.8% in the third spot, but European producers will slide to fourth place by the end of the century.

Other Industry Issues

Book-to-Bill Reports

The Semiconductor Industry Association (SIA) discontinued the book-to-bill statistical program, which was running for 20 years, in early January 1997, replacing it with the Global Billings Report (GBR). The book-to-bill ratio, once the most popular indicator of the semiconductor industry, measured the ratio of the dollar amount of orders received to the dollar amount of products shipped in a specific period of time. The value of the book-to-bill program had waned because it covered only the U.S. market. The new program reflects the industry's expanding focus on worldwide markets, and responds to the huge public demand for more information about semiconductor trends in other markets. The GBR should enable analysts to determine how chip sales are developing around the world.

Trade Issues

In 1996, an accord was reached by the U.S. and Japanese semiconductor industries to collect data, including market size, for reports their governments can use in bilateral consultations. The agreement called for the creation of a Semiconductor Council at the industry level, which would be composed initially of SIA and Japan's Electronic Industries Association. Industry associations from other countries would be eligible to join the Council provided that their respective countries have eliminated all semiconductor tariffs, are committed to do so, or have suspended those tariffs. Early in 1997, South Korea announced its plan to cut import taxes on semiconductors in the next two years and eventually lift them in 1999, in order to speed up its process in joining the Semiconductor Council.

Passive Components

Last year's dip for the passive components industry was an overcorrection from its robust, but unsustainable, growth in 1994 and 1995.

With the worldwide electronics industry expected to grow at a healthy pace for the rest of the decade, and international competition becoming ever more intensive, the U.S. passive components industry is presented with both opportunities and challenges.

A wide variety of products comprises the passive components category, including rigid printed circuit boards, connectors, capacitors, resistors, relays, switches, coils and transformers, and piezoelectric devices.

According to Electronic Outlook Corporation, U.S. passive components production totaled $19.1 billion in 1996, a 4.6% increase from the 1995 level. This was a considerable slowdown from two years of double-digit growth in 1994 and 1995, very much in line with trends in the broader electronic industry.

Connectors

Connectors create the electrical junctions or interconnections in virtually all electronic products. They comprise the second largest U.S. passive component market behind printed circuit boards (PCBs).

The heyday for the U.S. connector market from 1993 to 1995 will be remembered as a time of exceptional strength in U.S. components demand, caused by better Original Equipment Manufacturer (OEM) prospects, strengthened distributor activity, and inventory accumulation. Spurred by a gush in telecommunications-related activity and a relentless PC boom, U.S. production and demand jumped quite nicely in 1995. Demand growth moderated in 1996, and OEM purchases subsided considerably due to a significant inventory correction. The total production of connectors was estimated at over $6 billion in 1996, but growth was only in single digits. A market recovery is expected in 1997 and 1998, but lower prices are likely to prevail, especially since a strong U.S. dollar makes foreign imports significantly cheaper.

U.S. Connectors Market in 1996

	Output, $Mil	Growth rate, %
Non-captive Prod	5,831	3.7
Captive Prod	210	-0.8
Total Prod	6,040	3.6
OEM Purchases	6,459	5.3
Consumption	6,471	8.3
Exports	992	7.0
Imports	1,164	11.4

Source: Electronic Outlook Corporation

The major U.S. end-markets for connectors in 1996 were computer equipment (30%), communications (22%), electrical (21%), industrial/instrument (12%), military electronics (11%), and consumer electronics (2%). Aside from military electronics, which is likely to continue to be weak, connectors markets are expected to sustain average to better-than-average growth. Elsewhere, as world markets pick up strength in the next two years, U.S. connectors producers – the world leaders – will benefit more than producers of other types of passive components.

U.S. domestic connector producers are facing increasing competitive pressures from not only foreign manufacturers but also the offshore plants of U.S.-owned corporations. All companies are striving to stay competitive by exploring ways to design products more cost effectively and to leverage worldwide resources in view of changing cost advantages. The transfer of production to China, Mexico, and other low-cost regions is accelerating, and the strength of the U.S. dollar has only sped up this process. The search for lower-priced alternative materials is also an ongoing activity that is receiving significant attention as lower market growth rates squeeze profit margins.

Merger and acquisition activity continues in the U.S. connector industry in 1996. Thomas & Betts acquired Augat US recently, and KKR also took a major step toward buying Amphenol and staking a major position in the electronics business. Amp announced a consolidation of manufacturing plants as it adjusted to current market conditions. Amp completed a number of major acquisitions over the past several years, leaving it with the need to streamline its operations. As a result of its recent consolidation, the U.S. industry is more competitive.

Capacitors

Capacitors are used for filtering, tuning, coupling, isolating, and storing electrical energy. The primary end markets for capacitors are consumer electronics and automotive and computer equipment.

In 1994 and 1995, capacitor OEM demand accelerated with bullish OEM business. Prices shot up due to tight supply conditions, further aggravated by buyer anxiety and some double ordering. Capacitor demand soared in 1995, as several end markets grew rapidly, such as personal computers, telecommunications, and local area networks (LANs), even though production rates plateaued and began to retreat.

U.S. Capacitors Market in 1996

	Output, $Mil	Growth rate, %
Non-captive Prod	2,683	-2.0
Captive Prod	98	-7.0
Total Prod	2,781	-2.2
OEM Purchases	3,231	-4.7
Consumption	3,412	1.1
Exports	1,073	2.8
Imports	1,263	-10.0

Source: Electronic Outlook Corporation

In 1995, U.S. capacitor producers were able to enjoy nice sales and profits in a market where demand was running ahead of supply, which helped push prices upward. This came at a time when the U.S. dollar was still relatively weak, resulting in significantly improved profitability. It was particularly true for ceramic and tantalum capacitor manufacturers who faced stronger demand, higher prices and capacity constraints. The market turned upside down, starting with a brief inventory correction, in 1996 and prices tumbled. This is especially the case since significant double-ordering occurred by OEMs, who were overly concerned about key capacitor availability (tantalum, in particular).

In 1996, price weakness plagued the capacitor market, especially for tantalum capacitors. Lower profits and losses at manufacturers resulted in a smaller capital equipment budget in the near term. Much of the capital outlays in the near term are expected to be solely concentrated on expanding production in low-cost regions and scaling down or shutting down operations in the U.S., which have been and will continue to be hurt by the strength of the U.S. dollar. Overall, capacity is not expected to expand significantly over the next two years, which is anticipated to lead to tighter supplies and higher prices and possibly another cycle in 1999 .

The world OEM demand was weak in 1996 due to overstocked inventories, with North America and Western Europe posting negative growth and significantly lower capacitor prices. Nonetheless, in 1997 capacitor demand will turn up, and the growth rate should accelerate in each of the following two years and reach double digits in 1999.

As the business environment currently favors larger players, consolidation of the capacitor industry is expected to continue. Fewer but bigger companies will be seen in the next decade. Global diversification is also expected to continue. Multinational giants will increasingly dominate the marketplace. The capacitor industry will be more concentrated but more competitive on a global basis, with more moderate and more sustainable growth rates expected in the longer term.

Resistors

Overall, the U.S. resistor industry is mature, and profit margins are slim. In 1996, total resistor production was estimated at $1.1 billion, up only marginally from its 1995 level. The resistor market also faced an inventory adjustment in 1996, although it was relatively minor as compared with the cycles in the other passive components markets.

U.S. Resistors Market in 1996

	Output, $ Mil	Growth rate, %
Non-captive Prod	1,109	1.3
Captive Prod	52	-7.3
Total Prod	1,161	0.9
OEM Purchases	1,468	-3.3
Consumption	1,556	3.9
Exports	484	15.6
Imports	671	-7.4

Source: Electronic Outlook Corporation

Unexpectedly strong growth, due primarily to the surging broad passive components market, surprised the U.S. resistor market in 1994 and 1995. Strong demand, which led to spot shortages of parts late in 1995, and over-optimism on the part of buyers, which resulted in double ordering and an over-inventory situation, vaporized in 1996 as the market turned sour. OEM purchases fell for the year. The difference between domestic production and domestic consumption was due to inventory-building and faster growth in exports, as U.S. producers benefited from improved competitiveness overseas.

The market collapsed in the second quarter of 1996, completing a classic boom/bust inventory cycle. However, the cycle is expected to have a smaller impact on shipments than did the ones of the mid-1980s or early 1990s, because, fundamentally, equipment production is still increasing. The length of the cycle was certainly short by historical standards.

The near-term outlook for the U.S. resistor industry is fairly bearish. First, OEM growth will be weaker, and an excess of inventory will be on hand in the first half of 1997. Moreover, prices, which rose unexpectedly in the last few years, should come down as supply and demand move towards equilibrium. U.S. resistor producers will face a return to more normal market conditions in 1997, 1998, and 1999.

Among the major end markets, military electronics will remain weak as the defense budget remains under pressure, while consumer/automotive demand is lackluster. Computer and communications demand took off in 1994 and 1995, leading to the strong overall increase in resistor demand. This rapid growth rate cannot be sustained and will remain closer to historical averages in the long term. Nonetheless, the computer and communications sectors will continue to be the two major contributors to resistor growth, and the key locomotive of growth will shift from PCs to telecommunications.

The U.S. picture will be a subdued one over the next three years, while a gradually improving marketplace is developing overseas. U.S. resistor manufacturers must shift their focus onto faster growing and more profitable world markets to offset fairly saturated market conditions at home.

Relays and Switches

Relays

The U.S. relay market is primarily dependent on machinery, industrial electronics, and factory automation. The strength in U.S. manufacturing bettered U.S. relay prospects in 1995 and early 1996, with above-average growth rates for this type of passive component. However, overall 1996 performance was dragged by general weakness in cellular communication and consumer and automotive markets. An inventory correction also took place, in particular in the all-important communications markets.

Most damage was done in dry reed relays, which are widely used, and in cellular and other communications gear thanks to the inventory cycle and the ensuing slow-down in orders. Further weakness has occurred in wet relays designed for office business equipment and in solid state relays for instrumentation and industrial electronics end markets.

The U.S. relay market is expected to weaken further in 1997, then resume its normal growth for the rest of the decade. The long-term tendency away from electromechanical relays in electronics will continue, with solid state relays (SSRs) increasing market penetration. Increasing penetration for automotive electronics and industrial electronics continue to represent the main future growth opportunities.

Switches

U.S. switch production reflected robust U.S. domestic electronics industry performance in 1994 and 1995, and weaker prospects in 1996. Switch demand slowed significantly in consumer products, particularly appliances and automotive. However, industrial/process control and instruments, two of the largest switch users, were able to provide some stability for switch producers, while all other markets experienced a classic inventory cycle.

In 1997, the market is recovering after the slowdown in 1996. The long-term prospects for the industry point to average annual growth in line with historical averages. Solid state and software functions are still having an impact on the switch market, as are keyboards and optical and other non-contacting functions, which gradually are replacing mechanical functions. Despite the fact that their performance over the past few years has been very positive, switches generally lag the electronics industry as a whole. While standard switch functions stagnate, uses in sensor applications will expand, and the trend toward miniaturization and surface mounting will accelerate.

Overall Passive Components Market

One of the most significant impacts of the passive components market setback in 1996 is that price deterioration was more severe than expected. Prices will continue to be depressed in the near term, with demand still relatively weak and supply more than adequate. In addition, the U.S. dollar's continued strength against major currencies will aggravate the downward price pressures in the near term, putting U.S.-based manufacturers into very uncomfortable positions. This will eventually speed up the migration of production from the United States to offshore locations, with Mexico among the top alternatives.

Imports and exports grew by 38% and 41%, respectively, in 1995, but both declined in 1996.

The picture for subassembly is less encouraging for U.S. passive components producers. Considerable subassembly production overseas will also cut into component demand in the United States, as purchasers of components shift from traditional OEMs to subassembly manufacturers, a growing industry force in the years ahead. Passive suppliers must follow these new assembly locations to benefit fully from this industry trend, and also contend with the growing importance of worldwide distributors.

Over the next few years, on a worldwide basis communications equipment will replace computer equipment as the engine of growth for passive components demand. However, the U.S. passive components industry will be adversely affected by the increasing share of subassembly manufacturing that is permanently migrating overseas to low-labor-cost assembly facilities.

Chapter 20: Transportation Equipment

Motor Vehicles and Parts

Automotive manufacturing is one of the cornerstones of the United States industrial base. Motor vehicles and parts is comprised of five major product areas: automobiles (cars), light duty trucks, medium and heavy duty trucks, truck trailers, and motor vehicle parts. In 1996, shipments were valued at $323 billion, with automobiles and light duty trucks accounting for 63% of shipments, parts around 32%, and trucks, trailers, and some miscellaneous activity the remaining 5%.

The automotive industry directly employs over 950,000 workers, or more than 5% of U.S. manufacturing employment. The industry forms an important cog of the country's manufacturing base, consuming in a typical year 15% of the steel, 25% of the aluminum, and 75% of all the natural rubber purchased by U.S. industries. According to the Department of Commerce, every dollar of production of automobiles generates on average $2.50 of activity in the U.S. economy. Investment by the industry is substantial. In 1994, the automotive sector spent $16 billion, 8% of the manufacturing capital spending total.

Once given up for dead, the U.S. motor vehicle sector has undergone a startling resurgence in recent years. In 1996, there were 15.1 million cars and light trucks sold in the U.S. This was not a record, but it was the third straight year of sales around the very strong 15.0 million unit mark. In addition, there were a near record 411,000 medium and heavy duty trucks and 225,000 trailers sold in 1996. Of the 15.1 million light vehicles, 8.5 million were passenger cars, and a record 6.6 million units were light trucks. Giant U.S. corporations — General Motors, Ford, and Chrysler (the "Big Three") — that used to dominate the market were forced by the energy crises of the 1970s to make room for fuel–efficient Japanese imports. Now these Japanese producers are domestic players, having established a highly efficient production base in the U.S. and Canada. This base consists of plants with outright foreign ownership (transplant facilities, such as Honda's Marysville, Ohio plant) and of joint ventures operated in conjunction with a U.S. firm (such as the Nummi operation in California, which is owned jointly by GM and Toyota).

In 1996, Big Three sales amounted to 11.0 million cars and light trucks. Direct Japanese, European, and Korean imports totaled 1.8 million, and transplant producers, mostly Japanese, accounted for another 2.3 million. The low point in market share for the Big Three was 1990, when the combined share of GM, Ford, and Chrysler fell to 70%, and Japanese nameplates (imports and transplants) took almost 26% of the U.S. market. A combination of a revitalized product line, particularly light trucks, and a weaker dollar, has reversed the fortunes of the Big Three so that Detroit now holds almost 73% of the market, the Japanese 23%, and European and Korean producers the remaining 4%.

Between 1986 and 1996, the total value of shipments for motor vehicles and parts grew 5.0% per year, with 2.7% in real growth, and a 2.2% per annum rate of price increase. WEFA expects that the real value of shipments will average about 1.0% per year between 1996 and 2006.

Motor Vehicles and Parts
Growth in Sales (Line) and Volume (Bar)

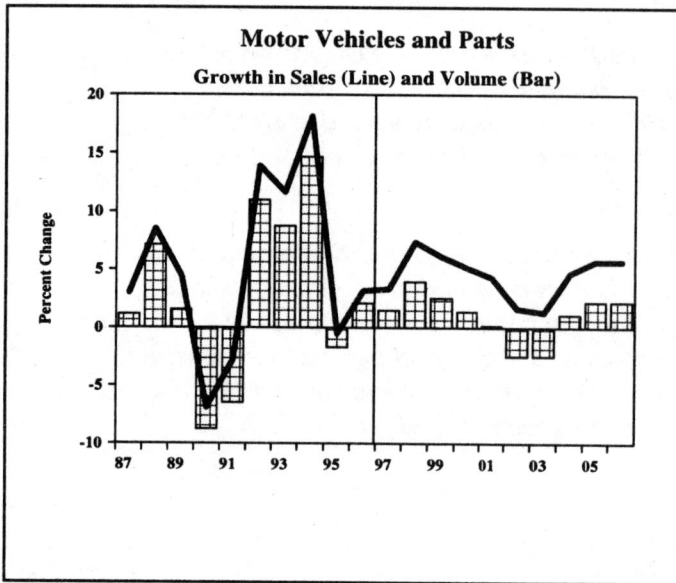

Motor Vehicles and Parts
Growth in Product Prices

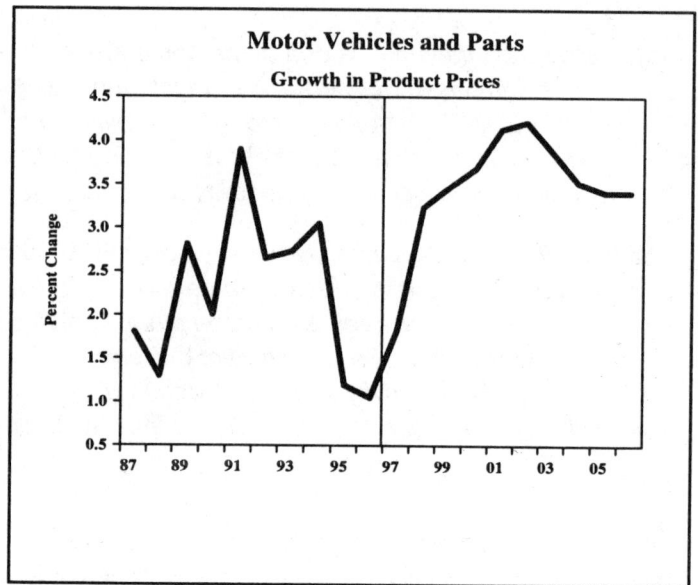

Motor Vehicles and Parts
  SIC 371

		1990	1991	1992	1993	1994	1995	1996	1997	1998	Compound Ann Avg Growth 1986-1996	1996-2006
Sales												
	Billions of $	216.21	210.10	239.30	267.21	315.74	314.10	324.03	334.77	359.28		
	% Change	-6.9	-2.8	13.9	11.7	18.2	-0.5	3.2	3.3	7.3	5.0	4.5
Volume	% Change	-8.8	-6.5	11.0	8.7	14.7	-1.7	2.1	1.5	4.0	2.7	1.0
Prices	% Change	2.0	3.9	2.6	2.7	3.0	1.2	1.0	1.8	3.2	2.2	3.5
Exports												
	Billions of $	35.96	39.40	46.35	51.85	57.03	60.92	63.26	65.30	67.19		
	% Change	4.4	9.6	17.6	11.9	10.0	6.8	3.8	3.2	2.9	11.1	4.7
Imports												
	Billions of $	86.15	83.73	90.52	101.06	116.76	123.25	128.70	137.89	150.16		
	% Change	0.6	-2.8	8.1	11.6	15.5	5.6	4.4	7.1	8.9	5.3	4.9
Apparent Consumption												
	Billions of $	266.40	254.42	283.47	316.42	375.48	376.43	389.47	407.36	442.26		
	Nominal % Change	-6.0	-4.5	11.4	11.6	18.7	0.3	3.5	4.6	8.6	4.4	4.6
	Real % Change	-7.9	-8.1	8.5	8.7	15.2	-0.9	2.4	2.7	5.2	2.1	1.1

Light Vehicles

Because of NAFTA, automotive production should be viewed from the perspective of North America. Each year, there is a tremendous volume of vehicles shipped from one country to another. There are 87 assembly plants in North America, of which 61 are in the United States, 13 in Canada, and 13 in Mexico.

North American light vehicle production was up 1.4% in 1996 to a record 15.2 million vehicles. Passenger car output of 8.2 million made up approximately 54% of the total build and declined 2.8% from 1995. Light truck production, at 7 million, experienced a 6.8% increase from the previous year to capture the remaining 46%. The accelerated trend by the Japanese to expand North American output at the expense of operations at home will be conducive to production growth throughout the next ten years. By 2000, output is expected to rise to 17.5 million units, and by 2005 North American output will reach 18.3 million units.

U.S. light vehicle production at 11.5 million units was down 1% from the previous year, mainly due to three work stoppages which idled several General Motors' plants during the year. Production is expected to increase 1.2% in 1997 to 11.7 million units, and 1998 should bring a 2.1% increase. In the long run, U.S. light vehicle output will stabilize at around the 12.5 million unit mark.

Consumer Affordability Outlook

Affordability pressures will slow light vehicle sales in 1997 and 1998. It took a massive amount of incentive dollars to keep activity at the 15 million unit rate at the end of 1996 and the early part of 1997, and today's more fragile market will find affordability pressures a problem. First–time buyers will increasingly turn to used cars, or simply stay on the sidelines, because of the high level of monthly payments. The family fleet will be scaled back because of affordability pressures. This means that manufacturers must be constantly aware of what is happening to the variables which shape the affordability environment: earnings, interest rates, sticker prices, incentives, and lease deals. The pressure will be constant to either hold the line on pricing or promote.

The following are the key factors shaping light vehicle affordability.

- New Vehicle Prices. Average new car and truck prices, when adjusted for incentives and leases, rose 1% in 1996, after a 1.6% decline in 1995 that was due mainly to shifts in the mix of vehicles sold. WEFA expects prices to move up over the course of 1997, as stickers are raised and rebates are reduced, and average a 4% increase. In the long term, prices will grow by about 3% to 3.5% per annum, considerably less than the 5% to 5.5% that was the historical norm.

- Auto Loan Rates. From the second half of 1995 through the first half of 1997, auto loan rates were very supportive of sales, running at around 9% at commercial banks and even lower rates available through dealers. However, the Federal Reserve began raising the Federal Funds Rate early in 1997, and commercial bank auto loan interest rates will creep up as a result. The creep will be modest, however, and rates will likely hover around 9.5%.

- Incentives. While the industry's drive in the early 1990s to wean the consumer from incentives and rebates was sensible, automakers discovered that some level of incentives is required in today's market to keep volume moving. According to CNW Marketing, total incentives (including dealer rebates, salesperson incentives, low rate auto loans, and leases) averaged over $2,800, or close to 13% of the base sticker price, in 1996. This was up from $2,450, or 12.2%, in 1995. We believe that incentive activity will move down from its January 1997 peak of $3,200, or 14.6% of base prices.

- Monthly Payments. The average monthly auto loan payment is expected to rise from about $400 currently to $450 by the year 2000, and rise further to $550 by 2005.

Leasing And The Used Car Market

Leases have become a key marketing tool employed by the automobile industry to promote sales. According to CNW Marketing and WEFA Automotive, leases accounted for roughly 7% of all consumer car and light truck purchases in the 1984–86 period. During this time, leases were the domain of the import luxury car sector. However, as the industry began to try to back away from traditional incentive programs, leases spread first to the family car market and then to light trucks. When a new set of tax laws eliminated the deductibility of auto loan interest, the subsidized lease became more attractive, both to buyers and to dealers looking for a way to move unwanted inventory. As recently as 1990, leases accounted for only 9% of the market. By 1992, lease penetration was close to 17.0%, and in 1994 it reached almost 26.0%. In 1996, lease penetration stood at a record 30.5% of all new light vehicle purchases. WEFA thinks that the rapid gains in penetration are likely over, and we expect leases to edge up only a bit further, to 35%, in the next ten years.

The industry now has to contend with reabsorbing the growing number of cars and trucks coming off lease. The 4.5 million units coming off lease in 1997 present some problems for the industry, but a number of factors are acting to lessen the impact in the near term.

- About 25% of off-lease vehicles are repurchased by the consumer who held the original lease.

- There is strong demand for younger used car models.

- Furthermore, because fleet programs have been de-emphasized, used car dealers are scrambling for vehicles.

- The used vehicle market is huge, is growing, and can be very profitable. In 1996, there were about 41 million used vehicles sold through dealers and by individuals, up from 34.4 million in 1990.

Manufacturers, in an attempt to control the supply of off-lease vehicles, have taken an active role in the used car market through their franchised dealers. However, the emergence of used car mega-dealers (such as AutoMax and Auto Nation), which use modern sales techniques and no-haggle pricing, has given automakers and traditional dealerships some unexpected competition.

The used car market, while recently hot, has begun to show some cracks. Sales leveled out in 1996, and used car prices have begun to decline. Manufacturers' restraint in 1997 model year pricing, along with their generous rebates, have played a major role in putting pressure on used car prices, and residual values on off-lease vehicles show signs of breaking.

In the longer run, there will be about 6 million cars and trucks coming off lease each year. If the economy continues to grow as WEFA forecasts and the automotive market remains reasonably robust as we expect, we believe that these units can be absorbed, but that residual values will likely be considerably lower. We expect the used car market to grow to about 44 to 45 million units in the early 2000s.

The advent of the mega-dealers has accelerated the consolidation trend in dealerships. In 1970 there were 31,000 franchised dealerships in the United States. By 1990, the number had fallen below 25,000, and currently there are about 22,000. Over the next few years, we expect to see another 2,500 to 3,000 dealers either absorbed into a buying group or simply out of business.

The Fleet And The Replacement Cycle

WEFA estimates that there were just over 197 million cars and trucks on the road (measured by total registrations) in 1996, or 2% more than 1995. This translates to 1.93 vehicles per household. The average age of the fleet has come down a bit, but still remains high. In the 1993–95 period, the age of the fleet stood at a forty-year high of 8.4 years, and it is now 8.2 to 8.3 years. Replacement demand improved in 1996 to roughly 11.5 million units, with scrappage rates (the number of cars and trucks not registered relative to total registrations) running at about 5.8%.

A significant move above 15 million light vehicle sales would require the re-emergence of more normal historical patterns in both ownership and scrappage:

- Replacement demand, as represented by scrappage, is larger when the fleet of vehicles in operation is old. However, the average age of the fleet is moving down as a result of recent strong sales levels, and the definition of old has changed as vehicle durability has improved. In the 1960s, scrappage rates averaged close to 8% per year. By the 1970s it had fallen to 7.0%, and in the 1980s it was down to 6.0%. Currently the scrappage rate is running at a very low 5.5%. The WEFA forecast assumes that scrappage rates will move up slowly over the next few years, and return to a still low 6% level by the year 2000, which implies replacement demand of about 11.5 million units per year on a trend basis.

- Desired fleet size changes with patterns of vehicle ownership, which WEFA expects to hover near 1.95 vehicles per household over the next two to three years and then edge up to 1.97. These ownership rates imply required additions to the fleet of 3.5 million units per year in the short run, with a slowing to about 3 million units a year in the longer run, when household formation growth slows. Both of these figures are considerably lower than the average fleet expansion of about 4 million units per year between 1970 and 1990.

- By 2000, the fleet of light vehicles should exceed 211 million cars and trucks. By 2005 there should be over 224 million vehicles on the road.

Sales Outlook

1996 was a good year for the U.S. automobile industry. Light vehicle sales were 15.1 million units, 2.5% better than in 1995. Light truck buying continued to drive the market, while the car sector remained a disappointment. Light trucks set a record once again in 1996, reaching the 6.6 million unit mark, up 7.8% from 1995, while car sales fell 1.7% to 8.5 million units. In all, cars lost a full three points of market share, falling to 56% of the market.

In the short run, the automotive forecast is shaped by the economy, Federal Reserve policy, and incentives. Sales were able to move up a notch in 1996 because of the robust economy and the industry's liberal use of incentives and rebates. With the Federal Reserve raising interest rates in 1997, we expect the economy to slow and sales to weaken a bit to 14.9 million units in 1997 and 14.6 million in 1998. The emergence of a replacement cycle at the end of 1998 will provide a boost to the market in 1999 and 2000.

The growth of transplant activity and the renewed popularity of Big Three models has cut the import share of the U.S. light vehicle market dramatically. Imports, which made up roughly 20% of the market in 1991, should capture 12% of the U.S. market in 1997 and between 11% and 11.5% over the next ten years.

Cyclicality

The automotive sector is a true "cyclical". Vehicles represent one of the largest single expenditures in the consumer's household budget, second only to housing. Since they have an extended life span, purchases of cars and trucks are readily postponed at the onset of any business contraction. In addition, the volatility of the market is exacerbated by competitive practices, particularly the use of incentives, leases, and fleet sales to rental companies.

The industry today is, however, better equipped to withstand a downturn than it has been at any time in the last 20 years. A wave of plant closures has all but eliminated excess capacity from the North American system. Cost cutting, outsourcing, and improvements in productivity have greatly strengthened the manufacturers' balance sheets. And, modern inventory management techniques have enabled producers to respond more quickly to changes in demand.

Foreign Trade

The international trade in motor vehicles and parts is a critical issue for U.S. foreign trade policy. In 1996 the U.S. trade deficit in motor vehicle and parts was $65.9 billion, compared to $49.9 billion in 1990. Almost 90% of this shortfall is made up of vehicles, and only 10% is parts. One critical and contentious issue has been the motor vehicle and parts trade deficit with Japan, which in 1996 stood at $29.7 billion.

While light vehicle imports from Japan have dropped significantly as Japanese producers expanded their productive capacity in North America, the 1.1 million light vehicles imported from Japan by the U.S. in 1996 still dwarfed the 122,600 American vehicles sold in Japan last year. Trade friction is the inevitable result, and in 1995 Japan and the United States signed the U.S. — Japan Automotive Framework Agreement. This agreement was designed to increase sales of U.S.-produced vehicles and parts to Japanese consumers and producers both here and in Japan. The treaty's progress has been slow and disappointing, and trade friction is again on the rise.

On most other fronts, the U.S. world trade picture has become quite favorable. Almost 80% of all cars and trucks sold in Canada are produced in the U.S., while 80% of Canadian output is sold here. With the North American Free Trade Agreement (NAFTA), Mexico has been included, increasing prospects for further growth and rationalization in North America. Recent initiatives have sought to bring Chile into this pact, and there are hopes of enlarging relations with the MERCOSUR countries (Argentina and Brazil).

North America is increasingly viewed as a good place to locate assembly plants, not only for serving North America, but also as a base for exports to other parts of the world. In 1990, the United States exported 285,000 new cars and trucks outside of North America. By 1996 this volume had jumped to 575,000, more than 12% growth per year on average. We expect exports of motor vehicles to rise by about 8% per year over the next five years.

Labor Issues

The U.S. automotive industry has entered a period of heightened labor conflict. In 1996, the United Auto Workers (UAW), as well as the Canadian Auto Workers (CAW) renegotiated their contracts with the Big Three. Chrysler and Ford managed to get through the process quietly, while GM could not. GM suffered three work stoppages: one local strike early in the year, one general strike with the UAW, and another with the CAW.

WEFA expects more labor unrest in the future, but the focus will shift from the national to the local level. Outsourcing and unionization of the component parts sector are the major areas of contention. In an effort to control costs, the Big Three are producing less of their componentry in-house. The parts supply firms are either largely non-union, or if unionized, earn wages that are considerably less than the in-house parts or assembly workers. The issue of job security is back on the table, as new production techniques continue to reduce the labor content of new models.

In addition, the industry's labor force is aging. By the year 2005, the Big Three will have to hire and train close to 200,000 new employees.

Globalization

The automotive industry is becoming more and more global. Not only is demand for new cars and trucks from developing countries expanding at a rapid pace, but their productive capability to supply this demand is also increasing by leaps and bounds. GM, Ford, and Chrysler all have announced very ambitious worldwide expansion plans. Asia (particularly China, India, Malaysia, Thailand, Indonesia, and the Philippines), South America, and Eastern Europe all have been targeted for a massive buildup in productive capacity. Foreign firms, most notably Toyota, Nissan, Kia, Hyundai, Daewoo, Peugeot, and Fiat have also committed massive amounts of capital to expanding overseas production facilities. Between 1996 and 2000, WEFA estimates that global auto production will grow by 4% to 5% per year, with South America, Eastern Europe, and developing Asia jumping by a phenomenal 8% to 12% per annum. Viewed from an output perspective, this translates into approximately 10 million more cars and trucks by the year 2000, and 10 million more additional units by 2005.

Energy And The Environment

At this time, there appears to be little threat to the automotive industry from energy and environmental restrictions. The industry received a well-deserved respite on March 29, 1995 when the California Resources Board (CARB), killed its mandate, which would have made it mandatory for manufacturers to begin selling electric vehicles in the state by 1998. In place of the mandate, the Board passed a "memorandum of agreement", which requires producers to slowly roll out electric vehicles until, by 2003, 10% of the California fleet is comprised of zero-emission vehicles.

The development of electrically-powered vehicles is currently a hot topic. General Motor's EV1 made its debut in December 1996, and because of stringent lease policies and a low mileage range, sales have been disappointing. Ford will begin production of the Ranger EV at the end of 1997 in Edison, NJ. Its range is between 35 and 50 miles, quite low compared to GM's 80-mile range for the EV1. GM expects annual output at 1,500 to 2,000 units. Chrysler, Toyota, and Honda are also dabbling with electronic vehicles, and most will debut in California due to alternative fuel legislation.

Fuel cell technology seems to be a far more appropriate and practical source of electric power than electric batteries for long term production. Hybrids, which are powered electrically in tandem with an internal combustion engine, would also be a logical choice for purposes of economies of scale. Mercedes–Benz and Chrysler have made significant strides in fuel cell technology. Despite all of the action, however, it will be well into the next decade before electric vehicles comprise even a minute share of total U.S. light vehicle sales.

It appears that changes in the Corporate Average Fuel Efficiency (CAFE) standards have been put on hold. There have been some rumblings about making light truck CAFE standards comparable to passenger cars, since vans and sport utilities are effectively passenger vehicles. While we don't see this as highly likely in the near term, such a change would severely impact light truck sales. Size, weight, and all important engine capacities (power and payload) would have to be substantially curtailed in order to get the fuel efficiency of the light truck fleet up to 28 miles per gallon from today's level of 20.

Medium and Heavy Trucks

The medium and heavy truck market includes vehicles over 10,000 pounds in Gross Vehicle Weight, or GVW, which includes the weight of both the truck itself and its recommended maximum contents. The market is segmented into size classes, defined by GVW and designated by a GVW or Class number from 3 to 8. The small commercial truck market (GVWs 3 and 4) ranges in weight from 10,001 pounds to 16,000 pounds. It includes large pickup trucks and low cab–over–engine trucks used primarily by contractors, small retailers and wholesalers, and the service industries. The midrange market covers GVWs 5 through 7, which consist of trucks and school bus chassis within the GVW range of 16,001 pounds. to 33,000 pounds. Midrange market trucks are used primarily for the distribution of a wide variety of products by manufacturers, wholesalers, retailers, and trucking companies. The heavy duty or GVW8 market covers trucks with a GVW rating of 33,001 pounds and over. The heavy duty market includes over–the–road tractors, and equipment that is used in heavy industrial applications such as construction, mining, and logging

Recent History

The 1990–91 recession was tough on the sales of mid-range and heavy duty trucks, as end–market activity and customer earnings took a tumble. Midrange market sales peaked in 1988 at 164,900 units and then fell to 139,800 units in 1989. Demand continued to slide over the next two years, falling 25% to 104,500 units by 1991. Heavy truck sales also peaked in 1988 at 148,400 units, but held up well the following year. The recession brought a sharp drop in manufacturing and construction activity, and motor carrier traffic fell sharply. Carrier profit margins came under pressure, and rising diesel fuel prices added insult to injury. Heavy truck sales dropped 16.5% in 1990 to 121,300 units and tumbled another 19% in 1991.

The small commercial truck market held up a bit better during this period. This occurred not because this segment of the truck market is immune to economic cycles, but because the products being offered in GVWs 3 and 4 were relatively new and siphoned off sales from the smaller classes, as equipment buyers looked to buy just the right amount of truck for specific vocational applications. Sales rose 4.6% in 1990 to 48,300 and then fell 6.5% the following year to 45,100 units.

The medium and heavy truck market did well coming out of the last recession. Sales of small commercial trucks more than doubled reaching 110,500 last year, as small business activity and earnings gained considerable ground and equipment buyers took advantage of a significant broadening of the product line. The midrange truck market benefited from solid growth in manufacturing, retail, and distributor activity and a replacement cycle in school buses. Sales rose steadily through 1995, reaching 134,400 units that year, a 37% increase from their 1991 low. As fleet replacement and expansion pressures began to subside, the demand for midrange trucks and buses eased off by 3% in 1996. The heavy truck market roared out of the recession, powered by solid gains in traffic, low interest rates, rising profits, and pent–up replacement demand, and posted record sales of 185,700 units in 1994 and 201,300 units the following year. Following this huge influx of new equipment, motor carriers took a breather and sales fell back to a still very respectable 170,000 units in 1996.

Market Shares

The small commercial truck market is dominated by Chrysler, Ford, and General Motors. Together these producers capture almost 83% of the market. Chrysler is number one with 36% of sales, followed by Ford with 33%, and GM with 14%. The remaining 17% is spread among Isuzu (8%), Freightliner (5%), Mitsubishi Fuso (2.5%), Hino, and Nissan Diesel.

In the midrange market, Navistar is king with 44% of the U.S. market. Ford and GM are second and third with 23% and 16% of sales, respectively. Freightliner rounds out the top four with 11% of the U.S. market. The remaining 6% of the market is spread among Isuzu, Mitsubishi

Fuso, Nissan Diesel, Hino, Mack Truck, Peterbilt, and Volvo–GM.

Freightliner has been the dominant player in the heavy duty market since 1992 and has steadily increased share since 1990. Last year Freightliner accounted for over 29% of U.S. sales, up from only 16% in 1989. In addition, Freightliner recently bought Ford's heavy truck business, which accounted for 9% of the U.S. market. PACCAR (Kenworth and Peterbilt) is second in size with 22% of sales. Navistar comes third in heavy–duties with a market share of just under 17%, but Navistar has been losing ground since 1992. Fourth place belongs to Mack Truck, which boosted its share in 1996 to slightly over 12%. Rounding out the major producers is Volvo–GM Heavy Truck with 9% of sales in 1996, down from 11.5% in 1995. Approximately 3% of the U.S. market goes to Western Star, a Canadian manufacturer, and a number of smaller specialty truck producers.

Forecast 1997–2006

The U.S. economy and most truck markets have surprised us on the upside in early 1997. The farm, retail, wholesale, and logging markets have done better than expected, and small businesses, which are key to the small commercial and midrange truck markets, have been optimistic about business conditions and have stepped up expansion and equipment acquisition plans. The strength in the U.S. economy, coupled with a solid recovery in Mexico and signs of life in Canada has translated into very solid gains in private and for–hire carrier traffic. Carrier profits have benefited from the strength in traffic as well as a downward trend in diesel fuel prices. With this as a backdrop, motor carriers have been somewhat more aggressive in their equipment acquisition programs.

We do not believe that the recent strength in the economy and key truck markets is a sign that a major new upswing in new equipment is underway. WEFA projects a fairly significant loss of forward momentum in the economy as 1997 progresses, and a considerably more moderate rate of expansion in 1998 than in 1997. Past history has proven that demand for new equipment gains ground when economic activity accelerates, and begins to falter when the pendulum swings the other way. We are not anticipating the kind of economic climate that would trigger anything resembling a major correction in the truck market, but we do expect equipment demand to lose some of its forward momentum as 1997 progresses, and then soften for a while next year.

Longer term, 1999–2006, economic and market fundamentals point to a period of healthy truck demand. Modest expansion is expected in key truck markets, including manufacturing, wholesale and retail trade, construction, and small business activity. Trucking companies will experience steady growth in tonnage which will require them to expand their fleets. Competition from a more streamlined and efficient rail system will force trucking companies to upgrade their fleets with state–of–the–art fuel–efficient equipment. A nagging shortage of qualified drivers will force trucking companies to continue to invest in equipment which provides increased creature comforts. Increases in efficiency, strong growth in intermodal service , and increased use of longer combination vehicles will dampen, to some extent, the demand for mid-range and heavy–duty truck tractors used to pull trailers and containers.

Summarizing The Forecast:

Small Commercial Trucks

U.S. retail sales will edge up by 1.0%–1.5% per year in 1997 and 1998. Longer–term we expect sales to advance by 2.5%–3.0% per year. The market is expected to get an added push, as equipment buyers continue to move up into these GVW ratings and truck makers continue to broaden their product lines to increase vocational appeal.

Midrange Market

Retail sales will decline 3% this year and 2% in 1998. Growth during the 1999–2006 period will average 2.5% per year. Within the market we expect a shift in buyer preference in favor of lower–cost vehicles rated in GVW 5 (16,001–19,500 pounds) at the expense of larger GVW 6 trucks.

Heavy Duty Trucks

Retail demand will drop by about 9% this year to 155,000 units, and then stabilize at about that level in 1998. A replacement cycle will allow sales to rise to 180,000 units by 2002. Sales will average about 160,000–170,000 units per year between 2002 and 2006.

Medium & Heavy Duty Trucks
U.S. Retail Sales
(000 Units)

Class	1994	1995	1996	1997	1998
GVWs 3–4	79.8	92.5	110.5	111.7	113.1
GVWs 5–7	122.7	134.3	130.2	126.0	123.3
GVW 8	185.7	201.3	170.0	155.0	154.0
Total	388.2	428.1	410.7	392.7	390.4

North American Factory Sales
(000 Units)

Class	1994	1995	1996	1997	1998
GVWs 5–7	130.0	44.2	123.4	124.5	122.0
GVW 8	225.2	245.1	191.8	183.5	184.7
Total	355.2	89.3	315.2	308.0	306.7

Truck Trailers

The demand for commercial trailers is driven largely by manufacturing activity, which involves the multiple moves of raw materials, intermediate goods, and finished products. Merchandise imports and construction activity also have an impact on the market. The major buyers of truck trailers include trucking companies and private fleets that are owned by manufacturers, retailers, merchant wholesalers, and distributors. The farm, mining, and logging sectors are major players in the market. Trailer manufacturers have increased their focus on Canada, Mexico, and the rest of Latin America in recent years, and will continue to do so in the years ahead. Exports account for 10%–15% of total shipments. Imports, primarily from Canada and Mexico, account for 15%–20% of the domestic market.

Van trailers account for about three–quarters of all shipments. Van trailers are generally used to carry general merchandise, food products, household goods such as furniture and appliances, and other manufactured goods. Platform trailers, low–bed heavy haulers, and dump trailers are closely linked to construction industry activity. Tank trailers are used to transport liquid chemicals, petroleum products, and food products.

Last year, the top 20 trailer manufacturers accounted for better than three–fourths of the industry's output. The recent peak year for trailer production was 1995. The top ten producers in that year were: Wabash National 42,424 units, Great Dane 36,514 units, Utility Trailer 25,066 units, Trailmobile 21,239 units, Monon Corp. 21,172 units, Strick Corp. 18,500 units, Fruehauf Trailer 16,753, Pines Trailer Ltd. 16,054 units, Stoughton Trailers 14,770 units, and Dorsey Trailers 12,276 units.

The trailer industry has gone through some major changes over the past year. After much bloodletting, the assets of Fruehauf Trailer, which for many years was the top trailer producer, were auctioned off. Monon Corporation was closed down by unpaid suppliers and eventually picked up by Wabash National. Finally, in early 1997 Great Dane Trailers, the number two trailer producer over the past three years, was purchased by the Crown family of Chicago. This family also owns Pines Trailers, which was also among the top ten trailer producers over the past three years.

Recent History

The 1990–91 recession saw shipments of truck trailers fall 33%. The 122,400 units shipped in 1992 represented the worst year for the industry since 1983, when 117,700 units were manufactured.

The slump in the economy and manufacturing activity during this period depressed truck trailer traffic. Private and for–hire carrier earnings were depressed by the weakness in traffic. Trucking companies were also hard–hit by high fuel prices. As equipment utilization rates fell and profits faltered, capital programs were shelved and then canceled altogether.

With the economy gaining ground starting in 1992, motor carrier traffic accelerated as manufacturing and construction activity rebounded. America's appetite for imported consumer and capital goods added to the traffic pool. The surge in trailer traffic provided the launching pad for a strong recovery in equipment demand. Robust traffic growth resulted in shortages in equipment in selected traffic lanes, and raised even greater fears that widespread shortages were in the offing. Financial conditions were also quite favorable due to the strength in the economy, the ability of trucking companies to raise freight rates, relatively benign diesel fuel costs, and low interest rates. Replacement buying programs were brought back to normal levels as the recovery took hold. This was soon followed by aggressive efforts to expand fleet capacity by adding large numbers of vans with enhanced carrying capacity, as well as other types of trailers.

One of the most striking things about the period after 1991 was the emergence of the 53 ft. dry van as the industry standard, replacing 48 ft. and 45 ft. vans as the equipment of choice. During this period, the vast majority of new van trailers purchases were 53 ft. units, which have about 18% more capacity than 45 ft. vans and about 10% more capacity than 48 ft. vans. In addition, many of the 53 ft. vans were high capacity units, equipped with plate walls and a low–profile design. Plate–wall trailers are constructed with outside supports rather than inside posts and allow an additional pallet of merchandise to be loaded. Low–profile vans take advantage of using smaller wheels, and allow more usable height within a van. Thus the actual carrying capacity of the van fleet was expanded dramatically.

Truck trailer shipments rose 35% in 1992 to 164,268 units and then jumped to 185,741 units the following year. The next three years saw trailer demand rise to unprecedented levels. Shipments surged ahead to a record 234,287 units in 1994, and then bested that performance with a whopping 279,144 units in 1995. With replacement and fleet expansion pressures easing in 1996, shipments fell back to 224,841 units. Prior to the 1994–96 period, truck trailer shipments had only exceeded 200,000 units three times, in 1974, 1979, and 1984.

The Outlook: 1997–2006

The adjustment in the trailer market is continuing this year and shipments are expected to finish 1997 at about 202,000 units. The relatively slow pace of economic ac-

tivity WEFA anticipates in 1998 will prevent any meaningful recovery from taking place, and shipments are expected to slip to 199,000 units.

Trailer demand should show steady improvement during the 1999–2002 period. WEFA is projecting real economic growth of 2.2% per year, on average, and industrial output is slated to grow by 2.5% per year. Based on our economic expectations we see activity in key trailer markets expanding by 2.6% per year. Growth in truck trailer tonnage will not be spectacular, but should be adequate enough to require additional fleet expansion. Furthermore, we expect replacement pressures to build during this period as the units that hit the highway during the early–to–mid 1990s come up for replacement. Motor carriers profits will not be spectacular during these years, but should be adequate to support additional investment in new equipment. Finally, we expect a downward drift to interest rates, and the Canadian and Mexican markets will also continue to provide support.

On balance, we expect complete trailer shipments to rise to 202,500 units in 1999, 208,400 units in 2000, 216,800 units in 2001, and 229,300 units in 2002. The latter part of the forecast period will see replacement pressures easing and fleet expansion proceeding slowly. During this time equipment utilization will improve due to expanded use of technology for tracking equipment location and scheduling front and back hauls. The trend to larger vans will continue to dampen unit sales to some extent. We expect truck trailer shipments to average about 210,000–215,000 units per year during the 2003–2006 period.

Motor Vehicle Parts

The automotive parts industry in this country is made up of over 5,000 firms, employing more than 710,000 workers, with a value of shipments in excess of $125 billion. There are two main sectors to the parts industry, original equipment parts (OEM), which are used in the manufacture of new cars and trucks, and the replacement market. General Motors (GM), Ford, and Chrysler all have in-house parts sourcing, which supply original equipment parts both for their own models and for other manufacturers, as well as replacement parts. In fact GM's Delphi Automotive Systems, which has revenues of about $26 billion, is the world's largest single parts producer. Ford Automotive Products, with roughly $16 billion in sales, is a strong second.

The Big Three, in an effort to control costs, have been de-emphasizing their in-house operations and doing more and more outsourcing. General Motors at one time made between 60% and 70% of its components in–house which in many cases could have been purchased cheaper from an outside parts supplier. GM has sold off many of its components divisions, and is in the process of transforming Delphi into a separate entity, so that it can compete more effectively in the OEM market.

The trend in the parts industry has been toward consolidation. Automakers are placing escalating demands on their supplier base, and component manufacturers are becoming responsible for the development, design, manufacture, and sometimes installation of entire component systems. For example, instead of having separate suppliers responsible for brake pads, brake drums, and brake shoes, one producer will furnish all of these components or a complete brake system. A single supplier is now often responsible for the entire vehicle interior, as opposed to the old way of separate suppliers for seats, carpeting, and upholstery.

The OEMs maintain constant pressure on parts suppliers to cut costs and have now moved to worldwide sourcing of parts. In 1996, U.S. parts imports exceeded $48 billion, up from $31.7 billion in 1990. On the other hand, the United States exported almost $41 billion, up even more from $23 billion in 1990. Mega mergers have been the parts industry's solution to this competitive pressure. In 1992, the top fifty OEM suppliers had total sales of $68 billion. In 1996, according to an estimate by Automotive News, the top fifty had sales of more than $120 billion. (Both figures include some non-automotive sales by these parts companies.) Vehicle manufacturers, wary of too much power being concentrated in the hands of their suppliers, have tried to discourage the merger mania, but they are unlikely to do more than slow the process.

Aircraft and Parts

During the 1986–96 period, aircraft industry shipments rose at a compound annual rate of only 0.1%. Aircraft and parts is certainly not a stagnant industry, despite showing little point–to–point growth during the past ten years. This performance is the direct result of violent swings in the two major industry segments, commercial aircraft and defense. During this period the aircraft and parts industry experienced a full cycle (first up, then down) in commercial transport demand, and has just recently begun to enjoy the early stages of another up–cycle. Equally important, the industry weathered the dramatic downsizing of the Defense Department and restrained spending by NASA and other government agencies.

We are in the early stages of a significant recovery in the commercial aircraft market. The upswing is driven by increasing pressure to replace older units still in service, the introduction of new models designed to meet the needs of specific traffic corridors, and strong growth that will require fleet expansion. The general aviation and civilian helicopter markets will expand modestly during the forecast period, supported by growth in corporate profits and increased regional business travel. The defense portion of the aerospace industry has been in the doldrums in recent years, as military downsizing occurred at an aggressive pace. However, discussions are underway for the next generation of military aircraft that will ensure air superiority for the United States into the next century. We expect defense–related aerospace to once again gain ground in the years ahead, and to accelerate through the middle of the next decade.

The WEFA forecast calls for aircraft and parts shipments to increase by 12% this year to $114.8 billion, and advance an additional 8% next year to $124 billion. Over the rest of the forecast period shipments should grow by 3.5%–4.0% per year.

The first half of the past decade saw industry shipments advance from $102 billion in 1986 to $132 billion in 1991, an increase of 29%, or nearly 6% per year, on average. Over the next four years, shipments fell 22% to $101.6 billion, as the civilian aircraft market dried up and the reductions in military outlays accelerated. The aircraft and parts industry reported sales of $102.5 billion in 1996. This represented an increase of only 0.9% above the 1995 level.

Civilian aircraft sales, including commercial transports, general aviation, and helicopters, rose by $21.7 billion from $15.7 billion in 1986 to $37.4 billion in 1991. Over the next four years, shipments dropped 36% to $24.0 billion in 1995. Civilian aircraft sales finally turned the corner last year as shipments rose between 8.0% and 9.0%. U.S. government spending for aircraft and missiles peaked at $23.4 billion in 1988 and then fell almost without interruption to $11.8 billion in 1995, a drop of 50%. Last year spending inched up by only 2% to $12 billion. U.S. government spending for space equipment stood at about $20 billion in 1986, peaked at almost $30 billion in 1992, and fell back to about $27 billion in both 1995 and 1996.

Foreign trade has remained a bright spot for the aircraft and parts industry. During the past decade, exports grew at an annualized rate of 8.7% and reached $51.1 billion last year. Imports have also exhibited strength, rising by 6% annually during this period but only reaching $13.6 in 1996. The United States has maintained a significant trade surplus, $37.5 billion in 1996, due to two key factors: Boeing's dominance in the commercial transport market; and strong demand overseas for military aerospace products. Swings in the commercial transport market have a profound effect on U.S. exports. The slump in the world commercial transport market depressed export levels during the 1992–95 period. Economic conditions and politics drive the demand for military exports, which did slump a bit in 1993 and 1994, but have gained ground over the last two years. Total aircraft and parts exports surged ahead by 19.7% last year supported by a 16% increase in foreign civilian sales and a whopping 32% jump in military exports. Imports of aircraft and parts also rose by 19.7% last year. Some growth was noted in imports of civil aircraft and aircraft engines, but the bulk of the increase came in parts and accessories, which account for about 55% of total imports.

The wild swings in aircraft and parts sales were reflected in industry after–tax profits which averaged $4.5 billion per year from 1987–90 and then dropped to $2.5 billion in 1991. The industry then posted a $1.8 billion loss in 1992. Restructuring has paid off in the past four years, and after–tax profits reached $7.3 billion in 1996.

We are in the early stages of a significant recovery in the commercial aircraft market. The upswing is driven by increasing pressure to replace older units still in service, the introduction of new models designed to meet the needs of specific traffic corridors, and strong growth that will require fleet expansion. The general aviation and civilian helicopter markets will expand modestly during the forecast period, supported by growth in corporate profits and increased regional business travel. The defense portion of the aerospace industry has been in the doldrums in recent years, as military downsizing occurred at an aggressive pace. However, discussions are underway for the next generation of military aircraft that will ensure air superiority for the United States into the next century. We expect defense related aerospace to once again gain ground in the years ahead, and to accelerate through the middle of the next decade.

The WEFA forecast calls for aircraft and parts shipments to increase by 12% this year to $114.8 billion, and advance an additional 8% next year to $124 billion. Over the rest of the forecast period, shipments should grow by 3.5%–4.0% per year. We are projecting growth in exports of 7% per year on average during the next decade, with overseas sales reaching $87 billion by 2006. Import growth is put at about 8% per year reaching $25 billion by 2006. The U.S. trade surplus in aircraft and parts will rise to $62 billion by the end of the forecast period.

Commercial Transports: Up, Up, and Away

After a long slump, the commercial aircraft market has turned the corner and is headed for much better times

ahead. The revival in commercial transports has been triggered by favorable passenger traffic prospects, a return to profitability by the airlines, pressure to replace the older planes in operation, and stringent noise pollution regulations.

The past ten years has brought a major cycle to the U.S. producers of commercial transports, Boeing and McDonnell Douglas. They are now beginning to experience the front end of another one. U.S. producers have also seen the European consortium Airbus become a major competitor. Deliveries by U.S. airframe manufacturers bottomed out in 1984 at 185 units and began to improve thereafter, rising to 357 by 1987. The market really hit its stride over the next five years, with deliveries averaging 500 units per year. Deliveries peaked in 1991 at 589 units and then edged off to 567 units in 1992. There is a long lead time between the ordering of new equipment and delivery, and there are stiff penalties for cancellation. New orders for aircraft had actually peaked back in 1989, but swollen backlogs kept airframe manufacturers humming for another three years.

The airline industry did not go through the 1990–91 recession unscathed. World airline traffic experienced a significant loss of momentum at the same time that deliveries of new commercial transports were peaking. The combination of sluggish traffic and a huge influx of capacity drove down load factors and severely weakened airline finances. During the 1990–92 period the world's airlines lost about $5 billion, and orders for new aircraft dropped like a rock over the next few years. U.S. airframe manufacturers reported deliveries of 408 units in 1993, 309 units in 1994, 256 units in 1995, and 269 in 1996.

Over the last four years, 1993–96, the airline industry has done well, reflecting the strength in the U.S. and world economies. World revenue passenger miles expanded by over 6% per year during this period. Airline profits have staged a very dramatic comeback.

- Strong demand for airline services has resulted in significant increases in load factors for U.S. and European airlines. Asia–Pacific airlines have reported some recent improvement in load factors. This tightening has given the airlines the leeway to boost fares 23% during the 1993–96 period.

- U.S. airlines also launched aggressive efforts to reign in labor and other operating costs. Jet fuel costs have been a bit more erratic, however, falling 13.5% between 1992 and 1994, edging up 2.5% in 1995, and then surging 22.5% in 1996.

- World airline operating profits turned positive for the first time in three years in 1993 reaching just under $2.5 billion. Profits rose to $8 billion in 1994, $14 billion in 1995, and $17.5 billion last year. U.S. air carriers posted record profits of $6.1 billion in 1996.

The revival in airline fortunes triggered a surge in new orders for commercial aircraft. U.S. airframe manufacturers announced orders for 456 new aircraft in 1995, up from 79 in 1994. Last year orders jumped to 717 new aircraft. (Airbus reported orders for 125 aircraft in 1994, 106 aircraft in 1995, and 336 aircraft in 1996.)

The commercial transport business has pretty much settled into a two horse race. Boeing remains the leader followed by the European consortium Airbus. McDonnell Douglas has been the weak sister in the industry for some time and last year a Boeing–McDonnell Douglas merger was proposed.

- At the end of last year, Boeing reported an order backlog of 1,418 planes, 781 destined for U.S. customers and 637 for foreign customers. Boeing recently signed contracts with Delta and American Airlines that lock these airlines into buying Boeing aircraft exclusively for the next 20 years, and Continental Airlines is considering a similar deal.

- McDonnell Douglas is still in the commercial aircraft business, but in a very limited capacity. At the end of last year McDonnell Douglas had an order backlog of 199 planes down from 212 a year earlier. Boeing's merger with McDonnell Douglas will give Boeing access to production facilities, engineering talent, and a stronger presence in Asia.

- Airbus Industries reported an order backlog of 753 planes at the end of last year up from 578 planes at the end of 1995. Airbus' backlog included orders for 303 planes placed by U.S. airlines, and 450 planes from foreign airlines.

The prospects for commercial transport demand are very favorable over the next decade. The orders already on the books will keep airframe manufacturers operating at a healthy pace over the near term, and the prospects for airline traffic and profits suggest that the current cycle will last for a while. The vast majority of the aircraft delivered over the next ten years will be for passenger service. However, strong growth is also expected in world cargo traffic, which will require the expansion of the freighter fleet. This will trigger some new orders with airframe manufacturers, but additions to the fleet will be largely filled by used passenger aircraft conversions. This healthy market for used passenger aircraft will only help convince the airlines that new plane purchases are a wise choice.

The outlook for U.S. and world air transportation, both passenger and cargo, is very favorable. World economic growth will be in the 3.0%–3.5% range. Growth in the United States, Western Europe, and Japan will be closer to 2.5%–3.0%, but that is more than adequate to keep air traffic expanding at a healthy clip, especially with increased support from overseas business travel. The real potential for air traffic, however, lies in China and the rest of Asia, Eastern Europe, Latin America, and Africa, where economic progress will be well above average, and airline services have a lot of room to grow. WEFA forecasts annual average economic growth during the next ten years as follows: China, 8.5%–9.0%, the rest of Asia except Japan, 6.0%–6.5%, Latin America, 4.5%–5.0%, Africa 4.5%–5.0%, and Eastern Europe, 4.5%. In addition to growth in personal and tourist travel, we expect a significant increase in business travel in these regions, as their trade with and investment from the major industrialized nations grows.

World revenue passenger miles will grow by 5.5%–6.0% per year on average over the next ten years, close to the 6% expansion rate achieved during the previous decade. Scheduled U.S. airline passenger traffic will grow by 4.5%, versus 5.7% per year over the last decade. U.S. airline cargo traffic should grow by about 6% per year, while world air cargo traffic expands by about 8% per year. World airline profits should remain on solid ground, with healthy growth in traffic providing the foundation. Furthermore, jet fuel prices are expected to taper off over the near term, and then expand by no more than 3%–4% per year. Finally, airlines should be able to raise fares with this strong demand, and will continue their efforts to hold the line on labor and other operating costs.

Strong growth in traffic will require fleet expansion over the next ten years. Airlines have been increasing load factors to handle traffic growth in recent years, but U.S.

and European airline load factors are already at record levels. Replacement demand will also remain strong. The average age of the world jet airplane fleet has been increasing rapidly in recent years, and is now approaching 14 years, up from 12 in 1992. In 1993, only four of the major U.S. airlines had fleets with an average age of over 10 years. Five years from now all 10 U.S. carriers will have fleets with an average age of over 10 years.

The requirement to meet stage 3 noise level standards will also have an impact on new plane purchases. In the U.S., the deadline for the quieter stage 3 noise levels is December 31, 1999. In Europe, the deadline is April, 2002. At the beginning of this year there were 3,252 aircraft in operation in the United States and Europe that did not meet stage 3 requirements. We estimate that a little more than half of these planes will be fitted with engine hushkits, but the remaining aircraft will either be diverted to service outside the United States and Europe or replaced.

We expect deliveries of commercial transports by Boeing, McDonnell Douglas, and Airbus to reach 600 units in 1997 up from just under 400 in 1996. Deliveries are projected to rise to 750 units in 1998, and then average between 650–700 aircraft per year. U.S. airframe manufacturers are expected to deliver 440 new planes this year, and 525 planes in 1998. Thereafter, we expect their deliveries to range between 450–500 aircraft per year.

Defense: The Worst Is Behind Us

Defense purchases of aircraft and parts lost considerable ground with the end of the Cold War and downsizing of the defense budget. U.S. government spending for aircraft and missiles peaked at $23.4 billion in 1988 and then fell almost without interruption to $11.8 billion in 1995, a drop of 50%. This spending inched up about 2% last year. Spending for aircraft peaked in 1988 at $18.2 billion and dropped 53% to $8.6 billion by 1995. Spending then rose by 3.5% in 1996. Government spending on missiles got a bump up $5.3 billion in 1990 and $5.5 billion in 1991 due to the Gulf crisis, but by last year had fallen back to $3.1 billion. Over the last three fiscal years, the number of aircraft approved for purchase fell from 324 in 1994, to 184 in 1995 to 181 in 1996. The fall off in the number of missiles was even more dramatic, from 8,331 in 1994, to 5,610 in 1995 and 4,548 in 1996. Defense and missile–related employment in the aircraft and parts industry began to decline in 1988 and has continued to fall. Employment peaked at 712,000 in 1987 and fell by 52% by the end of last year.

WEFA believes that the big reductions in defense spending are behind us, but we do not expect to see significant gains in spending anytime soon. However, the fact that we have gone from big declines in defense spending to much more subdued ones, and that we will eventually see modest increases in procurement, should be viewed as positive developments for the aircraft and parts industry.

Two major new military aircraft projects in the offing are the F–22 and the Joint Strike Fighter (JSF). The F–22, which will replace the Air Force's F–15, is largely being completed by Lockheed Martin, Pratt & Whitney, and Boeing, and is estimated at about $12 billion. The expected delivery of 438 F–22's is scheduled for 2003, and they could enter operational service by 2005. In comparison to the JSF, the F–22 is a small project. The JSF contract is projected to be the biggest contract in history, at close to $100 billion. An estimated 3000 planes will eventually be delivered, with all U.S. military services participating.

Aircraft and Parts
Growth in Sales (Line) and Volume (Bar)

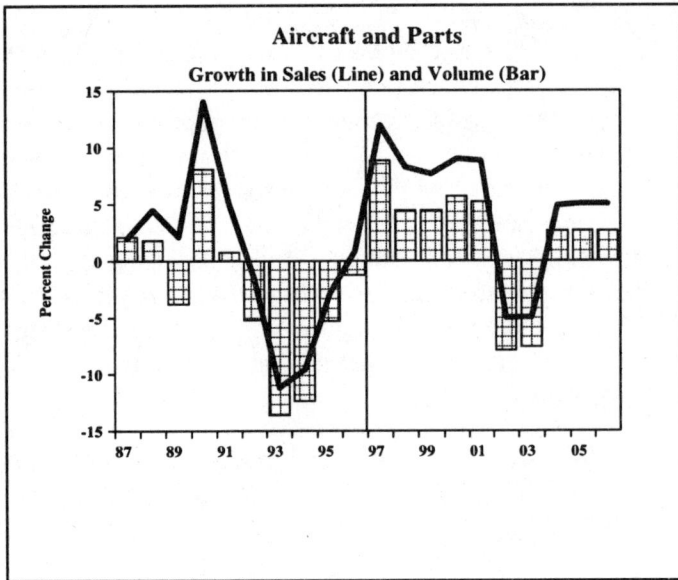

Aircraft and Parts
Growth in Product Prices

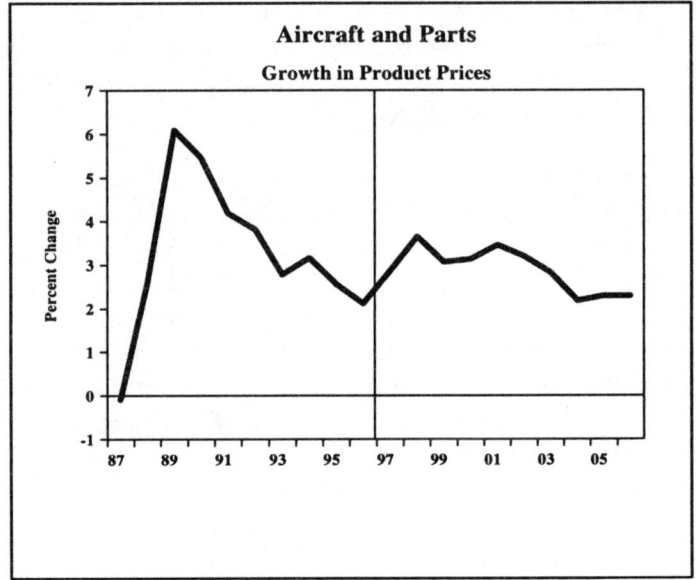

Aircraft and Parts
SIC 372

	1990	1991	1992	1993	1994	1995	1996	1997	1998	Compound Ann Avg Growth 1986-1996	1996-2006
Sales											
Billions of $	126.13	132.43	130.32	115.71	104.60	101.60	102.47	114.75	124.23		
% Change	14.0	5.0	-1.6	-11.2	-9.6	-2.9	0.9	12.0	8.3	0.1	4.9
Volume % Change	8.1	0.8	-5.2	-13.6	-12.4	-5.3	-1.2	8.9	4.4	-3.1	2.0
Prices % Change	5.5	4.2	3.8	2.8	3.2	2.5	2.1	2.9	3.6	3.2	2.9
Exports											
Billions of $	45.07	51.10	52.60	47.01	47.06	42.70	51.10	56.73	62.18		
% Change	17.7	13.4	2.9	-10.6	0.1	-9.3	19.7	11.0	9.6	8.7	7.0
Imports											
Billions of $	11.35	12.72	13.33	11.91	11.94	11.33	13.57	15.20	16.87		
% Change	11.2	12.1	4.8	-10.7	0.3	-5.1	19.7	12.0	11.0	6.0	8.1
Apparent Consumption											
Billions of $	92.41	94.06	91.05	80.61	69.48	70.23	64.94	73.22	78.91		
Nominal % Change	12.0	1.8	-3.2	-11.5	-13.8	1.1	-7.5	12.7	7.8	-2.9	3.8
Real % Change	6.2	-2.3	-6.7	-13.9	-16.4	-1.4	-9.5	9.6	4.0	-6.0	0.9

Boat and Ship Building and Repair

The boat and ship building and repair industry consists of establishments primarily engaged in building and repairing pleasure and commercial boats and ships. Marinas are not included in this category. Boat repair accounts for only about 5% of the consumer portion of this industry, while ship repair takes on a somewhat larger share of the commercial side of the business.

The surge in living standards following World War II generated a strong boom in demand for recreational boats in the United States during the 1950s. From the early 1960s through most of the 1980s demand grew at a healthy rate as the number of boats owned rose from 7 million in 1961 to almost 16 million by 1989, the peak of the boat building industry's strength. About 17 million pleasure boats are owned by Americans, a figure only modestly higher than the 16.3 million owned in 1991. Shipments in this industry peaked in 1988 at $5.9 billion and then went into steep decline for two years. The recovery since has been quite weak. A modest continuing recovery is expected, to be followed by little growth in the long term for pleasure boats.

The commercial ship–building industry has been on a long–run trend of consolidation since World War II. A bulge of building in the 1970s both over–supplied the market and provided an age cohort of vessels that are coming close to the end of their useful life. This aging fleet, along with renewed U.S. competitiveness and additional usable capacity created by U.S. Navy shipyard cutbacks, will bring growth to the commercial ship–building industry over the next decade.

Recreational Boats

Outboard motor boats are the largest category of the pleasure boat industry, representing almost half of all boats owned by consumers. This category has shown virtually no growth since 1989. In fact, inboard motor boats are the only category of pleasure boat to show any significant increase in sales since the industry's peak year of 1989. The larger and more expensive boats, such as inboard cruisers, were hurt severely by the recession in the early 1990s and the imposition in 1991 of a 10% excise tax. The tax was repealed in 1993, but the inboard cruiser market has yet to return to its earlier peak level.

Luxury items in general, and pleasure boats in particular, have some obstacles to overcome in today's U.S. economy. The segment of the income distribution that can afford a pleasure boat is not growing, and a larger proportion of the families in the higher income brackets requires two incomes to get there, which leaves less time for leisure activities. On the plus side, as the baby–boomers retire and finally have the time to enjoy such pursuits, there may be an offsetting rise in demand. On balance, however, it is our view that this business cycle's slump in the pleasure boat industry is the beginning of a period of more systemic weakness.

WEFA expects some firming in recreational boat prices in the near term as the recovery from the recession and tax episode continues, but in the longer term prices will reflect the trend toward soft sales.

Boats should be built near water, particularly the larger boats, and that is where their production is centered. The states of Florida and California continue to dominate the boat building and repair industry.

The size of businesses in the recreational boat building industry varies widely, with over half of the estimated 2,400 companies engaged in boat building employing four or fewer people. The bulk of the revenues is earned by a few large companies: in this case by the 100 or so companies that employ over 100 people. Paradoxically, the number of firms in the industry appears to have expanded during this period of sluggish demand since 1989. We expect this to reverse in the future with a gradual decline in the number of producers taking place. Employment in the industry has declined from its peak of 51,900 employees in 1988 to roughly 41,000 today.

There are risks to the pleasure boat industry both in the short term and over the long term. In the short term, pleasure boat builders have to deal with fluctuations in disposable personal income and the confidence of consumers. These issues become more worrisome as an expansion matures. In the long term, the risk centers on the availability of leisure time, and the inclinations and preferences of the population that can afford an expensive leisure activity.

Commercial Ships

U.S. flag vessels make up a mere 3% of the world merchant fleet. Panama, Liberia, Greece, Cyprus, and the Bahamas are the five largest registry flags, accounting for 46% of the world fleet. With the exception of Greece, these countries are "open registries" where a genuine link between registry country and nationality of the vessel owner is not required. The costs of registering a ship in these countries is significantly less than in the United States, hence U.S. flag vessels account for a small portion of the world fleet.

Freight–carrying vessels sailing under the U.S. flag include tankers, dry bulk, container, and roll–on/roll–off ships. Tankers account for more than 50% of total U.S. merchant capacity, and roughly 80% of the U.S. tanker fleet was constructed prior to 1980. Tanker ship construction surged in the 1970s, because of government financial assistance under the 1970 Merchant Marine Act and rising demand for transporting Alaskan oil. Other types of U.S. flag vessels have a similar age profile as tanker ships. The U.S. dry bulk fleet was mostly built prior to 1985, when exports of coal and grain were at high levels. Scrappage of U.S. ocean vessels is expected to accelerate during the next 15 years, as aging vessels reach the end of their useful life. The Oil Pollution Act of

1990 is also promoting tanker construction. This legislation mandates that only double–hull vessels are permitted to call on U.S. ports starting in the year 2010. Since most of the tanker fleet consists of single–hull vessels, the double–hull requirement is expected to spur shipbuilding over the next 15 years.

Inland and lake vessels face a situation similar to ocean ships, in that a large portion of these fleets are approaching retirement age. Roughly half of the dry cargo barge fleet was constructed between 1975 and 1984, and only 11% were built during the last five years. Since the life of a barge ranges from 20 to 30 years, a large number of retirements are expected during the next 10 years. A sizable portion of towboats, tugboats, and lakers (ships operating on the Great Lakes) are also expected to retire. Forty–four percent of the towboat/tugboat fleet is more than 25 years old and more than 40% of the laker fleet is 20 years old.

U.S. ship building capacity has declined significantly since World War II. There are approximately 20 shipyards currently in operation, one–third of which are engaged in Navy work. However, prospects may be improving for the U.S. ship building industry. One shipyard has received an order for two double–hull petroleum tankers. When complete, these ships will represent the first U.S.–built ocean commercial vessels for export since 1957. Thus, it appears that U.S.–built vessels may become competitive, and the large number of expected ocean vessel retirements should offer a growth opportunity for U.S. shipyards. The large number of expected retirements in the inland and lake fleets should also boost shipyard prospects. The ultimate number of ocean, inland, and lake vessels built in the United States will depend on expected returns to operating these vessels and the cost of U.S. vessels relative to alternative suppliers. However, ship building capacity may be constrained, at least in the short run, because of the industry's consolidation over the last 40 years.

Railroad Equipment

When all was said and done, 1996 proved to be a better year for rail equipment than was originally expected, despite the lack of demand for intermodal equipment. Powered by surging demand for covered hopper cars and a very solid tank car market, new car deliveries reached 57,877 units. This represented a decline of only 4.9% from the 60,853 units delivered in 1995, which had been the best year for the industry in well over a decade.

The demand for equipment during the forecast period will reflect a generally favorable outlook for rail traffic, improvements in car utilization, which will dampen demand to some extent, and the advanced age of the fleet.

The Age Of The Fleet

The advanced age of the freight car fleet will continue to be a key driver of new car demand. As a rule of thumb, WEFA identifies cars as potential candidates for replacement when they have more than 20 years of service. This is not to say that all cars over 20 years old will be replaced during the forecast horizon, but this is where the candidates for replacement reside. In general, cars within this broad age group, and those over 25 years old in particular, are nearing the end of their useful life, are beyond the point where rebuilding makes economic sense, and have been made obsolete because of improvements to new car technology and design.

When the average age of the fleet is rising or remains at a very high level, it is a sign that the pressure to replace equipment is mounting. Similarly, when the number of cars in the replacement pool (cars over 20 years) is growing or represents a significant portion of the total fleet, we view this as an indication that replacement demand will be strong during the next five years. As long as economic and market conditions have a favorable tilt, replacement programs will be allowed to proceed.

The most recent freight car age data suggest that replacement pressure remains strong and will continue to have a positive impact on new car demand during the forecast period.

- According to data from the AAR–UMLER file, the average age of the U.S. freight car fleet stood at 17.7 years at the beginning of 1997. The average age of the fleet has been relatively constant for the past four years, despite the huge influx of new equipment dur-

ing the recent buying cycle. However, at the end of the previous buying binge in the early 1980s, the average age stood at 13.8 years.

- The replacement pool (cars over 20 years old) now accounts for 41% of the U.S. fleet. UMLER data indicates that 23.5% of the cars in service are over 25 years old. At the end of the last buying cycle in 1982, 21% of the fleet was over 20 years old, and 13% was over 25 years old.

- The Canadian freight car fleet has an average age of 19.7 years. UMLER data indicates that 52% of the fleet is over 20 years old, and 26% of the fleet is over 25 years old.

- The average age of the Mexican freight car fleet currently stands at 22.2 years. UMLER data indicates that 60% of the fleet is over 20 years old, and 26% of the fleet is over 25 years old.

Freight Car Forecast: 1997–2006

New freight car deliveries will fall to about 43,000 units this year, a decline of 26%. The order backlog at the end of 1996 stood at a paltry 17,508 units, 46% below a year earlier.

- WEFA expects a significant loss of momentum in the covered hopper market in 1997, which alone accounted for 30,914 units delivered last year, or 53.4% of total new car installations. During the 1994–96 period, 64,000 new covered hoppers were added to the fleet and we believe a period of digestion is now in order.

■ Tank car demand should remain healthy, given the year–end backlog, traffic prospects, and the age of the fleet. However, we do expect new car demand to weaken, following back–to–back 11,600 units years in 1995 and 1996.

■ Coal cars have been a disappointment and any progress this year will be slow. Still, given the advanced age of much of the coal car fleet, we are hopeful that deliveries will improve somewhat.

■ Demand for mill gons and coil cars is also expected to drift down in 1997, following a period of very aggressive buying over the past few years. However, WEFA has a positive view of steel industry activity over the next year or two, and there may be more demand here than meets the eye.

■ Box car demand jumped above expectations in 1996, and should fall back to a level somewhere between its 1995 and 1996 levels. While box car traffic will be less than robust, replacement pressures should translate into new car orders.

■ The demand for non–intermodal flat cars appears to have additional life in it with lumber cars leading the way.

■ Finally, the intermodal market is likely to remain dormant this year, as the system continues to digest the huge influx of new equipment that hit the rails in recent years.

Beyond 1997, the freight car market will be relatively stable, with total new car deliveries ranging between 40,000–45,000 units. Improvements in car utilization rising out of the large rail mergers that have taken place, greater use of technology, and increases in average car carrying capacity will dampen fleet expansion. However, we do expect fleet expansion to take place in car types where traffic growth is the strongest and there is limited potential for improvements in car utilization, such as covered hoppers and tank cars. The advanced age of the fleet coupled with the enhanced carrying capacity of new cars, improvements in new car design, and increased competition between railroads and with truckers, will stimulate replacement buying throughout the forecast period.

The mix of new car demand should change dramatically during this period.

■ We anticipate that covered hopper deliveries will drift off and finally settle down at about 10,000–11,000 units by the end of the forecast period. Fleet expansion is expected to moderate considerably, but replacement demand will remain supportive.

■ At the same we expect a long–awaited revival in the intermodal equipment market, driven by steady growth in traffic and an end to the recent imbalance between equipment supply and demand.

■ Better days are also expected for coal cars, as coal production in the West increases and replacement demand mounts.

■ Deliveries of mill gons and coil cars should hold up pretty well. Steel industry activity will continue to gain ground, and steel scrap demand will expand at a healthy clip as the trend to the electric furnace method of production proceeds apace.

■ Box car demand will also hold its own supported by growth in auto parts and paper traffic, and pressure from shippers to improve service.

■ Finally, we expect tank car demand to remain strong, supported by modest fleet expansion pressures and solid replacement demand.

WEFA forecasts that total new car deliveries will edge off to 41,100 units in 1998, and then rise to 42,100 units in 1999, 43,800 units in 2000, and 45,400 units in 2001. Longer–term, new car deliveries should range between 40,000–45,000 units per year.

Our forecast may have some risk on the upside due to demand for equipment in Mexico. There is considerable potential demand for equipment south of the border. The privatization of the Mexican rail system is underway, and the outlook for the Mexican economy and the rest of Latin America is favorable. In addition, the advanced age of the Mexican freight car fleet means that it is in dire need of modernization and upgrading.

Railroad Equipment
Growth in Sales (Line) and Volume (Bar)

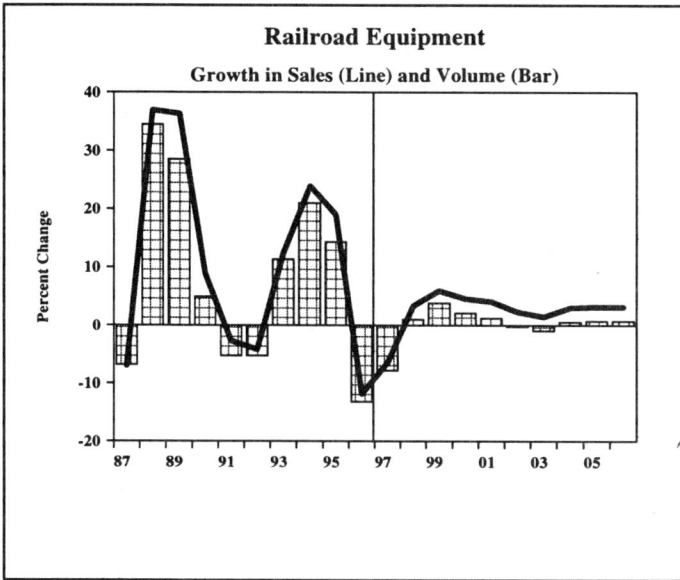

Railroad Equipment
Growth in Product Prices

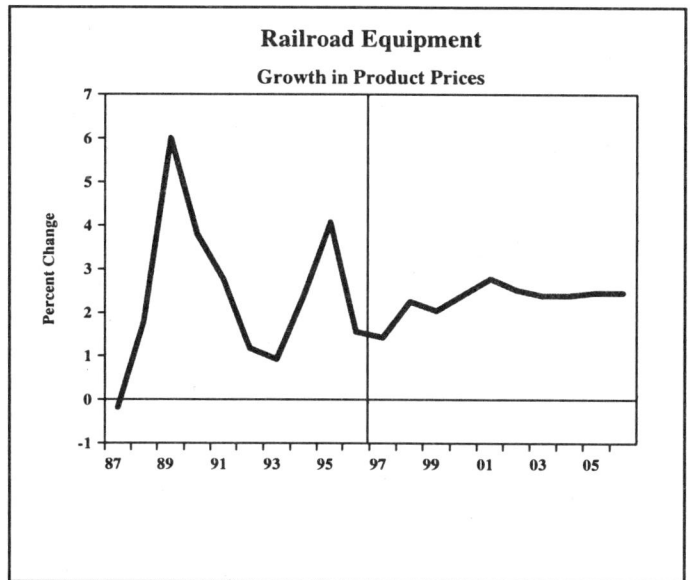

Railroad Equipment
SIC 374

		1990	1991	1992	1993	1994	1995	1996	1997	1998	Compound Ann Avg Growth 1986-1996	1996-2006
Sales												
	Billions of $	5.07	4.93	4.72	5.30	6.57	7.81	6.89	6.44	6.65		
	% Change	8.9	-2.7	-4.2	12.4	23.9	18.9	-11.9	-6.5	3.3	9.9	2.4
Volume	% Change	4.9	-5.3	-5.4	11.3	21.0	14.3	-13.2	-7.9	1.0	7.3	0.1
Prices	% Change	3.8	2.8	1.2	0.9	2.4	4.1	1.6	1.4	2.3	2.4	2.3
Exports												
	Billions of $	0.59	0.65	0.66	0.65	0.79	0.96	0.97	1.01	1.04		
	% Change	17.0	9.8	2.5	-1.9	21.0	21.7	1.3	3.8	3.2	6.0	2.2
Imports												
	Billions of $	0.65	0.57	0.64	0.65	1.03	1.22	1.22	1.25	1.31		
	% Change	-18.2	-12.2	12.0	1.4	59.5	18.4	-0.3	2.2	4.9	9.9	5.4
Apparent Consumption												
	Billions of $	5.13	4.85	4.69	5.30	6.81	8.08	7.13	6.67	6.91		
	Nominal % Change	3.7	-5.4	-3.2	12.9	28.6	18.5	-11.7	-6.5	3.6	10.6	3.0
	Real % Change	-0.1	-7.9	-4.4	11.9	25.6	13.9	-13.0	-7.8	1.3	7.9	0.7

20.23

Chapter 21: Instruments and Related Products

Instruments and Related Products

Instruments industry shipments totaled $150.6 billion in 1996, an increase of 3.7% from 1995. During the 1986–96 period, shipments grew at an average annual rate of 4.3%. Exports of instruments and related products grew by 10.9% in 1996 to $24.5 billion. Over the past ten years, exports have grown rapidly — 12.5% per year, on average. Traditionally, Japan, Canada, Western Europe, and Mexico have been the major destinations for U.S. exports, but in recent years China, the rest of Asia, and Latin America have become more important. Imports rose by only 7% in 1996 reaching $15.2 billion. Imports now account for about 11% of the $141 billion U.S. instruments market, up from 7% in 1990. Japan and the European Union are by far the major foreign suppliers of instruments to the U.S. market, accounting for about 50% of total imports. The trade surplus in instruments has almost doubled during the 1990–96 period, reaching $9.28 billion last year.

Domestic demand for instruments and related products will expand by about 5% per year during the next ten years to reach $211 billion by 2006. Imports are slated to expand by about 9% yearly, rising to $17.5 billion by the end of the forecast period. We expect imports to account for around 8.0% of the U.S. market by 2006. U.S. exports should advance by 8.5% per year totaling $29.5 billion by 2006. U.S. shipments of instruments and related products will total $166.5 billion by 2006, an increase of 5.5% per year.

The instruments industry includes a number of very diverse segments — search and navigation equipment, measuring and controlling devices, medical instruments and supplies, ophthalmic goods, and photographic goods. Each one of these categories marches to the beat of a different drummer, and reflects specific segments of the U.S. economy.

Measuring and Controlling Devices

The demand for automatic controls that regulate residential and commercial environments, industrial processes, and appliances is driven by activity in the housing, construction, manufacturing, and consumer durables markets. Shipments grew by nearly 8% per year, in nominal terms, during the 1986–96 period, reaching $45.4 billion in 1996. Over the next ten years, we expect shipments to expand by 5.5% per year, on average.

- New home construction will be relatively stable at about 1.4 million units per year during the next ten years.

- Nonresidential construction will reflect modest expansion of industrial, commercial, and electric utility capacity.

- Manufacturing activity and capital spending will proceed at an annual rate approaching 3% per year, in constant–dollar terms, in response to domestic and overseas demand. We expect the demand for industrial process controls and instruments to receive an added push as the pressure on manufacturers to improve productivity and efficiency remains intense.

- Consumer spending on appliances will expand by about 2% per year, and this will govern the growth in domestic demand for appliance controls.

- However, consumer income growth and demand for appliances will be much stronger in developing nations over the next decade, which will bolster export sales.

- Finally, measuring and controlling devices that find their way into defense and space equipment have been soft and will remain so.

Medical Instruments and Ophthalmic Goods

Shipments grew by 13.5% per year during the 1986–96 period. Sales of medical instruments rose from $19.6 billion in 1986 to $47.9 billion last year. This represented a whopping increase of over 14% per year and reflected the high cost of medical care in the United States and the increased use of high technology equipment in medical treatment. Shipments of ophthalmic goods advanced by 6.5% per year during this period reaching $4.6 billion last year. Our forecast calls for shipments of medical instruments and ophthalmic goods to rise to $99.5 billion by the end of the forecast period (1996), an annual increase of 9% per year, on average.

The medical instruments and ophthalmic goods industry is being influenced by a number of factors. Technology is allowing for the development of highly sophisticated diagnostic instruments, which usually carry a hefty price tag. Discussions on how to control medical costs are proceeding, and the debate at the federal, state, and local government levels is never–ending. There is evidence that progress has been made, but medical costs are still high and WEFA expects the growth in prices for medical equipment to moderate further during the coming decade. At the same time, the pressure to apply new technologies to medicine is not abating. On a more basic level, the population is aging and requiring more medical care.

The net result of all these factors is that the demand for medical instruments and ophthalmic goods in the United States will remain relatively strong. Overseas demand will also remain strong. Improving economic conditions in developed nations will have a favorable impact on demand. More importantly, economic progress in Asia, Africa, Latin America, and Eastern Europe will lead to efforts to improve the quality of medical care in these regions.

Photographic Goods

Photographic goods include cameras for commercial and consumer use, photocopying machines, and a whole host of products that are used to develop and process film. Shipments grew by just 2% per year during the past ten years. Last year shipments rose 2.4% to $22.4 billion. Prices of photographic goods have been relatively soft in recent years, rising just 0.2% annually between 1990 and 1996. Shipments of photographic equipment are slated to expand by about 4% per year during the next ten years.

Consumer photography is influenced by consumer confidence and income growth. Spending on vacation and recreational activities has been gaining ground in recent years, and this has had a positive impact on the equipment and supplies market. Expected growth in consumer disposable income of 2.0%–2.5% per year over the next ten years will provide subdued support to this segment of the market. However, an aging population with more leisure time and disposable income will provide a lift to sales.

The demand for photographic equipment and related products by the business sector has benefited from generally favorable economic conditions and healthy corporate profits. Spending for equipment and supplies is heavily influenced by the real estate, advertising, financial services, and entertainment industries. Corporate profits growth will benefit from expanding final sales, a downward drift in interest rates, and a corporate culture that promotes efforts to reign in and even reduce operating costs. Profits over the next ten years will be more than adequate to keep the commercial segment of the photographic goods market expanding at a decent pace.

Japanese producers have long been important in the U.S. photographic equipment market, and this is unlikely to change. Imports from Japan and the rest of Asia account for over 70% of sales of imported equipment and supplies in the United States. Export markets will provide support to domestic producers, but competition from European and Japanese producers in their home markets will remain intense.

Instruments and Related Products
Growth in Sales (Line) and Volume (Bar)

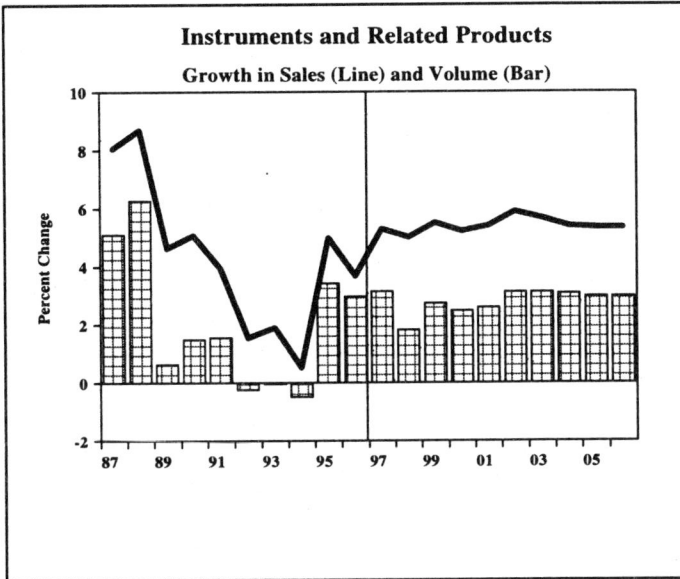

Instruments and Related Products
Growth in Product Prices

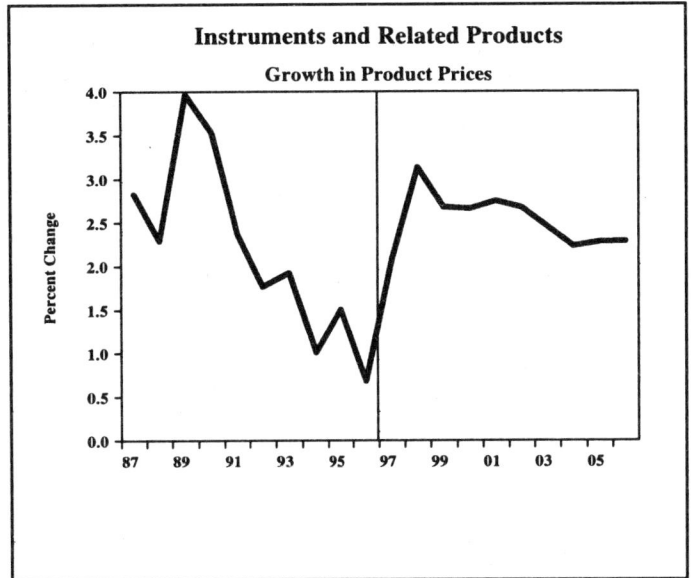

Instruments and Related Products
SIC 38

		1990	1991	1992	1993	1994	1995	1996	1997	1998	Compound Ann Avg Growth 1986-1996	1996-2006
Sales												
	Billions of $	128.02	133.09	135.11	137.66	138.38	145.27	150.61	158.58	166.50		
	% Change	5.1	4.0	1.5	1.9	0.5	5.0	3.7	5.3	5.0	4.3	5.4
Volume	% Change	1.5	1.6	-0.2	-0.0	-0.5	3.4	3.0	3.2	1.8	2.0	2.8
Prices	% Change	3.5	2.4	1.8	1.9	1.0	1.5	0.7	2.1	3.1	2.2	2.5
Exports												
	Billions of $	13.59	15.28	16.36	17.61	19.46	22.09	24.51	26.95	29.45		
	% Change	8.9	12.5	7.1	7.6	10.5	13.5	10.9	10.0	9.3	12.5	8.4
Imports												
	Billions of $	8.84	9.55	10.35	11.12	12.29	14.24	15.23	16.09	17.45		
	% Change	6.4	8.0	8.5	7.5	10.5	15.9	6.9	5.7	8.5	9.6	9.2
Apparent Consumption												
	Billions of $	123.27	127.35	129.11	131.18	131.20	137.42	141.33	147.72	154.50		
	Nominal % Change	4.8	3.3	1.4	1.6	0.0	4.7	2.8	4.5	4.6	3.8	5.3
	Real % Change	1.2	0.9	-0.4	-0.3	-1.0	3.2	2.1	2.4	1.4	1.5	2.7

Search and Navigation Equipment

The search and navigation equipment industry has been on a roller coaster ride over the past decade, reflecting the swings in activity in key markets. Shipments during the 1986–96 period declined from $33.7 billion to $30.2 billion, but peaked at $38.7 billion in 1991, which was a banner year for commercial aircraft production. We expect shipments to expand by 4.0%–5.0% per year during the next ten years.

The Defense Department and NASA represent the largest domestic markets for search and navigation equipment. As a result, search and navigation equipment lost considerable ground with the end of the Cold War and the downsizing of the defense budget. This reduction in military spending has forced many companies in this sector to either merge or sell pieces of their business that relied heavily on Pentagon spending. Many weapons and aircraft manufacturers saw this situation as an opportunity to become more vertically integrated.

■ Raytheon purchased three military electronic companies: Hughes, E–Systems, and Texas Instruments.

■ Northrop–Grumman bought Westinghouse.

■ Boeing acquired the electronic portion of Rockwell.

■ Lockheed Martin bought the electronics division of General Dynamics and defense electronics and systems integration businesses of Loral.

While the big reductions in defense spending are behind us, there is no reason to assume that spending will turn up significantly anytime soon. However, the fact that we have gone from big declines in defense spending to much more subdued ones, and that we will eventually see modest increases in procurement, should be viewed as a positive development for this industry segment.

Two good examples of new defense procurement that will help the search and navigation equipment industry are two military aircraft projects: the F–22 and the Joint Strike Fighter (JSF). The F–22, which will replace the Air Forces' F–15, is largely being completed by Lockheed Martin, Pratt & Whitney, and Boeing, and is estimated at about $12 billion. The expected delivery of 438 F–22's

(*Raptor 01*) is scheduled for 2003, and they should enter operational service by 2005.

In comparison to the JSF, however, the F–22 is a small project. The JSF contract is projected to be the biggest contract in history, at close to $100 billion. An estimated 3000 planes will eventually be delivered, with all U.S. military divisions participating.

Commercial aircraft is another major market for search and navigation equipment. This customer market posted very impressive production levels in the period between 1990 and 1992 and then fell into a slump that has only recently ended. The prospects for commercial aircraft, particularly over the next few years, are very encouraging, and this will have a positive impact on the demand for navigation equipment.

■ Strong growth in air traffic worldwide will certainly require expansion of air traffic control systems throughout the next decade.

■ There is also considerable concern about the quality of air traffic control systems in developing regions of the world, where the most dramatic gains in traffic will occur during the next ten years.

■ WEFA also expects aggressive efforts to modernize traffic control systems in traffic lanes that are currently well traveled and experiencing congestion and safety problems that will only worsen over time.

Commercial and personal use of Global Positioning System (GPS) navigation systems has been rising and will continue to provide support during the forecast period. Over–the–road truckers, railroads, and the shipping industry have already turned to satellite navigation and tracking systems that can pinpoint the location of equipment. This allows equipment owners to better monitor equipment utilization and more efficiently schedule traffic flows.

There also has been an increase in the use of GPS navigation systems in automobiles. Cadillac introduced its Onstar Navigation System about a year ago, Oldsmobile has its Guidestar system, and BMW, Toyota, and Nissan have all introduced similar systems in their luxury cars. Ford has indicated that it will offer a factory–installed GPS system on its Mondeo model in Europe in 1998. Rental car companies have been at the forefront of GPS navigation system movement. This is a trend that is expected to accelerate during the next ten years and will help to boost demand for search and navigation equipment.

Other segments made some modest gains as well: sales in simulation and training equipment were up 3.8%, and electronic warfare sales gained 3.2%. Simulation and training and electronic warfare equipment should both continue to grow, and are actually helped by restraint on military spending. Simulators have several key cost benefits that save fuel, weapons, and maintenance, and eliminate the risk of destroying a multi–million dollar weapon in training operations. Proficient ordinances, such as laser guided missiles, do a job that used to be more costly and less effective. In addition, there is a market for search and navigation equipment for upgrading older airplanes like the F–15, F–14, and F–16.

Some losers in this segments in 1996 were radar and sonar systems. Radar sales fell 0.3% while sonar sales slipped 3.6%. The fall–off in sonar systems is due to reduced requirements by the U.S. Navy as the Russian submarine fleet has been shrinking.

The ending of the Cold War had some devastating effects on many U.S. search and navigation equipment sectors. Looking to the future, although we may never see the same level of spending that we witnessed in the Reagan military buildup, the search and navigational sector should keep a steady positive growth in the years ahead.

Search and Navigation Equipment
Growth in Sales (Line) and Volume (Bar)

Search and Navigation Equipment
Growth in Product Prices

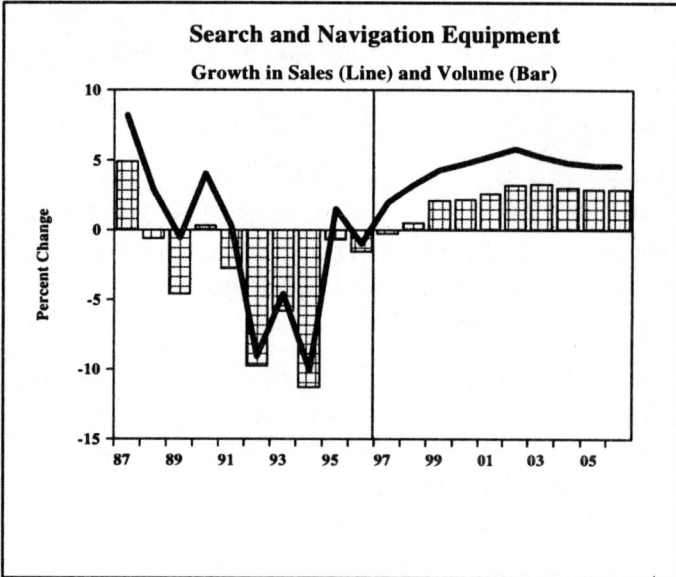

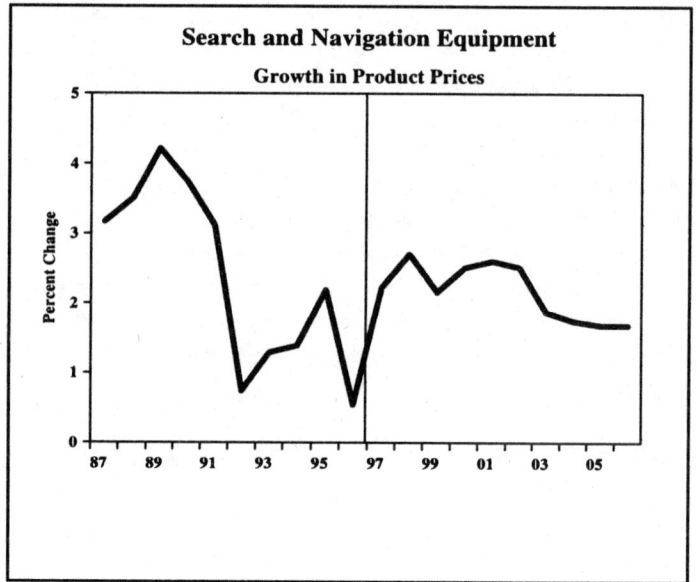

```
Search and Navigation Equipment
  SIC 381

                                                                                           Compound Ann Avg Growth
                         1990    1991    1992    1993    1994    1995    1996    1997    1998    1986-1996  1996-2006

Sales
          Billions of $  38.51   38.62   35.11   33.50   30.12   30.58   30.26   30.85   31.84
              % Change     4.1     0.3    -9.1    -4.6   -10.1     1.5    -1.0     1.9     3.2      -1.0       4.4

  Volume    % Change       0.3    -2.8    -9.7    -5.8   -11.3    -0.7    -1.6    -0.3     0.5      -3.3       2.2
  Prices    % Change       3.7     3.1     0.7     1.3     1.4     2.2     0.5     2.2     2.7       2.4       2.2
```

Chapter 22: Miscellaneous Manufacturing

Miscellaneous Manufacturing

Miscellaneous manufacturing industries include a number of small, craft–oriented industries, as well as several larger industries. The most important category is dolls, toys, games, and athletic and sporting equipment, with about 30% of total shipments. Fine jewelry and silverware accounts for 13% of the total, but this is misleading. Much of the value of the sales in this category is the cost of the raw materials (precious metals and gemstones), rather than value added of the industry itself.

The other miscellaneous category includes a variety of small industries, including brooms and brushes, signs, burial caskets, and other small and difficult–to–classify products. Signs and advertising specialties are the largest sub–industries in the other miscellaneous categories.

Many of the items in these industries are luxury or specialty items, and are therefore very dependent on economic conditions. Industries such as jewelry and toys are very vulnerable to business cycles, because they are entirely discretionary.

Miscellaneous Manufacturing Industries by Share of Total Shipments, 1994

Dolls, Toys, and Games	30.5%
Fine Jewelry	13.8%
Pens and Pencils	9.0%
Costume Jewelry	5.7%
Musical Instruments	2.4%
Other Miscellaneous	38.5%

Jewelry, Silverware, and Plated Ware

The jewelry, silverware, and plated ware industries are generally distinguished by their use of precious metals and gemstones. As a result, shipment levels and growth in dollar terms can be misleading. Large swings in raw materials prices can change industry shipment values without corresponding large changes in employment or actual industry production. Shipments grew rapidly in the 1980s, but dropped by more than 8% during the 1990–91 recession. Growth between 1992 and 1994 averaged about 3%. The industry is highly cyclical and its recovery usually lags behind those of other industries after recessions. Prices of raw materials, which are an important feature of this industry, rose quickly in 1993 and 1994, (helping to raise the value of shipments in those years) but have fallen slightly since then.

Musical Instruments

Shipments of musical instruments totaled about $1 billion in 1994. Exports account for about 25% of shipments, and imports provide an additional $900 million to domestic supply. The United States thus has a trade deficit in these items. Consumer spending on musical instruments currently totals about $2 billion per year. Spending on musical instruments has grown more slowly than income, and is highly cyclical.

Pens, Pencils, and Other Artists' Materials

Shipments of pens, pencils, and other artists' materials grew quickly in 1994 after several years of very slow or negative growth. This industry is very cyclical, and, in the past two business cycles, has recovered only several years after the rest of the economy. Domestic manufactures produced almost $3 billion in 1994. Exports accounted for 15% of total shipments, while imports equaled more than $500 million, about 17% of domestic sales.

Miscellaneous Manufacturing Industries: Brooms and Brushes, Signs and Advertising, Burial Caskets, Linoleum and Other Hard Surface Floor Coverings, and Others

Signs and advertising dominate this category, accounting for 37% of total sales. Other industries include a wide variety of consumer products and some service–industry products, such as beauty shop and barber supplies. As a whole, these industries are very volatile, with recent annual rates of growth in shipments ranging from 13% (in 1993) to 0.3% (in 1989). They are not very cyclical.

Shipments for all industries in this category totaled $6.4 billion in 1994.

Forecast

Most miscellaneous manufacturing items are discretionary, and many are even luxury items. As a result, the sector as a whole is very cyclical. Growing incomes, however, will fuel continued growth in the sector. In the absence of a recession, production growth will continue to be healthy, although strong import competition should be expected in some of the sub–industries, especially musical instruments and fine jewelry. Prices should grow at about the same rate as those of other manufactured items over the next 10 years. Short–term fluctuations in the price of jewelry should be expected, based on fluctuations in raw materials prices. Over the longer term, however, prices of these raw materials are unlikely to rise faster than other commodity prices.

Miscellaneous Manufacturing
Growth in Sales (Line) and Volume (Bar)

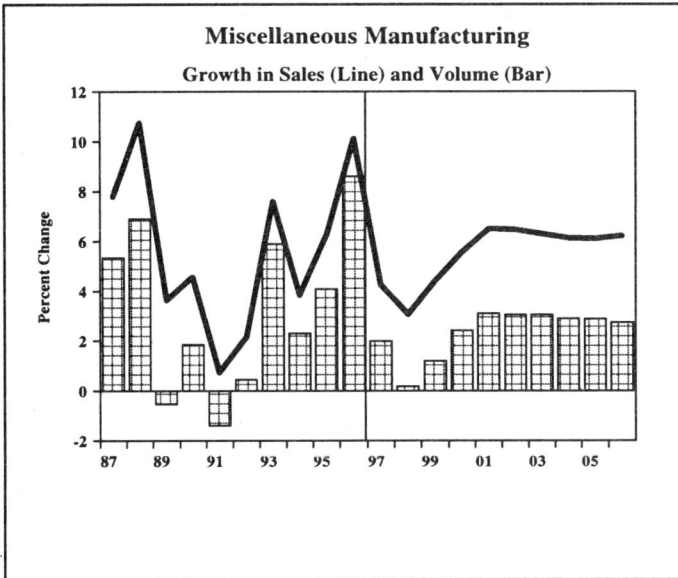

Miscellaneous Manufacturing
Growth in Product Prices

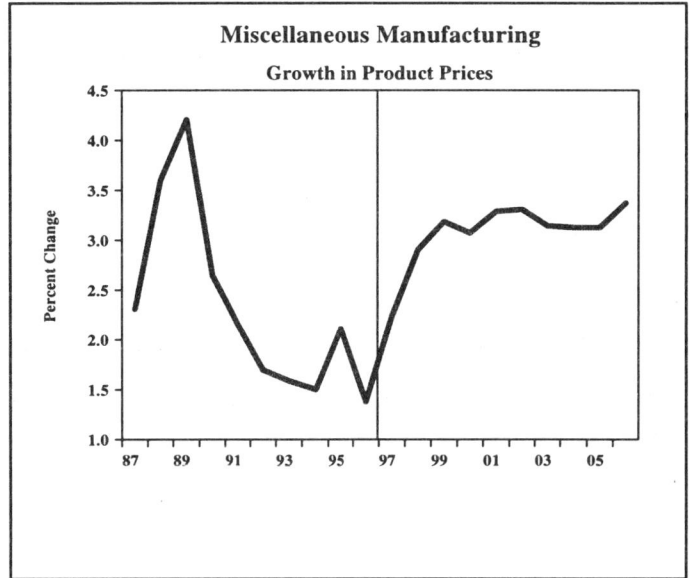

```
Miscellaneous Manufacturing
  SIC 39

                                                                                      Compound Ann Avg Growth
                        1990    1991    1992    1993    1994    1995    1996    1997    1998    1986-1996  1996-2006


Sales
        Billions of $   38.44   38.72   39.56   42.56   44.20   46.98   51.73   53.94   55.60
              % Change    4.6     0.7     2.2     7.6     3.9     6.3    10.1     4.3     3.1       5.7        5.5

   Volume    % Change     1.9    -1.4     0.4     5.9     2.3     4.1     8.6     2.0     0.2       3.3        2.4
   Prices    % Change     2.6     2.2     1.7     1.6     1.5     2.1     1.4     2.2     2.9       2.3        3.1

Exports
        Billions of $    8.94   10.45   11.56   12.30   13.47   15.06   16.74   18.22   19.59
              % Change   15.0    16.8    10.7     6.4     9.5    11.8    11.2     8.8     7.6      19.7        4.4
Imports
        Billions of $   26.34   26.22   29.63   32.64   34.31   38.16   42.14   45.88   48.58
              % Change    6.1    -0.5    13.0    10.1     5.1    11.2    10.4     8.9     5.9      10.0        6.6

Apparent Consumption
        Billions of $   55.84   54.50   57.62   62.90   65.04   70.09   77.13   81.60   84.59
       Nominal % Change   3.8    -2.4     5.7     9.2     3.4     7.8    10.1     5.8     3.7       6.0        6.3
          Real % Change   1.1    -4.5     4.0     7.4     1.9     5.5     8.6     3.5     0.7       3.6        3.2
```

22.3

Costume Jewelry

The costume jewelry industry is made up of establishments engaged in the manufacturing of jewelry composed of anything except precious metal, precious and semi–precious gemstones, goldplate, and gold–filled materials. Both the manufacture and retail sales of costume jewelry are important, because the activity of each affects the other.

In a recent study by the state of Rhode Island, costume jewelry was listed as the industry group losing the largest percentage of jobs in that state, and this finding is true in other states as well. Two key problems faced by the industry are low domestic demand and strong foreign competition.

Jewelry Demand

Demand for costume jewelry by American consumers is reflected in overall sales growth in U.S.–made jewelry over the past few years. In 1994, retail sales of American–made costume jewelry slumped, primarily in reaction to strong competition from less expensive, more fashion–trendy foreign–made necklaces, pins, earrings, and other novelty items. In 1995, all levels of the jewelry industry — retailers, designers and domestic manufacturers — reported a slight increase in sales, and growth continued in 1996.

Export demand is in general more healthy than the domestic market. Demand for U.S.–made costume jewelry in Japan, for example, is high because of high quality, good design, and low prices.

American jewelry manufacturers can also look forward to continued success in Mexico. Exports of American costume jewelry to Mexico have increased at a faster pace than total jewelry exports, making Mexico one of the United States' major markets for jewelry exports. The North American Free Trade Agreement's (NAFTA) elimination of tariffs on costume jewelry trade has contributed to U.S. producers' success south of the border. The U.S. Department of Commerce points to the jewelry industry as a major beneficiary of Mexico's increasing demand and standard of living.

Panama is another good market for U.S.–manufactured costume jewelry, primarily because the level of its own domestic production is very small. In Panama, American–produced jewelry tends to sell at higher prices than Asian goods because of its high quality. Relatively free trade also exists between the United States and Panama.

Supply

The demand for imported, less–expensive costume jewelry has affected the American suppliers' job market. In Rhode Island — a major jewelry manufacturing area — an estimated 1000 jobs were lost each year since 1982 as a result of competition with low–wage foreign producers. Also, as a result of this competition, the number of new domestic jewelry business starts have been declining in recent years. In 1995, the number of starts for new jewelry businesses dropped to 662 from 720 in 1994. In addition to demand competition, high labor costs have propelled some U.S. firms to consider producing their goods overseas.

Jewelry imports have been on the rise for twenty years. In early 1997, it was estimated that approximately 50% of jewelry sold in the United States was produced abroad. In general, the competition comes from countries with much lower wages than the United States. Price competition from foreign producers resulted in weak sales for American jewelers and increased business for foreign companies.

Shipments of inexpensive manmade gemstones from China and Russia have been on the upswing, causing not only a slip in the prices of many moderately–priced synthetics and highly–priced naturals, but also negatively impacting American jewelry makers. Highly– and moderately–priced natural and synthetic gemstones face competition in both pricing and appearance. The Asian–produced hydrothermal amethyst, for example, is very popular among consumers because of its uniformity in color and size — not to mention affordability. Although many of these less–expensive manmade pieces are clearly being marketed as "cheap synthetics," there is the possibility of these stones being mixed in with the supply of naturals, and sold at prices higher than their true value.

Industry Structure

The Jewelers Board of Trade estimated that in November 1996, 56 new jewelry firms started, while 17 failed. New starts were down by 15, while failures were up by 11, from November 1995.

Although many jewelry firms continue to suffer sales losses, one major costume jewelry maker, The Monet Group, based in New York, showed signs of improvement in 1996. When Monet's ornamental pieces began losing their appeal among consumers, the company decided to change not only its designs, but also its marketing approach. The turnaround, however, did not occur without some downsizing and cost–cutting. As a result, The Monet Group is one jewelry design firm that remains successful in a declining industry. Just last winter, Monet was licensed by Christian LaCroix, a Paris fashion design company, to begin producing its costume jewelry line in the United States, as an effort to balance out U.S. prices with those in Europe. The price of Christian LaCroix jewelry, when produced outside the United States, jumps 30% to 50% upon import into this country.

Meanwhile, American design firm Calvin Klein signed a licensing agreement with Vendome Yamada, Inc.— a Tokyo accessories firm — to begin producing and selling fashion jewelry in Japan.

The U.S. costume jewelry industry continues to experience an imbalance in merchandise trade, with higher imports than exports. Taxes on imports remain low, while in many countries U.S. exporters face high trade barriers. Although some American jewelers have lobbied for a quota on imports, others have looked toward technology and marketing improvements to increase sales overseas.

Conclusion

American costume jewelry manufacturers produce high–quality pieces, but not necessarily at a price low enough to prevent domestic consumers from demanding less–expensive imports. However, demand for American jewelry overseas is increasing, and American manufacturers see an opportunity to gain success in the export business, especially in countries like Mexico where NAFTA's elimination of tariffs on exported goods is in effect. Employment, however, may continue to decline, as lack of sales growth forces manufacturers to downsize, or, in extreme cases, close shop. Some American jewelry firms, however, are finding success as they venture into manufacturing agreements with overseas firms. Other companies are forecasting growth as a result of improved technology and stronger marketing techniques.

Value of International Trade of Costume Jewelry (millions $)

	1992	1993	1994	1995
Value of Imports to the United States	550	561	586	513
Value of Exports from the United States	121	135	148	150

Dolls, Toys, and Games

The toy industry (SIC 3944, which excludes dolls and stuffed toys) consists of established manufacturers of games and both mechanical and non–mechanical toys, including children's vehicles. The industry shipped almost $5 billion of manufactured toys in 1996 and is driven by family income, the state of the economy, and child demographics. The outlook for the three key segments of the population that use toys is crucial to the forecast for both total toys and the mix of product demand by age group.

Industry Demand

There are currently just under 20 million children under 5 years old, and that group of the toy buying (actually toy using!) population is expected to experience a modest decline over the next 10 years. The same modestly declining trend is also expected for the 5–to–9 year old segment of the population, which recently stood at 19 million persons. The third of the three key segments of the toy using population, 10–to–14 year olds, is the only one expected to show an increase in numbers over the next decade. This group, currently near 19 million, is likely to rise by just over 10% between now and 2005.

Consumer income and spending patterns in general are also important for this industry, and consumer spending gains over the next three years are forecast to be only modestly below their 1996 rate, averaging 2.2% per year in real terms. Expect demand for toys to slightly outpace the rate of real growth of personal consumption expenditures over the years just ahead. In addition, within the overall toy market, expect relatively stronger demand for games and other toys that appeal to the 10–to–14 year old segment of the U.S. child population versus those younger in age.

Toy shipments fell sharply during the early 1980s as the value of the dollar surged, making foreign–made products extremely competitive. Recovery began in 1987 and continued through 1993 when shipments turned soft again. Shipments for 1996, in current or undeflated dollars, were above their 1995 level, but remained very near the level achieved in 1982. Thus with modestly rising materials costs and hourly wage gains of just over 3% per year since 1986, maintaining profitability has been a challenge. Without extenuating circumstances, shipments — aided by modest domestic demand growth and favorable exports trends — should continue to recover beyond 1996.

Pricing Trends and Outlook

As is the case with many manufacturers who are encountering price pressure from their retail customers, the toy industry has experienced very modest gains in product pricing since 1989. Since that year price gains for toy manufacturers have averaged only 1% per year. This pressure comes from the intense competition from foreign manufacturers and from cost conscious parents, who themselves have been feeling the pinch from sluggish wages.

WEFA's projection is that the 1% trend in manufactured toy prices will continue over the next few years, providing little room for toymakers to maneuver. When 2.5% real growth is combined with projected price gains of 1%, we anticipate annual growth in toy shipments of about 3.5% per year over the next few years.

Supply Conditions

Toy manufacturing establishments are smaller than the average manufacturing facility, and it is estimated that there are about 850 establishments in operation in the U.S. The industry's shipments per establishment tend to run about 45% below those of the average manufacturer, but its cost per establishment is even lower, suggesting that toy manufacturers are more profitable than the average manufacturer. They accomplish this by using less capital equipment and by paying wages roughly 20% below that of the average manufacturer. So in spite of modest volume growth and sluggish output pricing, the toy manufacturing industry appears to be managing rather well.

In spite of the outlook for modest growth over the next few years, the toy industry is mature and most growth opportunities will be found overseas. In response to this longer term sluggish outlook, manufacturers are attempting to expand by acquisition rather than from–scratch greenfield expansion. The advantage here is that they are buying existing locations and products, as well as distribution leverage.

Major Trends Affecting The Outlook

While the toy industry is not as cyclical overall as are many other manufacturing industries, the turmoil within the industry — due to ever–changing fads and trends driven by the whims of 7 and 8 year olds — makes it something of a free–for–all. Important trends that will affect the industry in the near future are the following:

- Retail margins will continue to shrink as customers grow ever more cost conscious.

- Tighter shelf space will likely result from retail cost cutting, which will punish marginal and low volume products.

- There will be greater emphasis on multi–media products as the use of computers, and particularly CD ROM's, expand rapidly.

- Reliance on licensed products with television and movie tie–ins will continue, due to their advertising power.

- Production will continue to move abroad to take advantage of cheaper labor.

- The acquisitions trend will continue, since the market is mature.

- Exports will rise as foreign markets offer good potential.

- Established brands and classic products will be revitalized and squeezed hard, given the success of such products as Barbie, Monopoly, erector sets, and others.

Risks To The Outlook

The toy industry is a fickle industry, and periodic boom–bust cycles are always a threat to the kind of orderly market people like to expect. In addition, many products in this field have a short life cycle, and it is difficult to determine in advance which ones will give up the ghost early. Finally, the toy industry has but one major selling season, Christmas, which accounts for between 50% and 60% of annual sales. There is always the risk that something can upset this crucial selling season, particularly since it is driven by emotion and the confidence of the buying public in their economic situation — which is always subject to change.

Part 4: Transportation, Communications and Utilities

Chapter 23: Transportation

Railroad Transportation

The nation's railroads account for roughly 26% of U.S. intercity freight tonnage. The two major competing modes — truck and water — account for 46% and 14%, respectively. On a ton–mile basis, which reflects both tonnage and distance, these three modes stack up as follows: rail 40%, truck 27%, and water 15%. Over the past ten years, railroads have maintained their share of intercity tonnage. Railroads have gained ground in long–haul movements of various commodities allowing their share of intercity ton–miles to grow by over 10%. Railroad ton–miles grew by nearly 6% per year on average during the past ten years. Growth over the past five years has averaged 5.5%. Last year, revenue ton–miles grew by only 2%.

Background

The railroads changed their method of reporting traffic in 1988, separating commodity from intermodal traffic. Commodity traffic includes the number of freight cars loaded with coal, grain, chemicals, paper, lumber, metals, and other commodities. Rail commodity carloadings are influenced by U.S. production and import levels of individual commodities, modal competition, and the steady increases in the carrying capacity of freight cars.

Coal is king among rail commodities, accounting for 38.5% of total carloadings in 1996, and 37.5% during the 1988–96 period. Strong growth in coal production coming out of the Powder River Basin located in Wyoming and Montana has allowed rail coal traffic to gain considerable ground, since Powder River Basin coal is basically rail–captive. Rounding out the top ten rail commodities, chemicals and related products was a distant second accounting for 9% of traffic in 1996, followed by grain at 7%, motor vehicles and parts at 6%, metallic ores at 5%, crushed stone, sand, and gravel totaling 5%, metals at 4%, pulp and paper at 3%, waste and scrap at 3%, and stone, clay, and glass products at 3%.

Commodity carloads by major U.S. railroads stood at 17.55 million in 1988 and fell to a low of 16.83 million in 1992. Commodity loadings jumped to 17.85 by 1994 as the U.S. economy surged ahead. Since then, commodity traffic has drifted downward by 0.2% in 1995, and 0.5% in 1996 to 17.73 million. The decline in traffic last year can be traced to softness in loadings of the following commodities: grain (–10%), metallic ores (–2%), nonmetallic (–2%), grain mill products (–5%), food and kindred products (–8%), primary forest products (–9%), pulp and paper (–1%), coke, and stone, and clay, and glass prod-

ucts (–2%). This more than offset a 2% increase in coal loadings, and gains in crushed stone, sand and gravel, lumber, chemicals, petroleum products, metals, motor vehicles and parts, and waste and scrap materials.

Intermodal traffic measures the number of trailers and containers that are loaded on designated intermodal freight cars. These units travel the long stretch of their journey stacked on rail cars and are transported for short hauls on either end by truck. Manufacturing and foreign trade are the driving forces of this traffic, but the intensity of truck competition is very important, and intermodal service is most cost–effective in the heavily traveled east–west, north–south lanes.

The most striking development in intermodal traffic was the introduction in the early 1980s of articulated double–stack equipment. These were usually five connected platforms, each with the capacity to handle two containers stacked one on top of the other. Using this equipment, intermodal service has been moderately successful in pulling long–haul traffic off the highways. Shippers are increasing their use of rail intermodal service, but continue to complain about quality and delivery times. In most cases, truckers can still deliver a trailer or container load point–to–point faster than a combination of rail and truck. The more time–sensitive the load, the more likely it will go by truck alone rather than intermodally with a rail long–haul.

U.S. railroads reported intermodal loadings of 5.78 million units in 1988, comprised of 3.48 million trailers and 2.30 million containers. Trailer loadings, which are sensitive to domestic manufacturing, fell to 3.20 million units by 1991. Container traffic, on the other hand, grew steadily throughout this period as railroads aggressively marketed double–stack service. By 1991 the number of containers loaded had grown to 3.05 million. As the economy emerged from recession and foreign trade picked up steam, rail intermodal traffic began to gather momentum rising 6% in 1992 to 6.63 million. Trailer and container traffic grew 2% and 10%, respectively.

The following two years, 1993 and 1994, saw a dramatic surge in both trailer and container traffic. Economic fundamentals proved to be very favorable, as domestic manufacturing grew by over 9%, and foreign trade volume surged ahead by over 20%. At the same time, equipment and driver shortages plagued major trucking companies, and they directed as much traffic as they could onto the rails. This was also the period when rail–truck joint ventures proliferated. Railroads reported increases in trailer loadings of 6% in 1993 and 8% in 1994. Container loadings were even stronger, rising by 9% in 1993 and a whopping 19% in 1994.

Payback began in 1995, as economic growth slowed and the equipment shortage eased considerably. Trucking companies began to take delivery of large numbers of trucks and trailers in 1994 and this continued throughout 1996. Improvements in driver pay and working conditions may not have resulted in people lining up to become truck drivers, but retention rates did improve somewhat. Rail intermodal loadings fell back by nearly 2.5% in 1995 and managed a modest 2.7% increase last year. Trailer loadings were especially hard–hit, declining 7% in 1995 and 5% last year. Growth in container traffic slowed to a crawl, 1.6%, in 1995. However, growth in foreign trade volume of 7.5%, improvements in service, and aggressive marketing allowed container traffic to expand by 8.8% last year.

Mergers and Related Developments

Things have been happening in the rail industry at a speed never before imagined. The Union Pacific–Southern Pacific and Burlington Northern–Santa Fe mergers are history, and the breakup of Conrail is now in the works. There had been speculation on either CSX or Norfolk Southern making a run on Conrail for some time, the flush Northeast market being the prize. CSX struck first with a plan valued at $8.4 billion. Norfolk Southern quickly countered with an offer that exceeded $9 billion. After much discussion and hand–wringing a deal was cut that basically splits Conrail between CSX and Norfolk Southern.

The Burlington Northern–Santa Fe merger created a mega–railroad in the West that accounts for 21% of U.S. rail commodity traffic and 29% of intermodal loadings. The combined commodity loadings of the Union Pacific–Southern Pacific accounted for 26% of the total in 1996. UP–SP captured 32% of the intermodal traffic last year. CSX is a dominant player in commodity traffic with 21% of the total, but only a minor intermodal player with 8% of the market. Norfolk Southern can claim 14% of rail commodity traffic and 12% of the intermodal. CSX and Norfolk Southern will divide Conrail's 9% of commodity traffic and 14% of the intermodal market.

Another major railroad, Kansas City Southern (KCS) has been active in a very different way. KCS, in a joint venture with Transportacion Maritima Mexicana, S.A. de C.V., won the 50–year concession to operate the Northeast Line of Ferrocarriles Nacionales de Mexico. This represented the first stage in the privatization of the Mexican rail system. The Northeast Line handles about 40% of Mexico's rail traffic and is expected to benefit from strong growth in the Mexican economy and increased trade with the U.S. Kansas City Southern also won approval to acquire Gateway Western Railway Co. This creates a direct route for Kansas City Southern to St. Louis, the Southwest, and Mexico.

Eventually, the merger and purchase activity we have already experienced, and any other joinings that may occur in the future, will lead to a more efficient rail system. It does take time for the joined parties to fully rationalize their assets. The Burlington Northern–Santa Fe merger is a few years old and problems still abound. However, the result will be a more efficient, competitive, and shipper–friendly rail system. A more efficient rail system should translate into faster delivery times and should attract more traffic than would otherwise be the case.

Rail Traffic Forecast 1997–2006

Rail commodity traffic is slated to expand by 2%–2.5% per year during the 1997–2006 period. Support will come primarily from growth in coal, chemicals, grain, scrap metal, metal products, and paper. Intermodal loadings are forecast to grow by about 4% per year. This assumes that additional investment is made in new equipment and the intermodal infrastructure. Trailer loadings will be limited by stiff competition from truckers and will advance by only about 1% per year. Container traffic will benefit from strong growth in foreign trade and the further development of a domestic container business. Container loadings should grow by 5.5% per year. Railroad revenue ton–miles will continue to benefit from increases in length–of–haul, and should expand by 3% per year.

Railroad Transportation
Growth in Sales (Line) and Volume (Bar)

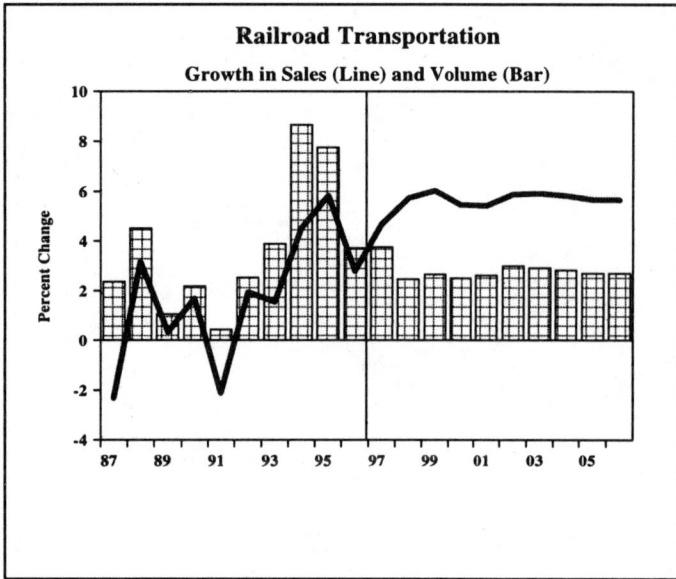

Railroad Transportation
Growth in Product Prices

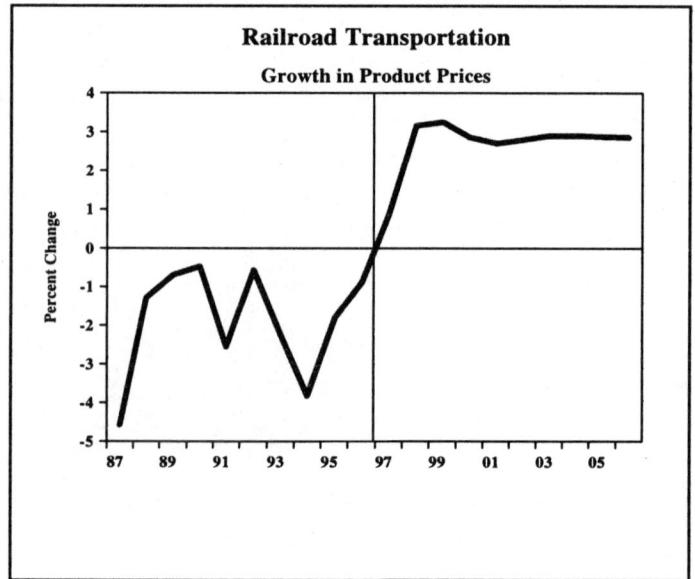

```
Railroad Transportation
SIC 40
```

		1990	1991	1992	1993	1994	1995	1996	1997	1998	Compound Ann Avg Growth 1986-1996	1996-2006
Sales												
	Billions of $	33.11	32.41	33.04	33.55	35.07	37.11	38.14	39.92	42.20		
	% Change	1.7	-2.1	2.0	1.6	4.5	5.8	2.8	4.7	5.7	1.7	5.6
Volume	% Change	2.2	0.4	2.5	3.9	8.7	7.8	3.7	3.8	2.5	3.7	2.8
Prices	% Change	-0.5	-2.6	-0.6	-2.2	-3.8	-1.8	-0.9	0.9	3.2	-1.9	2.7

Truck Transportation

Trucking is composed of two major segments, private and for–hire carriers. Truck traffic is influenced primarily by manufacturing activity and the multiple moves that occur as a result of transporting raw materials, intermediate goods, and finished products. Construction activity and the demand for imported goods also have their impact on truck traffic. Although air freight has made significant inroads in recent years, trucks still account for 70% of small package shipments. Trucks account for 46% of intercity tonnage and 27% of intercity ton–miles. Over the past ten years truck tonnage has grown by 6% per year, on average. Competition from rail in the long–haul market has intensified and truck ton–miles have expanded by only 5% per year, on average, during this period.

Private Carriers

Private fleets are owned and operated by businesses whose main purpose is not transportation. Many retailers, major food chains, building materials suppliers, and manufacturers own and operate their own fleets. We estimate that intercity truck tonnage is split between roughly 55% private carrier and 45% for–hire carrier. On a ton–mile basis, the mix tends to be closer to 50/50, because private carriers have more short–to–moderate haul loads, while for–hire carriers are dominant in long hauls.

Private fleets dominate the movement of food and kindred products, lumber and wood products, and building and paving materials. They handle roughly 30% of all chemicals, paper products, fabricated metal products, and other manufactured goods. In recent years, many private fleet owners, wanting to focus exclusively on their core businesses, have put their transportation needs in the hands of logistics companies. These companies handle all scheduling, hiring and firing, and equipment acquisition. During the past ten years, we estimate that private carrier tonnage grew by about 4.5% per year.

For–Hire Carriers

For–hire carriers are trucking companies which transport the freight of others. The for–hire segment includes truckload (TL) and less–than–truckload (L–T–L) carriers of general freight, as well as specialized carriers. Trucking company tonnage expanded by about 8% per year, on average, in the past ten years. During the same period, the American Trucking Association's truck tonnage index, which measures the intercity freight of large and small truckload and less–than–truckload carriers of general freight, grew by 10% per year, on average.

- Truckload refers to hauls with loads that fill a truck, usually in excess of 10,000 pounds. Major general freight truckload carriers include J.B. Hunt, Werner Enterprises, and M.S. Carriers. Over the past ten years, truckload carriers have experienced a slight decline, less than 1% per year, on average, in their revenue per ton–mile (a measure of price).

- Less–than–truckload refers to shipments of a quantity of freight less than required for the application of a truckload rate. This is usually below 10,000 pounds and generally involves the use of terminal facilities to break and consolidate shipments. Yellow Freight, Roadway Express, and Consolidated Freightways are major L–T–L carriers. UPS, the small package delivery company, would also fall into the L–T–L category. Less–than–truckload carriers have experienced an increase in their revenue per ton–mile of just under 1% per year in the past decade.

- Specialized carriers are trucking companies franchised to carry products which, because of size, shape, weight, or other inherent characteristics, require special equipment for loading, transporting, or unloading. Tank truck carriers hauling petroleum products and liquid chemicals, motor vehicle transporters, refrigerated commodities carriers, and moving companies fall into this category. Specialized carriers have experienced a 7.5% decline in revenue per ton–mile during the past decade.

Trucking company financial performance is heavily influenced by swings in economic activity and fuel costs. The loss of momentum in the economy that emerged in 1989, and the recession in 1990–1991, resulted in a marked deterioration in trucking company profits. As the pool of available freight dried up, trucking companies turned to rate discounting to attract freight to keep their equipment moving. This severely depressed carrier profits.

Adding insult to injury during this period was a sharp increase in diesel fuel prices. Fuel can account for 15% of a truckload carrier's operating costs. For L–T–L carriers, who carry the added cost of services at terminals where loads are broken up and consolidated, fuel represents about 8%–10% of operating costs. Retail diesel fuel prices had been in the $0.90–$0.96 cents–per–gallon range from 1986 to 1988 before moving up to $1.01 in 1989. The Gulf crisis pushed prices up to $1.21 in 1990 and they averaged $1.15 in 1991. Not surprisingly, the number of intercity trucking company failures rose by 36% in 1990 and another 15% in 1991.

Since the economy emerged from the last recession, trucking companies have done much better on the financial front. Traffic growth has been very strong. The ATA tonnage index grew by a whopping 13% per year, on average, during the 1992–96 period. Diesel fuel prices have generally been under control, and the spike in price started by the severe weather during the winter of 1996 has passed. Diesel fuel prices are now falling. During the period of higher fuel prices, major trucking companies turned to fuel surcharges to soften the blow. Freight rates did come under some pressure late in 1995 and into early 1996 as growth in the economy slowed down. However, the recent performance of the economy has been reflected in for–hire carrier tonnage, allowing trucking companies to turn the corner on the rate front. Competition between major national and regional carriers remains intense, but trucking industry finances are generally in pretty good shape.

Employment

The number of truck drivers in the U.S. has grown by roughly 2% per year over the past decade and now stands at about 2.9 million. Truck driving remains an area dominated by white males. Minorities account for less than 25% of total employment, and the share of women truck drivers has stabilized at 4%–5% in recent years.

Attracting and retaining high quality long–haul truck drivers has long been a problem for motor carriers. Working conditions generally leave much to be desired, character-

ized by long hours and much time spent away from home, and driver salaries are not at the top of the blue collar list. During exit interviews, drivers ususaly cite working conditions, rather than the pay scale, as their reason for leaving. Shortages of drivers have reached the critical point during periods of strong economic growth. That is when drivers are needed the most, but also when they have more job opportunities in other fields to lure them away. Recently, in order to make the job more attractive, there have been efforts to raise driver pay, increase the creature comforts within the truck cab, smooth out the ride by using better suspension equipment, and reduce the number of hours on the road and days away from home.

Truck Traffic Forecast

Truck tonnage is forecast to grow by about 4.5% per year on average during the 1996–2006 period. Manufacturing activity is also expected to expand by about 3% per year, on average. The movements of raw materials, intermediate goods, and final products that are associated with the manufacturing process will have a positive impact on trucking activity. Additional support will come as import volume expands by 4.5%–5.0% per year. Increased trade with Mexico will also prop up motor carrier traffic. Support from the construction sector will be modest.

We expect private carrier tonnage to expand by 3.5%–4.0% per year, as growth is limited by the trend among companies to turn to outside logistics companies for their transportation needs. For–hire truckers should experience tonnage growth of slightly over 5% per year. Competition from the railroads for long–haul traffic will intensify in the years ahead. The recent spate of rail mergers will result in a more streamlined and efficient rail system that will certainly attract more traffic. Furthermore, we expect the railroads to improve and aggressively market their intermodal service, which strikes at the heart of the long–haul truck market. Growth in rail intermodal will still require the use of trucks for drayage operations, which bring trailers and containers to and from rail heads, so truck tonnage will be only marginally impacted. Increased rail competition will not overwhelm the long–haul truck market, but will nibble away at the trucking industry's ton–mile market share. On the other side of the coin, we expect the railroads to continue to abandon unprofitable lines where traffic volumes are low, creating voids that trucking companies will be able to fill.

Truck Transportation
Growth in Sales (Line) and Volume (Bar)

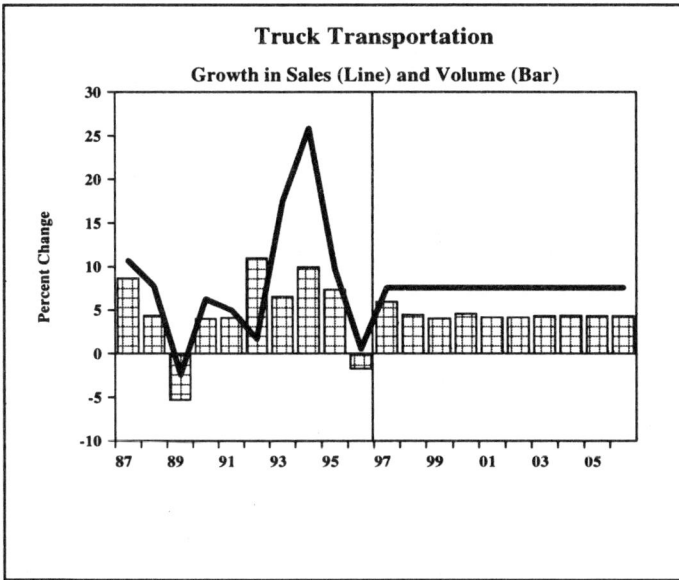

Truck Transportation
Growth in Product Prices

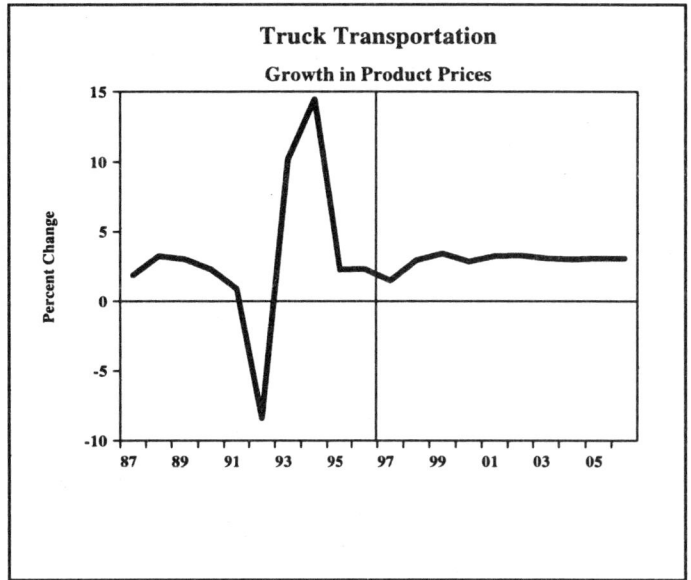

Truck Transportation
SIC 42

		1990	1991	1992	1993	1994	1995	1996	1997	1998	Compound Ann Avg Growth 1986-1996	1996-2006
Sales												
	Billions of $	129.76	136.23	138.50	162.60	204.62	224.65	225.88	242.98	261.37		
	% Change	6.3	5.0	1.7	17.4	25.8	9.8	0.6	7.6	7.6	8.0	7.6
Volume	% Change	4.0	4.1	11.0	6.6	9.9	7.4	-1.7	6.0	4.5	4.8	4.5
Prices	% Change	2.3	0.9	-8.4	10.2	14.5	2.3	2.3	1.5	3.0	3.0	2.9

Water Transportation

Internal waterways provide efficient, low-cost transportation for bulk commodities, with one out of every eight tons of domestically transported goods moving via these waterways. The Internal Waterway System consists of more than 25,000 miles of navigable channels, including the Inland Waterway System and the Intracoastal Waterway System. The Inland Waterway System consists of the Mississippi River and its major tributaries: the Arkansas River, the Illinois Waterway, the Missouri River, the Ohio River, and the Tennessee River. Other major rivers comprising this waterway system are the Black Warrior River and the Columbia-Snake River System. The Intracoastal Waterway System includes the Atlantic Intracoastal Waterway and the Gulf Intracoastal Waterway, and provides sheltered navigation routes along the Atlantic and Gulf of Mexico coastlines.

The Importance of River Cargoes

Internal waterways handled 925 million tons of cargo in 1994, up 4.8% from 1993. Total dry cargo (coal, grain, fertilizer, steel, and other non-liquid cargo) transported on waterways increased from roughly 275 million tons in 1979 to 400 million tons in 1995. Tonnage is generally highest during the fall months, when corn and soybeans are harvested and shipped to the Mississippi River Gulf for export. Waterway tonnage typically declines during the winter when the Missouri River and Upper Mississippi River are closed to barge traffic. Depending on weather conditions, other waterways may also be closed to navigation.

The Mississippi River accounts for roughly one–third of all traffic on the Inland Waterway System, followed by the Ohio River (26%), the Gulf Intracoastal Waterway (13%), the Illinois Waterway (6%), and the Tennessee River (5%). Coal is the most important cargo, accounting for 30% of internal waterway tonnage. Oil and oil products represent 26% of tonnage, with farm products and chemicals accounting for 14% each.

Coal

Open hopper barges are used to ship coal and other nonperishable products. More than 55% of coal production occurs in the Appalachian region, and most coal barge movements originate from terminals along the Ohio River and the Big Sandy River. Coal is shipped to power plants along major rivers and to export terminals along the Mississippi River Gulf and East Gulf. Most

coal exports depart from the Atlantic Coast, however, arriving at export terminals via rail.

Petroleum Products

Petroleum movements are a highly specialized market. Tank barges are used for these cargoes, and they are incapable of transporting alternative products such as grain or coal. Most petroleum movements originate at ocean ports and are delivered to inland terminals.

Farm Products

Covered hopper barges are used to ship perishable farm products and chemicals, including grains, oilseeds, and fertilizers. These barges can also haul coal if grain barge rates (prices) are sufficiently low. Grain and oilseeds, primarily corn and soybeans, represent more than 80% of farm product tonnage, and are a volatile component of total tonnage. Since 1980, the volume of grain transported on waterways has been volatile, ranging from 50 to 90 million tons. Most of this traffic originates on the Upper Mississippi River and Illinois River and is destined for Mississippi River Gulf ports, including New Orleans. Barges often carry fertilizer or forest products on the return trip to the Midwest, but most return empty in an effort to save time and maximize the number of southbound grain hauls in a season.

Industry Structure

The barge transportation industry is highly concentrated. Three carriers control 50% of the covered hopper barge fleet and 8 firms control 78% of these barges. Open hopper and tank barge ownership is also highly concentrated. The trend toward concentration is expected to continue, as grain firms and other shippers divest their water transportation assets. Other forms of vertical and horizontal integration are likely to continue. Not only does CSX own a railroad, but it is also the parent company of the largest barge carrier and a leading barge construction company.

Infrastructure

Dry cargo barges (open and covered hoppers) account for 86% of the 21,000 barges operating on inland waterways. Roughly half of these barges were constructed between 1975 and 1984, and only 11% were built in the last five years. A huge increase in hopper barge construction occurred in the late 1970s and early 1980s because of a surge in exports of coal and farm products. New tax rules included investment tax credits and accelerated write-offs, which helped further spur the construction boom. Tank barges have a similar age profile, with more than 75% of the fleet constructed more than 15 years ago.

Since the life of a barge ranges from 20 to 30 years, a large number of retirements are expected during the next 10 years. To meet future demand, barge construction must occur at the fastest rate since the 1970s. With prices of new jumbo open and covered hopper barges at $235,000 and $275,000, respectively, the industry will require $1.4 billion in additional capital by the year 2005. This investment will be necessary despite the fact that current barge rates are generally not high enough to justify or finance spending on the fleet.

The age of the locks on the Inland Waterway System also pose a problem for the industry. These structures are necessary to provide an adequate channel depth on some waterways, but many locks on the Mississippi River were constructed in the 1930s and 1940s. Individual lock capacities ultimately determine the overall capacity of internal waterways. Twenty-six locks stretch from Minneapolis to St. Louis, and most of these are standard locks measuring 600 feet in length. This size lock necessitates a tow of 15 barges to separate into two units to pass through the lock. The time spent disassembling and reassembling tows is both significant and costly. As a result, the U.S. Army Corps of Engineers is currently studying the possibility of lengthening locks on the Mississippi River. The costs of lengthening a single lock may be as much as $300 million, and there are also environmental factors to consider. One option might be for the industry to pay for lock renovations through higher fuel taxes.

Outlook

In the short term, capacity to ship cargo on the inland waterway system is fixed and demand is the main determinant of freight rates. Over the next two years, moderate growth is expected in exports of coal, grain, and oilseeds from the Mississippi River Gulf and Eastern Gulf. Consumption of petroleum and petroleum products is also expected to increase. Thus, demand for inland waterway shipping should grow during this period and higher freight rates are likely.

In the long run, rates must cover investments in new barges and towboats. A sizable portion of the barge fleet is going to reach retirement age during the next five years, but rates are currently inadequate to justify new investments. Demand for barge shipments is also expected to grow in the long run, placing upward pressure on rates. Capacity is expected to decline to the point where rates are high enough to replace retiring equipment. Volume is expected to remain relatively flat. Barge rates are expected to achieve 2.0% to 3.0% growth, as should industry revenue.

Water Transportation
Growth in Sales (Line) and Volume (Bar)

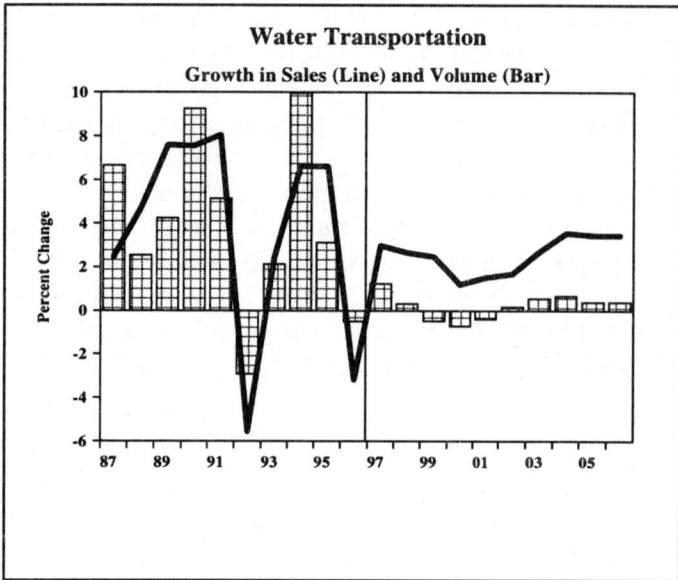

Water Transportation
Growth in Product Prices

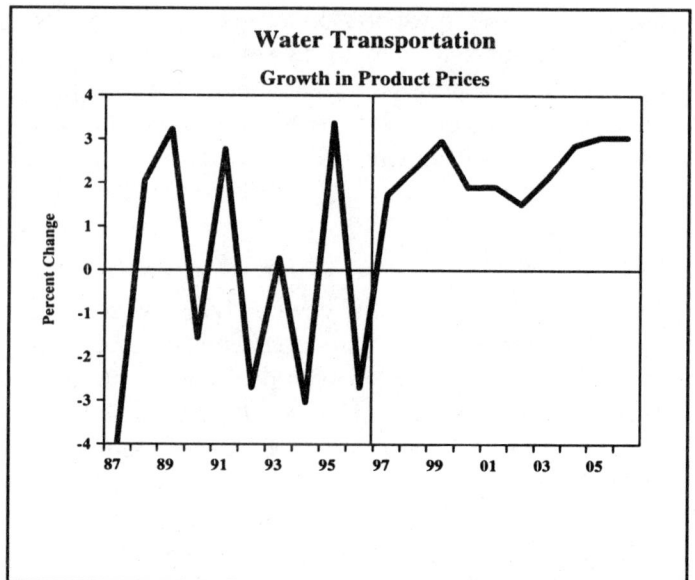

Water Transportation
SIC 44

		1990	1991	1992	1993	1994	1995	1996	1997	1998	Compound Ann Avg Growth 1986-1996	1996-2006
Sales												
	Billions of $	29.12	31.47	29.73	30.44	32.45	34.59	33.49	34.48	35.39		
	% Change	7.5	8.0	-5.5	2.4	6.6	6.6	-3.2	3.0	2.6	3.6	2.6
Volume	% Change	9.2	5.1	-2.9	2.1	10.0	3.1	-0.5	1.2	0.3	3.9	0.2
Prices	% Change	-1.6	2.8	-2.7	0.3	-3.0	3.4	-2.7	1.7	2.3	-0.3	2.3

Air Transportation

Revenue passenger miles reported by scheduled U.S. airlines grew by 5.6% per year, on average during the past decade. Domestic passenger traffic expanded by nearly 4%, while international traffic (non-domestic flights flown by U.S. airlines) grew by a whopping 14% annually. Rest–of–world (flown by foreign airlines) revenue passenger miles expanded by almost 6% per year over the past decade. U.S. airline cargo traffic grew by over 11% per year during this period, with air express companies such as Federal Express and UPS largely responsible for this growth. Air transport's share of the intercity small shipments business rose from 18% in 1986 to 28% in 1996. U.S. airlines reported a yield, that is, cents–per–revenue–passenger–mile, of 13.69 in 1996 up from 11.32 a decade earlier, an average annual increase of about 2% per year. World airline operating profits rose from just under $5 billion in 1986 to an estimated $17.5 billion last year. However, airline industry profitability during the past was characterized by wild swings, with positive numbers during the 1986–89 and 1993–96 periods on either side of a three–year stretch in 1990–92 which produced a lot of airline red ink.

The airline industry did not go through the 1990–91 recession unscathed. Domestic U.S. traffic grew by 3% in 1990, but declined by 2.4% the following year. International passenger miles jumped by 14.5% in 1990, and then slipped 2% in 1991. Rest–of–world traffic rose 6% in 1990 and dropped 3.6% the following year. U.S. airline cargo traffic grew by 2.5% in 1990 and declined 3% in 1991. As signs of life emerged in the economy, U.S. airlines reported growth in revenue passenger miles of 6.7% in 1992, with a 4.6% increase in domestic and a 13% jump in international. Rest–of–world passenger traffic grew by only 3% in 1992, as the world economy excluding the United States expanded at a paltry 0.9%.

Airline Profits

The loss of momentum in traffic that accompanied the recession in the early 1990s came during a period of very strong deliveries of new commercial transports. Deliveries of new aircraft began to heat up in 1988 and remained strong through 1992. U.S. airframe makers delivered 2500 new aircraft during this period. Airbus added another 581 planes. The combination of sluggish traffic and a huge influx of capacity drove down load factors (aircraft capacity utilization measures) and severely weakened airline finances. As a result, during the 1990–92 period the world's airlines lost about $5 billion.

Over the four years since 1992, the airline industry has done well, reflecting the strength in the U.S. and world economies. U.S. airline domestic and international revenue passenger miles have risen 20%, and rest–of–world airline passenger traffic has grown 28%. Last year alone, U.S. airline traffic grew by 5.9% and rest–of–world traffic expanded by 7%. Furthermore, U.S. cargo traffic has expanded 40% during the 1993–96 period, driven by continued strong growth in the small shipments business.

Airline profits have staged a dramatic comeback.

- Strong demand for airline services has resulted in significant increases in load factors among U.S. and European airlines. Asia–Pacific airlines have reported some recent improvement in load factors.

- This has given the airlines the leeway to boost fares 23% during the 1993–96 period.

- Airlines also launched aggressive efforts to reign in labor and other operating costs.

- In addition, jet fuel prices actually fell by 13.5% between 1992 and 1994, and edged up by only 2.5% in 1995. Jet fuel prices surged in 1996, however, by a whopping 22.5%.

World airline operating profits turned positive for the first time in three years in 1993, reaching just under $2.5 billion. Profits rose to $8 billion in 1994, $14 billion in 1995, and $17.5 billion last year. U.S. air carriers posted record profits of $6.1 billion in 1996.

Traffic Forecast

The prospects for U.S. and world air transportation, passenger and cargo, is very favorable. World economic growth will be in the 3.0%–3.5% range. Growth in the United States, Western Europe, and Japan, will be closer to 2.5%–3.0%, still more than adequate to keep air traffic expanding at a healthy clip, particularly with increased support from overseas business travel.

The real potential for air traffic, however, lies in China, the rest of Asia and the Pacific Basin, Eastern Europe, Latin America, and Africa, where economic progress will be well above average, and airline services have a lot of room to grow. Annual economic growth during the next ten years is projected as follows: China 8.5%–9.0%, other Asia and the Pacific Basin 6.0%–6.5%, Latin America 4.5%–5.0%, Africa 4.5%–5.0%, and Eastern Europe 4.5%. In addition to growth in personal and tourist travel, we expect a significant increase in business travel in these regions as the major industrialized nations look to increase their share of the pie in emerging markets.

Growth in cargo traffic in the United States and worldwide will expand as industrial activity and foreign trade continue to gain ground.

World airline profits should remain on solid ground, with healthy growth in traffic providing the foundation. Furthermore, jet fuel prices are expected to taper off over the near term, and then expand by no more than 3%–4% per year. Finally, airlines should be able to raise fares as demand remains strong, and will continue their efforts to hold the line on labor and other operating costs.

- World revenue passenger miles will expand between 5.5%–6.0% per year, on average, during the next ten years, close to the 6% expansion rate achieved during the previous decade.

- Scheduled U.S. airline passenger traffic will grow by 4.5% per year, on average, from 1996 to 2006 versus 5.7% per year for the 1986–96 period.

- Rest–of–world airline passenger traffic will expand by 6.0%–6.5% per year, on average, maintaining the pace achieved in the previous decade.

- Airline cargo traffic should grow by 6.0% per year, while world air cargo traffic expands by about 8% per year.

Transportation by Air
Growth in Sales (Line) and Volume (Bar)

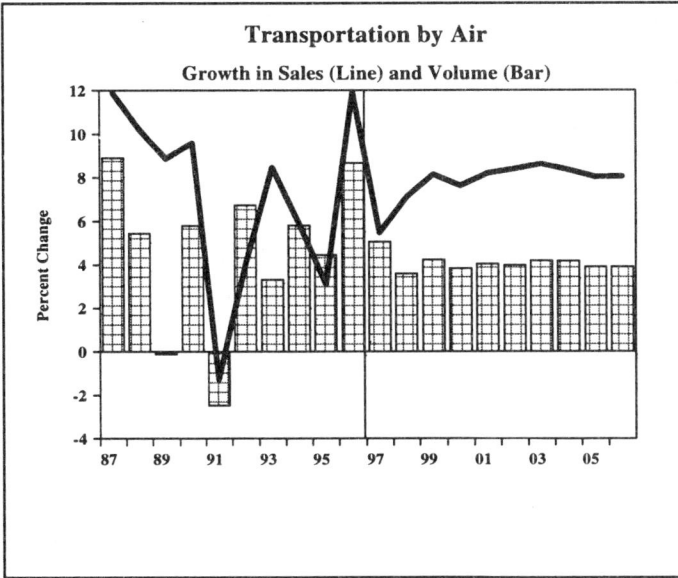

Transportation by Air
Growth in Product Prices

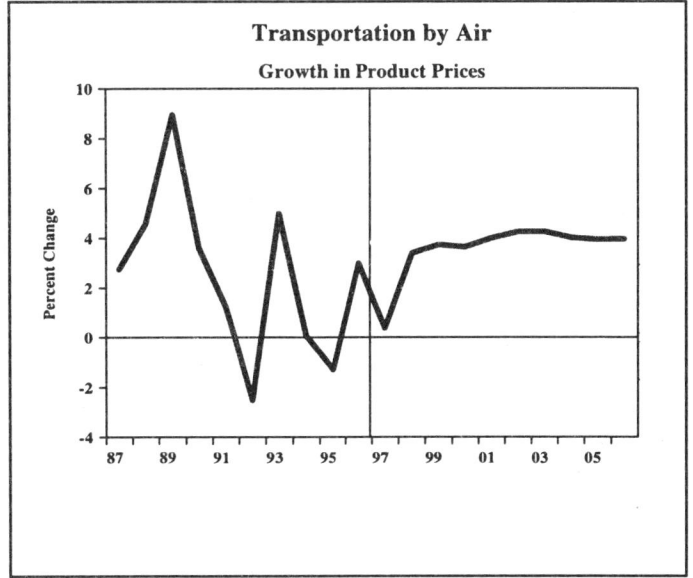

```
Transportation by Air
  SIC 45

                                                                            Compound Ann Avg Growth
                      1990    1991    1992    1993    1994    1995    1996    1997    1998    1986-1996  1996-2006

Sales
        Billions of $ 100.28  99.01  103.01  111.71  118.28  121.95  136.49  143.94  154.19
               % Change  9.6    -1.3     4.0     8.4     5.9     3.1    11.9     5.5     7.1        7.2        7.8

  Volume   % Change      5.8    -2.5     6.7     3.3     5.8     4.4     8.7     5.1     3.6        4.6        4.1
  Prices   % Change      3.6     1.2    -2.5     5.0     0.1    -1.3     3.0     0.4     3.4        2.5        3.6
```

Chapter 24:
Telecommunications

Telecommunications

The U.S. telecommunications industry remains poised for growth due to technological and regulatory change. The Telecommunications Act of 1996, which opens up the potential for genuine competition in local and long distance markets, has created a stream of merger, acquisition, alliance, and restructuring activity, and will continue to reshape the business landscape for the near future. Competition will lower prices and accelerate the transformation in services already underway. Increased demand for mobile communications, toll–free and 900 lines, and the explosion of the Internet and on–line services, combined with the expected marriage of computers, television, and telephony, will provide the need for further investment in high–speed lines, cellular telephone networks, and faster transmission gear. Growth in the number of lines and the intensity of usage will offset expected rate decreases, yielding continued growth prospects for the industry.

The U.S. telecommunications industry, which serves more than 94 million households and 25 million businesses nationwide, is expected to have revenues of $231 billion in 1997. The industry can be analyzed in its constituent parts of local, toll, toll–free (800/888), and cellular services.

Local Service

Until recently, every local exchange telecommunications market had one highly–regulated monopoly carrier. This local exchange carrier (LEC) provided service within its local access area and was subject to both state and federal regulation. LECs included the seven regional Bell operating companies and their 22 sub–regional operating companies, as well as approximately 1500 independent operating companies, mostly rural cooperatives.

Under the Telecommunications Act, regulations are eased on the existing LECs, but their monopoly status is gradually eroded. Traditional long–distance carriers (AT&T, MCI, Sprint, and others) as well as other LECs can compete for local customers. Competitive Access Providers (CAPs), companies which originally offered business customers special access services and interoffice transport services to long–distance carriers, can also enter the local access market. In addition, nontraditional providers such as cable television and wireless companies can enter the local access market.

With the threat of competition, residential local access revenues increased an estimated 2.9% in 1996, after increases of 5.7% and 6.0% in 1994 and 1995, respec-

tively. Residential local access revenue increases will remain in the vicinity of 3% through 1999. CAPs have provided a measure of competition in the business local access market since the mid–1980s. Consequently, revenue increases will slow less dramatically, but will remain in the 3% range.

Long–Distance Service

The long–distance market is also heavily influenced by the Telecommunications Act. Just as long–distance players can invade the local access market, so can local access providers, as well as CAPs, enter the long–distance business. While AT&T remains the dominant force in this market, its share has steadily eroded from 81.9% in 1986 to 55.2% in 1994. MCI and Sprint, together making up over a quarter of the market in 1994, have been the biggest beneficiaries of AT&T's decline, but a host of smaller firms, mainly resellers, have also sprung up.

Traffic is increasing in the long–distance market due to the various types of usage. Long distance now comprises data and fax traffic as well as voice. Growth in international calling has been strong for years as the U.S. economy has become increasingly globalized. As video and Internet usage increases, demand for long–distance service will remain robust. Despite price moderation, revenues in the consumer market increased an estimated 6.5% in 1996 and will continue to grow in excess of 6% for the next several years. Due to aggressive competition for large corporate accounts, business revenue growth will be more subdued, averaging 2.2% annually through 1999.

800/900 Services

The 800/900 market (which now includes 888) is one of the fastest growing telecommunications markets. 800 service is an incoming–only line, in which the cost of the call is typically paid by the receiver. In contrast, with 900 services the caller pays for access for a specific service such as a sports score. Initially, mail–order sales and catalog establishments were the dominant users of 800 services. However, toll–free numbers are now widely used for customer service centers and centralized sales and marketing activities at non–direct sale firms as well.

Portability of 800 numbers was required in 1993. Prior to that point, toll–free numbers were held by long distance carriers, making subscribers reluctant to switch carriers even for lower rates. Losing a prized number with a memorable mnemonic imposed significant business costs that lower rates would not offset. Portability increased competition, resulting in the lower costs that have been a major factor in the recent growth of the 800 market.

Technology has also fostered growth in this market. Originally, 800 numbers required dedicated telephone company lines, putting them out of the financial reach of most small establishments. The advent of switched inbound service allows 800 calls to be connected onto a firm's existing telephone lines, significantly reducing costs. Growth was so rapid that the telephone system ran out of 800 numbers, and 888 was added as a toll–free prefix in 1995.

Toll–free revenues increased 9.0% in 1993 and 16.6% in 1994. Decreased availability of numbers in mid–1995 until 888 came on line held 1995 revenue growth to 6.7%. However, toll–free revenues recovered, increasing an estimated 8.7% in 1996, and are expected to grow in the 6.5%–7% range annually through 1999. Toll–free growth will benefit from new applications for the service such as remote data processing driven by increased use of personal banking and finance options such as ATMs, credit card validation, and debit card terminals.

Regulation of the 900 market has affected its growth adversely. FCC requirements that 900 providers describe the cost and nature of their services, especially for services marketed to children under the age of 18, and that disputed 900 call billings be charged back to the service provider have increased the cost of such services. This has led a number of services, particularly at the higher priced end, to quit the business. Also, 900 numbers are not yet truly portable, limiting competition across carriers. The net result is that 900 revenues in 1996 are estimated to be less than those in 1991. While growth has returned to this market segment, it will not approach the attractiveness of the toll–free segment.

Cellular Service

By any measure, cellular service is the growth darling of the telecommunications industry. From an estimated 91,600 subscribers using about 350 cell sites and generating just over $350 million in revenues in 1985, this segment has mushroomed to an estimated 44 million subscribers utilizing 30,000 cell sites spending over $23 billion on calls at the end of 1996. Annual growth rates in this segment were better than 30% in 1994 and 1995, falling to a still impressive estimated 24% in 1996.

The growth is coming from new subscribers. New users are signing up at a rate of 28,000 per day, while the dollar amount of the average individual bill continues to drop. The wireless industry now directly employs in excess of 84,100 workers, and reports a total capital investment since 1983 of $32.5 billion, $8.4 billion of that in 1996 alone.

With only 17% of the U.S. population estimated to use a wireless telephone in 1996, there is still plenty of room for growth. Once only the domain of the business elite, declining prices and the convenience offered by mobile communications is making cellular service an indispensable tool for sales personnel as well as private individuals and families who are increasingly on the go. Despite anticipated competition from PCS and other mobile communications services, cellular telecommunications revenues should increase in the 17%–20% range through 1999.

The Internet and Other Technological Opportunities (Issues to Watch)

The rapid rise in the popularity of the Internet and in other on–line services poses a unique opportunity for the telecommunications industry. From virtually no individual usage prior to 1994, growth has exploded with an estimated 4 million households subscribing to Internet Service Providers (ISP) in 1996, and an expected 8.5 million in 1997. This is in addition to 13 million households subscribing to online services in 1996, up from less than 1 million in 1988. Clearly, some households have both Internet and on–line access. Estimates of Internet household penetration vary, but upwards of 24 million households may have Internet access by 2000. When business Internet use is factored in, the opportunity clearly becomes huge.

The current method used by most individuals for Internet access is via modem through a telephone line. Increased use of the Internet for e–mail, entertainment, and research has motivated many households to add a second or third telephone line dedicated to their computer. It has also fostered a tremendous increase in traffic on the existing telephone network. As Internet users demand ever more speed to push through large data files such as video, telecommunications providers will either need to step up with more capital investment (e.g., fiber optic cable) or technological innovation (e.g. affordable ISDN, ADSL, etc.), or they risk losing this business to cable or satellite communications companies.

So–called collaborative technologies also offer opportunities for the telecommunications industry. These include video–conferencing, telecommuting, and other forms of data sharing, such as allowing doctors at different institutions to simultaneously view a patient's medical records. There were about 50,000 video–conferencing systems in use in 1995, compared with 5,800 in 1992 and 3,000 in 1989. The video–conferencing market posted revenues of $2.4 billion in 1994, compared to $1.5 million in 1994. Some market specialists believe a fivefold drop in the price of video–conferencing systems (from 1994 prices) is in store, leading to potentially dramatic increases in the demand for such equipment. PC–based video–conferencing alone could hit $1 billion in revenue in 1997.

	1997	1998	1999
Residential — Local	24,654	25,413	26,185
% Change	3.2	3.1	3.0
Residential — Toll	44,669	47,435	50,327
% Change	6.3	6.2	6.1
Business — Local	24,263	24,979	25,706
% Change	3.0	3.0	2.9
Business — Toll	46,400	47,408	48,413
% Change	2.2	2.2	2.1

	1997	1998	1999
Local Service	48,917	50,392	51,891
% Change	3.1	3.0	3.0
Toll Service	91,069	94,844	98,739
% Change	4.2	4.1	4.1
Toll Free (800/888)	11,785	12,575	13,394
% Change	7.0	6.7	6.5
Cellular Service	28,438	33,729	39,605
% Change	20.3	18.6	17.4

	1997	1998	1999
Total – No Cellular	203,146	210,247	217,532
% Change	3.7	3.5	3.5
Total — With Cellular	231,585	243,976	257,137
% Change	5.4	5.4	5.4

Chapter 25: Utilities

Utilities

The Federal Energy Regulatory Commission's recent reform of the federal regulations governing the United States electricity industry will lead, without question, to far–reaching and systemic change affecting both the industry's basic operations and its structure. What are the implications of these reforms? And, more fundamentally, how will the new system work? Any intelligent attempt to analyze the future of the industry as a whole first requires a full understanding of both its historic and evolving structure.

Historic Structure and Regulation

Electricity in the United States is provided by a combination of investor–owned, federal, municipal, and cooperative electric utilities, together with nonutility power producers. The 250 investor–owned utilities (IOUs) dominate the United States industry, accounting for nearly 80% of all revenues from sales to end consumers, and historically providing transmission and distribution services through an exclusive franchise within a particular service area. Both federal and state agencies carry out regulatory functions, with state agencies controlling local issues including retail pricing and federal boards overseeing all interstate activities. Regulations governing the operation of utilities obligate them to provide reliable service to their customers, in return for which they benefit from regulated prices with a guaranteed fair rate of return.

The 2,970 government–run and co–operative utilities compose the remainder of the United States utility industry. The non–profit operations serve their local communities at cost, and in turn receive tax–exempt status and lower rates of financing. As opposed to investor–owned utilities, most of which generate their own power, over 50% of public utilities and co–operatives purchase their power from other sources, themselves serving as only transmission and distribution operatives. Among the various types of public utilities, states and municipalities provide 10% of the nation's electricity capacity; federally–operated utilities produce 9%; and co–operatives produce about 4%. Federal utilities primarily generate hydropower and then sell it wholesale to other electric utilities. Co–operatives, on the other hand, are member–owned and provide their services directly to those members.

Historically, retail power service was provided in the form of a bundled generation, transmission, and distribution package, with distribution carried out by a local utility in its franchised service area, under state and federal regulations. State regulatory agencies had jurisdiction over the certification of transmission, distribution, and most generating facilities. They oversaw utility franchise service territories and the pricing of "bundled" utility service to the utility's local retail customers. Federal regulators monitored wholesale interstate activities, interstate transmissions, and the licensing of hydro and nuclear facilities, of which the latter responsibility was carried out by the Federal Energy Regulatory Commission (FERC) and the Nuclear Regulatory Commission (NRC), respectively.

The Growth Of Competition

Regulatory reform did not come about spontaneously; on the contrary, many factors, several of which date back to the 1970s, together served as an impetus for change.

The evolving perceptions of members of both business and government involved in the electricity industry partly explain the move towards regulatory reform. First, deregulation in the natural gas, airline, and telecommunications industries heightened the belief that market forces could lower prices more effectively than regulators. At the same time, the traditional view of electricity as a natural monopoly began to change, as the growth of wheeling — — transporting electricity between utilities in the wholesale market —— led to a clear differentiation between the act of generation and that of transmission. Further, advances in technology have decreased what had previously been seen as an insurmountable initial capital investment for the construction of electric plants. In fact, smaller plants are now highly efficient and private financing is wholly possible. Taken together, these changes threatened the ideas at the very base of the electricity industry structure.

FERC Orders 888 and 889, which went into effect at the end of June 1996, put muscle on the skeleton structure the Energy Policy Act of 1992 (EPAct) had laid out. With these orders, FERC hoped to promote competition in the wholesale power market, correct undue discrimination in the use of wholesale transmission services, and establish standards by which utilities could recover stranded costs. The term "stranded costs" refers to the costs of power plants, power purchase contracts, and fuel supply contracts that will be uneconomical, and hence difficult to recover in a competitive market.

A primary tenet of FERC 888 requires utilities to unbundle their electricity services. Thus, rather than quote a package price, utilities are required to break down their fees into separate generation and transmission categories. Order 888 further mandates that all public utilities that operate transmission lines file open access transmission tariffs with FERC comparable to those tariffs the utility charges their own power customers, under the same terms and conditions of service.

Beyond filing such tariffs with FERC, Order 889 also requires open information. Through Real–Time Information Network (RIN), an electronic bulletin board, wholesale market buyers and sellers should all be able to access the same information on transmission prices and conditions for utilities nationwide. In fact, 889 requires public utilities to obtain data about their own transmission system the same way their competitors do, through RIN.

While the United States Congress and FERC have laid the groundwork for an increasingly open marketplace, many of the details have been left up to individual states to decide. Both the speed at which deregulation occurs and the extent to which open competition is permitted will be at the discretion of state regulatory commissions. Thus far, states with relatively high–priced electricity have progressed in their restructuring more rapidly, under pressure from large industrial and commercial customers. Leaders in reform include the states of California, Illinois, Massachusetts, and New Hampshire.

Regulatory Reform, Not Deregulation

An important differentiation to make when considering the changing face of the electricity industry is that the process occurring in this instance is regulatory reform, not total deregulation. At the close of the entire effort, regulation will remain at both the federal and the state level. A likely outcome, in the long run, is a generation industry with very limited regulation coupled with a heavily regulated transmission and distribution industry.

An integral part of regulatory reform involves the unbundling of electricity service so that generation, transmission, and distribution are all separate activities with separate fees. With the days of the vertically integrated electric utility numbered, the likely long–term result is specialization where three different types of companies would provide electric service to end–use customers: competitive unregulated generating companies, heavily regulated transmission companies, and moderately regulated distribution companies. Many utilities are already moving forward on this issue by aggressively pursuing the wholesale market and, in some cases, even preparing to split their operations.

Niagara Mohawk, for example, is now considering dividing itself into two separate segments. Presently facing a dim financial picture, partly as a result of stringent state regulations forcing it into contracts with more expensive independent power, the utility has close to $2 billion in estimated stranded costs. One plan being promoted by corporate management is called "PowerChoice" and would effectively split Niagara Mohawk into two separate companies, one generating and one transmission and distribution.

Although the number of utilities actually offering customer choice is extremely limited at this time, a significant number of utilities are engaging in greater wholesale wheeling. Northeast Utilities, for example, has been extremely aggressive in selling cheap wholesale electricity; over 20% of their generated electricity is sold on the wholesale market.

Industry Structure

Since 1992 there have been more investor–owned utility mergers than ever before in American history, as merging sheds its negative connotation and gains wider acceptance, being viewed in many cases as necessary for survival in the newly competitive industry. The trend extends beyond the investor–owned segment; electricity cooperatives also boasted a record number of consolidations between 1992 and 1995. By and large, these combinations have followed a "merger of equals" pattern, although prominent hostile bids have also occurred. Notably, deals with international companies have also gained in popularity: in 1995 there were an unprecedented number of mergers, acquisitions, and partnerships between U.S. and international corporations.

Why the sudden merger madness? Companies recognize that they must cut costs in order to compete. The economies of scale, increased efficiency, and elimination of duplicative processes that can result from company combinations are attractive to electric utilities concerned about the growing specter of regulatory reform. The "thing to do" in response to vast change in the industry is to merge. The current marcoeconomic situation —— favorable financial markets, modest economic growth, a universal trend toward globalization —— also provides an especially comfortable setting for mergers.

Another impetus to "mass merging" stems from the growing belief that, in order to survive in the future, an electric utility needs to start with a critical mass of customers.

Independent Power Producers

The 1978 Public Utilities Regulatory Policies Act (PURPA), adopted in large part to discourage domestic dependence on foreign oil, required utilities to purchase power from an outside source if the cost was equivalent to producing the electricity internally (a concept known as "avoided cost"). It spawned independent power producers across the country who grew rapidly through the 1980s and the first half of the 1990s, aided by strict regulations in some states that literally forced utilities to purchase power from them at higher rates. Although they currently provide around 10% of United States electricity, these nonutility generators are being threatened by competition and regulatory reform, especially because their power tends to be more costly than that produced by utilities: the average cost of nonutility power is 6.5¢/kwh, 2.6¢ more than the average cost for a utility. Independent power producers (IPPs) argue, however, that their higher costs are a result of having built many of the newer power projects which would have otherwise been capital projects of the utilities themselves, at a much higher cost. In either case, New York State, historically one of the most stringent in the country in terms of regulations favoring IPPs, recently ended its mandated price supports for IPPs, and New York utilities have responded by ending their IPP contracts. Niagara Mohawk has canceled more

than 80 contracts since 1992; New York State Electric & Gas has dropped 19; and Commonwealth Edison, 7 of its 22 total agreements with IPPs. This is demonstrative of a larger trend that will likely result in a smaller independent power producer industry.

Stranded Investment

Stranded costs are those costs arising from a reformed system that no longer gives a guaranteed rate of return on investments. Thus, stranded costs will be equivalent to the difference between the deregulated market price and the regulated revenue requirement. This will have a huge impact on electric utilities, especially those in the Northeast which have invested heavily in nuclear power and made other costly capital investments. The real impact will depend on the difference between the embedded costs and markets prices, how stranded costs are borne, and when effective deregulation occurs.

There is an inverse relationship between the time it takes for deregulation to take effect and the impact of stranded costs. First, building additional capacity is much less expensive now than it has been over the last twenty years; for example, during the 1970s and 1980s, average costs ran $1500 to $5500 per kW. Now it has been reduced to less than $1000 per KW in the case of gas, and now makers of coal–fired units are attempting to move toward that target. Furthermore, excess capacity is depressing bulk power prices at the same time that the industry works off its excess capacity. Finally, depreciation and inflation will also lessen the effect of stranded costs over time.

It is likely that state regulators will allow utilities to successfully recover a large percentage of their stranded costs, either through a transmission surcharge, a fee charged to end–use customers, or a combination of both.

Retail Sales Of Electricity

Electricity retail sales surpassed the 3 billion megawatt–hour (MWh) mark for the first time in 1995. This represents an impressive increase from the 291 million MWh recorded in 1950.

Electricity demand in the United States has consistently grown over time, but at a significantly declining rate of increase. There are numerous reasons for this trend, but as a general statement it is true that the strong electricity demand of 1950–73 was fostered by an ethic which maximized electricity use in the home as a means of reducing workload and increasing comfort (e.g., air conditioning), and promoted electricity consumption in the workplace (both commercial and industrial) as a means of increasing output. The "oil crises" of the early 1970s and the early 1980s increased the cost of using energy to the point that greater efficiency was called for in all sectors.

Electricity demand as measured on an annual basis has declined on only two occasions. In 1974, both the energy shortages and 25% electricity price increase caused by the oil embargo resulted in a slight 0.35% decline; in 1982, another oil price shock coupled with the worst economic recession in the United States since the depression of the 1930s combined to result in a 2.79% electricity demand reduction.

The four major sectors for electricity demand are classified as residential, commercial, industrial, and "other." The structure of the sectoral demand for electricity has changed dramatically over time. The period of the 1950s was dominated by an industrial sector twice the size of the residential demand base. Residential demand surpassed industrial sector sales in 1993 and continues to be the largest sector today.

Growth by demand sector has not been even, although all have essentially followed the same slope of decreasing sales rates. From the 1950s, electricity sales to all three sectors benefited greatly from expanded use of air conditioning. The residential sector's electricity use was supplemented by a growing array of electrical appliances. With the arrival of higher priced electricity in the early 1970s, increased efficiency in appliances and the greater use of insulation contributed to greater efficiencies in this sector.

The industrial sector pushed electricity–generated machinery in the 1950s and 1960s as a means of promoting higher production. With energy constituting such a large part of product cost, however, the higher prices of the post–1973 period led to a greater demand in plant efficiency as a means of cutting operating costs.

To a very large extent, the commercial sector has reflected the trends from both the residential and industrial sectors.

Electricity Rates

The declining "real" electricity prices from 1960 to 1973 were a major factor in stimulating the strong electricity demand which occurred during that time period. The oil price shock of 1974 began a trend of strong upward prices which continued, in real terms, until a decade later, in 1983.

The run–up in electricity prices during the 1974–83 period was due to a large number of factors, although precipitated largely by the 1973 oil embargo. Delivered fuel prices increased dramatically in all fuels as a result of the price pressure brought about by higher oil prices. Utility coal prices were higher not only because of higher demand, but also because Congress had passed the Clean Air Act of 1972 which mandated the use of higher cost, lower sulfur coal in new utility boilers.

There were also capital cost reasons behind the higher electricity prices of the post–embargo period. On the coal side, utilities were forced to install flue gas desulfurization equipment ("scrubbers") on all new plants as a result of the Clean Air Act Amendments of 1977. At the same time, the nation began to experience a rash of cost overruns among the rapidly growing ranks of nuclear power plants.

The reasons behind the electricity price decline since 1983 are similarly multi–faceted. Certainly, declining oil, coal, and natural gas prices have played a major role. Moreover, the growing penetration of nuclear power plants into electricity generation was able to contribute to lower electricity prices due to their low operating costs, in most cases offsetting their higher capital cost.

A major contributing factor to lower electricity prices since the early 1980s has been the very limited need by utilities to construct new plant capacity. Utility companies, in the 1970s, basing their projections on the high electricity demands of the 1950s and 1960s, had significantly overestimated the need for generating capacity and created an overcapacity situation that persists in some areas even today. As a result, a significant portion of new electricity demand during the 1980s and well into the 1990s has largely been met by existing power plants simply running at higher loads.

Forecast Of Electricity Trends

Electricity Sales

Electricity retail sales are expected to continue to slow their advance in the coming years, averaging about 1.7% growth over the forecast period. This is lower than the 2.6% annual average increases of the 1980s and the 2.1% annual changes of the first half of this decade, but still represents significant growth. Steady efficiency gains are projected to keep the rate of growth in total electric sales approximately 0.5% below the growth in the economy.

U.S. Electricity Sales Forecast (Annual Avg. Growth Rates)				
	1995–2000	2000–2005	2005–2010	1995–2010
Residential	1.62%	1.76%	1.89%	1.75%
Commercial	1.67%	1.81%	1.93%	1.80%
Industrial	1.58%	1.29%	1.38%	1.42%
Total	1.62%	1.62%	1.74%	1.66%

Capacity

With reserve margins still approaching 20% and with industry restructuring likely to push that number into the 16% range, there is still some excess capacity in the system to exploit before significant amounts of new capacity will be needed.

While this rate of projected growth is lower than historical levels, some forecasters hold even lower expectations. In part, their assumptions have included the rapid introduction of new energy–efficient capital in response to funded programs authorized under the Energy Policy Act of 1992. WEFA's assessment is that the potential impact of these programs has been overestimated, particularly in light of funding cuts which have reduced the projected level of the programs. In addition, the continued low electricity prices contained in our forecast themselves act as an incentive to higher demand growth.

In spite of the more rapid pace of growth in natural gas capacity additions, both coal and natural gas each gain about the same in total share of the capacity market by the year 2010. These 3%–4% gains each come at the expense of both nuclear and hydro, both of which are effectively stymied as far as meaningful new growth.

Electricity Capacity Changes by Fuel Type			
	1995	2010	% Chg
Coal	308	420	36.4%
Oil–Gas	234	335	43.4%
Nuclear	101	101	0.0%
Hydro	97	98	0.6%
Other	20	21	0.5%
Total	761	975	28.2%

Electricity Prices

Electricity prices remain generally flat in the WEFA forecast. In spite of slightly falling real O&M (operations and maintenance) costs, fuel costs rise slightly while the capital component remains steady.

While rates in general remain constant, the industrial sector rates tend to rise the most within a narrow range. As referenced previously, this is in large part due to the enormous price concessions already won by this sector.

Conclusions

This analysis has endeavored to portray a rapidly changing, dynamic power industry in the United States and, through reasoned assessment, point the directions in which it is headed. In an environment which is changing as quickly as this, it is difficult to single out the most volatile factors. Yet in the interest of attempting to provide an overall perspective as to the most significant risks, we have identified three key areas worthy of careful monitoring in the months and years ahead.

- *Technology.* The race between coal and natural gas equipment manufacturers to develop a highly efficient and low capital cost generating equipment will be crucial to the outcome regarding fuel choice.

- *Natural Gas Prices:* Proponents of natural gas use claim improved finding rates and other technological advances ensure prices may never rise in real terms; yet others caution regarding the tendency to base fu-

ture prices on today's cost of exploring only conventional sources.

- *Environmental Changes:* All of the likely environmental changes now being considered will favor the use of natural gas. The speed and extent to which these changes are adopted will have a profound impact on future fuel choice decisions.

Electric and Gas Utilities
Growth in Sales (Line) and Volume (Bar)

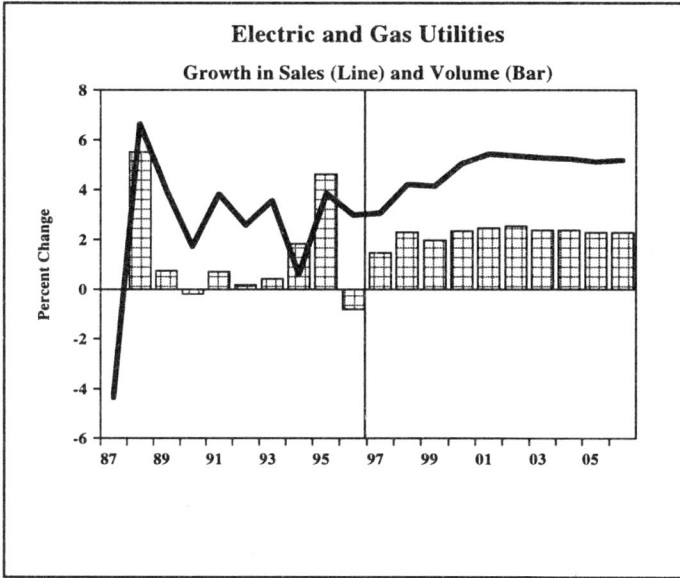

Electric and Gas Utilities
Growth in Product Prices

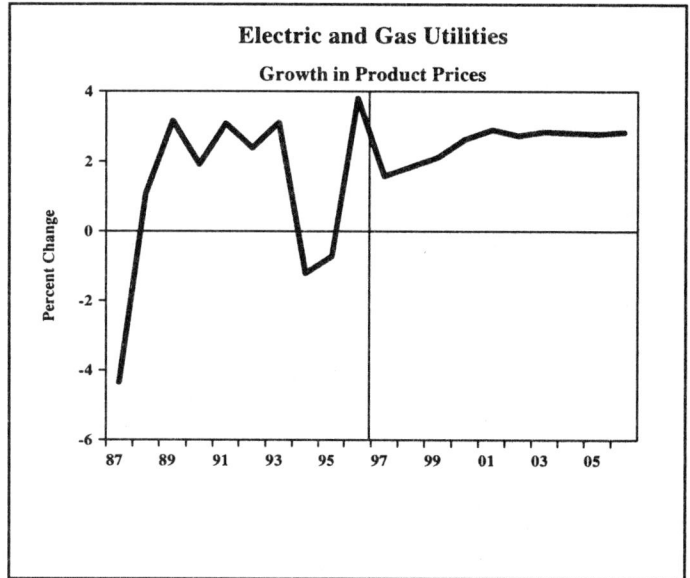

```
Electric and Gas Utilities
 SIC 49

                                                                              Compound Ann Avg Growth
                      1990   1991   1992   1993   1994   1995   1996   1997   1998   1986-1996 1996-2006


Sales
        Billions of $ 266.85 277.06 284.19 294.32 296.09 307.46 316.59 326.28 339.96
        % Change       1.7    3.8    2.6    3.6    0.6    3.8    3.0    3.1    4.2      2.5       4.8

 Volume  % Change     -0.2    0.7    0.2    0.4    1.8    4.6   -0.8    1.5    2.3      1.3       2.2
 Prices  % Change      1.9    3.1    2.4    3.1   -1.2   -0.7    3.8    1.6    1.9      1.2       2.5
```

Part 5: Wholesale and Retail Trade

Chapter 26: Wholesale Trade

Wholesale Trade

The wholesale industry is a large and diverse sector of the U.S. economy. According to the 1992 Census of Wholesale Trade, that year there were 386,609 firms operating 495,457 establishments in the industry, and their sales totaled $3.2 trillion. In 1996, there were 6.6 million people employed in wholesale trade, or 5.5 % of total nonfarm payrolls. The industry consists of a few large firms and many small ones. In 1992, of the 342,524 firms which operated for the entire year, 1,162 of them (or 0.3%) accounted for 53% of the industry's total sales; at the same time, 238,357 firms (70% of the total) accounted for only 6% of all sales.

Industry Structure

The products that wholesalers distribute to their customers are supplied by other firms in the manufacturing, mining, agricultural, and wholesale sectors of the economy. The wholesale industry has three categories — merchant wholesalers; manufacturers' sales branches and offices; and agents, brokers, and commission merchants. Of the three, merchant wholesalers account for the largest share of sales, employment, and number of firms.

Merchant wholesalers account for just under 60% of all wholesale sales, and at least 50% of all sales in each major product line, except motor vehicles and parts. Merchant wholesalers are distinguished from other types of wholesalers in that they actually take title to the goods. They may also sort, assemble, grade, and store them. Some also provide certain "value–added" services, such as packaging and labeling — a business strategy that is becoming increasingly important as thousands of wholesalers, selling products that are similar in quality and design, compete for customers. Sales by merchant wholesalers, the only wholesale data available on an annual basis, will be used here to illustrate the industry trends.

Other wholesale transactions involve agents or brokers, who sell supplier–owned products primarily to retailers and other wholesalers for a commission or fee, and manufacturers' sales branches and offices, which sell the parent manufacturer's products mainly to retailers and industrial users. The Census Bureau does not collect monthly or annual sales data for these wholesalers, and only benchmark reports are available every five years. According to the 1992 Census of Wholesale Trade, the latest report available, sales by manufacturers' sales branches and offices accounted for approximately 32%

of all sales by wholesalers, while agents and brokers accounted for about 11%. Agents, brokers, and manufacturers' sales branches represent a similarly small portion of total sales for each of the major wholesale product lines, with the exception of motor vehicles and parts.

Industry Trends

The wholesale trade industry has been a fast–growing sector of the U.S. economy in recent years. Measured in terms of value added, wholesale trade was the fastest–growing major sector during the period 1987–94. Over this period, while the overall economy (i.e., real Gross Domestic Product) grew at an average annual rate of 2.3%, value added in the wholesale trade industry grew more than twice as fast, at an average annual rate of 4.9%.

Merchant wholesaling firms account for nearly 90% of all wholesaling firms and constitute the dominant wholesale distribution channel for each of the major product lines carried by wholesalers: bulk commodities, capital goods, and all consumer goods, except motor vehicles and parts.

Sales by merchant wholesalers reached $2.4 trillion in 1996, up 6.0% from the 1995 total. Even after adjusting for inflation, the year–to–year gain was still a strong 4.3%. Indeed, during the five years of expansion since the 1990–91 recession, "real," or after–inflation, sales of merchant wholesalers have risen by about 4.5% on average per year. That compares with an average rate of increase in the overall economy during that period of 2.6%.

Alternative Channels Of Distribution

Despite the strong growth in sales of merchant wholesalers in recent years, those firms have been under increasing pressure from alternative channels of distribution. The most important alternative channels of wholesale distribution are direct manufacturer–to–retail arrangements, usually made by manufacturers under strategic alliances with major retail chain stores, warehouse clubs, discount stores, and home center stores. Other alternative channels include mail order, catalog sales, and direct sales from manufacturer to industrial user or from retailer to industrial users.

The value of products distributed through these alternative channels are lost sales as far as most wholesalers are concerned. Thus, the size of the current and potential market for wholesalers has been diminished by the volume of products distributed through the alternative channels.

Changes In The Industry

Intense pressures in the industry's competitive structure, in costs, and in other areas have caused significant changes in the wholesale trade business in recent years. For example, consumers and retailers are forcing changes in the beverage distribution system. Large retailers are demanding creative, contemporary, progressive changes to help them do a better job for consumers. Meeting these demands represents quite a change for beverage distributors, who historically have concerned themselves with delivery activities and have relied on their suppliers for marketing efforts. Now, a significant portion of the marketing burden has shifted to the wholesaler. According to one analyst, "the winners of the future will be wholesaler–and–supplier teams capable of marketing to consumers on a store–by–store basis."

Merchant Wholesalers: Annual

Indicator	1988	1989	1990	1991	1992	1993	1994	1995	1996	1997	1998
Sales, current dollars											
$ trillion	1.61	1.73	1.79	1.78	1.84	1.94	2.08	2.25	2.39	2.54	2.70
% change	9.3	7.2	3.8	−0.8	3.6	5.3	7.1	8.5	6.0	6.5	6.0
Sales, constant dollars											
$1992 trillion	1.72	1.76	1.78	1.77	1.84	1.92	2.03	2.13	2.22	2.33	2.41
% change	4.8	2.9	0.9	−0.4	3.9	4.3	5.8	4.5	4.3	4.8	3.8
Average Price											
level, 1992=100	93.9	97.9	100.7	100.3	100.0	100.9	102.1	106.0	107.8	109.6	112.0
% change	4.3	4.3	2.8	−0.4	−0.3	0.9	1.1	3.8	1.7	1.7	2.2

Merchant Wholesalers: 10–Year Trends
Average Annual Growth Rate

Indicator	1986–1996	1996–2006
Sales, current dollars	5.6	4.8
Sales, constant dollars	3.4	3.4
Prices	2.2	1.4

In another example of the ongoing changes in the wholesale trade business, global competition among chemical manufacturers has brought about more work for chemical distributors, as customers call for blending, reformulating, bar–coding, and quality control tests on top of repackaging. While manufacturers are working at cutting costs and enhancing efficiency, most of the needed improvements are passed on to distributors. While this redirects and expands opportunities for distributors, the greatest challenge lies in delivering the goods with the most service and at the lowest operating costs.

Once upon a time, chemical distributors were classic middlemen, buying in bulk, selling in parcels. Simple re-packaging was the extent of their hands–on product. To-day, distributors are not only repackaging as never be-fore, but blending, reformulating (as manufacturers shift to less hazardous products), bar–coding, testing, and performing other quality assurance chores — even safety and regulatory training. At the same time, a major result of manufacturers' determination to wring out every pos-sible supply–chain cost is to winnow the number of dis-tributors to an irreducible minimum and add to the tasks of the survivors.

Merchant Wholesale Sales, 1992–96, By Category
Billions of Dollars

	1992	1993	1994	1995	1996
Durable Goods	906.0	987.0	1,080.0	1,170.0	1,230.0
Motor vehicles and auto equipment	170.0	179.0	197.0	199.0	205.0
Furniture and home furnishings	33.1	34.9	36.7	39.3	41.4
Lumber and other construction materials	63.7	71.7	78.2	75.4	82.5
Sporting, recreational goods, and toys	139.0	159.0	166.0	191.0	226.0
Metals and minerals, except petroleum	76.6	80.3	92.6	100.0	97.4
Electrical goods	115.0	132.0	150.0	173.0	178.0
Hardware, plumbing and heating equipment	52.9	55.4	63.7	69.2	72.0
Machinery, equipment and supplies	149.0	161.0	170.0	181.0	183.0
Miscellaneous durable goods	106.0	114.0	128.0	145.0	145.0
Nondurable Goods	938.0	954.0	995.0	1,080.0	1,160.0
Paper and products	54.6	59.2	67.8	82.0	82.2
Drugs, drug proprietors and druggist sundries	66.8	72.2	83.5	93.5	99.9
Apparel, piece goods, and notions	67.7	70.2	72.6	71.9	77.1
Groceries and related products	278.0	286.0	289.0	301.0	309.0
Farm product raw materials	106.0	96.0	95.7	112.0	127.0
Chemicals and allied products	39.0	39.2	41.9	46.5	51.6
Petroleum and petroleum products	142.0	139.0	143.0	155.0	183.0
Beer, wine, and distilled alcoholic beverages	50.2	51.1	53.0	53.8	55.7
Miscellaneous nondurable goods	133.0	140.0	149.0	165.0	175.0
Total, all goods	**1,840.0**	**1,940.0**	**2,080.0**	**2,250.0**	**2,390.0**

Chapter 27: Retail Trade

Building Materials and Supply Stores

This segment of retail trade includes building materials stores, garden stores, hardware stores, paint and wallpaper stores, and mobile home dealers. The category is dominated by building material and supply stores, which account for half of all sales, and hardware stores, which account for an additional quarter of sales. Mobile home dealers account for only a small fraction of this category.

The aging of the population, combined with reduced population growth, will keep growth in sales at building supply stores very moderate over the next decade. The pent–up demand for remodeling and upgrading houses has largely worn off with the fast growth in home sales of the past few years. As a result, this sector will experience nominal sales growth of only about 3.0% over the next few years. Prices will also grow moderately, but faster than prices of most commodities. This will be the result of higher lumber prices and a changing (and more expensive) product mix which reflects environmental costs in this sector.

Demand Conditions

Building materials and supply stores sell to both professional and do–it–yourself builders. Spending for do–it–yourself projects tends to come from younger homeowners, while older homeowners prefer to purchase professional services. Since professional home remodeling is a fragmented industry made up of many small firms, both types of home remodeling result in retail sales at building supply stores.

Remodeling construction has been growing as a portion of total spending for residential construction. This trend will likely moderate in the near future, as the pent–up demand for remodeling and home improvements falls away.

An important demographic change is underway, however, which will affect the nature of sales in this market. Homeowners in the younger age brackets (25 to 34 years old) tend to do more work themselves, while older homeowners tend to purchase remodeling services. Many remodeling contractors purchase materials and equipment at retail building supply stores, but contractors have different requirements than homeowners. Building supply stores thus face the challenge of continuing to service their core business while increasing their appeal to these professional customers.

Supply Conditions

Stores in this category fall into two types. First are the major chains, such as Home Depot, Lowes, and Hechingers. Although these chains have grown, they still tend to be regional rather than national, and no one chain has more than a small portion of total sales for this industry. Total industry sales reached $133 billion in 1996, and Home Depot, the largest chain, reported revenues of $15.5 billion. Even the largest stores do not, therefore, dominate the market. This category also has many small stores. As a result, the average sales volume per store is considerably lower than in store types like general merchandise and food retailing, where chains take a larger share of the market.

Small stores have been able to keep a larger share of this market than in other areas, evidenced for example by the decline of small grocery stores as a share of food retailing. An important difference is the existence of marketing agreements and cooperatives that allow independent retailers to enjoy the advantages of national purchasing and marketing, while maintaining financial independence. Examples of such arrangements include Ace Hardware and TrueValue Hardware stores.

Chain stores will continue to move into this market aggressively, since there is evidently much scope for consolidation. Whether they can succeed in reducing the number of establishments in the face of the unusual cooperative arrangements in this sector remains to be seen.

Industry Structure

Cyclicality

The home building supply and hardware industry is typically very cyclical. During the 1990 recession, sales fell from a seasonally adjusted peak of $8.1 billion in June, 1990, to $7.1 billion at its lowest in January, 1991. This drop of over 10% was typical of the response of this industry to a recession.

Environmental Issues

Building supply stores face a number of challenges on the environmental front. The problem is not the stores themselves, but the nature of what they sell and how it is used. These stores are the major supplier of most of the toxic materials found in a typical house, including paint, glue, cleaners, and home–building products such as insulation, drywall, and others. Even when used correctly, many of these products can be dangerous or harmful to the environment, and, if used incorrectly, they can be directly harmful to people. In addition, consumers may cause environmental damage by disposing of the materials incorrectly.

While courts have not typically found retail stores legally responsible for the environmental impacts of building products, some of the major retailers would like to address this problem. The retailers are concerned about the image of the sector as well as the image of their own store. They are also concerned about possible regulation which would add to retailers' costs.

Specific environmental issues stores face include:

- *Lumber and its substitutes.* While lumber is a renewable resource, different types of lumber may be more or less environmentally friendly. With lumber costs rising, retailers will likely need to substitute other types of lumber (including faster growing species), and steel and plastic substitutes for traditional lumber.

- *Consumer education.* As consumers become more aware of environmental problems, retailers will need to supply more information about the environmental impacts of various products.

- *"Take–Back" items.* Stores that sell items that cannot be disposed of using normal methods will likely have to become collection points for the disposal of these items. Such items include used batteries, paint, and materials that constitute hazardous waste.

Environmental issues will pose a challenge in this competitive marketplace, because most stores will be unable or unwilling to invest in these areas if it will raise their costs above non–investing competitors. As a result, government regulation is very likely to eventually cover this area.

Outlook

The aging of the population, combined with reduced population growth, will keep growth in sales at building supply stores very moderate over the next decade. The pent–up demand for remodeling and upgrading houses has largely worn off with the fast growth in home sales of the past few years. As a result, this sector will experience nominal sales growth of only about 3.0% over the next few years. Prices will also grow moderately, but faster than prices of most commodities. This will be the result of higher lumber prices and a changing (and more expensive) product mix which reflects environmental costs in this sector.

Building Supply Stores: Major Indicators
Percent Change

Indicator	1988	1989	1990	1991	1992	1993	1994	1995	1996	1997	1998
Retail Sales, SIC 52	9.1	1.9	2.4	−3.6	10.2	8.7	11.7	2.2	5.7	4.0	2.6
Real Residential Construction Other than New Buildings	2.2	−5.2	−8.0	−10.3	18.7	9.9	9.4	2.6	4.1	1.8	2.9
Residential Construction, Deflator (Chained, 1992=100)	4.6	3.6	3.4	2.0	1.3	2.5	1.8	3.2	2.4	2.4	2.4

Building Supply Stores: Major Indicators
Average Annual Growth Rate

Indicator	1986–1996	1996–2006
Retail Sales, SIC 52	5.6	3.1
Real Residential Construction, Other than New Buildings	2.2	1.8
Residential Construction Deflator (Chained, 1992=100)	2.9	2.7

General Merchandise Stores

General merchandise stores are defined as retail stores which sell a number of lines, such as dry goods, apparel and accessories, furniture and home furnishings, small wares, hardware, and food. General merchandise stores are broken down into three major groupings: department stores, variety stores, and miscellaneous general merchandise stores. This sector of retail accounts for approximately 12.8% of all retail sales, and around 21.5% of all nondurable retail sales. General merchandise stores are one of the biggest components of overall retailing, and the second biggest retailer of nondurable goods, behind food stores.

With the massive restructuring undertaken by department stores in the 1990s, the general merchandise community looks healthy once again. Variety stores are still in significant trouble, but the relatively small portion of total sales which they comprise will limit their impact on the total for general merchandise stores. If miscellaneous merchandise stores are able to rebound from the decline in sales over the past few years, the general merchandise community will be in great shape. For now, sales and profits should remain relatively healthy.

Demand at General Merchandise Stores

Each of the three subdivisions of general merchandise stores has a different significance to overall industry sales. Department stores, by far the biggest of the three, account for over 88% of total employment, and almost 80% of total sales within this industry. A department store is defined as a retail store which carries men's and women's apparel, household appliances or other home furnishings, and various other lines. These stores are arranged in departments with individualized accounting. Department stores usually provide their own charge accounts, deliver merchandise, and maintain open stocks. In addition, department stores normally have more than 50 employees.

Sales at department stores fell during the late eighties due to the excellent performance of specialty stores, such as the Gap, and the rise of superstores, such as Home Depot and Best Buy. From 1985 to 1992, department store sales were a drag on overall general merchandise performance. During that period, sales growth at department stores averaged 5.4%, while sales growth at all general merchandise stores was 6.4%. Since the beginning of the 1990s, however, department stores have been making big changes, including downsizing, product changes, and mergers, which have allowed sales to grow more rapidly. During 1993–96, department store sales growth averaged 6.7%, compared to 5.7% for all general merchandise stores.

Major Components of General Merchandise Stores, 1996

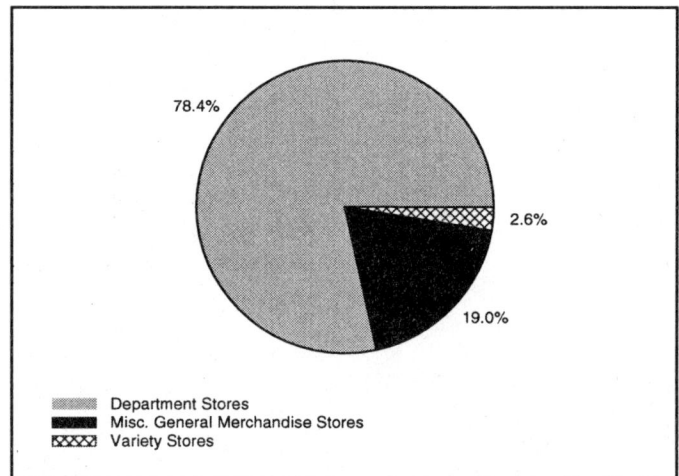

Variety stores, which are the smallest component in the general merchandise category, are defined as retailers who do not carry a complete line of merchandise, are not departmentalized, do not carry their own charge service, and do not deliver merchandise. Variety stores have been performing very poorly in recent years. Since the beginning of the 1990s, variety store sales have grown at an average rate of 1.1% per year. In addition, the share of sales for variety stores of all general merchandise sales has fallen from 7.2% in 1980 to 2.7% in 1996.

The growth of specialty stores and superstores is the major reason for the demise of variety stores. One of the major attractions of the variety store is lower prices. Since they do not carry complete product lines, however, they are especially vulnerable to superstores, which carry every product in a category and have relatively low prices. Employment at variety stores has suffered due to sluggish sales, dropping a whopping 48% since 1980. Unlike department stores, which were hurt in the late 1990s and rebuilt themselves in the 1990s, variety stores are still struggling to survive.

The final category under general merchandisers is miscellaneous general merchandise stores. Retailers in this subdivision are similar in structure to that of department stores, except they have fewer employees. Miscellaneous stores normally have fewer than 50 employees per store. Sales at miscellaneous general merchandise stores have struggled in the mid −1990s. Sales growth averaged 12.9% from 1982 to 1993, but have slowed significantly to a 2.9% average since then. The market share within general merchandise stores held by miscellaneous stores has remained significant, however, thanks to the strength of past sales and the demise of variety stores. Miscellaneous general merchandise stores' market share grew from 11.5% in 1980 to 20.9% in 1993, but has since fallen back to 19.3%.

Overall, general merchandise stores have increased market share in nondurable retail sales, and in total retail sales, since 1980. The strength of department stores in the 1990s and the strong performance of miscellaneous stores in the 1980s helped to increase the general merchandise market share of nondurable sales from 16.4% in 1980 to 21.5% in 1996. Since nondurable sales in general have decreased as a portion of total retail sales over that same period, the fact that general merchandise store market share of total sales has increased is a testament to the amazing rebound in department stores.

Although sales and market share at variety stores are likely to continue to decline, and the performance of miscellaneous stores has been weak in recent years, the healthy condition of department stores should keep overall sales at a respectable level. Since variety stores

constitute only about 2.5% of total general merchandise sales, their demise comes as a relatively small blow. Sales growth should be fairly stable for general merchandise stores in the near future. Faster growth could be possible if the stores in the miscellaneous category were to enact some of the changes undertaken by their department store counterparts.

General Merchandise Stores Have Been Increasing Their Market Share of Total Retail Sales, at the Same Time as Nondurable Sales Are Losing Their Market Share of Total Retail Sales

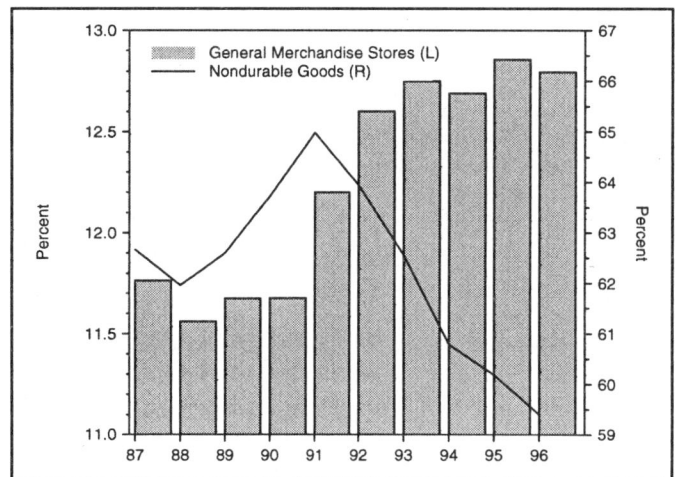

Supply

Like most corporate entities, general merchandise stores experienced a rash of mergers and acquisitions in the late 1980s and early 1990s. Most of the financially distressed stores have been acquired by more stable competitors. In addition, department stores, in particular, have undergone a major overhaul in the 1990s. Many stores have greatly downsized, cutting employees and closing unprofitable stores. The total number of competitors in the general merchandise industry has dropped over the past ten years, and the industry itself is much more sound as a result.

In addition, general merchandise stores have cut unnecessary administrative staff, changed product lines to more profitable areas, and overhauled existing managerial practices. Stores have also pumped up their commitment to customer service in an effort to increase customer loyalty. A recent survey of retailers found that 40% consider customer service as a primary source for differentiating their business from others. In general, the recent trend in general merchandise has decreased the number of competitors, but increased the appeal and profitability of the remaining companies.

Prices

Prices at general merchandise stores have been very soft since 1992. This has been made possible by the industry's low cost strategy and the cutbacks in employees and administrative expenses by department stores. Since 1992, general merchandise price inflation has averaged 0.7%; department store inflation has averaged 0.6%. Price inflation in both variety stores and miscellaneous general merchandise stores has averaged a slightly higher 1.1%.

The pricing situation for department stores is unlikely to change in the near future, especially since technological advancements have been implemented to make employees more efficient. At the same time, if variety stores and miscellaneous general merchandise stores wish to become more profitable, a similar strategy must be implemented, which would lower their price inflation. General merchandise inflation should therefore remain very low in the upcoming years.

Investment

Since general merchandise stores, and department stores in particular, have tried to improve their profitability in recent years, the amount of investment within the industry has risen. Renovations and improvements to existing stores and the building of new stores in more profitable locations have greatly increased the net value of the industry's property and equipment. In addition, there has been heavy investment in the introduction of new technology aimed at long-run productivity and profitability improvements.

The value of net property, plant, and equipment at general merchandise stores has increased by an average of about 9% per year in the 1990s, up from 7% in the 1980s.

Profits and Expenses

Profits at general merchandise stores have risen in the 1990s, as the industry has begun to reap the cost benefits of its consolidation and streamlining. Operating expenses at general merchandise stores increased by 5.5% per year from 1993–96, compared with a 10.4%

yearly increase during the weaker sales period of 1990–92. Profits increased from a $2.8 billion average during 1990–92, to a $6.9 billion average during 1993–96. Unfortunately, income as a percent of sales was stagnant over that period, and substantially lower than that of the 1980s. The main reasons for this weakness were the poor performance of variety stores and the mediocre performance of miscellaneous general merchandise stores.

The Productivity Issue

Employment in the general merchandise industry has experienced a lot of turmoil in the 1990s. Slow sales at miscellaneous and variety stores has necessitated cutbacks in employees. At the same time, the downsizing efforts of department stores also caused the elimination of jobs. From 1990 to 1992, employment at general merchandise stores fell by 1.2% per year. Since then, the excellent performance of department stores has helped employment grow at an average of 2.7% annually, which is slightly below the overall retail industry growth.

General Merchandise Store Productivity is Well Ahead of Total Retail Store Productivity in the 1990s

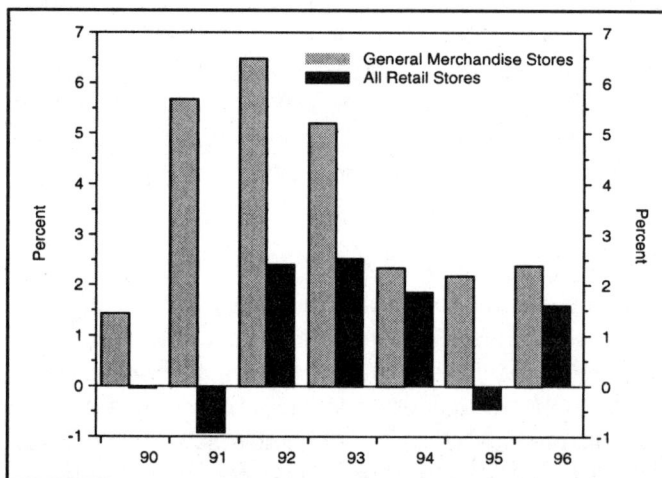

At the same time, productivity within general merchandise stores, defined as their ratio of real sales to employment has been well above that of the total retail population. The introduction of new technology and more efficient management, as well as increased sales and cutbacks in employment via downsizing, have enabled department stores to lead the productivity gains. The constant decline in variety store employment, on average more rapid than the sales decline, has also had some positive influence on the productivity average. Since

1990, productivity at general merchandise stores has increased at an average annual rate of 3.7%, much better than the mediocre 1.0% gain in productivity for all retail industries.

The Future Of General Merchandise Stores

With the massive restructuring undertaken by department stores in the 1990s, the general merchandise community looks healthy once again. Variety stores are still in significant trouble, but the relatively small portion of total sales which they comprise will limit their impact on the total for general merchandise stores. If miscellaneous merchandise stores are able to rebound from the decline in sales over the past few years, the general merchandise community will be in great shape. For now, sales and profits should remain relatively healthy. Miscellaneous store sales will be stable, department stores moderately strong, and variety stores declining, combining to a modestly growing total. Further gains in productivity through the implementation of technology will continue to increase profitability, and enable stores to keep prices low.

General Merchandise Store Indicators
Percent Change

	1988	1989	1990	1991	1992	1993	1994	1995	1996	1997	1998
Sales (Billions of Current $)	190.6	205.3	215.5	226.5	245.1	264.1	282.3	299.1	312.1	326.8	342.5
(% Ch)	5.3	7.7	4.9	5.1	8.2	7.8	6.9	5.9	4.4	4.7	4.8
Price Deflator (% Ch)	3.2	2.5	3.6	3.0	1.8	0.9	0.7	−0.1	0.3	0.5	0.8
Employment (% Ch)	2.6	2.9	−0.1	−3.4	−0.1	1.5	3.7	3.8	1.7	1.9	2.2
Productivity (% Change)	−0.6	2.2	1.4	5.7	6.5	5.2	2.3	2.2	2.4	2.8	2.7

General Merchandise Store Indicators: 10 Year Trend
Average Annual Growth Rate

	1986 −1996	1996 −2006
Sales	6.7	4.8
Price Deflator	1.9	1.1
Employment	1.5	2.0
Productivity (Inflation Adjusted)	3.1	2.5

Department Stores

Department store sales account for approximately 10% of total retail sales. However, department stores are the second largest retailer of nondurable goods behind food stores, accounting for close to 17% of total nondurable goods sales. A department store is defined as a store which carries men's and women's apparel, along with either major household appliances or home furnishings and various other lines. These lines are arranged in separate "departments" with the accounting on a departmentalized basis. The individual departments are collectively held under centralized management.

Department stores tend to be a significant source of sales due to the large variety of offerings, which allows for more convenience when shopping for more than one item. The lure of the department store is clearly convenience, and often lower prices. On the other hand, one of the biggest problems facing the department store industry is the lack of depth in individual product lines. For the most part, department stores offer generality, not specificity. A shopper wishing to purchase a particular product from a particular line may find that department stores offer a variety of lines, with very few products under each.

Demand

Retail sales at department stores slowed in 1996, after a strong 1995 year. Sales increased by 4.8% in 1996, following a 6.5% increase in 1995. Last year's growth was well below the large gains achieved early in the recovery, when growth averaged 7.8% from 1992 to 1994. Nondurable retail sales in general increased by 3.5% in 1996, and only 3.9% in the 1992-94 period. Department store sales have been relatively healthy so far in the 1990s, outpacing total retail sales every year but 1990.

Department stores have greatly increased their market share over the past six years, after a disappointing performance in the second half of the eighties. In 1989, department stores accounted for 9.3% of total retail sales, and 14.5% of nondurable sales. Since then, restructuring within the industry has led to continued gains in market share. In 1996, department stores accounted for 10.2% of total sales, and about 17% of nondurable sales. The rise of discount department stores played an important role in the direction of department stores. Discount department stores, such as Wal-Mart, have contributed to the overall growth of the industry by posting better than industry sales increases in every year of the 1990s. Market share of discount department stores in the total department store market rose from 7.2% in 1989 to 10.4% in 1996.

Department Stores' Market Share of Nondurable Retail Sales Has Expanded Since 1989

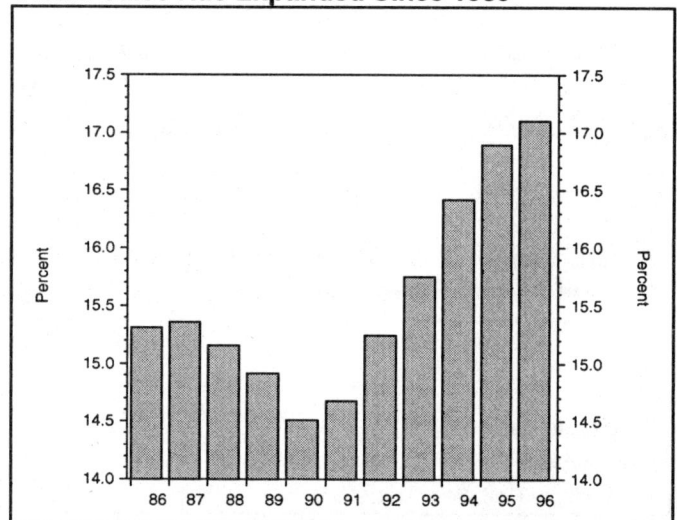

Consumer spending at department stores is likely to remain healthy in the near future. The turnaround in sales brought on by various managerial changes has allowed the industry to become more competitive in the 1990s. Technology advances and continuing change will keep costs, and therefore prices, down, which should lead to strong sales in the future.

Industry Structure

One of the major reasons for stronger department store performance has been the consolidation in the industry.

Many of the big names in the department store game not only downsized their operations in an effort to become more efficient and profitable, but also merged with other players in the industry. Federated Department Stores merged with rival giant R.H. Macy, at the time when Macy was under extreme financial distress. Many of the larger, more financially stable department stores have acquired or merged with less financially sound stores, improving poor profit margins, and resurrecting the department store industry.

Downsizing efforts are evident through such department store giants as Sears Roebuck, which cut sales and administrative costs from around 33% of revenues to around 25% via downsizing. In addition, Sears also lowered prices in order to compete better with discount and specialty stores, and focused its product range to include a wider variety of the more profitable lines, such as apparel. Specialty stores have suffered at the hands of the renewed department store trend, losing market share over the past six years.

Department stores face stiff competition from various other forms of retail businesses. Entities such as QVC, the Home Shopping Network, mail order catalogs, and now internet retailing have the ability to capture sales due to their convenience and ease. Consumers no longer have to spend hours waiting in check-out lines, fighting traffic, finding parking, or jostling with the Saturday afternoon shopping crowd. Nonstore retailers greatly increased their sales revenues in the early stages of the recovery, as shopper acceptance has increased. However, in 1995 and 1996, nonstore retailing sales increases were lower than those of department stores, and much slower than their own pace of a few years earlier.

Specialty stores are retail outfits that offer a collection of goods in a certain category line. One of the most popular and profitable areas is apparel. Stores such as The Gap and The Limited offer various lines of clothing, all with certain style and trend appeals that attract consumers who are conscious of fashion. Unlike in a department store, the lines of apparel at a specialty store are deep and well priced. Specialty stores helped boost apparel sales in the early part of the recovery, but have come under a lot of pressure recently from both department stores and a wave of new superstores.

"Category killers" or "superstores" are the latest trend in retail, and have the ability to seriously threaten department store sales. Home Depot, a large warehouse-like retail entity, offers anything and everything one could possibly want for the home, usually at prices much lower than its department store counterpart. These are called category killers because they sell practically every product offered in a particular retail category. Because they deal exclusively with one category of goods in large volumes, superstores can often acquire their goods more cheaply, and therefore have the ability to offer them to the consumer at lower retail prices.

In addition to the overwhelming number of products offered and lower prices, superstores have other attractions for the consumer. Barnes & Noble, a giant book superstore, offers food, music, and coffee with a sit-down area for enjoying the extras while reading something from the store. The stores attract customers based not only on their product offerings, but also on the spectacle of the store itself. The potential of superstores is evident by their rise from zero sales and no market share in 1986, to $550 million in sales and a 33.3% share of the nation's retail revenue in 1996.

Seasonality

Until recently, department stores relied heavily on the Christmas season (November-December) for much of their sales revenues. March and August, representing the Easter/spring clothing and back-to-school seasons, accounted for another large portion of sales. The seasonal nature of department stores is, of course, fairly similar to that of retail sales in general. The majority of spending is done near holidays, or the change of season, when apparel sales are particularly strong.

Department stores have made attempts, however, to spread sales out during the year, and have succeeded to a small degree. December sales accounted for 16% of total yearly department store sales in the 1980s, and averaged about a percentage point lower in the 1990s. Stores have begun introducing new items in January in an attempt to bring in more off-season business. In addition, department stores have begun to market more heavily throughout the year.

Prices

Department stores have used pricing as a means to compete more effectively with the growing number of discount and specialty retail stores. In particular, in an effort to combat the low prices offered by superstores, department store prices have been increasing only very slowly. During this recovery, from 1992 to 1996, department store prices increased at an average annual rate of only 0.6%. That compares to a much higher level of price inflation for the general retailing sector of 1.7%. This very low average reflects both the competitive pricing in traditional department stores and the rise in share of discounting department stores.

The competitive nature of the retail world suggests that price increases will remain moderate. The introduction of the low-cost superstores necessitates the continued practice of discounting. Technological advances will help department stores lower overhead, with new processes which continue to make industry employees more productive.

The Productivity Issue

One of the most important factors in the resurgence of department stores has been the implementation of technology. Many stores intend to, or already have implemented, various technological strategies to help control costs and become more efficient. Electronic price scanning equipment, point-of-sale computers, and automated inventory control tracking systems are some of the ways department stores have become more efficient. Sales tracking allows management to discover which stores sell what products best, and allows them to revamp inventory and floorspace strategies to take advantage of the information. Inventory tracking keeps products properly stocked without expensive bookkeeping (which requires costly man-hours), and eliminates the need for unnecessary warehousing costs.

Productivity, defined as price-adjusted sales per employee, declined for department stores in the late 1980s and early 1990s. Beginning in 1991, coinciding with the general turnaround in department stores, productivity began to grow, and its growth has been well above the general retail sector's productivity growth.

Productivity Growth in Department Stores Outpaced Retail Services in General Throughout the 1990s

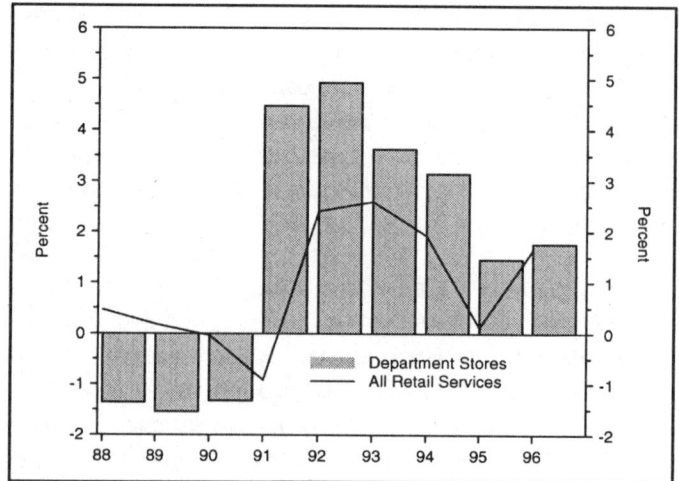

Productivity growth contributed greatly to the department store industry's turnaround in profit margins. This improvement is continuing, aided by ongoing investment in technology. The investment cost for technology can be fairly expensive, but it cuts down on many costs in the long run, and makes employees much more efficient.

The Future Of Department Stores

Thanks to the reorganizations of the early 1990s and the growth in successful discount department stores, the department store industry has come back to be a healthy part of the retail environment. The introduction of technology into management, sales, and administration will continue to make department stores more productive and more profitable in the future. However, department stores must be constantly aware of competitive threats from other retailers, especially superstores. Management must also take more steps toward matching offerings to consumer preferences, and making the shopping experience one that cannot easily be matched by another retail entity.

Major Department Store Indicators

	1988	1989	1990	1991	1992	1993	1994	1995	1996	1997	1998
Sales (Billions of Current $)	154.8	164.2	170.6	177.0	189.6	204.1	222.1	236.5	247.8	213.2	221.9
(% Ch)	4.6	6.0	3.9	3.8	7.1	7.7	8.8	6.5	4.8	4.6	4.6
Price Deflator (% Ch)	3.3	2.4	3.6	3.0	1.8	0.9	0.6	-0.4	0.1	0.6	0.8
Employment (% Ch)	2.6	5.2	1.6	-3.5	0.3	2.8	4.9	4.6	2.4	3.0	3.2
Productivity (% Ch)	-1.4	-1.6	-1.3	4.5	4.9	3.6	3.1	1.5	1.8	2.6	1.8

Major Department Store Indicators: 10 Year Trend
Average Annual Growth Rate

	1986-1996	1996-2006
Sales	5.9	5.4
Price Deflator	1.8	1.5
Employment	2.3	2.4
Productivity (Inflation Adjusted)	1.4	1.6

Food Stores

The industry segments grouped under the category for food stores include: grocery stores, meat and fish markets, fruit and vegetable markets, candy, nut, and confectionery stores, dairy products stores, retail bakeries, and miscellaneous food stores. Grocery stores account for about 95% of industry sales and nearly 90% of employment. Large chain–store companies operating supermarkets (full–line food stores with over $2 million in sales) dominate the grocery store category. Supermarket sales were over three–quarters of grocery store sales in 1996.

Retail establishments classified as food stores are primarily engaged in the distribution and sale of dry grocery items, canned goods, and perishable food items to the general public. Most food products are purchased for home preparation and consumption. Many establishments (especially chain supermarkets) also sell prepared meals, prescription drugs, tobacco products, small household appliances and housewares, health and beauty care products, pet–care products, and seasonal merchandise.

In 1996, retail sales at food stores were nearly $425 billion, a gain of approximately 3.5% over 1995 levels. Sales (which include food and nonfood items) are expected to increase by about 2% in 1997. Over 3.4 million people are employed in food–retailing industries.

WEFA forecasts retail food store prices will increase an average of 2.7% per year over the period 1996–2006. The implication of this price gain, combined with sales growth of 3.0% per year over the same period, is that real sales volume is forecast to grow by only 0.3% per year.

Demand Conditions

Expenditures on foods purchased for off–premises consumption, the principal determinant of retail food stores' core sales, grew by just over 4% in 1996. Growth in this category of personal consumption expenditures continues to trail gains in consumer incomes. Income growth is expected to be strong in 1997, up by more than 5%, but spending on food items for at–home consumption is forecast to grow only modestly by about 2% as other categories of spending crowd out food purchases. For the 10 years ending in 1996, retail sales at food stores increased an average of 3.6% per year in current dollar terms.

Changes in consumer tastes and lifestyles continue to erode sales of many traditional grocery items. Shoppers increasingly stop at food markets searching for hot meals for take–out, freshly baked breads and pastries, and nonfood items such as health and beauty care products. Consumer desires for "one–stop" shopping and convenience continue to drive growth rates for these value–

added product categories higher. Faster growth for non–traditional products means they will account for a growing share of total store sales over the next ten years.

For the period 1996–2006, expect retail sales at food stores to increase at an average rate of about 3% per year.

Long–Run Trends: Food Stores
Compound Annual Growth

	1986–1996	1996–2006
Retail Sales (%)	3.6	3.0
Price Index (%)	3.4	2.7

Supply Conditions

New store formats will continue to be constructed to target convenience–minded customers. Large supermarkets have set up in–store service counters (delis, snack shops, bakeries, flower shops, etc.) with separate checkout stations to speed up purchases of prepared take–out foods and other high value–added products and services. Grocery store size is increasing to accommodate changing consumer tastes.

In addition to changes in store format, technology initiatives in inventory management and new merchandising techniques have been aggressively deployed to reduce costs and raise productivity. Better management of the supply–chain continues to be the focus of most store operators. With an eye toward generating improved financial results, firms have been investing in cost–cutting systems to improve accounting and better coordinate supplier deliveries.

On the labor front, plans to increase the level of service in many markets have led to a shortage of cashiers, stockers, and deli counter help. Turnover is notoriously high in the food–retailing sector.

In 1996, there were 127,000 stores classified as grocery stores. Nearly 30,000 (23 %) of these stores were considered supermarkets (large full–line grocery stores with more than $2 million in annual sales).

Price Trends

Prices for items sold in retail food stores rose 3.3% in 1996 up from a 2.3% increase in 1995. Higher wholesale food costs for meats, dairy products, and grains associated with a drought–induced rise in agricultural products helped push the retail sales price deflator higher. Drops in wholesale food prices during part of 1997 should help hold the rise in the price index to about 1% for the year. For the ten years ending in 1996, food inflation has averaged 3.4% per year.

The central pricing issue facing the industry is the movement towards an everyday low pricing strategy at several large retailers. Consumers continue to demand value from retailer operators and appear increasingly unsatisfied with the advertised (and unadvertised) sales promotions typical of traditional food retailing. Competition from discounters and warehouse clubs which emphasize low prices has put pressure on food stores to adopt some form of low–price strategy.

Stores' private label brands can play an important role in the quest for value. These "house brand" products sell for less than the national brands, providing shoppers with a low–price alternative. Stores continue to increase the shelf space devoted to private–label products since they tend to carry fatter margins for retailers thanks to favorable supplier pricing.

Chains have also instituted affinity programs to reward loyal customers. Many stores now issue "clipless coupon" cards which customers present at the check–out counter to receive special pricing on featured promotional items.

Expect retail food store prices to increase an average of 2.7% per year over the period 1996–2006. The implication of this price gain, combined with sales growth of 3.0% per year over the same period, is that real sales volume is forecast to grow by only 0.3% per year.

Industry Structure

Food retailing has traditionally been considered a consumer staple industry, since many of the items purchased are deemed necessities. Swings in sales tend to be less volatile than changes in aggregate U.S. income. The industry is characterized by high fixed costs. Razor thin profit margins require continued sales gains to keep profits up. Weak sales growth in the early 1990s battered the financial statements of many retailers.

Chain grocery stores dominate the food–retailing sector. Top retailers include Kroger, American Stores, Safeway, Giant Food, and Winn–Dixie. The business environment is highly competitive, as the large retailers continue to try to grab market share from each other as well as from smaller independent grocery operators and establishments classified in other food retailing categories (e.g., meat and fish markets).

The proliferation of warehouse clubs has proven problematic for the chain grocery stores over the past ten years. Membership clubs have used a combination of low prices, limited selection, and a "no–frills" atmosphere to appeal to many value–conscious shoppers. Fortunately for the big chain supermarkets, overbuilding and consolidation in the buyers club industry has slowed new warehouse club construction. Food chains now appear to be holding their own against the clubs and discounters.

A new threat on the horizon, however, is the arrival of so–called "supercenters" that sell general merchandise and food. These new food/drug combination stores average more than 150,000 square feet (more than four times the size of the typical supermarket) and offer a wide variety of food and other merchandise. Whether retailers like Walmart & Kmart will be able to steal market share away from the grocery chains with these new supercenters remains to be seen.

Food retailers, particularly the large grocery chains, have proven to be able competitors. The outlook for the industry appears bright. New merchandising strategies and successful efforts to reduce costs should help push up profits and offset the effects of only modest increases in core food purchases in the years ahead.

Trends & Forecasts: Food Stores

	1988	1989	1990	1991	1992	1993	1994	1995	1996	1997	1998
Retail Sales (Bil $)	325.5	347.0	368.3	374.5	377.1	385.4	399.3	410.5	424.3	432.8	444.9
% Ch	5.2	6.6	6.1	1.7	0.7	2.2	3.6	2.8	3.4	2.0	2.8
Price Index (% Chg)	3.8	5.9	5.5	4.2	1.6	1.6	1.8	2.3	3.3	1.0	2.1

Trends: Food Store Categories
Retail Sales (Bil $)

	1988	1989	1990	1991	1992	1993	1994	1995	1996	1997	1998
Grocery	307.2	328.1	348.2	354.3	358.1	365.7	378.6	389.1	401.8	410.2	421.7
% Ch	5.6	6.8	6.1	1.7	1.1	2.1	3.5	2.8	3.3	2.1	2.8
Meat & Fish	6.2	6.4	6.1	5.8	6.0	6.0	6.1	6.0	6.0	–	–
% Ch	–0.2	2.4	–5.5	–4.1	2.9	1.2	1.0	–2.2	0.1	–	–
Fruits & Vegetables	1.9	2.3	2.7	2.7	2.1	2.2	2.2	2.1	2.3	–	–
% Ch	–19.3	23.6	17.5	–1.9	–20.9	5.7	–1.6	–2.1	2.3	–	–
Candy & Nuts	1.4	1.2	1.3	1.3	1.4	1.4	1.6	1.6	1.7	–	–
% Ch	6.6	–12.0	1.0	4.9	3.8	5.5	8.5	1.4	4.7	–	–
Retail Bakeries	5.0	4.8	5.2	5.5	5.7	5.7	6.1	6.5	6.7	–	–
% Ch	–3.8	–4.1	9.1	5.2	4.2	–0.6	7.2	6.3	2.4	–	–
Other (1)	3.8	4.2	4.9	4.9	3.8	4.3	4.7	5.2	5.9	–	–
% Ch	12.0	11.4	14.5	1.3	–23.0	12.5	10.7	10.2	14.0	–	–

Notes: (1) Includes dairy product stores, retail poultry stores, and miscellaneous establishments.

Gasoline Service Stations

Gasoline service stations are retailers whose revenue comes primarily from the sale of gasoline. Many gasoline stations sell convenience store (c–store) goods as well. Citgo owned the largest number of gasoline outlets in 1996, with 14,054 outlets in 46 states or 7.4% of the total. Following Citgo were Texaco, Amoco, Shell, and Exxon. In terms of revenue, the top five marketers were Mobil, Shell, Citgo, Exxon, and Texaco.

Total revenue of gasoline service stations was $157.2 billion in 1996, a 5.8% increase from the previous year. Growth in revenue, however, has been slowing over the past 15 years. Revenue grew at an annual average of 5.7% during 1980–89 compared with 2.2% during 1991–96. Similarly, employment in gasoline service stations has been growing but decelerating. In 1996, it reached 665,000, up 2.9% from the previous year.

Demand For Gasoline

According to the Department of Energy (DOE), average daily demand for gasoline in 1996 was 7.8 million barrels/day, up 0.7% from the previous year. Demand has been growing steadily, averaging 1.4% growth per year during the 1990s, largely driven by consumer demand. Consumer expenditure on gasoline increased 6.3% to $121.8 billion from 1995 to 1996. However, consumer expenditure on gasoline is shrinking as a percentage of disposable income, from 4.4% in 1980 to 2.2% in 1996. Gasoline prices were higher in 1980 than in 1996. There are offsetting factors at play in gasoline demand growth. While rising population and increasing numbers of vehicles have tended to increase the consumption of gasoline, other factors, especially more fuel–efficient vehicles, have mitigated it.

The total vehicles miles traveled increased from 1,527 billion miles in 1980 to 2,347 billion miles in 1994, a 54% increase. To a large extent, this was the result of a sharp increase in the number of vehicles over the past two decades. The number of registered vehicles increased from 139 million in 1980 to 197 million in 1996, a 41% increase.

Two factors contributed to such a dramatic rise in vehicle ownership.

- First was the growing size of adult population.

- Second, the proportion of families owning more than one vehicle increased from 52.7% in 1980 to 57.9% in 1990.

Consumption Expenditure on Gasoline and Oil

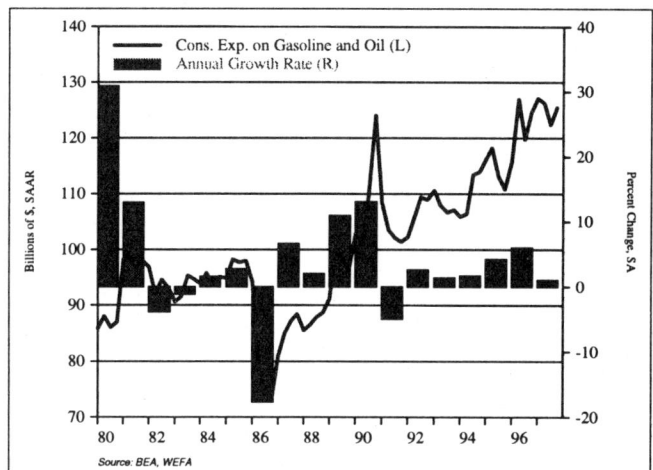

Source: BEA, WEFA

Also contributing to the rising vehicle mileage were demographic and geographic shifts. More people live in the sprawling suburbs today than in the previous decade, and tend to favor personal means of transportation to public transit. The impact of rising vehicle miles traveled was mitigated somewhat by better fuel efficiency of the vehicles produced. Average fuel economy in 1980 was 24.3 miles per gallon, and by 1996 it reached 28.2.

Consumer expenditure on gasoline and oil will increase at a slower rate than previously experienced, averaging about 2% per year.

Industry Structure

Gasoline stations face a number of challenges. First, the industry is very fragmented and intensely competitive. In 1995, the top five brands controlled 53,694 outlets, which represented just 27.5% of the total. Despite this national fragmentation., some companies have developed dominant positions in particular regions. For example, Arco controlled 25% of California's market in 1995, and the three next largest suppliers controlled another 45%.

Fortunately for consumers, there is intense competition at the retail level among the major brands and between them and independent marketers, outlets affiliated with major suppliers but not owned by them. Independent station owners must buy gasoline at the best possible price in a local or perhaps regional market; and then they must sell that product to car drivers at a profit while competing with gasoline stations as close as next door. Since gasoline is a commodity, retailers cannot differentiate their product to boost sales, so they have to compete with lower prices and increased services, a combination that hurts profitability.

U.S. gasoline stations are among the most productive in the world. U.S. retailers on average employ two people and sell 50,000 gallons of gasoline a month, compared with retailers in Japan, for example, which employ on average seven people and sell only 18,000 liters. However, prices are much lower in the United States than in Japan, and profit margins from gasoline retailing are tiny.

Components of the Price of a Gallon of Gasoline

Crude Oil	34.0%
Operation Costs	30.7%
Taxes	35.2%
Profit	0.1%

Source: PMAA, 1996

Since gasoline stations are marginally profitable, two distinct trends are occurring to increase their profitability. First, gasoline stations have started to diversify into other types of businesses like convenience stores and fast food restaurants. Second, major brands have started to merge or form alliances at the retail level to reduce costs by eliminating redundant administrative expenses and pooling prime real estate assets.

Convenient stores (c–stores) have become an integral part of many gasoline service stations, generating on average 25% of their total revenue. Tobacco and soft drink sales are particularly good for the bottom line. There is however another trend that negates the advantages of the c–store approach, and that is the growing number of gasoline stations with self–service pumps. Fully 88% of gasoline stations had self–service pumps in 1993 compared with 55% in 1980. Although self–serving drivers may not generate large margins, they help to turn inventory faster. As a result, the combination of self–service pumps with a c–store is more profitable than the traditional full–service format. Many gasoline retailers have also moved towards cobranding. Recently, Chevron and McDonald's announced that Chevron stations would share McDonald's sites. This format, like the c–store, tries to exploit the synergy that exists between fast food and gasoline retail.

Consolidation in gasoline retail has gained pace recently. Intense competition, stringent environmental regulations and rising crude oil prices have eroded gasoline stations' profits and forced many independent gasoline marketers to go out of business and many branded retailers to consolidate. Fortunately for the industry, government regulators have become more lenient toward vertical integration. Consequently, a record number of mega–mergers and alliances were announced in 1996. The number of total gasoline outlets declined by 19,874 outlets between 1992 and 1996.

Environmental Issues

Gasoline usage has important environmental implications, and thus, its sale is heavily regulated. Environmental regulations affect every aspect of gasoline retailing including production, transportation, storage, and distribution, and these regulations are becoming more stringent and costly.

The most important environmental regulation affecting gasoline service stations is the 1984 law requiring the Environmental Protection Agency (EPA) to monitor underground storage tanks (UST). USTs create health hazards because they can corrode, allowing gasoline to leak and contaminate soil and underground water. In 1988, EPA issued regulations setting minimum standards for new tanks and requiring owners of existing tanks to upgrade, replace, or close them by December 22, 1998.

Meeting the UST deadline is very costly for gasoline stations, at $125,000 to $150,000 per tank for clean–up. Where there is ground water contamination, the cost can escalate to $1 million. The upgrade cost is partly financed by the government through the Leaking UST Fund (LUST), but the money has not been forthcoming because of political wrangling in Washington. Despite the tightness of funds, the industry is moving to meet the guidelines.

Apparel Stores

Apparel stores are specialty stores that sell men's, women's, children's, and families' clothing as well as all types of shoes. Apparel stores are generally located in malls and strip–centers. The top ten apparel chains in order of revenue are The Limited, T.J Maxx, Gap, Melville Apparel, Woolworth, Burlington Coat, Ross Stores, American Retail Group, Eddie Bauer and Petrie Stores. The Limited led the pack in 1995 with sales of $7.9 billion, and the top ten accounted for just 27% of total industry sales.

In the short run, demand for apparel will be helped by income growth and consumers' confidence in the economy. The recovery of the mid–1990s continues and consumer confidence is strong. These positive factors will, however, be mitigated by rising consumer debt. Consumer debt as a percentage of disposable income has increased from 15.8% in 1985 to 17.0% in 1996. Though interest rates are not expected to increase much over the next year or two, higher debt will hamper consumers' ability to pay for new goods. Over the longer run, the demand for apparel will be determined by demographics and consumer buying habits. The aging population and frugal buying habits mean that growth in spending will remain subdued.

Industry Overview

Apparel stores' total revenue was $113 billion in 1996, an increase of 2% from the previous year. Revenue continues to grow, though at a slower pace than during the eighties. The average annual growth rate in revenue during 1991–96 was 3.0%, down from 7.5% during 1985–89.

While revenue growth is robust, employment growth is not. In fact, employment has been declining since the beginning of the 1990s. Between 1990 and 1995 it declined at an annual average of 0.9%, and in 1996, it declined 2.2% further to 1.1 million. The main reason for the decline in jobs is the changing nature of the apparel business. Increased competition and slowing consumer demand have forced apparel stores to cut costs and increase productivity. That has meant cutting workforce, either through layoffs or by complete closure of apparel businesses. The number of mall–based or strip center–based apparel stores has declined since its peak in 1994 due to bankruptcies, mergers, and acquisitions. According to Lazard Freres, the number of apparel stores was expected to fall from around 18,000 in 1994 to 15,629 by the end of the fiscal year 1996.

Demand For Apparel

The demand for apparel goods can be broken into several categories — men's, women's, boys', and infants' clothing, and footwear. Spending on women's and girls' clothing makes up almost half of the total spending on apparel. Men's and boys' clothing make up 31%, and footwear around 15%. Spending on women's apparel is proportionally higher because women generally purchase more variety of all three types of apparel — fashion, seasonal, and basic. Fashion products, which take 35% of the market, have an average of 10 weeks of product life. Seasonal products, with a 20–week product life, make up 45% of the market. Basic products sold throughout the year constitute about 20% of the market.

Components of Expenditure on Apparel 1996

Women's/Girls'	47.0%
Men's/Boys'	31.4%
Footwear	14.8%
Infants'	6.7%

Source: BLS

Consumer spending on apparel goods has been growing steadily over the past two decades, but recently its growth has slowed. The average annual growth rate in sales was 6.8% during the 1980s, compared with just 4.6% during the 1990s. As a percentage of disposable income, apparel has also declined, from 5.4% in 1980 to 4.7% in 1996. In fact, the share of nondurable goods overall in consumption has shown a downward trend, although spending on apparel has declined at a slower rate than spending on total nondurable goods. The discrepancy between rising consumer spending for apparel and apparel's falling share of disposable income is the result of two counteracting forces. Growing population and rising income have pushed up spending, but changing consumption patterns due to demographic shifts and consumer preferences have dampened it. Recent evidence shows that the latter has had a greater impact.

Apparel spending as a percentage of disposable income has fallen more precipitously since the beginning of the 1990s because of changing consumer habits. First, during the recession of 1991, apparel stores sharply marked down prices to get rid of their excess inventories. Consumers took this as a permanent decrease in price and continue to expect low price. Since apparel stores were facing intense competition from discount stores, they could not raise prices even after the recovery was well underway. Lower prices of apparel goods, however, did not increase the volume of goods sold, mainly because apparel is a necessity good; consumers buy what they need and not more than that. Secondly, consumers in the 1990s are not as fashion conscious as they were in the 1980s, and so they buy less high–end apparel. In addition, young adults spend more on fancy gadgets than on expensive clothes, while middle–aged consumers save more for their retirement and spend more on their children.

In the short run, demand for apparel will be helped by income growth and consumers' confidence in the economy. The recovery of the mid–1990s continues and consumer confidence is strong. These positive factors will, however, be mitigated by rising consumer debt. Consumer debt as a percentage of disposable income has increased from 15.8% in 1985 to 17.0% in 1996. Though interest rates are not expected to increase much over the next year or two, higher debt will hamper consumers' ability to pay for new goods. Over the longer run, the demand for apparel will be determined by demographics and consumer buying habits. The aging population and frugal buying habits mean that growth in spending will remain subdued.

Supply Of Apparel Stores

Specialty apparel stores are facing twin challenges. On the one hand, consumer expenditure on apparel is not growing as fast as during the 1980s. On the other hand, fierce competition from discount stores, sidewalk stalls, mail order, and electronic sales has hurt business. The market share held by specialty apparel stores has been declining over the past few years, falling from 21% in 1992 to 15% in 1996. Most of the share was lost to discount stores.

Intense competition has forced apparel stores to consolidate. Smaller and less financially sound apparel stores have either gone bankrupt or merged with larger and more financially secure chain stores. In the first quarter of 1996, Today's Man, Merry–Go–Around, and Country Seat Stores went into bankruptcy. Today's Man closed 26 stores while Merry–Go–Around closed more than 1000. Also closed during 1996 were 700 Edition Bros, 290 Charming Shoppes, and 600 Petrie Retail stores. Marshalls shut down 190 stores as a result of its merger with T.J. Maxx. Publicly traded specialty apparel retailers continue to grow faster in total sales than the industry as a whole, indicating a significant decline among independents and other privately–held apparel retailers.

While consolidation has weeded out weaker stores, it has not led to any significant rise in the market share for stronger ones. This is because apparel retailing is notoriously segregated geographically, with one or two chains dominating each region. Entrants face not only dominant retailers, but also an overcrowded marketplace. Although entry is not expensive, many go out of business before they are established.

Given intense competition from discount stores and limited room for expansion nationally, specialty apparel stores see much of their growth potential in foreign countries, particularly the emerging markets of Asia and Latin America. The trend toward foreign expansion is already starting. Gap generated 7% of its revenue from foreign sales in 1995 and that share could double by 2000. Similarly, The Limited generated 0.1% of its revenue from the international market in 1995, but foreign sales are expected to increase significantly in the next few years. The foreign contribution of total apparel sales for major retailers is expected to increase from 3% in 1995 to 11.5% in 2000.

Vanishing Middle–Market Retailers

One of the major challenges faced by apparel retailers is the growing income disparity in the population. Between 1970 and 1993, the share of national income of the lower 40% of households declined from 14.9% to 12.6%, while for the top 40% of households, it increased from 67.8% to 72.4%. The top 5% of households increased their share from 16.6% to 21.0% during the same period. Moreover, real income growth has slowed.

Slower income growth has made consumers thrifty and much more price–conscious about their purchases. Discount stores have recognized this trend and have successfully exploited it by making bargain hunting more popular with the middle class. In the process, they have lured price conscious consumers away from specialty apparel stores. Upscale apparel stores, like Saks Fifth Avenue, however, do not face those challenges. They have retained the loyalty of their high–income customers, who are more brand oriented than price oriented. In fact, such stores posted a big gain in revenue in 1996.

Income Distribution by Quintile

	Share of U.S. National Income					
	(By quintiles, or 20 percent segments of households)					
Year	Low 20%	2nd 20%	3rd 20%	4th 20%	Top 20%	(Top 5%)
1993	3.6	9.0	15.1	23.5	48.9	21.0
1990	3.9	9.6	15.9	24.0	46.6	18.6
1980	4.2	10.2	16.8	24.8	44.1	16.5
1970	4.1	10.8	17.4	24.5	43.3	16.6

Source: Bureau of Census

Middle–market apparel stores have begun to confront those challenges by targeting either bargain hunters or the brand hunters. For instance, Gap Inc. has remodeled its Banana Republic stores to make them more upscale and has increased the size of the chain by almost 50%, or 68 units, in the past five years. At the same time, in order to compete with discount stores, it has promoted a low–end chain, the Old Navy outlets. Both Banana Republic and Old Navy were among the most productive apparel stores in 1996.

In the short run, specialty apparel stores will follow a twin strategy. First, increase market share through mergers and acquisitions, exploiting the economies of scale. Second, arrest their declining market share in apparel at all levels of quality. Gap has provided a successful model for confronting both the discount stores and the high–end retailers. More specialty stores are expected to follow Gap's lead.

Pricing

Apparel goods prices have been decelerating steadily since the recession in 1990. Price deceleration began in 1991 when sales declined, forcing stores to unload their excess inventories through steep discounts. In 1992, apparel prices rose by less than 4.0% compared to 4.5% in 1990. By 1994, sales had picked up, but inventories continued to rise relative to sales, and prices fell. Apparel prices declined 0.2% in 1994 and 1.1% in 1995. After 1995, the industry's inventories–to–sales ratio declined, but prices kept falling.

Price Changes for Apparel

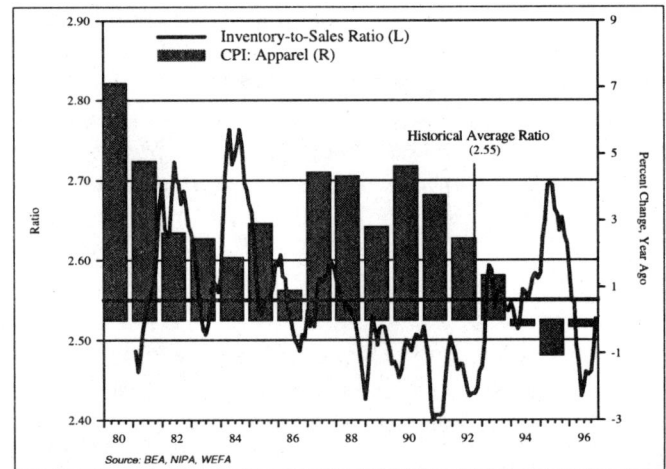

Source: BEA, NIPA, WEFA

Historically, a rising inventories–to–sales ratio led to falling prices, and vice versa, as firms responded to the ebb and flow of consumer demand. This is not the case in the 1990s due to structural economic and technological changes in the apparel stores.

First, the prevalence of efficient inventory management has reduced the costs of inventories. Equipped with Electronic Data Interchange (EDI), today's stores can communicate with their manufacturers instantly and manage their inventories more efficiently. Inventories are often purchased with credit, incurring costs to stores which rise with higher interest rates. Keeping inventories lean is best for profits and stores have made progress toward that goal.

Second, apparel imports are taking over the market. Almost half of the apparel bought in the United States is foreign–made, with China and Mexico the largest suppliers. Low labor costs and virtually no import duties have reduced the purchase price of apparel. The size of the apparel imports is exploding, and growing competition among foreign manufacturers has kept apparel prices down. In fact, the import prices of apparel goods are falling.

Third, consolidation in the industry has created giant retailers who exercise great buying power with manufacturers, keeping down purchase prices. The low purchase prices have been passed along to consumers since intense retail competition has made any significant price increase risky for retailers. Apparel prices will rise over the next few years, but will grow by significantly less than their historical average of 2.5% per year.

Furniture Stores

Furniture stores are defined as establishments primarily engaged in the retail sale of household furniture. These stores may also sell home furnishings, major appliances, and floor coverings. This includes beds and springs, cabinet work, kitchen cabinets, outdoor furniture, and waterbeds.

Competition for retail furniture dollars promises to be fierce for the remainder of the decade. Consumer spending for furniture is likely to slow considerably in growth, if not actually decline, over the next year or two as the housing market cools a bit and interest rates creep up. This will only prove to intensify the competition, so cost–cutting and consolidation will continue and pricing will be weak.

Furniture retailing is a quite cyclical, quite competitive industry, in which tight margins and a desire for cost–cutting have led to a wave of consolidation. The industry had two years of sales growth of 7% to 8% in 1993 and 1994, but gains have slowed since then. These stores face competition from a range of other retail establishments, including department stores, warehouse stores, and discount clubs.

The retail furniture industry used to be dominated by the small main street retailer. In the 1990s, on the other hand, more than one–third of the industry's sales were recorded by the top 100 furniture stores. Furniture consumers today are less quality sensitive than price sensitive, and the entry of large chain discount furniture stores into the market has taken market share from smaller local retailers. Larger retailers can use their size to put pressure on manufacturers to keep prices low.

After declining in the early 1990s, the number of employees at furniture stores has grown in the last three years. In 1995 employment grew by 6%, to 942,000, but in 1996 the growth slowed to 3.6%. Current trends in the industry suggest continued slowing in the growth of retail furniture employees, as consolidation leads to fewer larger stores.

Every Day Pressure On Margins

Furniture retailers have implemented 'every day low pricing' (EDLP) in recent years, in an attempt to wean consumers of incentive–induced binge buying. EDLP is supposed to erase consumer perceptions of large fluctuations in furniture prices, and therefore provide a steady stream of customers. However, EDLP has led many retailers into extremely tight profitability positions,

which can then lead to price wars for market share. In such a tight margin environment, firms must always keep sales volume up in order to survive.

Continued cost cutting by producers and retailers has led to the application of just–in–time inventory management in home furniture stores. This management has been in place since the beginning of the 1990s, and the sector's ratio of inventories to sales fell by almost 10% from 1990 to 1995.

Debt is a double–edged sword for furniture retailers. On one side, lower profit margins have forced many retailers into compromising debt situations. On the other side, many furniture purchases are bought on credit, including the use of store–specific credit cards issued by local banks. However, consumer credit availability is tightening, as a result of a rise in consumer bankruptcies and debt delinquency. This means the credit option will be a less flexible tool for furniture retailers, and any retailers who themselves extend credit may themselves face increasing collection problems.

Long–Term Prospects

Competition for retail furniture dollars promises to be fierce for the remainder of the decade. Consumer spending for furniture is likely to slow considerably in growth, if not actually decline, over the next year or two as the housing market cools a bit and interest rates creep up. This will only prove to intensify the competition, so cost–cutting and consolidation will continue and pricing will be weak.

Home Appliance Retailers

Home appliance retailers sell major appliances (stoves, refrigerators, and laundry equipment) as well as smaller appliances such as electric irons, coffee machines, and sewing machines. These stores often sell related items such as radios, televisions, and home computers.

Home appliance stores held their own in the 1970s and early 1980s against the competition from department stores and others. In 1985, home appliance stores accounted for 43% of total consumer purchases of home appliances. By the late 1980s, however, these stores started losing market share, and that trend has continued, although at a slow rate, through the present.

Home appliance stores will remain under competitive strain over the next few years. Competition from department stores, catalog operations, and general merchandise stores will keep margins low and prices down. In addition, sales growth will be very slow. As a result, the sector will likely see continued consolidation, including even takeovers by chains outside the sector.

Demand

Home appliance stores operate in a competitive environment where most competition comes from outside the specialty. These stores accounted for only 34% of total consumer purchases of household appliances in 1996. That number even overstates the influence of these stores, since it includes sales of items other than household appliances, such as computers, televisions, and radios.

Sales of household appliances are partially related to the housing cycle. When housing starts fall, sales at these stores do badly. Even when the housing market holds up, however, slow income and job growth can affect sales considerably. Thus, sales are even more volatile than total retail sales.

Home appliance stores held their own in the 1970s and early 1980s against the competition from department stores and others. In 1985, home appliance stores accounted for 43% of total consumer purchases of home appliances. By the late 1980s, however, these stores started losing market share, and that trend has continued, although at a slow rate, through the present. The major competition comes from certain department stores (especially those with catalog operations), home centers, and a variety of other outlets depending on the type of appliance. Small appliances are often sold at drug stores, while large appliances may be found at furniture stores, or bought through a contractor.

Appliance Stores Sell only a Fraction of All Appliances

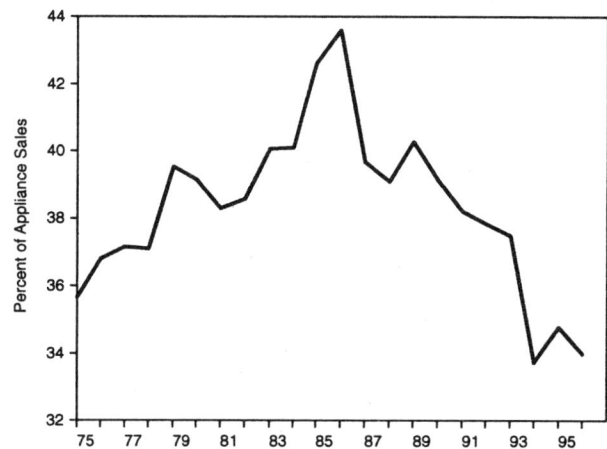

Source: Bureau of the Census (appliance store sales) and Bureau of Economic Analysis (consumer spending on appliances)

Appliance stores include both chain stores and a significant number of independent stores. If catalog/department stores are included, it is evident that appliance sales are generally dominated by very large, national chains. Sales within the narrow retail classification, however, are more evenly distributed, as chains that sell appliances remain relatively small. The average household appliance firm has 1.16 outlets, according to the *1992 Census of Retailing*, while the average retail firm has 1.21, the average building supply firm 1.22, and the average department store firm has more than 24 stores.

Pricing

Home appliance prices have risen more slowly than inflation over the past few years, and even fallen in some years. The business is very competitive, and manufacturers are constantly adding features to items in what is a mature marketplace. Competition at the retail level has intensified as well, with the growth in the non–appliance share of sales.

Environmental Issues

The major environmental issue in home appliances is faced by manufacturers. The Montreal Protocol has required the United States to cease manufacturing of chlorofluorocarbons (CFCs) and requires a phase–out of the hydrochlorofluorocarbons (HCFCs) currently in their place. CFCs were the main chemicals used as refrigerants, and HCFCs are the current replacement. Manufacturers have had to change many product designs, and will have to continue to put resources into adjusting to this change.

From the point of view of retail stores, the main issue involves the responsibility for disposal of old units. Retail stores generally exchange new large appliances for old appliances. Most old appliances are easily disposed of, and may even be worth a small amount of money. Disposing of refrigerators, however, has become considerably more complicated and expensive. The CFCs or HCFCs must be removed and correctly recycled or disposed of, an expensive process which may add to the retailer's liability. As a result, home appliance retailers can expect to continue to suffer increased costs because of environmental laws. Without the ability to raise prices, profit margins for these retailers will likely suffer.

Outlook

Home appliance stores will remain under competitive strain over the next few years. Competition from department stores, catalog operations, and general merchandise stores will keep margins low and prices down. In addition, sales growth will be very slow. As a result, the sector will likely see continued consolidation, including even takeovers by chains outside the sector.

Home Appliance Stores: Major Indicators
Percent Change

	1988	1989	1990	1991	1992	1993	1994	1995	1996	1997	1998
Retail Sales, Home Appliance Stores	12.2	7.6	1.2	1.4	5.8	13.8	17.9	14.5	6.8	−0.4	2.7

Home Appliance Stores: Major Indicators
Average Annual Growth Rate

	1986–1996	1996–2006
Retail Sales, Home Appliance Stores	9.0	1.4

Eating Places

Establishments classified as eating places include full–service restaurants, limited–service restaurants (fast–food outlets), commercial cafeterias, social caterers, and ice–cream stands. Sales of prepared food at hotel restaurants, supermarket deli–counters, sports complexes, and certain types of institutions are excluded. Sales of food and beverages at drinking places (pubs, bars, and taverns) are also excluded. Retail sales in drinking establishments account for about 5% of the combined sales of eating and drinking places.

Sales are nearly evenly divided between full–service restaurants and fast–food outlets. Together these two segments comprise approximately 95% of sales at eating places.

In 1996, retail sales at eating places reached almost $227 billion, a 2% increase over 1995 levels. Sales growth is expected to accelerate to 3.5% in 1997. For the period 1996–2006, expect retail sales at eating places to increase an average of 4.5% per year. Nearly 7.8 million people worked in locations classified as eating and drinking places. From 1991 to 1996, restaurant industry employment increased by one million jobs.

Demand Conditions

Consumption expenditures on purchased meals, the principal determinant of restaurant sales, grew by just over 2% in 1996. Growth in this category of personal consumption expenditures exceeded income growth in 1993 and 1994 and was only one–half percentage point below it in 1995. Expenditure growth slowed sharply in 1996 despite continued strong income gains. Income growth is expected to be strong in 1997 (up by more than 5%), and should carry spending on meals prepared away from home higher. For the ten years ending in 1996, retail sales at eating places increased by an average of 5.8% per year — the same as the growth rate for personal after–tax income.

One of the reasons consumers prepare less food at home and buy more ready–to–eat meals is because they have less time available for preparation. The share of the population that is employed outside the home for pay is at an all–time high, and still growing. Consumption of purchased meals has increased with the labor force participation of females, who traditionally have borne the responsibilities of at–home meal preparation.

The age profile of the population also affects which types of outlets are visited. As consumers age, they tend to switch to table–service restaurants and away from fast–food outlets. Some evidence also indicates that the frequency of restaurant visits declines with age. Six of ten 18–to–24–year–olds are restaurant patrons on a typical day. Only three of ten adults over 65 years of age are daily patrons. Since older population groups are projected to grow faster than other groups over the next ten years, fast–food outlets will have to increase marketing efforts to reach older consumers or risk declines in market share relative to table–service restaurants. For the period 1996–2006, expect retail sales at eating places to increase an average of 4.5% per year.

Long–Run Trends:
Eating Places
Compound Annual Percent Changes

	1986–1996	1996–2006
Retail Sales (%)	5.8	4.5
Price Index (%)	3.3	2.4

Note: Price index includes drinking establishments.

Supply Conditions

Over the past five years, eating establishments have sought to build volume through lower menu prices. This strategy worked in the absence of food cost pressures. Tight supplies for grains and lower meat production in 1996, however, contributed to a sharp increase, 4.5% in the year, in wholesale food costs. This cost increase put pressure on restaurant margins and led to selected price increases, but these averaged much less than the cost rise. Restaurant owners were forced to examine ways to reduce nonfood costs in an attempt to keep up profits.

Large chains have responded with initiatives aimed at lowering development costs for new sites. If successful, these cost reductions would ease the burden on new franchisees entering an already crowded market and allow expansion into smaller markets. Another tool the industry has used to hold down costs and expand menu selection is construction of dual–branded outlets. A Mexican menu might be paired with a complementary branded pizza or chicken franchise. The aim is to attract a broader mix of diners without the cost of two free–standing stores and a blurred menu identity.

One of the problems in the industry is overbuilding. Disgruntled operators and franchisees blame the overcapacity on the big chains (McDonald's, Boston Market, Wendy's, and Burger King) which often cannibalize sales at existing outlets when expansion plans run ahead of sales growth as has been the case over the past year. A battle for market share is shaping up with a shakeout likely. Currently, one in four retail outlets across the country is an eating or drinking place.

Price Trends

Labor (wages) and wholesale food costs are large inputs in restaurants' pricing plans; developments in both input markets tend to influence menu prices. In 1996, the price index for meals and beverages purchased at eating places jumped 2.6%, the fastest rate of increase in five years. The outlook for food cost inflation is better in 1997 than last year, and the effects of hikes in the federal minimum wage appear to be smaller than anticipated since tight labor markets would have bid up wages anyway. Still, many in the industry are sensitive to the cost effects of government proposals to expand health care coverage.

The customer response to many of the large chains' everyday "value pricing" plans is somewhat mixed. Most programs have emphasized price cuts on selected items or meal bundles. While these programs may build volume, they represent a threat to profits. Still, firms may have no choice since consumers have displayed limits on their willingness to pay, and price increases have cost business unless supported by more aggressive marketing.

Expect restaurant prices to increase an average of 2.4% per year over the period 1996–2006. Combined with sales growth of 4.5% per year over the same period, real sales volume is forecast to grow about 2% per year over the next ten years.

Industry Structure

Most eating places are small businesses and are unaffiliated with a large national restaurant chain. The two major market groups identified above, full–service (or table–service) restaurants and fast–food outlets, have very different degrees of sales concentration.

Data taken from the 1992 Census of Retail Trade (the latest available) indicate that fast food outlets are dominated by hamburger and pizza shops. These two categories accounted for nearly half of the outlets in the fast–food segment and almost 60% of sales. In contrast, the top two segments in the table–service category (Chinese and Italian restaurants) together accounted for only 19% of outlets and 14% of category sales.

In the restaurant industry, sales growth comes from construction of new outlets, acquisitions, and increases in existing sales. Given the overbuilding in many segments of the market, expect firms to emphasize programs which aim to bump up same–store sales. Promotional tie–ins with movie studios and toy manufacturers have enjoyed a fair degree of success in the past. Unfortunately, for every hit promotion there seems to be at least one that falls short of expectations.

International opportunities represent a key area of potential growth. Expansion–minded chains are currently targeting the Pacific Rim countries (e.g., China and southeast Asia). Untapped market potential is cited as the major reason for overseas development. This expansion will help U.S.–owned restaurant chain companies, but will not affect sales in the U.S. restaurant industry since the service will be "produced" abroad.

The outlook for food–service providers and restaurant operators is a bit cloudy. Sales are forecast to fall below income gains over the next few years. A battle for market share looms as overbuilding in certain segments will keep prices low and profit margins under pressure. Successful operators will be able to squeeze more costs out of their budgets and formulate a successful marketing strategy to differentiate themselves from the pack.

Trends & Forecasts: Eating Places

	1988	1989	1990	1991	1992	1993	1994	1995	1996	1997	1998
Retail Sales (Bil $)	157.1	167.2	178.7	182.6	187.8	201.4	211.4	222.3	226.8	234.7	244.4
% Ch	10.1	6.4	6.9	2.2	2.8	7.3	5.0	5.1	2.0	3.5	4.1
Price Index (% Ch)	4.3	4.7	4.8	4.1	2.2	1.9	1.8	2.3	2.6	2.6	2.3

Note: Price index includes drinking establishments.

Drug Stores

Retail establishments classified as drug stores are primarily engaged in the distribution and sale of pre-scription and non–prescription (proprietary) medicines, health and beauty care products, and seasonal merchandise. Many establishments (especially chain drug stores) also sell snack food, beverages, tobacco products, small household appliances, and housewares. Industry retail sales figures do not include the value of prescription drugs provided through in–hospital pharmacies and supermarket pharmacies.

In 1996, retail sales at drug and proprietary stores were nearly $90 billion, a gain of approximately 6% over 1995 levels. Sales (which include food and nonfood items) are expected to increase 5.3% in 1997. Over 600,000 people are employed in drug stores.

The forecast is for continued strong sales growth in the drug store sector thanks to favorable demographics in the prescription drug segment and an emphasis on expanded merchandise selection. Consolidation and implementation of new technologies will help cut costs and boost profits.

Demand Conditions

Consumer spending for items sold in drug stores is driven by outlays for prescription drugs, non–prescription medications, and health & beauty care products. Spending growth for these items has generally exceeded gains in nominal incomes over the past decade.

Demand for prescription drugs, a key expenditure category, is driven to a large extent by demographics and health insurance coverage options. With respect to demographics, the practice of modern medicine has come to rely more heavily on drug therapies than on many hospital procedures. The simple truth is that as people age, they get sick. And when they get sick, their physicians turn to medications to treat their problems. The over–65 population is expected to grow faster than younger groups for the foreseeable future, providing a stimulus to pharmacy sales.

Expansion of coverage also helps drive sales higher. The movement of Medicaid patients into managed care opens up a new market for drug stores. In the private sector, the spread of Pharmacy Benefits Management (PBM) companies has increased the incidence of prescription drug benefits for consumers. Interestingly, at pharmacies, cash sales are down while third–party and Medicaid sales have more than doubled since early 1992.

A desire for health & beauty care products to stay young–looking and fit has also spurred sales at many drug store counters. The post World War II baby boom generation's desire to cheat the aging process combined with demand for nutritional supplements — part of a fitness craze — should continue to provide support for sales gains in the future.

Shifts in consumer shopping habits, particularly the desire for convenience and one–stop shopping, provide an additional opportunity for store owners to boost sales by selling snacks and other merchandise to pharmacy patrons.

WEFA forecasts sales growth at drug stores to average about 5% per year over the 1996–2006 period. This growth rate compares with an average annual sales increase of 5.8% over the 1986–96 period.

Long–Run Trends:
Drug Stores
Compound Annual Changes

	1986–1996	1996–2006
Retail Sales (%)	5.8	5.0
Price Index (%)	4.6	3.9

Supply Conditions

In line with customer pleas for convenience and a new merchandise mix, drug store retailers are changing store layouts to accommodate drive–through pharmacies, expanded snack food shelf space, and value–added services such as one–hour photo–finishing. And it is not just the layout of the typical store that is changing. Store location decisions are also being affected. The hunt for new, more convenient locations has resulted in a migration away from smaller shopping mall stores towards larger, free–standing stores. Most large retailers are in the midst of expansion and remodeling programs.

Technology continues to play a critical role in firms' efforts to reduce costs. Pharmacy systems are often targets. The development of automatic prescription refill systems, establishment of computer links between doctors' offices and pharmacies, and computerized reordering procedures are all designed to free pharmacists for higher–value activities like customer counseling and interaction.

Technology initiatives have also focused on supply chain management issues: vendor delivery coordination, store stocking, and inventory control. In recent years, the industry has also undertaken a large investment campaign to outfit checkout counters with the latest in scanning and point–of–sale equipment.

Price Trends

Prices for items sold in drug and proprietary stores grew by 2.7% in 1996, their fastest growth rate in three years. The higher growth last year is mainly due to hikes in the cost of prescription drugs. Faster approval by the FDA of new drugs over the past few years resulted in a large number of new (and expensive) drug releases in 1996. In addition, many pharmaceutical firms are trying to pass along wholesale price hikes to make up for a very weak pricing environment in the 1991–94 period.

After taking a beating early in this decade, thanks to the spread of cost–conscious managed care providers who knocked down reimbursement rates, margins on pharmacy items are now holding steady. Although managed health care plans (PBMs) continue to expand, many of the plans are beginning to emphasize service dimensions other than price. These might include expanded coverage area or extra counter hours. About 70% of prescription sales are handled by third–party payment (with many prices set via negotiation).

Expect the retail sales price index for items sold in drug and proprietary stores to increase at a 3.9 compounded annual average rate during the 10 year period ending in 2006. The annual average change in the price index over the period 1986–96 was 4.6%. Slower growth in the price of prescription drugs is the factor most responsible for the deceleration in drug store inflation. The change in prices coupled with the expected 5% increase in sales dollars imply real shipments growth of just over 1% in the years ahead.

Industry Structure

Thanks in part to recently completed or pending mergers, the drug store industry is increasingly dominated by large retail chains. Top chain retailers include Walgreen, Rite Aid/Thrifty Payless, Revco/CVS, Eckerd/Thrift, and American Drug Stores. The first three account for over 60% of chain drug stores sales. The top ten chains control nearly 73% of all chain store sales and about half of all industry sales. The business environment is highly competitive, as the large retailers continue to try to grab market share from each other as well as from supermarkets, mass merchants, small independent pharmacies, and regional drug store chains.

Supermarket operators Kroger, Safeway, Winn–Dixie, and Albertson's have posed the biggest threat to traditional drug stores using combination food/drug stores. These stores are able to exploit the link in consumers' minds between nutrition and health. The retailers have also learned to leverage store foot traffic to increase sales of health and beauty care products.

Mass merchants like Walmart and Kmart may represent an even bigger threat to the drug stores. Both of these retailers have extensive pharmacy networks in their stores and would rank among the top ten drug chains in terms of pharmacy sales were they classified in that category. Mass merchandisers, discounters, and supermarket combo stores have been particularly hard on small, independent drug stores whose owners neglected to introduce new technologies and expand merchandise. Small drug stores have generally fought back by returning to the core pharmacy function in the hopes of carving out a high service niche.

For large chains, it appears that contracts with managed care providers are key to the new pharmacy economics. The wave of mergers (successful and unsuccessful) over the past two years that has created three industry giants is generally viewed as driven by the need to get bigger. Larger chains can offer the geographic reach and critical mass needed to service nationwide prescription benefit plan contracts.

Lobbying efforts by the National Association of Chain Drug Stores seek to convince states to loosen regulations restricting electronic transmission of prescriptions, raise the technician/pharmacist ratio, and include the pharmacist in drug therapy decisions. Success in these efforts would, in their proponents' eyes, eliminate old and artificial barriers to patient services (and translate into higher profits for drug store chains).

The forecast is for continued strong sales growth in the drug store sector thanks to favorable demographics in the prescription drug segment and an emphasis on expanded merchandise selection. Consolidation and implementation of new technologies will help cut costs and boost profits.

Trends & Forecasts: Drug Stores (SIC 5912)

	1988	1989	1990	1991	1992	1993	1994	1995	1996	1997	1998
Retail Sales (Bil $)	57.8	63.3	70.6	75.5	77.8	79.6	81.4	84.2	89.2	93.9	97.3
% Ch	6.8	9.5	11.4	7.1	3.0	2.4	2.2	3.5	5.9	5.3	3.6
Price Index (% Ch)	5.7	6.4	7.0	7.1	4.9	2.9	2.3	1.5	2.7	2.6	2.7

Catalog and Mail Order Houses

Catalog sales are generally made by sending or selling catalogs to prospective customers, taking orders by mail or telephone, and shipping goods directly to the buyer. Although some businesses specialize in catalog sales, many other retail companies maintain catalog divisions which may only account for a small portion of sales. Official statistics for this industry include only sales of firms primarily engaged in catalog sales. Catalog sales by firms not primarily engaged in this activity are not included in the official statistics.

Other direct marketing methods are not included in this specific industry. These include television sales, direct telephone marketing, and electronic sales through the internet.

Catalog Sales Have Grown Rapidly

Retail sales of catalog houses and related firms totaled $47.8 billion in 1996, or 2.6% of all non–automobile retail sales, versus 1.3% in 1982. The industry grew at a rapid pace in the 1980s, when catalog sales became popular for convenience and known quality. Catalog sales grew twice as fast as other non–auto retail sales between 1982 and 1996, and averaged more than 13% per year from 1983 to 1989. After the recession cut growth to about 4.5% in 1991, sales again took off. In the past two years, however, sales growth averaged only about 7%, only slightly better than the growth in other non–auto retail sales.

Catalog Firms' Share of Total Retail Sales Grew in the 1980s

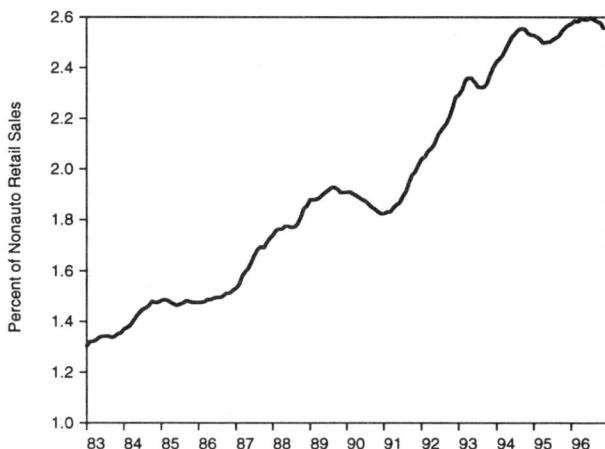

The retail sales figure for catalog houses does not include all catalog sales, however. A significant amount of retail catalog sales is chalked up by retailers that are not primarily catalog houses. In 1996, total catalog sales totaled $79 billion, or 50% more than official data for catalog houses. Total catalog sales grew at an annual rate of 8.2% between 1990 and 1996, considerably faster than total retail sales. In addition, total catalog sales have grown faster than sales of catalog houses, as more non–catalog companies have established catalog and sales–by–mail divisions in attempts to capture some of the sector's rapid growth.

The largest catalog operations by revenue are run by J.C. Penney (1994 revenues of $3.8 billion), and three computer companies: Dell, Gateway, and DEC direct. It is clear that many of the important businesses engage in more traditional retail selling, but have a division devoted to catalog sales. Even the biggest traditional retailers have catalog operations. Federated Department Stores, for example, has a small catalog operation (Bloomingdales by Mail) which accounts for $137 million of Federated's 1995 sales of $15 billion.

Pricing and Costs

The catalog sales industry is very dependent on printing and publishing costs, and mail costs. Printing costs rose more quickly than other prices in 1993 and 1994, reducing the industry's competitiveness with traditional retailing. In addition, the industry was hit with a 15% postal rate hike (for third class bulk mail) in January, 1995. Mailing rates have proven to be a particular problem for the industry, since they have been rising faster than inflation in the 1990s. Over the past ten years, bulk mail rates have risen at a 7% rate, more than double the overall inflation rate.

Printing Costs Rose Faster than Other Costs from 1993 to 1995

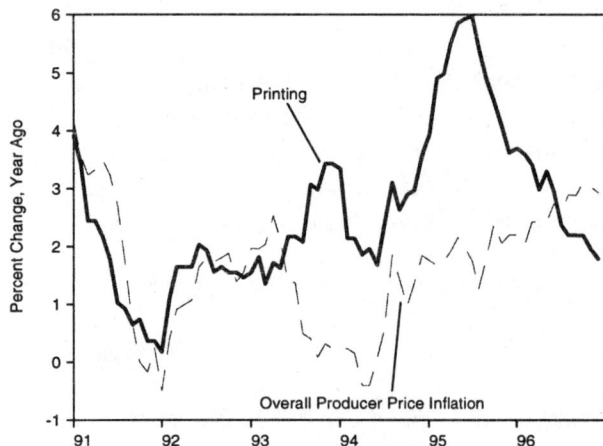

Catalog companies have responded in two ways to these cost pressures. First, they have reduced mailings and searched for ways to make mailings more effective through the use of more careful targeting and demographics, for example. Second, some companies have begun charging for catalogs, while allowing the catalog buyer a discount equal to the price of the catalog if an actual purchase is made. The price of these catalogs may be substantial; charges of $3.00 to $5.00 are typical. Charging for catalogs is more common among specialty retailers than among the largest companies (neither L.L. Bean nor Lands' End charge for catalogs), and it does not occur among the important electronics sector.

What They Sell

Catalog retailers account for about 60% of total catalog sales. Other industries that maintain a strong catalog sales presence include auto dealers and service stations (6% of the market), specialty retailers (3%), and food stores (2% of the market). Consumer catalog sales are concentrated in apparel and home goods, which accounted for over half of all consumer catalog sales in the 12 months ending June 1996.

A significant portion (40%) of catalog sales is made to businesses. Business–to–business catalog sales are dominated by catalog retailers, but also include printing and publishing (6% of the business market), government

enterprises (4% of the market), and chemicals and allied products (3% of the market).

Sales Forecast

Total catalog sales will continue to grow in the next few years at rates faster than the rate of growth of all retail sales. Growth will be slower than in the past, however, since the recovery in the market for consumer goods is more mature, and because catalog penetration may be reaching the saturation point. Catalog sales to businesses will grow faster than catalog sales to consumers, as this portion of the market has not been as fully penetrated. The portion of catalog sales accounted for by the catalog houses will continue to fall as non–catalog retailers continue to establish and grow catalog subsidiaries.

Substitution

Catalog companies face challenges from three other direct marketing methods: telephone sales, direct television sales, and internet sales.

- Telephone sales to consumers totaled $159 billion in 1995, or about 3% of total consumer spending. Telephone sales do not generally compete directly with catalog operations, however. Consumer telephone sales were concentrated in services — 50% of all such sales in 1995 were for financial or other services, and only 39% were in retail or manufactured goods.

- Direct television sales includes the home shopping networks, "infomercials" of various lengths, and traditional direct sales television commercials. Direct television sales to consumers totaled $9.5 billion in 1995, or about 25% of the value of total catalog sales to consumers. Most television sales are for retail items, with services accounting for only 15% of total sales.

- Estimates of internet sales (electronic commerce) in 1996 ranged from $140 million to $1 billion, a relatively small amount compared to catalog sales. Nevertheless, the traditional catalog industry has responded by establishing a presence on the internet, and even using it aggressively in marketing. This is in contrast to the industry's view of telemarketing and direct television sales, both of which have been largely ignored by the major catalog houses.

Other direct market sales are likely to grow faster than catalog sales over the next few years. The internet appears to be the only medium which directly competes with catalogs, however. The internet shares several characteristics with catalogs that distinguish these sales methods from television and telephone sales:

■ Both require a similar investment in the presentation of the merchandise, either for the catalog or for the internet page. Television and telephone sales present merchandise in very different ways.

■ The customer controls when and how to shop in both catalog and internet sales. By contrast, television and telephone sales techniques involve control by the seller.

Neither television or telephone provides a likely serious alternative to catalogs in the near future. The internet, however, will be an important alternative to catalog sales, and both catalog and non–catalog retailers can be expected to continue to expend resources on testing and improving internet sales.

Catalog Sales: Annual History and Forecast
Percent Change

Indicator	1989	1990	1991	1992	1993	1994	1995	1996	1997	1998
Total Catalog Sales	9.0	9.9	4.5	7.3	11.0	10.2	7.1	6.7	6.9	6.7
Consumer Sales	10.9	10.1	5.3	6.6	10.1	9.7	6.7	6.3	6.5	6.4
Business Sales	−16.2	9.7	3.3	8.4	12.4	11.1	7.8	7.4	7.5	7.2

Source: Direct Marketing Association and WEFA

Catalog Sales: Trend
Average Annual Growth Rate

Indicator	1988–1996	1996–2002
Total Catalog Sales	8.2	6.7
Consumer Sales	8.2	6.4
Business Sales	5.1	7.2

Source: Direct Marketing Association and WEFA

Part 6: Finance, Insurance, Real Estate, and Services

Chapter 28: Finance, Insurance, and Real Estate

Financial Services

The financial services industry is comprised of firms which provide some type of financial service to consumers, businesses, or government. These services may be related to the payments system and involve such specific products as checking accounts, electronic deposits or payment arrangements, and credit cards; the credit markets, including any of a wide array of specific types of loans; and, savings and investments, including all of the various forms that these may take. Historically, different types of financial services have been associated with different types of firms — depository and lending services have been associated with commercial banks and thrift institutions, for example, while services related to the issuance of, and investment in, financial securities have been associated with investment banks and securities brokers and dealers.

The traditional sharp distinctions between different types of firms providing different types of financial services have been disappearing rapidly in recent years, however, as a result of changes in regulations and technology. Banks now offer services traditionally offered only by securities firms, for example, and vice versa. Rapid advances in technology have even resulted in firms from totally different industries offering financial services, for example, when software firms become deeply involved in the payments system via developments in "home banking", through which people pay bills using personal computers. While the transformation of the financial services industry continues at a rapid pace, blurring the distinctions between traditiionally very different types of firms, those distinctions are still significant enough for it to make sense to look at different categories of firms. In the following, commercial banks, thrift institutions, credit unions, securities brokers, and mutual funds are reviewed.

Commercial Banks

After suffering through a difficult period in the early 1990s as a result of large loan losses concentrated in the real estate area, commercial banks recovered strongly by the middle of the decade. At the same time, as a result of regulatory and other changes enhancing economies of scale in industry, banking has been rapidly consolidating in recent years.

In 1996, insured commercial banks earned a record $52.4 billion, up 7.5% from 1995. The industry's basic measure of profitability, return on assets (ROA), rose to 1.19%, its second–highest ever (just slightly behind the 1.20% earned in 1993). In the late 1980s and early 1990s, banks were plagued by bad loans and weak performance. This turned around, and 1996 marked the fourth consecutive year of strong earnings.

Profits and Profitability of Insured Commercial Banks
1987 — 1996, annually

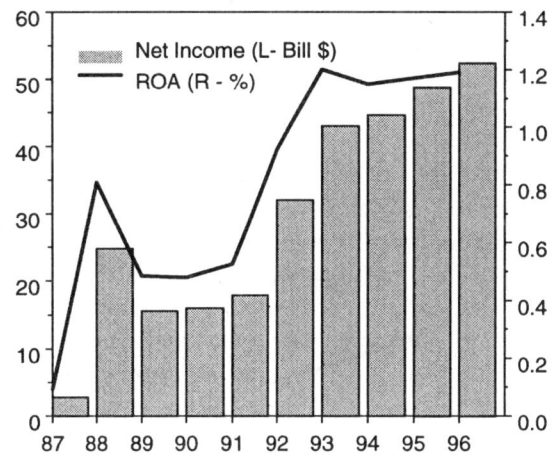

Total commercial bank assets increased by 6.2% in 1996, a slightly slower growth pace than the 7.5% and 8.2% gains achieved in 1995 and 1994, respectively. Loan volume rose by 8.1% in 1996, paced by increases in commercial and industrial loans and in residential mortgages. Although the growth in loans slowed in 1996 from the double–digit increases of the two preceding years, it was still strong, indicating that credit remained readily available. The past several years of strong loan growth stand in marked contrast to the experience in 1991–92, when loans on the books of commercial banks actually declined. At that time, banks were making loans only rather grudgingly, as they sought to strengthen their balance sheets which had been ravaged by massive volumes of bad loans.

While most asset–quality measures remained at relatively favorable levels in 1996, there were also clear signs of developing loan problems. Noncurrent loans (i.e., loans 90 days or more past due, or in nonaccrual status) are an example of how the good performance of an aggregate can mask underlying problems. The total of noncurrent loans declined slightly in 1996, falling to 1.1% of total loans, down from 1.2% in 1995, and by far the lowest level for this measure in the past ten years. In the early nineties, when banks were beset by bad loans, this ratio was as high as 3.8%. However, while noncurrent loans declined for most categories of loans, noncurrent consumer loans increased significantly. In addition, although noncurrent loans declined in 1996, delinquent loans (i.e., those with payments 30 to 89 days past due) jumped by 15.1%, led by a 24% increase in past–due credit–card loans and a 20% jump in delinquent commercial and industrial loans.

Net loan charge–offs of bad loans also increased in 1996, rising to 0.6% of total loans, up from 0.5% in 1995 — which was the lowest level for this measure in the past ten years. At their peak in 1991, bad loans that were written off by banks amounted to 1.6% of loans. Again, the problem of excessive consumer debt was reflected in banks' loan charge–offs in 1996, as charge–offs of bad credit–card loans — which jumped by 40% last year — accounted for 61% of total loan charge–offs.

As another sign of the much–improved health of the banking industry in recent years, the number of banks classified as "problem banks" has declined drastically. At the end of 1996, there were 82 institutions so classified, down from 144 at the end of 1995. This also represents a greater–than–ninety–percent decline from the 1,016 banks so classified at the end of 1991. Even more dramatic has been the drop in assets represented by "problem banks," which have fallen from $528 billion

(equal to 15.4% of total bank assets) in 1991, to only $5 billion (equal to just 0.1% of total bank assets) in 1996.

Assets of Problem Banks as a Percent of Total Bank Assets
1990 — 1996, annually

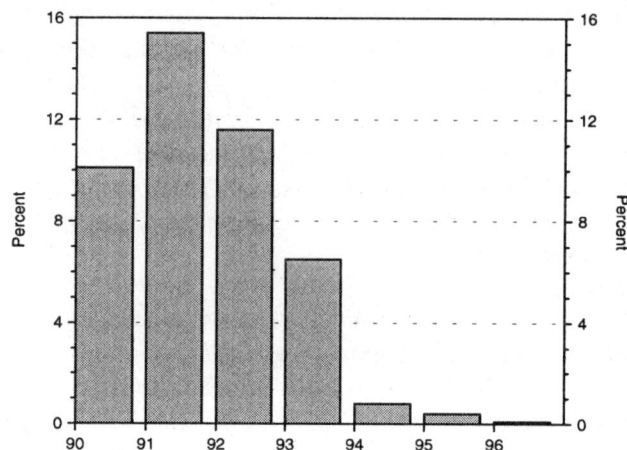

Consolidation of the banking industry continued in 1996, with the number of banks declining by 412 as the number of independent institutions eliminated through mergers continued to significantly outpace the number of new banks chartered. Over the past ten years, the number of banks in the United States has declined by one–third.

Number of Insured Commercial Banks
1986 — 1996, annually

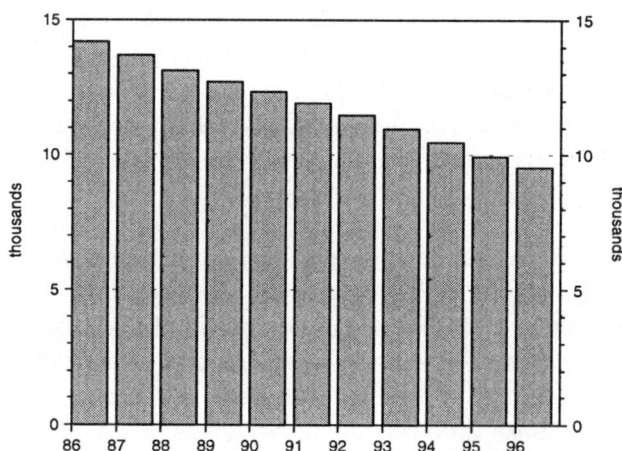

Thrift Institutions

The "thrift crisis" of the late 1980s and early 1990s officially ended in 1995 with the closing of the Resolution Trust Corporation. In the seven years of its existence, the

RTC sold or liquidated some 747 failed thrifts, representing approximately $450 billion in assets. Somewhat incredibly, following so close on the heels of that debacle, by 1996 the thrift industry had returned to a remarkably healthy state. Although the industry was considerably smaller than it was in the mid–1980s, in terms of both the number of firms and the assets which they represented, not only were earnings extremely strong last year but other key measures of industry health also registered highly favorable readings.

Total earnings of the thrift industry in 1996 were $4.8 billion. Although they were down from a record $5.4 billion in 1995, earnings were depressed by a one–time special premium assessed to recapitalize the Savings Association Insurance Fund (SAIF). Excluding the effect of that special premium, thrift industry earnings would have been $6.9 billlion last year, or 28% higher than they were in 1995. These favorable results were due in part to lower interest costs. In terms of profitability, the return on average assets in 1996 was a respectable 0.62%, down from 0.70% in 1995. Excluding the effect of the special premium, however, the thrift industry's "adjusted" ROA last year was an extraordinary 0.89%, the highest since 1962.

Thrift Industry Return on Average Assets (ROA)
1960 — 1996, annually

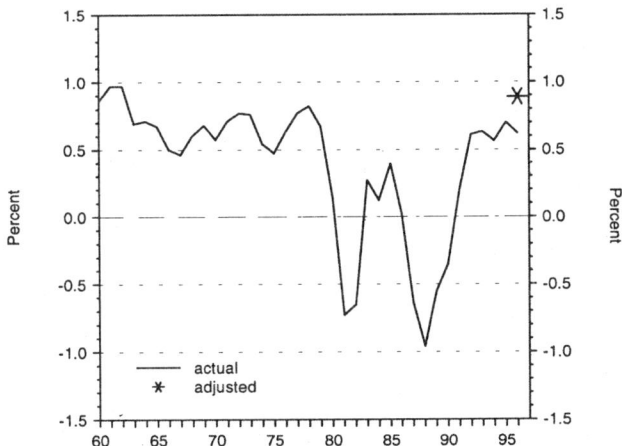

Balance sheet measures also track the return to health of the thrift industry by 1996. Although the equity capital ratio of the thrift industry declined slightly last year as a result of the SAIF special assessment to 7.92% at year–end, it remained close to the year–end 1995 record of 8.01% (at its depths during the 1980s, that ratio hovered around 3% for more than five years). Moreover, at the

end of 1996, there was only one thrift that was classified as "undercapitalized" to some degree according to FDICIA capital categories. Four years ago, at the end of 1992, there were 78 such institutions. At the same time, the percentage of thrifts that were classified as "well–capitalized" at the end of 1996 remained at ninety–seven; four years ago, only eighty–one percent of thrifts were so classified.

The number and size of institutions classified by the regulatory authorities as "problem thrifts" have diminished greatly. Whereas at the end of 1992 there were 203 such institutions, at the end of last year that number was down to only 29 (versus 41 at the end of 1995). Moreover, those problem thrifts which remain tend to be relatively small; altogether, their assets represented only 0.70% of total thrift assets (down from 1.4% at the end of 1995). This constitutes a dramatic improvement from four years ago, when the assets of problem thrifts represented 16.6% of total thrift assets.

Problem Thrift Assets as a Percent of Total Thrift Industry Assets
1992 — 1996, annually

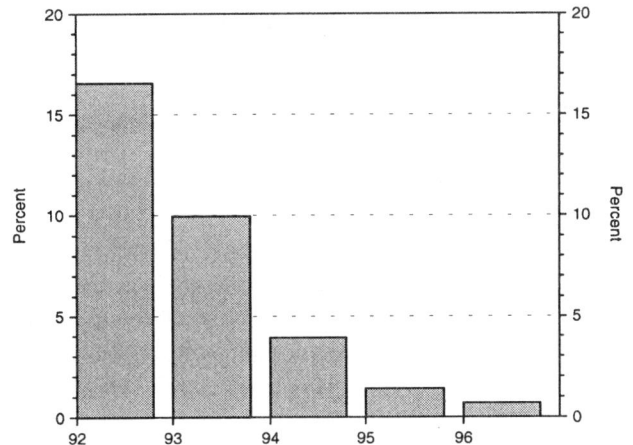

Measures of thrift industry asset quality also continued to improve last year. "Troubled assets" (i.e., the sum of noncurrent loans and repossessed assets) as a percent of total assets declined to 1.17% at the end of 1996, from 1.24% a year earlier. At the same time noncurrent loans as a percent of total assets eased to 0.86%, down from 0.88%. Both of these measures are significantly lower than they were four years ago.

Although the thrift industry was quite healthy in 1996, it continued to consolidate in terms of the number of thrift institutions, while its size in terms of total assets was little changed. The number of thrifts declined by about 7% last year, to 1,334. Over the past ten years, the number of thrift institutions has dropped by more than half: in 1986, there were 3,220 institutions. Much, but not all of that decline has been the result of consolidation within the industry through mergers and acquisitions. At the same time, the size of the thrift industry has shrunk in terms of its total assets, with some thrift assets written off and others acquired by commercial banks and other financial institutions. Although total thrift assets were essentially unchanged last year, since 1988 they have fallen by 45%.

Size Measures of the Thrift Industry
1986 — 1996, annually

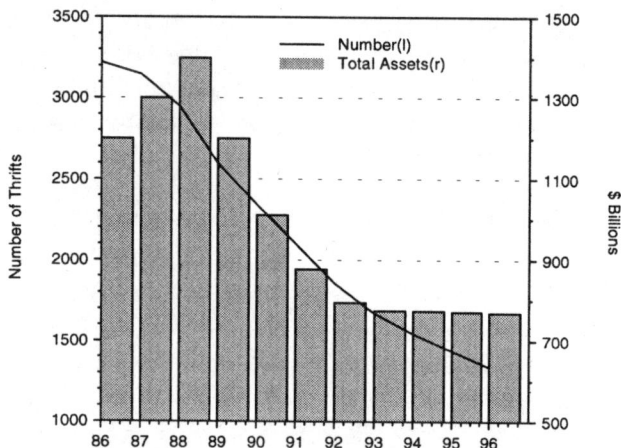

Credit Unions

Credit unions are cooperative financial institutions that provide saving and lending services to their members. In addition to basic services, large credit unions offer checking accounts, automated teller machines (ATMs), credit cards, individual retirement accounts (IRAs), and other services.

The National Credit Union Administration (NCUA), an agency of the Federal Government, insures approximately 12,000 credit unions that hold more than 95% of all credit union assets. NCUA examines and regulates most federally insured credit unions to ensure their safety and soundness. Approximately 500 credit unions are insured either privately or by states. State agencies regulate these state and privately insured credit unions.

Credit unions represent a relatively small share of the total financial services market. Of the total lending by

commercial banks, thrift institutions, and credit unions, for example, credit unions represented just under 6% at the end of 1996. Credit unions are most important in the market for consumer installment loans, such as personal, auto, and credit card loans. In that market, credit unions accounted for 12% of total loans outstanding at the end of 1996. Although credit unions represent a relatively small share of the total financial services industry, they have gained market share in recent years as regulations restricting their membership have been eased, and as they have charged lower fees, and offered to pay higher and charge lower interest rates than competing institutions.

Securities Firms

Securities firms perform various functions related to maintaining markets in financial securities, including short– and long–term debt instruments issued by governments and corporations, and equity issues of corporations. Their two principal functions are investment banking and acting as securities brokers and dealers. Firms which provide investment banking services assist businesses and governments in raising funds needed to finance capital expenditures and other spending, selling newly–issued stocks and bonds to individual and institutional investors.

In recent years, an important new type of debt issue has been for the purpose of "securitizing" mortgages and other types of otherwise illiquid loans (such as credit card receivables and car loans). Such issues effectively remove these illiquid assets from the books of commercial banks, thrift institutions, and other originators, through selling them to investors.

While investment–grade debt generally represents the largest dollar amount of offerings, substantial fees are also typically earned from high–yield bonds and equities. These latter instruments generate larger fees per dollar of issue sold, as they are generally riskier for investment banks to hold and also require more sales effort. While investment–grade debt might earn 50 cents in revenues for every $100 of issue value, comparable revenues for high–yield bonds might be $2 and for stocks $6.

The volume of all new securities (stocks and bonds) issued by corporations has increased significantly in recent years, rising from an average of $273 billion per year during 1986–90, to $533 billion per year during 1991–96.

In recent years, new bond issues have accounted for about 85% of new issues of corporate securities.

New Security Issues by U.S. Corporations, All Issues (stocks and bonds)
1986 — 1996, annually

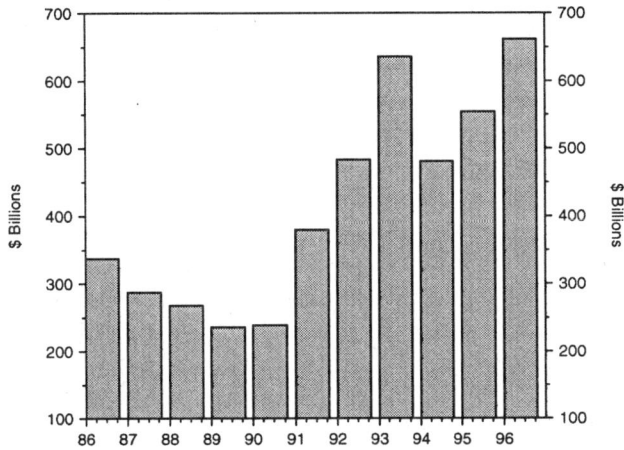

Securities dealers and brokers provide a "secondary" market for previously–issued securities, bringing securities buyers and sellers together. These firms maintain active markets for all kinds of marketable securities, including debt obligations of state and local governments, as well as those of the federal government, and corporate stocks and bonds. In recent years, as the volume of investments in financial securities has generally soared, so has trading activity in the securities markets. Trading volume on the New York Stock Exchange, for example, mushroomed from an average of approximately 160 million shares per day during 1986–90, to about 410 million shares per day in 1996.

Average Daily Volume on the New York Stock Exchange
1986 — 1996, annually

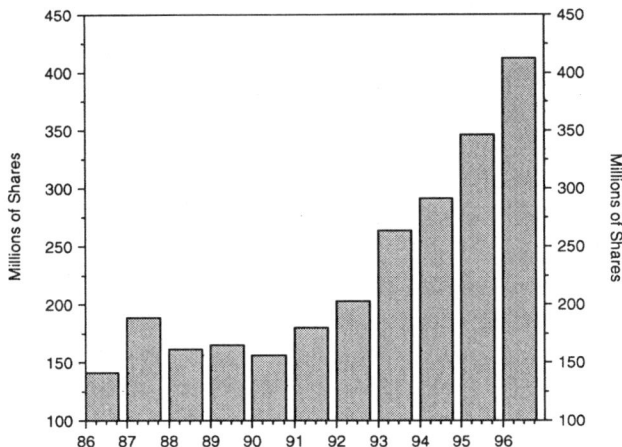

Mutual Funds

A mutual fund is a company that invests in financial securities on behalf of its shareholders. By combining the financial resources of shareholders, mutual funds offer small investors the ability to economically achieve the goals of professional money management and investment diversification. Professional money managers invest the fund's assets in a variety of stocks, bonds, or other securities selected from a broad range of industries, government agencies, and authorities. In effect, each mutual fund shareholder owns a percentage of the diversified portfolio created by the fund's money managers. The advantage of diversification is that, generally speaking, diversified portfolios of investments tend to be less risky than portfolios that are not diversified and are comprised of only a relatively few specific investments.

Mutual funds have stated investment objectives which are given in a fund's prospectus. The fund's managers select securities that they believe best meet their fund's objective. Investment objectives are usually described in terms of one or more main goals — such as "stability" (protecting shareholders' investment from loss), "growth" (increasing the value of shareholders' investment), or "income" (generating a regular stream of income through dividends).

The mutual fund industry consists of investment companies, each of which sells shares in one or more mutual funds. Investment companies sell shares directly to the public or through agents. Registered representatives of brokerage firms, insurance agencies, and financial planning firms, among others, sell shares in mutual funds as part of their overall financial service to clients. These funds usually add a sales charge, or "load," to the sale to compensate agents for their work and generate revenue for themselves. Organizations such as unions, associations, and retail stores also market mutual funds.

Many investment companies, however, sell shares in mutual funds directly to investors by mail and by telephone. These shares are often sold "no load" — that is, with no sales charge or only a nominal sales charge. Revenue for investment companies from these funds is usually provided by management fees based on size of assets or performance or both. Some expenses, such as marketing and distribution, can be covered directly by assets of the funds if these funds conform to government regulations.

Mutual funds must meet specific regulatory requirements. A mutual fund must register with the U.S. Securities and Exchange Commission (SEC), issue a prospectus giving a detailed report of its operations, and adhere to strict rules concerning accounting and valuation. A number of regulations exist to prevent conflicts of interest among officials of investment companies. State regulations and securities laws also govern mutual funds. Because of the fiduciary nature of mutual funds, their operations are subject to regulatory scrutiny.

As incomes of many households have risen to levels that can support significant saving, and as pension plans have shifted away from traditional plans entirely financed by employer contributions, to plans (such as 401K) that require contributions — and investment decisions — by employees, investment through mutual funds has soared in recent years. Moreover, when that trend is combined with sharply rising stock prices, which was the case in recent years, the result has been explosive growth in mutual fund assets.

Specifically, in the 10–year period from 1986 to 1996, total net assets of mutual funds has increased nearly five–fold, soaring from $716 billion at the end of 1986, to $3.5 trillion at the end of 1996. As spectacular as that growth has been, the growth of equity funds over that period has been twice as fast, as their net asset values have increased more than 10–fold — rising from $162 billion at the end of 1986 to $1.75 trillion at the end of 1996. As a result of that explosive rise, equity funds have become far–and–away the dominant type of mutual fund, whereas in 1986 investments in both bond and income funds, and in taxable money market funds, were greater than those represented by equity funds. Moreover, as investments in mutual funds have soared in recent years, so has the number of mutual funds. The number of mu-

tual funds more than tripled between 1986 and 1996, jumping from 1,840 to 6,293, with that growth approximately equally split between equity funds and bond and income funds.

Mutual Funds: Total Net Assets and Total Number of Funds
1986 — 1996, annually

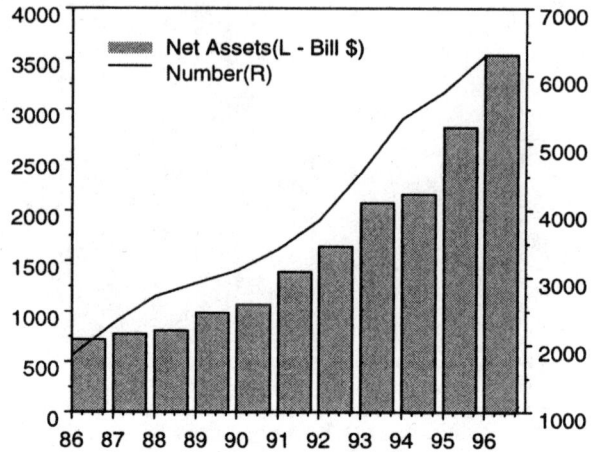

Financial Services: 10–Year Trends
SIC 60–62, 67
Average Annual Growth Rate

Indicator	1986–1996	1996–2006
Sales		
Current Dollars	6.9	5.7
Volume	3.6	2.2
Prices	3.2	3.5

Financial Services: Annual
SIC 60–62, 67

Indicator	1990	1991	1992	1993	1994	1995	1996	1997	1998
Sales									
$ billion	323.0	351.5	391.2	437.5	459.1	463.6	491.6	525.2	559.1
% change	8.9	8.8	11.3	11.9	4.9	1.0	6.1	6.8	6.5
Volume, % change	−0.3	−2.1	4.4	8.5	2.0	−1.1	2.4	2.8	2.3
Prices, % change	9.2	11.2	6.6	3.1	2.8	2.1	3.6	4.0	4.0

Insurance Services

The primary sectors in the insurance services industries are life insurers, property–casualty (P–C) insurers, and health maintenance organizations.

The tendency for property–casualty insurers to perpetually incur underwriting losses on insurance premiums written seems counterproductive but is not. When the cash received as premiums, which may be incurring an underwriting loss, is invested in a stock market that may be providing a total return of 15% or greater, the overall activity — underwriting loss plus premium investment income — often provides a healthy profit.

Life insurers have a different problem. During times of high interest rates, policy–holders increase borrowings against the cash value of their life policies at low rates. This deprives life insurers of that cash which could be profitably invested in financial markets, and makes life insurance an interest–sensitive sector.

For insurance providers in aggregate, we expect annual increases in sales volume (inflation adjusted) to average about 2% per year over the next ten years; a rate almost identical to that of the past ten years. Prices should rise at roughly 4.5% per year over the decade; a rate above that expected for most other industries but in line with the industry's historical trend.

Sources Of Demand

Preliminary figures suggest that premiums written by P–C insurers in 1996 were slightly below their 1995 level, and that a trend of only very modest growth in written premiums has been in place for almost a decade. Within that modest overall P–C trend, personal property–casualty underwriting performed well, while that for commercial lines grew more slowly. The commercial segment of the P–C business still has considerable excess capacity, which is negatively affecting pricing.

Life insurers experienced a good year in 1996, and many of the positive factors that sparked this performance should continue in 1997.

- Insurers are consolidating, gaining the earnings of other companies through acquisition.

- Cash flow is strong.

- While short–term interest rates are rising, the increase should not be more than 100 basis points.

- Profits are strong on variable annuity products. In fact,
  ⋯⋯ remain the key growth area in the life insur-

Health Maintenance Organizations (HMOs) have managed to hold ground despite fairly flat demand and a limited ability to improve pricing. One positive factor in this environment, however, has been the strength in outpatient services. In addition, despite a tough market environment, HMOs have made steady gains in market share by adding new services and watching costs closely. Consolidation continues in this industry too, driven by a need to reduce excess capacity and improve returns. Some price firming is likely as a result in 1997.

For the aggregate of all insurance providers, we expect annual increases in sales volume (inflation adjusted) to average about 2% per year over the next ten years, a rate almost identical to that of the past ten years. Prices should rise at roughly 4.5% per year over the decade, a rate above that expected for most other industries but consistent with the industry's historical trend.

Supply and Industry Structure

In the P–C insurance business, excess capacity and intense price competition continue. Strong investment returns and rising equity surplus has aided profitability within the industry and has boosted available cash. The competition to rake in more of this cash — which comes from underwriting premiums and is in turn invested profitably in the financial markets — has kept underwriting prices under pressure and has allowed the industry's excess of underwriting capacity to remain. This excess capacity is likely to continue as long as the financial markets stay healthy.

In the life insurance business, falling values of the industry's real estate and junk bond investments weakened the balance sheets of some firms earlier in the decade and made them prime takeover targets. Two companies that have grown substantially in recent years by selectively buying assets are SunAmerica and Conseco. Consolidation in the life insurance sector most likely will continue.

Trends Affecting The Outlook

Some insurers have narrowed their focus of operations, while others have bought competitors or expanded overseas in their attempts, in order to offset slowing premium growth. This consolidation trend has a while left to run in the insurance business. Modest wage increases and slow employment growth have slowed the growth of sales and premiums, and expansion by acquisition is seen as more prudent and less risky for insurers in an environment of sluggish demand.

A Supreme Court decision to let banks in towns with fewer than 5,000 people sell insurance products will begin the inevitable erosion of the barriers that have traditionally existed between banks and insurance companies. No doubt some banks will pursue joint ventures rather than building an insurance division from scratch, an arrangement which would actually expand the distribution network for insurance companies.

Risks To The Outlook

Risks to P–C insurers include, as always, unforeseen catastrophes like hurricane Andrew in 1992. Compounding this ongoing event risk is the fact that traditional sources of re–insurance (insurance bought by a property–casualty insurer to help reduce its risk for catastrophe payouts) have mostly dried up since hurricane Andrew. In addition, should the investment markets turn negative for any reason, those P–C insurers that have pursued written premiums too aggressively by pricing the business too low, could find themselves in serious financial trouble rather quickly.

Life insurers are also at risk to the health of the financial markets. Poorly performing markets will directly affect life insurers' profitability. An upward spike in bond yields — which would lower the value of the industry's bond portfolios — would severely erode investment income. Moreover, increased litigation remains a constant threat to the life insurance industry, particularly if punitive damages spread from those states that are already considered high risk to those that aren't.

For HMOs, the possibility of Medicare reform and/or cuts in provider payments presents an ever–present threat to the status quo. Enrollment growth is also critical for HMO success, but this need is in conflict with the need to hold the line on prices. Such conflicts will fuel further consolidation.

Insurance Services
Growth in Sales (Line) and Volume (Bar)

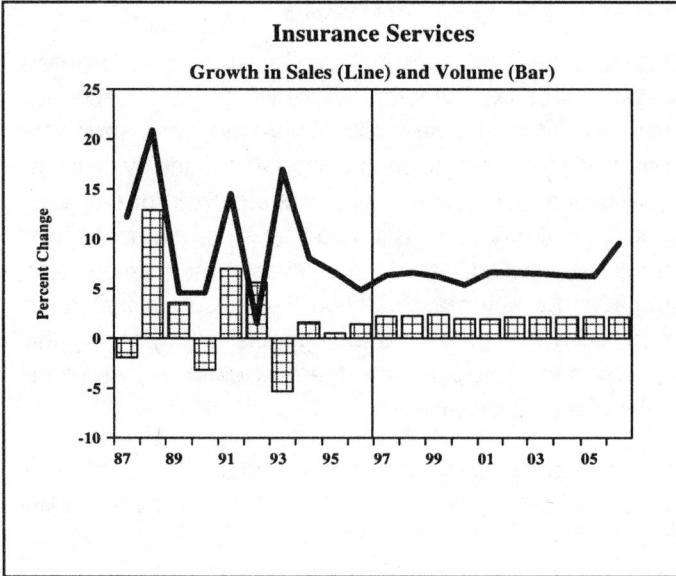

Insurance Services
Growth in Product Prices

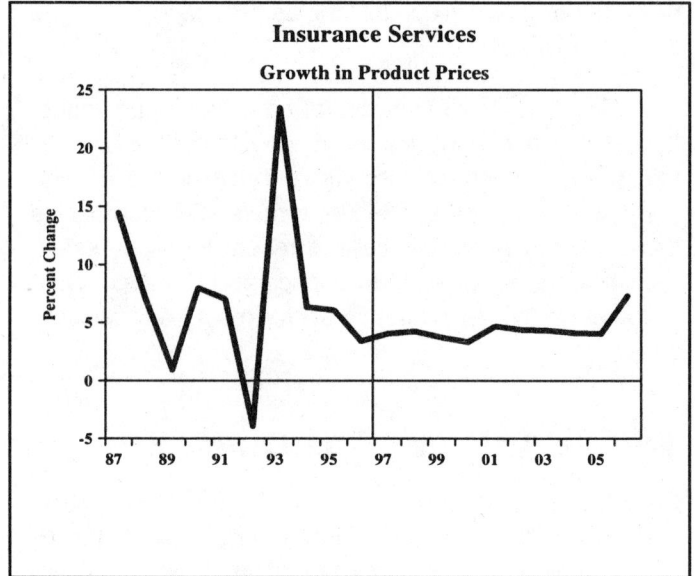

```
Insurance Services
  SIC 63-64

                                                                              Compound Ann Avg Growth
                      1990    1991    1992    1993    1994    1995    1996    1997    1998    1986-1996  1996-2006

Sales
        Billions of $ 228.49  261.73  265.77  310.84  335.84  358.08  375.47  399.41  425.73
        % Change      4.6     14.5    1.5     17.0    8.0     6.6     4.9     6.4     6.6       9.3        6.7

   Volume   % Change  -3.2    7.0     5.7     -5.3    1.6     0.5     1.4     2.2     2.3       2.1        2.2
   Prices   % Change  8.0     7.0     -3.9    23.5    6.3     6.0     3.4     4.0     4.2       7.0        4.4
```

28.9

Real Estate Services

The largest component of the real estate services industry is real estate agents and managers. Also included in this industry are lessors of railroad property, lessors of real property not elsewhere classified (n.e.c.), title abstract offices, land subdividers and developers, cemetery subdividers and developers, operators of residential mobile home sites, and operators of various types of buildings (nonresidential, apartments, and other buildings).

Inflation adjusted gains for the overall real estate services industry are likely to average less than 1% per year over the next few years as the U.S. economy slows and interest rates edge upward. Both short term cyclical and long term secular forces strongly suggest flatness in volume demand in the years just ahead.

Demand

Real estate agents and managers are primarily engaged in renting, buying, selling, managing, and appraising real estate for others. Every state requires that real estate brokers and agents be licensed, and that they complete educational courses and demonstrate their knowledge by passing examinations. Appraisers are often licensed and must also complete specialized training courses.

This subcomponent of the real estate services industry employs roughly 800,000 people dispersed among every state in the union. The health of the industry, as one would expect, varies with that of the housing industry. Sales of new homes were very strong in 1996, and sales of existing homes — which are of crucial importance to the real estate agency business — rose 7.5% in 1996. In the future, however, the aging economic expansion is expected to take its toll on this industry. Housing is one of the first industries to suffer when interest rates rise, and WEFA expects housing starts to be a bit lower in 1997 and 1998 as compared to 1996, and then remain flat for the next several years. Existing home sales should follow a similar trend.

Operators of non–residential buildings own and operate various types of non–residential properties, such as shopping centers, marinas, theaters, commercial and industrial buildings, and retail establishments. The overhang of excess commercial space and high vacancy rates beginning in the late 1980s, which carried over into the 1990s, resulted in serious problems for the industry. Cash shortages and mortgage defaults forced many into bankruptcy.

The commercial building bust of the late 1980s and early 1990s allowed large firms that had been financially prudent to buy up the assets of smaller operators at attractive prices. Office building vacancy rates nationwide peaked at 20.5% on an annual average basis in 1992, which was the height of the industry's woes. Some recovery occurred in 1993, however, and strong recovery followed in 1994 and 1995 as the national level vacancy rate dropped sharply to 14.3%.

At this point office and industrial building operators are doing well, since vacancy rates are down considerably from their 1992 levels. The excesses of the 1980s appear to have been avoided, for the most part, during the current economic expansion; and this should make another blowout like the late 1980s unlikely. WEFA expects stability, but not a lot of further growth, in this sector over the next few years as the U.S. economic expansion ages further. One key commercial space tenant, the retail trade industry, continues to consolidate, which tends to reduce space requirements. Rent increases on retail space have proven modest. Tenant sales have been flat; but the high bankruptcy rates of 1995 and 1996 in the retail industry have eased. Given expectations of continued market share gains by the giant discounters, at the expense of smaller operators, this sector should prove a sluggish source of demand for a few years yet.

Inflation adjusted gains for the overall real estate services industry are likely to average less than 1% per year over the next few years as the U.S. economy slows and interest rates edge upward. Both short term cyclical and long term secular forces strongly suggest flatness in volume demand in the years just ahead.

Supply Conditions

The supply of real estate agents is quite flexible, as agents are drawn into the business when home sales are strong and drift out of it when they are weak. While a great deal of money can be made as a real estate agent, the average full time agent, nationwide, earns less than $25,000 per year.

Prudent operators of non–residential buildings will avoid the excesses of debt that hammered the business so hard following the go–go years of the early and mid–1980s. Indeed, the firms that remain, having survived the shake–out of previous years, are likely to follow practices that promote more stability and reduce cyclicality within the industry.

The Forecast

For real estate agents and managers, the corporate emphasis on downsizing and cost reduction will continue to result in fewer company transfers and therefore fewer sales of existing homes. In fact, the downsizing of many higher level jobs in the U.S. economy and the slump in hiring at this level nationwide will keep gains in existing home sales rather meager in the years just ahead. Competition will continue to put pressure on commission rates, squeezing the incomes of agents and managers.

The major risk to real estate agents is higher interest rates. First, higher interest rates slow new housing sales, then they slow sales of interest–sensitive products like automobiles and appliances. These developments in turn slow, or reduce, employment, which hurts both consumer and business confidence levels. Lower levels of sales and investment in turn slow home sales even further. If business activity slows enough, recession could result. Thus, significantly higher interest rates are the biggest risk in the outlook for real estate agents.

The same risk holds for non–residential building operators. Higher interest rates will squeeze some of their tenants and put a portion of their revenues at risk. Recession, of course, would be worse, as it would hurt more companies in a wider number of industries.

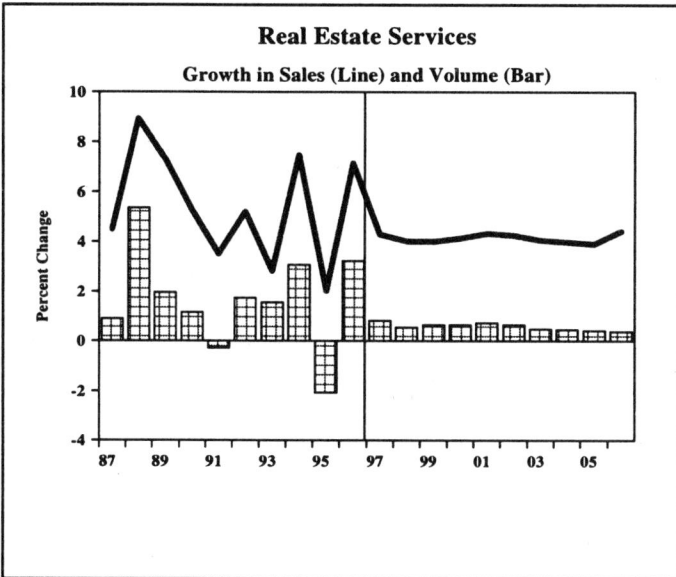

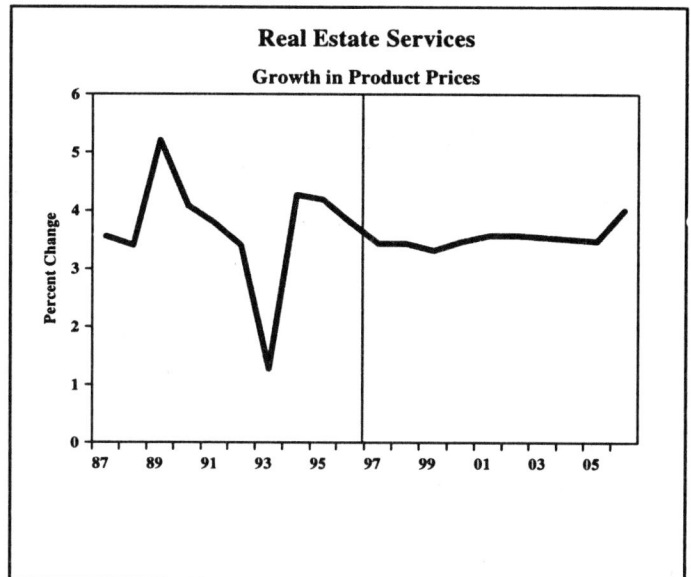

Real Estate Services

Growth in Sales (Line) and Volume (Bar)

Real Estate Services

Growth in Product Prices

Real Estate Services
 SIC 65

		1990	1991	1992	1993	1994	1995	1996	1997	1998	Compound Ann Avg Growth 1986-1996	1996-2006
Sales												
	Billions of $	867.93	898.38	945.05	971.88	1044.51	1065.68	1141.81	1190.66	1238.48		
	% Change	5.3	3.5	5.2	2.8	7.5	2.0	7.1	4.3	4.0	5.4	4.1
Volume	% Change	1.2	-0.3	1.7	1.5	3.1	-2.1	3.2	0.8	0.6	1.6	0.6
Prices	% Change	4.1	3.8	3.4	1.3	4.3	4.2	3.8	3.4	3.4	3.7	3.5

Chapter 29: Services

Business Services

Business services includes a wide variety of services, the largest of which is computer and data processing services, which is reported on separately. The other industry classifications in business services include: advertising; credit reporting agencies; mailing, reproduction, and stenographic services; building services; miscellaneous equipment rental and leasing; and personnel supply services. Apart from computer and data processing services, the largest sub–component of business services is personnel supply services, which includes employment agencies (about $4 billion in revenues per year) and temporary help agencies (about $26 billion in revenues per year). Building services ($10 billion) and advertising ($8 billion) follow in size.

For business services overall, we expect demand growth to exceed the U.S. all–industry average over the forecast period — as will price increases. Contracting service needs to independent vendors has become a way of life for American companies because of its convenience and flexibility.

Demand Conditions

Temporary help agencies have been one of the main benefactors of the downsizing and restructuring phenomenon of recent years. Firms have responded to competitive pressures by cutting full–time employment positions, and have turned to temp agencies to fill the gap in the short term. There are a number of benefits to using temporary workers that make the option attractive in spite of some of the negatives.

- The temporary worker typically earns less than a full–time worker, although the company is billed a higher amount to cover the fee to the temporary agency for supplying the worker. But the employer using such workers doesn't pay them benefits — such as health insurance, sick days, and vacation — and this more than offsets the somewhat higher total cost per hour over regular full–time employees.

- Temporary workers are only used when needed, which means they are not paid for down–time, as some full–timers are.

- There is no expense incurred for laying off or terminating temporary workers as there is with full–time employees.

In an environment of global competition, excess supply, and intense pressure to reduce costs, it is likely that the demand for temporary workers will continue to be strong. The proportion of U.S. workers that are temporaries will continue to rise over the forecast period. This will happen even if employment growth slows, as the trend toward greater use of temporaries — even in a stagnant economy — will continue.

Employment agencies have been impacted negatively by downsizing in recent years, and the reduced number of full–time positions available in some professions has forced many smaller specialized recruiters out of the business. Many of the surviving firms are focusing on hot areas of the labor market, such as computer processing professionals, or they are striving to find other ways to provide value to clients. Most find that competition within their industry remains intense. The industry is likely to continue to consolidate and shrink, but not in all occupations.

Initial figures suggest that 1996 was a good year for many advertising agencies, with total ad spending advancing by about 7% for the year. In the newspaper industry, gains in real estate ads and in the higher–margin category of employment ads fueled a strong year. Classified ads also did well in 1996 and are expected to do well again in 1997. While continued growth is expected in newspaper advertising in the years just ahead, the rate of growth will be slower than that of 1996. Magazine advertising showed some strength late in 1996, but ad pages were relatively soft for the year. An aging economic recovery suggests more modest advances in most types of advertising in the years just ahead.

For business services overall, we expect demand growth to exceed the all–industry average over the forecast period as will price increases. Contracting service work to independent vendors has become a way of life for many American companies because of its convenience and flexibility.

Supply Factors

There are few barriers to entry into the temporary agency business. The supply of such firms will continue to expand as the demand for temporary help increases. As the demand for temporary employees continues to move beyond traditional clerical jobs toward technical and professional jobs, the need for temporary agencies to provide training for the people they provide will increase.

The employment agencies' business is also an easy one to enter, but one that is quite competitive and not as promising in growth terms as temporary agencies. Competition has been pressuring fees lower and forcing some firms out of business. Employment shopping on the internet also poses a threat to employment agencies as well as to temporary agencies, but sites are not yet well developed and it will take some time for them to become truly competitive.

The Outlook

The nature of the American workplace has changed. Emphasis on productivity and cost reduction has been relentless for at least a decade, and the globalization of the economy — spurred by revolutions in computer and information technology, as well as the increased flexibility in capital markets — will keep unrelenting competitive pressure on most industries. Any device that can be used to reduce the cost of labor, whether hiring temporary workers, investing in new technology, or piling more work on the current workforce, will be given careful consideration.

The key risks for the business services industries are economic in nature. Services provided by both employment and temporary help agencies are provided to numerous industries and types of business, so anything that slows employment growth is likely to negatively impact business services — although employment agencies are likely to be hurt more than temporary agencies. Higher wages would slow business demand for workers as would higher interest rates. The same can be said for advertising: anything that slows the economy and employment growth is likely to have a negative impact on advertising expenditures. The automobile industry and retailing are important segments of demand for advertising services, and both are quite sensitive to overall consumer and economic trends.

The internet could bring changes to these industries in the future. Some advertising already appears on the internet; and some screening of employment recruits is also electronic.

Business Services
Growth in Sales (Line) and Volume (Bar)

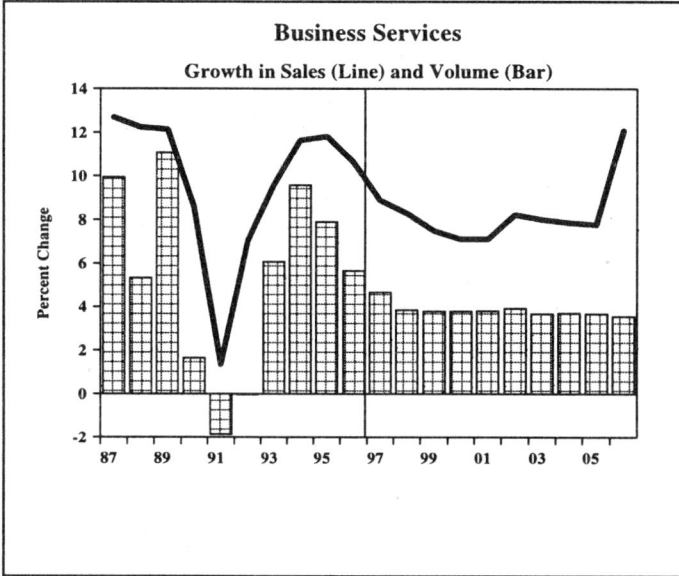

Business Services
Growth in Product Prices

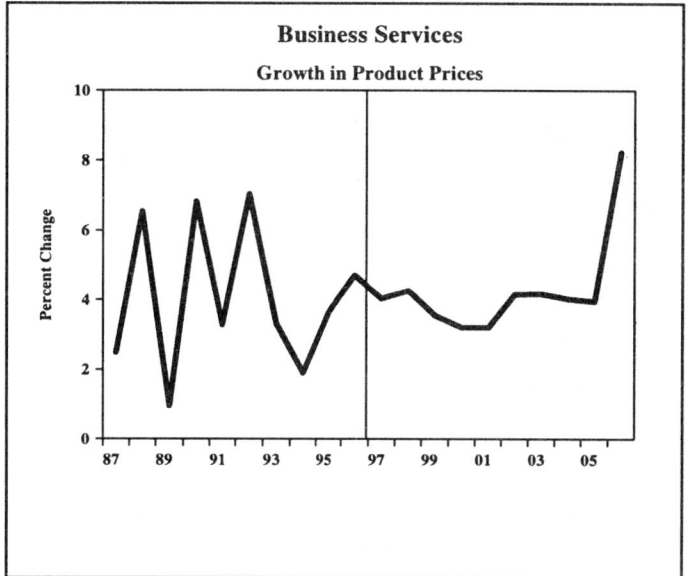

Business Services
SIC 73

		1990	1991	1992	1993	1994	1995	1996	1997	1998	Compound Ann Avg Growth 1986-1996	1996-2006
Sales												
	Billions of $	287.60	291.49	311.95	341.81	381.61	426.67	472.04	514.01	556.52		
	% Change	8.6	1.4	7.0	9.6	11.6	11.8	10.6	8.9	8.3	9.7	8.3
Volume	% Change	1.7	-1.9	-0.0	6.1	9.6	7.9	5.7	4.7	3.9	5.4	3.8
Prices	% Change	6.8	3.3	7.0	3.3	1.9	3.6	4.7	4.0	4.3	4.0	4.3

Computer Programming, Data Processing, and Related Services

The computer programming industry is comprised of companies that provide computer programming services on a contract or fee basis. Additional services are often provided, such as software design and analysis, modifications to custom software, and training clients in the use of custom software. Companies in the data processing industry provide computer processing and data preparation services. These services could include partial or full preparation of reports, data entry, or computer processing power or storage through timesharing computer services. The companies in these industries perform specialized business services for their clients more cheaply than the clients could have the work done in–house. Often the outsourcing cost advantage is due to economies of scale and specialization that make such operations cost–effective and profitable.

The computer programming and data processing services business has undergone a number of changes over the last decade. Future growth will come mainly from continued corporate outsourcing and from businesses' need for technical assistance with increasingly complex hardware and software decisions and support. Overall, WEFA expects gains of about 10% per year in revenues for this industry over the next two to three years, and then a gradual slowing in annual growth, due to maturation in the market, to the 7% to 8% range.

Demand Environment

The rapid growth in contract programming experienced in the 1980s eased somewhat in the early 1990s due to the increasing use of prepackaged software. This change was an inevitable part of the hardware evolution that brought more and more powerful desktop computers into offices and functions formerly serviced by mainframe computers. Despite this slowdown in its growth, the computer programming and data processing businesses remain healthy. Two important trends are still at work keeping programmers busy.

- First is the realization that it is expensive to hire permanent staff to keep up with rapidly changing technology and evolving hardware. It is often much cheaper to contract outside help in both the programming area and in the data processing (payroll, etc.) area.

- Second, the rapid development of electronic mail and networked computers has increased the need for computer systems expertise that only the largest firms can justify as internal cost.

On the negative side, computer–assisted software engineering tools, graphic user interfaces, and the continued popularity of prepackaged software for many applications have all been factors in the slowing of demand for custom programming services. These trends will continue, but on balance the circumstances that require specialized outside knowledge will spread enough to reinforce the trend toward the outsourcing of data processing work.

U.S. custom programmers are also in demand overseas, and the export of these services from the U.S. programming industry — the world leader in the field — continues to offer good possibilities.

Computer processing timesharing services have declined in recent years as networking hardware and software has advanced. However, some of the business lost goes to other parts of these industries, since a switch from timesharing may be a switch to outsourcing of the entire data processing function.

WEFA expects gains of about 10% per year in revenues for this industry over the next two to three years. After that time, annual growth will gradually ease to the 7% to 8% range as the market matures.

Supply Factors

In the mid–1990s it was estimated that there were over 4,000 companies and many more sole proprietorships in the United States offering computer programming and related services. Since the output produced in this industry is knowledge, and the business requires a relatively small outlay for capital equipment, there are few barriers to new companies entering the market. However, these small start–up operations also have high failure rates, as competition is intense and small companies have little in reserve for a rainy day.

In the early 1990s there were about 7,000 data processing services in operation, ranging from one–person shops to much larger corporations hiring several hundred people or more.

Both of these businesses have supported a large number of companies, including many small firms, largely through the dynamic environment that comes with rapidly changing technology. Logic suggests that as the pace of change slows, these industries will undergo a consolidation process to increase efficiencies and economies of scale. Constant pressure from clients to keep prices low will keep competitive pressure keen, particularly in the data processing services area.

Industry Trends

Despite some trends toward standardization and pre–programmed software, companies continue to turn to outside programming and data processing professionals.

It has simply become too expensive for some, particularly smaller concerns, to afford the staff and constant training required to keep up with constantly changing technology . In addition, labor markets for programmers are very tight in many parts of the country, making outsourcing more cost–competitive as well as a detour around hiring bottle-necks.

This industry is likely to face some softening in pricing power over the next ten years. Although firms find it somewhat more difficult to negotiate down the cost of purchased services as compared to goods purchases, there is persistent pressure everywhere to cut costs. In addition, the tight labor markets in the skilled occupations crucial to this industry will certainly push up payroll costs. It is the evolution of this squeeze that makes consolidation among firms in order to take advantage of the economies of scale more likely.

The Outlook and Forecast Risks

Data processing for payroll and other business functions is very dependent upon the course of the economy. A growing economy means more payroll checks, more invoices, and more business. With the U.S. economy in its sixth year of expansion and with interest rates rising, the pace of growth is likely to slow and the risk of recession to increase.

In the longer term, there is the risk that the lower costs and enhanced efficiencies of corporate computing via networks and client/server technology will make it feasible for companies to bring outsourced data processing functions back in–house. However, a much larger supply of workers with the appropriate skills would be required for this eventuality to occur.

Computer Software and Networking

This industry includes establishments engaged in the design, development, and production of prepackaged computer software. The software typically takes one of three forms: operating systems software, which determines how a computer operates; applications software, such as word processing or accounting programs; and utility software, which is designed to perform support functions for both operating systems and/or applications. This software can be for personal computers (PCs), mainframes, or minicomputers.

Computer software and networking are dynamic businesses that have taken a number of turns over the past decade. Future growth will come mainly from client/server applications and utilities — both from the mainframes or minis that power them and the PCs that connect to them — rather than from the traditional market for standalone units. WEFA forecasts gains of about 10% to 12% per year in revenues for this industry over the next two to three years, then a gradual moderation to a rate of roughly 8% to 9% per year after that.

Demand

Prepackaged software experienced explosive growth in recent years as the power and memory capabilities of personal computers expanded dramatically. In corporate applications, many functions that were previously run on larger computers, such as minicomputers or mainframes, are now being performed by smaller, but quite powerful personal or desktop computers. Moreover, many firms have come to the decision that writing their own programs is not cost effective, and they are therefore more interested in prepackaged software. On the negative side, however, the software market has been penetrating the market and maturing rapidly. Many users already have the bulk of the computer and software capability they need, and future growth will depend more on new business growth than in the past.

As PCs have become more powerful, software sales to mainframe and minicomputer users have stalled, even though they still account for a significant amount of total revenue for the firms that offer such products. The most important applications for these larger computers have been accounting and database management packages. More recently, however, the reorienting of mainframes to a central role in client/server technology has spurred sales of mainframe software for this application.

The trend toward networks and the client/server computing structure has also had a significant impact on the prepackaged software industry. With the spread of network servers has come new demands for software products that can run in many operating environments and network configurations. In addition, networking has opened up new opportunities for PC utilities software providers to give these machines the added features and functionality they need to take advantage of client/server efficiencies. Moreover, the demand for database management software continues strong, and has also been affected by the trend toward client/server setups.

In the PC market, the release of Microsoft's Windows 95 continues to generate demand for software products that provide applications and utilities to support it. Two areas that are particularly strong right now are maintenance related: virus–checking programs and diagnostic utilities. The large installed base of Microsoft Windows users provided a ready market for these products, and the brisk sales of Windows 95 have clearly added to it.

We must not overlook the impact of the primary force driving business today, and that force is downsizing or restructuring. During the recession of the early 1990s business continued to invest in new software, particularly in that which it felt would reduce costs or in some way make the firm more competitive in an increasingly competitive workplace. As the U.S. business recovery is now in its sixth year, the pressure to keep costs down, and even to cut them further if possible, has not abated. However, this frenzy by companies to expand computer capabilities quickly has no doubt borrowed some demand from the future, and growth will likely slow as the market matures.

The real question is whether technology will ever sit still long enough for the market to mature. Each time it appears that utilization of current applications is reaching a limit to penetration, new applications and expanded hardware capabilities pull the industry in yet another exciting direction.

Supply Factors

The price of hardware has come down dramatically in recent years, and the competition in prepackaged software has intensified. Together these developments have led to considerable price reductions on commercial software. Downward price pressure on these products will continue. This link with the hardware price and technology spiral dramatizes the similarities between the two industries. In both cases, it is a new wave of technology that makes the price of the old technology nose–dive, and it is these sudden changes in ground rules that make operating a business in these industries so treacherous.

Within the corporate server market, the battle between Microsoft's Windows NT and Novell's UNIX operating systems continues. Demand for both will likely continue to grow. Windows NT may grow faster because it is less expensive, but this more rapid growth is expected to take place at the lower–end segment of the server market where there is less complexity. UNIX remains a more robust operating system for high–capacity computers due to its support of a greater number of applications and better communications capabilities. However, technology changes can turn this competition on its head rapidly.

The Outlook

If chaos and confusion no longer reign in the information systems business, uncertainty still does. Technology continues to expand and change at a dizzying pace. The primary trend that will drive many others in the future is that of corporations continuing to cut costs to remain competitive. For many, particularly smaller firms, this may mean increased outsourcing of data processing functions. For others it will mean moving toward the powerful efficiencies of the client/server network. As the market for computers becomes more saturated, savvy software producers will have to stay on the leading edge of what the market wants to prosper.

The internet offers tremendous potential as commerce gears up to trip into cyberspace. Although it is already large, this is a fledgling business in terms of development and software, and much software remains to be developed. These windows of opportunity will have to be recognized and seized fast, however, because they will not remain open for long.

Risks to the software business in the past have not been so much cyclical as they are secular; but that may be changing. The benefits of computerization are such that firms have tended to go forward with hardware and software purchases even while the economy has been soft, since such purchases have tended to provide quick improvement to the bottom line. However, future recessions may have a more severe impact on the industry, since the market is more fully penetrated. During the next recession, the market for both hardware and software will be more mature and it may be easier to delay new purchases. This would result in a more cyclical industry than we have seen to date.

The most serious risk to companies in this industry is the rapidity with which technology is changing. Serious losses can be incurred by coming to the market slightly too late to take advantage of the latest trend, or by being left concentrated in the old technology that sells at a steep discount.

Equipment Leasing

Leasing is a method of obtaining the use of an asset without actually owning the asset. The length of time and cost involved in a lease agreement is predetermined. Finance leases and operating leases are the two most common methods. In a finance lease, the leasing company recovers all costs incurred plus a rate of return, with the lessee responsible for maintenance, taxes, and insurance. Operating leases are usually short–term, and the lessee acquires the use of equipment for a small portion of its economic or useful life. Other variations include: the leveraged lease, where the leasing company provides an equity portion of the equipment cost and lenders provide the balance; and the sale–leaseback, where a leasing company purchases equipment from the company that owns and uses it and then leases it back to that company.

Equipment leasing volume was put at about $169 billion last year, an increase of 11.6% above the 1995 level. Business investment in machinery and equipment grew by 7% in 1996, reaching $577 billion. Over the last ten years, equipment leasing grew by 8% per year, while total machinery and equipment investment expanded by 9.5% annually. Leasing's market penetration during this period peaked in 1989 at 34.3%, and hit a low of 28.1% in 1995. Last year, leasing accounted for 29.3% of total machinery and equipment investment, up from 28.1% in the previous year.

About 80% of U.S. companies lease all or some of their equipment. Leasing is particularly attractive to small and start–up companies that may not have the financial wherewithal to purchase equipment. Leasing allows for rental payments that are more in line with financial capability. It also provides access to equipment for companies that want to focus on their core business and view the ownership of certain types of equipment as incidental. Full service leasing provides operational and maintenance support. Finally, leasing is also an excellent way to satisfy equipment needs during peak periods of demand.

There are approximately 2,000 companies in the United States that provide leases. These include banks, independent leasing companies, and industrial finance companies. Equipment lessors own equipment worth more than $400 billion. Smaller companies tend to specialize in a certain type of equipment, but major leasing companies have a very broad equipment portfolio. Leasing companies are particularly active in the aircraft, computer and telecommunications, industrial and manufacturing, medical, construction and material handling, and rail and on–highway equipment markets. Captive leasing, that is leasing that is done by an arm of the equipment manufacturer, is common in agricultural equipment, construction machinery, commercial trucks and trailers, and office equipment.

Up to 25% of some types of medical equipment is leased. The value of computers leased was about $25 billion in 1996, or about one–third of total spending for such equipment. The commercial aircraft market has seen strong growth in leasing company activity in recent years. In 1986, 41% of the world's airlines owned all of their equipment, 15% leased, and 44% used a mix of the two. Last year, 16% owned all of their equipment, 42% leased, and 42% used a mix of the two. In recent years, between 35% and 40% of all medium and heavy trucks added to the fleet have been leased. A whopping 60% of passenger cars in corporate fleets are leased. Finally, major leasing companies, such as GE Rail Car Services and First Union Rail, control large portions of the nation's rail freight car fleet.

All types of equipment do not equally attract the eye of leasing companies. With the exception of the captive lessors, leasing companies have pretty much exited the agricultural equipment business. In 1980 there were over a half–dozen leasing companies in the Midwest with a very heavy focus on the farm equipment market. By 1995, after the farm crisis of the 1980s scared leasing companies, no leasing companies were pursuing the business. Recent improvements in farm sector finances have made the area more attractive to leasing companies, but they have not begun to aggressively court the business. Another area where leasing companies tread slowly is the restaurant business, where business failure rates are particularly high.

Forecast

WEFA forecasts that business spending for machinery and equipment will expand by 5.7% this year to $610 billion, and 4.8% in 1998 to $639 billion. In the longer run, spending should grow by roughly 5.5% per year, on average, reaching $912 billion by 2006.

- We expect computers and related equipment to post the strongest increases during the next ten years, driven by a steady stream of new and more capable products. Growth in communication equipment will remain healthy driven by efforts in the public and private sector to improve voice and data communication systems. Spending for computers and communication equipment is expected to expand by about 6.0% per year.

- Commercial aircraft is in the early stages of a cycle that will include replacement of existing older aircraft and a significant expansion of the fleet over the next ten years.

- A replacement cycle will stimulate demand for commercial trucks and trailers during the next few years, and demand will advance modestly thereafter.

- Rail equipment purchases will be influenced by expanding traffic and improvements in rail industry efficiency.

- Growth in spending for industrial equipment will reflect anticipated growth in manufacturing volume of 2.5%–3.0% per year which will trigger some industrial capacity expansion.

- Finally, corporate demand for passenger cars, and spending for construction and farm equipment will be modest.

Equipment leasing volume is forecast to expand from $169 billion in 1996 to $280 billion in 2006. While total investment in machinery and equipment will grow by just under 6% per year, on average, during the 1996–2006 period, we expect leasing volume to expand by close to 6.5% per year. By the end of the ten–year period we expect leased equipment will account for almost 31% of total spending.

Growth in leasing volume will reflect the strength we anticipate in demand for computers and communication equipment, two areas where leasing activity is well established. Additional support will come from the aircraft, rail, and over–the–road transportation markets where leasing already plays a major role. In addition, there will be steady growth in the leasing of medical equipment. Technology is allowing the development of highly sophisticated diagnostic instruments, which usually carry a hefty price tag, and the population is aging and requiring more medical care. The net result is that the demand for medical equipment will continue to expand at a healthy clip.

The equipment leasing business in the United States is part of a global industry, with more than half of the business now conducted in Europe and Japan. We believe leasing activity outside of the United States will also be expanding at a fast pace, driven by favorable world economic conditions. The Canadian economy is in the early stages of a solid recovery. The recovery in Mexico is well underway, and conditions in the rest of Latin America are also improving. The Japanese economy will expand by only about 2% this year, but the longer term growth rate is more along the lines of 2.5%–3.0% per year. China offers great opportunities with economic growth expected to remain close to 9% per year into the next decade. Opportunities will also abound in the rest of Asia. Finally, while economic growth in Western Europe will be modest, there is hope that the former Soviet Union and the rest of Eastern Europe will stage a recovery during the coming decade. All of this growth will be beneficial to the leasing industry, which has opportunities to increase market penetration as well.

Motion Pictures

The primary segments of the motion picture industry are: motion picture and video tape production, which includes the production of theatrical and non–theatrical motion pictures and video tapes for exhibition or sale; motion picture theaters; and home video rentals.

Sales of theater tickets (both domestic and foreign) and video cassette sales and rentals combined grew by about 7% in 1996, with the most rapid growth occurring in video sales. In the future, WEFA expects market penetration of VCRs to reach a level that will force a slowdown in the rate of growth of video sales. Revenue of the movie industry (the total in these three formats) should also see a moderating growth trend over the next few years from its current rate to one closer to 5% per year.

Demand

While there are many companies in the movie production business, five companies account for about 75% of the industry's revenues: Columbia, Disney, Fox, Universal, and Warner. Success in the industry requires three things: a wide distribution network, access to large amounts of capital, and the talent or luck to know what the market wants and to come to market with the right thing at the right time. The top 100 movies in 1996 brought $4.5 billion into box offices in the United States, up from $4.2 billion in 1995.

The portion of the industry that includes the sale (but not the rental) of video tapes has experienced strong growth in recent years and has even surpassed theater box office revenues by a wide margin. The rising cost of theater tickets, combined with lower prices for movies on video cassette, has provided a strong incentive for this reversal in market share — a movie can often be purchased a short while after its theater release for a price equivalent to two or three theater tickets. Sales of movies on video cassette rose strongly in 1996, reaching $5.7 billion. Movie rentals totaled another $2.5 billion, bringing the total revenue figure for videos — both sold and rented — to $8.2 billion in 1996, an increase of 11% over 1995. In 1996, 20th Century Fox became the third company to reach annual sales of video cassettes above the billion dollar level, behind Disney and Warner.

When the video industry was new, it was feared that the rental or purchase of movies on video would hurt theaters, but it seems to have simply broadened the market. Cable television is another distribution channel for near–new movies that was feared to hurt theaters, but its impact seems to have been positive. The biggest problem with movie production has long been the high initial outlay of cash necessary to produce a film. Expansion in the cable television industry has increased the demand for new movies to keep cable subscribers happy, and the large cable networks, like HBO and Showtime, have proven to be a considerable new source of financing. The networks' contribution even is timed correctly — they often buy the rights to movies before they have been produced. This influx of funds has allowed many smaller producers to make movies that they would not have otherwise made. In the process, video sales are surging, video rentals remain strong, and theater box office revenues are at record levels.

Motion picture theaters suffered a decline in total revenues from $6.2 billion in 1991 to $5.9 billion in 1992, but then sales recovered to $6.1 billion in 1993 and rose strongly to $6.5 billion in 1994. Despite the strength in video sales and rentals, as noted above, theaters continue to set records. Theaters are often the initial market for films, which then go on to video cassette sales and rentals, premium channels on cable television, and then traditional television stations. The ten largest theater companies in the United States operate almost half of the country's movie screens, with United Artists the largest of the ten by a wide margin. Some theater owners, however, have attempted to upgrade the theater experience by expanding concession options (which raises the portion of revenues they don't have to split with distributors) and by offering phone–ahead and credit–card ticket sales. The multi–screen theater complex seems to attract more customers through its wide selection of movies.

Internationally, sales of movies made in the United States are doing quite well, and in 1996 revenues from abroad again outpaced domestic sales. In contrast to domestic box office sales for the 100 best selling movies in 1996 of $4.5 billion, revenues from sales of U.S. movies by foreign box offices equaled $5.1 billion. The top overall seller in 1996 was *Independence Day*, which sold over $300 million in domestic theater tickets and the same abroad, bringing the film's total sales to roughly $700 million! Even the Kevin Costner movie *Waterworld,* considered a big disappointment in the U.S. market, sold very well overseas. When $9.5 billion in box office ticket sales, both domestic and foreign, is combined with $8.2 billion in video sales and rentals, 1996 was a very good year for American movie producers.

The Outlook

Sales of theater tickets (both domestic and foreign) and video cassette sales and rentals combined grew by about 7% in 1996, with the most rapid growth occurring in video sales. In the future, WEFA expects market penetration of VCRs to reach a level that will force a slowdown in the rate of growth of video sales. Revenue of the movie industry (the total in these three formats) should also see a moderating growth trend over the next few years from its current rate to one closer to 5% per year.

Major film studios have been drifting toward the elimination of the wholesaler as middle man and have instead been selling videos direct to retail outlets such as Wal-

mart, K–Mart, and Best Buys. This trend has proven profitable and is likely to continue. Another trend, resulting from the strength in video cassette sales, is increased shelf space for video for sale within video rental retail space. These companies, such as Blockbuster, the nation's largest, have concluded that video sales are profitable and don't compete with the rental business to the extent they had feared.

Cable based pay–per–view options remain a threat to video rentals, but not yet a large one. Pay–per–view viewing prices are equal to or often slightly above those for video rentals. They offer the convenience of eliminating the trip to the video store, but they have the drawback of offering only a single viewing with no pause options. In order for pay–per–view to become a serious threat to video rental, either prices will have to come down or flexible viewing options will have to become more widespread.

It is possible that the potential threat to theaters from video sales and rentals will eventually become a reality. The price growth in theater tickets is on a collision course with two other trends: lower prices of videos for sale and for rent and heightened cost–consciousness on the part of consumers. The motion picture market overall has developed enough momentum through these relatively new distribution outlets to grow sufficiently to support healthy growth in all the market segments, but slowing growth through saturation or weaker economic conditions would likely be felt disproportionately in movie theater ticket sales.

Health Services

Health services is one of the largest sectors of the U.S. economy. Consumer expenditures on health care services accounted for 16% of total consumer expenditures and 11% of Gross Domestic Product (GDP) in 1996. By comparison, total consumer expenditures on motor vehicles and parts accounted for only 3% of GDP. Employment in health services establishments totaled 9.6 million, or 8% of total establishment employment.

Health services spending can be broadly divided into four categories: professional services (including physicians, dentists, and other health professionals), hospital services, nursing home services, and insurance services. Hospitals account for 46%, or almost half of all health care spending, and professional fees account for another 40%. Nursing homes and insurance costs each total 7% of total health services spending. (Note that insurance costs in the table below are net of payments by insurance companies to providers.)

Health Care Services Spending by Type 1996

Hospitals	46%
Professional Services	40%
Nursing Homes	7%
Insurance	7%

Source: Bureau of Economic Analysis

Demand For Health Care

As is widely known, the demand for health care services has been growing rapidly in the United States in the past 20 years. From 1976 to 1996, health services spending, after accounting for inflation, grew at an annual average rate of 3.5%, considerably above the 2.9% growth in real consumption expenditures. As a result, health care spending is growing in importance in consumption and GDP, and consequently has become a target of major policy initiatives.

Three factors have driven the rise in health care spending:

- An increasing Federal role. Over half of all spending for medical care is financed by the Federal government or the state portion of the Medicaid program.

Health care spending is therefore closely related to the U.S. budget problem, and many of the risks to the outlook in this industry derive from efforts to close the budget gap by reforming the Federal medical entitlement programs.

- Technology. Medical research has progressed substantially in the recent past, allowing cures for conditions that were fatal only a decade ago. The breathtaking ability of medical science to diagnose and treat illness has been accompanied, however, by a rise in cost. Many of the new procedures and drugs are very expensive.

- Demographics. Older people use more medical care. The average consumer aged 75 years and older spent $2,787 on medical care in 1994, while the average consumer aged 25 to 35 years old spent only $1,086. The proportion of Americans who are older is growing steadily as birth rates fall and technology allows people to live longer.

During the very recent past, the growth in demand for health care services has slowed. After growing between 1980 and 1992 by almost 4% per year, spending adjusted for inflation on health care services has slowed to around 2% per year. This is the result of massive changes in the industry, as well as a slowdown in the growth of the elderly population.

In the near future, the inflation-adjusted growth rate of spending for health care services will likely pick up again.

The portion of the population aged 65 and over will start to rise more quickly in a few years, while the impact of managed care will fade. Technology and higher incomes will continue to drive spending in health care over the next 10 years.

Supply

Health care supply must be divided into market segments: the supply of professional workers, the supply of hospital beds, and the supply of insurance and management services. In the 1980s all expanded quickly as health care spending grew rapidly. Their fate in the 1990s has differed, however.

The Supply of Professionals

The delivery of health care services requires, perhaps more than in any other industry except education, highly trained professional workers. The major categories of professional health care workers are physicians and nurses. The supply of other types of workers, including occupational and physical therapists and physician's assistants, are growing rapidly, but these workers still make up a relatively small portion of the total professional workforce.

The number of physicians and nurses has been rising quite a bit faster than the overall population. The number of practicing physicians grew by 3% to 3.5% in the 1970s and 1980s, although this growth has slowed to about 3% in the past few years. (Figures for physicians by specialty are from the American Medical Association, *Physician Characteristics and Distribution in the U.S.*, annual.) Almost all of the growth in the number of physicians has been in specialists. The number of physicians in family practice grew only seven thousand (from 51 to 58 thousand) between 1970 and 1994, an average annual growth rate of only 0.5%.

The number of registered nurses has been growing faster than the number of physicians. In 1970 there were 750,000 registered nurses, but by 1994 the number had grown to 2.04 million, logging average annual growth of over 4%. (Figures for the number of nurses come from The National League for Nursing, *NLN Data Book*, annual.) The growth in the number of nurses is slowing a bit, but remains in the still-rapid range of 3% per year, despite an increasingly unstable job market at hospitals.

The Supply Of Hospital Beds

Hospitals are the second major category of health care service. Hospital capacity is usually measured by the number of hospital beds and by occupancy rates. In 1994, there were 1.128 million hospital beds in the United States, down from 1.550 million in 1972. Much of the decline took place in the 1980s, but the number of hospital beds has continued to decline in the 1990s. The number of hospitals has also declined, but much more slowly, so the average size of each hospital has fallen from 220 beds in 1972 to 177 beds in 1994.

The decline in the number of beds is a result of technology and pressure from health insurers. Both factors have contributed to turn inpatient procedures into outpatient procedures. Technology advances allow safer, less invasive surgery, and faster recovery from surgery. Insurers have questioned the length of stays generally required for many procedures, and in some cases have refused to pay to keep a patient in the hospital for longer than the insurer's physician advisors believe necessary. As a result of these trends, both the number of procedures performed and spending on surgery and hospital procedures have risen at the same time the number of hospital beds has declined.

Of more immediate importance to the industry is the consolidation of hospitals (and, to some extent, professional practices) into larger provider networks. For hospitals, this generally occurs through mergers. The number of hospital mergers and joint ventures has accelerated in the past few years, as organizations rush to achieve economies of scale in providing health care services. This has two results: first the number of independent community hospitals is declining, and second, the line between for-profit and non-profit hospitals is becoming blurred. For-profit hospitals remain a small segment of the market, accounting for only 8% of the revenues of all community hospitals. This number has been slowly growing, however, and for-profit hospitals can be expected to continue to play an important role in the current shake-out of hospital capacity.

Insurers and Health Maintenance Organizations

Insurers and Health Maintenance Organizations (HMOs) play a unique role in the American health care system. These organizations pay much of the actual bill on behalf of consumers. Traditional insurance plans allow consumers to purchase health care from any provider. The consumer then either directs the provider to bill the insurance company, or requests reimbursement after paying the provider. In general, such plans allow the consumer freedom in choosing health care options.

HMOs typically provide services directly. These organizations may even have their own staffs of physicians and other professionals, and their own hospitals. In other cases, the HMO contracts with certain providers, and the consumer must obtain health care through those providers. HMO providers must follow specific rules in treatment and referral; the rules vary among HMOs. HMO payments to providers may take the form of salaries, with bonuses for cost containment, or *capitation agreements*, in which the provider (hospital or professional partnership) agrees to a fixed price per patient, regardless of the actual treatment.

There are also hybrid HMO-insurance schemes in which certain providers are preferred because they have contracted agreements, but consumers may obtain partial reimbursement for treatment by non-preferred providers, for example.

As noted above, 7% of total health services expenditures pays for the services of these organizations. This is measured as the difference between the revenues of the insurance companies and HMOs, and their payments to providers. These services include the cost of salaries and wages for the clerical, management, and professional workers in the companies (except those involved in direct patient care), rents and other expenses, and the profits of the insurance companies and HMOs.

The insurance market, like the hospital market, is divided between for-profit and not-for-profit providers. HMOs are mostly private, but some of the not-for-profit insurers have created HMO subsidiaries. HMOs have been growing rapidly in recent years. From 1987 to 1995, the share of all insured covered by an HMO rose from 14% to 21% (Figures for the total insured population are from the Bureau of the Census; figures for HMO membership are from the Group Health *Association's National Directory of HMOs*, annual.) HMOs have gained market share in both the private and public sector. In the private sector, HMOs have proven to be able to keep costs from growing quickly, and have thus attracted the attention of corporate purchasers of health insurance. The public sector has found HMOs to be useful cost controls in both the

Medicare and Medicaid programs. Some elderly are now covered through Medicare payments to HMOs, a procedure which is designed to reduce costs to the federal government. States are moving aggressively to contract Medicaid services, especially those for poor families, to managed care providers. There is evidence that this is both cheaper and results in better health outcomes for this population.

Most of those covered by private health insurance are still covered by traditional plans, however. In 1995, 186 million people, or 70% of the population, were covered by private health insurance. HMO membership (including some people covered by government medical insurance) totaled 46 million in 1995, leaving at least 139 million people still covered by some type of traditional private health insurance.

As in the hospital sector, the insurance/HMO sector has been undergoing consolidation. This has taken several related forms:

- Mergers between health insurers, including mergers between traditional insurance companies and HMOs.

- The sale of not-for-profit health insurers to for-profit entities. This generally entails the creation of a foundation to hold and spend the surplus value earned by the not-for-profit partner in the transaction.

- The merging of roles as HMOs and traditional insurers begin to take on similar functions.

Pricing

Health care pricing has been at the center of a national debate for some years. As measured by the Bureau of Labor Statistics, the price of health care rose faster than overall consumer prices for many years. Higher medical costs have pushed up compensation costs for many companies, and left health insurance unaffordable for many smaller companies and individuals.

The sources of the higher medical inflation include:

- Fast demand growth, allowing providers to increase profits or surplus (for non-profit institutions).

- Technology-driven demand, as expensive (but effective) procedures came into general use. Note that this implies that the Consumer Price Index (CPI) measure of health care costs may be biased, because it may not pick up the improved quality of health care due to the new technology.

Medical Care Inflation Was Higher than Overall Inflation During the 1980s

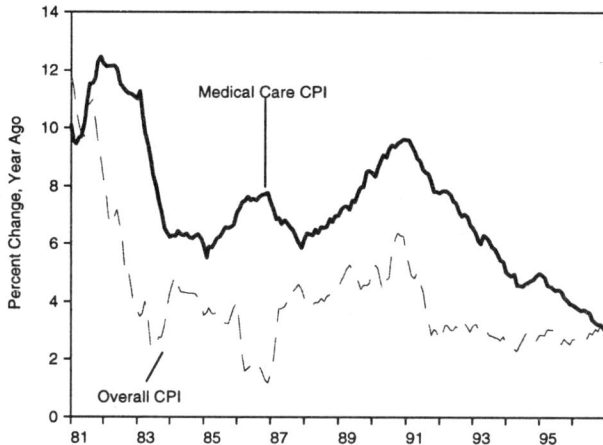

- The existence of the third-party payment system. Most health care payments are made not by the user, but by an insurance company, HMO, or government agency. This allows users to ignore the full marginal cost of using additional health care resources.

- The ethics and sociology of the health professions, which traditionally teach practitioners to ignore costs in making treatment decisions.

Experts have hotly debated the importance of each of these factors in pushing up medical care prices.

In 1996, the medical care CPI rose at a slower rate than overall consumer prices for the first time since 1980. This phenomenon appears to be the result of several years of aggressive action on the part of the employer-purchasers of health management and on the part of the health insurance organizations themselves. One symptom of this aggressiveness has been the rising proportion of people covered by HMOs instead of traditional health insurance.

Some of the most dramatic slowing in health care inflation occurred in 1996. As the portion of the public covered by managed care (HMOs and other preferred provider plans) grows, additional gains in cost cutting will become harder to obtain. The impact of technology and demand growth (from a larger portion of older people in

the population) will keep health care inflation about one percentage point above the general inflation rate in the near future.

Industry Structure

The Changing Organization of the Health Care Sector

The health care sector has traditionally been very fragmented, with professional partnerships, hospitals, managed care companies, insurance companies, and many others providing service, sometimes in overlapping pieces. The current wave of mergers among all types of health care organizations is creating two broad classes.

- *Health care provider networks* are based around hospitals. Often the lead hospital is a tertiary care and teaching facility in a large urban area, but this role may be taken by a for-profit hospital chain as well. Through ownership and partnerships with community hospitals and professional practices, the network becomes a complete provider of all health care services, from simple family practice to the most complex surgical procedures. These large provider organizations can obtain the benefits of economies of scale in management and marketing.

- *Health care management organizations* are based around insurance or managed care organizations. Their purpose is to police the provider networks, insuring that costs are kept under control and quality is maintained.

WEFA expects the future to bring continued rationalization in the health care sector as provider networks and management organizations become larger and perhaps start to merge into jumbo health care supplier organizations. The industry is sufficiently fragmented that this process will take a considerable time.

In this streamlined health care system, the final user of health care, the consumer, remains removed from the provider. The consumer typically obtains health insurance from his or her employer, who has contracted with a management organization. The management organization in turn contracts with one or more provider networks and pays the bills. As a result, the basic third-party payment problem, in which the users do not pay marginal cost, will remain a serious issue in health care.

Future structural changes in the industry will concentrate on this aspect of the industry. The health care management companies can be expected to intensify the following strategies to solve this problem:

- More careful review of payments.

- Oversight of providers' treatment decisions, and treatment guidelines based on cost. This will likely involve prohibiting certain procedures for certain people, essentially rationing health care.

- Additional copayments by patients.

From the patient's perspective these actions cost more on an out-of-pocket basis, reduce the choice available to consumers, and substitute bureaucratic rule-making for the traditional physician-patient relationship. The public will view such rationalization, therefore, as a deterioration in the quality of health care. This creates the largest risk in this industry: the risk that public pressure will increase government regulation and oversight of this entire sector.

The Important Role of Government

Government regulation continues to be a major risk for the industry. The failure of the Administration's health proposal in 1994 probably doomed the idea of a major, systematic overhaul of the health care system. Nevertheless, the logic of cost reduction will continue to collide with political reality, as consumer/voters who are removed from the financial realities of health care perceive a deterioration in the quality of health care services.

Politics enters the health care industry in two ways:

- Health care is heavily regulated by both the state and federal governments. State regulatory authorities include professional licensing boards, hospital authorities, and insurance regulators, and the Food and Drug Administration and other organizations enter the scene at the federal level.

- State and federal governments pay a large portion of health care costs, and as a consequence, are impor-

tant players in the market. Federal decisions about Medicare payment rates, for example, play an important role in medical services pricing. The movement by states toward managed care in Medicaid has had profound implications for providers who serve this population.

Frustrated consumer/voters are likely to turn to the political process to prevent cost-cutting from affecting the choice of physician and procedure inherent in the traditional insurance schemes. As more people enter HMOs, pressure for government intervention in the industry can be expected to rise. It is impossible to predict exactly how or when such intervention might occur. Politics, however, remains the most important risk facing the industry.

The Outlook For Health Care Services

Spending for health care services will grow substantially faster than the economy over the next ten years. Health care services spending in 1992 dollars will be driven by the growing population of the elderly and continued adoption of new technology, and will average about the same rate of growth as in the past ten years. We estimate that the population aged 65 and over will grow at about 0.9% per year over the next ten years, and health care spending adjusted for inflation will grow 3.4%. "Usage intensity" (*per capita* use of health care services) will therefore grow at about 2.5%, a rate similar to that seen in the past ten years.

Changes in the health care system will help keep prices down in the near future. At an average rate of 3.3%, health care inflation will remain below the 3.9% rate recorded in the last ten years. Continued efforts by health care management companies to keep costs down will help put a lid on health care prices. The greater the ability of the management companies to control costs, however, the greater the risk of government intervention in the form of more regulation or a government-led reorganization of the industry.

Major Health Care Sector Indicators: Annual
Percent Change

	1988	1989	1990	1991	1992	1993	1994	1995	1996	1997	1998
Real Consumer Spending on Health Services	4.5	2.6	4.7	3.1	4.0	1.9	1.5	2.3	2.1	3.3	2.7
Nominal Consumer Spending on Health Services	12.5	11.3	12.7	9.1	10.3	7.8	6.0	6.1	4.0	6.4	6.6
Medicare Spending	5.6	13.1	10.3	9.5	11.8	10.8	10.2	8.7	7.7	8.2	6.6
Medicaid Spending	10.4	14.4	20.2	32.4	20.4	10.5	10.7	8.8	6.0	7.5	6.6
Employment, Health Services Establishments	4.6	5.1	4.7	4.7	3.8	3.2	2.6	3.0	3.3	3.2	3.8
CPI, Medical Services	6.5	7.6	9.1	8.7	7.4	5.9	4.8	4.5	3.5	2.9	3.8

Major Health Care Sector Indicators: 10 Year Trend
Average Annual Growth Rate

Indicator	1986-1996	1996-2006
Real Consumer Spending on Health Services	3.2	3.4
Nominal Consumer Spending on Health Services	9.0	7.4
Medicare Spending	9.6	6.8
Medicaid Spending	14.1	7.3
Employment, Health Services Establishments	6.5	3.8
CPI, Medical Services	3.9	3.3

Legal Services

Legal services are performed in the United States through a variety of establishments. Private lawyers are by far the largest segment of the legal services industry, with firm sizes ranging from single to large corporations hiring hundreds of attorneys. It is estimated that private attorneys represent over three–fourths of the total number of practitioners in the legal profession. A second group of legal services is comprised of providers of public legal assistance, who work either as public defenders or in legal aid offices set up to assist those who can't afford the high cost of private legal counsel. A third group is government lawyers, who work for state, local, or federal government agencies and deal primarily with laws and regulations involved with government service. Fourth is a group of lawyers who work for nonprofit organizations and provide legal counsel in matters that relate to their particular organization's interests.

The aggressive cost–cutting that is so widespread in U.S. corporations is affecting legal services, and is likely to contribute to a modest slowdown in the rate of growth in industry revenue over the next decade. During the 10 years ending in 1996, revenues of legal services firms rose an average of 6.6% per year. Over the next 10 years, annual growth is likely to average about a percentage point slower. In addition, there may be considerably more volatility and dispersion of performance among the industry's sub–sectors with increased competition from non–traditional law firms.

Demand For Legal Services

The trend toward consolidation in many American industries has had a negative effect on the growth in demand for legal services. The smaller number of firms and increased cost consciousness at those firms limit the market to some degree and lead to heightened price sensitivity. Many clients balk at rates for legal services that range from $150 to $600 per hour, depending on the location and the service provided. This price sensitivity has also led to increased demand for fixed–fee structures, particularly for the less complicated legal services. The high fee structure and above–average fee inflation that the profession has enjoyed in the past is largely to blame for the emergence of a strong new wave of competition in the legal services industry.

Demand for legal services in support of Chapter 11 corporate restructurings has fallen off dramatically in recent years, but this decline has been offset by a rather dramatic surge in consumer bankruptcy litigation. Future demand growth areas for legal services include sexual harassment suits, sophisticated estate planning, and other types of elder law.

WEFA expects a modest slowdown in the rate of growth in legal services revenue over the next decade. During the 10 years ending in 1996 industry revenues rose an average of 6.6% per year. Over the next 10 years, annual growth is likely to average about a percentage point slower. In addition, there may be considerably more volatility and dispersion of performance among the industry's sub–sectors with increased competition from non–traditional law firms.

Industry Structure

Within large traditional law firms, cost control has already emerged as a key supply side issue. Some firms have slowed the fast–track route to partnership, and lower cost paralegal professionals are given more assignments that were previously given to lawyers. In fact, demand for paralegals should rise rapidly over the next decade as this trend extends throughout the industry.

Another supply–side development has been the spread of franchise law firms, which are often set up as storefronts in commercial strips or shopping malls. These firms are designed to handle basic standardized legal service at fixed fees that are well below those charged by the traditional partnerships.

The rise of legal temporary services has also brought a new brand of competition into the market for legal professionals and their services. The attractions of temporary legal help include: no benefits, no hourly fees, and no long–term commitment after a short–run problem is resolved. One such firm, headquartered in Sacramento and owned and operated by marketing professionals rather than attorneys, has opened about ten offices in California.

Another new form of legal services is the legal equivalent to a health maintenance organization, the prepaid legal service. This is a particularly attractive option for small firms that have a hard time affording traditional legal services. For a modest monthly fee, members of the plan have unlimited telephone access to legal professionals. When they need to hire legal counsel for litigation support or other projects, the rates are considerably lower than traditional fees. Montgomery Ward has such an operation that provides legal insurance for individual consumers.

The Outlook

The aggressive cost–cutting that is so widespread in U.S. corporations is affecting legal services, and is likely to contribute to a modest slowdown in the rate of growth in industry revenue over the next decade. Traditional law firms will encounter increasing competition from franchise and temporary firms, and clients will increasingly resist the billable hour format for purchasing legal services. Trends in the workforce will include increased usage of paralegals, as well as a longer and more difficult track from law school graduation to firm partner. Law firms will find some cost relief in better automation, achieved through increasing use of computers and improved management practices.

Legal Services
Growth in Sales (Line) and Volume (Bar)

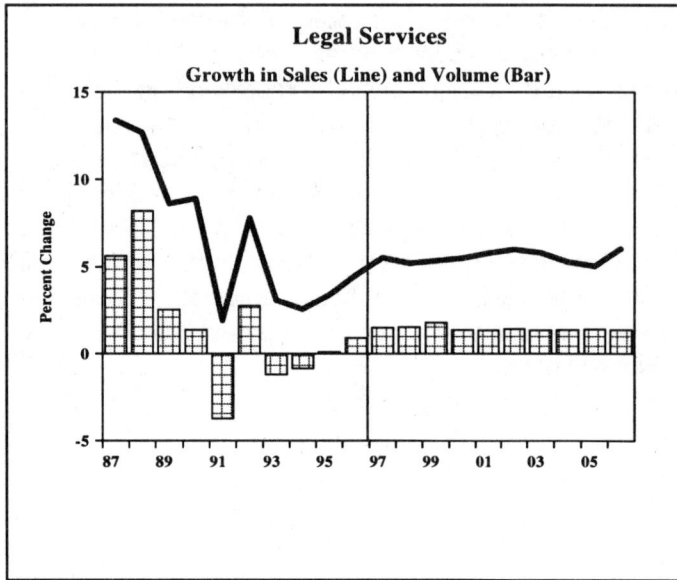

Legal Services
Growth in Product Prices

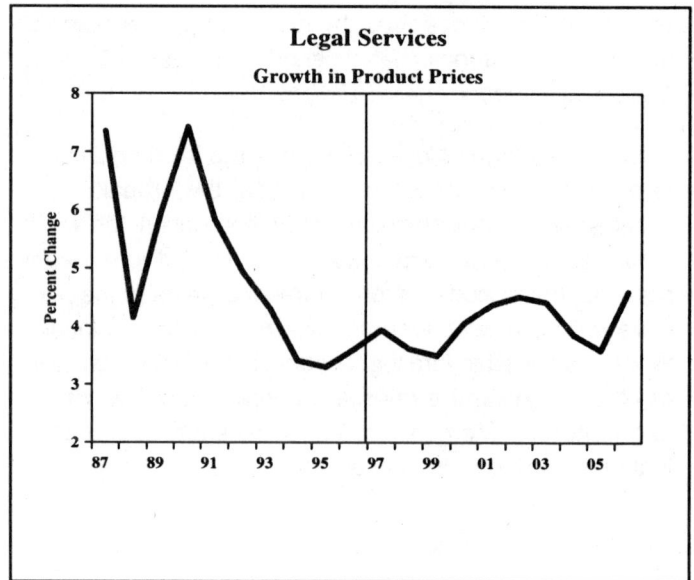

```
Legal Services
SIC 81

                                                                                            Compound Ann Avg Growth
                         1990    1991    1992    1993    1994    1995    1996    1997    1998    1986-1996  1996-2006


Sales
         Billions of $ 102.48  104.43  112.58  116.02  118.97  123.01  128.59  135.68  142.72
         % Change         8.9     1.9     7.8     3.1     2.5     3.4     4.5     5.5     5.2        6.6        5.5

  Volume  % Change        1.4    -3.7     2.7    -1.2    -0.8     0.1     0.9     1.5     1.5        1.5        1.4
  Prices  % Change        7.4     5.8     4.9     4.3     3.4     3.3     3.6     3.9     3.6        5.0        4.0
```

Educational Services

Educational services include both public and private educational activities. It includes: education at the elementary and secondary levels, both public and private; colleges, universities, and professional schools; vocational schools; educational courses by mail; and miscellaneous schools like music schools, drama schools, language schools, and exam preparation schools.

Over the next 10 years, high school enrollment will advance by 16.7% while that of elementary schools will grow by only 4% — virtually a reversal of the pattern observed over the last decade. Growing dissatisfaction with public schools — not only in terms of educational quality but also in terms of drug availability and the personal safety of students — will spark renewed interest in the private school option during the coming decade. Vocational and trade schools are likely to continue to do well over the next decade, particularly those providing training and skills in electronics and other areas where the occupational outlook is favorable.

Demand Factors

During the ten years from 1985 through 1995, enrollment in elementary schools (kindergarten through grade 8) surged as a bulge of children of baby boomers worked its way through the early years of the educational system. The number of students rose 17.9% over the decade, an average annual growth rate of 1.7%. Enrollment in secondary schools (grades 9 through 12), however, rose a much more modest 1.5% over the decade for an average annual gain of just 0.2%. In the coming decade, from 1995–2005, this experience will be reversed as the bulge of elementary school children moves on to high school. During that period, high school enrollment will advance by 16.7% while that of elementary schools will increase by only 4%.

For the ten–year period ending in 1995, private schools performed poorly. In the elementary area, where total population advanced the fastest, private elementary school enrollment rose only 5.6%, while public school enrollment advanced 20%. This may reflect affordability factors more than anything else. For high school age children the gap was even larger, as private secondary school enrollment fell by almost 7% during the decade ending in 1995. This slump in private enrollments should reverse in the future, and growth should be roughly equal to public school enrollment growth. Growing dissatisfaction with public schools — not only in terms of educational quality but also in terms of drug availability and the personal safety of students — will spark renewed interest in the private school option during the coming decade.

College enrollment advanced strongly during the last decade, and will do so again during the next ten years. The number of students enrolled in the nation's colleges advanced 16% during the ten years through 1995, and is projected to rise another 14% over the next ten. The same pattern between public and private schools will occur as in the earlier grades, although it will not be as pronounced. Private college enrollments rose less than those for public schools during the last decade, but will grow faster by a small margin over the next ten years.

There are about 3,000 vocational school establishments, a large majority of which are controlled by corporate entities. Most of these institutions do, however, qualify for some form of government education funding. The demand for vocational school services is likely to continue to grow in the years ahead. With the continuing trend of downsizing and the elimination of layers of management within the modern corporate structure, degrees in many typical business areas, such as marketing or general business administration, no longer offer the assured route to occupational success they once did. While a college education still pays off in the long run, there are clearly occupational categories, especially those with a high–tech orientation, that will pay off with more certainty. Training for some of these high–tech occupations is available from vocational schools, and this will help them in the future.

In addition, there is some demand for vocational and trade school retraining for displaced workers in a variety of both blue and white collar occupations. Overall, look for many vocational and trade schools to continue to do well over the next decade, particularly those providing training and skills where the occupational outlook is favorable.

Supply Factors

Modest growth in elementary enrollments will make it easy for school systems to adjust. The bulge in high school students, however, will be a more difficult problem. Strapped state budgets and overtaxed, and aging, constituent bases will make the construction and funding process more difficult than in the past.

However, new construction will definitely be required. Look for a combination of new high school buildings and expansions, increasing pupil–to–teacher ratios, and even greater criticism on the basis of safety and well–being of high school students.

Educational Services

Growth in Sales (Line) and Volume (Bar)

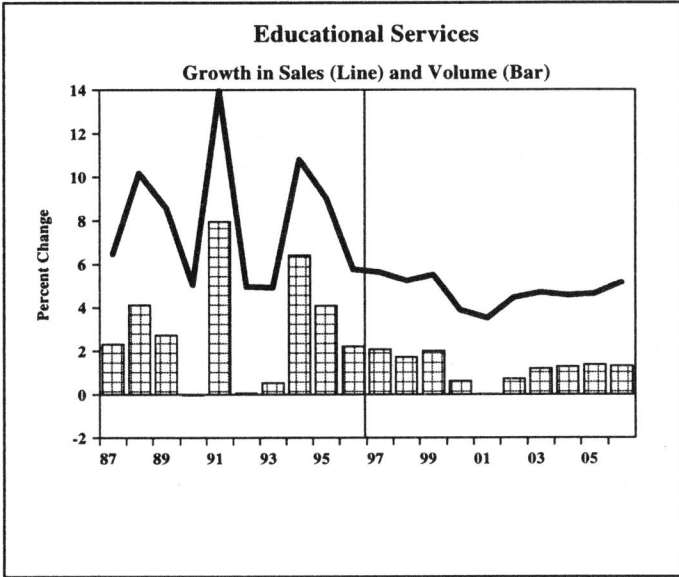

Educational Services

Growth in Product Prices

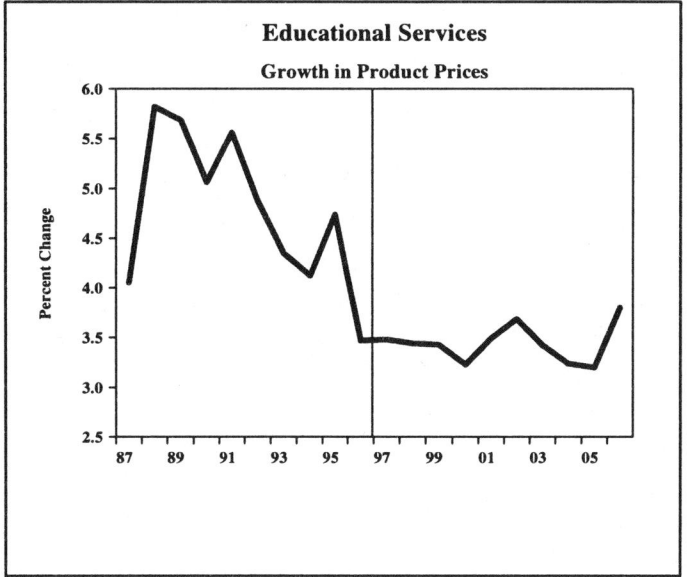

```
Educational Services
  SIC 82

                                                                          Compound Ann Avg Growth
                       1990   1991   1992   1993   1994   1995   1996   1997   1998   1986-1996  1996-2006


Sales
       Billions of $  63.16  71.98  75.54  79.24  87.81  95.72 101.24 106.93 112.52
       % Change         5.0   14.0    4.9    4.9   10.8    9.0    5.8    5.6    5.2      7.9        4.7

  Volume  % Change     -0.0    8.0    0.1    0.5    6.4    4.1    2.2    2.1    1.7      3.0        1.2
  Prices  % Change      5.1    5.6    4.9    4.3    4.1    4.7    3.5    3.5    3.4      4.8        3.4
```

Social and Membership Services

Social and membership services cover a wide variety of service organizations, including institutions providing welfare payments, job training and retraining, residential care for children and senior citizens, and re-election funds. Also included are business and professional associations that promote the interests of their members and religious organizations.

We expect a slowing of growth over the next 10 years for the groups within the social and membership services category. During the decade that ended in 1996, this industry advanced an average 8.3% per year in current–dollar terms. Over the next decade, however, we expect a slower rate of increase of about 5.5%, due to tight budgets at the consumer, business, and governmental levels.

Individual and family social services include family counseling and welfare services. Since the beginning of the decade, the number of people on welfare has surged, and annual expenditures have averaged growth of just above 10%. This has strained the system's finances. Single mothers accounted for roughly half of this increase, and many of them are teenagers. There appears to be no good solution to this problem in sight, but it does seem that any workable future solution — given projected numbers of recipients, expected financial resources available, and the political environment for the reform of public assistance programs — will require that some kind of work be done in exchange for most benefits.

Job–training vocational rehabilitation services include manpower training and vocational rehabilitation, and habilitation services for the unemployed, handicapped, and anyone with a job market disadvantage due to a lack of education, job skills, or experience. Job retraining will continue to require substantial resources since the technical skills required for success in the job market are changing rapidly. Those remaining on the job, however, will also need continuous training in order to keep their skills up to date. As competition for highly trained technical employees heats up, firms that don't keep workers' skills up to date, or that don't keep employment attractive, will lose those employees to other firms. Look for continued health in this sector of the industry over the forecast period.

Demand for child day care services over the next 10 years should slow a bit from recent rapid growth, because the population under five years of age will actually fall through 2000, and then rise only modestly by 2005. Offsetting the decline in the population pool will be continued increases in the share of families with all parents working. In many areas, the market for day care services is currently tight. Consumers of day care services are unhappy with the high rates of turnover in the industry caused by low wages, but are unwilling to pay more for services.

Residential care includes personal care for children and senior citizens where intensive medical care is not a major element. Rising demand for these services has squeezed budget–constrained government facilities at the same time that private nursing homes and rehabilitation chains are doing reasonably well. Demand for residential care for senior citizens will remain largely unchanged over the next decade as the percentage of the population over seventy years of age remains about the same. Beyond 2005, however, this percentage will begin to rise rather rapidly, and so will demand for residential care services.

Another segment of the industry includes other kinds of social services, such as advocacy groups, anti–poverty boards, community action and development groups, councils for social agencies, and regional planning organizations. Although the fund–raising efforts of this segment of the industry were assisted early in the decade by prominent entertainers, it has been one of the slower growing areas of social services, with revenues generally growing by less than 5% per year in current–dollar terms. Scandals over the misuse of funds, as well as concerns over political affiliation, have hurt contributions, as has the mood of American consumers who continue to be concerned about future employment and income.

Business associations and professional membership organizations include organizations engaged in promoting the business interests of their members, whether an industry or an occupation. These groups have increasingly developed ties to government and have established avenues to influence legislation in the direction they think is beneficial to their members. About 40% of these organizations have at least one lobbyist and one PAC (Political Action Committee) fund. The number of trade, business, and commercial associations rose strongly during the first half of the 1980s and then flattened out before actually declining during the first half of the 1990s. Look for only modest increases in the number of these organizations going forward, and for revenues within existing entities to rise slowly as members — both individuals and businesses — continue to experience tight budgets.

Political organizations are dominated by PACs. The Federal Election Campaign Act of 1971 brought PACs into existence in order to allow the pooling of funds and influence by a group. Given the rising cost of campaigning for office, PACs have increasingly come to dominate congressional elections. They also provide a significant advantage for incumbents, who receive a majority of PAC funds. This has given rise to some concerns that PACs influence legislation in an unfair way. Business PACs donate more than three times the amount of funds to election coffers than labor PACs contribute. These contributions are likely to continue to grow in the years ahead, unless campaign finance reform is enacted that changes the grounds rules under which these organizations operate.

Social and Membership Services
Growth in Sales (Line) and Volume (Bar)

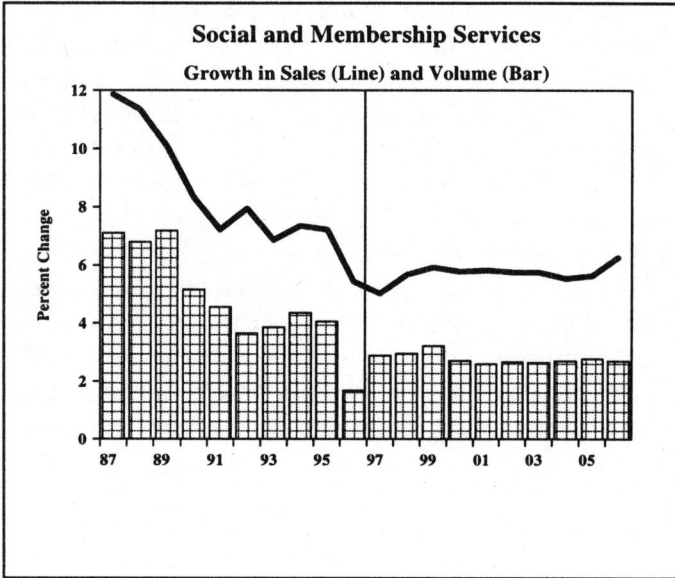

Social and Membership Services
Growth in Product Prices

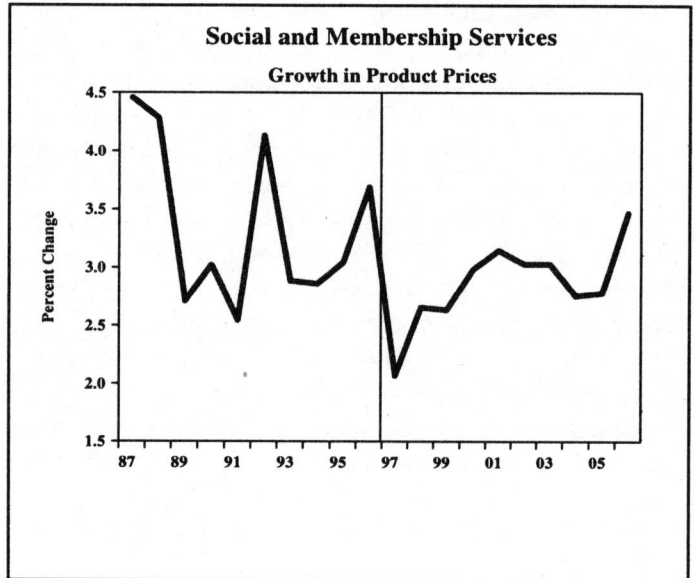

```
Social and Membership Services
 SIC 83-84,86

                                                                                    Compound Ann Avg Growth
                     1990    1991    1992    1993    1994    1995    1996    1997    1998    1986-1996 1996-2006

Sales
         Billions of $  146.23  156.77  169.21  180.81  194.08  208.08  219.38  230.39  243.48
            % Change      8.3     7.2     7.9     6.9     7.3     7.2     5.4     5.0     5.7       8.3       5.7

  Volume    % Change      5.2     4.5     3.7     3.9     4.4     4.0     1.7     2.9     2.9       4.8       2.8
  Prices    % Change      3.0     2.5     4.1     2.9     2.9     3.0     3.7     2.1     2.7       3.4       2.9
```

Engineering, Accounting, Research, and Management Services

This industry includes a broad variety of professional services that supply predominantly, although not exclusively, to business. The two largest components are engineering services and accounting services. The engineering services industry includes civil, mechanical, electrical and electronic, chemical, sanitary, industrial, petroleum, mining, aeronautical, and marine engineering, and comprises almost 30% of total sector revenues. Accounting services represent roughly 18% of total industry revenues. Other important industry subgroups are architectural services, research and testing services, management services, and management consulting services.

The growth in professional business services will likely be above the average of all industries in the United States over the next ten years, as it was over the last ten. Growth in sales is expected to moderate from the 8.5% per year averaged over the ten years ending in 1996 to 6.9% per year over the next decade. This still allows for healthy forecasted growth in real volume of 3.3% per year versus GDP growth of about 2.2%. The most rapid growth within the industry is likely to come in the accounting and management consulting subgroups.

Of the professional services included in this industry, engineering services were the hardest hit during the first half of the 1990s. In addition to the cyclical forces of recession and the secular forces of downsizing and foreign competition, the engineering profession also suffered from severe cutbacks from one of its most important clients — the defense industry. Cutbacks in procurement spending and in weapons development have taken a toll on these services, forcing many engineers to switch their focus to civilian industries. An additional problem for some engineering services firms is the ongoing revolution in information technology, which has shifted the base of economic growth away from physical commodities and toward information. This shift is good for electronic engineers, but not for most of the rest of the profession.

During the first half of the 1990s, revenues accruing to engineering service firms rose an average of only 2% per year. Education and training for engineers in many foreign nations has made great strides, and these professionals are finding it easier to compete with U.S. firms. In the future, growth will be healthy in certain types of electronic engineering and in environmental protection processes. However, the professions' other challenges will continue, and WEFA forecasts only modest gains for the industry overall.

Accounting, auditing, and bookkeeping services, in contrast to engineering services, grew rapidly during the first half of the 1990s, seemingly oblivious to the fact that a recession took place. Indeed, revenues rose modestly in both 1990 and 1991, the years when many other professional service businesses were losing sales. Large accounting firms have broadened their range of services well beyond traditional accounting services. Small firms, on the other hand, have found it productive to specialize in more narrow fields where they can be more efficient and compete effectively with the large firms through lower overhead. Middle size accounting firms, in contrast, have been pinched between the big firms, which offer services the mid–size firms can't, and the small firms, many of which have become very competitive in narrow niche areas. There is still strong demand for accounting services. A strong market for initial public offerings and ongoing merger and acquisition activity create demand for accounting services. In addition, there are institutional and knowledge–based barriers to imports of accounting services. Moreover, outsourcing will continue to help accounting services firms grow.

Management and management consulting services will also do well over the forecast horizon. These firms rose almost as fast as accounting services firms over the last five to ten years, and have in fact done somewhat better since 1993. Management consultants provide operating counsel and assistance to the management of private, nonprofit, and public organizations. Services offered include strategic planning, financial planning and budgeting, information systems planning and design, human resources, marketing counsel, and production planning. The economic trends that propel accounting services also help management services and consulting. Hiring a consulting firm is quite often less expensive than maintaining in–house staff, and it is temporary. Look for a continuation of the favorable trend in this industry in the years ahead.

Architectural services firms were hit hard during and immediately following the recession of 1990–91, and the industry is still struggling. The downturn in demand for architectural services in the early 1990s was not just a cyclical slump, but also reflected the unwinding of the overbuilding in commercial construction that occurred in the late 1980s. Demand has recovered from this slump only slowly, and this business suffered through 1994. However, commercial construction has picked up in the last two years, and it is expected to grow modestly in the future. Future demand for highway and bridge architectural services is likely to be strong as Federal transportation spending increases, as will demand for services related to hazardous waste projects and environmental facilities in general.

The growth in professional business services will likely be above average over the next ten years, as it was over the last ten. Growth is expected to moderate from the 8.5% per year averaged over the ten years ending in 1996, to 6.9% over the next decade. This still allows for healthy forecasted growth in real volume of 3.3% per year versus GDP growth of about 2.2%.

Engineering, Accounting, and Management Services
Growth in Sales (Line) and Volume (Bar)

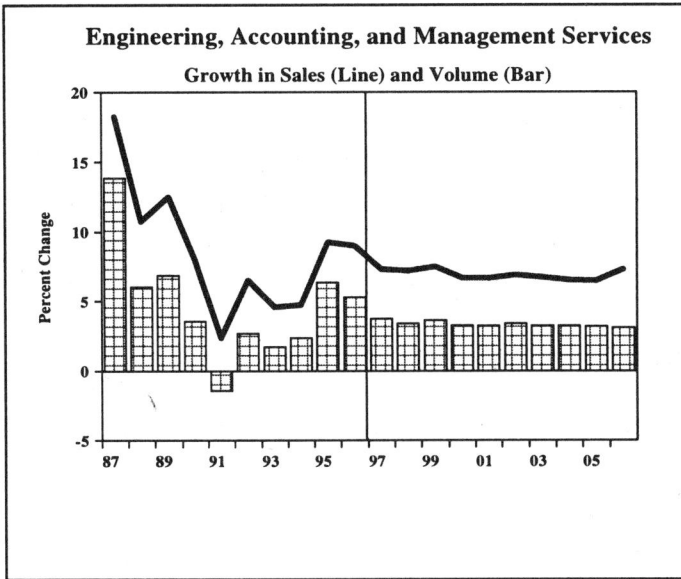

Engineering, Accounting, and Management Services
Growth in Product Prices

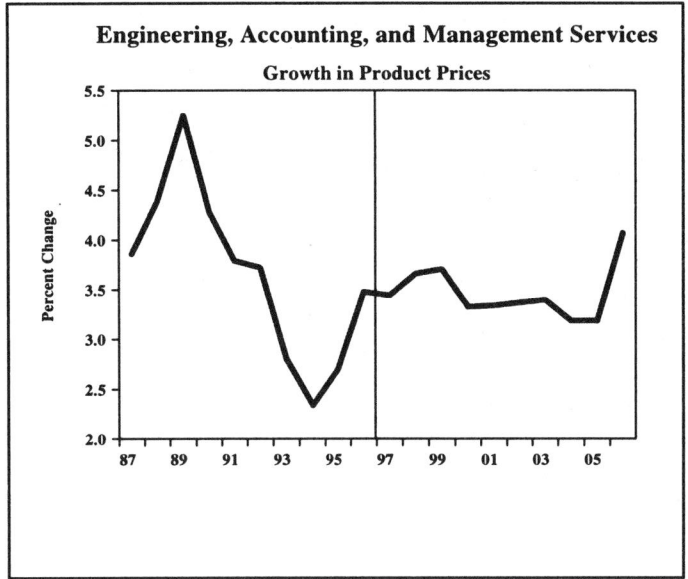

```
Engineering, Accounting, and Management Services
  SIC 87

                                                                                  Compound Ann Avg Growth
                     1990    1991    1992    1993    1994    1995    1996    1997    1998    1986-1996  1996-2006

Sales
        Billions of $  222.62  227.84  242.70  253.82  265.86  290.41  316.43  339.55  363.98
        % Change       8.0     2.3     6.5     4.6     4.7     9.2     9.0     7.3     7.2       8.5        6.9

  Volume   % Change    3.6    -1.4     2.7     1.7     2.3     6.4     5.3     3.7     3.4       4.7        3.3
```

Chapter 30: Environmental Technologies and Services

Environmental Technologies and Services

The environmental equipment industry includes industrial air pollution control equipment, water and wastewater systems, solid waste recycling, and hazardous and toxic waste technologies. Because the environmental equipment industry includes many diverse products, services, and technologies, it is extremely difficult to estimate market size or trade in environmental goods and services. The United States is the world's largest producer and consumer of environmental goods and services, accounting for roughly 40% of the world market.

While environmental equipment is purchased by many industries, the bulk of this equipment is purchased by the utilities industry, followed by chemicals and allied products, petroleum and coal products, paper and allied products, and primary metals.

During the first half of the 1990s, capital expenditures for pollution abatement equipment rose an average of 6% per year. WEFA expects annual domestic expenditures to increase in the 5% to 6% range over the next decade, with spending for air pollution slowing and that for water pollution systems picking up. Moreover, we expect the U.S. Department of Energy to shift its sizable budget more in the direction of remediation (restoring polluted sites to their prior condition) and away from study projects. Export opportunities for United States companies in this industry are substantial, as both Eastern Europe and Asia are becoming increasingly concerned about the quality of their environment.

Demand Conditions

Of the three major areas of pollution equipment — air, water, and solids — spending during the first half of the 1990s was concentrated on air pollution equipment, which increased at an average annual rate of almost 14% per year. Much of this was in response to the Clean Air Act Amendments of 1990, which required substantial reductions in a wide variety of hazardous air pollutants. During the same period expenditures on solid contained waste equipment rose strongly early in the 1990s, only to fall off toward the middle of the decade. Water pollution equipment was the laggard, as spending remained relatively flat throughout the period.

In the future, the growth of air pollution expenditures will likely slow, while spending for water systems increases. New tax legislation enabling towns to issue 20–year tax exempt bonds to finance new and upgraded water systems will lead to strong demand for water systems equipment, since the demand for clean water in residential, municipal, and industrial applications remains strong. The water purification industry is fragmented, and consolidation is occurring. The resulting larger firms, because of their greater resources and experience with various regulatory authorities, may be able to respond more quickly to this demand for clean water going forward. New wastewater treatment technologies will continue to replace, where feasible, conventional activated carbon absorption and air stripping systems that merely transfer pollutants from one medium to another.

Waste management encompasses products for collecting and transporting solid waste, landfill policies, treatment and disposal of toxic wastes, and recycling. The trend in U.S. sanitary landfill practices is toward fewer but bigger solid waste sites. Landfill sites today require sophisticated design and construction procedures, quality assurance/control oversight and documentation, and rigid monitoring and reporting of site operations. Small landfill sites are being phased out because of the difficulty in complying with increasingly complex regulations. Consequently, solid waste is being hauled longer distances to larger disposal sites.

In the hazardous waste area, future solutions will be focused in processing and disposing rather than shipping and burying. The use of technologies such as putting waste through high–temperature electric arcs and ionizing remediation will increase.

During the first half of the 1990s, capital expenditures for pollution abatement equipment rose an average of 6% per year. Looking ahead over the next decade, WEFA expects domestic expenditures for this equipment to advance in the 5% to 6% range on average per year, with spending for air pollution slowing and that for water pollution systems picking up. Moreover, we expect the U.S. Department of Energy to shift its sizable budget more in the direction of remediation (restoring polluted sites to their prior condition) and away from study projects. Export opportunities for United States companies in this industry are substantial, however, as both Eastern Europe and Asia are becoming increasingly concerned about the quality of their environment.

The Trade Situation

As international concern over pollution grows, demand is expected to be strong for U.S.–made environmental equipment. An additional factor raising international sales expectations is the interest in pollution abatement by international banking organizations, such as the World Bank, which are increasingly tying the availability of funds to a willingness to upgrade environmental standards. The United States retains a healthy trade surplus in pollution equipment, and that advantage is expected to continue. Areas where demand is expected to be strong include Asia — particularly Hong Kong, Taiwan, and Korea — where the commitment to environmental protection and remediation is strong and rising. Other countries that will be customers of pollution abatement equipment in the future include many in Eastern Europe and in the Southeastern Asian (ASEAN) nations.

Appendix
Definitions and Sources

Historical Data

The key historical database used in this book is that developed for WEFA's U.S. Industrial Analysis Service. It contains the consistent time-series data required to build the model used in that service's forecasts, at quarterly frequency. The data for the most part begin in the late 1960s, and at the time of this writing in the spring of 1997 included actual historical figures through the fourth quarter of 1996.

The database covers 130 U.S. industries. Not all of its coverage has been included in this book, but on the other hand additional sources have been used in some sections. These are noted as used, unless they are available through one of the U.S. government's standard statistical releases.

The key government sources used are the following.

- U.S. Department of Commerce, Bureau of Census: Census of Manufactures; Census of Services; benchmark input-output tables; Manufacturers' Shipments, Inventories, and Orders; Merchandise Trade.

- U.S. Department of Commerce, Bureau of Economic Analysis: National Income and Product Accounts

- U.S. Department of Labor, Bureau of Labor Statistics: Employment and Earnings; Producer Price Indexes

- Federal Reserve Board of Governors: Industrial Production Indexes

- U.S. Department of Agriculture

- U.S. Department of Energy

Sales

In the manufacturing sectors, the figures displayed in dollar terms as sales are actually the value of industry gross production in current dollars. These are derived mainly from the Manufacturers' Shipments, Inventories, and Orders data released monthly by the Commerce Department. Gross value of production is defined as the value of shipments plus the value of the change in finished goods inventories. (Finished goods inventories are estimated at a quarterly frequency by WEFA using a combination of published monthly total inventories by in-

dustry and published annual-frequency inventories by stage of fabrication by industry.)

For the industries outside of manufacturing, the data come from a variety of sources. A complicated patchwork of information is required to build up measures for these industries that are both

- Consistent with those for manufacturing in definition and

- As timely as those in manufacturing, in this case through 1996.

In general, however, all service industry sales figures are benchmarked to the 1977, 1982, and 1987 input-output tables' values of total output. The 1987 table is the most current available with the full detailed statistics required, at the time of this writing. Their trends through time before, between, and after these points are developed either from another government data source, such as construction put-in-place, or from a trade association or other private source. An example of such a private source is the Air Transport Association, from which statistics for trends in passenger and freight air transport are derived.

In many cases, the sources for non-manufacturing sectors are not as timely and current as those for manufacturing. If the preferred data are not up to date, we take advantage of the highly labor-intensive nature of many service industries and use trends in labor compensation as estimates for sales in very recent historical periods.

The dataset that results from these calculations is unique and proprietary to WEFA for use by clients of its Industrial Analysis Service, as are the details of the methodology of its construction.

Data referenced as "volume", or "real sales", or "sales in constant dollars" are simply the sales figures described above deflated with the industry's price index described below.

Prices

Price indexes for industries are derived wherever possible from Producer Price Indexes (PPIs) for industry groups from the Bureau of Labor Statistics (BLS). PPIs are matched as closely as possible to the aggregation of industries included in the industry sales measure, are extended back through time where necessary through linkages with the historical trends in BLS' PPIs by commodity, and are rebased to equal 100 in 1992.

In some cases, most often in service sectors, PPI data are not available, or available for only a brief period of recent history. When PPI data does not exist or is insufficient, we resort to the patchwork of sources described above in the description of sales data. In all cases, we search for a consistent indicator — a measure of selling price at the producer level in that industry. In a very few cases, where the service is sold directly to consumers, a consumer price index is used. All data are converted to index form, with 1992 equal to 100.

Imports and Exports

The data for imports and exports were developed specifically for this book, and are not routinely updated and forecast in support of WEFA's U.S. Industrial Analysis Service as the other data are.

This data is matched to the best aggregation of commodity-based imports and exports statistics from the monthly Department of Commerce Merchandise Trade data releases. For industries where the match was not good, trade data were omitted from the book.

Additional Sources

In addition to the sources described above, the analysis for certain industries quotes other sources of data.

One source that is used for a number of the electronic sectors is Electronic Outlook Corporation (EOC). For some of these sectors, the analysis and some tables (noting EOC as a source) are based in part on the research and forecasts produced by:

Electronic Outlook Corporation
418 Mississippi Street
San Francisco, California 94107.

Forecasts

The forecasts presented in this book were developed by WEFA staff in support of various WEFA industry services, including the U.S. Industrial Analysis Service, Agricultural Services, Energy Services, Steel Services, Automotive Services, Capital Goods and Freight Transportation Services, Cost Planning Services, Real Estate and Construction Service, and others. All are the most recent forecast available in April and early May 1997, and are consistent with WEFA's April U.S. Economic Outlook and First Quarter 1997 World Economic Outlook.

The forecasts are developed using four key tools:

- WEFA's huge historical database, derived from government and private sources, up-to-date, and including more than 5 million time series;

- WEFA's econometric models of the world, the United States, the United States as defined by all its industries, and various specific industries;

- WEFA's economists, top analysts hired to build the models and to monitor and analyze events that the models cannot represent; and

- WEFA's forecast process, which ties all of the models together mathematically and electronically, and brings all the economists together in a consistent framework of forecast assumptions and world-view.

Index

(Chapter names are in bold.)